The Cambridge Social History of Modern Ireland

Covering three centuries of unprecedented demographic and economic changes, this text-book is an authoritative and comprehensive view of the shaping of Irish society at home and abroad from the famine of 1740 to the present day. The first major work on the history of modern Ireland to adopt a social history perspective, it focuses on the experiences and agency of Irish men, women and children, Catholics and Protestants, in the north, south and the diaspora. An international team of leading scholars surveys key changes in population, the economy, occupations, property ownership, class and migration as well as considering the interaction of the individual and the state through welfare, education, crime and policing. Drawing on a wide range of disciplinary approaches and consistently setting Irish developments in a wider European and global context, this is an invaluable resource for courses on modern Irish history and Irish studies.

EUGENIO F. BIAGINI is Fellow of Sidney Sussex College Cambridge and Professor of Modern and Contemporary History, University of Cambridge.

MARY E. DALY is President of the Royal Irish Academy and Professor Emerita of Modern History, University College Dublin.

[handwritten inscription] To Tom with best wishes Eugenio Biagini Mary Daly

The Cambridge Social History of
Modern Ireland

EDITED BY

Eugenio F. Biagini
University of Cambridge

and

Mary E. Daly
University College Dublin

CAMBRIDGE
UNIVERSITY PRESS

CAMBRIDGE
UNIVERSITY PRESS

University Printing House, Cambridge CB2 8BS, United Kingdom

One Liberty Plaza, 20th Floor, New York, NY 10006, USA

477 Williamstown Road, Port Melbourne, VIC 3207, Australia

4843/24, 2nd Floor, Ansari Road, Daryaganj, Delhi – 110002, India

79 Anson Road, #06–04/06, Singapore 079906

Cambridge University Press is part of the University of Cambridge.

It furthers the University's mission by disseminating knowledge in the pursuit of education, learning, and research at the highest international levels of excellence.

www.cambridge.org
Information on this title: www.cambridge.org/9781107095588
10.1017/9781316155271

First published 2017

Printed in United Kingdom by TJ International Ltd. Padstow Cornwall in 2017

A catalogue record for this publication is available from the British Library.

Library of Congress Cataloging-in-Publication Data
Names: Biagini, Eugenio F., editor of compilation. | Daly, Mary E., editor of
    compilation.
Title: The Cambridge social history of modern Ireland / [edited by] Eugenio
    Biagini (University of Cambridge), Mary Daly (University College Dublin).
Description: Cambridge, United Kingdom ; New York, NY : Cambridge University
    Press, 2017.
Identifiers: LCCN 2016049339| ISBN 9781107095588 (hardback) | ISBN
    9781107479401 (paperback)
Subjects: LCSH: Ireland – Social conditions. | Ireland – Economic conditions. |
    Ireland – Population – History. | Social change – Ireland – History.
Classification: LCC HN400.3.A8 C35 2017 | DDC 306.09415–dc23
LC record available at https://lccn.loc.gov/2016049339

ISBN 978-1-107-09558-8 Hardback
ISBN 978-1-107-47940-1 Paperback

Contents

Figures

Maps

Tables

Contributors

Juliana Adelman, Lecturer in History, Dublin City University

Colin Barr, Senior Lecturer in Modern British, Irish and British Imperial History, University of Aberdeen

Guy Beiner, Lecturer in Modern History, Ben Gurion University of the Negev

Eugenio F. Biagini, Professor of Modern and Contemporary History in the University of Cambridge and a Fellow of Sidney Sussex College Cambridge

Andy Bielenberg, Senior Lecturer in History, University College Cork

Sarah-Anne Buckley, Lecturer in History, National University of Ireland Galway

Sean Campbell, Reader in Media and Culture, Anglia Ruskin University, Cambridge

Catherine Cox, Lecturer in History, University College Dublin

Niall Cunningham, Lecturer in Human Geography, Durham University

Mary E. Daly, Professor Emerita of Modern History at University College Dublin and President of the Royal Irish Academy

David Dickson, Professor of Modern History at the Centre for Irish, Scottish and Comparative Studies of Trinity College Dublin

Terence Dooley, Professor of Modern History, Maynooth University, National University of Ireland

Lindsey Earner-Byrne, Lecturer in History, University College Dublin

Mark Finnane, Professor of History, Griffith University

John FitzGerald, Adjunct Professor in Economics, Trinity College Dublin, formerly Research Professor, Economic and Social Research Institute, Dublin

Irial Glynn, Lecturer in Modern History, Universiteit Leiden

Ian Gregory, Professor of Digital Humanities, Lancaster University

Andrew Holmes, Lecturer in Modern Irish History, Queen's University Belfast

Kevin Kenny, Professor of Modern History, Boston College

Maria Luddy, Professor of Modern Irish History, University of Warwick

Patricia Lysaght, Professor Emerita in Irish Folklore, University College Dublin

Angela McCarthy, Professor of Scottish and Irish History and Associate Director of the Centre for Irish and Scottish Studies, University of Otago

D. A. J. MacPherson, Lecturer in History, University of the Highlands and Islands

Tim Meagher, Associate Professor of Modern History and University Archivist, Catholic University of America in Washington

William Murphy, Lecturer in the School of History and Geography, Dublin City University

Caoimhe Nic Dháibhéid, Senior Lecturer in Modern History, Sheffield University

Daithí Ó Corráin, Lecturer in Modern Irish History, Dublin City University

Ian O'Donnell, Professor of Criminology, University College Dublin

Diarmuid Ó Giolláin, Professor of Irish Language and Literature, Concurrent Professor of Anthropology, University of Notre Dame

John O'Hagan, Professor of Economics, Trinity College Dublin

Eunan O'Halpin, Bank of Ireland Professor of Contemporary History, Trinity College Dublin

Ciaran O'Neill, Ussher Assistant Professor in Nineteenth-Century History, Trinity College Dublin

Gearóid Ó Tuathaigh, Professor Emeritus in History, National University of Ireland Galway

Henry Patterson, Emeritus Professor of Irish Politics, University of Ulster

Susannah Riordan, Lecturer in History, University College Dublin

Sarah Roddy, Lecturer in Modern Irish History, University of Manchester

Ellen Rowley, School of Architecture, University College Dublin and Tenement Museum Dublin Project, Dublin City Council

Joseph Ruane, Emeritus Professor of Sociology, University College Cork

Paul Rouse, Lecturer in History, University College Dublin

Peter Solar, Emeritus Professor of Economics, Vesalius College, Brussels

Roger Swift, Emeritus Professor of Victorian Studies, University of Chester

Jennifer Todd, Professor of Politics, University College Dublin

Diane Urquhart, Reader in Modern Irish History, Institute of Irish Studies, University of Liverpool

Bronwen Walter, Professor Emerita of Irish Diaspora Studies, Anglia Ruskin University, Cambridge

County map of Ireland

Editors' Introduction

What is social history? In this introduction we refrain from offering an analytical and systematic concept of the discipline for two main reasons. The first is that this book is a collective endeavour and the authors whom we have gathered here reflect a variety of approaches and methods. We affirm and celebrate such plurality of voices, believing that there is much to learn from listening to one another, for the age of the 'grand theories' is happily over. The second reason is that, for us, social history – and particularly this book – is not a point of arrival, but a point of departure. It is open-ended, it is a programme, a springboard for the rewriting of the history of the Irish. It is methodologically eclectic, open to cognate disciplines (geography, sociology, demographics, economics), and, if not *histoire totale*, it is at least interested in grasping the totality of human experience in society. Its totalising quest of meaning is a project, rather than a narrative.

Why do we start with the central decades of the eighteenth century? Though any chronological starting point would be more or less arbitrary, 1740 is significant for Ireland's social and economic history because it marked the beginning of a devastating famine. It was a catastrophe. It is not as well remembered as the one which started in 1845, partly because it did not have any immediate or long-term political consequences and was never incorporated into the grand narrative of national struggle. However, it deeply affected large numbers of people in a more direct and drastic way than political events such as the 1800 Act of Union.

Irish historiography, whether 'nationalist', 'revisionist' or 'post-revisionist', has traditionally been dominated by a concern for political history, with a focus on the national question. To an extent, the latter has affected also the way historians have explored social and economic topics, for example by stimulating excellent research on the Great

Famine, emigration and the Land Wars.[1] While there has long been a parallel scholarly interest in less obviously 'political' issues – a tradition spearheaded by historians such as Connell, Cullen and Akenson[2] – it is only in recent decades that there has been a substantial development in the study of a wider range of social and economic formations and phenomena. These include works on issues which used to be almost 'taboo' – such as class and sex – but also the social and cultural analysis of religious minorities and the questioning of the failure of the Irish state to sustain economic and social growth during the first generation since independence.[3]

This development has been vigorous and many-folded, yielding a rich crop of historical monographs on various problems long neglected by Irish historians – from urbanisation to elite formation, industrial development and the history of minorities. However, we do not have, as yet, any synthesis bringing together the results of this new way of looking at the Irish past. Partly as a consequence, these studies have not created the momentum which in other countries – already in the 1960s – resulted in 'social history' challenging received narratives.[4] In the *Cambridge Social History of Modern Ireland* some of the scholars who have been, and are, reshaping the landscape of history reflect on the result of recent monographic research and offer a comprehensive new interpretation of the country's history since 1740. Our emphasis is on economic and social change, our focus on people and cultures, instead of institutions and political ideologies, but this is not 'history without politics'. On the contrary, politics is always present in our analysis, with reference, for example, to the impact of political and administrative factors on social practices, attitudes to welfare, family planning, women's employment, child benefits and civil rights. While Irish migration was primarily driven by socio-economic and demographic forces, the timing of migratory flows and the destinations of emigrant Irish were influenced by wars and political decisions in the countries of destination. The Union with Britain shaped the evolution of education, health

---

1 For example, D. Fitzpatrick, *Politics and Irish life, 1913–21: provincial experience of war and revolution* (Dublin, 1977) and P. Bew, *Land and the national question in Ireland, 1858–1882* (London, 1978).

2 K. Connell, *The population of Ireland 1750–1845* (Oxford, 1950); K. Connell, *Irish peasant society* (Oxford, 1968); L. Cullen, *Six generations: life and work in Ireland from 1790* (Cork, 1970); L. Cullen, *The emergence of modern Ireland, 1600–1900* (London, 1981); D. Akenson, *The Irish education experiment: the national system of education in the nineteenth century* (London. 1970).

3 M. Silverman, *An Irish working class: explorations in political economy and hegemony, 1800–1950* (London and Toronto, 2001), M. Luddy, *Prostitution and Irish society, 1800–1940* (Cambridge, 2007) and D. Ferriter, *Occasions of sin: sex in twentieth-century Ireland* (London, 2009); F. Campbell, *The Irish Establishment 1879–1914* (Oxford, 2009); I. D'Alton, *Protestant society and politics in Cork 1812–1844* (Cork, 1980); C. Ó Gráda, *Jewish Ireland in the age of Joyce: a socioeconomic history* (Princeton, 2006); D. Keogh, F. O'Shea and C. Quinlan (eds.), *Ireland in the 1950s: the lost decade* (Dublin, 2004).

4 With a few exceptions, such as M. E. Daly, *Social and economic history of Ireland since 1800* (Dublin, 1981); T. Brown, *Ireland: a social and cultural history, 1922–2002* (London, 2003); C. Clear, *Social change and everyday life in Ireland 1850–1922* (Manchester, 2007); M. E. Daly, *Sixties Ireland: reshaping the economy, state and society, 1957–1973* (Cambridge, 2016).

and welfare, and any account of the social history of twentieth-century Ireland must take account of the impact of the formation of two separate governments after 1922.

Though contributors to the present volume adopt different methodological and historiographical strategies, they all share a sense that Irish history is best understood in a wider European and indeed global context. They challenge the insular, introspective paradigm of an Irish *Sonderweg*, and adopt an inclusive, eclectic and comparative approach, which borrows widely from a wide range of disciplines, including historical demography, literary criticism, social anthropology, archaeology, economics, sociology, social geography and the history of science.

Moreover, because the *Cambridge Social History of Ireland* focuses primarily on people, rather than institutions, its remit goes beyond the shores of the island: the diaspora, mass emigration and, generally speaking, movements of people in and out of the country are part of our subject. As is well known, there are many more people of Irish descent living overseas than in Ireland itself. They belong in the present history, because they have always played an important role in the economic, social and political development of the 'Ould Sod'. They helped to shape a worldwide Irish 'imagined community', encompassing both the diaspora and the Irish who stayed behind, especially those who contemplated emigration as a manageable option for either themselves or some family members. Thus, though often unwilling pioneers of globalisation, the Irish contributed powerfully to the creation of that quintessentially global entity, the 'English-speaking' world – one in which the language was a *lingua franca* rather than a symbol of nationality and identity.

This book is designed to be a tool to unpack Ireland's social and cultural history in its global as well as national significance. We hope that it will inspire our readers, in the words of W. B. Yeats, to 'go forth … and seize whatever prey the heart long for, and have no fear. Everything exists, everything is true, and the earth is only a little dust under our feet.'

Cambridge and Dublin, St Patrick's Day 2016

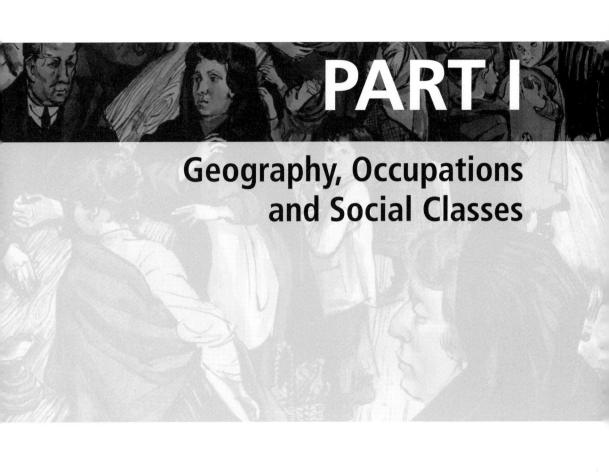

PART I

Geography, Occupations and Social Classes

1

Irish Demography since 1740

John FitzGerald

1.1. Introduction

The demography of Ireland presents an unusual picture when compared, not only with our nearest neighbour, but also with other European countries. The dramatic fall in the population in the nineteenth century caused by the Great Famine, followed by near stagnation for much of the twentieth century, makes Ireland exceptional. However, probably the most striking feature of Irish demographic change over the past two and a half centuries has been the role played by very large migratory flows.

One of Ireland's leading statisticians, writing in 1935, bravely provided estimates of the future population to 2016.[1] His 'high' forecast for 1996 was very close to the actual outturn of 3.6 million. However, he went on to conclude that 'it would appear that the population of An Saorstát is unlikely to exceed 3,700,000 during the next 80 years'. Already at 4.6 million, it exceeds this forecast by a quarter, highlighting the dramatic shift in demographic fortunes that Ireland has experienced in recent years.

Section 2 of this chapter describes the data sources that are available. Section 3 considers the demographic changes that occurred over the period 1740 to 1850, while Section 4 describes the changes in the subsequent 160 years to 2010. As well as considering demographic change on the island of Ireland, taken as a unit, where possible this chapter also analyses demographic developments in both Northern Ireland (the north) and the Republic of Ireland (the Republic).

---

1 R. C. Geary, 'The future population of Saorstát éireann and some observations on population statistics', *Journal of the Statistical and Social Inquiry Society of Ireland*, 15 (1935/6), 15–35.

1.2. The Data

The 1926 census for Ireland collected estimates of the population from the late seventeenth century until the first full census for the island in 1821. Most of these estimates were based on hearth tax returns. However, as even contemporary analysts indicated, the estimates from these different sources were defective. Their reliability was affected by changes in the definition of exempt dwellings and also changes in the process of revenue collection. Connell analysed these data and provided a set of population estimates for the eighteenth century. However, his estimates also suffer from some problems. More recently, Dickson et al.,[2] using additional information, considered the reliability of individual tax returns, producing revised estimates of population in the eighteenth century.

The collection of consistent data on an annual basis for births, deaths and marriages only began in 1864. The paucity of reliable data on these vital statistics in the period up to 1864 makes the analysis of demographic change more difficult for the period to 1860.

Since 1821, there has been a census at least every decade. The first three censuses (1821, 1831 and 1841) may have involved some under-recording. In these early censuses an attempt was made to fill gaps in demographic data by asking questions about marital status and also about births and deaths over the previous decade. However, it was clear to contemporaries that these data, which were based on recall at the time of the census, were increasingly unreliable the further back in the decade they refer to.[3]

From 1864 to the present day, the annual *Report of the Commissioner for Births, Deaths, and Marriages*, now referred to as the *Vital Statistics* (for simplicity it is referred to in this chapter as the *Commissioners' Reports*), published data on births, deaths and marriages. This publication has changed little in content over the century and a half since 1864. As with all such nineteenth-century data sources, there are questions about their reliability. However, the internal consistency of the data suggests that they are reasonably reliable from the first publication for 1864.

One area where continuing problems were reported was in the recording of their ages by spouses at the time of their marriage. While in the 1860s up to 45 per cent of spouses recorded their actual age at marriage, this had fallen to about 12 per cent by the early years of the twentieth century.

When combined with the censuses, the *Commissioners' Reports* provide a pretty comprehensive set of data. While estimates are published of the numbers emigrating, the statistics omit emigration from Ireland to Great Britain. For the century

---

2 D. Dickson, C. Ó Gráda and S. Daultrey, 'Hearth tax, household size and Irish population change 1672–1821', *Proceedings of the Royal Irish Academy. Section C*, 82c, 6 (1982), 125–60, 162–81.
3 Census of Ireland (1851), part 6, XLIX.

Table 1.1. Estimate of population in the eighteenth century (millions)

	Ireland	
	Low	High
1706	1.75	2.06
1712	1.98	2.32
1725	2.18	2.56
1732	2.16	2.53
1744	1.91	2.23
1749	1.95	2.28
1753	2.20	2.57
1791	4.42	
1821	6.8	7.2[1]
1831	7.7	
1841	8.2	8.4
1851	6.5	6.5

SOURCE: Dickson et al., 'Hearth tax, household size and Irish population change'
NOTE: [1] Including an adjustment in 1821–41, as suggested by Lee 1981.

after the Great Famine, Geary suggests that emigration to Britain was approximately 50 per cent of the emigration to the USA. However, as discussed later, on the basis of the census and of data for births and deaths, the numbers emigrating can be derived residually for the inter-censal periods. In turn, these estimates can be compared with the published estimates of the numbers emigrating to give an indication of emigration to Britain.

For Northern Ireland similar data are generally available from the *Annual Report of the Commissioners for Births, Deaths and Marriages.* However, there are fewer censuses for the north and they provide more limited information than the censuses for the Republic. In addition, there is not a continuous series for emigration from the north covering the period since 1922.

To make up for the limitations in the pre-1864 data an alternative approach, using a simple demographic model, was employed. The life tables for 1926[4] were modified to reproduce the published life expectancy figures back to 1871. Using the resulting model, the population for 1841 to 1881 was predicted and compared with the actual population. This facilitates the testing of different assumptions on life expectancy and births.

4 Census of Ireland (1926), vol. V, part 1, tables 22 and 23.

1.3.   Demographic Change, 1740–1850

The best source of information on the population in the eighteenth century is the hearth tax returns. To the extent that they provide a reliable indicator of the number of dwellings, they are the basis for estimating the population. Dickson *et al.* concluded that the tax returns for the first half of the eighteenth century and for 1791 are more reliable than the returns for the intervening years. On this basis they prepared revised population estimates for a range of years from the beginning of the eighteenth century through to the 1821 census (Table 1.1). Because of the uncertainty associated with these data, where appropriate, the authors provide a high and a low estimate of the population.

As shown in Table 1.1, between 1732 and 1744 there was a dramatic drop in population due to a major famine in the intervening years. Most of the fall in population was probably due to excess deaths, because emigration in the early eighteenth century was still quite limited. As shown in the table, in the second half of the eighteenth century and continuing to 1821, the Irish population grew very rapidly, maybe at a rate of 1.6 per cent a year. Thereafter, the population growth rate slowed to 0.9 per cent a year between 1821 and 1831 and to 0.6 per cent a year between 1831 and 1841. The Great Famine of the 1840s resulted in a truly dramatic fall by an average of between 2.3 and 2.5 per cent a year.

By the end of the eighteenth century there was already very extensive emigration from Ireland, mostly from the north. Connell estimated that emigration between 1780 and 1845 amounted to 1.75 million. Mokyr and Ó Gráda suggested that between 1815 and 1845 alone, 1.5 million people left Ireland, a much higher emigration rate than was suggested by the annual estimates published in the censuses. Mokyr and Ó Gráda, in their 1984 work, confirm Connell's hypothesis that marital fertility was high in the eighteenth century. They also suggest that the age at marriage was quite low in 1800: between twenty and twenty-two, rising to twenty-four to twenty-five by the 1840s.

The traumatic effects of the famine years of the late 1840s produced a dramatic change in the population. The upheaval was so great that, even with better data, it would be very difficult to estimate the composition of the demographic changes between 1840 and 1850; with the limited data available to supplement the censuses, a number of researchers have done extensive work to elucidate the key details of what happened.[5]

Table 1.2 shows the census population figures for 1841 and 1851. To the population estimated in the census is added an estimate for under-recording derived from Lee. If marital fertility had been the same as it was in the 1860s, then there would have been more than 2 million births between 1841 and 1851. Mokyr estimated that the

5 Summarised in J. Crowley, W. Smyth and M. Murphy, *Atlas of the Great Irish Famine* (Cork, 2012).

Table 1.2. Derivation of excess deaths due to the Great Famine

		Thousands
Population 1841 – census	+	8,175
Population adjustment (Lee 1981)	+	300
Births at 1860s marital fertility	+	2,034
Births – effects of famine (Mokyr 1983)	–	350
Emigration – official statistics	–	1,235
Emigration to Great Britain (Miller 2012)	–	300
Deaths – at 1871 life expectancy	–	1,167
Deaths – famine related	–	905
Population 1851 – census		6,552

SOURCE: Author's estimates.
NOTE: The estimated life tables for 1871 are applied to the detailed age data from the 1841 census, deriving an estimate of the number of 'normal' deaths. This estimate is based on the assumption that life expectancy in 1841 would have been similar to that in 1871, were it not for the Great Famine.

effect of the famine was to reduce the number of births by between 0.3 and 0.4 million. The numbers reported to have emigrated to countries other than Britain over the decade amounted to 1.25 million, to which must be added an estimate for emigration to Britain of between 0.2 and 0.3 million.

If life expectancy in the 1840s had been identical to that in 1871, then there would have been about 1.17 million deaths. When these estimates are combined with the census population for 1851 they would suggest 'excess' deaths due to the famine of around 0.9 million. This is similar to the estimate of 'excess' deaths of 1 million.

1.4.   Demographic Change, 1850–2010

Figure 1.1 shows an estimate of the population over three centuries. It is based on the Dickson *et al.* estimates for the eighteenth century, linked to the annual series published in the *Commissioners' Reports* and its successor publications. It illustrates the dramatic changes that have taken place over three centuries, the most notable being the shock arising from the famine of the 1840s.

The Irish population fell nearly every year between the Great Famine and the end of the nineteenth century. In the case of what is now the Republic, there was only one year in the second half of the nineteenth century when the population did not fall. In the case of Northern Ireland, while the population also fell between 1851 and 1901, there were seventeen years when the population actually increased.

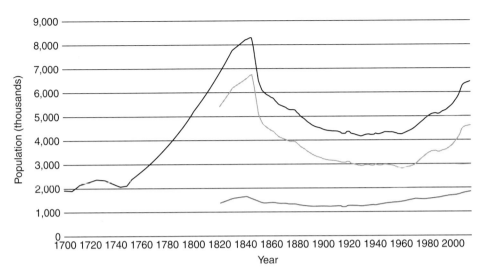

Figure 1.1 Irish population, 1700–2014 : Ireland (top), Republic of Ireland (middle) and Northern Ireland (bottom).

The population in the Republic fell in forty-five of the years between 1901 and 1961, whereas in Northern Ireland the population rose pretty continuously. This difference in experience reflected different rates of economic development in the two jurisdictions after 1922. It was only in the years immediately after the First World War, and again in the Depression years of the 1930s and during the Second World War that emigration from the Republic was halted or reversed. The very poor economic performance of the Republic in the first forty years of independence meant that the standard of living on offer in Britain was much superior to what was available in Ireland.

As a result, between 1850 and 1960 the population in the Republic fell by an average of 0.4 per cent a year, whereas in the north the population in 1960 was almost identical to what it had been just over a century earlier. From 1960 to 2014 the position has altered, with the population in the Republic growing by 0.9 per cent a year and that in Northern Ireland by 0.4 per cent a year.

1.4.1. Survival Rates in Ireland

For what are now the Republic and Northern Ireland, Figures 1.2 and 1.3 show the proportion of each cohort born between 1830 and 1890 that survived to a given age, taking account of the combined effects of emigration and deaths. The exceptional emigration and the dramatic increase in the death rate during the famine years had a devastating effect on the cohort born in the Republic between 1831 and 1840: by the age of thirty, less than 30 per cent were still alive and living there. However, as the century progressed, the death rate decreased rapidly from its famine peak, and emigration also fell, reflecting improved economic conditions. Thus, for the cohorts born in the 1870s

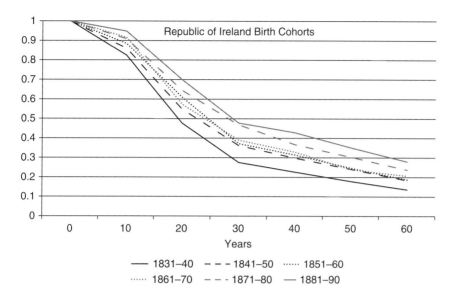

Figure 1.2 Survival rates of birth cohorts, Republic of Ireland, nineteenth century

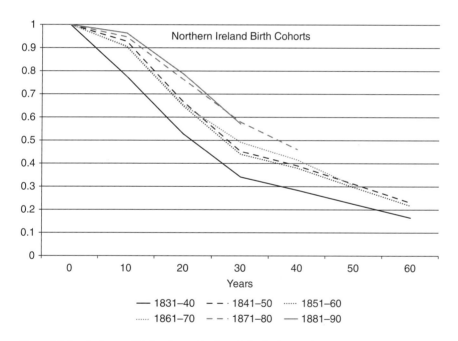

Figure 1.3 Survival rates of birth cohorts, Northern Ireland, nineteenth century

and the 1880s, almost 50 per cent were still alive and living in Ireland at the age of thirty.

In the case of Northern Ireland, as shown in Figure 1.3, there was a slightly lower rate of attrition for the 1830s birth cohort, with just over 30 per cent alive and living in Ireland thirty years later. However, for the 1870s and 1880s birth cohorts, 60 per cent

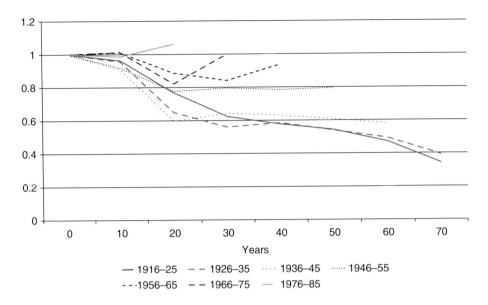

Figure 1.4 Survival rates of birth cohorts, Republic of Ireland, twentieth century

were still in Ireland thirty years later, significantly higher than the 50 per cent figure for the Republic. As life expectancy was similar, or possibly even lower, in the north, the difference was due to lower emigration from Northern Ireland.

Figure 1.4 shows survival rates for the twentieth-century birth cohorts for the Republic.[6] This shows that the cohort born between 1916 and 1925 was rather different from subsequent cohorts. Because they came to adulthood in the 1930s and 1940s, at a time when emigration was much more difficult, 80 per cent of them were still living in Ireland twenty years after their birth. For those born in the period 1926–45 only 60 per cent were still living in Ireland twenty years later: they were affected by the very high emigration in the late 1940s and the 1950s. It is interesting that thirty years after they were born there was little difference in the survival rate for all three of these cohorts: a significant number of the 1916–25 cohort emigrated at an older age in the 1950s when labour market opportunities opened up in the UK.

For the cohort born between 1946 and 1955 the experience was very different from that of all previous cohorts: 80 per cent of them were still living in Ireland fifty years after their birth. The key difference in their experience was the fall-off in emigration in the late 1960s and early 1970s when they reached adulthood. For the 1966–75 cohort, many left in the emigration surge in the late 1980s but, by the time of the 2011 census, many had also returned (or been replaced by immigrants). In the case of the most recent cohort considered here, those born between 1976 and 1985, the number living in Ireland today is significantly greater than the number of those who were born there, reflecting very high rates of immigration in the 2000s.

6 The data for the north don't permit a similar analysis.

1.4.2. Life Expectancy

Rather than looking at death rates, which are affected by the age structure, a more useful measure is life expectancy at birth. Table 1.3 shows female and male life expectancy at birth for the Republic, Northern Ireland, and England and Wales from 1871. In 1871 both male and female life expectancy was significantly higher in Ireland than in England and Wales. This reflected the rural nature of the population in Ireland, with significantly higher death rates being experienced in urban areas throughout the British Isles.

If the life tables based on the 1871 life expectancy figures are applied to the population in 1851 and 1861, they reproduce almost exactly the recorded number of deaths in the relevant inter-censal periods. This suggests that there was little change in life expectancy between 1851 and 1871.

Male life expectancy in England, which had been lower than in Ireland in 1871, caught up with the Republic by 1926. Thereafter, it increased more rapidly than in the

Table 1.3. Life expectancy at birth (years)

	Male			Female		
	Ireland	England and Wales		Ireland	England and Wales	
1871	49.6	41.2		50.9	44.5	
1881	49.4	43.8		49.9	47.0	
1891	49.1	44.3		49.2	47.8	
1901	49.3	48.1		49.6	51.9	
1911	53.6	45.1		54.1	55.2	
	Republic		Northern Ireland	Republic		Northern Ireland
1926	57.4	57.3	55.3	57.9	61.3	55.7
1936	58.2	60.8	57.7	59.6	65.1	58.6
1941	59.0	58.2	58.7	61.0	66.3	60.0
1951	64.5	66.9	66.0	67.1	72.1	67.8
1961	68.1	68.2	67.8	71.9	74.2	70.2
1971	68.8	69.2	67.3	73.5	75.4	70.5
1981	70.1	71.3	69.6	75.6	77.2	72.8
1991	72.3	73.6	72.6	77.9	79.0	75.6
2001	75.1	76.2	75.5	80.3	80.7	78.0
2006	76.8	77.7	76.4	81.6	81.8	78.9

Republic up to 1951.[7] In the case of Northern Ireland, male life expectancy exceeded that in the Republic in 1951. From 1971 onwards male life expectancy in England has been generally one year greater than in either the North or the Republic.

Female life expectancy in England was below that in Ireland in the nineteenth century. However, with rising female life expectancy in England from the late nineteenth century, the English rate converged with the Irish rate in the early years of the twentieth century. By the mid-1920s the position had been reversed, with female life expectancy in England exceeding that in Ireland and continuing to rise much more rapidly. The data for Northern Ireland in 1926 show that female life expectancy there was even lower than in the Republic. For the rest of the twentieth century female life expectancy in Ireland lagged behind English levels. It was not until 2001 that female life expectancy in Ireland caught up with that in England, and life expectancy in the north today is still more than two years lower than in the Republic or England.

Table 1.4 shows infant mortality (deaths in the first year of life) since 1864 in the Republic, Northern Ireland, and England and Wales. The rate was consistently lower in

Table 1.4. Infant mortality (deaths per 1,000 births)

	Republic of Ireland		Northern Ireland		England and Wales
	Total	Non-marital	Total	Non-marital	Total
1864	98		99		153
1870	103		70		160
1880	112		115		153
1890	92		103		151
1900	105		118		154
1910	89		108		105
1920	78	344	94	188	80
1930	68	251	68	140	60
1940	66	246	86	167	56
1950	46	78	40	65	30
1960	29	71	27		22
1970	19		23		18
1980	11		13		12
1990	8		8		8
2000	6		5		6
2010	4		6		4

7 A more detailed comparison of life expectancy in the twentieth century in Ireland and Northern Ireland is available in M. Hall, 'Mortality in Ireland 1901 to 2006', *British Actuarial Journal*, 18, 2 (2013), 436–51.

Ireland than in England in the second half of the nineteenth century, reflecting much lower mortality rates in rural areas. There was little change in the rate of infant mortality up to 1900 in Ireland or England. However, from 1900 onwards a steady decline began in all jurisdictions. By 1920 the rate in England had fallen to the Irish rate. Thereafter it fell more rapidly, so that it was below that of the Republic until 1970. More recently it has been at a similar very low rate in all jurisdictions.

In the first *Commissioners' Report* published by Saorstát Éireann in 1923, a new section was introduced showing that infant mortality for non-marital children was exceptionally high. In the following year the Northern Ireland report published similar data. In the Republic in 1920 more than a third of such children died in their first year; in Northern Ireland the proportion was just under a fifth compared with 13 per cent in England.

While the *Commissioners' Reports* never expressed opinions over their 150 years of publication, the 1923 report exceptionally opined: 'These rates must be regarded as excessive.'[8] It went on to document the fact that the vast bulk of these deaths occurred in institutions across the country. The reports continued to give details on the infant mortality of non-marital children up to 1940 and, as shown in Table 1.4, it remained at an incredibly high level. It was not until the 1950s that the death rate had fallen substantially, approaching the rate for urban areas.

One of the most important contributors to the rise in female life expectancy over the past century has been the dramatic fall in maternal death rates. As shown in Table 1.5,

Table 1.5. Maternal death rates (per 100,000 births)

	Republic of Ireland	Northern Ireland	England and Wales	Scotland
1864	679	541		
1880	713	646		
1900	645	632	467	474
1920	548	787	403	636
1940	367	422	274	450
1951	164	109	84	109
1960	58	44	39	34
1970	31		18	19
1980	7	7	11	14
1990	4		1	6
2000	2		6	15
2011	3	16	6	8

8 Saorstát Éireann, *Annual Report of the Registrar General of Marriages, Births and Deaths* (1923), xxiii.

the maternal death rate was very high in Ireland in the second half of the nineteenth century, around 700 per 100,000 births. As mothers had, on average, five children, the probability of a mother dying in childbirth was greater than 3 per cent.

In the twentieth century the maternal death rate in England and Wales was well below that in Ireland. While the rate declined in both jurisdictions, the rate in England continued to be lower than in the Republic until 1980. Since then the rate has been very low throughout the islands, with the rate in Ireland today being marginally the lowest. In Northern Ireland there was a particularly rapid decline in the death rate between 1941 and 1951, coinciding with the introduction of the National Health Service. It remained lower there than in the Republic until 1980, by which stage it had reached the very low level common across Europe today.

1.4.3. Births and Fertility

Figure 1.5 shows the birth rate since 1864 for the Republic of Ireland, Northern Ireland, and England and Scotland. The birth rate in Ireland in the second half of the nineteenth century was much lower than in either Scotland or England. In the period 1911–26 the birth rate was at an all-time high in Ireland, approaching the rate in England and Scotland. However, since then the birth rate has declined across the British Isles – albeit the decline was much more gradual in Ireland.

An important feature of the Irish birth rate is that the vast bulk of children were born to married women. It is only since 1970 that there has been a dramatic increase, both north and south, in the proportion of births taking place outside marriage. The fact

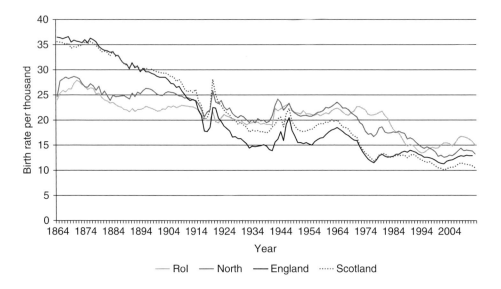

Figure 1.5 Birth rate, per thousand

that during most of the period since the famine nearly all births occurred to married women means, first, that the proportion of women marrying before the age of forty-five played an important role in determining how many children were born. Secondly, the age at which women married was also crucial in determining completed family size.

The different factors affecting fertility in the Republic are summarised in Table 1.6. Firstly, the proportion of women aged 35–44 ever married peaked in 1851 at around 85 per cent. For the following eighty-five years it fell continuously to reach a low of 70 per cent in 1936. From 1936 to 1981 it rose to reach a new peak of 89 per cent in 1981. Since that date it has again fallen, reflecting a changing approach to marriage.

Because most children were born to married women, the decline in the proportion of women marrying was a very important factor in the decline in fertility in the nineteenth century. However, the fall in the numbers marrying over the past thirty-five years has not affected fertility. Increasingly marriage has become a consequence of motherhood rather than its precursor; the factors affecting fertility today must be analysed in a different way.

The second important factor affecting completed family size is the age at which women married.[9] The data on this are less reliable than the census data on the proportion of women married. As discussed in Mokyr and Ó'Gráda, the average age at marriage of women had already begun to rise before the famine, reaching almost 25 in 1851. However, on the basis of the sample of data published in the *Commissioners' Reports*, the age at marriage ranged between 24 and 24.5 over the rest of the nineteenth century. Thereafter it began to rise, reaching a peak of 28 in the late 1940s, falling again to 25 in 1971. Today it has risen to an exceptional level of 32.5. However, from 1970 onwards marriage has become increasingly divorced from decisions on fertility.

Table 1.6 shows the marital and non-marital birth rates.[10] The marital birth rate rose from around 0.25 per woman per year in 1841 to 0.31 in 1871, remaining at a high level to 1911. Thereafter there was a slow decline until 1961 and a very rapid decline thereafter. On the basis of this birth rate, the average number of children that a married woman would have is a function of the age at marriage. The number of births per woman, calculated in this way, rose from 5.2 in 1841 to a peak of 6.5 in 1871, largely because of the rise in marital fertility. Thereafter it fell slowly to 1961, and precipitously thereafter.

A crude measure of fertility is shown in Table 1.6 as the 'potential number of children'. This is derived by taking the average number of births to women aged between 20 and 45 and multiplying it by 25 – an estimate of the reproductive years for that female population. As shown in the table, it was 3.7 in 1841. However, by 1851 it had fallen to 3.2, possibly as a consequence of the effects of the famine. It peaked in 1871 at 4.2, the same rate as in 1961.

9 For the period to 1911 the age at marriage is for the island as a whole. Figures for Northern Ireland are not available.

10 Births are divided by the number of married and unmarried women aged 20–45.

Table 1.6. Republic of Ireland – fertility behaviour

	Women ever married 35–44 years old (%)	Birth rate		Average age at marriage	Married women average children	Births/women	Potential no. of children	Total fertility rate
		Marital	Non-marital					
1831				23.8				
1841	82.8	0.251	0.008	24.4	5.18	0.150	3.7	
1851	84.8	0.251	0.008	24.9	5.04	0.127	3.2	
1861	81.5	0.251	0.008	24.1	5.23	0.133	3.3	
1871	80.2	0.314	0.005	24.2	6.53	0.169	4.2	
1881	80.8	0.285	0.005	24.5	5.85	0.145	3.6	
1891	77.2	0.294	0.005	24.5	6.03	0.137	3.4	
1901	75.7	0.292	0.004	25.1	5.81	0.124	3.1	
1911	71.8	0.307	0.005	25.9	5.85	0.133	3.3	
1926	70.5	0.272	0.006	26.0	5.17	0.126	3.1	
1936	69.8	0.260	0.007			0.119	3.0	
1946	70.0	0.272	0.010	28.0	4.62	0.138	3.4	
1961	77.3	0.273	0.016	26.9	4.95	0.170	4.2	3.8
1971	82.5	0.140	0.089	25.0	2.79	0.122	3.1	4.0
1981	88.6	0.116	0.128	25.3	2.29	0.120	3.0	3.1
1991	88.5	0.113	0.096	26.9	2.04	0.107	2.7	2.1
2002	83.1	0.119	0.059	29.5	1.85	0.090	2.2	2.0
2011	72.9	0.121	0.041	32.5	1.51	0.074	1.9	2.0

Possibly the best summary measure of fertility is the total fertility rate (TFR) shown in Table 1.6. It shows the number of children that a woman would have if she experienced the then current age-specific fertility rates over her reproductive years. (As can be seen from the table, the alternative 'potential number of children' tracks the TFR over the period from 1961.) However, the TFR is only available from the late 1950s. Between 1961 and 1971 the TFR suggested a completed family size of between 3.8 and 4 children. After that it fell rapidly over the twenty years to 1991, when it reached 2.1. In England and Wales the TFR fell from 2.8 in 1961 to 1.9 in 2011, slightly lower than the Irish rate, but still significantly higher than for most of the rest of the European Union (EU).

Table 1.7 shows the same data for Northern Ireland. In each case the age at marriage up to 1926 is, perforce, that for the island as a whole. In the case of Northern Ireland the marital birth rate between 1841 and 1861 was much higher than in the Republic.[11] However, it began to fall in 1911 and it fell much more rapidly than in the Republic over the rest of the twentieth century. Throughout most of the period, the non-marital birth rate, while low, was higher than in the Republic.

As shown in Table 1.7, the 'potential number of children' per woman in Northern Ireland was much higher than in the Republic in 1841. It remained higher in 1851, probably reflecting a less severe impact from the famine. As in the Republic, the measure peaked in 1871, in this case at 3.9. Thereafter, as in the Republic, it fell steadily. However, from 1926 onwards fertility fell more rapidly in Northern Ireland than in the Republic. It is only since the beginning of the twenty-first century that the TFR has converged for the two parts of the island.

1.5. Emigration

In the second half of the nineteenth century the rate of emigration from Ireland, as a proportion of the population, was more than double that of any other European country.[12] In Table 1.8 the data for emigration are shown from two sources. The first, referred to as 'census', is derived residually from the change in the population between censuses, allowing for births and deaths. This estimate includes emigration to Britain. The 'Vital Statistics' measure is that published in the *Commissioners' Reports* (and in the CSO Vital Statistics). Up to the 1920s this series excludes emigration to Britain.

Given the fact that this latter measure excludes emigration to Britain, the two estimates are surprisingly close for the nineteenth century: one would have expected the census-based estimate to have been significantly higher than the Vital Statistics measure.

11 This may also have reflected an earlier age at marriage.
12 T. Hatton and J. Williamson, 'After the famine: emigration from Ireland, 1850–1913', *Journal of Economic History*, 53, 3 (1993), 575–600.

Table 1.7. Northern Ireland – fertility behaviour

Year	Women ever married 35–44 years old (%)	Birth rate		Average age at marriage	Married women average children	Births/women	Potential no. of children	Total fertility rate
		Marital	Non-marital					
1831				23.82				
1841	68.1	0.298	0.014	24.4	6.2	0.174	4.4	
1851	79.1	0.298	0.014	24.9	6.0	0.153	3.8	
1861	63.9	0.298	0.014	24.1	6.2	0.132	3.3	
1871	61.7	0.293	0.020	24.2	6.1	0.154	3.9	
1881	60.0	0.292	0.012	24.5	6.0	0.137	3.4	
1891	56.4	0.301	0.011	24.5	6.2	0.134	3.4	
1901	52.4	0.285	0.008	25.1	5.7	0.125	3.1	
1911	56.3	0.268	0.010	25.9	5.1	0.128	3.2	
1926	65.7	0.232	0.011	26.0	4.4	0.121	3.0	
1936	65.4	0.200	0.010			0.108	2.7	
1951	74.7	0.194	0.008			0.120	3.0	
1961	80.0	0.161	0.019			0.117	2.9	
1971	87.0	0.103	0.107			0.104	2.6	
1981	89.9	0.078	0.158			0.097	2.4	2.6
1991	86.6	0.079	0.091			0.083	2.1	2.2
2002	77.7	0.098	0.057			0.077	1.9	1.8
2011	65.0	0.123	0.044			0.074	1.8	2.0

Table 1.8. Net emigration (thousands)

	Ireland		Republic of Ireland		Northern Ireland	
	Census	Vital Stats	Census	Vital Stats	Census	Vital Stats
1831–41						
1841–51		1,235				
1851–61	1,328	1,226				
1861–71	1,209	772	946	584	253	
1871–81	688	621	523	380	165	
1881–91	733	771	593	553	139	
1891–01	452	434	386	347	66	
1901–11	329	346	259	240	70	
1911–26	498	276	398	187	100	
1926–36	225		169	177	56	35
1936–46	225		186	187	39	
1946–51	160		129	112	31	
1951–61	494		405	400	89	
1961–71	186		129	170	57	38
1971–81	0		−108	−100	108	111
1981–91	259		210	202	49	47
1991–01	−115		−122	−86	7	3
2001–11	−386		−349	−407	−37	−38

Over the twenty years from 1850 to 1870, emigration amounted to more than 2.5 million. While it slowed in the following twenty years from 1870 to 1890 to 1.4 million, this was still much greater than the natural increase in the population. The emigration rate was much higher for the Republic than for Northern Ireland, reflecting the much greater success of the latter's economy, centred on Belfast.

For the 1911–26 period the emigration implied by the census is substantially greater than the *Commissioners' Reports* would imply, suggesting major emigration to Great Britain from both parts of Ireland. As the *Commissioners' Reports* suggest very low emigration during the First World War, this would indicate substantial emigration to Britain immediately before and after independence.

The 1926–46 period saw a fall-off in emigration from the Republic, reflecting the closure of the US labour market, depressed conditions in Britain during the 1930s and the Second World War. For Northern Ireland, its lower level of emigration through to the late 1960s reflected a superior economic performance.

The 1970s saw exceptional emigration from Northern Ireland, counterbalanced by net immigration into the Republic of equal magnitude. This was the first recorded period of sustained immigration in the Republic. It reflected better economic performance on entry to the European Economic Community (EEC) and the relocation from the north of substantial numbers of people, as a result of the disturbances. For the first time the immigration into the Republic also included a significant return flow of emigrants from earlier decades. Fahey et al.[13] show that by 1991 between 25 and 35 per cent of third-level graduates in Ireland were returned emigrants.

There was significant emigration from the Republic in the second half of the 1980s. However, with rapid economic growth in the 1990s many of these emigrants returned. As the growth continued throughout the decade there was also a major influx of well-educated foreign immigrants. EU enlargement in 2004 saw an even bigger influx of immigrants from the new member states over the period to 2007. Once again, the collapse in the economy in 2008 saw a reversal of the inflow.

Over the past two centuries the fluctuations in emigration have reflected changes in relative economic conditions in Ireland and in foreign labour markets. However, the oscillations in economic growth in recent decades have been the greatest since the mid-nineteenth century and, as a consequence, the fluctuations in migration have also been very large.

FURTHER READING

Connell, K. H. *The population of Ireland, 1750–1845* (Oxford, 1950).

Daly, M. E. *The slow failure, population decline and independent Ireland, 1920–1973* (Madison, 2006).

Delaney, E. *Demography, state and society: Irish migration to Britain, 1921–1971* (Montreal, Kingston, Ont. and Liverpool, 2000).

Lee, J. 'On the accuracy of pre-famine censuses', in M. Goldstrom and L. Clarkson, *Irish population, economy and society: essays in memory of K. H. Connell* (Oxford, 1981), 37–56.

McAfee, W. 'The pre-famine population of Ireland: a reconsideration', in B. Collins and P. Ollerenshaw (eds.), *Industry, trade and people in Ireland, 1650–1950* (Belfast, 2005).

Mokyr, J. *Why Ireland starved* (London, 1983).

Mokyr, J. and C. Ó Gráda. 'New developments in Irish population history, 1700–1850', *Economic History Review*, 37, 4 (1984), 473–88.

Ó'Gráda, C. *Ireland: a new economic history 1780–1939* (Oxford, 1994).

13 T. Fahey, J. FitzGerald and B. Maitre, 'The economic and social implications of demographic change', *Journal of the Statistical and Social Inquiry Society of Ireland*, 27 (1997/8), 185–222.

2

Occupation, Poverty and Social Class in pre-Famine Ireland, 1740–1850

Peter M. Solar

In Ireland, before the Great Famine, most people lived in the countryside and worked in agriculture. The conquest and land transfers of the sixteenth and seventeenth centuries had created a simulacrum of English rural society. As in England, the land was owned by an elite of several thousand proprietors who kept some of their property in gardens, parks and forests, but cultivated little of it. They rented most of the land, especially the good land, in holdings of viable size to a larger class of tenant farmers. These farmers cultivated the land with the help of a much larger class of labourers. Where rural society in pre-famine Ireland differed markedly from that in England was in the situation of these labourers, who grew their own food rather than working for wages. Their growing numbers in the late eighteenth and early nineteenth century, aggravated by Ireland's peculiar status within what became the United Kingdom, made for an increasingly precarious and impoverished existence for the bulk of the Irish population.

This characterisation of pre-famine rural society needs to be qualified to take account of the impact of rural manufacturing activity in the north of the country. During the eighteenth century that part of Ireland north of a line between Drogheda and Westport became one of Europe's major producers of linen textiles. Rural industry was most heavily concentrated in eastern Ulster, but its tentacles increasingly reached westward and southward. The result was a society where, compared with the south, farm sizes were smaller and non-agricultural income more important to both farmers and labourers. This area was prosperous for much of the eighteenth century, but rural linen producers suffered in the early nineteenth century when competition from the British cotton industry limited the demand for their product and when flax spinning was mechanised and became increasingly concentrated in Belfast.

In 1700 Ireland was among the least urbanised countries in western Europe and it fell further behind during the next century and a half. Measures of the degree of urbanisation are somewhat arbitrary, but cut-offs of 5,000 and 10,000 inhabitants are quite common. Moreover, population estimates for some Irish towns in the eighteenth century remain uncertain. Based on the existing figures, Ireland at the start of the eighteenth century had a similar share of its population living in such cities as did eastern and northern Europe, represented here by Germany and Sweden (Table 2.1). But it was well behind highly urbanised areas such as the Low Countries and southern Europe, represented here by Italy. In 1700 Ireland was less urbanised than Great Britain, though the difference is not particularly striking. However, Ireland did not participate in the UK's singularly rapid urbanisation during the Industrial Revolution, except by supplying migrants to Britain's growing cities.

Table 2.1. European urbanisation, 1700–1850 (share of total population)

	Cities >5,000		Cities >10,000	
	1700	1850	1700	1850
Ireland	8	8	6	8
Great Britain	14	37	11	36
France	10	16	9	13
Netherlands	35	30	31	28
Belgium	26	25	23	20
Italy	22	25	16	20
Germany	7	11	5	9
Sweden	3	7	3	5

SOURCES: City populations: Centre for Global Economic History Urbanisation Hub (www.cgeh.nl); total populations: Clio Infra (www.clio-infra.eu).
NOTE: The Irish population figures have been adjusted to be in line with the estimates in D. Dickson, C. Ó Gráda and S. Daultrey, 'Hearth tax, household size and Irish population change 1672–1821', *Proceedings of the Royal Irish Academy*, Section C, 82C (1982), and the 1841 total has been substituted for that in 1851.

More than 90 per cent of Ireland's pre-famine population thus remained in the countryside. Since the larger cities were located on the coast, much of the interior had little in the way of towns, even towns of fewer than 5,000 inhabitants. In County Carlow, in the relatively prosperous south-east, only 17 per cent of the population in 1841 lived in settlements of a thousand persons or more. In County Leitrim, in the poorer north-west, the share was only 3 per cent. County Armagh, at the heart of the east Ulster linen industry, lay in between, with 11 per cent. By contrast, the English counties of Wiltshire and Derbyshire, both with relatively low rates of urbanisation, had 22 and 27 per cent of their populations living in such towns of more than a thousand inhabitants.

In the countryside most Irishmen worked in agriculture. In 1841 the share of those over age fifteen with agricultural occupations was 72 per cent in Carlow and 85 per cent in Leitrim. Even in Armagh 60 per cent of males were recorded as working in agriculture, though some of them may have also been weaving linen cloth. In that county 23 per cent had primary occupations in textile manufacturing, but in Carlow and Leitrim the textile shares were less than 3 per cent. Agricultural occupations were much less dominant in England. In Wiltshire only 48 per cent of males over age twenty had agricultural occupations and in Derbyshire only 24 per cent.

Outside agriculture and textile manufacturing males in rural Ireland were occupied quite diversely. Shoemakers, tailors, carpenters and blacksmiths, together with many lesser trades, accounted for 7–12 per cent of all those employed. Male domestic servants accounted for another few per cent, as did merchants and dealers of all sorts. Professionals, mostly schoolteachers and clergymen, amounted to about 1 per cent.

Although almost all adult males declared or were assigned occupations in the census, far fewer women were recorded as having occupations and this varied considerably across counties. It thus makes more sense to calculate the share of the total adult female population in various occupations. In 1841, 31 per cent of all females over age fifteen had textile occupations in County Armagh. The share was even higher, at 41 per cent, in Leitrim, but far lower, at 7 per cent, in Carlow. In Armagh and Leitrim another 6 per cent of women were domestic servants and 2 per cent had agricultural occupations, some of whom were farmers but most were labourers. In Carlow the share of domestic servants was 11 per cent and that in agricultural occupations almost 12 per cent. Many of the larger numbers employed in agriculture may have been involved in dairying, a speciality of the south-east.

In such a predominantly agricultural society land was a key asset, so the ownership of land and access to it were central concerns. The confiscations and transfers of the sixteenth and seventeenth centuries had left the ownership of land concentrated in the hands of a largely Protestant elite. Large chunks of land were in corporate hands. The London livery companies owned most of County Londonderry. Trinity College Dublin and its Provost had estates scattered around the island, amounting to more than 200,000 acres. The Ecclesiastical Commissioners and the Incorporated School Society had dispersed holdings on a smaller scale. But most Irish land was in the hands of a relatively small number of aristocrats and gentry. In both counties Armagh and Carlow just ten proprietors owned about a third of the county; in County Leitrim the share of the top ten reached 40 per cent. In these counties less than 5 per cent of the land was owned by those who occupied it, and most of these holdings were relatively large.[1] So there were almost no peasants in pre-famine Ireland, at least in the sense that they owned the small farms that they operated.

1 These figures are from Griffith's Valuation, which was carried out between 1848 and 1864, but pre-famine concentration should not be significantly different.

Sometimes the owners had effectively alienated control of their property, creating a sub-stratum of quasi-proprietors. In the late seventeenth century and early eighteenth century some landowners, probably in order to raise large sums of capital, granted leases in perpetuity, for 999 years and for three lives renewable. Other owners, including Trinity College Dublin, found it convenient to devolve the management of their lands to intermediate tenants. Such practices created lessees who were effectively proprietors and who then sublet the property, often for long terms, to working farmers. Such middlemen were often, perhaps unfairly, stigmatised by contemporary commentators, but some were part of what Kevin Whelan has described as 'an underground Catholic gentry'.[2]

Although some large estates had home farms to supply the needs of the Big House, the cultivation of almost all Irish land was managed by tenant farmers. From the seventeenth century the relationship between landlord and tenant had become increasingly governed by the written lease. In the eighteenth century the most common terms were three lives, if the tenant was Protestant, and twenty-one or thirty-one years, if the tenant was Catholic. In the early nineteenth century three-life leases were still being given, but terms of one life, or one life or twenty-one years, were becoming more common. These terms were quite long: a three-life lease could sometimes run for more than fifty years; a one-life lease for more than thirty. At least in terms of lease length, insecurity of tenure, a common complaint in post-famine Ireland, was not a problem for farmers in the pre-famine period.

Tenure was also secure because these long leases were generally renewed to sitting tenants. In the north the right to renewal was a feature of what became known as 'Ulster custom', but it was the norm in the south of Ireland as well. Continuity of tenure was often in the landlord's interest. Even where it wasn't, changes in tenancy, if regarded as unfair, could be the cause of rural unrest. Both landlords and incoming tenants could face violence or the threat of violence.

Seventeenth- and early eighteenth-century leases often required tenant farmers to consolidate land into regularly shaped parcels and to enclose these parcels with walls and hedges. This reorganisation was largely carried out privately, by contrast with England, where legislation was often required. The reclamation of land in uplands and bogs under the pressure of population growth during the eighteenth and early nineteenth century created a more chaotic structure of holdings in these areas.

The result of this leasing system in the south of Ireland was a landscape in which most of the good agricultural land was organised and maintained in reasonably good-sized holdings. The statistics of farm size before the famine are uncertain, but the share of land in the south of Ireland on holdings of more than 20 acres must have been in

2 K. Whelan, 'An underground gentry? Catholic middlemen in eighteenth-century Ireland', in J. S. Donnelly and K. A. Miller (eds.), *Irish popular culture, 1650–1850* (Dublin, 1998), 118–72.

excess of two-thirds. Such farms were generally far smaller than those of hundreds of acres to be found in southern England and the Parisian basin, but they were comparable to holdings in north-west England and were generally larger than those in the Low Countries and in many parts of France.

Although there was some specialised grazing in the Irish midlands, most farmers in pre-famine Ireland practised mixed farming. Land was rotated through several tillage crops, then laid down to grass for several years. This period of pasture renewed the soil and provided grazing for cattle and sheep. Cattle were kept in the south-east and south-west primarily for dairying, with calves and young cattle sold off to the midlands where they were reared and fattened for sale in urban markets. Until the 1820s much of the beef produced was salted and barrelled for export. The introduction of steamships created a trade in fat livestock across the Irish Sea to the industrial cities of Britain. From the late eighteenth century Irish farmers also increasingly exported wheat, oats and barley to the British market.

On holdings where tillage exceeded a few acres, the labour of the farmer and his family was usually insufficient, so external labour was needed. The way in which this labour was hired may have been unique to pre-famine Ireland. Instead of paying wages, either in cash or in kind, the farmer gave over part of his potato field for the labourer to cultivate. Its produce was typically enough to feed a family and to raise a pig or two. In return for this short-term access to land – the potato field changed each year – the labourer helped cultivate and harvest the farmer's cereal crops. In this system little or no money changed hands, though farmers sometimes helped labourers finance the purchase of other goods.

At harvest time additional workers were sometimes needed. Here farmers relied on another source of labour. During the eighteenth and early nineteenth century uplands and bogs were becoming increasingly populated. Hard work was needed to bring these lands into cultivation as well as to sustain their productivity thereafter. In places such as the Aran Islands the soil was essentially created using seaweed and other materials. On mountainsides the remnants of terraced cultivation can still be seen. In such areas smallholdings prevailed and life was precarious. Additional sources of income were welcome. One of these was harvest labour, initially in the lowland parts of Ireland, then increasingly in Britain. On the eve of the famine up to a hundred thousand Irish men, and sometimes women, spent several months each summer following the harvest in England from south to north.[3]

Rural society in the south of Ireland was thus tripartite: landlords, tenant farmers, labourers. In a county such as Carlow the number of significant proprietors – those with a few hundred acres or more – numbered perhaps a hundred or so. As for farmers,

3 C. Ó Gráda, 'Demographic adjustment and seasonal migration in nineteeth-century Ireland', in L. M. Cullen and F. Furet (eds.), *Ireland and France, 17th–20th centuries* (Paris, 1980), 181–91.

the census of 1841 enumerated 4,682 adults, which corresponds quite closely to the number of holdings of more than about 10 acres, a size in the pre-famine period that probably called for non-family labour, depending on family size and the mix of pasture and tillage. Farmers with large holdings – say, more than 60 acres – amounted to fewer than a thousand. Tenants with holdings of a few hundred acres, who might have been as well off as some of the lesser proprietors, numbered fewer than a hundred. Labourers were far more numerous: in 1841 they numbered more than 15,000 in County Carlow. Some of these labourers would have been sons and daughters of tenant farmers. Although after the famine agricultural labourers came to be primarily family members, before the famine this family labour was probably in the minority.[4]

The situation in the north of Ireland was different from that in the south in several respects. Despite the quality of agricultural land in the north being generally inferior, population density was much higher. In 1841 there were almost twice as many persons per acre in County Armagh as there were in County Carlow. Differences in population density traced a particularly distinct frontier between the north and the rich grazing areas of the eastern midlands. Northern parts of County Meath had densities of 250 persons per acre and more; southern parts, 100 and less.

In the north there were also far more farmers relative to labourers. Whilst there were three times as many male labourers as farmers in County Carlow, there were only half again as many in counties Armagh and Leitrim. A far larger share of these would thus have been family members. There were more farmers because there were far more small farms. Roughly three-fifths of the land in Armagh and Leitrim was held in parcels of smaller than 30 acres, and holdings of 5–10 acres were quite common.

Small farms went hand-in-hand with domestic textile manufacturing. The ability of households to generate income from spinning and weaving allowed them to make the common desire for secure access to land a reality. They could pay higher rents than those who only wanted to farm the land, especially when, as in much of the north, it was poorly suited to agriculture. Landlords recognised the contribution of domestic industry to their rent rolls and encouraged the development of scutching mills and bleach greens in the countryside and of markets in nearby towns.

In addition, the linen industry relied primarily on flax grown in Ireland and both the cultivation of flax and its preparation prior to spinning were highly labour-intensive activities well suited to small farms. This did not necessarily mean that flax was cultivated, spun and woven in the same household. In fact, there was considerable local and intra-regional trade in both flax and yarn. As the linen industry grew during the eighteenth century, spinning and, to a lesser extent, weaving spread from its heartland in east Ulster into south-west Ulster, north Leinster and north Connacht. By 1800

---

4 D. Fitzpatrick, 'The disappearance of the Irish agricultural labourer, 1841–1913', *Irish Economic and Social History*, 7 (1980), 66–92.

weavers in counties Armagh and Down could draw on supplies of yarn from as far away as County Mayo.

The linen industry was a great source of prosperity in the northern countryside during the eighteenth century. Weavers could aspire to a small farm held by lease directly from the landlord. They and their families lived in decent, though still modest, housing and had a diet that was richer and more varied than that of rural labourers in the south. On their small farms they could grow potatoes and oats and keep a cow and some pigs and poultry. Some of the produce was sold locally, but much was consumed on the farm. The linen industry did have its ups and downs, and in periods of depressed trade some weavers emigrated, often to America. But overseas travel in the eighteenth century was expensive and the predominance of Ulstermen in early Irish emigration to North America should be seen as a consequence both of relative prosperity and of widespread landholding since the sale of tenant right could finance the passage.

The heyday of the Irish rural textile industry was probably reached sometime in the first decade of the nineteenth century. From the 1780s linen cloth was increasingly being supplanted in many uses by cotton cloth. The early mechanisation of cotton spinning and the advent of much cheaper raw cotton from the United States put downward pressure on yarn and cloth prices. This had diverse effects on Ireland. One was to eliminate exports of linen yarn to Britain, where it was used to make mixed cotton and linen fabrics. More generally, competition among fibres affected the returns to linen production. In the 1790s and 1800s this led some weavers in County Down to shift over to cotton cloth production. This was a short-lived respite, which ended as cotton weaving was mechanised in Britain from the 1810s.

Competition from cottons continued to depress the earnings of flax spinners and linen weavers during the early nineteenth century. Flax spinners in the countryside were further hurt when from 1825 it became possible to produce fine linen yarn by machine. Production of yarn became concentrated in factories, most of which were located in and around Belfast. But the 1841 census still recorded half a million female spinners, of which only 10,000 or so were employed in factories. Mechanisation had not entirely driven out hand-spinning, though it would largely do so during the following decade. Power-loom weaving of medium to fine quality linen cloth did not become feasible before the 1850s, so hand-loom weaving persisted in the countryside. But it was far from dynamic. Although trade in linen cloth from Ireland was given a modest boost by the spread of mechanical spinning, over the long term it grew very little. From the 1790s to the early 1830s exports remained at around 40 million yards; in the late 1830s and early 1840s they rose to around 55 million. Production of linen cloth in Ireland is likely to have grown even more slowly than exports, and may even have declined, as Irish consumers began to use imported cottons instead of domestically produced linens.

The troubles of the linen industry meant that inhabitants of the northern countryside were certainly becoming worse off during the early nineteenth century. This was the view of the local worthies who supplied information to the Irish Poor Inquiry in the early 1830s. It also shows up in the striking growth in agricultural trade from northern ports after the French wars. Oats, butter and pork, previously consumed in northern households, were increasingly exported to the British market. In the late 1810s and 1820s emigrants from Ireland still came disproportionately from the north. But, again, emigration was a sign of relative prosperity. In terms of housing and diet, east Ulster, at least, still showed up better than much of the south on the eve of the famine.

The rural south matched neither the boom in the north during the eighteenth century nor its bust during the early nineteenth century. But in both parts of the country the trends in agriculture were similar. Since there are no good series for agricultural output, inferences need to be drawn from prices, wages and rents. In the late 1770s Arthur Young recorded agricultural wages at many places in Ireland; in the early 1830s witnesses to the Irish Poor Inquiry supplied comparable information for many more places. Together these sources suggest that nominal agricultural wages rose by 30–50 per cent over this half-century or so, and other sources suggest that nominal wages remained stable until the famine. During the same period agricultural prices rose by 50–80 per cent, with the size of the increase depending on how much weight is given to potato prices. These figures, imprecise as they are, suggest that, measured against the prices of what they produced (and what they consumed for the most part), labourers may have barely kept up but probably fell behind. This is not very surprising, given large increase in rural population over this period. It might even be suspicious that wages did not fall more relative to prices. But the interpretation of real wage movements is difficult in a world where for most transactions the wage was more a unit of account than a unit of payment. Very little information survives concerning how much short-term access to land labourers received in exchange for their labour, and almost none that would help trace changes over the long run.

What is more surprising is that land rents may also not have kept up with agricultural prices during the late eighteenth and early nineteenth century.[5] In measuring land rents it is important to distinguish between the current value of the land, what it would bring if it could be rented anew, and the rent actually due to the landlord. The latter depended on when the land had been let; with the long leases prevalent in pre-famine Ireland this could have been decades earlier. Samples of rents at new letting on estates in various

5 This discussion of the trends in rent per acre is based on large samples from estate records in six regions of Ireland. The first results, which prefigure the others, can be found in P. M. Solar and L. Hens, 'Land under pressure: the value of Irish land in a period of rapid population growth, 1730–1844', *Agricultural History Review*, 61 (2013), 40–61.

parts of the country show that nominal rents increased by only 40–60 per cent. With price increases of 50–80 per cent, real rents at new lettings may well have been falling.

At first glance the observation that agricultural prices may have risen more rapidly than both wages and rents would suggest that agricultural productivity was falling from the late eighteenth century. The returns from the sale of agricultural produce became the incomes of landlords and labourers. If over time the prices of the inputs rose less rapidly than the price of the output, then there must have been less to sell relative to land and labour used to produce it. However, there is a missing element here, which is the return to the labour, skills and capital of the tenant farmer. For agricultural productivity to have been maintained, the return to farmers would have had to have risen faster than prices, indeed considerably faster. Although substantial farmers were a relatively prosperous class in pre-famine Ireland, little is known about the trends in their incomes. Few farm accounts complete enough to calculate income survive and none over long periods. Studies of the trends in the building of farm houses or in emigration by farmers might someday cast light on what was happening to this largely hidden class.

The conclusion that agricultural productivity in Ireland was indeed falling during the late eighteenth and early nineteenth century does become more plausible in light of what happened during the famine. The disappearance of almost a third of the rural labour force between the early 1840s and the late 1850s led to a much less pronounced decline in agricultural output. Since there are no signs of major technological changes over this period, the implied productivity growth could be seen as an unwinding of a pre-famine decline.

These trends conceal important shifts in the distribution of agricultural income during and after the French wars. Both real wages and real rents fell from the 1780s to the early 1810s, with the result that this may have been the heyday of tenant farmers. But the impact of these changes could vary greatly. A landlord with many leases up for renewal during the wars could see large increases in his nominal income; one without could see little change at all, with a correspondingly large fall in his real income. The post-war deflation reversed the process, as real wages and real rents rose until the early 1830s. Unless landlords had let large quantities of land at the high wartime rents, which usually led to abatements or reletting in the late 1810s and early 1820s, their nominal rentals continued to rise as old leases fell in and deflation brought a significant shift in the distribution of the returns to agriculture from farmers back to landlords.

If agricultural productivity in Ireland was falling before the famine, this has two important implications. The first, and most obvious, is that per capita income in the rural economy was falling, a fall only reinforced in the north after 1800 by falling returns from linen production. The second is that somewhere in agriculture agents were passing up the opportunity for higher incomes. Resources were being used less efficiently: the question is how and why.

A start can be made by looking at the state of agricultural labourers. Evidence from the Poor Inquiry and from contemporary observers shows that labourers had only rudimentary housing and few household goods. Their clothing was often second-hand. Most of their resources went towards securing enough to eat. They cultivated potatoes either on farmers' fields or on smallholdings on marginal lands. Although some of these potatoes were fed to pigs and poultry, these animals were rarely eaten, being sold to pay the rent on smallholdings or to finance modest purchases of salt, buttermilk and other consumer goods. The bulk of the potato crop was eaten in the household. Only in Ulster did cereals figure prominently as a supplement to potatoes.

The predominance of the potato in the diet and in the household budget of Irish rural labourers had no counterpart elsewhere in Europe. Potatoes were certainly grown in other countries, and in some regions, such as Flanders, the Netherlands and Silesia, they formed an important element in the diet. But they were rarely the sole staple. This can be seen by comparing the shares of the arable land devoted to potato cultivation in the early 1840s. In Belgium, Prussia, Austria and the Netherlands potato cultivation occupied 10–14 per cent of the arable; in France it was only 6 per cent. But in Ireland the share was more than 30 per cent. Since grain imports were largely non-existent before the famine and large shares of the Irish wheat and oats crops were exported to Britain, the share of the potato in consumption was even higher.

Why did the Irish depend so heavily on the potato? One reason may be that Ireland's wet and cool climate was more favourable to potatoes than to cereal crops, especially wheat. Another reason may be the early commercialisation of Irish agriculture and the openness of the Irish to dietary innovation. The most common explanation is that Irish labourers had become simply much poorer than those elsewhere, as the consequence of rapid population growth. But there is another factor that has been overlooked and that arises from Ireland's peculiar relationship with Britain. From the late eighteenth century Ireland's rural economy had become increasingly oriented to British markets and with the creation of the United Kingdom it became part of a common tariff regime. The system of agricultural protection, of which the Corn Laws were a major, though not the only element, gave Irish farmers privileged access to the British market. But it also meant that agricultural prices were much higher than on the continent. Bread, the staple of continental labourers, was relatively expensive in Britain and Ireland. Although the wages of an agricultural labourer in Flanders could buy roughly the same quantity of potatoes as those of an Irish agricultural labourer, the Flemish labourer could buy almost twice as much bread.

The potato diet did prove to be nutritious and reasonably reliable. The Irish were relatively tall, a sign of good nutrition. But for all the merits of the potato, Irish agricultural labourers were probably living at close to a subsistence wage. This may be a reason why wages did not fall more relative to prices. The question then arises: how was the growing rural population absorbed at this subsistence wage? One answer is that during the last decade or two before the famine many were not. As passenger fares fell, emigration became possible for those further down the social scale and larger and larger numbers left for Britain and America. Others sought sources of income outside Ireland. The growth in harvest migration to Britain allowed many smallholders from the west of Ireland to stay on the land.

One important way in which the growing population was accommodated in Ireland was through the reclamation of marginal lands. During the eighteenth century landlords tended to overlook such initiatives, though in the early nineteenth century some tried to bring some order to these parts of their estates. In policy circles reclamation was seen as a way of dealing with surplus population and was even encouraged, notably by road construction in the west. Whether intensive potato cultivation was the best use of these lands is an open question. The importance of harvest migration, begging and other sources of non-agricultural income suggests that farming on its own could not pay the rent. Many of these areas were used for rough grazing after the famine.

The other main way in which rising numbers were absorbed in Ireland was through farmers undertaking more tillage. This required more labour than grazing or dairying and, given the usual crop rotation, more land under potatoes to be parcelled out to labourers. Irish exports of wheat and oats grew rapidly during the early nineteenth century. But it is not clear that growing more cereals in a period during which price trends were persistently in favour of beef and butter was the most productive use of the land.

This account suggests that Irish landlords and farmers may have been forgoing income in two ways. They lost because land was not being allocated to its most productive uses. This loss vanished into the air, showing up as the fall in productivity. They may also have lost because they were providing land to labourers and smallholders at less than their contribution to production.

Why did landlords and farmers accept these losses? The easy answer is that they feared the wrath of the labouring poor. When cereal prices were low, for example, in the early 1830s, and some farmers tried to shift from tillage towards pasture, outbreaks of agrarian unrest were not unusual. Yet agrarian unrest was sporadic and often regionally specific. Whilst it may have heightened class differences between farmers and labourers, there are few indications that farmers lived in a constant state of fear. On the contrary, there is considerable testimony to their generosity and hospitality. It seems more plausible to think that farmers would have been accommodating when faced with other members of their community whose subsistence depended on obtaining land on which to grow potatoes.

The solidarity of landlords is less easy to explain. The prevalence of long leases meant that they rarely had effective control of their property. They, too, may have preferred a quiet life, since replacing sitting tenants was another incitement to agrarian unrest. In the early nineteenth century some landlords did realise that clearing their estates of surplus population might be a profitable investment. Although large-scale evictions were rare before the famine, schemes of subsidised emigration became more common. The incentives to get people off the land were heightened by the imposition of a poor law on Ireland in the 1830s. But subsidised emigration remained relatively rare, as it was an expensive investment, open only to those with the capital, initiative and organisational capacity to undertake it.

The vulnerable groups in Irish rural society – widows and orphans, the sick and the old – depended on the widespread availability of land on which to grow potatoes. Evidence to the Poor Inquiry shows that there were few institutions in rural Ireland dedicated to their support. Some received doles from church collections and from farmers, but they relied primarily on family and friends, who themselves needed access to land.

On a western European scale pre-famine Ireland was notable for its quite limited development of institutions for the relief of the poor during the early modern period. In most other countries from the sixteenth century onward localities were responsible for their poor and took care of them, more or less generously, through local collection of funds. Such solidarity had its limits and these were often delineated by laws and customs defining who belonged to the local community and was thus eligible for support. The most highly organised system of poor relief, at the other extreme from Ireland, was to be found just across the Irish Sea. Under the pre-1834 poor law England had a national and relatively generous system of relief that was locally administered and locally financed through the collection of a tax on property.

Pre-famine Ireland, by contrast, depended on the informal solidarity of rural society. Such solidarity may help to explain how the country accommodated such rapid growth in population. Although fertility showed some signs of falling in the 1820s and 1830s, it remained high by European standards. Life expectancy was also relatively high and there were few signs of the sort of crisis mortality that Malthus and his followers might have expected. Whilst the natural rate of growth remained high, after the Napoleonic wars an increasing rate of emigration helped slow down the growth in numbers in Ireland. Of course, everything changed in 1845 when the introduction of the potato blight led to an unanticipated, exceptionally severe and permanent fall in potato yields. In the short term it reduced labourers to penury and left farmers with few means to help them. In the longer term it eliminated the need for the hidden solidarity that lay at the heart of pre-famine rural society.

FURTHER READING

Much of this chapter is based on ongoing research on the pre-famine economy. Key sources for any discussion of occupations and poverty are the 1841 census and the Poor Inquiry of the mid-1830s.

Almquist, E. L. 'Prefamine Ireland: the theory of European proto-industrialization: evidence from the 1841 census', *Journal of Economic History*, 39 (1979), 699–718.

Clarkson, L. A. and E. M. Crawford. *Feast and famine: a history of food and nutrition in Ireland, 1500–1920* (Oxford, 2001).

Crawford, W. H. *The impact of the domestic linen industry in Ulster* (Belfast, 2005).

Cronin, M. *Agrarian protest in Ireland, 1750–1960* (Dundalk, 2012).

Cullen, L. M. *The emergence of modern Ireland, 1600–1900* (London, 1981).

Dickson, D. 'In search of the old Irish poor law', in R. Mitchison and P. Roebuck (eds.), *Economy and society in Scotland and Ireland, 1500–1939* (Edinburgh, 1988), 149–59.

Geary, F. 'Deindustrialization in Ireland to 1851: some evidence from the census', *Economic History Review*, 51 (1998), 312–41.

Kennedy, L. and P. M. Solar. *Irish agriculture: a price history* (Dublin, 2007).

Kennedy, L. and P. M. Solar. 'The rural economy, 1780–1914', in L. Kennedy and P. Ollerenshaw (eds.), *Ulster since 1600: politics, economy and society* (Oxford, 2012), 160–76.

Moran, G. *Sending out Ireland's poor: assisted emigration to North America in the nineteenth century* (Dublin, 2004).

Solar, P. M. 'The Great Famine was no ordinary subsistence crisis', in E. M. Crawford (ed.), *Famine: the Irish experience, 900–1900* (Edinburgh, 1989), 112–33.

Solar, P. M. 'Poor relief and English economic development before the Industrial Revolution', *Economic History Review*, 48 (1995), 1–22.

Solar, P. M. '*Why Ireland starved* and the big issues in pre-famine Irish economic history', *Irish Economic and Social History*, 42 (2015), 62–75.

3 Famines and Famine Relief, 1740–2000

Mary E. Daly

The Irish famine of the 1840s ranks among the greatest natural disasters in modern history, and it is generally seen as a major dividing line in the history of modern Ireland. Yet Ireland experienced not one but two acute famines in little more than a century. The famine of the 1740s, though largely forgotten, probably killed an even higher proportion of the population. The fact that Ireland experienced two major famines within a century was mainly due to poverty, but the inadequacy of relief systems, or unresponsiveness – especially when compared with elsewhere in western Europe – is also noteworthy.

3.1. Famine or its Absence, 1740–1840

Ireland escaped lightly during the major European food crises of the 1690s and the early eighteenth century. However, 'twenty-one months of bizarre weather', beginning in December 1739, which affected a large area of northern Europe, resulted in a major crisis. The Great Frost of 1740 was the longest period of extreme cold in modern European history. In Ireland 1741 was known as *blian an áir* – the year of the slaughter. Frozen waterways disrupted trade and business: water wheels could not function, so milling came to a halt. Potatoes, which had traditionally been left in the ground until needed, were destroyed, so households had to rely on oatmeal; many consumed the seed grain and seed potatoes reserved for the coming season. Dublin food prices rose sharply during the summer of 1740, but as the new season crops were small and late, prices peaked again in December 1740, prompting food riots. Cattle and sheep perished from lack of fodder; many horses died because of an epizootic disease. In some areas livestock numbers did not recover for many years, and many under-tenants were ruined by the crisis, if they didn't die. The famine ended with a bumper harvest in 1741.[1]

The primary cause was the damage caused to crops by acute weather, but the lack of food imports, because of extreme weather in Europe, was a contributory factor. Burials in Dublin city in January–February 1740 were three times the normal figure. In St Catherine's parish burials from January 1740 to the end of September 1741 were double those of previous years. Few death registers survive for rural Ireland, but, comparing hearth tax records for 1732 and 1744, Dickson, Ó Gráda and Daultrey conclude that the population loss 'was of the order of 16 percent', which was higher than in the 1840s. In Munster, the worst-affected province (because of greater dependence on the potato), one-quarter of the population may have died, but Ulster was less affected because the diet was more reliant on oatmeal and because the expanding linen industry provided the means to buy food.[2] Little information survives about numbers dying from starvation; however, there are extensive reports of epidemics, including smallpox – a disease where mortality is unrelated to nutrition – typhus, typhoid, and 'bloody flux' or dysentery. Only dysentery, which may be caused by eating diseased and unsuitable food, is directly related to food scarcity.

J. D. Post showed that despite acute food shortages throughout northern Europe, only Norway, Finland and Ireland experienced a significant increase in deaths. He concluded that Ireland's 'national mortality crisis however was rooted more in the inadequate welfare and relief measures than in the absolute per capita shortage of food. The national epidemics were inescapably tied to the wave of itinerant vagrants and beggars who crowded into the towns.'[3] In contrast to other affected countries, Ireland had no system of poor relief. Many towns and cities set up schemes to distribute food and fuel. In the countryside responsibility fell on Church of Ireland clergymen and local landlords. Towns tried to ban beggars from entering, for fear of disease, and some relief schemes were restricted to residents or by religion. The remarkably high mortality indicates that relief was seriously inadequate. Yet this famine had no discernible impact on public policy, though farmers took steps to protect potatoes from future winter frosts.

This proved to be a short-lived crisis. The economy was expanding rapidly and the spread of commercial activity enabled Ireland to overcome subsequent years of scarcity by importing food. Between the 1750s and the 1790s Ireland recorded the fastest rate of population growth in Europe. According to Macafee, 'only England appears to

1 D. Dickson, *Arctic Ireland: the extraordinary story of the Great Frost and forgotten famine of 1740–41* (Belfast, 1997); L. M. Cullen, 'The Irish food crises of the 1740s: the economic conjuncture', *Irish Economic and Social History*, 37 (2010), 1–23.
2 D. Dickson, C. Ó Gráda and S. Daultrey, 'Hearth tax, household size and Irish population change, 1672–1821', *Proceedings of the Royal Irish Academy. Section C*, 82c, 6 (1982), 125–8.
3 J. D Post, *The last great subsistence crisis in the western world* (Baltimore and London, 1977), 177, 225–6.

come close'.[4] In 1950 Connell suggested that the population was rising because of a 'gap in the famines'. Dickson presents a more complex picture. Peaks in Dublin food prices indicate acute shortages in the late 1760s, 1772–4, 1782–4, 1794–6, 1800–1, 1812–13 and 1816–18; the most severe crisis was in 1800–1. These price rises coincided with above-average numbers of burials in surviving parish registers in north Leinster. Nevertheless higher rural incomes and readily available food imports, plus a buffer stock of potatoes (when potatoes were scarce, pigs went unfed and were slaughtered early), prevented a repeat of the1740s crisis. Local authorities and voluntary bodies were more active in importing and distributing food, though the Irish Parliament and government continued to play a minor role in crisis relief. The Dublin administration was more active after 1800, importing food and supplementing local funds, an involvement prompted more by fears of unrest than by a new concern for the poor. Excess mortality in the crises of 1800–1 and 1816–17 is estimated at 40,000 on each occasion.[5] In 1822, 1826 and 1831 food crises in the west of Ireland prompted the formation of local committees. They secured government funding plus substantial support from private English philanthropists. Relief funds supported public works, the provision of cheap imported food, and seed potatoes. By 1831, however, according to O'Neill, private philanthropists proved less sympathetic and landlords were disengaging from local committees. Distress was reported again in western areas in 1835, 1837, and in 1842 when a number of midland and Ulster counties appeared on the list.[6] The recurring crises might suggest that Ireland was becoming more vulnerable to food shortages; alternatively those in the past had attracted less public attention. There is no evidence of a significant spike in mortality in the years before the Great Famine.

By 1841 the population was 8.1–8.5 million, compared with 1.9–2.2 million in 1744. The increase was greatest in the north-west – from Galway to Derry. It was least pronounced in what Smyth describes as 'the long-settled stable world' that included most of Leinster, east Ulster, and more prosperous parts of Munster, where middling and large farms were not subdivided and social controls restricted marriage – as happened in much of northern and western Europe.[7] The highest growth was in areas where domestic textiles were important – hence the northerly counties – and on marginal land, which was cleared, settled and subdivided. By 1841, however, domestic textiles were in decline, leaving thousands of households without a cash income. In Ulster population

4 W. Macafee, 'The pre-famine population of Ireland: a reconsideration', in B. Collins, P. Ollerenshaw and T. Parkhill (eds.), *Industry, trade and people in Ireland, 1660–1950: essays in honour of W. H. Crawford* (Belfast, 2005), 76.

5 D. Dickson, 'The gap in famines: a useful myth?', in E. M. Crawford (ed.), *Famine: the Irish experience, 900–1900* (Edinburgh, 1989), 96–111.

6 T. O'Neill, 'The state, poverty and distress in Ireland, 1814–45', Ph.D. thesis, University College Dublin, 1971.

7 W. J. Smyth, 'Mapping the people: the growth and distribution of the population', in J. Crowley, W. J. Smyth and M. Murphy (eds.), *Atlas of the great Irish famine* (Cork, 2012), 15.

growth fell sharply from the 1820s, because of rising emigration. But in Connacht, west Munster and other upland areas the population continued to rise. The living standards of Ireland's poor were falling, and the proportion of labourers occupying tiny plots continued to rise. By 1841 they constituted more than one-quarter of the population. They faced weeks of near-starvation every year, when the old potato crop was exhausted and there was little agricultural work available; during that time they depended on begging and charity. Living in one-room cabins, clothed in rags, with nothing to spare, they lacked the resources to survive a major food crisis. Nevertheless this does not mean that a crisis on the scale of the Great Famine was inevitable.

3.2.   The Great Famine

Since the 1990s the famine of the 1840s has been the subject of a remarkable volume of publications, covering local, national and transnational aspects, making it probably the best-researched pre-twentieth-century famine. Detailed investigations of famine mortality, its causes and incidence, and the differences in the operations of individual poor law unions have proved highly informative about the specific impact of the famine, and the contrasts between the Irish famine and more modern food crises. The main debate continues to focus on British relief policy and the degree to which senior British politicians and officials used the famine as an opportunity to transform rural Ireland. Like the famine of the 1740s, the Great Famine coincided with a major food crisis in northern Europe, also caused by potato blight. This increased the competition for grain imports, while again offering scope for comparisons between responses in Ireland and elsewhere.

The immediate cause is not contested. Potato blight, which was rife in the Low Countries in the early summer of 1845, spread to the south of England, and reached the east coast of Ireland in September. However, the early crop had been saved and some areas were unaffected. In 1846 the blight destroyed most of the crop, leaving little seed potato for planting the following year. The small crop of 1847 was largely blight-free, though blight returned in 1848. In the 1840s, according to Austen Bourke, 4.7 million labourers, cottiers and smallholders relied on the potato as their staple food, consuming 75 per cent of potatoes used for human consumption.[8] Solar, building on Bourke's work, concludes that while the failures in 1845 and 1848 were 'extreme' though not unprecedented, 'the 1846 failure … seems to be in a class by itself'. In the years 1846–50, the quantity of food produced in Ireland and available for domestic consumption was almost one-quarter less than in 1840–5; the 1846–7 shortfall was significantly higher. Grain imports exceeded exports by a ratio of nine to one.[9] This refutes

8 A. Bourke, 'The use of the potato crop in pre-famine Ireland, in J. Hill and C. Ó Gráda (eds.), 'The visitation of God'? The potato and the great Irish famine (Dublin, 1993), 97–9.
9 P. Solar, 'The Great Famine was no ordinary subsistence crisis', in Crawford, Famine, 115.

the argument made by the Young Ireland leader, John Mitchel, that this was an artificial famine, with food exports far outstripping imports. Food, mainly livestock, *was* exported, which enabled farmers to buy imported grain to feed their families. Banning livestock exports would not have fed starving labourers, unless some elaborate mechanism was implemented, and the money would have been better spent on cheaper grain. But preventing grain exports, in the autumn of 1846, before the arrival of mass imports of grain, could potentially have saved lives, as could a ban on brewing and distilling, as Daniel O'Connell demanded. By late January 1847, however, quantities of imported grain greatly exceeded exports. The major challenge posed by the potato failure was to provide a substitute for the staple food of a majority of the population, who had not previously purchased their staple diet. This demanded unprecedented imports of food, and a mechanism to make food available to the poor, either to purchase or without payment.

3.2.1. Relief Policies

Famine relief cannot be divorced from the political, social and ideological context of the 1840s: the Union of Britain and Ireland; British perceptions of the state of Ireland; Britain's transition to free trade and the debate over repealing the Corn Laws; the failure of O'Connell's campaign for repeal, his ideological battles with Young Ireland and his death. Earlier writings tended to contrast the more benign relief regime of 1845–6, when Sir Robert Peel's Conservative government was in office – best summarised in a contemporary quotation from the *Freeman's Journal*, that 'No man died of famine during his [Peel's] administration'[10] – and the harsher attitude of the successor Liberal government. Cecil Woodham-Smith's best-selling *The Great Hunger* was not alone in highlighting the role of Sir Charles Trevelyan, Chief-Secretary to the Treasury, whose book *The Irish Crisis*, originally published anonymously in 1847, gave ample evidence to support this indictment. Peter Grey's research has modified this picture significantly.

By the 1840s, the reports of the 1830s Poor Inquiry and the Devon Commission, and recurrent requests for relief, had reinforced a perception of Ireland as a country with a flawed economic system, where emergency relief merely perpetuated poverty. The potato blight was seen as confirming these views: a 'visitation' from providence which highlighted the need to transform rural Ireland. Peel linked Irish famine relief with repealing the Corn Laws. Grey notes that he 'combined an element of free trade opportunism with a serious concern for what he hoped would be a long-term replacement of peasant potato subsistence with the purchase of imported grain (purchased in the marketplace by proletarianised wage-labourers)'.[11] He claims that the distinction

10 *Freeman's Journal*, 5 April 1847, quoted in R. D. Edwards and T. D. Williams (eds.), *The Great Famine* (Dublin, 1957), 272.
11 P. Grey, *Famine, land and politics: British government and Irish politics, 1843–1850* (Dublin, 1998), 76.

between Peel's government and Russell's in terms of famine relief and attitudes towards Ireland have been overstated.

Peel provided grants for relief works and arranged for the secret purchase of £100,000 worth of maize and rice to control rising food price. But relief works and food depots did not open until the spring of 1846. In the first year of a partial famine, most families had something to sell or pawn, enabling them to buy food. Private imports of maize – which had been little used in Ireland before that time – helped to fill the shortage. By contrast Russell's government was confronted with a massive food shortage by the autumn of 1846. Admittedly their attitude was ungenerous: they offered loans for relief works, not grants, to deter excess demand. They assumed that rising food prices would encourage farmers to sell surplus stock and encourage imports by merchants. Ó Gráda has concluded that markets worked effectively during the famine (which has not always been the case in more recent famines in developing countries). Nevertheless the consequences were disastrous. Irish merchants were slow to place orders, and given an international shortage, potential imports went elsewhere.[12] It was only in late January 1847 that significant imports began to arrive. Soaring prices meant that wages offered on relief works were too low to feed a family.

In the winter of 1846-7 malnutrition, appalling weather and fever epidemics meant that relief works were probably killing people rather than saving lives. Newspaper reports in Britain and internationally of starving workers collapsing on relief works or people dying on the roadside forced the government to rethink its approach. Relief works began to close in March, and were replaced by a programme offering free cooked food. While this was probably the correct decision, a gap of six or more weeks between closing relief works and opening food kitchens left many poor families without any assistance. Donnelly claims that in June 1847, approximately 15 per cent of those dismissed from relief works and their families were not receiving food relief.[13] Soup kitchens eventually fed up to 3 million people in the summer of 1847 (workers on relief schemes probably supported an average of five, so soup kitchens actually relieved fewer people than public works at their peak). The kitchens closed when the new potato crop appeared. Relief works cost a total of £4.8 million; the soup kitchens £1.7 million. In those parts of Europe which were affected by the blight, relief efforts were directed by municipalities, and generally consisted of a combination of food aid, controls on food prices, relief works and the prohibition of vagrancy and begging.[14] The contrast with Ireland is evident – firstly, in the emphasis on a local response, and secondly, in the greater reliance on providing food or controlling the food market.

12 C. Ó Gráda, *Black '47 and beyond: the great Irish famine in history, economy, and memory* (Princeton, 1999), 134–49.
13 J. S. Donnelly, *The great Irish famine* (Stroud, 2001), 85.
14 C. Ó Gráda, R. Paping and E. Vanhaute, 'The European subsistence crisis of 1845–1850: a comparative perspective', in Ó Gráda, Paping and Vanhaute (eds.), *When the potato failed* (Turnhout, 2007), 30.

3.2.2. The Poor Law and Evictions

While much of the debate has concentrated on the relief programmes and food trade in the years 1846–7, the most questionable decision taken by a British government was to end all special relief measures in the autumn of 1847, placing all responsibility on the poor law. The only concession to the poorest unions was a proposal that more prosperous Irish unions would be surcharged to provide a subsidy. However, this fiscal transfer was restricted to the island of Ireland, and when Ulster poor law guardians protested, the proposal was dropped. The story of the Irish poor law during the famine years involves high-level political and ideological issues, and more local aspects. A recent paper by Charles Read suggests that Russell's government was committed to providing continuing support for Irish famine relief, but the financial crisis of 1847 made it difficult to raise a national loan, forcing them to place the entire burden of relief on Irish property. This debate will continue.[15]

Ireland had no national system of poor relief until shortly before the famine, when the country was divided into 130 unions, each with a workhouse, providing places for 100,000 poor, sick or elderly inmates. The system was not designed to cope with a national crisis such as famine. The poor law was based on a local property tax, so poorer areas with potentially the greatest demand and lowest tax base would carry the heaviest burden. In contrast to England, Irish unions were precluded from granting outdoor relief. The first workhouses opened in the 1840s, but local resistance meant that the system was only fully operational in 1845. Workhouses had plenty of vacant spaces until the autumn of 1846 – indicating that distress was manageable in the first year of the blight. Overcrowding began in the late autumn of 1846, and by January 1847 the horrors of the famine-era workhouses were unfolding.

The Poor Law Extension Act, passed in the spring of 1847, recognised that those who were destitute had a basic right to support, and it permitted unions to grant outdoor relief. But an amendment proposed by the MP for Dublin, Sir William Gregory (a protégé of Peel), provided that relief would not be given to anyone holding more than one-quarter acre of land. The 1847 Act marks the point when the poor law became wholly responsible for relieving Irish distress. It can be seen as the ultimate expression of the dictum that 'Irish property should support Irish poverty'. As landlords were responsible for paying the poor rate on holdings valued at less than £4, removing smallholdings would reduce their rates bill, while the Gregory Clause left smallholders facing a choice between starvation and abandoning their land. A select committee of the House of Commons found that between November 1847 and July 1850, landlords and

15 C. Read, 'Laissez-faire, the Irish famine and British financial crisis, c. 1846–50', Paper presented to Irish Quantitative Historians conference, January 2015.

middlemen in the Kilrush Union in West Clare ejected roughly 12,000 people from their homes, 17 per cent of the 1841 population. Clare had the highest recorded rate of evictions.

The Irish Constabulary only began to collect eviction statistics in 1849. However, more than 140,000 families were served with ejectment proceedings in the years 1846–8, though not all will have been evicted. Constabulary statistics, which may be an under-estimate, record 48,740 permanent evictions between 1849 and 1854, approximately 250,000 people. Donnelly suggests that 'this number may represent only half of those disposed formally and informally from 1846–54'.[16] In Clare evictions appear to have been a response by insolvent landlords, who were no longer receiving rents from destitute small tenants. However, the records of the Encumbered Estate Act, which was introduced in 1849 to make it easier for insolvent landowners to sell their property – yet another measure introduced to assist the creation of a solvent, capitalist Irish landowning class – show that estates sold under this legislation were already insolvent before the famine.

Poor law statistics offer the best evidence of the long-tailed impact of the famine. In 1847 a total of 417,139 people were relieved in workhouses; this figure rose to 610,463 in 1848 and peaked at 932,284 in 1849. Outdoor relief peaked at 1,438,042 in 1848. In 1850, 805,702 were relieved in the workhouses and 368,565 received outdoor relief. By 1852 the number of inmates relieved was 504,864 (still significantly higher than in 1847), but only 14,911 received outdoor relief. Studies of individual workhouses reveal differences in admission policies and varying responses to national and local crises. Before the famine a majority of Enniskillen inmates arrived alone, but by 1847, the union appears to have given priority to family groups and only one-fifth of those admitted arrived alone. Women were more readily granted admission to workhouses than men; many family groups consisted of women and children. Although a majority of inmates in Enniskillen in 1845–7 were under fifteen years old, orphaned or deserted children accounted for only 6–7 per cent of admissions in Enniskillen, Inishowen and Parsonstown, perhaps because these exceptionally vulnerable children were unable to secure a place. Some unions responded relatively swiftly to overcrowding and fever, by opening auxiliary workhouses and separate fever hospitals or introducing outdoor relief – even before it was permitted under the 1847 Act. However, many unions in north-east Ulster refused to provide outdoor relief, claiming that it was not needed. The only union in Leinster not to do so was Parsonstown; this decision is consistent with the union's record of neglect and maladministration.[17]

16 Donnelly, *Great Irish famine*, 156–7; Ó Gráda, *Black '47*, 44–5.
17 On workhouses and famine deaths, see J. Mokyr and C. Ó Gráda, 'Famine disease and famine mortality: lessons from the Irish experience' and T. W. Guinnane and C. Ó Gráda, 'The workhouses and Irish famine mortality', both in T. Dyson and C. Ó Gráda (eds.), *Famine demography: perspectives from the past and present* (Oxford, 2002), 19–43 and 44–64; M. E. Daly, 'Something old and something new: recent research on the great Irish famine', in Ó Gráda, Paping and Vanhaute, *When the potato failed*, 59–78.

3.2.3. Famine Deaths

Civil registration of deaths and births was only introduced in the 1860s; however, the 1851 population census asked households to list those who had died over the preceding decade, and the year and cause of death. Given that the famine wiped out entire families, and many emigrated, these returns are incomplete. Mokyr and Ó Gráda estimated that 1.9 million people died between 1846 and 1850 – double the figure given in the 1851 returns. Almost half of these deaths would have occurred irrespective of the famine, so the excess mortality was 1.1 million. The death rate more than doubled. Mortality was significantly higher than in more recent famines in developing countries. Dysentery, diarrhoea and fevers accounted for a majority of deaths. Deaths from dysentery and diarrhoea were related to food shortages, because starving people ate seaweed, decomposing animals and inadequately cooked maize meal, though dysentery was also spread by poor hygiene. The high incidence of typhus, typhoid and relapsing fever was a consequence of social disruption. Fevers spread through migration, overcrowding in towns, cities, workhouses and emigrant ships, and the collapse of normal hygiene standards. Starving people spent their available money on food, not on soap; they conserved energy by not hauling water or saving turf; clothes or bed clothes were sold or pawned, leaving people huddled together in louse-ridden rags. Malnutrition caused by lack of food reduced immunity to, and increased mortality from, tuberculosis and respiratory diseases.

One in ten died from starvation or diseases directly related to starvation, such as dropsy (famine oedema) or marasmus, a wasting disease most common in children. Children and the elderly were at greatest risk of death – as they were in the absence of famine. Almost half of recorded deaths from starvation and one-third of deaths from diarrhoea were in children under ten. Women were at less risk of dying than men; female advantage was greatest in relation to starvation and starvation-related illnesses, because the female body is better able to survive food deprivation, but fewer women than men also died of fever. At the time there was little understanding of how infectious diseases were transmitted, and sanitation was primitive. While there were few doctors in the areas worst affected by the famine, it is not clear what they could have done to save lives, given the state of knowledge. Better knowledge of how infectious diseases are spread meant that there was no rise in infectious diseases during the Second World War famines in Leningrad and the Netherlands.

18 Ó Gráda, *Black '47*; R. Scally, *The end of hidden Ireland: rebellion, famine and emigration* (Oxford and New York, 1995).
19 The term was first used by Samuel Plimsoll in his campaigns to improve the safety of ships. My thanks to Dr Cian McMahon for alerting me to this.

The poor were at greatest risk of dying, though the rich were not spared. Doctors and clergymen who ministered to famine victims contracted fever and some died. The death rate in Connacht and Munster was roughly double that in Ulster and Leinster. One-quarter of deaths occurred in workhouses, prisons and hospitals, and these are the best documented. While workhouse deaths reflect local conditions, they can be revealing about the quality of management, making it possible to distinguish between well-run unions and those that neglected or even starved inmates. Indicators of quality of care include the numbers dying from hunger-related diseases – such as marasmus, which is not infectious – and whether inmates who died of fever had been recently admitted – presumably already ill – or had contracted the infectious disease in the workhouse. The proportion dying from infectious diseases was significantly lower in Wexford – a county less affected by famine – than in Mayo. Peaks in mortality often occurred when a work-house was overcrowded, but the risk of infection and death could be reduced by opening auxiliary workhouses or fever sheds. Some guardians were more responsive to doing this than others. Almost one-quarter of deaths in Parsonstown were caused by maras-mus, and this was four times the average for other workhouses; there were allegations that staff stole the children's food. In Enniskillen, another negligent workhouse, 12.2 per cent of men and 9.9 per cent of women died from marasmus, or dropsy – in essence, of starvation. Two-thirds of those who died in Parsonstown in 1849, the majority from infectious diseases, had been in the workhouse for three to six weeks, which suggests that they contracted the disease there. More than two-thirds of those dying from dys-entery in Ennistymon in1850–1 had been in the workhouse for four weeks or more.

3.2.4. Crime

Famines generally bring a rise in minor crime and Ireland was no exception. Food riots were a feature of the autumn of 1846. Grain stores were sacked; ships carrying food either in or out of Ireland were attacked. The large quantities of coins in transit to pay relief workers encouraged a wave of robberies: overseers on relief works were occasionally threatened by groups of men who were denied jobs. There was a sharp rise in convictions for thefts of food – potatoes, turnips, sheep, etc. – and in convictions for vagrancy and prostitution, but there were few major public-order incidents. Some desperate people may have viewed a criminal conviction as a free emigrant ticket – convict transportation to Australia. Dublin prisons had more first-time offenders and more non-Dubliners than either before or after the famine, and the famine criminals appear to have been taller and therefore better nourished. But chronic malnutrition is associated with listlessness and lack of energy, which makes it difficult to mount a seri-ous challenge to authority. In the decades before the famine it is possible that threats of retaliation from secret societies deterred landlords, agents or large farmers from carrying out evictions. Statistics suggest that this deterrent did not apply during the famine years. Only one landlord, Denis Mahon of Strokestown, was murdered during these years.[18]

3.2.5. Emigration

Although many Irish emigrant communities tend to ascribe their existence to the famine, emigration had reached all parts of Ireland, and regular emigration routes to North America and Britain were well established by 1840. If that had not been so, fewer would have emigrated and more people would probably have died in Ireland. The highest rates of emigration in the decade 1841–51 were in south Ulster and north Connacht, which were badly affected by the decline in domestic textiles, and adjacent to areas where emigration was well established. The famine accelerated the spread of mass emigration, especially in Connacht and Munster. Most emigrants financed their passage either through family remittances, or by selling what they owned; however, some landlords, notably Denis Mahon and the Earl of Lansdowne, provided assisted passages in order to clear their estate of smallholders, as did some poor law unions that wished to reduce the number of inmates. But assisted emigration, whether by the poor law or landlords remained the exception.

Many accounts of famine emigration refer to 'coffin–ships', yet the term only came into use in the 1870s.[19] Mortality among Irish emigrants to New York between 1836 and 1853 was 2 per cent, which was similar to that of German emigrants. Passage to Canada was cheaper: ships were older and poorly regulated, so they attracted poorer emigrants. At the height of the famine one-fifth of emigrants to Canada died; many of them were buried at Grosse Ile quarantine station. Between 1846 and 1851, 250,000 Irish emigrants travelled to Liverpool each year, the majority en route to North America or other parts of Britain, though the poorest and the sickest remained. Irish emigrants were accused of spreading fever. Newspapers expressed shock at their appalling condition, and the cost to local taxpayers of caring for them. There were similar responses in Glasgow, Manchester and other cities where Irish emigrants gathered. But many recently arrived emigrants who sought relief from a poor law union were shipped back to Ireland. Neal concluded that the cost to local ratepayers in Liverpool and other cities that attracted large numbers of emigrants was not "'crippling' or 'disastrous'", though their arrival brought long-term social costs.[20]

20 F. Neal, *Black 47: Britain and the famine Irish* (Basingstoke, 1998); Crowley *et al.*, *Atlas of the great Irish famine*, Section VI; W. J. Vaughan (ed.), *A new history of Ireland, vol. V: Ireland under the Union, 1 (1801–70)* (Oxford, 1989), chs. xxix, xxx, xxxi.

3.2.6. Aftermath and Memory

The 1851 census recorded a population of 6.5 million, 1.6 million fewer than in 1841. The population continued to fall until the 1930s. The decline was concentrated among the poorest sections of the community, those with little or no land, and in the west and south-west, and in south Ulster where domestic textiles had disappeared. Almost three-quarters of holdings under 1 acre disappeared between 1845 and 1851, as did more than half of holdings of 1–5 acres and more than one in three holdings of 5–15 acres. Despite the lower population, post-famine Ireland was no longer self-sufficient in food. Maize meal became a staple in the diet of the poor in the spring and summer months; potato yields never reached the pre-famine levels, mainly because of persisting blight. The share of agricultural output from crops declined, though that would have been expected with the repeal of the Corn Laws.

It has often been argued that the Irish population responded to the famine by ending the subdivision of holdings and the practice of early and near-universal marriage. But evidence suggests that before the famine, middling and larger farmers did not subdivide holdings, and they adopted a prudent approach to marriage. In the decades immediately after the famine, communities in the west of Ireland continued to marry at an

Figure 3.1 Ruins of famine village, Achill Head, by Robert French (1841–1917). Lawrence Photograph Collection. Courtesy of the National Library of Ireland.

early age and the marriage rate remained high. However, the numbers emigrating were undoubtedly higher, because famine emigrants were funding emigrant passages for family members. The persistence of pre-famine marriage practices in poorer western communities conforms to Ó Ciosáin's interpretation of the accounts of the famine collected by the National Folklore Commission. Many suggest that their particular community escaped relatively lightly compared with others, or that those who died were strangers – indicating a reluctance to acknowledge the poverty of their community. Local landlords were recalled either as relatively benevolent, or for their hard-heartedness, but there is little evidence that the British authorities were blamed for the disaster. The famine was seen as divine retribution – perhaps for wasting plentiful potatoes in the past; there are stories of personal charity and miraculous responses to such charity. Ó Ciosáin concluded that the folklore record 'implies that the experience of the famine did not produce any radical or fundamental change in perceptions, in psychology or in culture'. He rejects arguments that the famine resulted in traumatic suppression of memories, which manifested itself in alcoholism and mental illness in later generations.[21] There is also increasing evidence of continuity of religious practice in these communities, and although Irish-speakers accounted for a disproportionate number of emigrants and famine deaths, their culture and community survived.

The years 1859–64 brought an almost biblical combination of freak weather, blight and animal diseases, prompting fears of another famine. But despite a succession of poor harvests and an absence of any major relief programme, there was no significant rise in deaths. Donnelly suggests that cheap maize plus an effective network of importers and shopkeepers (which probably emerged because of the 1840s famine) kept people alive, the latter by offering food on credit, though often at exorbitant cost. There were fears of another 'near-famine' in the late 1870s, which was caused by yet another severe outbreak of blight, plus bad weather and falling agricultural prices. Distress and food shortages were reported in 1880–2, 1882–3, 1885–6, 1890–1, 1894–5, 1897–8 and 1904–5, though they were mainly confined to communities along the western seaboard and there is little evidence of any significant loss of life.[22] Nationalists gained electoral control of poor law unions from the 1870s and they responded to reports of distress by providing extensive outdoor relief and other forms of assistance, often in defiance of Local Government Board regulations. The Irish administration tended to treat reports of famine conditions with scepticism. But the political pressures exercised by nationalist politicians both locally and in Westminster secured a succession of special relief programmes: seed potatoes, food supplies, relief works and extra subventions to the

21 N. Ó Ciosáin, 'Famine memory and the popular representation of scarcity', in I. McBride (ed.), *History and memory in modern Ireland* (Cambridge, 2001), 111.
22 J. S. Donnelly, 'The Irish agricultural depression of 1859–64', *Irish Economic and Social History*, 3 (1976), 33–54; T. P. O'Neill, 'The food crisis of the 1890s', in Crawford (ed.), *Famine*, 176–98.

poorest unions. The Congested Districts Board was established in 1891, with the goal of ending these recurrent crises by promoting a programme of social and economic development, though periodic crises continued. The last report of famine in the west was in 1924, when it was linked with the abolition of the Congested Districts Board by the new government of the Irish Free State. Higher incomes, the ability to buy food, and a more politically responsive local and national government ensured that, while crops failed, there was no significant rise in deaths.

The nationalist indictment of British famine relief – best captured in the writings of John Mitchel – concentrated on the question of food exports, and claims that this was an artificial famine: that there was more than sufficient food available to feed the population. By the 1870s constitutional and revolutionary nationalists cited the famine and Ireland's continuing population decline as a justification for Home Rule or complete independence. In April 1920, during a meeting of the First Dáil attended by an American delegation, a succession of deputies recited the populations of their constituencies on the eve of the famine, and their current populations, to demonstrate the link between economic and demographic decline and the Union with Britain.

The famine happened during a time of religious confrontation. Proselytisation and 'souperism' form part of the surviving folk memory and they featured in the mass evictions in Clare. There is also evidence of cross-denominational co-operation in relief efforts, and while the overwhelming majority of victims were Catholic, Ulster Protestants were not spared. But there was no shared history of the famine: its aftermath brought an upsurge in denominational tensions, both in Ireland and in Irish communities overseas. The famine was obliterated from unionist political discourse and unionist memory, and from the narratives constructed by Ulster Scots emigrants in Canada and elsewhere.

The sesquicentenary of the famine in the 1990s prompted an extensive commemorative programme throughout Ireland and internationally, and many assertions that the famine had hitherto been forgotten, but an absence of memorials or formal commemorations does not necessarily indicate amnesia. Throughout the nineteenth and the twentieth century the famine was frequently invoked: when the government urged rural communities to grow food and harvest turf during the Second World War, during debates on emigration, and more recently by campaigners seeking funding for development or relief in developing countries, or creation of new links with the Irish diaspora. In the 1960s Irish diplomats in the USA saw the success of Cecil Woodham-Smith's *The Great Hunger* as an opportunity to connect with affluent long-established Irish Americans. The centenary of the famine passed largely unnoticed – the government commissioned a scholarly history, and the Gaelic Athletic Association (GAA) played the 1947 all-Ireland Gaelic football final in New York. The current interest in the famine, especially in its local or diasporic impact, may reflect the distance between contemporary Irish society and the famine and its consequences.

FURTHER READING

Connell, K. H. *The population of Ireland, 1750–1845* (Oxford, 1950).

Crawford, E. M. (ed.). *Famine: the Irish experience, 900–1900* (Edinburgh, 1989).

Crowley, J., W. J. Smyth and M. Murphy (eds.). *Atlas of the great Irish Famine* (Cork, 2012).

Dickson, D. *Arctic Ireland: the extraordinary story of the Great Frost and forgotten famine of 1740–41* (Belfast, 1997).

Grey, P. *Famine, land and politics: British government and Irish politics, 1843–1850* (Dublin, 1998).

Kinealy, C. *This great calamity: the Great Famine, 1845–52* (Dublin, 2006).

Ó Gráda, C. *Black '47 and beyond: the great Irish Famine in history, economy, and memory* (Princeton, 1999).

Ó Gráda, C., R. Paping and E. Vanhaute (eds.). *When the potato failed* (Turnhout, 2007).

Vaughan, W. J. (ed.). *A new history of Ireland, vol. V: Ireland under the Union, 1 (1801–70)* (Oxford, 1989).

4 Languages and Identities

Gearóid Ó Tuathaigh

4.1. Introduction

This chapter will consider two distinct but, certainly in the Irish historical context, interlocking understandings of language as a constitutive element of the social. Firstly, the ideological dimension: the significance of language in the construction of a distinct sense of peoplehood or nation. This will principally entail an examination of the origins and later elaboration of the idea of cultural nationalism in Ireland. Secondly, we will consider the related – but distinct –issue of language as cultural practice. Here the central concern must be the historically exceptional case of Ireland's major vernacular shift from Irish to English, beginning in the seventeenth century and with the centuries under review in this volume being the decisive period.

4.2. Language in the Construction of a Distinct Sense of Peoplehood

The ideological dimension of language surfaces strongly during the Tudor conquest of Ireland. Earlier attention to language in the medieval frontier between Gaelic and Anglo-Norman settlers, while generally aimed defensively at preventing the Anglo-Normans from being thoroughly assimilated into majority Gaelic culture, had, nevertheless, fixed what would prove to be an enduring 'cultural value frame' on the two languages, Irish and English. This frame identified the native Irish (language and general culture) as degenerate and English as the – at the time endangered – language of civility. This categorisation became more aggressively articulated in the conquest of Ireland during the Tudor and early Stuart monarchies, with military and political conquest rationalised in terms of a superior people and culture overcoming a more backward one, and with English as the language of the new political and civil order being introduced and, as necessary, imposed. New settlers or planters constituted a key element of the new civility.

For some of the leading apologists for the new English order and its civilising mission – such as Sir John Davis – language as the marker of civility/loyalty (English) and degeneracy/rebelliousness (Irish), and as constitutive of character and culture (individual and collective), was central to the legitimation of the conquest and plantations. Conversely – in this early modern *Kulturkampf* – the defenders of the Gaelic order came to articulate a version of Irish national 'identity' in which language and religion combined as the basis of legitimate authority, with a narrative of Gaelic 'high culture' – as practised by its custodian mandarin poets, genealogists and lawyers – contrasted with the vulgar culture and language of the upstart newcomers – English in speech. This early formulation fused Catholicism and the Irish language as the twin bases for legitimate authority, and insisted on a denial of legitimacy to the new English order, that is, to Protestantism and the English language.

This ideological construct would prove enduring in Gaelic literature. In the period between Aughrim and the Great Famine, the transmission of the essential core of the legitimist Gaelic view remained remarkably steady and intact.

However, already by the seventeenth century religion was the more potent marker of communal identity in Ireland. Religious loyalty was the basis of loss and gain – in land, position and privilege – in a conquest that saw a Protestant ascendancy securely established, with a Catholic majority harbouring an unquenchable resentment, encoded in a historical narrative of victimhood. The mobilisation of popular resentment at historical wrong, constantly rearticulated in terms of contemporary social and economic grievances, would be on the basis of such confessional rather than linguistic loyalty.

Currents of late eighteenth-century cultural nationalism (drawing on Fichte, Herder and others) found disciples in Ireland, notably in the writings of Thomas Davis (1814–45), cultural nationalist and leading propagandist of the Young Ireland movement of the 1840s. But, for Davis, as for a succession of later advocates of language essentialism in their claims for Irish nationalism, the medium of their advocacy and propaganda was English. 'The spirit of the nation' might reside in its Gaelic roots, but the case for it would be made through English. Indeed, the newspaper founded by Davis and his fellow Young Irelanders – *The Nation* – became the most influential organ for stirring propaganda – 'patriotic' history, popular songs, myth and legend – for Irish national sentiment, doing so virtually entirely in English. This was the paradox that exercised – and exasperated – the founder of the Gaelic League, Douglas Hyde, later in the century.[1]

1 J. E. Dunleavy and G. W. Dunleavy, *Douglas Hyde* (Berkeley and Los Angeles, 1991); for Hyde's key texts, see Douglas Hyde, *Language, lore and lyrics*; edited by B. Ó Conaire (Dublin, 1986).

The crux of this paradox was simple but profound. From a relatively early stage in the seventeenth century, the Gaelic ideology – of denial of legitimacy to the new order and prophecy of restoration to dominance of Irish as part of a Catholic restoration – was increasingly at odds with the socio-cultural 'facts on the ground', at least in so far as these pertained to language use. English was replacing Irish as the main vernacular of Ireland. The destruction of the Gaelic order, the dispersal or social eclipse of its leaders and mandarin class, the construction of a new apparatus of government and adminis-tration with English as its medium, together with the continuing influx of Protestant immigrants – all shaped the cultural revolution of the seventeenth century. It is claimed that 'English was firmly established as the language of the elite by the beginning of the seventeenth century', and that 'by the fourth decade of the seventeenth century the tide in the ongoing linguistic ebb and flow between Irish and English in Ireland was flowing strongly in favour of the latter'.[2] The advance of English, reflecting the logic and reality of the new power structures, was socially from the top down, and moved from east to west and from the towns out to the countryside.

4.3.   Language as Cultural Practice

Cultural practice was at odds with the constancy of the reiterated message of linguis-tic essentialism within the Irish-language narrative. As the surviving Catholic lead-ership gained a foothold in the new order, and as an advancing Catholic middle class emerged in trade and commerce throughout the eighteenth century, the language of their homes, hopes and progress was English. The vernacular shift from Irish to English was well advanced by the second quarter of the eighteenth century among those who had ambitions to advance and succeed. As a recent study concludes:

> What is apparent is that as Ireland was slowly absorbed during the course of the eighteenth century into an economy whose language was English, into a cultural milieu which deemed English the superior language, into an administrative (including legal) system which conducted itself through English, and into a political world whose discourse was conducted in English, the incentives to acquire English to converse, and to learn to read and to write English to function effectively in an increasingly literate world became compelling.

Thus, 'as the end of the eighteenth century approached, it was manifest that English had replaced Irish as the vernacular of choice over much of the country'.[3]

Eighteenth-century Ireland has been described as a pervasively bilingual or diglos-sic society, a description that requires some qualification. Certainly, Irish scribes were familiar with English texts and periodical publications. A cohort of the Protestant elite

2 J. Kelly and C. Mac Murchaidh (eds.), *Irish and English: essays on the Irish linguistic and cultural frontier, 1600–1900* (Dublin, 2012), 21, 15.
3 Ibid., 'Introduction', 32; for emerging research, see N. Ó Ciosáin, 'Gaelic culture and the language shift', in L. M. Geary and M. Kelleher (eds.), *Nineteenth-century Ireland: a guide to recent research* (Dublin, 2005), 136–52.

showed interest in native relics and antiquities, including Irish manuscripts, taking pride in the glories of an ancient civilisation.[4] In the doings of everyday life, for land-lords or their agents, merchants, pedlars, revenue police or the like, a knowledge of Irish remained useful – if not essential – for effective dealings with the lower peas-antry. At fairs and markets and popular social gatherings in the countryside and rural towns, the acoustic of Irish was probably pervasive.[5] Pastoral needs determined that in largely or exclusively Irish-speaking districts priests needed competence in Irish. Interest in Irish (and patronage of its scribes) animated exceptional remnants of the older Catholic noble families and a minority of clergymen.[6]

But, for all that, there was a gross inequality in standing and an utter contrast in the prospects of the two languages as vibrant vectors of cultural practice. English was the language of power, prestige, success and opportunity. Increasingly it was the language of the majority church, of trade and commerce, the law and administration. Literacy – specifically, the expanding print culture – provides firm evidence of the underlying cultural imbalance. It is estimated that between 1700 and 1750 some 9,000 English-language titles were published in Ireland, compared with only four Irish-language titles; for the years 1751 to 1800, the figures were 16,000 English-language titles com-pared with 19 Irish-language. A spike in Irish-language titles (to 150) in the 1800–51 period was followed by a virtual collapse in the post-famine decades.[7]

Literacy in official census data meant literacy in English. Self-reported competence in language must be treated with caution (given the anxieties and social aspirations inevitably at play). But by 1841 almost half of those over five claimed an ability to read English; this rose from the 1850s and by the 1911 census was close to 90 per cent. Schools were key sites of the language shift. The hedge (or 'fee') schools catering for the majority Catholic population were – allowing for variability in their character – over-whelmingly dedicated to teaching English and, at the behest of parents, discouraged the use of Irish. As a more formal Catholic network of schools developed from the later eighteenth century, the exclusive use of English in elementary education intensified.

It is true that there was considerable activity in manuscript compilation in Irish right up to the eve of the Great Famine, supported by an assortment of patrons – bishops, antiquarians, a group of Belfast cultural activists interested in promoting the Irish lan-guage as an aspect of pre-famine civic enlightenment.[8] But this hardly compensated for

4 Among the fruits of this new spirit was the founding of the Royal Irish Academy in 1785, 'to advance the stud-ies of science, polite literature, and antiquities'.
5 B. Ó Cuív, 'Irish language and literature, 1691–1845', in W. E. Vaughan and T. W. Moody (eds.), *A new history of Ireland, vol. IV: Eighteenth century Ireland* (Oxford, 1986), 374–473, is the authoritative survey.
6 Ibid.; also L. Gibbons and K. O'Conor (eds.), *Charles O'Conor of Ballinagare: life and works* (Dublin, 2015). For a study of how bilingualism operated, see N. M. Wolf, *An Irish-speaking island* (Madison, WI, 2014).
7 Kelly and Mac Murchaidh, *Irish and English*, 29, 39, 56.
8 Ó Cuív, 'Irish language and literature'; B. Ó Buachalla, *I mBéal Feirste Cois Cuain* (Dublin, 1968).

the relative dearth of Irish-language material in the print culture. A crucial variable in the literacy situation was the role of religion and the churches. Here, Ó Ciosáin's verdict is apposite: 'Literacy in a language which is not the language of the state or the language of trade and commerce is rooted in religious usage, and its extent is largely determined by the attitudes and actions of institutional churches.'[9]

The whole domain of religion – pastoral care, devotional practice and catechetics – was central to Irish social life. The established (episcopal) Church of Ireland – despite a sprinkling of members, clerical and lay, who showed an interest in native culture and antiquities – was overwhelmingly a church of the English language. The controversial exceptions were the members of evangelical missions to the Irish poor, active from the early nineteenth century and bitterly opposed by a resurgent Catholic Church. But the crucial factor in determining the issue of language use in religious worship was the disposition of the Catholic Church – the church of the majority.

In contrast to the situation in Wales or in Scotland – where the dominant religious culture and local churches were largely bulwarks of the indigenous Celtic languages in their heartlands – in Ireland the Catholic Church, as it recovered from the dislocation of the penal era, embraced English as the appropriate and most effective medium for its mission to the people.[10] Of course, pastoral needs dictated that in many dioceses effective ministry required some competence in Irish – certainly for direct communication with the lower peasantry. Some bishops were more attentive than others to these particular pastoral needs.[11] A clutch of catechisms, sample sermons and a very exceptional book of popular devotional literature supply further evidence of the use of Irish within the devotional life of the Catholic Church up to the famine.[12]

Moreover, while bishops encountered difficulties ensuring proficiency in Irish among the priests trained in the seminaries of continental Europe up to the end of the eighteenth century, thereafter the Irish seminaries (chiefly Maynooth) made no coherent effort to prepare clergy for pastoral duty through the medium of Irish. The Maynooth-trained priests undoubtedly included many competent Irish-speakers, and some who later used Irish in pastoral work.[13] But this was considered by all parties to be a transitional measure – until English percolated down to the lower peasantry.

---

9 N. Ó Ciosáin, 'Pious miscellanies and spiritual songs: devotional publishing and reading in Irish and Scottish Gaelic, 1760–1900', in Kelly and Mac Murchaidh, *Irish and English*, 270

10 For an overview, see V. E. Durkacz, *The decline of the Celtic languages* (Edinburgh, 1983); G. Jenkins (ed.), *The Welsh language and its domains, 1801–1911* (Cardiff, 2000).

11 See B. Ó Conchúir, *Scríobhaithe Chorcaí, 1700–1850* (Dublin, 1982); A. Heussaff, *Filí agus Cléir san Ochtú hAois Déag* (Dublin, 1992); G. Ó Tuathaigh, 'An Chléir Chaitliceach, an léann dúchais agus an cultúr in Éirinn, *c.*1750–*c.*1850', in P. Ó Fiannachta (ed.), *Léann na Cléire* (Maynooth, 1986), 110–39.

12 See Ó Ciosáin, 'Pious miscellanies and spiritual songs'.

13 N. M. Wolf, 'The Irish-speaking clergy in the nineteenth century: education, trends, and timing', *New Hibernia Review*, 12, 4 (Winter 2008), 68–83.

There was a further incentive: the missionary horizon of the Irish Catholic leadership throughout the world of the expanding British empire and later the wider Anglophone world. Irish Catholicism may have suffered discrimination at home in the penal era, but even before the absorption of Ireland formally into the British state by the Union of 1801, the Irish shared in the expanding British empire and, over time, the Irish would become the main source of clergy for the growing Catholic settlements throughout that empire. For missionaries as for the emigrant throng of the nineteenth century, English was the priceless asset for their future progress.

However complex the conjunction of factors driving the language shift, the direction was firmly set by the end of the eighteenth century. The concentration of population increase among the base of the rural society meant that the actual number of Irish-speakers increased in the period 1770–1845. But, as Fitzgerald's pioneering estimates demonstrated, this masked the underlying pattern of the language shift. His calculations of language transmission patterns from the 1770s to 1901 indicated that only 28 per cent of children born in the 1830s grew up with a knowledge of Irish. Moreover, while upwards of 40 per cent of the population may have been Irish-speaking in 1800, only 15 per cent, perhaps, were monoglot Irish-speakers. Intergenerational transmission of Irish was weakening, as need and opportunity for acquiring English percolated downwards and westwards.[14]

To the social and intergenerational dynamics of the language shift there was also a geographical dimension. Approaching the end of the eighteenth century, Connacht and Munster were still solidly Irish-speaking, with significant (if contracting) wedges of Irish-speakers across south Ulster and north Leinster and smaller pockets elsewhere. But the language frontier was moving in one direction only, with English advancing and replacing Irish, generally within a two- or three-generation span.

Clearly, the pattern of the language shift was already firmly embedded by the time of the Union of 1801. But the expanding role of the state under the Union was itself a major accelerator of the shift, extending its range and penetration throughout the nineteenth century: notably in policing, welfare and education. The rate of language shift was already accelerating in the opening three decades of the nineteenth century. The establishment in 1831 of a centralised, state-run and English-mediated system of elementary education was not the instigator of language change that some later language revivalists claimed, though the more uniform and systematic inculcation of English through the 'national schools' in later decades cannot be discounted.[15] A no less

14 G. Fitzgerald, 'Estimates for baronies of minimal level of Irish speaking amongst the successive decennial cohorts, 1771–1781 to 1861–1871', *Proceedings of the Royal Irish Academy*, 84C (1984), 117–55; Fitzgerald, 'Irish-speaking in the pre-famine period: a study based on the 1911 census data for people born before 1851 and still alive in 1911', *Proceedings of the Royal Irish Academy*, 103C, 5 (2003), 5–283.
15 For early difficulties, see M. E. Daly, *Social and economic history of Ireland since 1800* (Dublin, 1981), 111–18.

potent agent of popular socialisation through English was the mass politics of Daniel O'Connell in the twenty years before the famine – conducted overwhelmingly through English in all parts of the country.[16]

Estimates for the number of Irish-speakers in the immediate pre-famine period require caution, varying, as they do, from 1.5 million to as high as 4 million. Working backwards from an adjusted 1851 census figure, we might surmise that a figure of more than 3 million Irish-speakers in 1845 would not be unrealistic, given the heavy famine mortality among the poorest classes of the rural population and in the western half of the country.[17] The Great Famine decimated the rural underclass. Geographically and socially, the poorer areas and communities of the west – where Irish was strongest as a community language – were especially badly ravaged. But the acceleration of the shift became apparent in the census figures from 1851, the census of that year containing a 'language question' for the first time.[18] (See Table 4.1.)

Problems with the positioning (and clarity) of the 'language question' in the early censuses contributed, among other factors, to the under-reporting of Irish-language competence, in some estimates by as much as 40 per cent in 1851, so that the number of Irish-speakers in that year may well have been above 2 million. Likewise, the language data for the immediate post-famine censuses may also be underestimates. But, however imprecise the actual census data may be – at least up to the 1880s – the pace and pattern of the language shift was unmistakable.[19]

Table 4.1. Irish-speaking population, 1851–1901 ·

Census date	Total population	Speakers of Irish only		Total Irish-speakers	
		No.	%	No.	%
1841	8,175,124	Not enumerated		Not enumerated	
1851	6,552,365	319,602	4.9	1,524,286	23.3
1861	5,798,564	163,275	2.8	1,105,536	19.1
1871	5,412,377	103,562	1.9	817,875	15.1
1881	5,174,836	64,167	1.2	949,932	18.2
1891	4,704,750	38,121	0.8	680,174	14.5
1901	4,458,775	20,953	0.5	641,142	14.4

SOURCE: Table and calculations in Hindley, *The death of the Irish language*, 19.

16 O. MacDonagh, *O'Connell: the life of Daniel O'Connell 1775–1847* (London, 1991), 7–14.
17 Estimates extrapolated from Fitzgerald, 'Estimates for baronies of minimal level of Irish speaking' and from R. Hindley, *The death of the Irish language* (London, 1990), 13–20.
18 M. Ó Gliasáin, *The language question in the Irish census of population* (Dublin, 1986).
19 Hindley, *The death of the Irish language*, 19.

Continuing heavy emigration to the Anglophone world proved a powerful incentive for acquiring English – and for seeing no further utility in retaining Irish. At home, increasing retail penetration (facilitated by the expanding railway network), post offices, commercial travellers and a growing presence of religious personnel, with an infrastructure of education and welfare – all hastened the advance of English. The state itself – in addition to its already formidable presence since the 1830s – brought the schemes of the Congested Districts Board to the remotest Atlantic communities from the 1890s and pensions would follow more than a decade later. Even in the still strong Irish-speaking enclaves of the Atlantic rim, neither geographical remoteness nor socio-economic disadvantage could offer long-term insulation against the advance of English, with all the powerful vectors of social intercourse at its disposal. A monolingual English-speaking Ireland seemed a relatively close prospect. The consensus view was captured in the bureaucratic note accompanying the 1871 census: 'there can be no error in the belief that within a relatively few years Irish will have taken its place among the languages that have ceased to exist'.[20]

Remarkably this did not happen. A surge of cultural nationalism from the late nineteenth century produced a movement for the preservation of Irish as a living vernacular (and, for the more ambitious activists, its 'restoration' as a vernacular among the population at large). In short, the language revival movement sought to halt abandonment of the language in its heartlands (or Gaeltacht) and to reverse the by now deeply embedded process of replacing Irish with English, thus bringing cultural practice into alignment with the ideological proposition that the ancestral Irish language was essential to an authentic claim for a distinctive Irish nationality or identity. This movement and its project would deeply influence many of the first generation of leaders of the new self-governing Irish state after 1922, prompting them to embark on a remarkable experiment in language 'revival'.

Beginning with the exertions of the Society for the Preservation of the Irish Language (founded 1876), Irish first gained a foothold as an optional subject at second level for Intermediate examinations. But the Gaelic League – founded in 1893 by the scholars Douglas Hyde and Eoin MacNéill – built a more formidable support-base and lobbied more effectively than any earlier cultural organisation. Its objectives were the preservation of the existing Irish-speaking population, the extension, through education, of the use of Irish throughout the country, and the creation of a modern literature in Irish. The League not only established a serious Irish presence in print culture, but, more vitally, made headway in the education system.

In primary schools Irish became an ordinary subject and a new Bilingual Programme was introduced in 1904. More controversially, Irish was made obligatory

---

20 Cited in T. Crowley, *The politics of language in Ireland, 1366–1922: a sourcebook* (London and New York, 2000), 165.

for matriculation in the new National University in Ireland.[21] By 1922 some Irish was being taught in almost a quarter of all schools in the country. Yet, notwithstanding this impressive progress by the League, it did not succeed – even in the heyday of its influence – in arresting or even slowing the language shift to English. In fact, the years 1891–1926 saw a decline of 18 per cent in the total number of Irish-speakers, with continuing contraction in the language heartlands or Gaeltacht.

4.4. New States, Language and Identity

With the Anglo-Irish settlements of 1920–2, two states were established in Ireland, with totalising, and mutually exclusive, official narratives of identity. In Northern Ireland the dominant unionist majority asserted the essential Britishness of their heritage and identity: there was no prospect of the Irish language finding acknowledgement in official culture or policy. For a section of the nationalist minority, an attachment to the Irish language was a valued aspect of their national, as distinct from religious, identity. But it found little expression within the public sphere of their society. Recalling the binary terms of thinking on language and identity in Northern Ireland, Seamus Heaney later confessed that 'I tended to conceive of Irish and English as adversarial, as either/ or conditions rather than both/and ...'[22]

On the other hand, the new independent Irish state was determined to assert a distinct Irish cultural identity. A cohort of the new political leaders had been Gaelic League activists and assumed that one of the main tasks of the new Irish state would be to achieve the League's objectives, 'maintaining and extending' the use of Irish as a living vernacular. Accordingly, Irish was given recognition as 'the national language' in the first Irish Free State constitution, a status strengthened in the 1937 constitution, which declared Irish the 'first official language'. The actual language policy of the new government adhered closely to the strategy and priorities already devised by the Gaelic League: 'a strong emphasis on education policy, teaching methods, teacher training, developing a standard language and promoting a creative literature, securing the employment of competent Irish-speakers in the public service, and maintaining the Irish-speaking heartland'.[23]

The state's revivalist commitment was most aggressive in the education system; ensuring the acquisition of basic competence in Irish in the schools was the overriding objective. Irish was made a compulsory subject in all schools at elementary and second

21 T. A. O'Donoghue, *Bilingual education in Ireland, 1914–1922* (Perth, 2000); G. Ó Tuathaigh, 'The position of the Irish language', in T. Dunne (ed.), *The National University of Ireland: centenary essays, 1908–2008* (Dublin, 2008), 33–43.

22 S. Heaney, Introduction to *Boewulf: a new translation* (London, 1999), xxiv.

23 P. Ó Riagáin, *Language policy and social reproduction: Ireland 1893–1993* (Oxford, 1997), 9

level and as medium of instruction for other subjects in elementary schools. In the 1920s and 1930s Irish was made a compulsory subject for passing examinations (and being awarded certification) at the second level. From 1925 competence in Irish was required for recruitment to general grades of the civil service. High visibility for Irish in the naming of state agencies and offices, streets and public spaces, and symbolic use by prominent personages on formal occasions sought to enhance the prestige of the language.

Other, more modest initiatives were launched in publishing, theatre and in the fledgling state radio service. The standardisation and modernisation of the language – grammars and dictionaries – made progress, if often rather slowly. Specialist dictionaries of terms appeared in the 1920s, followed by a standard spelling guide in 1945, a standard grammar in 1953, an official English–Irish dictionary in 1959 and an official Irish–English dictionary in 1977.

The first wave of enthusiasm – from the revolutionary generation of state-builders – seemed to promise progress. By the early 1950s more than half the combined total of primary and secondary schools were using Irish as a medium of instruction, for at least part of the curriculum. But this was to prove the high point: by the 1960s the tide was ebbing rapidly on this experiment. More fundamentally, however, throughout the state apparatus of government and in the wider civic society, the evidence was unmistakable that cultural practice had stubbornly resisted being brought into alignment with declared state ideology. This was not surprising: in an open society and a liberal-democratic state, a cultural practice as fundamental as language use could not be altered merely by regulation or exhortation. Political leadership did not lead by example: the business of government, the legislature, the judiciary and administration (central and local) continued to function virtually exclusively through English, as did the vital spheres of commerce and religion.[24]

Competence without need or opportunities for use, and incessant exhortation without practical example, together with the seemingly irreversible melting away of the core Gaeltacht communities, inevitably bred disillusion with the state's declared commitment to the revival project and also – from the 1950s – growing opposition to the compulsory status of Irish in educational certification and in recruitment to the public service and other areas.

By the 1960s 'restoration' had been replaced in state rhetoric and policy by an elusively imprecise commitment to 'bilingualism'. The state increasingly retreated from a proactive position to one of seeking to respond (within narrow resource limits) to

---

24 For detailed consideration of this process, see G. Ó Tuathaigh, 'The state and the Irish language: an historical perspective', in C. Nic Pháidín and S. Ó Cearnaigh (eds.), *A new view of the Irish language* (Dublin, 2008), and, 'Language, ideology and national identity', in J. Cleary and C. Connolly (eds.), *The Cambridge companion to modern Irish culture* (Cambridge, 2005), 42–58.

demonstrable public demand, seeking at best to stay in step with public attitudes rather than driving a cultural agenda. In the early 1970s, requirements of competence were dropped for state certification of Leaving Certificate and for entrance to and promotion within the civil service. Expansion of access to second- and third-level education laid emphasis on meeting the challenges of economic and technological development and made only the most perfunctory obeisance to the place of the Irish language within the emerging education infrastructure.

The entry of Ireland to the European Economic Community (EEC) in 1973 did not generate – as some had hoped – a new context of multilingual normalcy conducive to improving attitudes and prospects for a renewed commitment to Irish. Consistent with the dominance of neoliberalism from the late 1970s, the notion of 'choice' in an open marketplace proved increasingly inhospitable to such state-supported cultural interventions of a linguistically protectionist kind that the vulnerable Irish language required for survival. A leading sociolinguist mused whether the attitude of the state towards Irish in the 1970s might be characterised as one of 'benign neglect'.[25]

However, the most grievous failure of the declared state policy was the failure to maintain, still less to strengthen, a sustainable Irish-speaking core community within the Gaeltacht. In 1926 the report of a government-appointed Commission of Enquiry into the predicament and prospects of the Gaeltacht captured the daunting legacy of linguistic fatalism with which the new state was confronted: 'Those who spoke it traditionally saw no avenue of advancement open to them or their children without English. Thus, it came to be accepted that the language was destined to pass.'[26]

The report of 1926 made many recommendations aimed at reversing these attitudes and constructing a sustainable Irish-language heartland: socio-economic interventions, ensuring state services through Irish in the Gaeltacht, a thorough overhaul of education provision. In the decades that followed a number of these recommendations were implemented, but generally partially and piecemeal, and with little effect on the underlying pattern of language shift. The continuing ravages of emigration and the relentless penetration of English resulted in the uninterrupted contraction of the Gaeltacht. The weaker residual pockets of native Irish-speakers died out; even in the strongest enclaves erosion continued, exacerbated by the massive emigration crisis of the 1950s (a net outflow from the state of more than 400,000 in that decade), in which the western periphery suffered major losses.

Thus, by the late 1950s – as an intergenerational shift in political leadership coincided with a major reappraisal of the project of economic protectionism, and as economic performance (rather than cultural essentialism) became the touchstone of

---

25 Ó Riagáin, *Language policy and social reproduction*, 23.
26 *Report of Coimisiún na Gaeltachta* (Dublin, 1926), 10.

Irish patriotic endeavour – a reconsideration of the Irish revival project was overdue. A new government commission (which sat from 1958 to 1963) restated the original belief in Irish as the essential marker of the nation's identity and made numerous recommendations aimed at building on progress already made and remedying defects in policy implementation and shortage of resources.[27] But the ideological and cultural context had changed fundamentally from the early decades of the century.

To suggest – as some Irish-language activists did from time to time – that simple bad faith or a lack of political resolve could account for the failure to sustain and to expand a vibrant Irish-speaking community in twentieth-century Ireland, would be to ignore the historical circumstances in which the Irish experiment in language 'restoration' was attempted. There could be no cultural protectionism in an open society such as Ireland from the extraordinary cultural hegemony of English as a world language, increasingly – as the twentieth century advanced – reflecting the global reach of the United States in popular entertainment, information technology and mass consumerism.

The Irish language predicament was not unique in the world. From the early modern period, in Europe, centralising national states (especially those constituting the metropole of expanding global empires) inexorably exerted linguistic hegemony over subordinated national communities within the state – as the experiences of Breton, Catalan, Basque and Galician testify, together with the Celtic languages of the British state. The centralising intention and capacity of the metropolitan state was the key determinant in each case. In Scandinavia, the interplay over the centuries between changing contours of power, hierarchies of cultural esteem and national sentiment determined the survival and relative strength of the languages of the region. The timing and specific historical circumstances of the Irish state's language revival project of the early twentieth century are fundamental to any understanding of its prospects and outcome.[28]

At the dawn of the twentieth century, before an Irish national state was established, the Irish were already a diasporic people, distributed overwhelmingly throughout the Anglophone world. Emigration to English-speaking countries would remain a central fact of Irish demographic and social history throughout most of that century. Again, for the majority of Irish Catholics, their religion provided a powerful, historically rooted sense of identity – which did not need further linguistic affirmation. The state itself – with its symbols, rituals and membership of international bodies – conferred an assured sense of Irish identity and national pride. Furthermore, with the international prestige attached to Irish writers in English from the 1920s – Yeats, Joyce, Shaw – the English

27 *An Coimisiún um Athbheochan na Gaeilge: An Tuarascáil Dheiridh* (Dublin, 1963).
28 The unique circumstances of the revival of Hebrew in the new Israel make it an inappropriate case for comparative purposes. For comparative perspectives, see R. Grillo, *Dominant languages: language and hierarchy in Britain and France* (Cambridge, 1989); D. Nettle and S. Romaine, 'Vanishing voices: the plight of the Celtic languages in global context', in M. Lloyd Jones, *First Language* (Llandysul, 2006).

of Ireland was more likely to be accepted as an authentic medium for 'Irish literature'.[29] At a popular level, the fame of John McCormack and his repertoire of 'Irish' songs, of Irish faces and voices in Hollywood and in the world of sport, entertainment and city politics in the USA, all fortified Irish confidence in English as a world language it had made 'its own'.

Indeed, in the light of these trends in global communications and the increasingly disengaged stance of the state in relation to Irish language policy, the more remarkable development was the growth from the 1980s of a bottom-up movement of popular demand for Irish-language schooling at primary and, in time, at second level – not least in the rapidly growing urban centres. But these new school-centred networks were now, clearly, those of a language minority seeking rights and facilities from a virtually neutral state, rather than the vanguard of a state-driven strategy of language change. Crucially, these recent networks have yet to establish the base for what the Irish-language revival failed to generate in the twentieth century: a sustainable urban community within which Irish dominates all the main arteries of social life.[30]

The changed context of state policy and its new emphasis on public attitudes is also relevant to new impulses and initiatives operating within the Gaeltacht from the later 1960s. A cohort of mainly young, educated Gaeltacht men and women (stimulated by 'civil rights' movements and rhetoric from the USA and Paris and, closer to home, Northern Ireland) mobilised politically, demanding a more radical response from the government to the predicament of their communities, as Irish-language communities under threat. They achieved results: a dedicated Gaeltacht radio station (1972), a substantial Gaeltacht development authority, with elected membership (Údarás na Gaeltachta), and a state-supported Irish-language television service (1995), all with their headquarters in the Galway Gaeltacht. These infrastructural props undoubtedly inculcated a more positive attitude towards Irish, now a source of employment, opportunity and progress for at least a cadre of young Gaeltacht broadcasters, entrepreneurs and educationalists.[31]

But even as employment prospects improved during the intervals of Irish economic growth from the last quarter of the twentieth century, unchecked in-migration, together with vigorous tourism development, added to the already powerful forces driving the advance of English within the surviving Gaeltacht enclaves. From the early twenty-first century a series of research reports documented clearly the accelerating weakening of the transmission of Irish, as a home or community language, to children and young

29 Yeats was awarded the Nobel Prize for Literature in 1923, Shaw in 1925.
30 For a concise survey of the 'voluntary' Irish-language sector, see *Treo 2000: Commission to examine the role of the Irish language voluntary organisations* (Dublin, 1997).
31 See, for example, I. Watson, *Broadcasting in Irish: minority language, radio, television and identity* (Dublin, 2003); B. Delap, 'Irish in the media', in Nic Pháidín and Ó Cearnaigh, *A new view of the Irish language*, 152–63.

adults in the Gaeltacht. Intergenerational transmission of ancestral cultural practice seemed close to final rupture in the remaining Gaeltacht heartlands.[32] In the early twenty-first century a belated Language Act (2003) gave some legislative substance – in terms of the delivery of state services through Irish to the dispersed and base Irish-speaking community – to the constitutional status of Irish. Its provisions promised to provide employment opportunities and incentives to an increased use of Irish in the state sector, but were unlikely to fundamentally alter the forces that have determined the firmly embedded cultural practices of language use in Ireland.

The communal violence that convulsed Northern Ireland from the late 1960s was rooted in issues of rights, ethnicity and identity, in which language was always likely to feature. Ethno-religious identities defined the polarisation, but cultural assertiveness – markedly in the working-class republican enclaves of Belfast and Derry – came to include demands for public recognition of the Irish language in the political and cultural accommodations being proposed for ending the thirty years of conflict. The 1998 Belfast Agreement committed the parties to 'understanding and toleration' in respect of cultural diversity, including language. Giving institutional and practical expression to this commitment, in the everyday lives of a divided community, is likely to continue to demand patience and restraint from all sides.[33]

By the second decade of the twenty-first century, the Irish language enjoyed a valued symbolic place in the rituals and ceremonial rites of the Irish state, an uneven presence in many domains of its civil life, and a more cautious presence in certain public domains (e.g. broadcasting, education, the arts) in Northern Ireland. It is unlikely that the foreseeable future will see a formal renunciation by any Irish government of the ideological identification of Irish as a significant (but not essential) marker of a distinctive Irish nationality. But, in the realm of cultural practice, whether a vibrant community of Irish-speakers (based on the developing urban networks of secondary bilinguals or on the dangerously fragile remnants of the Gaeltacht heartlands, or both) can be sustained and secure intergenerational transmission of Irish as a living community language into an indefinite future, must remain an open question.

FURTHER READING

Canny, N. 'The formation of the Irish mind: religion, politics and Gaelic Irish literature, 1580–1750', *Past and Present*, 95 (May 1982), 91–116.

32 See, for rich evidence, C. Ó Giollagáin, S. Mac Donnacha, F. Ní Chualáin, A. Ní Shéaghdha and M. O'Brien, *Comprehensive linguistic study of Irish in the Gaeltacht* (Dublin, 2007).
33 J. M. Kirk and D. P. Ó Baoill (eds.), *Linguistic politics: language policies for Northern Ireland, the Republic of Ireland, and Scotland* (Belfast, 2001); A. Mac Póilín (ed.), *The Irish language in Northern Ireland* (Belfast, 1997).

Crowley, T. *War of words: the politics of language in Ireland, 1537–2004* (Oxford, 2005).

Cunningham, B. *The world of Geoffrey Keating: history, myth and religion in seventeenth-century Ireland* (Dublin, 2000).

Daly, M. E. *The slow failure: population decline and independent Ireland, 1920–1973* (Madison, WI, 2006).

Daly, M. E. and D. Dickson (eds.). *The origins of popular literacy in Ireland: language change and educational development, 1700–1920* (Dublin, 1990).

de Brún, P. *Scriptural instruction in the vernacular: the Irish Society and its teachers, 1817–1827* (Dublin, 2009).

Delaney, E. *Demography, state, and society: Irish migration to Britain, 1921–1971* (Liverpool, 2000).

Hutchinson, J. *The dynamics of cultural nationalism: the Gaelic revival and the creation of the Irish nation state* (London, 1987).

Kelly, A. *Compulsory Irish: language and education in Ireland, 1870s–1970s* (Dublin, 2002).

Mahon, T. G. *Grand opportunity: the Gaelic revival and Irish society 1893–1910* (Syracuse, 2008).

Molony, J. N. *A soul came into Ireland: Thomas Davis 1814–1845: a biography* (Dublin, 1995).

Morley, V. *Ó Chéitinn go Raiftearaí* (Dublin, 2011).

Ó Buachalla, B. *Aisling Ghéar* (Dublin, 1997).

Ó Buachalla, S. *Education policy in twentieth-century Ireland* (Dublin, 1988).

Ó Ciosáin, N. *Print and popular culture in Ireland, 1750–1850* (Basingstoke, 1997).

Palmer, P. *Language and conquest in early modern Ireland* (Cambridge, 2001).

Quinn, J. *Young Ireland and the writing of Irish history* (Dublin, 2015).

Whelan, I. *The Bible war in Ireland: The 'Second Reformation' and the polarization of Protestant–Catholic relations, 1800–1840* (Dublin, 2005).

5 Catholic Ireland, 1740–2016

Colin Barr and Daithí Ó Corráin

5.1. 1740–1878

5.1.1. Church and Society

In 1730, everyone agreed that Ireland had too many priests. The Catholic bishops thought so; Rome thought so; and the Irish government certainly thought so. Although exact numbers are hard to recover, Emmet Larkin estimated that there were in that year perhaps two thousand Catholic priests engaged in parish work in Ireland.[1] A substantial proportion of these were friars (Franciscans and Dominicans), whose numbers had been steadily recovering after their effective expulsion in 1698. To the bishops, the friars appeared at best an ungovernable drain on scarce resources and at worst a source of scandal, and they frequently complained of them to Rome; to the government, Ireland seemed to be teeming with priests of all kinds, and they feared for the Protestant state. Perhaps ironically, it was Rome that took action.

In 1742, the Propaganda Fide (the Roman congregation with responsibility for the mission territories, including Ireland) limited each Irish bishop to twelve ordinations in his lifetime without regard to local need or the size of the diocese; although some exceptions were eventually allowed, in theory and to a degree in practice the archbishop of Dublin had no more ordinations than did the bishop of Achonry. In 1750, Rome turned its attention to the regular clergy, ordering that prospective friars had to undergo at least a year's novitiate on the continent before they could be received. This substantially increased costs, thus drying up the supply of men attracted by the

1 E. Larkin, *The pastoral role of the Roman Catholic Church in pre-famine Ireland, 1750–1850* (Dublin, 2006), 27.

opportunity to become a priest quickly and cheaply in Ireland. The bishops were also permitted to compel friars to become parish priests, which invariably meant the best and most committed were diverted from conventual life to parochial work. The result was that by 1840 the number of friars in Ireland had declined by some 77 per cent, or from around 800 to some 180 members.[2] The collapse was particularly severe after 1800, and by the time of the Great Famine the secular clergy dominated the Irish Catholic Church to an extent unseen almost anywhere else in Europe.

Until 1789, a longstanding network of Irish colleges in Europe supplied some forty priests a year for the Irish mission. This allowed for a slow growth in clerical numbers and ensured that the Irish church was fully abreast of liturgical, theological and devotional developments elsewhere. When the French Revolution closed these colleges, the flood of clerical refugees to Ireland masked the near-complete destruction of seminary training. This was met on a relatively ad hoc basis by several of the Irish bishops, and on a formal one by the Irish government when in 1795 it chose to endow the Royal College of St Patrick at Maynooth, County Kildare, to provide what was hoped would be a loyal priesthood.[3] Although Maynooth and a handful of the diocesan colleges proved enduring successes, it took time for them to replace the numbers once trained on the continent, and longer still to address the absolute need for priests among a rapidly growing population that was overwhelmingly Catholic. (From 1770 to 1840, the number of priests climbed from approximately 1,600 to 2,400, while the population grew from perhaps 2.6 million to more than 6.5 million.) That left pre-famine Ireland with a ratio of one priest to 2,750 people nationally, but with regional variations that ranged from 1:2,150 in the prosperous archdiocese of Dublin to 1:3,080 in the impoverished archdiocese of Tuam. In Europe the ratio ranged from 1:750 in Catholic Austria to 1:900 in Protestant Prussia. The French bishops believed the ideal ratio was 1:650.[4] This shortage shaped Irish Catholicism for the better part of a century.

The question of whether Ireland underwent a 'devotional revolution' in the decades after 1850 has dominated academic debate since Emmet Larkin first advanced the concept in 1972.[5] Did Archbishop Paul Cullen of Dublin make the Irish, in Larkin's phrase, 'practising Catholics'? What Larkin meant was that Cullen and the hierarchy succeeded in imposing a Tridentine model of parish-based administrative and devotional practice only after 1850.[6] It is undoubtedly the case that Irish Catholicism had developed its own local peculiarities, and that these were not fully extirpated until the second half of the

2 Ibid., 29–30.

3 See P. Corish, *Maynooth College* (Dublin, 1995).

4 Larkin, *Pastoral role*, 9–10.

5 E. Larkin, 'The devotional revolution in Ireland, 1850–1875', *American Historical Review* (June 1972), 625–52.

6 The most effective criticism of Larkin's thesis was T. McGrath, 'The Tridentine evolution of modern Irish Catholicism, 1563–1962: a re-examination of the "devotional revolution" thesis', *Recusant History*, 20 (1991), 512–23.

nineteenth century. It also seems clear that active participation in Catholic life – as meas-ured most easily, although still imperfectly, by attendance at Mass – was strikingly weak given what came later. Despite criticism, David W. Miller's estimate that by the 1830s rural Mass attendance was probably on average no more than 40 per cent has largely been sustained. There were of course regional variations: attendance was better in Leinster than further west or north-west, for example.[7] More people went to church on Sunday in towns than in rural areas. There seems to have been a class element, with rural labourers being less inclined than more established farmers to participate in the sacramental life of their church, whether out of hostility or preference, or because they were ashamed of their poverty and feared the collection plate.[8] Predominately Irish-speaking areas seem to have been less conventionally devout than English-speaking ones. Some sacraments, such as baptism, marriage and extreme unction, were highly valued and eagerly sought: no matter how overworked or otherwise unsatisfactory a priest was, he was expected to attend to the sick or dying. Others, such as confession and (especially) confirmation, were less attended to. Catholicism was and remained deeply embedded among the vast majority of the Irish population, but it was not always *Roman* Catholicism.

Irish religious practice in the pre-famine years was marked not only by relative dis-engagement from what might be termed the official church, but also by local practices that ranged from the idiosyncratic to the heterodox. Instances of the latter included a robust belief in the world of the fairies and other magical creatures and a concom-itant willingness to credit the efficacy of magic more generally. Such beliefs were still widespread in rural Ireland in the first half of the nineteenth century, and lingered on, as the burning of Bridget Cleary in 1895 sharply demonstrated.[9] They can still be glimpsed in rural topography. Unsurprisingly, magical practices also overlapped with or were overlaid by Catholic ones, whether via the adoption of pre-existing sacred sites such as holy wells or places of pilgrimage such as Croagh Patrick, or the deployment of Catholic symbols or implements in magical rituals like the lie-detecting crozier of County Mayo.[10] But as Vincent Comerford has pointed out, the underlying beliefs were *common* ones in Ireland, and not limited to the rural Catholic population, nor indeed to Catholics.[11] What was uniquely Catholic – and uniquely Irish – was the custom of 'stations', in which sacraments were administered, and dues collected, in private homes on a rotating basis. A direct result of the shortage of both priests and suitable ecclesias-tical buildings, stations slowly retreated as the provision of both increased.

---

7 See D. Miller, 'Mass attendance in Ireland in 1834', in S. Brown and D. Miller (eds.), *Piety and power in Ireland, 1760–1960: essays in honour of Emmet Larkin* (Belfast, 2000).

8 S. J. Connolly, *Priests and people in pre-famine Ireland, 1780–1845* (Dublin, 2001 [1982]), 103.

9 A. Bourke, *The burning of Bridget Cleary: a true story* (London, 1999).

10 Connolly, *Priests and people*, 116.

11 R. V. Comerford, 'Irish confessional relations', in C. Barr and H. Carey (eds.), *Religion and greater Ireland: Christianity and Irish global networks, 1750–1950* (Montreal and Kingston, Ont., 2015), 50.

In one sense the debate over Larkin's thesis has missed the point. As Thomas McGrath and others pointed out (and Larkin accepted), there were signs of change in Ireland long before 1850, whether measured by the building of churches and chapels, the foundation of confraternities and sodalities, the establishment of religious orders, the introduction of Roman devotions, the astonishing success of Father Mathew's temperance campaign, or the rough measure of attendance at Sunday Mass. These were particularly notable in the east from the early 1820s, and in the dioceses of energetic and reforming prelates such as Daniel Murray of Dublin and James Doyle of Kildare and Leighlin.[12] Murray, for example, oversaw a substantial campaign of church building in Dublin and served as midwife to the birth of, among others, the Loreto Sisters, Sisters of Mercy and Irish Vincentians. Important groups such as the Presentation Sisters, the Dominican Sisters and the Irish Christian Brothers were established even earlier. Renewed and well-funded Protestant missionary activity from the 1820s further concentrated Catholic minds.[13] But Larkin's point still stands: in 1850, Dublin, Kildare and their like remained the exceptions. The Catholic hierarchy did not have the personnel to provide, let alone impose, their preferred forms across the island. As the number of priests slowly rose, and the number of people sharply fell, this became increasingly possible. There was little point in a bishop fulminating against stations (or misbehaviour at wakes) if he could not provide a resident parish priest or a suitable parish church; and it was no sign of resistance to episcopal authority to believe in the efficacy of a holy well if there was no one to guide your devotions in more conventional directions. As for the fairies, the advent of the national system of education in 1831 slowly but inevitably reduced the power of their world, even if that came too late for Bridget Cleary.

5.1.2. Making a 'Roman' Catholic Nation

The appointment in late 1849 of Paul Cullen as archbishop of Armagh marked an important change in the course of Irish Catholicism. Born to a prosperous family in County Kildare in 1801, Cullen had been sent to Rome in 1819, where with the exception of three short holidays he remained until his elevation to the primatial see. In Rome, he had secured the patronage of the future Pope Gregory XVI, and through him appointment as rector of the recently revivified Irish College. In that role he became the official representative of the Irish hierarchy at the Holy See, and the unofficial agent of Irish bishops abroad as they sought advantages over their French, German, Scottish or Portuguese rivals.[14] An unapologetic enthusiast for the liturgical, theological,

---

12 For Doyle, see T. McGrath, *Religious renewal and reform in the pastoral ministry of Bishop James Doyle of Kildare and Leighlin, 1786–1834* (Dublin, 1999).

13 I. Whelan, *The Bible war in Ireland: The 'Second Reformation' and the polarization of Protestant–Catholic relations, 1800–1840* (Dublin, 2005).

14 See C. Barr, '"Imperium in imperio": Irish episcopal imperialism in the nineteenth-century', *English Historical Review* (2008), 611–50.

architectural, educational and devotional life of papal Rome, Cullen sought to import Italy into Ireland. Tired of the serial rows within the Irish hierarchy over such issues as charitable bequests and university education, Rome sent Cullen with the authority of an apostolic delegate and orders to convene the first national synod of the Irish Catholic Church.[15] Duly held in August 1850 in the County Tipperary town of Thurles, the synod built on precedents established by Roman-trained Irish-American bishops in Philadelphia and Baltimore to standardise every aspect of the administrative life of the church, from the placement of baptismal fonts to the powers, responsibilities and financial arrangements of the parish clergy. The Synod of Thurles marked the full-throated introduction of Tridentine Roman Catholicism into Ireland. Cullen's own translation to the archdiocese of Dublin two years later cemented it.

As archbishop of Dublin, Cullen exercised unprecedented power. This largely flowed from his mastery of Roman politics, which allowed him to extend his reach beyond his own ecclesiastical province, which was one of four, and into nearly all of Ireland's twenty-eight dioceses. His primary mechanism was arranging for the replacement, retirement or removal of bishops who did not meet his standards for energy and good practice; very few episcopal appointments occurred between 1850 and Cullen's death in 1878 without his express approval or at least acquiescence. The primary exception was in the archdiocese of Tuam in the west, where Archbishop John MacHale mounted a determined resistance against Cullen and all his doings. He was, for example, one of only two Irish bishops to oppose papal infallibility at the first Vatican Council in 1870, while Cullen wrote the dogma itself. MacHale outlived his antagonist by three years, and it is no accident that older forms of devotional practice and ecclesiastical organisation endured the longest in Tuam.

There were other regional variations, in particular in the north-east where Catholics found themselves in the minority, and often substantially so. Through most of the period, Catholics made common if uneasy cause with Presbyterians who also felt marginalised in an avowedly Anglican state. This was most obviously true in the years leading up to the rebellion of 1798, but it endured, if not always comfortably, until home rule became a realistic possibility. In 1868, for example, Catholics and newly enfranchised working-class Presbyterians combined to elect for Belfast a notorious Orangeman pledged to the cause of disestablishing the Church of Ireland. The city's increasing and increasingly violent sectarianism made such accommodations difficult, but they remained possible through the 1870s. Although the ever-present risk of violence or Orange provocation made northern Catholics warier, more insular and more discreet about public displays of faith, it did not prevent them from pursuing a similar programme of

---

15 See D. Kerr, *Peel, priests, and politics: Sir Robert Peel's administration and the Roman Catholic Church in Ireland, 1841–1846* (Oxford, 1984) and *'A nation of beggars?': priests, people, and politics in famine Ireland, 1846–1852* (Oxford, 1998).

institution-building as elsewhere on the island. This can be seen, for example, in the steady erection of the massive St Patrick's Cathedral in Armagh, which was finally completed in 1904.

On whatever measure, institutional Catholicism exploded in the mid-Victorian era, and the devotional lives of Irish Catholics came more and more into line with Roman practice. The remarkable popular piety of the twentieth century had its roots not in the penal era, but in Cullen's. In material terms, Cullen and the other Irish bishops built an astonishing number of parish churches, which if rarely beautiful were certainly commodious and invariably in conformity with Tridentine norms. Convents spread across the island, led by the Sisters of Mercy but including many other groups of women, some contemplative, some not, committed to education at every level and of every class, to nursing, and to orphanages or asylums. As Larkin put it, 'cathedrals, churches, chapels, convents, monasteries, seminaries, parochial houses, episcopal palaces, schools, colleges, orphanages, hospitals and asylums all mushroomed in every part of Ireland' in a building boom that lasted from Cullen's arrival to the late 1870s.[16]

To a degree, and especially in Dublin, the vast Catholic infrastructure dedicated to the poor was built in direct response to a new wave of Protestant evangelisation targeted at urban Catholics.[17] Margaret Aylward, for example, formed a group of pious women dedicated to visiting the workhouses of Dublin which grew into a religious order (the Holy Faith Sisters) with several schools and a system of fostering in preference to the institutionalisation of orphaned or abandoned children. When Aylward was imprisoned for refusing to return a Catholic child to its mother for fear of its spiritual fate, Cullen enthusiastically supported her.[18] Under Cullen the church tried to provide the institutional and moral framework to keep Catholics and Protestants socially, spatially and sexually separate at every stage of life.

In those areas in which the state retained nominal control, such as primary education and poor relief, the Catholic Church strove to gain effective supervision of its members. The open, almost entrepreneurial, nature of the national system of education made this possible: despite relentless complaints from the hierarchy, the majority of national schools were for all practical purposes Catholic, and overseen by priests. Cullen also assisted with or approved the foundation of secondary schools, many run by resurgent religious orders. In 1878, the British government instituted (with Cullen's approval) a system of payment by results for students in such schools. By allowing state money to flow to denominational schools, the Intermediate Education Act subsidised Catholic education at all levels throughout the country. The sole exception was higher education, where Cullen's experiment (with John Henry Newman) in founding

16 E. Larkin, *The historical dimensions of Irish Catholicism* (Washington, DC, 1997), 27.
17 See M. Moffitt, *The Society for Irish Church Missions to the Roman Catholics, 1849–1950* (Manchester, 2010).
18 J. Prunty, *Margaret Aylward: lady of charity, sister of faith, 1810–1899* (Dublin, 1999).

a Catholic university in Dublin proved a signal failure.[19] The workhouses were a greater challenge, although Cullen and the other bishops worked hard to ensure the segregation of morally compromised inmates (unmarried mothers, prostitutes, drunkards) from the 'deserving' poor.

The second half of the nineteenth century also saw the effective return of the religious orders to Ireland. Some, such as the Jesuits, had been in place before Cullen's appointment. Others, such as the Franciscans and Dominicans, had never left, although their numbers and activities had been severely constrained. Cullen used his position of apostolic visitor to all the religious in Ireland to encourage new orders and reform established ones. The Franciscans, for example, were almost entirely (and somewhat reluctantly) remade under his orders. By 1856, they had some fifty-five friars living in sixteen convents and they continued to expand into the twentieth century.[20] But Cullen preferred newer orders such as the Vincentians and Redemptorists, with their Roman devotions and nationwide campaigns of parish missions. These utilised charismatic preaching and liturgical display to encourage people to approach the sacraments, and then enrolled them in confraternities or sodalities to keep up the enthusiasm after the missionaries had moved on. By Cullen's death, nearly every Irish parish outside Tuam had hosted at least one such mission. Their success did much to standardise Irish devotional and liturgical life around norms that Cullen and his protégés had themselves learned in papal Rome. Religious women were also encouraged and supported, and rapidly became an important and omnipresent provider of social and educational services throughout Ireland. When Cullen arrived in 1850, there were some 1,500 female religious in Ireland. When he died in 1878, there were more than 3,700.[21]

Under Cullen – who became Ireland's first cardinal in 1866 – the Irish Catholic Church definitively solved its manpower crisis. The number of priests increased by some 700 in absolute terms, while the ratio of priests to people fell from 1:3,300 in 1850 to 1:1,100 in 1870. As with the increase of religious women, this was achieved against the backdrop of a substantial export market for Irish clergy. With its newfound ability to reach into every corner of the island and to provide both a resident priest (or often priests) and suitable churches, the parish became the centre of Irish Catholic life. In it, new devotions, mostly of Roman origin, were encouraged. As Larkin put it, 'the rosary, forty hours, perpetual adoration, novenas, blessed altars, *Via Crucis*, benediction, vespers, devotion to the Sacred Heart and to the Immaculate Conception, jubilees, triduums, pilgrimages, shrines, processions, and retreats' all flourished under the

---

19 C. Barr, *Paul Cullen, John Henry Newman, and the Catholic University of Ireland, 1845–65* (Notre Dame, IN, 2003).

20 P. Conan OFM, 'Reforming and seeking an identity, 1829–1918', in E. Breathnach, J. MacMahon OFM, and J. McCafferty (eds.), *The Irish Franciscans, 1534–1990* (Dublin, 2009), 108–9.

21 E. Larkin, *The historical dimensions of Irish Catholicism*, 77.

watchful eye of the parish clergy or missionary priests.[22] Devotion was channelled and encouraged not only through missions and Sunday worship, but also through pious organisations, holy medals, beads or pictures, or the increasing volume of religious texts produced by a thriving Catholic book trade. Most of these had existed in Ireland, in some form and in some places, before Cullen arrived in 1850. But Cullen achieved change on such a scale that Larkin's use of the term 'revolution' must surely be justified.

5.2.   1878–2016

5.2.1.   Clergy and Culture

By Cullen's death in 1878 an increasingly confident Irish church was characterised by a strong allegiance to Rome, a vast institutional presence through its control of Catholic education, health and welfare homes, a disciplined clergy under episcopal control, a remarkably high level of religious practice among the laity and a thriving 'spiritual empire' abroad. The Cullenite model remained largely intact for the next century during which four relative constants may be observed. The identification of faith and nationalist political identity, first harnessed by Daniel O'Connell, strengthened during the various efforts to end the Union and emerged triumphant in independent Ireland. Catholicism was also a core element of identity in France, Spain and Italy but identification alone could not prevent a steady decline in church allegiance in those countries. The Irish case was different because Catholicism was a key component in the struggle for political independence and in the subsequent state-building project. A second constant was the church's longstanding interest, irrespective of political jurisdiction after 1921, in the sensitive area of education and to a lesser extent health. Control of education was regarded as essential if Catholic faith and values were to be transmitted to future generations. The third was an obeisance to the legally constituted government, support for order, social stability and constitutionalism. Lastly, a pervasive culture of clericalism, at the heart of the unprecedented crisis in which the church is now mired, prevailed. This championed a clerical elite, institutional loyalty, conformity, anti-intellectualism and resistance to change. The decline in the authority and pre-eminent position of the Catholic Church, the rise of secularism and efforts to dismantle legislative and constitutional support for a Catholic ethos can be traced to the early 1960s. Although identification with Catholicism and religious practice in Ireland remained atypically high, survey evidence since the 1970s has revealed dramatic changes in the nature of being Catholic. As elsewhere, scandal has engulfed the Irish Catholic Church since the 1990s. Yet despite the dramatic failure of leadership and the loss of power,

22 Ibid., 77–8.

Figure 5.1 Archbishop Byrne blessing the foundation stone of an extension of the Whitefriar Street School, n.d. Preserved in the Dublin Diocesan Archives.

credibility and moral authority of the institutional church, 84.2 per cent described themselves as Catholic in the 2011 census. This suggests that Catholicism remains an integral, if difficult to define, aspect of Irish identity.

5.2.2.   Church and State

In his influential study David Miller has charted the efforts of the Catholic Church to remain on terms with both the 'state' (the British government) and the 'nation' (the Catholic population) in the final decades before independence.[23] In return for advancing its interests – the university question was particularly fractious until resolved by the creation of the National University of Ireland (NUI) in 1908 – the church would bestow its legitimacy on state and nation alike. But it was not a neutral arbiter and backed nationalist aspirations in the belief that the nation would eventually supplant the British imperial state. This required considerable political dexterity and moral and theological ambiguity on the matter of rebellion. From the 1880s until 1916 a majority of the nation was represented by the Irish Parliamentary Party (IPP) which sought Home Rule for Ireland. An informal but highly effective clerical–nationalist alliance,

23 D. W. Miller, *Church, state and nation in Ireland, 1898–1921* (Dublin, 1973).

cultivated by Parnell, was disrupted by the IPP split. It re-emerged, however, when the party was reunited under Redmond in 1900. There were limits to the political influence of the church just as there was a variety of political standpoints within the hierarchy and among the clergy. Church authority was accepted without demur in matters deemed to be within the ecclesiastical domain such as education or health. But where land (perhaps the greatest Irish obsession) and politics were concerned the church had little choice but to demonstrate that it was of and with the people. Secular clergy and some bishops were therefore sympathetic to tenant agitation during the Land War (1879–82) and subsequent Plan of Campaign despite Vatican disapproval. Archbishop William Walsh was concerned for the plight of the workers during the 1913 Lockout and Ireland's small urban working class was not divorced from belief and practice in the manner of large segments of the same class in Europe. The third Home Rule crisis (1912–14) demonstrated the limitations of the hierarchy's political influence. Redmond largely ignored its concerns about the financial and educational aspects of the measure. His acceptance of partition in 1914 alienated the northern bishops and their flock who feared their interests would suffer under a unionist government in Belfast. This was the beginning of a rupture with the IPP as the church adapted itself to a political landscape profoundly altered by an inoperative Home Rule measure, disenchantment with the First World War, and the 1916 Rising. The church's traditional abjuration of violence, so evident in its response to Fenianism, was moderated between 1916 and 1918 by the shift in popular opinion occasioned by ill-conceived government policy in the aftermath of the Rising and embodied in the new nationalism of Sinn Féin. The church's alignment with majority nationalist opinion was demonstrated during the massive protest campaign against conscription in 1918 which the hierarchy declared was 'against the will of the Irish nation'. During the War of Independence clerical opposition focused on the violent methods employed but not on the goal of independence.

A majority of Catholic Ireland supported the Anglo-Irish Treaty which granted a significant measure of self-government but not a republic and could not prevent civil war. The Catholic Church played an important role in securing popular legitimacy for the fledgling Irish Free State. Prompted by the government, in October 1922 the hierarchy expressed horror at the destruction and loss of life and maintained that 'no one is justified in rebelling against the legitimate government … set up by the nation and acting within its rights'. In the aftermath of the conflict, Catholicism and the reification (if not active use) of the Irish language provided a sense of shared identity and cohesion clearly distinct from Protestant Britain.[24] Remarkably little hostility was shown to the church even by republicans excommunicated during the civil war. During the uncertainties of the 1920s the church offered the new state continuity, stability and an extensive infrastructure with more than 13,000 clergymen and nuns. In return, a

24 P. Corish, *The Irish Catholic experience: a historical survey* (Dublin, 1985), 244.

financially bankrupt government was content to see the church consolidate and extend its institutional presence in the realms of education, health and welfare with minimal interference – a pattern which continued until the 1960s. The well-established nine-teenth-century archetype of pillarisation in these spheres continued as before. The Catholic Church was more secure and more confident than at any previous time; it had little to fear from rival churches and enjoyed close links with the state. The situation was very different in Northern Ireland where the experience of Irish Catholicism before the 1960s was marked by a sense of being in but not of the state. Antagonism initially characterised relations between church authorities, who had a political importance as spokesmen for the minority, and the northern administration. After the Second World War the opportunities occasioned by the welfare state saw the northern Catholic bish-ops adopt a more pragmatic approach as they moved from highlighting the injustice of the state to injustices within it. There was never any question that the political border would compromise the unity of the Catholic Church whose map image remained an all-Ireland one.[25] Abroad, Catholic Ireland's missionary activity, both male and female, continued to prosper whether following the British empire into Africa and Asia, the Maynooth Mission to China (founded in 1916) or serving the Irish diaspora from Birmingham to Brisbane. This laid the basis for concern with the developing world from the 1960s. It paved the way for non-governmental organisations (NGOs) such as Concern, established in 1968, and Trócaire, the Irish church's official overseas develop-ment agency founded in 1973, with its distinctive Lenten collection boxes.

5.2.3. Moral Monopoly?

The Irish Free State was not a theocracy but Catholicism was 'effectively transformed into a civil theology'.[26] That the political culture had a pronounced Catholic ethos was inevitable given the Catholic educational formation of successive generations of Irish elites in politics, business and public service, and an extraordinary level of religious homogeneity. The 1926 census revealed that Catholics comprised 93 per cent of the population. As Tom Inglis has argued, a Catholic habitus – a way of thinking and act-ing in conformity with a systematic view of the world – permeated all social classes and religious capital facilitated the acquisition of economic, political or social capital.[27] And so during the first fifty years of independence both church and state leaders, irrespective of political party, shared a desire to develop the country according to a philosophy of Catholic nationalism. In this sense the coming to power of Fianna Fáil

---

25 See D. Ó Corráin, *Rendering to God and Caesar: the Irish churches and the two states in Ireland, 1949–73* (Manchester, 2006), 43–69.
26 D. V. Twomey, *The end of Irish Catholicism?* (Dublin, 2003), 32–3.
27 T. Inglis, *Moral monopoly: the rise and fall of the Catholic Church in modern Ireland* (Dublin, 1998), 11–12.

under de Valera in 1932 was marked by a sense of continuity in church–state relations. The new government demonstrated its loyalty to Catholicism during the 31st Eucharistic Congress, a showpiece of global Catholicism, held in Dublin in June 1932. Unlike France or Italy, no anticlerical party emerged in Ireland and this reflected the failure of left-wing politics to develop. Until the 1960s there was an informal consensus between political and religious leaders but ministers did not submissively dispose as the bench of bishops proposed. For example, diplomatic relations were opened with the Vatican in 1929 despite the opposition of the hierarchy and the Dunbar-Harrison case in 1931 demonstrated the resolve of the Cosgrave government to reject the imposition of religious tests against non-Catholics.[28] Too much has been made of the 'mother and child' debacle in 1951 which was less a church–state crisis than an internal government one. Two years later, firmer leadership on the same issue by Fianna Fáil negated the opposition of the Irish Medical Association (doctors' fears about fees were central to the 1951 saga) and an episcopal impulse to embed certain Catholic principles in social legislation.

Figure 5.2 Priest speaking to farmer by gate, n.d. but *c.* 1910. Image from the Wiltshire Collection. Courtesy of the National Library of Ireland.

28 See D. Keogh, *Ireland and the Vatican: the politics and diplomacy of church–state relations, 1922–1960* (Cork, 1995), 36–92; J. J. Lee, *Ireland 1912–1985: politics and society* (Cambridge, 1989), 161–7.

Significant elements of the Catholic moral code were enshrined in law, particularly in the areas of sexual morality and family relations. Conservatism remained a feature of most aspects of Irish life between the 1920s and 1950s. For this reason the censorship of films (1923) and publications (1929), the prohibition of divorce (1925) and a ban on the importation and sale of contraceptives (1935) were broadly favoured by all the Christian churches. Many commentators have overstated the influence of Catholic social teaching – in particular *Quadragesimo anno* (1931) which reinvigorated the Catholic social movement through its emphasis on solidarity and subsidiarity – on the 1937 constitution. Recent legal scholarship has criticised that view and emphasised the extent to which the document reflected secular values such as respect for individual rights and separation of the church and state.[29] Famously, article 44.2.1 acknowledged 'the special position' of the Catholic Church as the guardian of the faith professed by the great majority of citizens. Such recognition was common in other Catholic countries but the 1937 constitution did not establish the Catholic Church or describe it as the one true church. Instead it guaranteed not to endow any religion. The 'special position' clause was deleted with minimum fuss in a referendum in 1972 under the shadow of the Northern Ireland Troubles. The most important manifestation of the new Catholic social teaching in this period was Muintir na Tíre, a community development organisation founded by Father John Hayes in 1931.

Between the 1920s and the 1950s the institutional church was at its most dominant, and devotional practices by a devout and deferential laity, in addition to weekly attendance at Mass, were at their most visible and numerous. These activities included benediction, membership of confraternities and sodalities, pilgrimages, parish missions, processions, the rosary, stations, novenas, reading abundant devotional literature, devotion to the Sacred Heart, the cult of the saints and their relics, and Marian devotion (the cult of Mary was well established before independence as the fascination with Knock and Lourdes testifies). At an official level, the absence of a civic ceremonial resulted in a reliance on Catholic ceremonial such as special masses for the opening of the Dáil and other occasions. Visitors to Ireland, both lay and clerical, were struck by the extent to which Irish life was imbued with the language, symbols and rituals of Catholicism. Despite the legislative and moral protectionism afforded by censorship, this period was none the less a time of vigilance and fortress Catholicism. Sermons and pastorals warned relentlessly of the menace of atheistic communism at home and abroad, proselytism, evil literature, indecent Hollywood movies, immodest dress, courting in public, excessive drinking, secularism, materialism, 'leakage of the faith' among Irish emigrants, and, in particular, the craze for pleasure. Dance halls, or more accurately the

---

29 G. Hogan, 'De Valera, the constitution and the historians', *Irish Jurist*, 40 (2005), 293–320.

Figure 5.3 Industrial tribute to Our Lady in Tonge & Taggart factory, Dublin, *c.* 1954. Image copyright J. Walsh. Courtesy of the Dublin Diocesan Archives.

opportunities they afforded for sexual immorality, were the greatest clerical obsession. Patrick Kavanagh's fictional character Tarry Flynn, poet and bachelor farmer, greatly admired the Catholic religion 'because it kept girls virtuous until such time as he'd meet them'.[30] The hierarchy's approach to the laity was authoritarian, prescriptive and dogmatic. In spite of the hothouse climate, there were dissenting voices which maintained that Irish Catholicism was less secure than it appeared in the face of the rising tide of secularism. In 1959 one priest warned that an increasingly middle-class Ireland was 'trying to make do with a peasant religion' instead of 'a religion to fit our needs'.[31] This was due in part to the absence of theology in Ireland, as the discipline remained a clerical preserve. The prohibition of a theology faculty was a condition of the hierarchy's support for the establishment of the NUI in 1908. This helps explain why Ireland has generally lacked a Catholic philosophical tradition in public discourse.

30 P. Kavanagh, *Tarry Flynn* (London, 1978 [1948]), 11.
31 J. Kelly, 'Solid virtue in Ireland', *Doctrine and Life*, 9, 5 (1959), 120, cited in L. Fuller, *Irish Catholicism since 1950: the undoing of a culture* (Dublin, 2002), 61.

5.2.4. Modernisation and Crisis

Change and modernisation were the zeitgeist of the 1960s and they gradually dissolved the defensive walls surrounding Irish Catholicism. Over the past half-century a variety of factors combined to transform Irish society and the place of religion within it. From the premiership of Lemass onwards, the state prioritised economic growth over the simpler Catholic nationalist vision which had prevailed since independence. The establishment of a national television service in December 1961 was the most significant instrument of modernisation. Coupled with the relaxation of the laws on censorship, programmes such as the *Late Late Show* facilitated the questioning of traditional structures of authority and over time reduced the influence of priests, bishops and even popes. The expansion of the market and the media in subsequent decades 'ushered in a new habitus that was based on liberal-individualism, materialism and consumerism, the very things against which the Church had preached so vehemently for generations'.[32] The shift from God and self-denial to Mammon and consumption was spectacularly evident during the 'Celtic Tiger' era. The changing position of women was also crucial in modernising Ireland, particularly from the 1970s onwards. Irish women challenged the patriarchal nature of Irish society and traditional church teaching on birth control and on the natural role of woman as mother and home-maker. Inglis contends that the Irish mother played a vital role in the development and transmission of Irish Catholicism from generation to generation. Once women were able to access alternative sources of power through the workplace and public life, a key pillar of the church's ideological control was removed.[33]

The Second Vatican Council (1962–5) generated an expectation of change in the religious sphere which was ultimately unfulfilled. It sought *aggiornamento*, the bringing of the church up to date. Proceedings were extensively reported by the media and Catholic Ireland greeted the key deliberations – on the nature of the church as the people of God, the collegiality of the bishops and lay participation in the mission of the church – with optimism. By contrast, the Irish ambassador to the Vatican described the hierarchy's attitude as 'the reverse of exuberant'.[34] The bishops were wary of change lest it undermine their *magisterium* or endanger the faith and morals of the laity. Hence, John Charles McQuaid, the formidable archbishop of Dublin, reassured a congregation that 'no change will worry the tranquillity of your Christian lives'.[35] Ireland did not witness the fractious division over alterations to liturgy, theology, church governance and

---

32 T. Inglis, 'Individualism and secularisation in Catholic Ireland', in S. O'Sullivan (ed.), *Contemporary Ireland: a sociological map* (Dublin, 2007), 68.
33 See Inglis, *Moral monopoly*, 178–200.
34 Ó Corráin, *Rendering to God and Caesar*, 203.
35 Ibid., 206.

ecumenism that occurred in other European countries and in North America, but the local implementation was legalistic and narrow. As Vincent Twomey put it, 'unthinking to the end, a provincial and submissive Church simply and obediently carried out the instructions coming from Rome that unintentionally but effectively dismantled their own, deeply cherished version of Catholicism'.[36] Aside from participation as Eucharistic ministers and readers, the laity remained on the margins, the failure to permit women to play a significant role at all levels of decision-making within the church continued, and it took years before a dialogue was opened between the conference of priests and the hierarchy. Advances in inter-church relations, a key aim of the Council, occurred largely due to the violence of the Northern Ireland Troubles.

The extension of educational opportunity, particularly at second level, produced a population no longer willing to accept dictation on issues considered matters of individual conscience. This was evident in the Irish response to *Humanae Vitae*, Pope Paul VI's contested encyclical in 1968 which reaffirmed traditional church opposition to artificial means of birth control. A survey by Mícheál Mac Gréil in 1977 revealed a gulf between the orthodox beliefs of the Vatican and those of the faithful in respect of artificial contraception (63 per cent disagreed that it was always wrong), celibacy (46 per cent agreed that priests should be allowed to marry) and homosexuality (43 per cent agreed that it should be decriminalised).[37] Another study found that slightly less than half did not fully believe in the devil and hell, an indication that the habitual fear of eternal damnation was waning.[38] The survey findings indicated that the higher the level of educational attainment, the lower the level of orthodox religious belief, acceptance of church teaching and attendance at confession. In this sense the papal visit in 1979, when an estimated 2.7 million people greeted John Paul II, was less a celebration of Catholic Ireland than an unsuccessful attempt to slow down the inroads made by materialism and secularism. This was underlined by legislative and constitutional change, and by a collapse in vocations.

For much of the twentieth century Ireland was unique among western countries in not permitting abortion, contraception or divorce. The hierarchy held the traditional line on these issues, but for the first time in 1973 openly acknowledged that the state should not be the guardian of private morality. In Britain and the United States change in this sphere occurred over a century, but in Ireland seven 'moral issue' constitutional referendums on abortion and divorce were held between 1983 and 2002. They were preceded by the legalisation of contraception in 1979, as a result of a Supreme Court ruling in the McGee case, with further extensions in 1985 and 1992. The insertion of an

36 Twomey, *Irish Catholicism*, 35–6.
37 M. Mac Gréil, *Prejudice and tolerance in Ireland* (Dublin, 1977), 411.
38 M. Nic Ghiolla Phádraig, 'Religion in Ireland: preliminary analysis', *Social Studies: Irish Journal of Sociology*, 5, 2 (1976), 120.

ambiguously worded pro-life amendment in 1983 was carried by a two to one majority in a poll of only 54 per cent. In the wake of the 'X' case which ruled the risk of suicide as grounds for abortion, three concurrent referendums in 1992 affirmed freedoms of travel and information about abortion services but not the risk of suicide as grounds to allow an abortion. The latter position was reaffirmed in a further referendum in 2002. Concerns about property rights and pressure from the pulpit led 63 per cent to reject divorce in 1986. Nine years later divorce was narrowly approved. The so-called liberal agenda during this tumultuous period was a reflection rather than a cause of change.

Between 1966 and 1996 vocations to all forms of religious life fell from 1,409 to 111, a decline of 92 per cent.[39] This was most acute among religious orders, some of which will disappear. The number of diocesan clergy has also contracted drastically. In 1984 there were 171 ordinations; in 2006 there were 22. In 2012 just 12 seminarians began their training for Ireland's 26 dioceses, the lowest number on record. During the 1990s seminaries in Dublin, Thurles, Kilkenny, Waterford and Carlow closed; only the national seminary in Maynooth remains. At a parish level, an ageing and declining cohort of priests have increasing demands on their time and energy. Greater lay ministry will be required to sustain the church into the future. Without the human resources to staff the myriad hospitals, welfare homes and schools, the church's institutional presence has contracted. Increased running costs, greater state involvement and professionalisation of services have prompted a withdrawal of religious in welfare and medical institutions. The church still exerts immense influence on the education system through its patronage, management and ownership of 2,841 primary schools (90 per cent); in addition, about half of post-primary schools are under denominational control. But there is a growing demand for a plurality of models of provision and a school system better aligned with the needs of a more diverse population.[40]

The secularisation of Catholic Ireland is not easy to measure or expound. While census evidence has demonstrated a steady identification with Catholicism, religiosity has changed significantly. In 2011 84% of the population identified themselves as Catholic, a decline of just 10% since 1971. This has less to do with disaffiliation than with the significant immigration of other religious denominations since the 1990s. Attitudinal research reveals a divergence between high levels of belief and declining formal religious practice. Mac Gréil found that just 3.9% of respondents in 2007–8 did not believe in the existence of God and that six of every seven reported some level of 'closeness to God'. Similarly, in 2008 the International Social Survey Programme found high levels of belief in heaven (90%), life after death (75%) and miracles (65%).[41] By contrast,

---

39 Inglis, *Moral monopoly*, 212.
40 *Forum on patronage and pluralism in the primary sector: report of the forum's advisory group* (April 2012).
41 M. Mac Gréil, *Pluralism and diversity in Ireland: prejudice and related issues in early 21st century Ireland* (Dublin, 2011), 462; P. Share, M. Corcoran and B. Conway, *A sociology of Ireland* (4th edn, Dublin, 2012), 335.

between 1974 and 2008 there was a sharp decrease in attendance at weekly Mass (from 91 to 43%), monthly Holy Communion (from 66 to 43%) and monthly confession (from 47 to 9%).[42] Mac Gréil's study revealed significant differences in weekly Mass attendance by age cohort (19.7% of 18–25 year olds attended compared with 83.1% of those over 71), location (29.5% in urban areas with a population of more than 100,000 but 62.7% in rural Ireland) and educational attainment (75.7% of those with primary education or less compared with 34.1% with third-level education). Most striking was the finding that confession was 'dying out', further indication of the erosion of the church's ideological power. One-third of Catholics never go to confession, only 28% go 'several times a year', and slightly less than half of 18–40 year olds had given up going altogether.[43] A number of reasons for an increasing detachment from the institutional church can be advanced. Participation rates, historically regarded as uniquely high, may simply be converging with other European and western countries. Unquestionably, the number with a genuine faith commitment has shrunk. Understanding of the basic tenets of Catholicism has become so poor that even in seminary training a propaedeutic year is being introduced.[44] Secondly, the church in contemporary Ireland has little influence over public opinion, the state and the media. Indeed, the last has become the chief supplier of alternative value systems. The media has also provided an intense critique of religious institutions which were once above public scrutiny. Thirdly, the divergence between the church and the general population on social and moral matters has continued to increase. For instance, the percentage of non-marital births has increased from 4% in 1977 to 31.4% in 2005.[45] In May 2015 a referendum on same-sex marriage was approved by 62%. Fourthly, an increasing number of Irish Catholics may belong but not fully believe, for whom Catholicism is part of a socio-cultural identity expressed in key rites of passage from cradle to grave such as baptism, marriage and last rites. Lastly, the clerical sex abuse scandals and the church's inadequate response have been intensely corrosive.

Since the 1990s scandal has besieged the Irish Catholic Church. The emotional, physical and sexual abuse of children by a minority of clergy and religious was revealed in a cascade of harrowing inquiry reports: Ferns (2005), Ryan (2009), Murphy (2009) and Cloyne (2011) among others. They revealed a failure of leadership, hypocrisy and a dysfunctional authoritarian institutional culture more concerned with avoiding scandal and secrecy than with protecting the vulnerable. The betrayal of trust has undermined the credibility and moral authority of the institutional church. A pastoral letter of apology from Pope Benedict XVI in March 2010 was too little and too late. The scale of

---

42 Mac Gréil, *Pluralism and diversity*, 447.
43 Ibid., 448–9, 454.
44 J. Littleton, 'Being a Catholic in Ireland today', in J. Littleton and E. Maher (eds.), *Contemporary Catholicism in Ireland: a critical appraisal* (Dublin, 2008), 17.
45 B. Hilliard, 'Family', in O'Sullivan, *Contemporary Ireland*, 88.

clerical abuse may have appeared greater because decades of crimes were investigated in a relatively short period of time. The institutional church does not stand indicted alone. The Irish state and society also colluded by their failure to safeguard the marginalised. Since the 1990s the church has put in place stringent child protection guidelines. The scandals have overshadowed the invaluable work of priests, religious and Catholic voluntary organisations such as the Society of St Vincent de Paul to ameliorate economic hardship and social inequality. Over the longer term the scandals were 'just the final act in a long play of structural transformation' which has denuded the power and influence of the church.[46] As an institution, the Catholic Church currently labours under the challenges of coping with the past and salvaging its precarious position to find a relevant role in contemporary Ireland.

FURTHER READING

Barr, C. '"Imperium in Imperio": Irish episcopal imperialism in the nineteenth century', *English Historical Review* (2008), 611–50.

Barr, C. *Paul Cullen, John Henry Newman, and the Catholic University of Ireland, 1845–65* (Notre Dame, IN, 2003).

Bhreathnach, E., J. MacMahon and J. McCafferty (eds.). *The Irish Franciscans, 1534–1990* (Dublin, 2009).

Bourke, A. *The burning of Bridget Cleary: a true story* (London, 1999).

Comerford, R. V. 'Irish confessional relations', in C. Barr and H. Carey (eds.), *Religion and greater Ireland: Christianity and Irish global networks, 1750–1950* (Montreal and Kingston, Ont., 2015).

Connolly, S. J. *Priests and people in pre-famine Ireland, 1780–1845* (Dublin, 2001 [1982]).

Corish, P. *The Irish Catholic experience: a historical survey* (Dublin, 1985).

Corish, P. *Maynooth College* (Dublin, 1995).

Forum on patronage and pluralism in the primary sector: report of the forum's advisory group (April 2012).

Hogan, G. 'De Valera, the constitution and the historians', *Irish Jurist*, 40 (2005), 293–320.

Inglis, T. *Moral monopoly: the rise and fall of the Catholic Church in modern Ireland* (Dublin, 1998).

Keogh, D. *Ireland and the Vatican: the politics and diplomacy of church–state relations, 1922–1960* (Cork, 1995).

Kerr, D. '*A nation of beggars?*': *priests, people, and politics in famine Ireland, 1846–1852* (Oxford, 1998).

Kerr, D. *Peel, priests, and politics: Sir Robert Peel's administration and the Roman Catholic Church in Ireland, 1841–1846* (Oxford, 1984).

46 Inglis, 'Individualism and secularisation', 68.

Larkin, E. *The pastoral role of the Roman Catholic Church in pre-famine Ireland, 1750–1850* (Dublin, 2006).

Littleton, J. and E. Maher (eds.). *Contemporary Catholicism in Ireland: a critical appraisal* (Dublin, 2008).

McGrath, T. *Religious renewal and reform in the pastoral ministry of Bishop James Doyle of Kildare and Leighlin, 1786–1834* (Dublin, 1999).

McGrath, T. 'The Tridentine evolution of modern Irish Catholicism, 1563–1962: a re-examination of the "devotional revolution" thesis', *Recusant History*, 20 (1991), 512–23.

Mac Gréil, M. *Pluralism and diversity in Ireland: prejudice and related issues in early 21st century Ireland* (Dublin, 2011).

Mac Gréil, M. *Prejudice and tolerance in Ireland: based on a survey of intergroup attitudes of Dublin adults and other sources* (Dublin, 1977).

Miller, D. *Church, state and nation in Ireland, 1898–1921* (Dublin, 1973).

Miller, D. 'Mass attendance in Ireland in 1834', in S. Brown and D. Miller (eds.), *Piety and power in Ireland, 1760–1960: essays in honour of Emmet Larkin* (Belfast, 2000), 158–79.

Moffitt, M. *The Society for Irish Church Missions to the Roman Catholics, 1849–1950* (Manchester, 2010).

Nic Ghiolla Phádraig, M. 'Religion in Ireland: preliminary analysis', *Social Studies: Irish Journal of Sociology*, 5, 2 (1976), 113–80.

Ó Corráin, D. *Rendering to God and Caesar: the Irish churches and the two states in Ireland, 1949–73* (Manchester, 2006).

Prunty, J. *Margaret Aylward: lady of charity, sister of faith, 1810–1899* (Dublin, 1999).

Share, P., M. Corcoran and B. Conway. *A sociology of Ireland* (4th edn, Dublin, 2012).

Whelan, I. *The Bible war in Ireland: the 'Second Reformation' and the polarization of Protestant–Catholic relations, 1800–1840* (Dublin, 2005).

Whyte, J. H. *Church and state in modern Ireland, 1923–1979* (Dublin, 1980).

6

Protestants

Andrew R. Holmes and Eugenio F. Biagini

6.1. Introduction

The Protestants of Ireland are a complex community, made so by social, denominational, political, economic and geographical factors. Since the early seventeenth century, there have been tensions between, on the one hand, Church of Ireland Protestants in the south, the self-styled natural leaders of Ireland with their ties to the land and the state, and, on the other, Presbyterian-dominated Ulster with its tenant farmers, industrial character and often cantankerous disposition. Of course, this simplistic dichotomy obscures social and economic divisions within both communities and the numerically small but dynamic subculture of Protestant churches and sects that have contributed much to the development of the island. Given its often bewildering variety, historians have struggled to describe the complexity of this group.

6.2. Confessional State, Enlightenment and Rebellion, 1740–1800

Ireland in the 1740s, according to S. J. Connolly, was an *ancien régime* society in which religious inequalities were inseparable from social hierarchy and landownership. The dominance of the members of the established episcopal Church of Ireland was predicated on the rights of landed property, not the rights of numbers. The religious allegiance of the Irish population had been determined in the previous century by population movements rather than conversion. Three-quarters to four-fifths of the population were Catholic and though various Protestants were at certain times compelled to make common cause, Irish religious divisions were not simply binary – tensions between

Protestants were as important and contributed to the remarkable events of 1798 when Presbyterian rebels in Ulster joined with Catholic insurgents in the south to overthrow in part the political, social and economic ascendancy of episcopal Protestants. The confessional divisions expressed during the Williamite wars had largely subsided by the 1740s. The Age of Reason had cooled somewhat the religious temperature of the previous century, though it was the 'good behaviour' of Irish Catholics during the Jacobite risings of 1715 and 1745 that is perhaps more important. The penal laws played their part, but those against Catholic religious practice quickly entered abeyance whereas those concerned with landownership were rigorously enforced.

The state of the established church presents a mixed picture. It monopolised privilege and power, yet suffered from low self-esteem, partly because it was unable to function as a national church. Because it became a central part of the Protestant state and society, it was exploited and often taken for granted by its erstwhile supporters in Parliament. The close connection between the landed elite and the clergy fed anticlericalism. Pluralism and non-residence were rife at a parish level, and around 1750 in Waterford, Cork and Kerry, 126 of 340 church buildings were in a ruinous condition.[1] Yet, neither non-residence nor pluralism necessarily entailed pastoral neglect as many clergymen simply lived in a neighbouring parish or employed a curate. There were well-intentioned voluntary attempts to deal with problems and the church was able to deliver for the religious needs of its members, if not for the population in general. Close links with the land also meant first-hand experience of the problems and potential of rural Ireland. Improving clergymen promoted agricultural progress and contributed to revive the fortunes of the Dublin Society (Royal since 1820), established in 1731 to promote agricultural and industrial improvement.

Appointments and promotions within the church were based on both patronage and proven ability, and though the church suffered political subordination after 1714, the political appointees were not necessarily inept. For instance, Charles Agar (1735–1809), *de facto* leader of the church during the late eighteenth century, was appointed bishop of Cloyne in 1768 and archbishop of Cashel in 1779, largely because of his political and social connections, yet he was a dutiful bishop and ensured that pastoral provision was strengthened through resident clergy.[2] As Toby Barnard has written, the 800 or so clerics who manned the church were deemed gentlemen, yet they were certainly not a cohesive group and had a variety of experiences, backgrounds and, above all, incomes. As in England and Scotland, the life of the parish combined secular and sacred functions.[3] The parish was a unit of government and had formal roles to play, such as road

1 S. J. Connolly, *Divided kingdom: Ireland, 1630–1800* (Oxford, 2008), 273.

2 Connolly, *Divided kingdom*, 275.

3 T. C. Barnard, 'The eighteenth-century parish', in E. FitzPatrick and R. Gillespie (eds.), *The parish in medieval and early modern Ireland* (Dublin, 2006), 297–324.

repairs and poor relief, yet it also defined social roles by creating a local elite of office-holders. The Irish parish was never as powerful administratively as in Britain and the confessional imbalance led to parishes being amalgamated to raise a reasonable stipend. Catholics and dissenters could hold parish office, but evidence is only suggestive for the former and Presbyterians had their own coherent system of church courts.

By the early eighteenth century there were about 6,000 Quakers, around 2,000 Baptists, and a much smaller number of other Protestant dissenters, including refugees from Catholic Europe (see Chapter 26 on 'Minorities').[4] By far the largest group of Protestant dissenters were the Presbyterians who dominated the north-east. By the 1780s, it was estimated by one sympathetic observer that there were around 514,800 Presbyterians in Ireland, despite the emigration of thousands to the American colonies.[5] Other forms of dissent declined – Quakers had between 5,000 and 6,000 members in 1750, but Baptist numbers had collapsed from around 2,000 in the 1720s to 500 by 1800.[6]

Presbyterians remained the main Protestant alternative to the established church. They had a distinctive form of church government and a distinctive social profile as the backbone of the denomination was composed of substantial tenant farmers. The economic upturn from the 1750s meant that Presbyterians were well represented amongst merchants, businessmen and skilled textile workers, and, more generally, were better educated and better housed than their Catholic and episcopal neighbours. The coherence of the community was challenged in the 1720s when an internal debate in the Synod of Ulster over whether subscription to the Westminster Confession of Faith should be enforced prompted a small secession of so-called New Light Presbyterians. This group reflected the mood of the Age of Reason and came to characterise the leadership of the Synod, yet its dominance was shallow as it was confined socially and geographically amongst the better-off sections of Presbyterian society. Though conservative Presbyterianism suffered in the Synod of Ulster with the eclipse of the Old Light party, it was revived and considerably extended elsewhere by the arrival of Seceder Presbyterian preachers from Scotland from the 1740s. The Secession spread rapidly and by 1818 there were 114 congregations. Seceders were especially popular amongst recent Scottish immigrants in the south and west of Ulster and were seen as a vibrant alternative to the allegedly lax Synod of Ulster. For the very small number who wanted an even more rigid form of Presbyterianism, they could become Covenanters or Reformed Presbyterians who believed in the perpetual obligation of the Scottish

4 T. Barnard, 'Identities, ethnicity and tradition among Irish dissenters, c.1650–1750', in K. Herlihy (ed.), *The Irish dissenting tradition, 1650–1750* (Dublin, 1995), 33n.

5 I. R. McBride, *Scripture politics: Ulster Presbyterians and Irish radicalism in the late eighteenth century* (Oxford, 1998), 227–8.

6 Figures from Connolly, *Divided kingdom*, 283.

Covenant of 1638 and the Solemn League and Covenant of 1643. Irrespective of which group they belonged to, Presbyterian ministers received their university education in Scotland, and this set them apart from both the clergy of the established church and the general population. On the other hand, education overseas was something they shared with the Roman Catholic clergy, who were generally trained in France until the 1790s.

In the eighteenth century the European influence was also evident in the development of new varieties of Protestantism. Moravians and Methodists owed their existence to the international origins of the evangelical awakening, being part of a movement of spiritual renewal amongst Protestants that had its origins in the early eighteenth century amongst persecuted Protestant minorities in central Europe. This evangelicalism soon acquired a transatlantic dimension, as illustrated by the Great Awakening in colonial America and the rise of Methodism in England. Over the next century and a half this regenerated Protestantism with its emphasis on personal conversion and its missionary zeal. The Moravian itinerant preacher John Cennick arrived in Ireland in 1746 at the invitation of Baptists in Dublin. By the early 1750s there were thirty to forty Moravian preachers serving ten chapels and more than two hundred societies. Methodism proved more popular. John Wesley first visited Ireland in 1747 and returned twenty-one times over the next forty years, focusing largely on areas of Protestant strength owing to his opposition to Catholicism, though he opposed Presbyterian Calvinism almost in equal measure. Methodist preachers, some of whom were women, faced significant local opposition. From the 1770s onwards the centre of Methodism moved northwards.

Until the 1840s, Dublin boasted the only university in the country. This accounted for the high concentration of professionals among the Protestant population in the capital that continued well into the late nineteenth century. In social terms, university graduates ranked more highly than the merchants, reflecting the political influence of lawyers and clergymen. The development of a wide range of manufacturing activities – breweries, sugar-refineries, and especially the woollen and the linen industries – boosted employment opportunities and brought about a major expansion of the business elite and the Protestant artisan 'class' in Dublin, Cork and Belfast. Everywhere dissenters – including Quakers and Congregationalists – played leading roles. Soon, observers contrasted their resourcefulness and energy with the allegedly more laid-back attitude of the members of the Catholic and established churches, a perception that reflected the greater social visibility of the poor within these latter denominations because they encompassed a wider cross-section of society. In any case, business success provided the sinews of future power, though stability was threatened by the migration of workers from the surrounding countryside – a phenomenon which reached significant levels during famines and crop failures. In Ulster, textile production until the 1820s was still a domestic activity, with farming families supplementing their income by spinning and weaving. Combined with their strong dissenting traditions, this gave northerners a level of cultural and economic independence which contributed to their self-confidence and collective image.

Such self-confidence was expressed during the imperial crisis of the late 1770s, when middle-class Presbyterian Ulster joined forces with Church of Ireland patriots to demand the recognition of the status and rights of the Kingdom of Ireland. A hardening of identities also occurred at a grassroots level in Ulster with the formation in 1795 of the Orange Order. In this context of Ascendancy and revived sectarianism, frustrated reformers increasingly felt that only radical political reform would deal with the inequalities of the Irish state. As a consequence, in October 1791 the Society of United Irishmen was formed in Belfast. All but one of the founder members were middle-class Presbyterians from mercantile backgrounds whose declared intention was to unite with Episcopalians and Catholics to gain wholesale and inclusive political reform. The United Irish society was transformed over the following years from a political pressure group to a movement for revolutionary separatism owing to the outbreak of the war between Britain and France and the failure of the government to introduce further political reform by 1795. The 1798 rebellion was a potent mixture of the high ideals of the Enlightenment and traditional sectarian antagonism, and ended disastrously as Irishmen fought and killed each other in significant numbers.

6.3. Reform, Protestant Union and Religious Revival, 1800–80

The dislocation of the 1790s across Europe prompted reform and revival within western Christianity. Amongst Protestants, this manifested itself through evangelicalism: Ireland became a mission field, Methodism in south Ulster experienced a remarkable revival in the wake of the rebellion, and Presbyterians promoted itinerant preaching.[7] Evangelicalism unlocked the potential of the Protestant laity through voluntary missionary and philanthropic effort, though church leaders had to tread a fine line between fostering zeal and maintaining control. During the first three decades of the century, the Church of Ireland was under pressure to reform perceived abuses through official inquiries and potential legislation, a process that would eventually lead to disestablishment in 1870. Yet efficiency and reform were also the watchwords of evangelicals and other conscientious churchmen who sought to address pluralism, non-residence and the provision of adequate church buildings. The structures of the church were streamlined through the Church Temporalities Act of 1833, which, amongst other measures, appointed ecclesiastical commissioners to channel much-needed funds.

7 The standard account, followed below, is D. Hempton and M. Hill, *Evangelical Protestantism in Ulster society 1740–1890* (London, 1992).

Presbyterianism underwent the same process of internal reform, though in this case it included the expulsion in 1829 of non-Trinitarian ministers from the Synod of Ulster. Methodism experienced serious internal difficulties caused by the need to organise and formalise a protean religious movement, and in 1816 the denomination split over the administration of the sacraments.

Paralleling these developments, there was a missionary awakening, which was unprecedented and primarily motivated by religious conviction, though the balance between religious conversion, social improvement and political identity was complex. The various voluntary religious societies gave Irish evangelicals a sense of purpose, and links with British evangelicals brought much-needed financial and moral support. Evangelicals targeted 'superstition' and 'ignorance' by encouraging education through preaching, teaching and bible distribution, a process that culminated in the Second Reformation of the 1820s. This was primarily a Church of Ireland event in the south of Ireland, though it did affect the southern edges of Protestant Ulster. As shown by Irene Whelan, evangelical landlords such as the Farnhams of County Cavan, the Lortons of north Roscommon, and the Rodens of Tollymore in County Down took up the challenge to extend the Church of Ireland across the island for religious and social reasons.

These efforts provoked opposition from groups within and without the churches. There was a backlash from politically liberal members of the established church and High Churchmen. Irish Catholics were especially offended and during the late 1820s through to the 1840s, many Protestants went on the political defensive as successive governments sought to make the minority established church more palatable to public opinion by reforming its abuses. Amongst other developments, this led to the secession of some ultra-Protestants from the Church of Ireland, including John Nelson Darby, founder of the so-called Plymouth Brethren. Darby and his fellow millenarians believed that the threats to the Protestant constitution were signs that Christ's Second Coming was imminent. 'True' believers should keep their 'purity' until the tribulation had occurred, holding unstructured services 'from house to house', weekly 'breaking the bread' (Acts 2:46).

This crisis also produced a political and religious alliance between Episcopalians and Presbyterians in defence of the Union and the Protestant character of the state against Whig reforms and resurgent Catholicism. Championed by Henry Cooke (1788–1868), the dominant figure in nineteenth-century Presbyterianism, this vision to unite evangelical religion and conservative politics was supported by Church of Ireland Protestants and many Presbyterians, yet it was rejected by the overwhelming majority of his ministerial colleagues. They shared his evangelical beliefs and unionist instincts, but remained distinctively Presbyterian and liberal in politics, demanding legislative redress for farmers' grievances against Church of Ireland landlords.[8]

8 A. R. Holmes, 'Covenanter politics: evangelicalism, political liberalism and Ulster Presbyterians, 1798–1914', *English Historical Review*, 125 (2010), 340–69.

Many Protestants were victims of the famine, or fled the pressure of high taxation when the government shifted the burden of relief on to local taxpayers, a development which – as Charles Read has recently suggested – contributed considerably to middle-class emigration in the late 1840s,[9] though others seized the opportunity to be active in both evangelism and social work. Missions to Catholics in the west of Ireland had been undertaken by the Church of Ireland from the early 1830s and these efforts eventually culminated in the formation of the Irish Church Missions to the Roman Catholics in 1849. Angry claims were made by Catholics that conversions to Protestantism had been bought by these societies on the promise of food – a practice widely known as souperism. Though these claims were denied, Protestant missions provoked significant controversy and effectively ended their ability to convert Catholics in any number. By contrast, disinterested philanthropy was widely admired and gratefully received. It was especially characteristic of the Quakers, who were praised by all sides for their commitment to those in need irrespective of their background.

The famine period also saw a brief but significant recrudescence of Protestant populism. The Orange Grand Lodge was reconstituted in August 1847 after an eleven-year hiatus and when the Young Ireland rising occurred in 1848 the Orange Order was keen to display its loyalty. However, an Orange procession in July 1849 at Dolly's Brae near Castlewellan in County Down led to a significant number of Catholic fatalities and the passage of the Party Processions Act (1850) that banned party parades. This disreputable behaviour, coupled with religious reasons, meant that many Protestants, especially Presbyterians, before the 1870s opposed the Order as socially disruptive and disreputable.

Meanwhile, the social dynamics of Irish Protestantism had been transformed by the industrialisation of the north-east, especially in Belfast with the linen and shipbuilding industries. While these developments are discussed elsewhere in the present volume, here it is important to note that industrialisation was driven by a number of Protestant business firms, the most famous of which was Harland and Wolff, established in 1861 by a Scottish-educated businessman and a Hamburg-born Jew who later converted to Protestantism. In Dublin, the much older Guinness breweries provided a parallel – at least in terms of the close connection between Protestantism and entrepreneurial spirit – as did a number of Quaker ventures, the most famous of which is Jacob's. Economic change brought prosperity, but also produced significant social problems in urban areas through overcrowding, poor sanitation and infectious disease, accompanied by a hardening of sectarian divisions in Belfast that were expressed in periodic outbursts of vicious rioting.

9 C. Read, 'Laissez-faire, the Irish famine and British financial crisis', *Economic History Review*, 69, 2 (2016), 411–34 and 'British economic policy and Ireland, *c.*1841–53', unpublished PhD thesis, University of Cambridge (2016), ch. 5.

Figure 6.1 Gathering the crowds in Ireland: Methodist open air meeting, n.d. but *c.* 1885. Courtesy of the Methodist Archives of Ireland, Edgehill College, Belfast.

Against this background, the growing influence of evangelicalism led to a remarkable revival in 1859, part of a general religious awakening that began in the USA and would spread to the UK and parts of the British empire.[10] Supporters claimed more than a hundred thousand conversions and a significant improvement in public morality. For instance, the Twelfth of July was remarkably peaceful in 1859 – a reminder that sectarianism and religious fervour were often two distinct phenomena. Yet the revival was chaotic and the clergy struggled to control innovations such as male and female lay preachers and the physical manifestations that accompanied some of the conversions. Furthermore, many of the numerical gains and improvements in morality proved short lived. For instance, the Presbyterian General Assembly heard in 1862 that intemperance was as bad as ever and that Belfast alone had 525 public houses. In addition, the dominance of mainstream Protestant denominations was weakened somewhat as the revival led to the growth of smaller groups who demanded a more visible commitment from their members. The census records for the province of Ulster show that the number of persons in the 'Other' category – which included

10 The following paragraph is based on A. R. Holmes, 'The Ulster revival of 1859: causes, controversies and consequences', *Journal of Ecclesiastical History*, 63 (2012), 488–515.

Baptists, Independents and Brethren assemblies – rose from 20,443 in 1861 to 35,098 a decade later, while the number of Presbyterians declined by more than 26,000. Later in the century, other groups such as the Salvation Army began to appear in Ireland along with interdenominational evangelical groups such as the YMCA and the Faith Mission.

The renewal of Protestant culture more generally was reflected in the establishment, in 1859, of the *Irish Times*, which became the most prestigious and best-established Protestant newspaper in the south. Despite the committed conservatism of the paper's founder, Lawrence E. Knox (1836–73), and its first two editors, the *Irish Times* supported radical causes, such as land reform and the extension of the parliamentary franchise to working men. It also championed the established church – by English

Figure 6.2 William Young, Methodist colporteur, Co. Cork, n.d. but end of the nineteenth century. A colporteur was a travelling bookseller (selling cheap bibles and tracts) and a missionary. Young, an Irish-speaker, enjoyed a long and successful career. Courtesy of the Methodist Archives of Ireland, Edgehill College, Belfast.

standards a quintessentially 'Tory' concern – but did so in the conviction that the Episcopalian elite were the harbingers of the 'real' progress of Ireland, whether moral or material, in the elevation of the standard of life among the labouring classes, in the general diffusion of education, in the security of property and of the fruits of the poor man's industry'.[11] In Ulster, the gospel of Protestant 'improvement' was articulated in a number of newspapers, including the *Northern Whig*, the *Banner of Ulster* and the *Derry Standard*.

Such concerns chimed with the social activism of the Protestant churches, which the revival had greatly stimulated. A remarkable network of voluntary societies was established by Protestants to meet the spiritual and practical needs of the Irish population – Sunday schools, temperance, education, bible and tract distribution, clothing and poor relief. These offered spiritual regeneration and 'moral elevation'. Social control was not absent, though the cross-class appeal of respectability, personal morality and self-improvement was more important. Between the wealthy and the poor – and between the middle classes and the rest – the glue was evangelicalism. A good example is the Protestant Orphan Society (POS). First established in Dublin in 1828, it rapidly spread to the rest of Ireland as local committees were set up to fundraise and administer a system which proved both cheap and effective. The POS strategy was based on boarding out children to rural families, paying a host 'nurse' an annual contribution to the costs. In this way they tried to protect children from the social stigma of becoming institutionalised (which might affect their employability in later life) and, simultaneously, encourage them to develop thrifty habits and a work ethic. In any case, the POS's resolve to keep as many orphans as possible out of the workhouse was also driven by social anxieties. 'Respectability' – that touchstone of Victorian middle-class values – was the ultimate goal in the children's education. More than the symbol of prudish Victorianism, 'respectability' was about developing attitudes, aspirations and skills which could eventually help children to secure and hold down a job and become 'independent'. Thus the values that the POS tried to inculcate into its children reveal the priorities and the mindset of the Church of Ireland community and how they hinged not necessarily on the Big House, but on communitarian individualism.

From the start, the POS was also concerned about protecting the orphans' religious identity and fostering their faith. It is interesting to see that Protestant leaders were no less preoccupied than their Catholic colleagues with protecting their own flock from the snares of souperism under the poor law. Such fears may have been exaggerated: new research by Simon Gallaher and others shows that guardians were carefully patrolling

---

11 *Irish Times*, 27 March 1859.

Figure 6.3 Class divides. Rich and poor Protestants: shooting party, Clonbrook House, end of the nineteenth century. Clonbrook Collection. Courtesy of the National Library of Ireland.

denominational boundaries within the workhouse, especially as far as children were concerned. However, for foundlings and orphans anti-proselytism regulations were more ambiguous.

The working-class communities that received church aid were not passive recipients and used these services for their own ends. Indeed, the POS itself was started by craftsmen. Such individuals sent their children to Sunday schools to gain basic literacy skills or avail them of the rites of passage without committing their families to church membership. One of the most significant aspects of this associational culture was the involvement of middle-class women. Many of the women involved were content to see their activity as an extension of their domestic roles as dutiful daughters, wives and mothers, but others developed skills and a public profile that would otherwise have been denied them. In some instances, such as those of Isabella Tod (1836–1896) and Margaret Byers (1832–1912), this activism led to political involvement in campaigns to repeal the Contagious Diseases Acts and extend the franchise, as well as opposition to Home Rule.

Figure 6.4 Class divides. Rich and poor Protestants: Peter Doherty, colporteur in Skibbereen, and a couple interested in acquiring New Testaments and Methodist tracts. Courtesy of the Methodist Archives, Edgehill College, Belfast.

6.4. Home Rule, Partition and the Exodus of Southern Protestants

Religious revival renewed zeal and self-confidence that were to prove important preparation for the various trials that Protestants would face between disestablishment in 1870 and partition. Disestablishment turned the Church of Ireland into a voluntary body governed by synods representative of both clergy and laypeople at the diocesan and national levels. An enormous effort was made to equip the church for the task ahead, and this resulted in the development of an institution and culture which were more and more distinctively Irish.

The years between 1880 and 1886 saw the radicalisation of the land campaign and the agitation for Home Rule. Its renewal in 1910–14 polarised the country and within six years resulted in partition. The issue cannot be understood without its religious dimension, though it concerned issues that were primarily political and cultural, rather than theological. Moreover, while most Protestants opposed Home Rule, many feared partition and disapproved of extreme unionist rhetoric, including the signing of the Ulster Covenant in September 1912. According to David Fitzpatrick, about a quarter of northern Protestants refused to sign it, and the proportion was even higher among ministers and clergy, particularly from the predominantly evangelical Methodists, whose ministers (because of the itinerant system) had first-hand knowledge of life in the south and were less inclined to demonise Catholics.

The fear that 'Home Rule' might mean 'Rome Rule' – undiluted clericalism – was not eased by the Catholic Church, which at the time was confidently asserting views that were widely repugnant not just to Protestants, but also to supporters of 'modern' and liberal ideas in general. The *Ne Temere* papal decree (1908) – which reaffirmed Catholic discipline on mixed marriages by prescribing that any offspring should be brought up as Catholics – added further fuel to the flames. It was so emotive because it was associated with issues of identity, freedom of choice and 'liberty'. In this context, the 1907 controversy over J. M. Synge's *The Playboy of the Western World* is also of some relevance. Though not himself religious, the author hailed from a prominent evangeli-cal family. The play was part of his 'photographic' exploration of the Irish character: it caused nationalist riots when it was performed at the Abbey Theatre in Dublin because it represented Gaelic peasants as rather commonplace people, mainly concerned with the daily struggle against the boredom and parochialism of village life, rather than with great political ideals. Northern Protestants read such developments as further confir-mation of the insidious and intractable nature of Catholic nationalism.

The Great War brought about a short-lived pan-Irish, cross-community solidar-ity which was, however, soon poisoned by politics and then killed off by gunmen in 1919–21. This was accompanied by an intensification of sectarian strife, a development which paralleled similar crises in other partitioned regions of Europe: everywhere the disintegration of multinational empires resulted in communal conflicts. In both south and north, and especially in Ulster, this was accompanied by an evangelical revival and, interestingly, an inverse correlation developed between the intensity of religious obser-vance and a tendency to be involved in paramilitary violence.[12] For, as N. H. Douglas

---

12 A. R. Holmes, 'Revivalism and fundamentalism in Ulster: W. P. Nicholson in context', in D. W. Bebbington and D. C. Jones (eds.), *Evangelicalism and fundamentalism in the United Kingdom during the twentieth century* (Oxford, 2013), 253–72.

has noted, even though 'religion reflects cultural difference … strong religious beliefs, held within each culture group, act as a constraint upon violence' because they 'emphasize the sanctity of human life and erect a moral barrier against the use of violence'.[13] At the same time, such was the strength of the Orange Order, that unionist leaders and clerics felt it necessary to join even when they did not share its agenda. One example is Bishop Fredrick MacNeice: in 1912 he had refused to sign the Covenant and in the 1930s he campaigned for a more irenic approach to the ethnic/confessional divide, but he decided to become an Orangeman because, as David Fitzpatrick has shown, he felt that this was the only way to reach out to the unchurched Protestant working class.

Northern Ireland faced a variety of formidable obstacles, and in 1922 sectarian rioting in Belfast had claimed the lives of almost 500 people and forced a further 23,000, mostly Catholics, from their homes. Remarkably, however, the government under the leadership of Prime Minister James Craig quickly established an effective administration and parliament, though it was dominated by Protestant unionists in part because northern nationalists refused to recognise the state. According to Buckland, 'Craig's cabinet was neither vindictive nor deliberately oppressive, and it was often well intentioned, but it was too responsive to the claims of its supporters and thus unable to correct the imbalance in the state created by the minority's opting out.'[14] Its readiness to pander to sectarian pressures was influenced by fear of the rise of cross-community, working-class support for Labour. Populist rhetoric and a defining of Northern Ireland in contrast to both the Catholic nationalist south and the 'treacherous' English ruling elite became increasingly important as unemployment and social deprivation spread during the decades of the Great Depression. Such attitudes were readily echoed by the Unionist government. For example, in April 1934, speaking in the northern parliament, Craig boasted that he was 'an Orangeman first', and that 'we are a Protestant Parliament and a Protestant State' in contradistinction to de Valera's version of a Gaelic and Catholic Irish Free State.[15]

Craig's statement (often misquoted as proclaiming 'a Protestant parliament for a Protestant people') raises the issue of whether Northern Ireland can be called a 'confessional state'. Certainly there was and could be no return to traditional confessionalism, as the constitution of Northern Ireland, the Government of Ireland Act, did not permit a state church. But other questions must also be raised. For example, was the dominance of Protestantism enshrined in law? Does confessional refer to an ethos, a set of unwritten assumptions and one-party rule by the Unionist Party? Was it expressed through discrimination against the Catholic minority? Most northern Protestants

13 N. H. Douglas, 'Cultural pluralism and political behaviour in Northern Ireland', in C. H. Williams and E. Koffman (eds.), *Community conflict, partition and nationalism* (London, 1989), 77.
14 P. Buckland, *The factory of grievances: devolved government in Northern Ireland, 1921–39* (Dublin, 1979), 222.
15 Cited in ibid., 72. Cf. H. Patterson, *Class conflict and sectarianism* (Belfast, 1980), 144.

felt, in Patrick Mitchel's words, 'at ease in Zion', assuming both the legitimacy of the state and a British allegiance. The Catholic minority and their grievances were largely ignored by all Protestant churches, and there was little critical reflection on the relationship between the church and unionism before the late 1950s. While the parliament buildings at Stormont were being completed, the House of Commons and Senate met in the Presbyterian College, Belfast until 1932, and two Presbyterian clergymen, Robert Corkey and Robert Moore, held cabinet posts. The Protestant churches, with the critical aid of the Orange Order, were able to amend Lord Londonderry's 1923 Education Act by diluting the non-denominational character of education. Yet for all their influence in education, the churches made little impact in terms of persuading the government to introduce local option to further the cause of temperance and failed to succeed in promoting film censorship.[16]

In the south, despite the Orange Order being active and present in various areas, overt displays of Protestant sectarianism were uncommon, partly because the minority were in no position to challenge Catholic supremacy. In fact, about one-third of southern Protestants had left the Free State by 1926. The causes of such an exodus

Figure 6.5 Rossnowlagh Parade, Co. Sligo, 2013. This is the only Orange march regularly held in the Republic. Credit: Eugenio Biagini.

16 J. W. Hill, *Cinema and Northern Ireland: film, culture and politics* (London, 2006), 47–77.

have always been controversial. The First World War, long regarded as having decimated the community, primarily affected the 'officer class', that is the gentry, which
then suffered economic setbacks when they lost part of their estates through the completion of land purchase in the 1920s. Likewise, the trade war with Britain (1932–8)
hit hard both landowners and large farmers, many of them Protestant. As for the rest
of the Protestant community, historians disagree on the causes of the fall in numbers.
Economic pressure played a role: for example, shopkeepers in garrison towns, such as
Athlone, were undermined by the disappearance of most of their customers when the
British army left in 1922. Likewise, the shrinking of the civil service and the allocation
of the functions of the poor law to religious organisations meant fewer employment
opportunities for university graduates, both Catholic and Protestant, with the latter
also suffering because of the new Irish-language test requirement.

However, it is the extent to which revolutionary violence further contributed to such
decline that has been at the centre of the liveliest historiographical debate since Peter
Hart published his work on County Cork, where thirteen Protestants were killed by
the IRA in one night and many others fled fearing persecution. Violence of varying
intensity raged in other parts of the country as well, though it is difficult to establish
the extent to which 'sectarian' – rather than political or agrarian – motivations inspired
it. However, it is not clear whether fear of attacks was the prime cause of the Protestant
exodus or affected national trends. Working on the records of the Methodists, David
Fitzpatrick has argued that their decline had little to do with violence, but instead was
due to failure to reproduce themselves or attract new supporters as the old generation
passed away. However, examining evidence from a wide range of denominations, other
scholars reach different conclusions. Andy Bielenberg's estimate that at least 16 per cent
of the Protestant demographic decline was due to 'involuntary' emigration is the most
plausible figure,[17] but even he does not fully account for the grey area between 'involuntary' expatriation caused by well-attested persecution, and that caused by 'softer'
forms of community pressure ('there's more than one way to skin a cat', as Emma says in
Jonathan Burgess's play *The Exodus*). Low-intensity intimidation could be very effective
in scaring away farming families in contested areas, including the midlands and border counties. Likewise, village shopkeepers were vulnerable to boycott and economic
pressure: it would be interesting to investigate in how many towns high-street shops
changed hands in the 1930s, as Protestants were 'persuaded' to sell and leave.

For the Protestants who opted to remain in the Free State, the challenges were numerous and affected not only their economic prospects, but also their national identity.
They were now a royalist (if not even a loyalist) dissenting religious minority – 'the ten
per cent' – within a country primarily defined by republican, Catholic, Anglo-phobic

17 A. Bielenberg, 'Exodus: the emigration of southern Irish Protestants during the Irish War of Independence
and the civil war', *Past and Present*, 218 (2013), 199–232.

imperatives. The Protestant experience was one of intimate marginalisation. Deidre O'Byrne has studied how this was expressed in works of fiction and autobiography, which reveal the imaginary of a community which felt like 'exotic fruits' within 'walled gardens'. The most celebrated of such writers are Edith Somerville, Martin Ross (alias Violet Martin) and Elizabeth Bowen. The last embodied the cosmopolitan parochialism of a caste and a generation: her life and writing were shaped by the intellectual atmosphere of London and Oxford, and were rooted in a quintessentially Irish world defined and confined by Big Houses – such as her own Bowen Court (County Cork). Many such houses were destroyed – 'executed', as she puts it in *The last September* (1929) – deeply shaping the outlook of the survivors. Loss, isolation and the sense of fighting a losing battle are also conveyed by the works of Archbishop Gregg's daughter, Barbara Fitzgerald: *We are besieged* (1946) and the posthumous *Footprints upon water* (1983). The gender dimension of such an experience is significant also because the survival of the community depended on the informal culture of the church, the interrelationship of religious and social, as well as gender, identity in everyday life, in parish activities and charitable work.

Protestant schools were the key institutions that allowed for the preservation of community identity, and it is much to the credit of successive Irish governments that they were granted generous terms which enabled them to prosper. However, the emphasis on

Figure 6.6 Eamon De Valera at the opening of a Protestant school in Booterstown, 1957, with Canon Ernest Bateman (at the centre) and Archbishop George Otto Simms. Courtesy of *The Irish Times*.

the Irish language in the curriculum caused opposition and protest from both parents and school managers, especially in the border counties, while in 1926 the *Irish Times* went as far as recommending the withdrawal of church schools from government control. Nevertheless, from 1928, under its new head, E. C. Hodges, the Church of Ireland Training College adopted a more pragmatic and co-operative approach, which helped to reconcile the minority to the linguistic policies of the state. More awkward was the ethos of textbooks, which 'casually equated gaelicisation, nationalism and Catholicism and portrayed England's historical role in Ireland in exclusively pejorative terms'.[18]

In this context, the Catholic Eucharistic Congress, held in Dublin in 1932, came as a major challenge. It was the high-water mark of Catholic nationalism and its claim to be the authentic voice of Ireland. The Protestant response included a reassertion of their claim on the true legacy of St Patrick, who had landed in Ireland fifteen centuries earlier. Most Church of Ireland Irish leaders – including Archbishops Bernard and Gregg (the president of the committee to celebrate the 1,500th anniversary of St Patrick's arrival) – insisted on the Episcopalian identity of the 'historic' Patrick. Affirmed at the 1932 Church of Ireland conference, such interpretation was further elaborated by N. J. D. White in his contribution to Walter Allison Phillips's controversial *History of the Church of Ireland* (1934). This work in itself had been conceived as an attempt to reassert the church's claim on the Patrician legacy. Even the date of the publication had been originally planned to coincide with the response of the church to 'Roman' propaganda.

In general, however, Protestants were less assertive. An implicit choice was made in order to focus on the community's immediate material concerns, prioritising issues on which they hoped to build broad local coalitions with the Catholic middle class, even if this involved appeasement or quietism over *national* issues. This was no new departure reflecting post-independence weakness: instead, it was the implementation of a strategy which the minority had adopted from the late 1890s, particularly in local elections. Inevitably, religiously divisive concerns came to the forefront from time to time – for example, censorship and the prohibition of divorce. However, Protestants were divided on some of these issues, with the Methodists actually *welcoming* the puritanical trend in family law and the discipline of the press. Moreover, the Free State government was committed to the protection of constitutional rights and generally eager to retain the support of the minority, which included so many members of the business, insurance and banking elite, whose services, skills and investments were more necessary than ever now for the new country to prosper. This was reflected in the minority's resilience within Ireland's elite. Thus, despite heavy emigration, by 1926 Protestants accounted for more than 50% of the bankers, 40% of the lawyers, 20% of doctors, 20% of large

18 M. Relihan, 'The Church of Ireland, the state and education in Irish language and history, 1920s–1950s', in D. Raftery and K. Fisher (eds.), *Educating Ireland: schooling and social change, 1700–2000* (Dublin, 2014), 161.

farms, and 20% of all managers in businesses. Two years earlier, one of the institutions with which they were often associated – the Freemasons – had celebrated its two hundredth anniversary in great style in Dublin's St Patrick's Cathedral: more than three thousand brethren attended a service led by three bishops of the Church of Ireland and chaired by the Primate, Archbishop D'Arcy.[19] The Freemasons continued to flourish as suggested by the accounts of their network of benevolent institutions, which entered the twenty-first century in robust health. By then, Catholics had again started to join the organisation.[20] As one of its leaders claimed in 1938, '[t]he immense power exercised by Freemasonry is to be found in the great principle of Brotherhood to all men, whether Jew or Gentile, Christian or Mohammedan'.[21] It was quite a statement to make in an allegedly confessional Ireland, but it must have sounded like music to members of minority groups.

Different was the experience of the working and lower middle classes, which more than other social groups suffered the effects of *Ne Temere*. For as long as it was enforced (it was replaced in 1970 by the less stringent *Matrimonia Mixta,* but survived in local practice until much later), this decree contributed to perpetuating segregation at the level of leisure and socialisation, within schools, clubs and sports associations, which enabled members of the bourgeoisie to find suitable partners. These institutions were essential to the community's survival, but many poor Protestants had no easy access to such a socially selective system. For artisans and small farmers the choice was often between remaining unmarried or submitting to the *Ne Temere*. Couples who challenged the system tended to emigrate in order to avoid community backlash. What could happen when these rules were flouted was illustrated by the 1957 Fethard-on-Sea Boycott (County Wexford). The event provoked parliamentary debates in Dublin, Stormont and London, secured global media coverage and showed that Dublin was as impotent as Stormont in the north when it came to community-backed sectarianism. As for the Protestants, while the Methodists remained quiet, the Church of Ireland was in abject submission. Only in the north were the churches up in arms: there the episode, together with the IRA Border Campaign (1956–62), was taken as evidence of the threatening and oppressive nature of what was regarded as the southern 'Catholic State for a Catholic People'. As for the Catholic Church, it won only a Pyrrhic victory, for its role in society came under critical public scrutiny for the second time in a decade, following the damaging 1951 'mother and child' episode (when its hierarchy was perceived to oppose essential welfare legislation in order to retain control of the care for pregnant women).

19 R. E. Parkinson, *History of the Grand Lodge of Free and Accepted Masons of Ireland, vol. II* (Dublin, 1957), 258.
20 *Masonic Benevolent Institutions. Report and Financial Statements of the following: Masonic Girls Benefit Fund; Masonic Boys Benefit Fund; Masonic Welfare Fund; Masonic Havens Limited; Masonic Trust Company and Radcliffe Masonic Housing Association Limited, for the year ended 31st December 2001* (NLI).
21 S. Leighton, *History of Freemasonry in the Province of Antrim* (Belfast, 1938), 249.

From the late 1950s, the onset of a more ecumenical mood made such episodes less frequent, but not unthinkable. Southern Protestants welcomed the change, which gradually improved inter-communal relations. However, in the north, ecumenism was divisive because its benefits were less obvious to the man and woman in the pew, while any dilution of confessional principles was resisted as woolly, upper-class liberalism. Ulster Protestant anti-elitism had always found powerful spokesmen who could express the fears and concern of their followers in such abusive and inflammatory language that church authorities could hardly tolerate it. For example, in 1951 the Presbyterian authorities denied the use of denominational premises to a young fundamentalist preacher named Ian Paisley (1926–2014), whose firebrand denunciations of 'Rome' and 'heresy' within the Protestant churches themselves were becoming a source of public embarrassment. Undeterred, Paisley established his own denomination, the Free Presbyterian Church, and embarked on a life-long crusade against the evils of what he denounced as a decadent society and apostate Protestant churches.

6.5.   Troubles, Pluralism – and Renewal? 1968–2016

In the 1960s Northern Ireland entered a period of economic difficulty. Under pressure from foreign competition, the shipyards, on which the Belfast economy had relied so heavily for a century, incurred significant setbacks. The empire, another pillar of Northern Ireland's sense of identity, was being rapidly dismantled and its associated values discredited. Such unsettling changes coincided with the rise of the ecumenical movement (Vatican II, 1962–5), which threatened deep-rooted northern Protestant certainties. Together, these developments generated insecurity and anxiety. Neither the official Protestant churches nor the Unionist Party knew how to handle such a rapidly evolving situation. Ian Paisley, a man not known to be assailed by doubt, rejected theological liberalism and the watering down of dogmas, but reasserted comforting cultural certainties, offering a rough-and-ready alternative in both religion and politics. In a society in which the working-class movement was divided and the Labour Party weak, Paisley increasingly became the voice of the Protestant working classes. Like his adversary, Archbishop McQuaid in Dublin, he denied the need to change and insisted that there would be 'No surrender!' Unlike McQuaid, however, he was not prepared to step down when times changed. Paisley's brand of unionism would eventually come to dominate Northern Irish politics, though the same cannot be said of his fundamentalist religion which alienates more evangelicals than it attracts. The 2011 census showed that only 10,068 people described themselves as Free Presbyterians in comparison with 752,555 other Protestants.[22]

22 www.nisra.gov.uk/census/2011/results/detailed-characteristics.html, accessed 14 May 2015.

By contrast, in their relationship with the state and nationalist narratives, southern Protestants had always cultivated a prudent distance and this made them readier to embrace change. Thus, though the churches were not partitioned, within Protestantism there was a clear divergence between north and south. From 1968, women's liberation and the Troubles further highlighted profound differences within the Church of Ireland. These were amplified by asymmetrical demographics, with a majority of its members living in the north, but with the south retaining considerable influence within the representative bodies, particularly the General Synod.

However, while southern figures such as Archbishop Otto Simms (1910–91) and the Baptist leader Robert Dunlop (1938–2014) were in many ways 'ahead of their time', they were not without counterparts in Northern Ireland. One notable example is the Methodist Eric Gallagher (1912–99), who started to engage with the IRA in the 1970s, a time when most people thought only in terms of a military solution to the Troubles. In a more systematic way ECONI (Evangelical Contribution on Northern Ireland) addressed the question of how to retain belonging while rejecting sectarianism. Started in 1986, by 1991 ECONI involved about one-third of all Protestant congregations in the north and two hundred evangelical leaders. Even among those who did not engage in a radical rethink of the relationship between Protestantism and Ulster culture, there were leaders who facilitated practical change. For example, the Presbyterian Roy Magee (1930–2009), a prominent evangelical in the Presbyterian Church, used his influence to persuade loyalist paramilitaries to accept a ceasefire in 1994. Robin Eames (b. 1938) – who, as archbishop of Armagh during the last, difficult phase of the Troubles, was criticised by liberals for not taking a firmer stance on the Orange marches – became co-chairman of the Consultative Group on the Past in Northern Ireland (2007–9), whose mission was to help communities achieve reconciliation.

Women's ordination was adopted without much fuss in 1990, when the Church of Ireland followed the example set by the Methodists in 1973 and the Presbyterians in 1976, but more conservative denominations refused to consider the issue. Even within the churches there was a remarkable variety of political and social opinion, including divergent attitudes to issues such as gay and lesbian lifestyles. Yet, on the whole, at least in the south, the Irish church was more successful in dealing with its differences than many of its counterparts within the worldwide Anglican Communion. As the Catholic Church was rocked by child abuse scandals, Protestant institutions which had cared for children and single mothers did not escape unscathed, with the cases of the Bethany Home and the Westbank Orphanage sparking off bitter and protracted debates. These involved allegations about systematic neglect and contributed to the wider debate about the health and nutrition standards for children in public care and, more generally, the relationship between the state and the private/religious sector.

Meanwhile, old distinctions and traditional denominations were challenged by the rapid growth of the Charismatic Movement and especially the Pentecostal churches. From modest beginnings in 1908, after establishing itself as a primarily northern, conservative denomination, Pentecostalism expanded into a new, island-wide reality from the end of the century, with the arrival of non-European immigrants, including Africans, Latin Americans and Roma.[23] The last are distinguished from the Travellers (see chapter 26, below) not only by their ethnic origin, but also because of their religion: according to a survey by the Health Service Executive (HSE), 70 per cent of Roma are Pentecostal.[24] Overall, Pentecostalism in Ireland grew by more than 150 per cent between 2002 and 2006 and continues to expand at a rate in excess of 20 per cent per year. By 1991 more than 16,000 people declared themselves to belong to 'Christian (unspecified)' groups. According to Andy Pollak, the *Irish Times* religious correspondent, '[the] majority of these people are certainly members of smaller evangelical churches, sects, and "house" churches.'[25] Much of such Pentecostal growth was due to immigration (see Chapter 33 below). Inner-city areas – such as that around Parnell Street in Dublin – became 'little Africas', and this has been reflected by the curious phenomenon of 'Findlater' Presbyterian Church and other institutions of Irish middle-class religiosity becoming increasingly multicultural. Many Africans, however, worshipped in Pentecostal communities run by immigrants for immigrants. As Abel Ugba notes, the 'acceptance and recognition members find in these churches help to restore the sense of self-worth they had experienced in their home countries.'[26]

All of this came with an overall Protestant demographic recovery, to such an extent that by 2002 their number in the Republic was almost 40 per cent higher than in 1991. Apart from immigrants, there were converts and other adherents – both permanent and temporary, for in an increasingly post-Catholic south people became more relaxed about crossing confessional boundaries, even if only to explore other forms of Christianity or belief. In the north, by contrast, church membership was in steady decline. Thus, by 2016, while the churches remained unpartitioned, Irish Protestantism was developing in different directions. In particular, it was divided on social and ethical issues – such as attitudes to gay and lesbian Christians – with the northerners taking a more conservative view than their co-religionists in the Republic.

---

23 A. McCann, *Charismatic Christians in the Church of Ireland: a historical and theological introduction* (Saarbrucken, 2015); J. Robinson, *Pentecostal origins: early Pentecostalism in Ireland in the context of the British Isles* (Milton Keynes, 2005).

24 See http://hse.ie/eng/services/Publications/SocialInclusion/InterculturalGuide/Pentecostalism/profile.html, accessed 8 August 2016.

25 A. Pollak, 'C of I decline not as great as it was thought', *Irish Times*, 26 April 1994, 6.

26 A. Ugba, 'African Pentecostals in twenty-first-century Ireland: identity and integration', in B. Fanning (ed.), *Immigration and social change in the Republic of Ireland* (Manchester, 2007), 178.

FURTHER READING

Akenson, D. H. *Discovering the end of time: Irish Evangelicals in the age of Daniel O'Connell* (Montreal and Kingston, 2016).

Barnard, T. *A new anatomy of Ireland: the Irish Protestants, 1649–1770* (New Haven and London, 2003).

Biagini, E. F. '"Patrick, the first churchman" in the Protestant vision of Ernest Bateman of Booterstown (1886–1979)', in J. Hill and M. Lyons (eds.), *Representing Irish religious history* (London, 2017), 211–28.

Biagini, E. F. 'A challenge to partition: Methodist open-air work in independent Ireland, 1922–1962', *Bulletin of the Methodist Historical Society of Ireland*, 19, 34 (2014), 5–44.

Connolly, S. J. *Divided kingdom: Ireland, 1630–1800* (Oxford, 2008).

Connolly, S. J. *Religion and society in nineteenth-century Ireland* (Dundalk, 1985).

Cooper, J. *The Protestant Orphan Society and its social significance in Ireland, 1828–1940* (Manchester, 2015).

Crawford, H. *Outside the glow: Protestants and Irishness in independent Ireland* (Dublin, 2010).

D'Alton, I. *Protestant society and politics in Cork, 1812–1844* (Cork, 1980).

Daniel, G. *Transforming post-Catholic Ireland: religious practice in late modernity* (Oxford, 2016).

Deignan, P. *The Protestant community in Sligo, 1914–49* (Dublin, 2010).

Fitzpatrick, D. *Descendancy: Irish Protestant histories since 1795* (Cambridge, 2014).

Hempton, D. and M. Hill, *Evangelical Protestantism in Ulster society 1740–1890* (London, 1992).

Holmes, A. R. 'Religious conflict in Ulster, c. 1780–1886', in J. Wolffe (ed.), *Protestant–Catholic conflict from the Reformation to the 21st century: the dynamics of religious difference* (Basingstoke, 2013), 101–31.

Holmes, A. R. *The shaping of Ulster: Presbyterian belief and practice 1770–1840* (Oxford, 2006).

Holmes, R. F. G. *Henry Cooke* (Belfast, 1981).

Kaufmann, E. P. *The Orange Order: a contemporary Northern Irish history* (Oxford, 2007).

Kirkpatrick, L., *Presbyterians in Ireland: an illustrated history* (Dublin, 2006).

McBride, I. R. *Scripture politics: Ulster Presbyterians and Irish radicalism in the late eighteenth century* (Oxford, 1998).

McDowell, R. B. *The Church of Ireland, 1869–1969* (London, 1975).

Maguire, M. 'The Church of Ireland and the problem of the Protestant working class in Dublin, 1870–1930s', in A. Ford, J. McGuire and K. Milne (eds.), *As by law established: the Church of Ireland since the Reformation* (Dublin, 1995), 195–203.

Megahey, A. *The Irish Protestant churches in the twentieth century* (Basingstoke, 2000).

Mitchel, P. *Evangelicalism and national identity in Ulster 1921–1998* (Oxford, 2003).

Moffitt, M. *Soupers and jumpers: the Protestant missions in Connemara, 1848–1937* (Dublin, 2010).

Moffitt, M. 'Identity issues: what sources show', *Journal of Irish Society for Archives* (2014), 12–22.

Roulston, R. 'The Church of Ireland and the Irish state: institution, community and state relations, 1950–1972', unpublished PhD thesis, University College Dublin, 2010.

Roulston, R. 'Reassessing the Church of Ireland's relationship with the Irish state in education: an archival approach', *Journal of Irish Society for Archives* (2014), 51–62.

Walker, B. M. *A history of St George's church, Belfast: two centuries of faith, worship and music* (Belfast, 2016).

Walker, B. M. and C. Costecalde. *The Church of Ireland: an illustrated history* (Dublin, 2013).

Whelan, I. *The Bible war in Ireland: the 'Second Reformation' and the polarization of Protestant–Catholic relations, 1800–1840* (Dublin, 2005).

White, J. *Minority report: the anatomy of the southern Irish Protestant* (Dublin, 1975).

Wilson, T. K. *Frontiers of violence: conflict and identity in Ulster and Upper Silesia, 1918–1922* (Oxford, 2010).

7

Town and City

David Dickson

7.1. An Occluded Past

In 1820 the first history of the town of Galway was published in Dublin. Its author, James Hardiman, lawyer, archivist, antiquarian and pioneering folklorist, saw it as a work of revelation, demonstrating the rich and heretofore hidden antiquity of 'the capital of Connaught', an urban world brought low over the previous two centuries by penal laws and mercantilist legislation, which now in a more enlightened age was entering a renaissance. Hardiman noted the extraordinary absence of urban history-writing in Ireland compared with Britain, where 'almost every village and hamlet … can boast of its history'. Whatever the truth about that, he was correct in noting the absence of Irish work. Yet within a few years, his Galway history shared the shelf with Warburton, Whitelaw and Walsh's *Dublin* (1818), and with seven other Irish urban histories. These were substantial antiquarian and topographical works, but unlike the contemporaneous county statistical surveys sponsored by the Dublin Society, they were not in any way co-ordinated, and their authors were drawn from across the religious spectrum. None was unduly partisan, local pride of place it seems masking the divisive passions of the age.[1]

1 S. McSkimin, *The history and antiquities of the county and town of Carrickfergus …* (Belfast, 1811); J. Warburton, J. Whitelaw and R. Walsh, *History of the city of Dublin …* 2 vols. (London, 1818); J. Stuart, *Historical memoirs of the city of Armagh …* (Newry, 1819); J. Hardiman, *The history of the town and county of Galway …* (Dublin, 1820); [G. Benn], *The history of the town of Belfast …* (Belfast, 1823); R. H. Ryland, *The history, topography and antiquities of the county and city of Waterford* (London, 1824); L. C. Johnston, *History of Drogheda …* (Drogheda, 1826); P. Fitzgerald and J. J. McGregor, *The history, topography, and antiquities, of the county and city of Limerick*, 2 vols. (Dublin, 1826–7); F. H. Tuckey, *The county and city of Cork remembrancer …* (Cork, 1837). For Hardiman's views: *Galway*, v–viii. The only attempt to survey systematically the principal Irish cities in the nineteenth century was A. Marmion's *The … port cities of Ireland* (London, 1855), a privately published venture that went through four editions.

The irony is that this moment of optimistic self-reflection in Irish urban history marked not so much a renaissance but rather the end of a long period of urban regeneration. In the case of the largest Irish cities, Dublin and Cork, this process had commenced in the seventeenth century, concurrent with the elaboration of English mercantilist legislation, but in the case of other port cities, county towns and regional centres, urban growth became the prevailing national trend from approximately the middle years of the eighteenth century, when of course formal religious discrimination was still in full force. Hardiman was right to talk of the eclipse of early modern Galway, but wrong to characterise it in primarily political terms. And now in the 1820s, with Anglo-Irish free trade and currency union being fully implemented and with Catholic emancipation on the cusp of achievement, Hardiman's optimism was to prove misplaced: the tide would recede once again for Galway and indeed for most of the other larger Irish towns. They were close to their zenith in terms of population, reaching a human scale not to be surpassed in some cases until the second half of the twentieth century.

Given the subsequent recession and long stagnation in urban populations, it is quite understandable that in twenty-first-century public discourse Irish 'urbanisation' and Irish 'modernisation' are often linked together, with the country – outside the northeast – seen as a late and reluctant urbaniser, its older towns and cities perched on the geographical rim, shallow, even exotic cultural implants that only took root in the twentieth century. Indeed Lynn Lees's pioneering 1977 paper with its seductive title 'The Irish countryman urbanized', a study of Irish settlement in London and Philadelphia during and after the Great Famine, has coloured a generation of writing about the Irish diaspora that was predicated on the assumption that Irish emigrants were not just by definition rural dwellers but were unfamiliar with urban life and urban ways.[2] Throughout the history of long-distance Irish emigration the great majority leaving the country were of course from a rural background, but that needs to be qualified in several ways: in the generation or two before the Great Famine the proportion migrating from Irish cities and towns, especially to Britain, was substantial; further back in time, migration from the Irish countryside to Irish towns and cities, especially in the south, was of far greater importance than was emigration (although this is very hard to quantify). And, most fundamentally, the many-sided impact of Irish towns on rural society (in terms of material culture, retail commercialisation, language change, religious practice, education and popular politicisation) was extremely pronounced on the eve of mass migration (that is, by the 1830s), and that impact was far more pronounced than even half a century earlier, a process rather late in western European terms, but very evident none the less.

2 L. H. Lees, 'The Irish countryman urbanized: a comparative perspective on the famine migration', *Journal of Urban History*, 3 (1977), 391–408.

By the time of the first completed census in 1821 the proportion of Ireland's population recorded as living in towns and cities of more than 2,000 inhabitants (a low threshold of urbanisation) was 13.5 per cent. We have no earlier estimates to compare this with, but it is plausible that the urban share had climbed from very low seventeenth-century levels to reach this proportion in the late eighteenth century, and that the spurt in rural population growth and the rustication of industrial employment during and after the French wars may have stabilised the ratio. That remains speculative. The share of total population in towns and cities was virtually unchanged twenty years later in 1841 (at 13.9 per cent). But, thereafter, the reported share rose in each decennial census to reach 33.5 per cent by 1911. That of course masks the fact that national population was declining throughout the period: 99 of the 139 towns and cities that had a population of 2,000 or more in 1841 were actually smaller seventy years later in 1911. Urban population recovery over much of the country only resumed in the 1930s, and in some cases not until the 1960s.[3]

The striking underemphasis of the urban dimension in Irish social history reflects this long demographic stagnation. Nineteenth-century change, whether for good or ill, was evident primarily in the countryside, and the distant eighteenth-century cycle of urban growth was obscured by the subsequent prolonged stasis, in complete contrast to the almost explosive growth of cities across much of western Europe after the 1870s. There were of course regions of slow urban growth in every country, but the Irish cycle seems to have been unusually intense and enduring. Admittedly the physical fabric of nineteenth-century Irish towns and cities changed a great deal – in terms of the expansion of urban sites, the slow improvement of utilities, the renewal of the housing stock, and a far richer diversity of public and commercial buildings (from the competing array of new churches to theatres, workhouses, branch banks, public libraries, railway stations, market houses and town halls). But the prevailing assumption in much of the historiography has been that Ireland simply does not feature in the history of modern European urbanisation, and that Irish towns and cities had relatively weak agency in post-medieval Irish history, whether in terms of the political struggle, the devotional revolution, the language shift or the wider modernisation of cultural practices and material comforts. And in the nationalist narrative, towns with their pervasive Protestant and anglicising legacies were places to be conquered or, at

---

3 *Abstract of the population of Ireland … 1821, Accounts and papers* (Parl. Papers, 1824 [12]); A. J. Fitzpatrick and W. E. Vaughan, *Irish historical statistics: population, 1821–1971* (Dublin, 1978), 27–41. Note that Fitzpatrick and Vaughan issued a strong warning as to the 'slippery nature of municipal statistics' and the uneven quality of their urban population data, given the illogical and changing conventions as to town boundaries, adding 'anyone who is tempted to study town populations in detail will find much … to quarrel with': ibid., xviii–xix. I have nevertheless followed their figures in this chapter.

best, were no more than passive sites of contention in the long rise of Irish democracy and self-determination. Compounding this strain of anti-urbanism in the early twentieth century, Catholic writers linked Irish city life with moral degeneracy, socialism, atheism and the horrors of communism. The fact that it was a Protestant nationalist MP, Stephen Gwynn, who wrote the first substantial and quite sympathetic history and guidebook to Irish cities in 1915 is an indication of just how unusual a politician the author was.[4]

7.2. The First Cities

Throughout post-medieval Irish history, the top ten urban centres, with the exception of Kilkenny, were maritime ports, located strategically on estuaries or on the tidal sections of navigable rivers and functioning as trans-shipment points between fairly well-defined hinterlands and overseas buyers and suppliers. These ports were all trading nodes, and those who did business there were a mix of indigenous merchant elites and external agents, some of whom chose to settle and intermarry. That cultural mix altered markedly, moving from the situation in the early seventeenth century, when indigenous and largely Catholic trading families were utterly dominant in the port towns, to that of a century later when mainly immigrant and overwhelmingly Protestant families, originating from England or Scotland, Holland or France, controlled wholesale business, local government and urban property development. That in turn reflected both the formal exclusion of Catholics from local government and corporate bodies, and the wider revolution in landownership. Thus we find that during the cycle of urban growth – beginning in the early seventeenth century in the case of Dublin, a little later in the cases of Cork and Belfast, and in the eighteenth century for other ports on the east and south coasts – the local commanding heights were Protestant; among the cities, only Limerick and Hardiman's Galway were partial exceptions. Protestant dominance was weakening long before 1800, but the memory of Protestant control over the principal eighteenth-century towns helped ensure that in nationalist historiography urban history (other than the heroic episodes of siege warfare) hardly featured. This cultural estrangement from the urban past was reinforced by the long and bitter struggle over

4 For explorations of Irish anti-urbanism, see D. Corkery, *The hidden Ireland* (Dublin, 1924), 19–20; M. Goldring, *Pleasant the scholar's life: Irish intellectuals and the construction of the nation state* (London, 1993), 65–77; S. A. Royle, 'Industrialization, urbanization and urban society *c.*1850–1921', in B. J. Graham and L. J. Proudfoot (eds.), *An historical geography of Ireland* (London, 1993), 258–60; M. Horgan, 'Anti-urbanism as a way of life: disdain for Dublin in the national imaginary', *Canadian Journal of Irish Studies*, 30, 2 (2004), 38–47. For Gwynn: *The famous cities of Ireland* (Dublin, 1915).

Irish municipal reform, the winning of which in 1840 Daniel O'Connell was happy to celebrate as a great Catholic victory, the metaphorical storming of the citadel.[5]

In that era of religious polarisation, parallel systems of social, educational, welfare and civic organisation were evident in most Irish towns and cities, reflecting the intensity of denominational and party rivalries. Yet eighteenth-century cities and large towns, divided by class, craft, gender and much else, did not display such overt religious segmentation. It is true that alternative Catholic structures (schools, charities, friendly societies, confraternities, recreational associations) were developing late in the century in some cities, but they were usually poorly resourced, and clerical disapproval of non-denominational or Protestant-controlled organisations was rarely strident. Informal associational culture may have been Protestant dominated, but was rarely exclusive.[6] Furthermore, urban divisions within the Protestant world were at times more pervasive than those between Protestant and Catholic, whether between Calvinist dissenters and Huguenot conformists in Dublin, or between Anglican and Presbyterian leaders, lay and clerical, in the city of Derry, who for several generations vied for local dominance. And the statutory exclusion of Catholics from trade guilds and corporate government, which had mattered a great deal in the late seventeenth century when the battery of anti-Catholic legislation was constructed and elaborated, had little economic meaning by the time Catholic relief was beginning in 1778: many trades had by then outgrown guild-style regulation, and the privileges of urban freedom now meant far less in practice. How else could a new Catholic middle class have emerged in eighteenth-century Irish towns, as Maureen Wall argued many years ago, if there was no such space within which to trade and prosper?[7]

Wall's evidence was drawn from Dublin, Galway and the Munster cities in the main. Their demographic expansion in the course of the eighteenth century is surprisingly strong. Thus in Jan de Vries's survey of *European urbanization 1500–1800* (1984), which plotted the growth trajectories of 379 European cities achieving a population of

5 J. H. Andrews, 'Land and people, *c.*1685', in T. W. Moody, F. X. Martin and F. J. Byrne (eds.), *A new history of Ireland,* vol. III: *Early modern Ireland 1534–1691* (Oxford, 1976), 472–6; L. M. Cullen, 'Economic development, 1750–1800', J. H. Andrews, 'Land and people, *c.*1780' and R. B. McDowell, 'Ireland in 1800', in T. W. Moody and W. E. Vaughan (eds.), *A new history of Ireland,* vol. IV: *Eighteenth-century Ireland 1691–1800* (Oxford, 1986), 181–2, 259–63, 666–9; O. MacDonagh, *The emancipist: Daniel O'Connell 1830–1847* (London, 1989), 202–9; J. Hill, *From patriots to unionists: Dublin civic politics and Irish Protestant patriotism 1660–1840* (Oxford, 1997), 362–76; D. Dickson, *Dublin: the making of a capital city* (London, 2014), 337–9.
6 C. Begadon, 'The renewal of Catholic religious culture in eighteenth-century Dublin', in E. Magennis, E. Ní Mhurchadha and P. Walsh (eds.), *New perspectives on the penal laws* (Dublin, 2011), 227–48.
7 M. Wall, 'The rise of a Catholic middle class in eighteenth-century Ireland', *Irish Historical Studies,* 11, 42 (1958), 91–115; T. Barnard, 'The cultures of eighteenth-century Irish towns', in P. Borsay and L. Proudfoot (eds.), *Provincial towns in early modern England and Ireland …* (Oxford, 2002), 208–9, 21; D. Dickson, *Old world colony: Cork and south Munster 1630–1830* (Cork, 2005), 166–9, 276–7; D. A. Fleming, *Politics and provincial people: Sligo and Limerick 1691–1761* (Manchester, 2010), 42, 58–60 131–3.

10,000 inhabitants, Ireland features hardly at all before 1700, but by 1750 Dublin in his estimate was the fourteenth largest city in Europe (on a par with Berlin) and – perhaps even more remarkable – Cork a respectable twenty-fourth, with six other Irish cities featuring by 1800. The estimates on which his rankings were based are soft (the Dublin figure should be revised significantly upwards, Cork downwards), but the point stands that a small number of Irish towns seem to have raced up the European rankings in the eighteenth century.[8]

There were a number of other latecomers in de Vries's dataset, all either capital cities or Atlantic ports (or both). Dublin's European status is the least surprising and was longer in the making: it began its ascent at the end of the sixteenth century with the reassertion of English authority over the whole country, and within a generation the city had become the exclusive hub for financial, legal and other services; parallel to this a capital-centred web of wholesale trade began to develop. Then in the later seventeenth century Dublin's physical and demographic expansion became more apparent, reflecting the mushrooming of its craft workshops and high-end services and its popularity as the place of winter resort for the post-Cromwellian upper classes. The city's growth in the eighteenth century was less hectic, but its position as national warehouse and national workshop, once achieved, seemed almost unassailable. The road system radiated out from the city, the fledgling postal system was Dublin-centred, and the earliest coaching services reflected this. New toll roads (from the 1730s) and the first canals (from the 1740s) promised to reinforce Dublin's growth, allowing for the more efficient transport of foodstuffs and fuel eastwards. Meanwhile the Irish parliament, fitfully underwriting capital expenditure on infrastructure in and around Dublin, privileged Dublin's needs over provincial concerns. Even in the absence of such infrastructural investment, Dublin's economic primacy would probably still have been the most striking feature of Irish urbanisation until the early nineteenth century. It was utterly dominant in publishing and the dissemination of print, and was therefore pivotal in shaping the emerging bourgeois culture, north and south: metropolitan tastes and fashions (themselves largely imported from London or Paris) determined what circulated among provincial readers and what tempted provincial consumers.[9]

The denial of direct access to colonial supplies until the concession of 'free trade' in 1779 was never as important as Irish critics of English mercantilism maintained. Earlier repeal would have made a difference, but the salient point is that the growth of French, Portuguese and Spanish markets for Irish provisions and linen, and the long-term dynamism of British colonial markets for Irish staples, had sustained employment growth in the southern ports, in Cork in particular, where its streets in autumn flowed

8 J. de Vries, *European urbanization 1500–1800* (London, 1984), appendix 1.
9 Andrews, 'Land and people, *c*.1780', 256, 263; T. Barnard, 'The world of goods and Co. Offaly in the early eighteenth century', in W. Nolan and T. P. O'Neill (eds.), *Offaly: history and society* (Dublin, 1998), 371–92.

with bullocks' blood. The three Munster cities, Limerick, Waterford and Cork, together with Belfast, Newry and Derry, prospered as never before as centres of foreign trade. But (with the partial exception of Limerick) they did not follow Dublin to become centres of upper-class seasonal consumption, and all relied to a greater or lesser extent on Dublin for financial and legal services. Employment and business activity centred on the basket of export commodities that they could command from their respective hinterlands, processing and packaging them for export, and doing so largely but not exclusively on external account. And the big local players in overseas trade generally moved from counting house to country house over one or two generations, with relatively few ploughing their assets back into civic or industrial investment, although gentrification may have been more pronounced in the south than in the north of the country.[10]

Prior to 1800 the principal towns in the north did not witness growth like those in the south. Belfast's population at that time, some 19,000, was about a third of that of Cork and a tenth of Dublin's, and a much smaller proportion of Ulster's population in 1821 lived in towns (7.0 per cent) than was the case in either Leinster (19.7) or Munster (18.8).[11] Yet Belfast in some respects represented the urban future more than did its southern rivals. True, unlike them, it was a seigneurial town, its corporate governance and parliamentary representation controlled by the Chichester family, and it was the most active member of that family, the first Marquis of Donegall, who was directly involved in the improvement of the town between the 1760s and 1790s: he made leasing decisions that reshaped the street system, incentivised speculative building and reordered the markets, and he underwrote the construction costs of several major public buildings and a regional infrastructural project (the Lagan Navigation).[12] In that sense Belfast, like dozens of much smaller urban centres across the four provinces, from Ballina (County Mayo) to Bagnelstown (County Carlow), Cookstown (County Tyrone) to Mitchelstown (County Cork), was propelled forward at a critical moment by proprietorial enthusiasm. But, as was so often the case, seigneurial commitment to a long-term development strategy was rarely maintained over the long term, and the translation of urban estate plans into brick and stone could be very slow, held back by litigation, economic fluctuations, or delays in the expiry of critical leaseholds. Few landlord-inspired urban projects were complete failures, but success for the most part reflected the entrepreneurial actions of lessees, helped by the patience of estate agents. But there can have been few cases where tenant ambitions outgrew those of their patron quite so quickly as in Belfast. The presence of lessees willing and able to

10 Barnard, 'Eighteenth-century Irish towns', 199–202, 207.
11 *Census of Ireland, 1821.*
12 S. J. Connolly, 'Improving town, 1750–1820', in Connolly (ed.), *Belfast 400: People, place and history* (Liverpool, 2012), 162–72.

speculate, build and improve brown- or green-field sites was always the prerequisite for successful development, as demonstrated elsewhere at this time (in Newton Pery in Limerick, or on the Fitzwilliam and Gardiner estates on the east side of Dublin city), but what was distinctive about Belfast was the withering away during Donegall's life-time of both proprietorial influence and municipal control, and the emergence of less formal structures of local administration and civic organisation. These representative structures mirrored economic power in the bustling bourgeois community, with its strong educational ethos, religious diversity, and complex web of cross-channel and transatlantic family links. 'The Boston of Ireland' (a term that was coined in 1782) had more than its lively political culture in common with the New England capital.[13]

Belfast shared with Cork and Waterford a heavy dependence on provisions exports and textiles. But in its hinterland, flax and linen production took far deeper root and with that a vast demand for food and services. The remarkable growth of the linen trade across Ulster raised rural incomes above those in other provinces, stimulated small-town development and restrained the growth of poverty in the back lanes of Belfast or Derry. The artisan population in both towns was relatively small and variegated, and large workshops and manufactories did not appear until the 1790s. However, at that point Belfast became the first Irish centre to experience rapid immigration of mill workers (associated initially with the cotton industry), the first chapter in an astonishing nineteenth-century saga of factory-based industrialisation that had many European but no Irish parallels.[14]

The sedate growth of the northern ports prior to the 1790s if compared with those in Munster, notably Limerick and Cork, is at first sight puzzling. The vestigial demographic evidence suggests that population growth across Ulster was stronger than that in the other provinces until late in the eighteenth century; transatlantic migration (however much it is adjusted upwards) can only have absorbed a fraction of this growth. So if there was no drift to the Ulster port towns, it suggests that the carrying capacity of the proto-industrialising countryside and the network of small towns and villages were expanding fast enough until the final years of the century to discourage that drift. Limerick and Cork by contrast had teeming ghettoes long before this and showed abundant signs of environmental degradation – on the urban margins in the case of Cork, within the city in Limerick's case. Both had large craft sectors but also the pervasive presence of street poverty. This did not happen in eighteenth-century

13 Ibid., 172–4; D. Dickson, 'Large scale developers and the growth of eighteenth-century Irish cities', in P. Butel and L. M. Cullen (eds.), *Cities and merchants: French and Irish perspectives on urban development, 1500–1800* (Dublin, 1986), 109–23; A. Thomas, *Derry-Londonderry, Irish Historic Towns Atlas* 15 (Dublin, 2005), 5–6; R. J. Morris, 'Urban Ulster since 1600', in L. Kennedy and P. Ollerenshaw (eds.), *Ulster since 1600: politics, economy and society* (Oxford, 2013), 127.
14 Connolly, 'Improving town', 173–4.

Waterford, perhaps because the urban system in the south-east was quite distinctive: three of the country's largest inland towns were within a thirty-mile radius of Waterford: Kilkenny, Carrick-on-Suir and Clonmel, with the first two housing large artisan populations engaged in woollen manufacture. But the kind of rural textile industry present across most of Ulster never developed in the southern countryside, despite several false dawns, and more than elsewhere there was intense seasonal underemployment in Munster affecting all those below the cattle-owning tenant-farmer class. It was this underclass who provided not just the harvest migrants to Leinster and further afield and the fishermen for the Newfoundland cod banks, but also the inflow of 'cellar-tenants' into the Munster cities and the labour required there during the autumn cattle-slaughtering frenzy.[15].

The southern cities were predominantly Catholic through the era of urban growth, the main Ulster towns overwhelmingly Protestant. In the case of Dublin, Protestant and Catholic numbers were roughly even around 1750, but were tipping towards a Catholic majority. By then artisans, servants and the great unskilled were overwhelmingly drawn from within Dublin's predominantly Catholic hinterland, whereas the more lucrative openings in the capital city (in wholesale trade, the professions and public office) drew in the younger sons of propertied families from across the country (not least Ulster), and these longer-distance migrants were disproportionately Protestant, thereby maintaining Dublin's heterogeneous religious character far into the nineteenth century.[16]

But the contrasting religious make-up of Irish cities was not evident to the eye, and there were no culturally distinct ghettoes (Derry's extramural Bogside was the only part of the city with a Catholic majority, but its distinctive character lay in the future). Architectural fashion showed no distinction between north and south: tree-lined malls and richly fitted assembly rooms had appeared in the most larger towns by the 1780s, constructed usually on local initiative. By then the brick-fronted terrace, first appearing in early eighteenth-century Dublin, had become the standard but highly adaptable carapace for bourgeois living, presenting a chaste image to the street and sometimes containing a tour-de-force of neoclassical decoration within. Only the 'Gothic' merchant houses in Galway survived the purge of 'barbarous' old buildings.[17]

15 L. A. Clarkson, 'The Carrick-on-Suir woollen industry in the eighteenth century', *Irish Economic and Social History*, 16 (1989), 23–41; L. Proudfoot, 'Markets, fairs and towns in Ireland c.1600–1853', in Borsay and Proudfoot, *Provincial towns*, 83–90; Dickson, *Old world colony*, 135–47; J. Crowley, R. Devoy, D. Linehan and P. O'Flanagan (eds.), *Atlas of Cork city* (Cork, 2005), 149–67; D. Fleming, 'Limerick's eighteenth-century economy', in L. Irwin and G. Ó Tuathaigh (eds.), *Limerick: history and society* (Dublin, 2009), 159–62, 165; Morris, 'Urban Ulster', 160–5.

16 D. Dickson, 'The demographic implications of Dublin's growth 1650–1850', in R. Lawton and R. Lee (eds.), *Urban population development in western Europe from the late eighteenth to the early twentieth century* (Liverpool, 1989), 178–89; Connolly, 'Improvement', 174–5.

17 Andrews, 'Land and people', 262–3; Thomas, *Derry-Londonderry*, 5–6.

7.3.   The Shaping of the Irish Urban System

The wider history of Irish towns spanning the long cycle of growth between the 1690s and the 1840s has been concerned with three interrelated issues: how far older urban forms shaped the location and physical evolution of market towns; the relative importance of landlords in initiating and shaping that process; and the impact of other agencies on urban destinies, specifically the role of the monied tenantry within such towns and the expanding tentacles of the state after 1800. Brian Graham and Lindsay Proudfoot's major project evaluating Irish 'urban improvement' in this era created a database of town and village plans based on the Ordnance Survey c.1840; they estimated that 'in excess of 750 provincial towns and villages throughout Ireland displayed morphological evidence of formal planning intent and/or infrastructural modernization'. Projecting back from such mid-nineteenth-century evidence to determine the dating of standardised patterns of building plot, regularity of street alignment or geometric configuration of marketplaces is a somewhat hazardous enterprise, but they concluded that most of the formal interventions evident in the maps were recent, and that only a fifth of the towns and villages in the database inherited some of their planned character from medieval or early modern plantation origins.[18]

That implies that some degree of urban planning was remarkably prevalent across the country during the long eighteenth century. But Graham and Proudfoot gave convincing evidence that landlord intervention, once regarded as the overriding factor in urban growth, was only part of a far more varied story, with estate policies rarely explaining long-term urban outcomes. Few municipal corporations were themselves developers in this era: even in Dublin the management of corporate property had for the most part passed to long-term leaseholders, and the only substantial land-bank was on the foreshore of Dublin Bay. The strategic redevelopment of the centre of Dublin, achieved by the Wide Streets Commissioners in the 1780s and 1790s, was only possible because it was championed and managed by the most powerful politician of the day (John Beresford), and could never have been realised by the city corporation if it had been so minded. But Beresford was in his grave before many of his 'metropolitan improvements' were actually built.[19]

The key to securing change on the ground was indeed a public or private landlord's willingness to defer profit and concede long leases, and this seems to have

18 L. J. Proudfoot, 'Property, society and improvement, c.1700–c.1900', in Graham and Proudfoot, *Historical geography of Ireland*, 234–8; B. J. Graham and L. J. Proudfoot, 'Landlords, planning and urban growth in eighteenth- and early nineteenth-century Ireland', *Journal of Urban History*, 18 (1992), 319–26.
19 Dickson, *Dublin*, 218–25, 275–9.

become almost standard on urban estates by the late eighteenth century, encouraging tenant-led property speculation at a time of rising economic expectations. Indeed without the rise in tenant farmers' incomes from the 1750s, the long-term growth of Anglo-Irish trade from about the same time, and the seemingly inexorable rise in rural population, the fashion for urban improvement would not have got very far. Even in the green-field case of Westport, County Mayo, 'the most elaborately planned of smaller Irish towns' which was laid out in the 1780s, the Marquis of Sligo's very real enthusiasm was important only at the beginning of the project and as a local stimulus to other would-be urban 'improvers' such as Lord Lucan at Castlebar; they were both fortunate to be active when the Mayo economy was in a benign phase of growth. Similarly in the case of Tullamore in the midlands, which was substantially redesigned and leased out after the fire of 1785, the first Earl of Charleville had a very real impact at a formative moment, but his family were in financial trouble when, a generation later, their town was growing from strength to strength, a clear beneficiary of the extension of the Grand Canal. There were indeed a few towns where proprietorial purses were deep enough to ride out recession and to permit a strategic approach to urban estate management spanning more than a single generation: the Downshire estates, which included six towns in three counties, and the Devonshire estates, which included five south Munster towns, provide some of the best examples of prudent development.[20]

7.4. Involution and Evolution of the Modern Irish City

There were eighteen cities and towns recording a population in excess of 10,000 in 1841. Thirteen of them were ports, and some were the recent beneficiaries of the steam-packet revolution and the implementation of free trade, secondary centres that were able to challenge the old dominance of the big ports and their merchant houses: Drogheda, a medieval port long eclipsed by Dublin, was now a thriving conduit for food exports to Lancashire and was also benefiting as the most southerly extension of the linen economy while it passed from handicraft to factory production; Wexford re-emerged as a coastal shipping and fishing hub; in the west, the skylines of Tralee and Sligo witnessed a competition between grain warehouses, flour mills, breweries and new church spires. Of the inland towns Kilkenny was still the largest, but its once powerful handicraft textile industry was by 1841 a thing of the past; however, unlike other former textile towns such as Carrick, Bandon and Mountmellick, Kilkenny remained a commercial

---

20 M. Craig and the Knight of Glin, *Ireland observed* (Cork, 1970), 106; M. Byrne, 'Tullamore: the growth process', in Nolan and O'Neill, *Offaly*, 592–617; B. Clesham, 'Lord Atlamont's letters to Lord Lucan about the Act of Union 1800', *Journal of the Galway Archaeological and Historical Society*, 54 (2002), 31–2.

centre serving a rich agricultural region, its newspapers (led by the redoubtable *Leinster Journal*) the most widely circulating in the south-east.[21]

Probably seventeen of the eighteen urban leaders had a predominantly English-speaking citizenry by the mid-nineteenth century (to judge by the 1851 census), and much earlier in the case of some. The language in the markets and the docks was of course another matter, and there was a somewhat stronger influx of the rural poor once the big urban workhouses were completed, an influx drastically swollen in the crisis years after 1845. Just under three-fifths of the migrants to Dublin city in 1841 came from the old hinterland counties of Kildare, Wicklow and Meath, and it was much the same for other cities; it was the poor of Donegal who helped give Derry city a (small) Catholic majority by 1831.[22]

By 1911 the population of twelve of the group of eighteen was smaller than in 1841, and in the case of five (Armagh, Carlow, Carrick, Drogheda and Kilkenny – all in the eastern half of the country), their numbers had shrunk by more than a quarter.[23] Of provincial towns registering a modest increase over their 1841 populations, each was arguably a special case: Dundalk in being a railway hub and engineering centre for the Great Northern system, Wexford in having developed a distinctive niche in light engineering and farm machinery manufacture, Waterford as a transport hub and centre of innovation in food processing, and Derry having become the largest centre of shirt-making in the world (or so it claimed). But the general picture was one of demographic decline: of the largest 152 Irish towns in 1911, 102 were smaller than in 1841, and of those recording growth more than half were in Ulster, and principally in the Lagan valley.[24]

Irish towns and cities had already been negatively affected by declining rural incomes from the 1820s and by the destructive centripetal effects of the Industrial Revolution in the era of steam and steel. There was short-term growth during and immediately after the famine in most towns (evident in the 1851 census), reflecting short-distance migration by those financially ruined by the crisis, some destined for the back lanes and some for the workhouse, but this migration left little legacy in the age of sustained high emigration. And insofar as urban population decline in the later nineteenth century meant the thinning of fourth-class housing from Irish towns, the elimination of putrid courts and thatched back alleys, the change had a positive side. Urban social structure by 1900

---

21 A. Marmion, *The ancient and modern history of the maritime ports of Ireland* (London, 1855), passim; Fitzpatrick and Vaughan, *Irish historical statistics*, 28–41; D. Dickson, 'Inland city: reflections on eighteenth-century Kilkenny', in W. Nolan and K. Whelan (eds.), *Kilkenny: History and society* (Dublin, 1990), 340–4. On the handful of new factory villages established in early and mid-nineteenth-century Ulster associated with the linen trade: Royle, 'Industrialization, urbanization', 277–8.

22 *Census of Ireland for … 1851, part VI* (Parliamentary Papers, 1856 [2134], xlvii); K. Miller and B. Gurrin, 'The Derry watershed: its religious and political demography 1622–1999', *Field Day Review*, 9 (2013), 40; Dickson, *Dublin*, 309.

23 Fitzpatrick and Vaughan, *Irish population statistics*, 28–41.

24 Royle, 'Industrialization, urbanization', 286–7.

was substantially different from the 1830s: a huge decline in the diversity of crafts and a halving or more of the proportion of urban males engaged in manufacturing, a very visible growth in shopkeepers and publicans, and the expansion of service employment, notably in education, transport and security. Hinterlands were haemorrhaging certainly, but despite years of sharp recession rural incomes were now rising, and in an era of branch banking and rising literacy, with poor law, then parliamentary, politics entering every farmhouse, town and countryside were becoming integrated as never before. The shopkeeper and the strong farmer were in many cases close allies in politics as in business, and the local government of all towns was transformed in a series of statutory reforms, taking it from corporate and proprietorial control into the hands of the ratepayers, or at least the dominant local traders, by the end of the century.[25]

But the outstanding changes by 1911 were at the top of the urban hierarchy: Dublin and Belfast, which over this time had become rival primates, competing for economic territory if not cultural influence. Belfast's population in the years 1841–1911 had grown fivefold (from 75,308 to 386,947), and now exceeded that of Dublin if defined by formal municipal boundaries. However, 'Greater Dublin' (the term did not yet exist) embraced a coastal commuting zone from Howth to Dalkey, which together with the autonomous townships contiguous to the old city had a recorded population in 1911 of 404,214. However, if 'Greater Belfast' is taken to include Holywood, Lisburn and Greenisland, the northern conurbation was touching half a million by 1911. These cities were sprawling over vastly more land than in 1800: Dublin then had been almost entirely contained within the line of the new canals; Belfast had not even crossed the Lagan. Now, a century later, lower density living came with the mass suburbanisation of the middle classes, an exodus driven by the usual mix of Victorian fashion and efficient trams, and accentuated in Dublin's case by the hope of lower taxes, lower morbidity, cleaner air and more salubrious neighbours. That said, Dublin's population had grown by little more than a half between 1841 and 1911 (from 252,653 to 404,214), a poor showing compared with its northern rival. However, the more important point is the contrast between the inexorable growth of these primates and the very modest performance or actual decline of nearly every other large urban centre. Dublin and Belfast between them contained just over half of all residents in the >10,000 urban sector in 1841; by 1911 they contained 72 per cent of 'urban Ireland', and 18 per cent of Ireland's total population.[26]

25 M. Murphy, 'The economic and social structure of nineteenth-century Cork', in D. Harkness and M. O'Dowd (eds.), *The town in Ireland* (Belfast, 1979), 125–39; M. E. Daly, *Social and economic history of Ireland since 1800* (Dublin, 1981), 100–3; S. Clark, *Social origins of the Irish Land War* (Princeton, 1979), 122–38, 262–76; Morris, 'Urban Ulster', 130–3.

26 Fitzpatrick and Vaughan, *Irish population statistics*, 28–41; F. W. Boal, 'Big processes and little people: the population of metropolitan Belfast 1901–2001', in Boal and S. A. Royle (eds.), *Enduring city: Belfast in the twentieth century* (Belfast, 2006), 59–62; S. A. Royle, 'Workshop of the empire, 1820–1914', in Connolly, *Belfast 400*, 222–6.

Figure 7.1 Belfast from the air, 1939. Courtesy: HOYFM. 674, © *Belfast Telegraph* Collection, Ulster Folk & Transport Museum.

This utterly dominant status of the two cities emerging in an era of wider urban stagnation can be explained in many ways. Transport developments (most obviously the twin-fan layout of the Irish railway system) greatly enhanced the wholesale functions of the two cities, Belfast extending across and beyond nine-county Ulster, Dublin projecting its commercial dominance over Munster as never before, helped by the structure of the banking system, the concentration in Dublin of the higher professions, higher education, the newspaper press, parliamentary political organisation and all the delights of the proliferating department stores, serving capital and country.[27]

At the time when Belfast's vast Edwardian city hall was being erected on the site of the old White Linen Hall (*c*.1906), its unionist sponsors were happy to trumpet the contrast between the economies of Belfast and Dublin: the one a Protestant-run world with British-style industrialisation built on linen and shipbuilding, sectors for which Belfast had achieved a global reputation by 1900, manned by a skilled labour force (of both genders) housed in purpose-built back-to-backs superior to those in many British

27 L. M. Cullen, *An economic history of Ireland since 1660* (London, 1972), 140–8; M. E. Daly, 'Dublin city in the nineteenth century Irish economy', in Butel and Cullen, *Cities and merchants*, 54–61; Dickson, *Dublin*, 317–27, 347–8.

cities; the other a Catholic–nationalist dominated city, with a warehouse economy, a few strong industries, and a vast unskilled labour force housed in the older quarters of the inner city, filling the recycled houses of the rich departed.[28] The contrast was real enough, but searching for the similarities can be revealing.

Their size alone meant that the two cities were culturally far more hybrid than their respective hinterlands. They were the sites for significant Jewish settlement from the 1880s, and the overall proportion non-Irish born (mainly located in the middle classes), while low by international standards, was high by Irish, notably in the case of Belfast where 7.5 per cent of the 1901 population had been born outside the island.[29] But in assessing their role in the gathering crisis surrounding Home Rule and its armed rejection, one should try and imagine what the political mobilisation of Protestant Ulster would have been like without Belfast's financial, commercial and reputational success. Belfast's extraordinary nineteenth-century growth had been achieved by persuading prospective migrants in the two most Protestant counties in the country to travel not to Clydeside or to Canada but to the town on their doorstep, and Belfast's east Ulster and Protestant character was not maintained by accident or unknowingly. But if the industrial aristocracy of Belfast shaped and powered popular unionism, they also contributed by default to its uniquely violent urban sectarianism, in embryo from the 1840s, and on full display in the horrors of the early 1920s. The long-practised manipulation of the partially reformed structures of Belfast corporation, the sectarianism of both workplace and neighbourhood, left very bitter legacies.[30]

But in Dublin too, twentieth-century popular politics was germinated in a nineteenth-century sectarian seedbed. It was a city of cross-hatching divisions – spatially, between the reformed and nationalist city corporation and the suburban townships where power was either in unionist hands or shared, and economically, between sectors in Protestant control (like most of the large alcohol and food-processing firms, the railways, the banks, law and the higher branches of the public service), and sectors firmly Catholic (most of the retail sector, the huge cattle trade, education and medicine). But the sheer size and complexity of Dublin made it also the arena for counter-cultural initiatives – whether the Gaelic League, the Celtic Revival, socialism or Larkinite unionism. And as Yeates has observed of the 1916 Proclamation of the Republic, 'it could not have been drafted, let alone adopted … anywhere in Ireland but Dublin.'[31]

28 S. Gribben, 'An Irish city: Belfast, 1911', in Harkness and O'Dowd, *The town in Ireland*, 203–20; Daly, *Social and economic history*, 105–7; Royle, 'Workshop of the empire, 1820–1914', 199–237.

29 Daly, 'Dublin in the nineteenth-century Irish economy', 61–3; S. J. Connolly and G. McIntosh, 'Whose city? Belonging and exclusion in the nineteenth-century urban world', in Connolly, *Belfast 400*, 266–7.

30 P. Ollerenshaw, 'Business and finance, 1780–1945', in Kennedy and Ollerenshaw, *Ulster*, 184–8; Connolly and McIntosh, 'Whose city?', 237–71.

31 P. Yeates, *A city in wartime: Dublin 1914–1918* (Dublin, 2011), 93.

Perhaps the most enduring similarity between the two primates only became evident later in the twentieth century. With partition and the creation of the 'two Irelands', public policy had the (apparently) unintended consequence of strengthening the relative importance of the two cities within their respective jurisdictions. In the Free State, the cumulative effects of protection and industrial sponsorship worked in Dublin's favour up to the 1970s, with Greater Dublin holding 19.7 per cent of the state's population in 1936, but 28.6 by 1971. Public investment in housing and the final eradication of Dublin's inner-city slums was one of the real (albeit delayed) achievements of political independence (the record of town councils across the provinces in clearing their ghettoes was generally less impressive).[32]

Belfast's dominance, both commercially and demographically, became so pervasive that Northern Ireland was almost a city-state by the time of the Matthew report on regional planning in 1964, although Belfast's dominance was accompanied by very conservative attitudes in relation to the social and housing problems thrown up by the city's declining economic fortunes. By 1971, some 35 per cent of the province's population was living in the Belfast urban area. To tackle this bloated city, decentralisation was prescribed in the 1964 Matthew report, and the construction of the new city of Craigavon in the Lagan valley a mere 27 miles from the centre of Belfast was agreed; it was deservedly a white elephant. Craigavon was, however, the forerunner of a series of more successful satellites constructed around Greater Dublin in subsequent decades. Together these new towns marked a resumption of urban genesis after a lapse of more than a century. But in both Belfast's Ireland and Dublin's Ireland, town and regional planning was something provided by outsiders, championed by minority voices, imposed on politicians, and compromised or subverted by political and electoral calculation, with profoundly ugly consequences for the new urban communities across Ireland in the next generation.[33]

FURTHER READING

Borsay, P. and L. Proudfoot (eds.). *Provincial towns in early modern England and Ireland …* (Oxford, 2002).

Butel, P. and L. M. Cullen (eds.). *Cities and merchants: French and Irish perspectives on urban development, 1500–1800* (Dublin, 1986).

Campbell, F. J. M. *The Irish establishment, 1879–1914* (Oxford, 2009).

---

32 Dickson, *Dublin*, 508–15, 536–8.

33 Daly, *Social and economic history*, 202–3; D. G. Pringle, 'Urbanization in modern Ireland', in W. Nolan (ed.), *The shaping of Ireland: the geographical perspective* (Cork, 1986), 176–81, 184–7; S. O'Connell, 'An age of conservative modernity, 1914–68', in Connolly, *Belfast 400*, 271–316; Morris, 'Urban Ulster', 133–4, 136–7; Dickson, *Dublin*, 475–9, 509–11.

Clark, P. and R. Gillespie (eds.). *Two capitals: London and Dublin 1500–1840* (Oxford, 2001).

Clarke, H. (ed.), *Irish cities* (Cork, 1995).

Connolly, S. J. (ed.). *Belfast 400: people, place and history* (Liverpool, 2012).

Cullen, L. M. *Economy, trade and Irish merchants at home and abroad, 1600–1988* (Dublin, 2012).

Daly, M. '"An alien institution?" Attitudes towards the city in nineteenth- and twentieth-century Irish society', *Etudes Irlandaises*, 10 (1985), 181–94.

Dickson, D. *Dublin: the making of a capital city* (London, 2014).

Fagan, P. 'The population of Dublin in the eighteenth century … ', *Eighteenth-Century Ireland*, 6 (1991), 121–56.

Graham, B. J. and L. J. Proudfoot. *Urban improvement in provincial Ireland 1700–1840* (Athlone, 1994).

Harkness, D. and M. O'Dowd (eds.). *The town in Ireland* (Belfast, 1979).

Kelly, J. and M. J. Powell (eds.). *Clubs and societies in eighteenth-century Ireland* (Dublin, 2010).

McManus, R. *Dublin 1910–40: shaping the city and the suburbs* (Dublin, 2002).

Morris, R. J. 'Urban Ulster since 1600', in L. Kennedy and P. Ollerenshaw (eds.), *Ulster since 1600: politics, economy and society* (Oxford, 2013), 121–39.

Ó Gráda, C. *Jewish Ireland in the age of Joyce: a socioeconomic history* (Princeton, 2006).

Potter, M. *The municipal revolution in Ireland: a handbook of urban government in Ireland since 1800* (Dublin, 2011).

Royle, S. A. 'Industrialization, urbanization and urban society c.1850–1921', in B. J. Graham and L. J. Proudfoot (eds.), *An historical geography of Ireland* (London, 1993), 258–92.

8 The Farmers since 1850

Paul Rouse

The translation of dreams into realities is no easy task.[1]

In the years after 1850, the prosperity of agriculture was central to Irish economic development. This centrality underpinned a social position that was founded on the rise of tenant farmers in the nineteenth century and in the triumph of peasant proprietorship in the early twentieth century. The nature of the Irish political revolution and the subsequent partition of the island further influenced the lives of farmers and their position either side of the border. The entry of both the Republic of Ireland and Northern Ireland into the EEC in 1973 was also significant in changing farming in Ireland. Into the new millennium, farming remained a vital industry in Ireland, despite the substantial diminution of the importance of agriculture on the island.

8.1. The Triumph of Livestock, 1850–79

Irish agriculture, wrote Raymond Crotty, is influenced by climate, system of land tenure and demand for its products.[2] Seemingly oblivious to patterns of land tenure, though, the cattle trade dominated after 1850 through the comparative advantage arising from climatic conditions and the proximity of the British market. The trade in cattle across the Irish Sea was underway by 1600 and was so attractive it was suggested that Ireland seemed destined for conversion into vast cattle walks while its population might be transferred to provide a helot class in England. The caustic exaggeration of such suggestions does not disguise the essential truth of the enduring romance between cattle and Irish land.

I would like to thank Leanne Blaney, Brian Casey and Alan Matthews for their comments and assistance.
1 L. Skinner, *Politicians by accident* (Dublin, 1946), 34.
2 R. D. Crotty, *Irish agricultural production, its volume and structure* (Cork, 1966), 1.

Figure 8.1 Farmer with three donkeys. Wiltshire Collection. Courtesy of the National Library of Ireland.

The decades immediately before the Great Famine of the 1840s had seen both pastoral and tillage farming in Ireland struggle under falling prices, but tillage, with its higher inputs, proved less profitable than grass, thriving, as ever, with little encouragement under Irish conditions. Most critically, cattle prices held more firmly than tillage ones as demand on the British market ebbed from cereals towards livestock. This trend continued after the Great Famine. Britain's policy of free trade encompassed unlimited food importation on a comparative cost basis and on the lines best suited to the British economy. Imported American grain on an improving transport network worsened the corn market, while Irish agriculture bowed to the imperatives of climate and allowed natural conditions to provide enough grass at negligible cost to feed livestock. Increasingly, it was beef rather than dairying, hampered by a shortage of winter feed and traditionally inefficient seasonality, which held sway in the new order. The result was that in the years between 1847 and 1876, the cattle population rose by almost 60 per cent and the sheep population by more than 80 per cent.[3]

3 The statistics used in this chapter are taken from Crotty, *Irish agricultural production, its volume and structure*; S. J. Sheehy, J. T. O'Brien and S. D. McClelland, *Agriculture in Northern Ireland and the Republic of Ireland* (Dublin and Belfast, 1981); K. A. Kennedy, T. Giblin and D. McHugh, *The economic development of Ireland in the twentieth century* (London, 1988); Mary E. Daly, *Industrial development and Irish national identity, 1922–1939* (Syracuse, 1992); Central Statistics Office, *Farming since the famine: Irish farm statistics 1847–1996* (Dublin, 1997); P. O'Hara, *Partners in production? Women, farm and family in Ireland* (Oxford, 1998); A. Matthews, *Farm incomes: myth and reality* (Cork, 2000); P. Rouse, *Ireland's own soil, government and agriculture in Ireland 1945–65* (Dublin, 2001); D. W. Alexander and M. Drake, *Breaking new ground: fifty years of change in Northern Ireland agriculture 1952–2002* (Belfast, 2002), T. Hennessy and A. Kinsella, *40 years of Irish farming since joining the European Union: a journey with the Teagasc National Farm Survey 1972–2012* (Galway, 2013); *Census 2011: Ireland and Northern Ireland* (Dublin, 2014); *Compendium of Irish agricultural statistics 2013; Annual statistical review of Northern Ireland agriculture.*

This shift in the structure of the agricultural economy had, of course, a profound impact on Irish farmers. The number of people who now made their living on the land declined spectacularly. The number of rural labourers fell from at least 700,000 in 1845 to 300,000 by 1910. The agrarian classes just above the labourers also declined in huge numbers; this was a demographic rupture that appears to have originated in the years before the famine, but it was that cataclysm which defined its nature. Between 1845 and 1910, those who farmed less than five acres of land fell from 300,000 in number to 62,000. In the same period, the number of farmers holding between five and fifteen acres fell from 310,000 to 154,000. The fact that the farmer with up to fifteen acres did not vanish as conveniently as the labourer, or the cottier, had an enduring impact on Irish life over the following century. That toehold of land was protected with unrelieved zeal until the family line was ended through emigration or failure to marry. Allowing for that, this class of farmer – as surely if not as spectacularly as the labourer – had now lurched into a steady, unrelenting decline. In tandem with this decline, the decades after the famine saw tenant farmers become the largest social group in rural society and their interests grew increasingly important. These farmers ultimately benefited from clearances and consolidation in the years after the famine. As R. V. Comerford has noted, the years 1850–70 saw the prices for cattle, mutton, pork and butter increase by up to 50 per cent.[4] Progressive tenant farmers were carried into prosperity on the back of this agricultural boom. Landlords,

Figure 8.2 'Donegal natives', undated. Courtesy of the National Library of Ireland.

4 R. V. Comerford, 'Ireland 1850–1870: post-famine and mid-Victorian', in W. E. Vaughan (ed.), *A new history of Ireland: Ireland under the Union* (Oxford, 1989), 372–95, at 381.

too, benefited from the increase in rents that often followed a rise in prices, but it was the rise in importance of prosperous tenant farmers – farming ever larger tracts of land – that underpinned what eventually amounted to a social and political revolution.

8.2.   The Politics of Proprietorship, 1879–1921

Recast demographics, the assertion of the primacy of livestock and the rise of tenant farmers created the context in which a drive towards peasant proprietorship developed an irresistible momentum. This 'dynamic element of structural change' dominated the political landscape in the closing decades of the nineteenth century as the agrarian movement joined constitutional and revolutionary nationalism in the unprecedented unity of the Land League. Beginning with the 'Land War' in 1879, agrarian protests linked ideas of economic advancement with a rhetorical challenge to the legitimacy of landlordism. Mass meetings and boycotting were joined with murder and intimidation, and ultimately, the government capitulated with a series of land acts culminating in 1903 with the Wyndham Act. These acts – remarkable internationally for the relative ease by which the transfer of landownership occurred – provided, in essence, long-term government loans allowing many tenants to buy the land they farmed and the tenure system became one of peasant proprietorship. By 1916, 64 per cent of agricultural holdings were owner-occupied, as compared with a mere 3 per cent in 1870; expropriation spelled the inevitable demise of the class of Anglo-Irish landowners and confirmed that the future of Irish farming belonged now to small farmers.

Peasant proprietorship failed to inspire an improvement in productivity. There was no dramatic or even significant effect on efficiency, investment or land use. J. J. Lee noted how the land activist Michael Davitt had initially promoted land nationalisation with tenancy secured by a reasonable standard of efficiency, but 'the farmers were not impressed. There would be no nonsense about efficiency as far as they were concerned … They had not fought the land war to be crucified on the cross of their efficiency.'[5] Ultimately, peasant proprietorship brought a stability of output which shaded into stagnation.

The difficulty was, of course, that peasant proprietorship had been presented by its advocates as something of a panacea for Irish farmers. This notion was decried by only a few observers, notably James Connolly, who argued in 1897:

> The agriculture of Ireland can no longer compete with the scientifically equipped farmers of America … Have our advocates of peasant proprietary really considered the economic tendencies of the time and the development of the mechanical arts in the agricultural world? … The day of small farmers … is gone and wherever they are still found, they find it impossible to compete with the mammoth farmers of America and Australia.[6]

5 J. J. Lee, 'The Land War', in L. de Paor (ed.), *Milestones in Irish history* (Cork, 1986), 114.
6 R. M. Fox, *James Connolly: the forerunner* (Tralee, 1946), 39.

Connolly's dismal prognosis was rejected by others and the early years of the twentieth century did bring institutional innovation, both realised and imagined. The principal reformer in Irish agriculture was the Unionist MP Horace Plunkett, who worked in, and wrote on, the co-operative movement and the establishment of a Department of Agriculture and Technical Instruction in Dublin in 1899. In the course of his 1904 treatise, *Ireland in the new century*, Plunkett outlined his interpretation of the problems facing Irish agriculture, the requirements to solve these problems and the means to meet those requirements. Stripped of its self-aggrandisement and crass generalisations on the Irish character, the book offered an insightful analysis of Irish agriculture at the beginning of the twentieth century. Like Connolly, Plunkett stressed that peasant proprietorship alone would not bring prosperity to Irish agriculture. He posited, however, that a well-organised co-operative movement offered the means to compete against the large-scale farming operations of the New World and the more organised productivity of other countries in the old one. Plunkett argued that, as foreign competition was not about to disappear, but would rather intensify, Irish farming would have to reform itself, or perish.

Noting the ready markets now available in growing industrialised cities, Plunkett wrote of the importance of the 'regular consignment of food in large quantities of such uniform quality that the sample can be relied upon to be truly indicative of the quality of the bulk. Thus the rapid distribution of produce in the markets becomes as important a factor in agricultural economy as improved methods of production or cheap and expeditious carriage.' To this end, the Irish Agricultural Organisation Society was established to offer a co-operative outlet to assist smallholders. While he commented disapprovingly that Irish people had 'an extraordinary belief in political remedies for economic ills', Plunkett none the less cast an envious eye on European countries where 'state intervention has undoubtedly done much to render possible a prosperous peasant proprietary by, for example, the dissemination of useful information, admirable systems of technical education in agriculture, cheap and expeditious transport, and even state attention to the distribution of agricultural produce in distant markets.'[7]

There was optimism that the Department of Agriculture and Technical Instruction – in conjunction with the co-operative movement – could play such a role in Ireland, that it would give free play to 'a reawakening life'. This was never realised. The co-operative movement showed early prosperity but lost its government funding in a political wrangle and failed to take firm hold. It stumbled onwards but never attained the vibrancy of continental movements. Similarly, the new department enjoyed little success. On the grounds of assisting in the improvement of output alone, it did not justify the expectations that had attended its inauguration. None the less, the issues raised by Plunkett and what he perceived as being the needs of Irish farms were repeated at will

7 H. Plunkett, *Ireland in the new century* (London, 1904), 20–1, 51, 180, 231.

through the century that followed. Pleas for land redistribution, education, technical efficiency, marketing, transport, co-operation, innovation and a balanced economy – as the century began so would it continue. There was, however, the occasional glimpse of what might be achieved. Although neither co-operation nor the establishment of a Department of Agriculture succeeded in substantially raising the prosperity of Irish farmers, the competing powers of Europe had greater success. Exports of farm produce, food and drink rose from £41.6 million in 1914 to £78.3 million in 1918 without ever threatening to fully exploit the lack of competition from Danish and Dutch exports.

By then, political unrest in Ireland had brought a new dimension to the agricultural scene. Drawing on the doctrine of James Fintan Lalor, who had written that a strong and independent peasantry was the only base on which a people could be improved or on which a nation could safely rest, the rhetoric surrounding the Easter Rising of 1916 was suffused with the imagery of agrarianism. Inevitably, it strove to offer all things to all men – the landless man was to be given land, the small farmer was to have his holding increased, and the larger farmer was to have his position safeguarded. That the remaining landlords would be stripped of their holdings was a given, but if the rebels were to make good on their commitments, they were now faced with the challenge of not merely freeing Ireland, but extending its landmass.

Some were not prepared to await either eventuality; the rural poor sensed their moment had arrived and it was not long before labourers and small farmers were rallying to the old battle hymn of 'The land for the people.' Whether seeking conacre or the aggrandisement of smallholdings, the motivating force was the seizure of land. From 1917 onwards, estate redistribution, cattle driving, ploughing and stripping, and general agrarian unrest were in full swing. Elsewhere, farm labourers organised in trade unions and threatened strike action.

Patriotism is rarely more sharply displayed than when founded in acute self-interest and for the strong farmer, too, freedom was often defined in economic not constitutional terms. Some reacted to the groundswell of land agitation by covertly participating to further expand their own property and wealth; others founded the Irish Farmers' Union to defend their existing position. The republican movement was moved to intervene with a headlong rush to the middle ground in an attempt to preserve unity and earn respect for responsible leadership. A Dáil Éireann decree was issued on 29 June 1920 stating 'That the present time when Irish people are locked in a life and death struggle with their traditional enemy, is ill-chosen for the stirring up of strife amongst our fellow countrymen; and all our energies must be directed towards the clearing out [of] – not the occupiers of this or that piece of land – but the foreign invader of our country.'[8]

8 G. Ó Tuathaigh, 'The land question, politics and Irish society', in P. J. Drudy (ed.), *Ireland: land, politics, and people*, Irish Studies 2 (Cambridge, 1982), 167–89, 170–1.

Special Land Courts were set up by the Dáil to curtail the activities of the more radical and to enforce, through the IRA, such redistribution as could most easily be effected.

Through the years of the Irish Revolution, in the construction of an alternative vision to the one offered by the 'traditional enemy', Gaelic revivalists and revolutionary nationalists alike presented the small farming ideal as the genuinely Irish existence. Far from the squalor of industrial cities and their degrading factories, the Irish would create a vibrant rural landscape of small homesteads and thriving cottage industries. Political independence would ensure the agricultural prosperity which would drive this buoyant, self-sufficient economy. Detail was ignored as excessively divisive. Rather, all were assured that economic progress was an essential by-product of independence. Rhetoricians, calmly ignoring market forces, claimed that legislative freedom would signify arrival at Babylon – and there basking on the shores would be Irish farmers and farm labourers.

8.3.   Selling Beef to John Bull, 1922–39

The partition of Ireland carried obvious consequences for Irish agriculture. In the new Irish Free State, the opposing sides in the civil war had not merely divided on matters constitutional – economics were of definite importance. Notwithstanding the danger of oversimplifying the equation given the cross-class allegiances of both sides, opponents of the Anglo-Irish Treaty enjoyed their greatest support amongst the labourers and smallholders of the south and west. Agrarian radicals tended to find a more accommodating home in anti-Treaty forces than in the government party which was dominated by the more conservative elements of society, most notably by large farmers. A radical restructuring of Irish agriculture may not have occurred in any event, but civil war and its legacy brought the rejection of any restructuring at all.

The new government – constituted in a political party as Cumann na nGaedheal – effectively disregarded the social and economic sloganeering which had attended the path to political independence when faced with the realities of government. The primacy of agriculture was enshrined as the government accepted that the economy depended on farming for general prosperity, that agricultural prosperity depended on the export market, that that market essentially comprised Britain, and that by far the most profitable Irish product in Britain was cattle exported on the hoof. Policy revolved around these essential verities; the new Minister for Agriculture, Patrick Hogan, said in 1924: 'National development for Ireland in our generation at least is practically synonymous with agricultural development.' This meant the championing of farmers continuing to do almost precisely what they had done in the decades before independence.

George O'Brien, Professor of National Economics at University College Dublin, neatly summed up the status of farmers in independent Ireland by describing how the state was designed to maximize farmers' income, because the farmers being the most important section of the economy, everything that raised their income raised the national income of the country. Prosperity among farmers would provide the purchasing power necessary to sustain demand for non-agricultural goods and services, and it was useless to encourage secondary industries unless the primary industry was in a position to purchase their products.[9]

During the 1920s, the state did introduce a number of initiatives. A series of acts established systems of inspection and control on Irish farm produce, the Dairy Disposal Company was established to acquire co-operatives in trouble and the Agricultural Credit Corporation was designed to offer loans to individual farmers. Against that, there were no guaranteed prices, no protective tariffs and no subsidies; farmers were left free to follow the market for good or ill. The Land Commission was established in 1923 and charged with transferring the land of the remaining large estates from the remaining landlords to smallholders. The Land Commission also took over the work of the Congested Districts Board in rearranging farm holdings in the western region. In general, the Land Commission was given only limited powers and limited resources – it was to redistribute land but it was to do so without interfering with property rights and at minimal cost.

The life of Irish farmers changed hardly at all while Cumann na nGadheal were in government, but the ascent to power of Fianna Fáil in 1932 promised something entirely different. One of the founding aims of Fianna Fáil was to provide for the greatest possible number of families to live on the land through greatly intensified redistribution. There were promises also to reassert the notion of self-sufficiency in food production – meaning, of course, that tillage would have to be prioritised ahead of cattle. This realignment from cattle farming to tillage farming was fundamental to the wished-for success of Fianna Fáil policies. The substitution of intensive for extensive farming was seen as the key to a revitalised rural society by allowing smallholders improve their incomes and larger farmers to employ more labourers, thus stemming emigration and the drift from the land. A concerted campaign was launched to encourage farmers to convert to tillage production. A bounty was offered for calf skins, subsidies were introduced for wheat and sugar beet, import controls were imposed on sugar and tobacco, and relief was offered on rates in proportion to the amount of non-family farm labour used. This attempt to restructure farming in Ireland saw the government increase spending from 24 per cent of GNP in 1931 to 30.3 per cent in 1933, before averaging 30 per cent for the remainder of the decade. Agricultural spending claimed 46 per cent of this increase, with a further 23.3 per cent allocated to land redistribution.

Economic 'war' – originating from the decision by the Irish government to withhold the payment of land annuities to the British exchequer – was yet another factor

9 G. O'Brien, 'Patrick Hogan: Minister for Agriculture 1922–32', in *Studies*, 25 (1936), 37.

to consider. By November 1932 duties of 30 per cent ad valorem were placed on the principal Irish agricultural exports to Britain. The imposition of this duty exacerbated the challenges faced by Irish farmers as Britain moved from free trade to protectionism through the introduction of import quotas and tariffs in the wake of the Great Depression. The establishment in Britain of marketing boards for milk, bacon, pigs and potatoes, as well as the introduction of a guaranteed price for wheat in 1932, altered the free trade landscape which so recently had appeared immune to change. Worst of all for Irish farmers, Britain imposed strictures on the import of cattle. The price of fat cattle had been in decline through the 1920s and early 1930s and – under pressure to assist its own farmers – Britain placed quantitative restrictions on the import of cattle. Between 1929 and 1934 the export of live animals fell in value from £19.7 million to £6.1 million and that of animal-derived foodstuffs fell from £14.5 million to £5.2 million.

It was none the less most revealing that by the end of the 1930s, almost nothing had changed in agriculture south of the border. Buoyed by subsidies, the wheat acreage had increased from 22,000 acres to more than ten times that amount and the area under sugar beet grew from 13,000 acres to 51,000 acres. These expansions supplied 30 and 60 per cent of the national requirement, respectively, but the overall acreage under tillage in 1939 was only 2 per cent higher than it had been in 1932. Despite the struggles in the sector, the number of cattle in the country had actually increased during the 1930s. Southern Irish farmers continued to cling to livestock. This reality was recognised in the 1938 Defence, Financial and Trade Agreements with Britain. Another reality was revealed in these agreements: Britain was committed to the concept of 'orderly marketing' of agricultural products. In the course of the negotiations, the British Minister for Agriculture, W. S. Morrison, told the Irish delegation that since 1930 'powers have been secured and an organisation built up to prevent unregulated imports of agricultural products which would threaten the stability of markets … No-one now had a free entry into the agricultural markets of this country.' The Irish had sought agreement that the quantities fixed for the import of Irish produce would enable the country to export the whole of its surplus production to the British market.[10] The great difficulty with this was that southern Irish farmers were now operating in a market where British producers were receiving guaranteed prices for cattle, and the price the Irish would receive was pegged rigidly below these. The advantage of comparative costs did not now appear quite so wholesome.

For the farmers of the six counties of Ulster that became Northern Ireland, the free flow of agricultural goods with Britain remained unimpeded under the protectionist policies introduced in the 1930s. There was no politically inspired policy of expanding the acreage under wheat and the result was that it continued to decline, as did the

10 P. Rouse, *Ireland's own soil: government and agriculture in Ireland 1945–65* (Dublin, 2001), 19.

acreage under potatoes and other crops. Instead, 'under the policy of free grain imports and supported prices' farmers in Northern Ireland were encouraged to produce more pigs and more poultry, crucially obtaining the prices paid by the British Ministry of Food.[11] Despite the disparity in policy and output, the structure of agriculture in Northern Ireland remained much the same as it did in the Republic. As James Meenan wrote in 1948, 'the Land Acts had produced the same type of farm' either side of the border, with 39 per cent of farms comprising 15 acres in Northern Ireland compared with 31 per cent south of the border, 27.6 per cent between 15 and 30 acres compared with 26.9 per cent in the south, 17.1 per cent between 30 and 50 acres compared with 18.6 per cent in the south, and 4.1 per cent of farms consisting of more than 100 acres compared with 8.7 per cent in the south.[12] The upshot was that farming in Northern Ireland was even more dependent on small farms, worked by family labour. In the context of global change in the years after the Second World War this had a profound impact on the long-term prosperity of Irish farming.

8.4.   The Death of the Peasantry, 1940–70

In 1943 a Northern Ireland Agricultural Enquiry Committee was appointed to advise on the future development of farming and agriculture-related industries. The Committee, presided over by Lord Justice Babbington, proposed a greater concentration on the production of milk for human consumption and urged intensification in the processing of agricultural produce: 'Our best hope of successful economic development lies in making the maximum use of our agricultural products as the basis of our industry and trade. Indeed, of no country is it truer to say that agriculture constitutes the basis of economic life than of Ulster.'[13] The Agriculture Act (1947) was critical for farmers in Northern Ireland in providing for agricultural price support arrangements through the provision of guaranteed prices and assured markets for products. This was supplemented in 1955 with the introduction of special financial assistance (a 'Remoteness Grant') to assist in supporting farmers by means of cattle headage payments, and silage and fodder-crop payments. The establishment of the marketing boards for pigs and milk, for instance, further enhanced prosperity. The result was the continued expansion of 'farmyard enterprises' involving pigs and poultry.[14] By 1960 pig numbers in Northern Ireland had increased sixfold in little more than three decades, while poultry numbers increased by one-third. By contrast, pig numbers in the Republic of Ireland were unchanged, while poultry numbers actually decreased by one-third. And all the

---

11 Sheehy *et al.*, *Agriculture in Northern Ireland and the Republic of Ireland*, 20.
12 J. Meenan, 'Agriculture in Northern Ireland', *The Irish Monthly*, 76, 904 (Oct. 1948), 440–8, at 442.
13 *Reports of the Agricultural Enquiry Committee, 1947*, 121.
14 Sheehy *et al.*, *Agriculture in Northern Ireland and the Republic of Ireland*, 2.

while the numbers of cattle in the north continued to grow and grow, increasing by some 67.6 per cent between 1926 and 1960. Ultimately, farmers in Northern Ireland now had the benefit of systems 'that engendered a greater sense of security throughout farming, increased profitability, and so gave farmers confidence to invest in their enterprises'.[15]

To prepare for the post-war world, the southern Irish government had also instituted a radical reassessment of farming. Agreement on the 'deplorable state' of agriculture was accepted by all and was crystallised in the words of a government official who wrote of 'appalling hardship and poverty' and of 'agricultural slums'.[16] A government commission produced a series of sectoral reports which amounted to a damning indictment of the failures of farming, both in its pattern and in its levels of production, and ended with a majority report which noted:

> The condition of many farms in this country is deplorable. Outlying fields usually show deterioration as they recede from proximity to the farmyard .... For various reasons, some subjective, others fortuitous, the fertility of thousands of farms is now so low that they yield but the barest maintenance to their occupiers and frequently subsistence is obtained by annual lettings or the repeated sale of hay, or by part-time alternative employment; judged by modern standards of agriculture, such land is derelict.[17]

There remained a commitment to build Irish prosperity around farming in the post-war years, however. This is revealed in a trade agreement with the United Kingdom in 1948, where negotiations inevitably returned time and again to the price and quantity of live cattle that would be exported from Ireland. It was revealed also in the manner that Ireland chose to use its Marshall Aid money (provided by way of loan rather than grant aid). In 1950, Richard Mulcahy, the leader of Fine Gael (the largest party in the new inter-party government), said: 'We have always accepted the supremacy of agriculture in the nation's economy. Emphasis has been given to this by the government's decision to do what no other government has undertaken, namely to invest almost the whole of the funds available in the rehabilitation of the land of the country.'

As a result of this investment in what became known as the Land Rehabilitation Project, it was planned to increase agricultural output by 22 per cent in four years. This was the investment which was intended to kickstart the Irish economy and to bring prosperity through the 1950s. The plan was a failure. In the end, the increase for the entire decade was 2.5 per cent. Worse than that, the volume of agricultural exports rose by just 0.5 per cent. There was a range of reasons for this, not least the fact that the Land Rehabilitation Project was entirely undercut by other aspects of government policy. For example, it was still government policy to break up large farms and estates and to

15 Alexander and Drake, *Breaking new ground*, 16.
16 Rouse, *Ireland's own soil*, 25.
17 *Commission of inquiry on post-emergency agricultural policy* (1945), 78.

create small farms in their place, despite every study conducted in Ireland and internationally showing that agricultural output could be increased on large farms, but rarely
on small ones. The core ambition of this policy of land redistribution was to establish
as many families as possible on the land. The problem with it was that the size of the
small farms created by the state was so small – never more than 50 acres – as to render
them not just incapable of expansion, but increasingly incapable even of survival. After
1945, 25,800 small farms were created by the Irish government. It would be a mistake
to imagine that this small farms policy was something which was dreamed up by ideologues and imposed by the state on an unwilling Irish public. The cherished dream
of many in rural Ireland was to obtain the biggest farm possible, but the first goal was
to obtain any sort of a farm at all. You see this in the letters received by TDs (*Teachtaí
Dála*, members of the Dáil) throughout the 1950s. One woman, for example, wrote to
the Limerick TD Donnchadh Ó Briain to plead the case of her son who, she said, was
'married with one child and currently farmed eight acres of craggy land, which you
may understand is hard to make a living on. I wonder if you can do anything for him
to get a few more acres.'[18]

In a broader sense, the second reason for the failure of Irish agriculture was the want
of adequate education. To properly modernise Irish farming, a basic level of agricultural education was required. Indeed, a basic level of general education was required.
However, as late as 1964 83 per cent of Irish farmers had received only a primary school
education. Every year, 7,000 farmers' sons left school to go into farming, but only 200
received any instruction in agriculture. In the 1930s there had been a proposal to
establish 500 agricultural instruction schools across the country with a view to providing agricultural education to those leaving national schools. This was rejected by
the Catholic bishops who wrote to the Department of Education to say that this was an
unnecessary extension of state control into education. It was further stated that in many
households families were so poor that they needed the children to go and work and so
they didn't have the resources to go to such schools. And, finally, the bishops wrote that
from the moral point of view there was an inherent danger in allowing boys and girls
between the ages of twelve and sixteen to travel unsupervised to school together. In the
wake of church objections, the government abandoned the plan and the education of
Irish farmers remained basic.

Ultimately, even if Irish land policy had been appropriate and even if education
standards had been excellent, what the Irish were trying to do flew straight into the
face of the prevailing winds of the rest of the western world, where workers were being
freed from the land to provide labour for industrial development. This drift from the
land had been underway from the nineteenth century, but its momentum accelerated

---

18 University College Dublin Archives, Donnchadh Ó Briain Papers, P83/175(2), Madge Ranahan letter, 15 Feb. 1961.

significantly after the Second World War, facilitated by increased mechanisation of farming and the electrification of farms. Across the world – in every modern society – farmers (especially small farmers) were being pushed to the margins. As Eric Hobsbawm put it: 'The most dramatic and far-reaching social change of the second half of the twentieth century and the one which cuts us off forever from the world of the past is the death of the peasantry.'[19] The policy of successive Irish governments was to try and resist that process and the result was complete failure. There was a mass exodus from the countryside. In 1945, 522,000 men worked on southern Irish farms; twenty years later in 1965 that number had fallen by almost half to just over 300,000. One by-product of this was that in contrast to trends elsewhere in the world, the proportion of female farmers in the Republic of Ireland increased throughout the twentieth century, reaching 15.8 per cent in 1951; 40 per cent of these were aged over sixty-five. Almost invariably this was not by way of female empowerment or the assertion of economic independence; rather it was that women had been left in possession through the death and emigration of all male relatives. This was despite the fact that more women emigrated from rural areas than did men as part of a process which saw the abandonment of the land by the children of small farmers. This exodus was the most eloquent of statements that the vision of a prosperous farming society had been entirely shattered; the south of Ireland was 'a land half-farmed, a people fleeing in despair'.[20] The same was true also for Northern Ireland where the drift from the land was equally remorseless. In the second half of the twentieth century, the total agricultural workforce fell from 152,314 in 1951 to 56,362 in 2001. Just as in the south, the watershed decade was the 1950s when some 40,000 left the agricultural workforce. It is a further striking testimony to the decline of the importance of agriculture in Northern Ireland that by 2001 the 56,362 working in agriculture included 15,786 part-time farmers and 11,090 part-time, casual or seasonal labourers. Ultimately, alternative agricultural policies north or south of the border proved futile in protecting employment in farming.

8.5.   Dreams of Europe since 1970

Farmers' incomes rose after 1970, but, significantly, the gap between those in agricultural and those in non-agricultural employment widened considerably as industrial workers continuously increased their purchasing power. Across the western world states sought to support farmers and to contain the growing disparity of income between families living in rural and in urban areas. Central to those attempts in Ireland from the early 1970s was entry into the European Economic Community (EEC). Following the

19 E. Hobsbawm, *The age of extremes: the short twentieth century, 1914–1991* (London, 1994), 284.
20 *Irish Farmers' Journal*, 11 Jan. 1958.

accession to the EEC of both the Republic of Ireland and the United Kingdom in 1973, farming was reshaped by much higher levels of protection provided by the Common Agricultural Policy (CAP) through price support and trade barriers, the application of quota systems and by a series of directives from the European Commission relating to farm structure. Irish farmers benefited from the range of measures included in the CAP. Indeed, by the end of the millennium the Republic of Ireland had enjoyed the highest transfers to its farmers of money from Europe through a plethora of schemes including market-price supports, headage payments and premia payments. Funds from Europe were complemented by payments from the Irish exchequer, and by 1998 direct payments made up 56 per cent of aggregate farm income in the Republic of Ireland and passed 70 per cent in the new millennium; there was no denying that entry into the EEC had greatly increased the prosperity of farmers.

Despite this, between the 1960s and the 1980s, the number whose principal occupation was farming declined by almost 2 per cent per annum in the Republic of Ireland, although many held on to the land and there was relatively little consolidation of farms. Farm households fell from 22 per cent of total population in 1973 to less than 5 per cent in 1997, and the numbers were continuing to fall sharply. With more than a quarter of Irish farms considered incapable of generating a viable income from farming alone, the importance of part-time farming increased considerably during the 1970s and became crucial to the survival of many farming units. By the mid-1990s 27 per cent of farmers had jobs away from the farm, with this percentage reaching 41 per cent on small farms. Further, 16 per cent of farmers' wives also held off-farm employment. The boom of the 'Celtic Tiger' years confirmed this trend as more and more people made their living away from the land.

In Northern Ireland, entry into the EEC brought further subsidies and grants on top of the ones provided domestically, but the basic structure of farming remained relatively unchanged. More than 80 per cent of farms in the 1990s were beef production operations that revolved around small herds. Dairy farming was also significant with milk accounting for 29 per cent of gross agricultural output in 2001. As Derek W. Alexander and Michael Drake note, 'eggs and poultry meat were still the most concentrated enterprises on Northern Ireland farms at the end of the 1990s': almost 99 per cent of laying hens were found on just 106 farms, while all of the nearly 9 million broiler chickens were raised on 280 farms.[21]

Nothing revealed the enduring economic importance of farming in Ireland quite as dramatically as the periodic crises that afflicted the industry. From the BSE/CJD scandal of 1996 to the Foot and Mouth Disease outbreak in 2001 and on to the meat adulteration saga of 2013, the upheavals in agriculture brought sectoral and national

---

21 Alexander and Drake, *Breaking new ground*, 106.

disruption on a large scale. All of those crises were partially related to the globalised nature of modern agriculture and the challenge that this presents has changed the nature of modern farming. The new millennium has seen a significant modification in the twentieth-century practice of price supports, tariffs and quotas, and the development of a global marketplace increasingly dominated by larger companies that operate on a transnational basis. The 'sustainability agenda' was also increasingly important with its focus on water pollution, biodiversity loss and the retention of landscape features. Further, it remains to be seen what impact the decision to withdraw (at least in part) support for farmers has on farming practice in Ireland. The reform of the CAP, including, for example, the abandonment of milk quotas in 2015, carries both threats and opportunities for Irish dairy farmers. It is equally unclear to what extent global farm trade will be influenced by a growing emphasis on safety, quality and environmental standards. On a local level, the buying power of large supermarket chains also presents a significant challenge to farmers who have seen their profit margins diminished by relentless price wars and, in certain instances, destroyed by below-cost selling.

Farming remains invested with a significance that travels beyond economics. North and south of the border, farmers continue to enjoy a status that in part reflects the importance of food supply to every modern state, but is also a legacy of political, cultural and social forces and events. There is no denying the relative decline in the percentage of people who make their living from farming in Ireland, however. By 2011 the census was recording that agriculture, forestry and fishing accounted for just 8.2 per cent of male employment and 1.2 per cent of female employment in the Republic of Ireland, and 3.7 per cent of male employment and 0.7 per cent of female employment in Northern Ireland. The importance of the wider agri-food sector has ensured that farming and farmers continue to matter, albeit in a much smaller way than at any time in history. Global trends and the sands of time have proved impossible to stem, let alone reverse, and agrarian Ireland has continued its long fade.

FURTHER READING

Alexander, D. W. and M. Drake. *Breaking new ground: fifty years of change in Northern Ireland agriculture 1952–2002* (Dublin, 2002).

Crotty, R. D. *Irish agricultural production, its volume and structure* (Cork, 1966).

Daly, M. E. *The first department: a history of the department of agriculture* (Dublin, 2002).

Dooley, T. '"The land for the people": the land question in independent Ireland, 1923–73 (Dublin, 2004).

Drudy, P.J. (ed.). *Ireland: land, politics, and people*, Irish Studies 2 (Cambridge, 1982).

Gillmor, D. A. 'The political factor in agricultural history: trends in Irish agriculture, 1922–85', *Agricultural History Review*, 37, 2 (1989), 166–70.

Hennessy, T. and A. Kinsella. *40 years of Irish farming since joining the European Union: a journey with the Teagasc National Farm Survey 1972–2012* (Galway, 2013).

Matthews, A. *Farm incomes: myth and reality* (Cork, 2000).

Rouse, P. *Ireland's own soil: government and agriculture in Ireland 1945–65* (Dublin, 2001).

Sheehy, S. J., J. T. O'Brien and S. D. McClelland. *Agriculture in Northern Ireland and the Republic of Ireland* (Dublin and Belfast, 1981).

Vaughan, W. E. *Landlords and tenants in mid-Victorian Ireland* (Oxford, 1994).

9 The Irish Working Class and the Role of the State, 1850–2016

Henry Patterson

9.1. The Working Class and Colonialism

We know considerably more about the various aspects of the history of the Irish working class than we did twenty years ago when the editors of *Saothar*, the journal of the Irish Labour History Society, commented that the Irish tradition of labour history was relatively weak and 'less than generously served by academe'.[1] The implicit comparison was with the historiography of the trade union movement and the Labour Party in the UK. In the intervening years there has been an increase in the number of books and articles published on the Irish working class and labour movement, but it is still a stream compared with the torrent of work on political and cultural history. Although labour history in the UK has to a large extent become an unfashionable ghetto in academia, it still maintains a much more substantial presence than its Irish counterpart.

Nevertheless, perhaps because of the relative lack of scholarly work on the Irish working class, there has been a tendency for the scholarship that does exist to emphasise the centrality of colonialism as an explanation for the weakness of labour and socialist parties and ideologies in Ireland as compared with Britain and other European states, particularly in the 1880–1914 period. A considerable part of the literature on the Irish working class remains explicitly or implicitly structured by a colonial framework of analysis. Although this framework has been challenged in other areas of Irish history,[2] the development of labour and working-class history was largely unperturbed by the

1 F. Devine and E. O'Connor, 'Saothar, labour history and the future', *Saothar, Journal of the Irish Labour History Society*, 1, 22 (1997), 3–5.
2 S. Howe, *Ireland and the empire: colonial legacies in Irish history and culture* (Oxford, 2000).

Figure 9.1 'Pig strike', Waterford, 1901. Wiltshire Collection. Courtesy of the National Library of Ireland.

'revisionist' versus 'anti-revisionist' debate. This reflected not so much the development of some alternative macro-analysis of Irish history from 'below' as the fact that most contributions to the field were focused on discrete issues, regions and localities.

Thus J. W. Boyle in what remains the most substantial scholarly history of the Irish labour movement in the nineteenth century[3] noted that, at the level of trade union-ism, Ireland had a history of organisation that, for considerable periods of time, devel-oped in a similar fashion to what was happening on the other island. Combinations of journeymen developed in the eighteenth century as the power of guilds weakened, manufactures developed and the gap between masters and journeymen widened. In the late eighteenth century there was no marked difference in organisation, objectives and activities between Irish and British trade clubs and societies. They were local in character, composed of skilled craftsmen, and hampered by broadly similar forms of legislation against combinations. In some trades, clubs in both islands exchanged information on wage and price lists and provided relief to members 'on the tramp' in search of work.[4] Similarly, work people who combined faced a hostile legal framework

---

3 J. W. Boyle, *The Irish labour movement in the nineteenth century* (Washington, DC, 1988).
4 Ibid., 7–25.

in Ireland as in Britain and similarly benefited from the repeal of the Combination Laws in 1824. As communications improved in the second half of the nineteenth century British amalgamated unions increased their Irish membership by setting up new branches or absorbing existing Irish societies. This process accelerated with the 'new unionism' for the hitherto largely unorganised groups of unskilled workers from 1889 onwards.[5] By the end of the century the great majority of organised Irish workers were in British-based unions, and even when an Irish Trades Union Congress (TUC) was formed in 1894 it was not as an assertion of the specific needs and autonomy of Irish workers, but conceived as supplementing the work of the British TUC which often did not have time to devote to specifically Irish issues.

However, Boyle claimed, and this has been heavily emphasised more recently by Emmet O'Connor, that this unity of labour across the Irish Sea was more apparent than real. Its superficiality lay in its ignoring the issue of Ireland's 'colonial' status and what O'Connor refers to as its 'capitalist colonisation'.[6] For writers like Boyle, O'Connor and Joe Lee, the very structure of trade unionism, its reliance on what is depicted as a British model of development, was in O'Connor's view so inappropriate to Irish conditions that its adoption could only be a product of what he refers to as 'mental colonisation'. This chapter, while not denying the importance of colonial legacies in understanding the history of all social classes in Ireland, argues that rather than being held back by inappropriate type of trade unionism, the success or failure of different sections of the Irish working class in pursuing their economic class interests reflected the nature of uneven economic development on the island and, in particular, the decline of most centres of manufacturing industry from the 1820s onwards. Boyle's and O'Connor's analysis of the weakness of the Irish labour movement explains it by its refusal to engage with the issue of national independence and the ending of the Union. Both, although in nuanced and intelligent ways, are supporters of the analysis of James Connolly, that no Irish labour movement, let alone the broader Irish working class, could realise its interests except in some alliance with Irish nationalism.[7] O'Connor argues that the support of Irish trade unions for nationalism in the post-Union period was a rational response to capitalist colonisation and the process of deindustrialisation. It was the arrival of British 'new unionism' in the 1890s that led to a 'profound mental colonisation' and the strategic dead-end of attempting to build up a labour movement independent of nationalism.[8] For him the refusal of urban trade unionists to work from

---

5 E. O'Connor, *A labour history of Ireland 1824–1960* (Dublin, 1992), 7–55.
6 E. O'Connor, 'Labour and politics 1830–1945: colonisation and mental colonisation', in F. Lane and D. Ó Drisceoil, *Politics and the Irish working class, 1830–1945* (Houndmills, Basingstoke, 2005), 28.
7 J. Connolly, 'A plea for socialist unity in Ireland', reprinted in The Cork Workers' Club, *The Connolly/Walker controversy: on socialist unity in Ireland* (Cork, n.d.), 2.
8 O'Connor, 'Labour and politics', 30–1.

within the nationalist movement was one of labour's great strategic failures. He quotes the president of the ITUC in 1900: 'We are not ashamed to admit that we took as our model the procedures and methods which resulted in bringing material benefits for the workers of England during the past quarter of a century.'[9]

In contrast was the philosophy of the Irish Transport and General Workers Union founded by James Larkin in 1909: 'Are we going to continue the policy of grafting our-selves on the English trades union movement, losing our identity as a nation in the great world of organised labour?'[10] Eighty years later Joe Lee would echo this sentiment in his history of Ireland where he argued that the Free State inherited a structure of trade unionism based closely on the British model, and added, 'It may be wondered how well it served either Ireland or the Irish working class.'[11] This begs the question of what is meant by the 'British model' or the 'English trade union movement'. The major empirical histories of British trade unionism from Clegg, Fox and Thompson's[12] to Alastair J. Reid's more recent history have insisted on disaggregating notions of some unitary working class or labour movement in favour of different types of occupational experience, each producing its own outlook and form of organisation. Thus, for exam-ple, Reid identifies three main groups: assembly workers, process workers and general workers. Each group was characterised by a specific type of trade union reflecting the nature of the labour processes in which they were involved.[13] Assembly workers, such as boilermakers, various types of engineering workers, printers, carpenters, etc., were mainly concerned with building products from a number of components. These work-ers usually learnt their trade through apprenticeships and were able to exercise some control over entry to their trade; as a result they were well paid and able to provide their own welfare funds. They were organised in craft unions and were confident that they could look after their members' interests without outside interference. Process workers were involved in the processing of a single raw material through various stages: in the mining of coal or iron ore, in smelting of metals or spinning of textile thread. They picked up the skills on the job and were relatively easily replaced. As a result they found it more difficult to maintain welfare funds and permanent trade unions, and were more dependent on government intervention. The third group were those who performed general manual labouring tasks and needed little more than physical strength. Often migrants from the countryside, they were employed on very short-term contracts, received the lowest pay and needed a distinctive type of organisation which Reid calls federal unionism.

9 Ibid., 31.
10 Ibid., 33.
11 J. J. Lee, *Ireland 1912–1985: politics and society* (Cambridge, 1989), 89.
12 H. A. Clegg, A. Fox and A. F. Thompson, *A history of British trade unions since 1889,* vol. I: *1889–1910* (Oxford, 1964).
13 A. J. Reid, *United we stand: a history of Britain's trade unions* (London, 2004), ix–x.

In Ireland as in Britain the early history of trade unionism was dominated by craft unions, greatly strengthened in the north-east from the mid-Victorian period by the expansion of the shipbuilding and engineering industries. As in the rest of the UK the main groups of Irish process workers – largely female workers in the linen and textile trades – were difficult to organise without external support, whether from government or, in the case of Belfast and Derry, from the trades council and British organisers. It was not until the early 1890s that some groups of general labourers in Belfast and Dublin began to be organised by the British-based National Amalgamated Union of Labour. Later on in the Edwardian period, dockers in Belfast, Dublin and other Irish ports would begin to be organised by the National Union of Dock Labourers. The integration of the two economies, particularly in the period after the Great Famine, was reflected in the way that Irish unions participated in the periods of expansion of the British movement: 1850s to 1870s and 1890s to 1920s. A wage survey conducted by the Fiscal Inquiry Committee in 1923 indicated that by 1914 skilled workers in Ireland were paid almost as much as their British peers. However, the gap in wages between skilled and unskilled workers in the towns was substantial, and even worse off were Irish agricultural labourers.[14]

This reflected the island's distinctive economic profile in the post-famine period as consolidation of agricultural holdings and a shift from tillage to pasture radically diminished the demand for rural labour, while at the same time the manufacturing sector in the south experienced a severe crisis precipitated by the flooding of the Irish market by cheaper goods from English firms.[15] By the end of the nineteenth century, if food and drink are excluded, the south of Ireland was virtually without industries.[16] In 1911 the proportion of the Irish labour force employed in manufacturing was 10.2 per cent whilst in Belfast the figure was 37.3 per cent.[17] In the second half of the nineteenth century, outside Ulster the majority of waged workers were engaged in agricultural work and the great mass of them unorganised.

The depressing effect of this reservoir of labour from the countryside on wage rates for the unskilled was evident throughout the island. Thus in Belfast, the wage divide between craftsmen and labourers was profound. In 1905 weekly wage rates for skilled engineering workers averaged between 37 and 39 shillings – higher than the average for similar workers in ten other UK shipbuilding areas. In sharp contrast the average wage of labourers was between 15 and 18 shillings, whilst the average for labourers in other areas was between 18 and 23 shillings.[18] In Belfast's largest employer of labour, the linen industry, although

14 C. Ó Gráda, *Ireland: a new economic history 1780–1939* (Oxford, 1994), 237–9.

15 L. M. Cullen, *An economic history of Ireland from 1660* (London, 1972), 147.

16 Ó Gráda, *Ireland: a new economic history*, 313.

17 J. Lynch, 'The Belfast shipyards and the industrial working class', in F. Devine, F. Lane and N. Puirséil, *Essays in Irish labour history: a festschrift for Elizabeth and John W. Boyle* (Dublin, 2008), 135.

18 Ibid., 137.

Figure 9.2 York Street Mill, Belfast, girls ornamenting white linen goods. Image courtesy of the National Library of Ireland.

there was an upward movement in wages between the 1830s and the end of the century, only a small minority of the labour force, primarily men in what were seen as skilled occupations and as overseers, could earn enough to support a family. Flax-dressers and tenters had unions from the early 1870s, whilst linen-lappers and flax-roughers were unionised from 1890.[19] The wages of women, girls and juveniles, the bulk of the workforce, were still pitiably low at the beginning of the twentieth century.[20] Writing of female linen workers in the Edwardian period, Adelaide Anderson, one of the first female factory inspectors, claimed that wages 'did not rise above 7 or 8 shillings a week out of which came deductions for disciplinary fines, charges for damage or purchase of damaged articles so that for many young women 5 to 6 shillings per week was nearer the mark'.[21]

19 H. Patterson, 'Industrial labour and the labour movement', in L. Kennedy and P. Ollerenshaw, *An economic history of Ulster 1820–1939* (Manchester, 1985), 173.
20 E. Boyle, 'The economic development of the Irish linen industry', PhD thesis, Queens University of Belfast, 1979, 166.
21 A. Anderson, *Women in the factory: an administrative adventure 1893–1921* (London, 1922), 84.

When trade unionism became a possibility for these workers it was as part of a UK-wide upsurge of militancy associated with the spread of new unionism, which in the form of the Newcastle-based National Amalgamated Union of Labour began to organise in Belfast in 1890 and within a few years had nine branches and two thousand members. The Gasworkers and General Labourers Union also established eight branches in the same period. This was the context in which the London-based Women's Trade Union League sent a group of organisers to Belfast to work with the local trades council in establishing unions amongst female spinners and weavers.[22] However, the union that emerged from this effort, the Textile Operatives Society of Ireland, never managed to organise more than a small section of potential recruits and in 1914 only about 10 per cent of the labour force in linen was organised.[23]

Just as the spread of unionism to the unskilled in the early 1890s was part of the broader explosion of new unionism throughout the UK, the irruption of conflict in the docks and streets of Belfast and Dublin between 1907 and 1913 needs to be seen in the context of a broader pattern of mounting industrial discontent in Ireland and Britain. The fiery young orator, James Larkin, was sent to Belfast as an organiser for the National Union of Dock Labourers to take advantage of the fact that the British Labour Party was having its conference there to begin the process of organising the Irish ports.[24] The upsurge of militancy and syndicalist and industrial unionist ideas associated with the Belfast dock strike of 1907, the formation of the Irish Transport and General Workers Union (ITGWU) by Larkin in 1908 and the titanic conflict between Dublin employers and members of the union during the Lockout of 1913 are clearly key events in the history of Irish labour. However, they should not be conscripted into a nationalist narrative: as Colin Whitston has noted, 'it cannot be fully described, nor its significance fully understood, as a purely Irish event'.[25]

Although the ITGWU was defeated, the union did not disappear and 1913 set the ground for the permanent organisation of the most marginalised sections of the working class. After 1914 in Ireland as in the rest of the UK the wages of unskilled workers, men and women, rose more than those of skilled workers, a product of the tightening of the labour market produced by the First World War.[26] Trade union membership soared: from fewer than 100,000 in 1916, numbers of members affiliated to the Irish Trades Union Congress more than doubled to 225,000 in 1920.[27] The ITGWU was in

22 H. Patterson, *Class conflict and sectarianism: the Protestant working class and the Belfast labour movement 1868–1920* (Belfast, 1980), 30–1.
23 Patterson, 'Industrial labour and the labour movement', 174.
24 O'Connor, *A labour history of Ireland*, 70.
25 C. Whitston, 'The 1913 Dublin Lockout and the British and international labour movements', in F. Devine (ed.), *A capital in conflict: Dublin city and the 1913 Lockout* (Dublin, 2013), 27.
26 Ó Gráda, *Ireland: a new economic history*, 436.
27 O'Connor, *A labour history of Ireland*, 95.

the vanguard of the upsurge in wage militancy amongst labourers in towns and countryside, but British-based unions also expanded in this period: one important example is the unionisation of the predominantly female workforce employed in the Derry shirt and textile industry. Up until the war, unionisation had only developed significantly amongst the largely male workforce employed in shirt and collar cutting who composed around 10 per cent of the industry's labour force. However, in 1917–18 a substantial number of female workers from the shirt assembly and finishing factories joined the British-based Amalgamated Society of Tailors and Tailoresses (ASTT). By the end of the war a predominantly Catholic workforce was organised by two British-based unions with the shirt and collar cutters now in the United Garment Workers Union (UGW).[28]

What was the relation between the expansion of trade union organisation and wage militancy and the radicalisation and militarisation of Irish politics in this period? O'Connor has emphasised the role of a Larkinite 'syndicalist' ideology in encouraging labour militancy and a potential radical social republican dimension to the Irish Revolution.[29] However, Fitzpatrick's analysis points to the more mundane economic roots of trade union expansion: a buoyant agricultural economy and a tight labour market.[30] It is certainly the case that the central role played by James Connolly in both the struggles of the ITGWU and the Easter Rising encouraged a nationalist narrative of the relationship between political radicalisation after 1916 and the possibilities of radical social and economic change in Ireland. But just as the employers who locked out their workers in 1913 were supporters of the Irish Parliamentary Party and Home Rule, Arthur Griffith and many other radical nationalists were bitterly hostile to Larkin for importing supposedly foreign notions of class conflict to Ireland, and as Niall Whelehan points out, 'the goals of the nationalist movement were not significantly restructured to accommodate ideas of social justice'.[31]

9.2. The Working Class, Religion and National Identity

To the extent that Irish workers were mobilised by mass political ideologies in this period, their allegiances polarised them whatever interests they shared at an economic level. Those trade unionists and socialists who argued for the primacy of class over nation would, despite the upsurge of class militancy, find themselves at best

---

28 A. Finlay, 'Trade unions and sectarianism among Derry shirt workers 1920–1968', DPhil., University of London, 1989, 99.
29 See O'Connor, *A labour history of Ireland*, 94–116.
30 D. Fitzpatrick, 'Strikes in Ireland 1914–1921', *Saothar*, 6 (1980).
31 N. Whelehan, 'The Irish Revolution 1912–23', in A. Jackson (ed.), *The Oxford handbook of modern Irish history* (Oxford, 2014), 623.

marginalised and at worst persecuted and expelled from their workplaces. In the classic works of Irish labour history this was explained by reference to the manipulation of religious prejudices by employers and landlords. However, more recent work has located the explanation in the fact that the Irish working class had deeply rooted traditions of economic class consciousness and religious and national identity.

This was most obvious in Belfast. Its rapid expansion in the nineteenth century, from a town of 20,000 to (in 1911) a city containing Ireland's main centre of manufacturing with a population of 387,000,[32] was accompanied by regular outbreaks of sectarian riots and confrontations. Initially such confrontations reflected inward migration from rural Ulster that brought with it established patterns of feuding between Protestant and Catholic secret societies, the Peep of Day Boys and the Defenders, later Ribbonmen and Orangemen. Clashes of Ribbonmen and Orangemen occurred in many parts of Ulster in the 1820s, a time of heightened tension associated with the 'Second Reformation' (an attempt by Protestant missionaries and voluntary societies to convert Catholics) and this tension was also apparent in Belfast with 'Twelfth' riots occurring in 1822, 1824 and 1825.[33]

These sectarian tensions were from the 1830s overlain by a proto-national conflict in the aftermath of Catholic emancipation and the implications of the democratisation of the British state for Ireland's place in the Union. Catherine Hirst has shown how the unionist/nationalist divide amongst Belfast's working class dates from the 1840s when Protestant and Catholic workers were involved in campaigns for and against repeal of the Union. From the 1830s Protestant working-class areas felt the increasing influence of evangelical ministers who, in Hirst's words, 'legitimised existing sectarian attitudes, inflamed potentially riotous situations and mobilised them in support of the Union'.[34] By 1860 the Catholic proportion of the town's population had reached one-third and its politics were characterised by a strong identification with the development of nationalist and reform movements in the rest of the island. The serious rioting of 1864 which lasted for eighteen days and during which twelve deaths occurred had been precipitated by a large contingent of Catholics attending a mass demonstration in Dublin for the unveiling of a monument to O'Connell. During this period Catholic workers were attacked in some linen mills and factories and on the Queen's Island works of Harland and Wolff the shipwrights went on strike to demand the dismissal of Catholics who they claimed had given information to the police about shipyard workers involved in the rioting.[35]

32 S. A. Royle, 'Workshop of the empire, 1820–1914', in S. J. Connolly (ed.), *Belfast 400: people, place and history* (Liverpool, 2012), 200.
33 S. J. Connolly and G. McIntosh, 'Whose city? Belonging and exclusion in the nineteenth-century urban world', in Connolly, *Belfast 400*, 245.
34 C. Hirst, 'Politics, sectarianism and the working class in nineteenth century Belfast', in Lane and Ó Drisceoil, *Politics and the Irish working class*, 65.
35 Patterson, *Class conflict and sectarianism*, xvii.

Whilst these divisions would debilitate attempts to develop a cross-sectarian Labour party, their negative effects on trade unions can be exaggerated. An example is the Derry shirt workers. According to the 1911 census Protestants made up 43.8 per cent of the town's population and accounted for 65 per cent of male shirt workers, whilst Catholics were 56.2 per cent of the population and 67 per cent of the female shirt workers.[36] A number of factories were identified as 'Protestant' and others as 'Catholic', but in the majority the workforce was mixed. The workers were from time to time involved in sectarian confrontations, usually around the time of the annual Relief of Derry celebrations.[37] However, sectarian affiliations did not determine or indeed significantly influence workers' behaviour in relation to unions. If the predominantly Protestant collar cutters joined the UGW it was because they regarded the ASTII as a 'women's' union – in other words the decision was motivated by gender not religious or political affiliation. The complex relationship between union membership and political and sectarian divisions can be illustrated by the Derry shirt cutters strike in 1920 – the only industry-wide strike and the only sustained conflict between workers and employers in the history of shirt production in Derry. It involved the predominantly Protestant, male shirt cutters who struck for parity with English cutters organised by the UGW. The ASTII opposed the strike which led to the laying off of most of their members in the city.[38] Although it was denounced by the Derry Trades Council and the local nationalists as part of a strategy of cross-channel unions to kill off one of Ireland's few successful industries, the Derry dockers, predominantly Catholic and nationalist/republican in politics, supported the strike by refusing to move any shirts for export or to handle any imported raw materials for the industry. They were largely organised by the Amalgamated Transport and General Workers' Union. Peadar O'Donnell, soon to play a leading role in the IRA campaign in Ulster and at the time of the strike the ITGWU organiser in the area, also opposed the strike, adding that he wanted to 'smash every British-based union in Ireland'.[39] Although the strike failed, the fall-out was a boost for the UGW as the bulk of the female members of the ASTII transferred to it because they were dissatisfied with their own union's failure to support them when they were locked out during the strike. The ITGWU was only able to attract a minority of the female workers and these were all Catholics, but the bulk of female workers chose the British-based union on the purely pragmatic grounds that its capacity to look after them was seen as superior. Similarly an attempt by the recently established Ulster Unionist Labour Association to set up a loyalist trade union for textile workers failed miserably. The strike took place soon after the city had experienced severe sectarian violence and

36 Ibid., 84.
37 Finlay, 'Trade unions and sectarianism', 93–5.
38 This account of the strike is based on ibid., 99–129.
39 Ibid., 108.

at a time of extremely high political tensions. But what is striking is how, despite the attempts of local unionists and republican radicals like O'Donnell, the workforce put its economic class interest first.

For all the disruptive effects of nationalist revolution and unionist counter-revolution leading to the creation of two new states on the island, workers continued to maintain a framework of trade union organisation largely unaltered. This would be one of the main complaints of leading Fianna Fáil politicians in the 1930s and 1940s when a concerted attempt was made, with the support of the leadership of the ITGWU, to expel British unions from the Free State. Although protectionism would lead to some expansion of employment opportunities in the 1930s, the longer-term importance of the British labour market for maintaining living standards in Ireland by providing unemployed workers with an exit was reasserted in the 1940s and 1950s and was a standing refutation of the limitations of nationalist political economy. Even so, although Irish living standards (in the thirty-two counties) had been catching up with Britain between the mid-nineteenth century and the 1920s, in the inter-war period this process of convergence ceased in the Irish Free State. UK growth rates were slightly higher than those in the Free State during the inter-war years, while in the two decades after 1939 the growth rates of both countries were roughly equal. Overall Irish performance was quite poor relative to the UK between 1922 and 1960.[40]

In this context Connolly's decision to participate in the Easter Rising had disastrous long-term effects on the possibility of an independent labour politics in the new Irish state. The legacy of 1916 was a profound tension between the original trade union base of the party and the determination of both Connolly and Larkin to provide a Labour Party for nationalist Ireland. The decision not to contest the pivotal 1918 election reflected the unwillingness of the leadership of the party to confront the apparently relentless upward surge of popular support for Sinn Féin. For a brief period in the 1920s with a socially and economically conservative government in power and republicans marooned in abstentionism, Labour saw a significant increase in support. However, once the republican mainstream entered the Dáil, the difficulties for Labour in differentiating its politics from those of Fianna Fáil, in its most leftist phase, proved insurmountable.[41] Pulled towards republicans by Connolly's legacy and terrified of adopting more radical policies given the power of a virulently anti-socialist Catholic Church, the party in the 1930s at times appeared a miserable appendage of Fianna Fáil. Although part of the support of the working class for Fianna Fáil was determined by its nationalist militancy, it was its combination of protectionism, state-sponsored

---

40 A. Bielenberg and R. Ryan, *An economic history of Ireland since independence* (London, 2013), 189–90.
41 See analysis of the dilemma of Irish Labour in P. Bew, E. Hazelkorn and H. Patterson, *The dynamics of Irish politics* (London, 1989), 142–5.

industrial development and modest welfarism which led to the fact that by 1939, in the words of Cormac Ó Gráda, 'In Dublin Fianna Fail had become the party of the working class'.[42] However, as Dunphy has noted, this was not inevitable: it reflected a disastrous decision by Labour and many of the unions which 'found themselves thanking Fianna Fail for the modest social welfare provisions … and then wondering why these measures led to increased working class and trade union support for the governing party'.[43]

However, Fianna Fáil's ascendancy was directly linked to its ability to portray itself as a progressive, left-of-centre, political force, and during the Second World War that image became a distinctly tarnished one. The declaration of the Emergency was accompanied by the outlawing of strikes and the imposition of a Standstill Order on wages which contributed to a fall in real wages of 30 per cent between 1939 and 1943. During the Emergency the cost of living rose by two-thirds and wages by a third, ensuring that pre-war real wage levels were not achieved again until 1949.[44] Fianna Fáil had angered many in the labour movement with the 1941 Trade Union Act limiting the right of unions to negotiate and strike, and the 1943 election was a blow to the party: its vote dropped by 10 per cent and it lost ten seats. The Irish Labour Party gained ten seats and for the first time since the formation of the state, it established a serious presence in Dublin. In fact that challenge would have been greater but for emigration. At least 100,000 and perhaps as many as 150,000 emigrated to the UK during the war years, and another 50,000–70,000 volunteered for the British armed forces. The vast majority were young, unskilled workers. As Donal Ó Drisceoil notes of these figures: 'The absence of so many young unemployed workers helped to weaken the potential for radical working class politics'.[45] Bill Kissane is one of those who have depicted emigration as a crucial barrier to the development of class politics: 'Polarised class conflict could never happen if the Irish working class was content to improve its position in other countries'.[46] Perhaps as crucial was the effectiveness of a strident Fianna Fáil inspired and church-supported anti-communist crusade against those in the unions and Labour Party who opposed the government's attempt, in league with the leadership of the ITGWU, to expel British-based unions from the Republic. The result was the disaffiliation of the ITGWU from the Labour Party, the formation of a rival Congress of Irish Unions and a National Labour Party, and the absence of any Labour challenge to Fianna Fáil dominance until the 1960s.

42 Ó Gráda, *Ireland: a new economic history*, 441.
43 R. Dunphy, 'Fianna Fail and the working class, 1926–38', in Lane and Ó Drisceoil, *Politics and the Irish working class*, 258.
44 H. Patterson, *Ireland since 1939: the persistence of conflict* (London, 2007), 65.
45 '"Whose emergency is it?" Wartime politics and the Irish working class, 1939–45', in Lane and Ó Drisceoil, *Politics and the Irish working class*, 266.
46 Quoted in Lane and Ó Drisceoil, *Politics and the Irish working class.*, 2.

9.3. The Working Class through Revolution, Civil War and Partition

Writing in the 1930s, the prominent Northern Irish Labour politician Harry Midgley had summed up the challenge to those of a Connollyite tradition represented by the north's Protestant working class: 'The Ulster Protestant will not, under present conditions, be interested in the question of Irish Nationalism. He is a Britisher in sentiment and outlook. During the whole of his lifetime, he has lived in such an atmosphere.'[47] Connolly's own experience in Belfast as an organiser for the ITGWU in the 1910–14 period had led him to refer to them as 'the least rebellious slaves in the industrial world' and privately to the city as an 'Orange hole'.[48] However, while Connolly's frustration is understandable given the visceral and at times violent opposition which socialists experienced in the fraught conditions of Ulster at the time, his analysis was flawed. For as Hobsbawm noted about Belfast and other situations where working classes were divided along religious or national lines, 'the force of class experience was such that the worker's alternative identification with some other group in plural working classes – as Pole, as Catholic … narrowed rather than replaced class identification'.[49]

Thus there was a relatively strong trade union movement, and in the Edwardian period, a serious attempt to develop a local bastion of the Labour Representation Committee with William Walker as its standard bearer. However, it was no coincidence that Walker came nearest to winning a parliamentary seat in north Belfast, when Home Rule was temporarily off the agenda and when the local Conservatives were under fire for not being vigorous enough proponents of ultra-Protestant and Orange interests.[50] Conflicting national and religious identities did not exclude class consciousness but were almost insurmountable obstacles to political class consciousness. Only when constitutional issues receded in importance could economic class issues develop a challenging political salience. Of course neither of the dominant political parties in the two states which emerged in the 1920s had an interest in allowing such class identifications to remain unchallenged.

Belfast experienced a formidable display of workers' industrial power during a mass engineering workers' strike for a 44-hour week in January 1919 and the Ulster Unionist Party had to create a working-class organisation, the Ulster Unionist Labour Association, to try and prevent the defection of the Protestant working class to Labour or socialist politics.[51] However, the developing IRA campaign in the south and west

47 Quoted in G. Walker, 'The Northern Ireland Labour Party 1924–45' in Lane and Ó Drisceoil, *Politics and the Irish working class*, 236.
48 Patterson, *Class conflict and sectarianism*, 83.
49 E. J. Hobsbawm, *The age of empire 1875–1914* (London, 1987), 120.
50 A. Morgan, *Labour and partition: the Belfast working class, 1905–23* (London, 1991), 60–90.
51 Ibid., 229–49.

of Ireland and the unionist counter-mobilisation transformed the shipyards and engineering factories from sites of class conflict to scenes of ethnic cleansing as Catholic workers and 'disloyal' Protestant labourites and socialists were expelled during the intensifying sectarian violence from July 1920.

The new Northern Irish government, although it emphasised its determination to use the state as a bulwark against nationalism and republicanism, was in fact more concerned with the threat of intra-Protestant conflict along class and sectarian lines. The relative success of Northern Irish Labour candidates and Independent Unionists in the 1925 election for the Belfast parliament provoked the abolition of proportional representation to ensure that elections became plebiscites on the continued existence of the state.[52] As importantly, and although it caused concern amongst a section of the unionist elite, the governments of Sir James Craig and his successors showed no desire to use devolution to set Northern Ireland on a divergent economic and social path from Britain. Instead, and after significant arguments with the Treasury, they ensured the maintenance of welfare payments, including unemployment benefit, at the same level as in the rest of the UK. Extra resources were also extracted from Westminster to shore up the Harland and Wolff shipyard during the dire conditions of the early 1930s: in 1932 more than fifty thousand workers were unemployed in Belfast.[53] An active minority of communists and Labour Party members were involved in the mass protests against the niggardly relief payments made by the Belfast Board of Guardians. The unemployed workers' movement in 1932 was a brief moment of cross-sectarian working-class solidarity which did succeed, after serious rioting, in extracting better rates of relief, but did not prevent serious outbreaks of intercommunal violence in 1935.[54] Here, a large share of responsibility lay with government ministers who indulged organisations like the Ulster Protestant League, which demanded that employers only take on loyalists, and in a time of significant sectarian tension lifted a precautionary ban on Orange parades leading to ten days of rioting and ten deaths in 1935.[55]

The Second World War and the post-war welfare state brought a new impetus to the British strain of Labourism associated with William Walker and now embodied in a Northern Ireland Labour Party (NILP) which moved decisively to embrace partition in 1949, losing its nationalist and Connollyite wing in the process.[56] It had been the strong performance of Labour in Belfast in the 1945 elections that convinced the Unionist

---

52 C. Reid, 'Protestant challenges to the Protestant state: Ulster unionism and Independent Unionism in Northern Ireland, 1921–1939', *Twentieth Century British History*, 19, 4 (2008), 419–45.

53 C. Norton, 'Creating jobs, manufacturing unity: Ulster unionism and mass unemployment', *Contemporary British History*, 15 (Summer 2001), 9–10.

54 A. C. Hepburn, *A past apart: a history of Catholic Belfast 1850–1950* (Belfast, 1996), 183.

55 G. Walker, 'Protestantism before party: the Ulster Protestant League in the 1930s', *Historical Journal*, 28 (1985), 961.

56 The most comprehensive history is A. Edwards, *A history of the Northern Ireland Labour Party* (Manchester, 2009.)

administration, against its basic inclinations, to fully embrace the welfare state. In an Irish context of economic crisis and high levels of emigration in the 1950s, the Northern Ireland Labour Party seemed set for a breakthrough, but its success was to prove brittle. Like the more liberal elements of the Unionist Party, the NILP, like Walkerism before it, relied on the relative quietism of Irish nationalism after the collapse of the anti-partition campaign in the early 1950s. However, nationalism was being reformulated not jettisoned. More fundamentally, the labour movement was still disproportionately Protestant, and did nothing to address the fact that the limited Catholic presence in trades such as engineering, shipbuilding and printing had declined further between 1910 and 1951.[57]

As the 1960s dawned, the labour movement in Northern Ireland seemed to be on an upward trajectory, while that in the Republic stagnated. However, the crisis in the Northern Irish state and the subsequent 'Troubles' were to effectively destroy Labour politics, although not the trade union movement. In contrast the shrugging off by the Irish state of its protectionist straitjacket created the conditions for an expanding union movement and a more confident Irish Labour Party that, after jumping from 8 per cent to 28 per cent of the vote in Dublin in the 1960s, predicted that 'The Seventies will be Socialist'.[58] Whether, as some of its more radical currents argued, it should have built up an independent leftist presence in the Dáil and not entered coalition government with a much larger party, Fine Gael, is a moot point as in embracing coalition it acted in line with a deeply rooted conception of itself as a 'national' not a 'class' party. It was certainly the case that after the end of the post-war boom in the international economy in 1973, its commitment to coalition and 'responsible' government led to a haemorrhaging of support to more radical formations, first the Workers Party and more recently Sinn Féin.

In Northern Ireland, the disappearance of the NILP as a political force did not prevent the working class from being insulated from the Thatcherite revolution in the rest of the UK, as British ministers calculated that public expenditure cuts and sharp rises in unemployment might increase support for political extremism and terrorism.[59] Thus, although the heartlands of the Protestant working class were devastated by deindustrialisation and the destruction of previously solid community networks, new employment opportunities opened up in expanding service industries and a large public sector. All the main parties in the north were, during the Troubles, united in Keynesian responses to the region's economic problems. This has been maintained since the return of devolved institutions, with both the largest parties, the Democratic Unionist Party (DUP) and Sinn Féin, opposed to the UK government's austerity policies since 2010.

57 Hepburn, *A past apart*, 100.
58 M. Gallagher, *The Irish Labour Party in transition: 1957–82* (Dublin, 1982), 89.
59 M. J. Cunningham, *British government policy in Northern Ireland 1969–89* (Manchester, 1991), 226.

In 2013 levels of trade union density were significantly higher in the Republic and Northern Ireland than in most other European states with the exception of Scandinavia.[60] This evidence of a relatively strong economic class consciousness was, as it had been throughout most of the nineteenth and twentieth century, quite compatible with deeply conflicting national and religious identities. In 2016 as in 1860 class consciousness was more likely to be expressed within an ethnic bloc than to challenge the fundamental logic of ethno-national politics in itself.

FURTHER READING

Boyle, J. W. *The Irish labour movement in the nineteenth century* (Washington, DC, 1988).

Cronin, M. *Country, class or craft: the politicization of the skilled artisans in nineteenth century Cork* (Cork, 1994).

Devine, F., F. Lane and N. Puirseil. *Essays in Irish labour history* (Dublin, 2001).

Edwards, A. *A history of the Northern Ireland Labour Party* (Manchester, 2009).

Lane, F. and D. Ó Drisceoil. *Politics and the Irish working class 1830–1945* (Basingstoke, 2005).

O'Connor, E. *A labour history of Ireland 1924–1960* (Dublin, 1992).

Patterson, H. *Class conflict and sectarianism: the Protestant working class and the Belfast labour movement 1868–1920* (Belfast, 1980).

Silverman, M. *An Irish working class 1800–1950* (Toronto, 2006).

60 Department of Business, Innovation and Skills, *Trade union membership in 2013*, available at www.gov.uk./government/uploads/system/uploads/attachment_date/file/313768/, accessed 30 March 2015.

10 The Big House

Terence Dooley

10.1. Introduction

By the nineteenth century there were in the region of four thousand Big Houses of varying architectural sizes, shapes and styles in Ireland. These were the country residences of Irish landlords, the focal points of extensive landed estates, the rental incomes of which provided for their building, embellishment and annual upkeep. They had their origins in the tower houses and medieval fortified castles of the Norman era, but their architectural form had evolved over time to the semi-fortified structure of the seventeenth century, to eventually the defenceless houses which characterised the apogee of Big House construction in the eighteenth century.[1] The most significant building boom of *c*.1720–40 came in the aftermath of the defeat of the Catholic threat in the wars of 1689–91, the introduction of the penal laws after 1695, and the culmination of the social engineering process that resulted in the almost complete transfer of landownership out of native Catholic hands to Protestant landlords. The construction of defenceless Classical and Palladian mansions by the emergent wealthy and landed elite signalled their confidence in the future stability and economic prosperity of the country, but it was also a powerful and symbolic signifier of their specific social and political ambitions and agendas of future control and power.

Over time, the physical prominence of the Big House on the Irish landscape became imprinted on the collective identity of the dispossessed who, especially after the

---

1 Introductory essays to all of these phases can now be found in R. Loeber, H. Campbell, L. Hurley, J. Montague and E. Rowley (eds.), *Art and architecture of Ireland, vol. IV: Architecture 1600–2000* (Dublin, New Haven, London, 2014).

emergence of Irish nationalism in the nineteenth century, denounced them as foreign and imperial, the manifestations of colonial oppression and decadence. Their high demesne walls (more characteristic of aristocratic mansions), built to offer privacy and security, were deemed further symbols of the exclusive elitist culture of those who lived behind them. The popular appeal of this orthodox nationalist representation of the Big House worked to the detriment of future understandings of the true complexities of its role in the Irish countryside. It is only in recent years that the nuances which governed the relationships between landlords and tenants have been revealed.

10.2. Construction and Functionality

While Big Houses were to be found in almost every parish of rural Ireland, Matthew Stoute's illuminating map of planned landscapes in the nineteenth century clearly indicates they were more densely situated in the agriculturally prosperous areas and very often where wealth co-existed with impressive scenic beauty as along the Blackwater valley in County Cork. In contrast, there were fewer houses located in the backward and impoverished west or in the province of Ulster where landed estates tended to be larger than elsewhere, thereby giving rise to fewer houses.

Many of the houses of the early eighteenth century were modest in size, simple and functional, but as the decades progressed and landlord prosperity grew, so did their ambitions to emulate their social peers in England. From roughly 1720 to 1740, rising rents and a dramatic increase in banking, credit facilities and low interest rates provided the incentives to induce landlords to invest massively in the construction of such great houses as Castletown, Carton, Russborough and Powerscourt. These were all enormous, complicated architectural structures in which every household function and social nuance was planned for. As David Dickson has noted, they were built 'to impress social peers (and, perhaps more importantly, pretentious inferiors) as to a family's substance, standing and taste, and to provide for their genteel neighbours a venue for conspicuous hospitality, social intercourse and polite recreation'.[2] Physical spaces for the family, guests and servants were all carefully delineated. In the multitude of spaces of the great houses, servants were very clearly segregated to basements, kitchen wings and top-floor sleeping accommodation and only the upper servants came into contact with the family in clearly defined spaces such as entrance halls and dining rooms.[3]

2 D. Dickson, *Old world colony: Cork and South Munster 1630–1830* (Cork, 2005), 95.

3 The role and lives of servants in the Irish country house have yet to be rigorously examined, but to a large extent this has been dictated by the paucity of sources; however, see T. Dooley, '"Till my further orders": rules governing servants at Carton in the mid-eighteenth century', in T. Dooley, P. Cosgrove and K. Mullaney-Dignam (eds.), *Aspects of Irish aristocratic life: essays on the FitzGeralds and Carton House* (Dublin, 2014), 106–17.

Figure 10.1 The magnificent dining hall at Glin Castle, Co. Limerick. Courtesy Madam Olda Fitzgerald.

The reason was very clearly suggested by the eminent architect Isaac Ware, who commented in his *A complete body of architecture* (1758):

> the kitchen is hot, the sculleries are offensive and the servants hall is noisy; these therefore we shall place in one of the wings. This is the conduct of reason; the housekeeper, the clerk of the kitchen, and other domestics of the like rank, will thus be separated from the rabble of the kitchen; they will be at quiet to discharge their several duties, and they will be ready to attend the master or lady.[4]

That said, scholars of the Irish country house are only beginning to illuminate how the more complicated architectural structures reflected patterns of life, to interrogate the social and familial attitudes upon which they were planned, to investigate their functionality as socio-economic power structures, and to appreciate that Big Houses cannot be studied in isolation simply as architectural artefacts or repositories of fine arts. They cannot be separated from the families who commissioned them, their wealth and tastes, and their changing fortunes (more often declining after the eighteenth

---

4 I. Ware, *A complete body of architecture, vol. III* (Farnborough, 1971; originally issued in parts, 1756–7), 413.

century than rising). Nor can house and family be separated from the history of the landed estate or the wider social, political and economic circumstances which provided for their construction and running and ultimately their demise.[5] Moreover, there is an acknowledged need to address certain lacunae, for example the role of women. Emerging scholars are now beginning to focus on the role of marriage, matriarchy and house management, how women acted as socialites and hostesses, and as influential players in the political, cultural and social lives of the Big House.[6] It is an area rich in research potential.

The historiography of the Big House tells us relatively little about how much they cost to build and complete in terms of interior and exterior demesne and landscape embellishment, nor, indeed, does it illuminate ancillary issues such as the state of the Irish building trade in the eighteenth century, what the construction of a country house meant to a local economy, or how the planning of them as architectural structures contributed to wider technological advancement.[7] Most of the great houses did not stand still, a frozen monument to a particular era; instead houses such as Bantry and Lismore Castle, both composites of a variety of styles fashionable at different periods, clearly illustrate that the Georgian or even earlier construct had to be modified to fit later Victorian trends and to cater for very different manners and attitudes.

A good deal more is known about the material culture of the Big House (in large part because of the excellence of journals such as *Irish Architectural and Decorative Studies* published annually under the auspices of the Irish Georgian Society). From the outset, it was imperative for owners that their houses should be decorated with all that was fashionable, that they should become the repositories of valuable works of art, and their libraries rich in books and curios. However, this need to impress in the eighteenth century came with a long-term price for the future. Ostentatious displays of opulence and the social desire to self-promote eventually led to long-term unsustainability; put simply, the initial construction and embellishment costs placed enormous financial and even practical challenges and burdens upon future generations, burdens which became unbearable as soon as the economic system which gave rise to Big Houses came under threat.[8]

What recent historiography has shown is that before the advent of the Land League and separatist nationalism, there was a much more complicated relationship between

---

5 See, for example, W. Laffan and K. Mulligan, *Russborough: a great Irish house, its families and collections* (Dublin, 2014).

6 M. O'Riordan, *Women of the Irish landed class, 1860–1914: home, family, and society* (forthcoming).

7 For further potential research areas, see T. Dooley, *The Big Houses and landed estates of Ireland: a research guide* (Dublin, 2007).

8 T. Dooley, *The decline of the Big House in Ireland* (Dublin, 2001); O. Purdue, *The Big House in the north of Ireland: land, power and social elites, 1878–1960* (Dublin, 2009).

rural Ireland and the Big House than the traditional narrative conceded (as, indeed, there was between Ireland, Britain and the empire as a whole).[9] While the more nuanced narrative does not deny that rapacious landlords existed or that the system which gave rise to the opulence of their Big Houses was morally and socially flawed, it more carefully examines the complex social structures in the countryside and – local case studies are important in this respect – reveals the interdependent relationships between landlords, large farmers, the small town elite and the Catholic clergy that existed in the interests of social stability.[10]

On aristocratic estates paternalism very often worked to the benefit of the tenant community (but subject to a number of variables, not least of all the personality of the landlord). The fact that the local Big House was a major employer in any locality with economic spin-offs for local businesses and services has often been overlooked. For example, in the town of Maynooth in County Kildare, which for most of the eighteenth and nineteenth centuries was the home to Ireland's only ducal family – the FitzGeralds, Dukes of Leinster – economic considerations gave rise to a deferential dialectic where landlords and larger tenants observed unwritten codes of mutual respect. This dialectic was most clearly articulated in the presentation of addresses to the landlord on the coming of age of his heir. When the landlord accepted the address (or 'the gift') he acknowledged the moral contract that the gesture entailed, the fulfilment of certain duties and responsibilities – social, political, religious and economic – deemed essential to prosperity and wider social stability.[11] The changing rhetoric of addresses from the 1880s reflected imminent shifts in power, and when that power eventually passed to nationalists the previous existence of any deferential dialectic was generally consigned to the scrapheap of memory. But even in the 1920s evidence of its existence and the loss of paternalism on the Leinster estate was clearly articulated in the local newspaper when news circulated that Carton and its remaining lands had been lost to an English property developer:

> Any severance of the FitzGerald family with the management of the Leinster property will be greatly regretted in Kildare, where despite the fact that the land has been largely sold to tenants they still retain large interests in the ground rents and many buildings and homes in practically all the towns being held from them. Very extensive employment is given on

---

9 C. Shepard, "'I have a notion of going off to India": Colonel Alexander Porter and Irish recruitment to the Indian Medical Service, 1855–96', *Irish Economic and Social History*, 41, 1 (2014), 36–52; T. Foley and M. O'Connor (eds.), *Ireland and India: colonies, culture and empire* (Dublin, 2005).

10 T. Dooley, *The decline and fall of the Dukes of Leinster: love, war, debt and madness* (Dublin, 2014); R. V. Comerford, 'The Land War and the politics of distress, 1877–82' in W. E. Vaughan (ed.), *A new history of Ireland, vol VI: Ireland under the Union, 2 (1870–1921)* (Oxford, 1996), 26–52.

11 Dooley, *The Dukes of Leinster*, 11–14; K. McKenna, 'Power, resistance and ritual: paternalism on the Clonbrock estates, 1826–1906', unpublished PhD thesis, Maynooth University, 2011, 118; H. Newby, 'The deferential dialectic', *Comparative Studies in Society and History*, 17 (1975), 139–64.

the demesnes, tillage being intensive and a splendid class of livestock bred. Being a resident family a very deep interest was taken in the welfare of the employees, who are comfortably housed and well treated.[12]

10.3.   Decline in the pre-Independence Period

The history of the decline of the Big House can be written as a narrative of the cumulative impact of one major crisis after another; decline was more a long drawn-out illness than a sudden heart attack. There were houses which long before the end of the nineteenth century had become the early victims of irresolute and spendthrift heirs, too fond of gambling and other extravagances to marshal finances in such a way as to secure the future of their houses and estates. More were the victims of economic troughs over which their owners had little control. While a systematic analysis of house turnover during the Georgian period has yet to be undertaken, and while the history of the country house and the Great Famine has yet to be written, we do know that the latter crisis resulted in scores of houses coming up for sale in the Encumbered Estates Courts after 1849. While there was a period of recovery in the post-famine decades and plenty of evidence of Big Houses being remodelled and embellished in the 1860s and 1870s, the socio-economic system that had given birth to them was no longer viable in the long term and the era of their affordability had come and gone. During the 1880s, the agricultural downturn and all that consequently came with it – the rise of the Land League, the Land War, agrarian agitation, rent strikes, the legislative lowering of rents under the 1881 Land Act – placed landlords under immense financial pressure. As Irish land was no longer safe collateral, the old landlord expedient of borrowing to overcome financial difficulties ceased. Landlords had, therefore, less to spend on the running and maintenance of their houses and so the age of dilapidation began. Elizabeth (Daisy) Fingall recalled her home, Danesfield, in the 1880s: 'My memory of the Drawing Room at Danesfield is that it was a shabby, rather faded room, and very little used … There were what-nots about the room, with bits of old china on them and shells and such things, and an Ottoman on which one might sit as uncomfortably as in a railway station waiting for a train.'[13]

After 1882 with the passing of the Settled Land Act (Ireland), the age of stripping houses of their contents to fund house maintenance and, indeed, family survival also began. The Act allowed for the sale of family heirlooms and thus art collections and other forms of material culture accumulated over generations were sold to meet debts

12 *Leinster Leader*, 17 June 1922.
13 Elizabeth, Countess Fingall, *Seventy years young* (London, 1937), 22

Figure 10.2 Derrylahan House, Co. Offaly (then King's County), burned in July 1921 by the IRA. Courtesy Offaly Historical and Archaeological Society.

and were dispersed to the four corners of the world, a phenomenon that would continue for decades to come. In the mid-1920s, William Randolph Hearst (1863–1951), 'the great accumulator', bought the contents of Carton House in Kildare and shipped them to one of his homes in Santa Monica, California, where he also had the salvaged dining room, reception room and drawing room from the eighteenth-century Burton Hall in County Clare. Hearst also bought the magnificent seventeenth-century staircase from Eyrecourt in Galway from White Allom in 1927. Olwen Purdue has shown that this phenomenon also existed in Northern Ireland after partition.[14] The 2014 exhibition 'Ireland: crossroads of art and design, 1690–1840', held in the Art Institute of Chicago, provided stunning evidence of the accumulation of Irish country house goods by the American wealthy elite in the twentieth century. From the 1890s, country house owners in Britain and Ireland came under sustained pressure from increased taxation. Even during the First World War landed families who were emotionally impoverished by personal tragedies also became the economic victims of harsh death duties. A notable example was the Acton family of Kilmacurragh House, Rathdrum in County Wicklow. On 25 September 1915 at the Battle of Loos, Charles Annesley Acton was killed and the estate passed to his only surviving brother, Reginald. Reginald fought on and was killed at the Battle of Ypres in Belgium eight months later on 22 May 1916. As their father had died in 1908, it meant that over an eight-year period Kilmacurragh had to

14 Purdue, *The Big House in the north of Ireland*, 135–7.

face three significant bills for death duties that aggregated 120 per cent of the value of the estate. The financial pressure became too much to bear for Reginald's young widow, and after two hundred years of residence the Acton family left Kilmacurragh and the house subsequently fell into dereliction.[15]

Another major catalyst in decline was the consolidation of the ideology that promoted land as the basis of the nation, where landownership became related to the other great national issues of identity and independence. In the 1880s, with the rise of Irish nationalism and the Celtic Revival, the Irish nation was reinvented as nationalist, Gaelic and Catholic: the rhetoric of nationality became concerned with justifying possession of the land, and because landlords, predominantly Protestant in religion and unionist in politics, were supposed to be of different stock from the rest of the population, they were excluded. By extension, country houses were identified and demonised by nationalists as symbols of everything the new political order wanted to overthrow; as R. V. Comerford puts it, the stately mansion was 'regarded as a relic of oppression and some form of affront to the nation'.[16] Such negative populist perceptions were embedded in the social memory of confiscation and redistribution of lands at the very time that Irish politics was being polarised along politico-religious lines.

10.4.   Challenges to Survival

During the War of Independence and civil war, 1920–3, approximately three hundred houses were burned in the twenty-six county area that now constitutes the Irish Republic. Counties with the highest rates of burnings, such as Cork and Tipperary, also tended to be the areas of most violence during the two phases of conflict.[17] No more than half a dozen houses were burned in the area of Northern Ireland. Olwen Purdue has shown that this low rate can be attributed to the significant differences in the social, political and demographic conditions which historically pertained in the region.[18]

The motivations for the burnings may be summarised as follows: to punish owners who had offered their houses as billets to the crown forces; IRA reprisals for the actions of the British forces against the property of alleged Sinn Féin and IRA supporters; because owners showed their support for the British authorities; because of the antipathy towards Big Houses from individual IRA leaders such as Tom Barry in Cork; and, not least of all, for agrarian reasons, some harking back to grievances from the Land

15 My thanks to Fidelma Byrne for the information on the Actons.
16 R. V. Comerford, *Ireland* (London, 2003), 46.
17 Dooley, *The decline of the Big House in Ireland*, 171–207.
18 Purdue, *The Big House in the north of Ireland*, 145–51.

Figure 10.3 Tudenham, Co. Westmeath, one of the spectacular Irish country house ruins still visible in the Irish landscape. Courtesy George Gossip.

War era, others more immediately grounded in the desire to acquire and redistribute demesne and other estate lands still in landlord hands.[19] This last motivation was particularly strong during the civil war when almost three times more houses were burned than during the War of Independence.

However, it needs to be recognised that a single motive may not be enough to explain the destruction of individual houses; very often there were complex interlocking

19 See also J. S. Donnelly Jr., 'Big House burnings in County Cork during the Irish Revolution, 1920–21', *Éire-Ireland*, 47, 3–4 (Fall/Winter 2012), 141–97; C. J. Reilly, 'The burning of country houses in Co. Offaly during the revolutionary period, 1920–3', in T. Dooley and C. Ridgway (eds.), *The Irish country house: its past, present and future* (Dublin, 2011), 110–33.

reasons. It might seem the case that a house was burned during the War of Independence because it was owned by a British military officer and, therefore, deemed a legitimate reprisal target by the IRA, but unless the full circumstances of social, political and agrarian activities in the locality, both at the point in time of burning and in the historical past, are explored, one cannot be certain that there were no other extenuating reasons. James S. Donnelly claims of the burning of Castle Cooke in County Cork, the residence of Colonel William Cooke-Collis, that 'his own and his family's military eminence' provoked the IRA into burning it as a counter-reprisal, but he also concedes that 'There is some evidence that his extensive agricultural operations aroused local hostility and inspired covetousness among local farmers.'[20] Clearly, therefore, more searching questions have to be asked of the IRA's selection process. If the IRA was going to burn a house in a locality as a counter-reprisal and there were four or five available to them, why choose one over the others? If houses were burned solely because of an owner's loyalism and British military tradition, how did so many survive? After all, there were very few country houses that did not have a British military tradition. Most obviously, why was Currygrane in Longford not burned during the War of Independence given that it was the home of Field Marshal Sir Henry Wilson?[21]

Very few burned houses were rebuilt. Neither the compensation on offer nor the socio-political climate of Ireland after 1922 proved enticing to former landlords. In 1923, Lord Glenavy pointed to more practical reasons in the Seanad: 'Nobody was anxious to have a building reinstated in its old form. It had grown out of their needs and they wanted a different style of architecture.'[22] The generous terms of the 1903 Wyndham Land Act had provided a respite to landlords after a long period of economic depression and retrenchment and allowed them to enjoy the *belle époque* of the Edwardian era, but the post-war global economic depression decimated investment portfolios while simultaneously taxes were rising at unprecedented rates. It became obvious that nothing had been more important to the survival of the Big House than the great land banks that had supported them in the past.

The objectives of the 1923 and succeeding land acts emphasised that the cultural heritage significance of eighteenth-century planned landscapes and demesnes meant very little to successive governments that were attempting to address the rural concerns of the uneconomic smallholders and the landless. The compulsory acquisition of demesne and untenanted lands for the relief of local congestion led to the abandonment and demolition of scores of Big Houses. This does not imply that the Land Commission had an official brief to demolish them; it did make attempts to sell several

20 Donnelly, 'Big House burnings', 182.
21 Currygrane was to be burned during the civil war but that was an entirely different set of circumstances in a very different time, even if it was only separated chronologically from the War of Independence by a few months.
22 Quoted in *Irish Times*, 14 Apr. 1923.

houses such as the magnificent Nash-designed Shanbally Castle in Tipperary, but purchasers were scarce, and even those who could afford to purchase were not interested in houses denuded of the extensive parkland required to offer privacy. And land-hungry locals were not prepared to barter good agricultural land for the preservation of the house. That said, there was a small stock of houses bought by wealthy Americans such as Castle Hyde in Cork and Glenveigh in Donegal which ensured their survival, while a significant number, including Ballyfin, Emo Court, Kylemore Abbey and Moore Abbey, were acquired by religious orders and turned into schools, convents and monasteries. Inevitably, when those houses were modified to fulfil their new functions, their historical and architectural integrity was compromised.

As tends to be the case in a post-colonial society, it was difficult for the new political elite to stomach any symbol of what they had fought to overthrow. There was no place in the Irish national patrimony for the country house or, indeed, within the definition of Irish heritage as set out in the National Monuments Act of 1930. Round towers and monastic sites were deemed the archetypal symbols of Ireland's golden age, while the erasure of Georgian architecture from the landscape was, to many, the best way to erase memories of a colonial past.

Big House owners who remained in Ireland came to realise that cultural exclusion would be difficult to avoid. When Elizabeth Bowen wrote her classic memoir in 1944 she pondered how her home, Bowen's Court, had been constructed of native stone but 'imposed on seized land [and] built in the ruler's ruling tradition', essentially questioning whether the Big House could ever become part of the national patrimony, and, indeed, metaphorically suggesting the ambiguity of identity faced by her class. In a similar vein, her contemporary, Elizabeth (Daisy) Fingall, wrote of Killeen Castle:

> The front of the house seems to have had a blank look, the windows staring across the country like blind eyes. It is a look that the windows of Irish country houses often have, as though indeed that was the spirit inside them, the spirit of the colonist and conqueror, looking out across the country which they possessed but never owned.[23]

Political (and public) antipathy to the Big House undoubtedly created immense challenges for the minority of original owners who decided to stay on in Ireland after independence, but it was the ubiquitous debilitating economic circumstances that made their sustainability very difficult. In 1932, the *Irish Times* was unambiguous about where it felt the fault for decline lay: 'The dead hand of the State lies heavily on the great houses. Depleted incomes make their maintenance difficult enough, but high taxation and death duties render the passage of a great house from father to son almost impossible.'[24] Moreover, a changing world meant also that servants and estate

23 Fingall, *Seventy years young*, 29.
24 *Irish Times*, 7 Nov. 1932.

employees, including craftsmen, became less and less affordable with the result that the physical infrastructure of houses deteriorated at a rate much faster than ever before. It became expedient to demolish houses or to abandon them. There are no definitive estimates of how many, but it certainly ran into hundreds.[25] *Vanishing country houses of Ireland* (1988) listed sixty and fifty respectively for Counties Dublin and Galway alone.

The marginalisation of the old landed class in the Free State/Republic was in contrast to their situation in Northern Ireland where, as Purdue has shown, they continued to retain a more prominent position in society and politics. This was facilitated by the different Protestant demography there. Historically, Ulster Protestant tenants may have shared the same agrarian grievances as their Catholic counterparts, but a shared religious, political and cultural outlook left landlord–tenant relations less fraught in the north-east, especially after the land and national questions merged in the late nineteenth century and Protestant tenants became more inclined to throw in their lot with landlord unionists.[26] Along with their strong links to both the unionist movement and the Orange Order, northern Big House owners operated in a state where political and private attitudes to the landed class were less resentful. They could be more honest in their loyalism and less reticent about revealing their attachment to the crown, British public schools and the armed forces. While Purdue does concede that Big Houses in Northern Ireland suffered from economic decline for similar reasons to those in the Free State/Republic – investment losses in the 1920s, taxation and the impact of the 1925 Northern Ireland Land Act[27] – she contends that 'careful management, strict economies or simple good fortune' as well as 'a crucial sense of identity and purpose' prolonged the life of the Big House in the north-east.[28]

Moreover, owners in Northern Ireland had a state apparatus to look to in the form of the National Trust. In time this provided a compass for the government in the Republic but it was still some decades away. While the government found it appropriate to reimagine two houses – Derrynane, the home of Daniel O'Connell, and Avondale, the home of Charles Stewart Parnell – so as to fit with the national narrative, the mere mention of Georgian architecture in government buildings was more likely to excite antagonisms. This was evident in the antipathy towards the Irish Georgian Society when it was first founded in 1957. It was portrayed as an elitist organisation for the preservation of an elitist culture. In 1970 Kevin Boland, Fianna Fáil Minister for Local Government, made it clear that his department saw the clearance of Georgian slums in Dublin as a matter of social concern and not preservation.

25 For a catalogue of these, see D. FitzGerald (The Knight of Glin), D. J. Griffin and N. K. Robinson, *Vanishing country houses of Ireland* (Dublin, 1988).
26 Purdue, *The Big House in the north of Ireland*, 3.
27 Ibid., 109.
28 Ibid., 239–40.

I make no apology whatever for saying that the physical needs of the people must get priority over the aesthetic needs of Lord and Lady Guinness and Deputies Dr FitzGerald, Dr Browne, Dr Desmond and all the other Deputy Doctors that we have. I make no apology for saying that, desirable as is the preservation of old buildings of architectural merit, while I am Minister for Local Government and while the needs of the people for housing, water and sewerage services remain unfulfilled, not one penny of the capital allocation that it is possible to make available to my department will be spent on such preservation, desirable as it is.[29]

10.5.   The Struggle for Preservation

Preservationists had to find an alternative means to influence a change in political attitudes and so they began a campaign to convince the wider public that country houses owed as much to Irish influence as to English oppression and that the Irish 'nation' would be at a great loss if any more were destroyed. Reports and publications began to refer to the 'losses to the national heritage' that were imminent. A house such as Clonalis in County Roscommon was promoted as 'the home of the descendants of the last high kings of Ireland, the O'Conor Don, and his Irish manuscripts and books dating from the thirteenth century'. In 1988, Desmond FitzGerald, the 29th Knight of Glin, attempted to dilute the colonial influence when he wrote in *Vanishing country houses of Ireland*: 'Even if the upper classes were considered "foreign", the craftsmen and builders were Irishmen. The naïve assumption that these houses are to be seen as merely memorials to outdated colonialism should be resisted because they are in fact treasure houses of Irish skills.'[30] After Ireland joined the EEC in 1973, the architectural significance of the Big House could be re-presented in a much wider European context. This was a significant milestone for another reason: accession to the EEC required Ireland's adherence to international charters and conventions intended to inform and influence government policy and legislation for protecting the architectural heritage and, of course, it also unlocked generous funding opportunities.[31]

From the beginning of the twenty-first century Irish governments have clearly improved policies towards future preservation. However, it is interesting that national(ist) sentiment still dictates to a large extent how an Irish country house and its histories are presented. This is clearly evident in some of the major houses opened to the public such as, for example, Fota in County Cork, managed by the Irish Heritage Trust, an organisation established by the Fianna Fáil government in 2006 with a mandate to protect Irish heritage properties for the future benefit of Irish society.

29 *Dáil Éireann Debates*, vol. 245, 11 Mar. 1970, 168.
30 FitzGerald *et al.*, *Vanishing country houses*, 28.
31 For more on this, see T. Dooley, 'National patrimony and political perceptions of the Irish country house in post-independence Ireland', in T. Dooley (ed.), *Ireland's polemical past: views of Irish history in honour of R. V. Comerford* (Dublin, 2010), 192–212.

The Trust commissioned *Aspects of Fota*, supported by funding from Fáilte Ireland, which declared in a chapter entitled 'The Land Wars' that Arthur Hugh Smith Barry (1843–1925) 'emerged relatively unscathed and with his reputation as a fair man intact'. However, the leading expert on the Plan of Campaign, Dr Laurence Geary, describes the agitation on the Smith Barry estate as 'the most malicious, rancorous and truc-ulent of all struggles' associated with that period of the Land War. At the time the *Tipperary Nationalist* newspaper denounced Smith Barry as 'the arrogant aspirant of the title Lord Barry-No-More ... unblushing and unscrupulous rack-renter ... vain-glorious little bashaw'. *United Ireland* described him as 'the pernicious little noodle of a Cork landlord' and one commentator, W. J. Lane, went as far as to compare him to Jack the Ripper.[32] It would obviously have made for a more historically accurate narrative to reveal the fact that Smith Barry was the instigator of one of the most vicious standoffs between landlord and tenant during the Land War, but it was obviously deemed by the authors a risk too far to take. Their apprehension probably stems from a fear that if a Big House is not presented as being authentically Irish (whatever that means) then the people will not come, that attitudes towards it will remain negative or, even more importantly, that state funding will not be made available.

Similarly, *Russborough: a great Irish house, its families and collections* (2015) has a foreword by President Michael D. Higgins in which he states that a sympathetic con-nection 'between nation and architectural heritage is ... reflected in the long and enduring relationship that existed between Russborough and the Irish people'.[33] Yet, in the main body of the book, the story of the offer of the house to the nation as a gift in 1929 is at complete odds with this assertion. The offer was declined on the advice of a Department of Finance report that concluded:

> So far as the Minister has been able to gather neither Russborough House nor the family con-nected with it has ever been associated with any outstanding events or personalities in Irish history. Accordingly, the interest which the place possesses is only its interest to the connois-seurs of architecture, plus whatever interest it has as illustrating a certain phase of social life in Ireland. Opinions differ as to the aesthetic merits of the Georgian as a style of architecture, but, the period being relatively modern, good specimens of it are sufficiently numerous both in this country and in England to render state action to preserve this one superfluous.[34]

10.6.　Conclusion

It is now taken as a given that there is an onus on the Irish state or local authorities to safeguard or at least recognise the cultural benefits of country houses. But the state has now probably taken over as many country houses as it ever will. It has been strategic in

---

32 Quotations from L. M. Geary, *The Plan of Campaign 1886–1891* (Cork, 1986), 120–1.
33 W. Laffan and K. Mulligan, *Russborough: a great Irish house, its families and collections* (Dublin, 2015), xii.
34 Department of Finance memo, 24 Feb. 1921 (NAI, Dept of An Taoiseach files, S5935), quoted in Ibid., 228–9.

Figure 10.4 Enniscoe House, Crossmolina, Co. Mayo, one of the few surviving Irish country houses in private possession. Courtesy of Ms Susan Kellett.

its choice: Castletown is arguably the most important house in Ireland; Kilkenny Castle is located in Ireland's most vibrant city; Rathfarnham and Farmleigh are situated in the country's capital; Muckross and Glenveigh are in two of the most beautiful and tourist orientated areas of the country. The Office of Public Works has been commendable in preserving these houses and transforming them into major cultural heritage tourist attractions. It has faced immense challenges in the changing economic and political contexts of the late twentieth and early twenty-first century. It has done well to balance the protection of the built heritage with depleted funding as a result of Ireland's economic meltdown.

A few very important Irish Big Houses have survived either because of massive private investment (for example, Ballyfin, Castle Hyde, Castletown Cox) or because they have become commercialised (Adare, Ashford, Carton, Dromoland). Russborough was one of those fortunate to have been saved by something of a mixture of both. Initially it was private benefaction but more recently it has also had to adapt and evolve. It has entered into necessary partnerships. It has commercialised. Russborough today encapsulates the pragmatic approach that is necessary for a country house in Ireland to survive. That is not to say that it doesn't continue to face everyday challenges of sustainability, a continuous struggle to ensure its long-term future. This it has in common with the ever declining number of houses which have survived in original ownership (such as Bantry, Birr Castle, Enniscoe, Hilton Park). The question mark in the title of this author's 2003 report, *A future for Irish historic houses? A study of fifty houses* (2003) was intended to convey the serious nature of a problem that unfortunately has yet to be adequately addressed.

FURTHER READING

Barnard, T. C. *Making the grand figure* (New Haven and London, 2006).

Craig, M. *The architecture of Ireland from the earliest times to 1880* (London, 1982).

Dickson, D. *Old world colony: Cork and South Munster 1630–1830* (Cork, 2005).

Dooley, T. *The Big Houses and landed estates of Ireland: a research guide* (Dublin, 2007).

Dooley, T. *The decline and fall of the Dukes of Leinster: love, war, debt and madness* (Dublin, 2014).

Dooley, T. *The decline of the Big House in Ireland* (Dublin, 2001).

Dooley, T. *A future for Irish historic houses? A study of fifty houses* (Dublin, 2003).

Dooley, T. and C. Ridgway. *The Irish country house: its past, present and future* (Dublin, 2011).

Dooley, T., P. Cosgrove and K. Mullaney-Dignam (eds.). *Aspects of Irish aristocratic life: essays on the FitzGeralds and Carton House* (Dublin, 2014).

FitzGerald, D. (The Knight of Glin), D. J. Griffin and N. K. Robinson. *Vanishing country houses of Ireland* (Dublin, 1988).

Laffan, W. and K. Mulligan. *Russborough: a great Irish house, its families and collections* (Dublin, 2014).

Loeber, R., H. Campbell, L. Hurley, J. Montague and E. Rowley (eds.). *Art and architecture of Ireland, vol. IV: Architecture 1600–2000* (Dublin, New Haven, London, 2014).

McParland, E. and N. Robinson (eds.). *Heritage at risk* (Dublin, 1977).

O'Kane, F. *Landscape design in eighteenth-century Ireland* (Cork, 2004).

Purdue, O. *The Big House in the north of Ireland: land, power and social elites, 1878–1960* (Dublin, 2009).

11

The Changing Role of the Middle Classes in Twentieth-Century Ireland

Joseph Ruane and Jennifer Todd

11.1. Introduction

There is an extensive literature on elites and the middle classes in the two parts of Ireland during the twentieth century, but it is uneven by discipline, theme, methodology and time period, and most studies focus only on one part of the island. The dominant historical narrative of twentieth-century Ireland is written in terms of the conflicting projects of unionism and nationalism, their division of the island, the states they built and their subsequent trajectories; discussion of class fills out the narrative. Our analysis foregrounds class as a key analytical category in the making and managing of political divisions and in subsequent developments. We focus on three periods – the late nineteenth century to partition in 1921; 1921 to the transitional period of the 1950s–1960s; the 1960s to the present.

We give particular attention to the middle class. The concept is notoriously fuzzy and yet unquestionably useful.[1] Viewed in the broadest sense, it is the class that occupies the space between the upper (landowning or industrialist) and the lower (working or landless) class. In Ireland's case – as indeed in other European countries – it includes a large section of farmers, a rural middle class, which is discussed elsewhere in the present volume. Viewed more narrowly, it refers to a largely urban-based commercial, white-collar and professional stratum with a relatively high educational level and distinctive lifestyle and values. We find Bourdieu's concepts of cultural, symbolic, social and economic capital valuable in defining the resources which give the middle class, and the various strata within it, very different degrees of control over their conditions

1 For a discussion, see R. Crompton, *Class and stratification: an introduction to current debates* (Cambridge, 1998), 150–60.

of life, work and familial reproduction, and very different interests and values, than other classes and strata.[2]

The middle class, broadly understood, possesses sufficient capital to escape the absolute want and dependence of the working class, but without the manoeuvrability or security of those above them. The middle class more narrowly conceived has a further characteristic: the close, reciprocally supportive, relationship that often exists between it and the state. It may be critical of some state policies, but it accepts the state's legitimacy; it staffs the state's middle and higher levels and carries out many of its functions; in return the state provides it with the resources, particularly education, on which it depends. In what follows, we draw on both meanings, sketching the broad span of middle classes at different periods and focusing also on the changing role of the state-centred middle class, more narrowly conceived.

11.2. Class and Partition

Ireland at the turn of the twentieth century had a class distribution at once even and uneven: the aristocracy, gentry, middle class (from higher professionals to small retailers and clerks) and multiple layers of farm families were present throughout the island, while the major industrialists and skilled and unskilled industrial workers were concentrated in the north-east. The north-east had been densely settled in the seventeenth-century plantation, it remained the most Protestant part of the island, and it stayed in the United Kingdom when the rest seceded. This territorial and political division was achieved by the conflicting mobilisations of two ethno-religiously distinct populations in defence of their religious, ethnic, economic, national, political and cultural interests. The convergence of identities and interests was so powerful that to bring class into the explanation may seem superfluous. Yet it was important and had long-term consequences.

Ireland was integrated into the British state through a set of interlocking socio-spatial relationships that constituted a hierarchy of valuation and position along a set of intersecting dimensions: religion, ethnicity, economic capital of different forms, cultural capital, political perspectives.[3] Within Ireland Catholics found themselves subordinate to Protestants (themselves highly differentiated) on each of these dimensions. Class was one aspect of the hierarchy of relationships, and while Irish Catholics were to be found at all class levels, they tended to have lower positions within each class and they were disproportionately present in the lower classes. So, for example, Protestants were over-represented in the civil service and judiciary, particularly at the higher ranks,

2 P. Bourdieu, *Distinction: a social critique of the judgement of taste* (Cambridge, MA, 1984), 53–92, 114–25.
3 These relationships were centred spatially on the south-east of England, symbolically on the monarchy, and socially on a (changing) British elite, spreading out from there across the entire British world.

and in the private professions of medicine and law, although by the early twentieth century Catholics were making inroads even in the senior ranks.[4]

For most of its history the economic basis of this socio-spatial order was ownership of land, though trade and banking played an ancillary role. Industrialisation potentially challenged this order by introducing new groups – industrialists, an expanded middle class and working class – with different interests and cultural resources. In the Irish case, Jackson traces the retreat of the landowning class during this period.[5] There was a parallel rise of the middle classes, nationalist throughout most of the island. In the north-east, however, the overwhelmingly Protestant character of industrialisation created a distinctive class configuration: the biggest industrialists quickly allied with landowners in the interests of social stability and Union.[6] The Protestant middle class and smaller business class soon followed.

The expansion of the middle class was made possible by the development of university education in the second half of the century, when the Queen's Colleges (Belfast, Galway and Cork) and Newman's Catholic University in Dublin started to produce graduates in many disciplines, with professions such as the law, medicine and the civil service providing new opportunities and outlets. Graduates included both Protestants and Catholics, men and women. The poor law (which became a more benign and professional set of social support structures as the century progressed) and (from 1891) the Congested Districts Board sustained demand for engineers, teachers, doctors and nurses. With the extension of education to women, the size and structure of the Irish middle class changed considerably, so that, as Pašeta has observed, on the eve of the First World War there was a new and professionally trained middle class ready to take over the running of the country.

The Third Home Rule Bill (1912) was constitutionally and socially conservative; it proposed a quite minor political and institutional arrangement within the existing hierarchical socio-spatial order. But for Ulster unionists – and the mass of Ulster Protestants – it represented a sufficient threat to their industrial prosperity, religious freedoms that cultural status that they mobilised against it. Nationalists counter-mobilised. The First World War broke out before the Act could be implemented, creating further instability and the conditions for the Easter rebellion of 1916. The rebellion and the harsh British

---

4 L. W. MacBride, *The greening of Dublin Castle: the transformation of bureaucratic and judicial personnel in Ireland 1892–1922* (Washington, DC, 1991), argues that by 1921 the administration and judiciary were dominated by Catholics and nationalists. S. Pašeta, *Before the revolution: nationalism, social change and Ireland's Catholic elite 1879–1922* (Cork, 1999) concurs and also argues that Catholics had come to dominate the private professions. The extent and speed but not the fact of Catholic advance is disputed by Fergus Campbell in *The Irish establishment: 1879–1914* (Oxford, 2009).

5 A. Jackson, 'Irish unionism: 1870–1922', in D. George Boyce and A. O'Day (eds.), *Defenders of the Union: a survey of British and Irish unionism since 1801* (London, 2001), 115–36.

6 A. Bielenberg, 'The industrial elite in Ireland from the Industrial Revolution to the First World War', in F. Lane (ed.), *Politics, society and the middle class in modern Ireland* (Houndmills, Basingstoke, 2010), 157, 163–5.

response began a process of polarisation that finished with the division of the island, the establishment of Northern Ireland with a devolved government and parliament within the Union (1920), and the creation of the Irish Free State (1922).

On the Ulster unionist side, mobilisation was not a communal movement in which class dissolved, but a cross-class one based on an implicit contract: that when the nationalist challenge was defeated and power was in the hands of the Protestant upper classes, the interests of the Protestant working class would be taken care of. The honouring of this contract became the condition of the new state's political stability. The Protestant middle class supported the alliance without being part of the contract.

The class dynamic in the south was very different. The Democratic Programme of the First Dáil of 1919 had promised a new beginning, and contained an implicit class bargain. But even at the time it had limited support. Nationalists – the elite and the wider population – were as divided on the social question as the constitutional one. The constitutional division could not be circumvented and the matter was settled by civil war. The social question was in varying degrees denied, sidelined or postponed until the principal enemy – the British government and its unionist supporters – was dealt with.

The argument is frequently made that independence was a political revolution, rather than a social one.[7] There is a sense, however, in which independence was a social revolution: it completed the marginalisation of the Anglo-Irish. The Anglo-Irish are generally seen within a cultural, religious and political frame: the descendants of English planters, predominantly Protestant, and the traditional upholders of British rule in Ireland. But they were also the traditional upper class. The attacks on them, and in particular the burning of their houses, were motivated in the first instance by military and political considerations, but class was inescapably part of the meaning for perpetrators, victims and observers alike.[8]

Independence also came at a cost to the middle class. The contraction of the civil service and the rigorous policy of cuts to public expenditure after 1922 curtailed the income, influence and employment opportunities of the professional and university-educated middle class for at least a generation. In the early 1920s, Trinity College and the Royal College of Surgeons (which managed to hold on to its title and its link with its British counterpart) were worried first and foremost about their members' prospects and fought to retain access to the wider imperial professional networks. We may see this less as a matter of imperial ethos than as a question of class survival.

---

7 For examples, see J. Knirck, *Afterimage of the revolution: Cumann na nGaedheal and Irish politics, 1922–32* (Madison, WI, 2014), 255.

8 This was inevitable where grand houses, stocked with the wealth of generations and accoutrements of fine living, were being burned by rebels of modest backgrounds and limited means. For examples, see J. Donnelly, 'Big House burnings in County Cork during the Irish Revolution, 1920–21', *Éire-Ireland*, 47, 3–4 (2012), 141–97.

11.3. From State-Building to Post-War Modernisation: from the 1920s to the 1960s Transition

Viewed in terms of wealth, income and status, the Irish Free State was composed of four broad strata. At the bottom were unskilled rural and urban workers and farmers on very small holdings, many of whom (particularly west of the Shannon) lived on the margins of subsistence. Above that were farmers on economically viable holdings, small shopkeepers, clerks, lower state employees and the skilled working class, who were on low incomes but were not impoverished. Above that were farmers on substantial holdings of good land, owner-managers of medium-sized businesses, managers of large businesses, higher state employees and professionals, who lived in reasonable comfort.[9] Finally, there was a small upper stratum consisting of wealthy business families, the owners of very large farms and the residual gentry.[10]

The economy was overwhelmingly agricultural, with 54 per cent of the working population employed in agriculture, 13 per cent in industry (of whom 10 per cent were employed in manufacturing), and 33 per cent in services.[11] The large size of the agricultural sector meant that farmers were the major economic interest group and that the rural world (including the small farm sector) was an important cultural influence. But the middle classes provided the political and cultural elite, staffing the higher levels of government, civil service, liberal and teaching professions, the media, and church authorities.[12] By the 1920s the professions were predominantly Catholic and nationalist. The relative Protestant percentage of the civil service decreased, not least because of the Irish-language qualification, but Protestants remained over-represented in the professions and judiciary.[13] The small wealthy stratum was not a major political force:[14] its economic concerns were attended to but the new political elite was firmly in control.

9 For changes in occupational categories from the 1920s to the 1950s, see R. Breen, D. Hannan, D. Rottman and C. Whelan, *Understanding contemporary Ireland: state, class and development in the Republic of Ireland* (Houndmills, Basingstoke, 1990), 53–69.

10 For the business sector in the 1950s, see P. Kelleher, 'Familism in Irish capitalism in the 1950s', *Economic and Social Review*, 18, 2 (1987), 75–94.

11 K. Kennedy, 'The context of economic development', in J. H. Goldthorpe and C. T. Whelan (eds.), *The development of industrial society in Ireland* (Oxford, 1992), 13.

12 The political elite came overwhelmingly from the lower professions and small business class; D. M. Farrell, 'Age, education and occupational backgrounds of TDs and "routes" to the Dail: the effects of localism in the 1980s', *Administration*, 32, 3 (1984), 323–41.

13 Twenty per cent of Supreme Court judges were Protestant through the first fifty years of the state (MacBride, *Greening*, 310–11) and representation in the other liberal professions remained steady, falling only in medicine and dentistry, although even there remaining above the percentage of the working population (K. Bowen, *Protestants in a Catholic State: Ireland's privileged minority* (Kingston, Ont., 1983), 80–6).

14 Its weakness derived in part from the fact that it was disproportionately Protestant and ex-unionist and wary of asserting itself. Drawing on the research of Dr Patricia Kelleher, Joy Rudd reports that in the 1950s one-third of the top ninety-five companies were owned by ex-Ascendancy landed families. See J. Rudd, '"Cast a cold eye": a sociological approach', in J. Genet (ed.), *The Big House in Ireland: reality and representation* (Dingle, 1991), 41.

The immediate priority of the first Cumann na nGaedheal government was to secure the state and build a functioning administrative system. Having built it, they chose to limit its size and scope, keeping taxes and expenditure as low as possible, and leaving key functions (education, health) in the control of the churches and voluntary bodies. Despite the pre-independence Sinn Féin promise of an interventionist state, their developmental and social effort was very limited. The existing policy of free trade was maintained, with increased agricultural output and exports intended to be the growth motor for the economy. There was a small expansion in agricultural and industrial output, with emigration at a level above that of preceding decades. The rise in GNP per capita was not negligible: 3 per cent per annum between 1926 and 1931.[15] Social provision remained meagre and in some areas was reduced.

Fianna Fáil, in government from 1932, was energetic and radical on all fronts, constitutional, economic and social.[16] The most important economic policy shift was from free trade to protectionism. This was done partly for nationalist reasons, but also to increase employment and reduce emigration by replacing industrial and agricultural imports with home produce. A wide range of tariff and non-tariff restrictive measures were imposed. Industrial output increased by nearly 50 per cent between 1931 and 1938, as did industrial employment. Agricultural output fluctuated but overall remained stable, and the increase in GNP (10 per cent) was small.[17] Fianna Fáil also expanded social provision, focusing in particular on rural and urban housing.

The immediate post-war period saw a rapid expansion in industry that then levelled off. Agriculture remained stagnant. Large numbers were now leaving the land, and the slowly expanding industrial sector was unable to absorb them. By the end of the decade, more than 400,000 people had emigrated and the population had reached its lowest level since 1851. The overall growth rate in the 1950s was less than 1 per cent per annum in GDP, and Irish GDP per capita fell from 75 per cent of the EU average to 60 per cent.[18] Social expenditure rose but much less than in Britain where a national health service and welfare state were being put in place. Self-sufficiency as an ideal had been abandoned, but protection remained in place, including limitations on the foreign ownership of Irish firms. The political conditions for abandoning it were emerging, but slowly.

Explanations for the slow growth of the economy and the limited social provision of these decades frequently stress the role of nationalism and Catholicism.[19]

15 K. A. Kennedy, T. Giblin and D. McHugh, *The economic development of Ireland in the twentieth century* (London, 1988), 38–9; J. Haughton, 'Historical background', in J. O'Hagan and C. Newman (eds.), *The economy of Ireland: national and sectoral policy issues* (10th edn, Dublin, 2008), 14–16.

16 M. Daly, *Industrial development and Irish national identity 1927–39* (Syracuse, 1992), 59–60.

17 Kennedy *et al.*, *Economic development*, 46–7; Haughton, 'Historical background', 18.

18 Haughton, 'Historical background', 19–20.

19 See especially T. Garvin, *Preventing the future: why was Ireland so poor for so long?* (Dublin, 2004), 20–48.

Nationalism was certainly a major influence on policy in the 1930s,[20] but it was less important in the 1920s and 1950s. The influence of Catholicism on individual economic behaviour at any stage is open to question; more important was the church's opposition to an interventionist state. Moreover, the impact of nationalism and church doctrines on policy was mediated by the class position of those elites – political and religious – who made policy. Farmar conveys the self-absorption, sense of entitlement and traditional gender roles of the middle class of this period,[21] while Ferriter attributes much of the policy inertia of the 1950s to their complacency.[22] A similar argument could be made for the 1920s, and again for the 1930s when the political elite lived in relative comfort while advocating 'frugal comfort' as the ideal for the strata below.[23]

Political elites could have designed better policies, but given the limits they had set to the state's role, it is not clear how much more could have been achieved. The stagnation of the agricultural sector rested on a low input–low output system of Irish farming based on the balance of factor and market prices; for the individual farmer, the gains to be made from investing in a more intensive system were likely to be small and the risks considerable.[24] Regardless of the disincentive of protection, businesses faced the challenge of a small domestic economy with limited aggregate demand and foreign markets that required capital and entrepreneurial skills to access; rather than undertake the risk, it made sense to stay small and to manage the local market to their advantage.[25]

In Northern Ireland, the unionist governing elite – big business, landowners and upper middle class with a very modest sprinkling of lower groups[26] – built the civil service, security forces, policy-making practices and democratic procedures of a regional state, in the process negotiating its relation to the British centre. It did this in a society where ethno-religious and national division had been intensified by partition and where, particularly among Protestants and unionists, class conflict was overt. It honoured its class bargain, protecting Protestant jobs from Catholic competition, and the state from nationalist subversion. The Orange Order – itself an avenue for (male) lower-class voice as well as traditional authority – was a key part of the new regime,

20 Daly, *Industrial development*, 63–74.

21 T. Farmar, *Privileged lives: a social history of middle class Ireland 1882–1989* (Dublin, 2010). The radical feminism of the revolutionary period was marginalised in the new Ireland.

22 D. Ferriter, '"The stupid propaganda of the calamity mongers"? The middle class and Irish politics, 1945–97', in Lane, *Politics, society and the middle class*, 271–88.

23 Farmar, *Privileged lives*, 144–5.

24 For an experiment, see R. Crotty, *A radical's response* (Dublin, 1988), 1–17; also R. Crotty, *Irish agricultural production: its volume and structure* (Cork, 1966).

25 On their successful efforts, see T. Garvin, *News from a new republic: Ireland in the 1950s* (Dublin, 2010), 125–52.

26 J. F. Harbison, *The Ulster Unionist Party 1882–1973* (Belfast, 1973), 99, 109–11.

with seats in the ruling Unionist Council and with every unionist prime minister and 95 per cent of unionist MPs members.[27]

The state combined conservatism in overall political and economic policy with clientelist populism on a multiplicity of particular issues.[28] There was little social intervention, and no serious attempt to deal with poverty until the post-Second World War period. The beneficiaries of clientelism were numerous – Protestant clergy had their interests accommodated in education and public symbolism, unionist notables kept their local power-bases through the state's gerrymandering of constituency boundaries, unionist localities benefited from the relatively meagre available state funding.

These policies produced regime stability but also social stasis[29] and made a coherent economic policy difficult to develop and sustain. The need for such policy was becoming urgent. Partition had been a means to protect the industrial economy with its core of linen, shipbuilding and engineering. Changing patterns of world trade thrust this cluster of industries into long-term decline and the unionist government needed to find ways to compensate. Working-class discontent was rising and increased dependence on British funding was exposing the government to new political pressures.

Catholics kept to their own world after partition. They had a middle class of doctors, teachers and retailers not much smaller proportionately than the Protestant middle class, though with less wealth and lower status.[30] The relative Catholic position in the higher civil service, the police and even the private professions weakened significantly in the new state.[31] Catholic and nationalist politics was largely the preserve of lawyers and small business with a strong clerical input; and they were notoriously ineffective in changing state policy or challenging unionist dominance. Their quiescence would end just at the time when a more active state-led development project was fracturing the unionist elite and the Protestant class alliance.

Unionist politics held the state together, but not all unionists participated in it. There was a broad swathe – including most of the professional middle class – who, though unionist, kept their distance from Orangeism, political unionism and the loyalist working class. They could be relied upon to vote for the Unionist Party but otherwise their political participation was minimal. They focused instead on their jobs and

27 H. Patterson and E. O. Kaufmann, *Unionism and Orangeism in Northern Ireland since 1945: the decline of the loyal family* (Manchester, 2007), 28–43; Harbison, *Ulster Unionist Party*, 95.

28 P. Bew, P. Gibbon and H. Patterson, *Northern Ireland 1921–1994: political forces and social classes* (London, 1995), 56–63.

29 D. P. Barritt and C. F. Carter, *The Northern Ireland problem: a study in group relations* (London, 1962), 153.

30 A. C. Hepburn, *A past apart: studies in the history of Catholic Belfast 1850–1950* (Belfast, 1996), 88–112, 148–9.

31 Hepburn, *Past apart*; John Whyte, 'How much discrimination was there under the unionist regime 1921–68?', in T. Gallagher and J. O'Connell (eds.), *Contemporary Irish studies* (Manchester, 1983). P. Bew, P. Gibbon and H. Patterson, *The state in Northern Ireland: political power and social classes* (London, 1979), 77 note that 'the number of Catholics in the higher ranks of the NICS [Northern Ireland civil service] dropped consistently throughout the late '20s and early '30s'. Nor was the gender balance significantly better than in the south.

families and lived relatively comfortable lives. They were closely interconnected, with links formed through shared schooling in the highly class-selective grammar schools, and later in work-related networks.[32] They valued their linkages to the wider British sphere, and there was a constant drain of their members into it. Their interest in the state centred on education, particularly the grammar schools, and when their interests were challenged they flexed their collective muscle: in the 1940s, to ensure that the grammar schools retained 20 per cent fee-paying places; in the 1960s, to resist the introduction of comprehensive education.[33] They constituted a potential political resource which Terence O'Neill would try to harness for his modernising project in the late 1960s.

The transition from the 1950s to 1960s was a critical juncture for the two societies. By the 1950s, the Republic had completed its state- and nation-building project. The hope of reunifying the island had faded, but a sovereign Irish state now existed. The major challenge was economic: very slow growth, recurring balance of payments crises, a new surge in emigration, a population that continued to fall, and GDP per capita falling further behind other European economies. There had been policy errors, but there was an underlying problem: it was an economy without an internal development dynamic and high tariff barriers insulated it from that of the rapidly developing international economy. The realisation that this could not continue was growing, but political resistance to dismantling protection delayed change until the end of the decade. Once the decision was made, it happened very fast.

In Northern Ireland, the 1950s and 1960s saw an increase in the confidence and optimism of the unionist middle class.[34] Northern Ireland had earned its place in the post-war 'free world' and the Union was bringing benefits in educational and welfare reforms, new hospitals and bigger schools, beside which the Irish state appeared stagnant. The middle class was a particular beneficiary of these developments. On the other hand, industrial decline was continuing, unemployment was rising and there had been a surge in the Northern Ireland Labour Party vote.[35] Government strategy was to attract inward investment and to diversify employment through infrastructural funding by the British state, although its practice was indecisive and slow.[36] When Terence O'Neill took more decisive steps to modernise the polity and the economy, unionist unity fractured.

---

32 J. Whyte, *Interpreting Northern Ireland* (Oxford, 1990), 30–2.

33 D. H. Akenson, *Education and enmity: the control of schooling in Northern Ireland 1920–1950* (Newton Abbot, 1973), 190–2; E. Cave and J. Dallat, 'Education: step by step or out of step', in M. Connolly and S. Loughlin (eds.), *Public policy in Northern Ireland: adoption or adaption* (Belfast, 1990), 303–22.

34 A. Gailey, *Crying in the wilderness: Jack Sayers: a liberal editor in Ulster 1939–69* (Belfast, 1995), ix.

35 Bew *et al.*, *State in Northern Ireland*, 114–19.

36 G. Walker, *A history of the Ulster Unionist Party: Protest, pragmatism and pessimism* (Manchester, 2004), 147–50.

11.4. The Reconfiguration of Elite Politics and Class Relations, 1960s–2016

Up to the 1960s the developmental paths of the two states on the island seemed quite similar. Each had faced early crises and had overcome them; each had completed its task of state-building. Each had encountered economic difficulties and was now prioritising modernisation and development. When the two prime ministers, Terence O'Neill and Sean Lemass, held their first official meeting in Stormont in January 1965, it was possible to present it as a meeting of two leaders of equal political standing facing the same kinds of challenges. It would soon become clear that the two states were on very different tracks and that the gap between them was widening.

In 1960 over a third of the population of the Republic was still employed directly in agriculture (37%) and less than a quarter (24%) in industry, while the ratio of trade (exports and imports) to GNP was 64.5%. By 2011 the percentage employed directly in agriculture was 5%, in industry 20.9%, and in services 74.1%, while the ratio of trade to GDP was 186.5% in 2010. The trend in GDP growth was uneven: it averaged 4% per annum between 1962 and 1969, 4.6% between 1970 and 1979, 1.6% between 1980 and 1989, 6.7% between 1990 and 1999, and 5.9% between 2000 and 2006.[37]

The major sources of growth were foreign direct investment (FDI) and EU membership. FDI was secured by strong promotional efforts and favourable incentive packages. The first wave came in the 1960s and consisted mainly of low-paying, mass production industries; a second wave, beginning in the late 1980s, consisted of firms in the advanced sectors of micro-electronics, chemicals and pharmaceuticals, and in financial services. Entry into the EEC (later EU) in 1973 brought higher agricultural prices, increased investment, concentration of holdings and reduced numbers in agriculture. It also brought regional and structural funds to support investment in infrastructure, including education. The effects of both – FDI and EU membership – worked their way through the rest of the economy.

At the height of the 'Celtic Tiger' (1990s and 2000s) the Irish achievement was much praised internationally and the Irish political and civil service elite took credit for having worked out so successful a development model. Despite its successes, the model has two key weaknesses. Firstly, it rests on an exceptional level of dependence: more than 80 per cent of the incomes of Irish farmers now come from direct EU subsidies, while foreign-owned firms account for close to half of manufacturing employment and over 80 per cent of Gross Value Added.[38] Secondly, it is high risk: success depends

37 A. Bielenberg and R. Ryan, *An economic history of Ireland since independence* (Abingdon, 2013), 130, 143, 191, 202. World Bank National Accounts Data, data.worldbank.org, accessed 14 January 2017.

38 CSO, *Business in Ireland 2011* (2013), 50–2; European Commission, *Farm Economy Focus: Ireland* (2014), available at http://ec.europa.eu/agriculture/rica/database/factsheets_en.cfm#lnyear, accessed 10 August 2016.

on successfully monitoring and managing the impact of powerful and often volatile investment and financial flows.[39] The failure to deal with the consequences of global financialisation was the underlying condition of the property and banking bubble of the 2000s and the crash of 2008.[40]

The crash put the trends of the preceding period into reverse. GDP fell by 3% in 2008, by 7% in 2009, by 0.4% in 2010; recovery began in 2011 with growth of 0.7%.[41] Unemployment rose from 4.7% in 2007 to 14.3% in 2011.[42] In the same period the ratio of government debt to GDP went from 25% in 2007 to 110% at the end of 2011.[43] It has since fallen, but its repayment will depress incomes and growth for decades. The crash also cost the state its economic sovereignty which has yet to be fully restored. It bankrupted the banks whose debts the government had chosen to underwrite and these transferred to the sovereign debt. In 2010 a combination of depleted revenues and high international bond rates forced the government to apply for emergency funding from the EU, European Central Bank (ECB) and International Monetary Fund (IMF).

The transformation in the economy and educational system from the 1960s saw a corresponding transformation of the class structure. Internal growth and recruitment from the classes above and below has made the middle class the single largest class,[44] more layered than in the past, spread across all sectors of the economy, and culturally hegemonic. Women were increasingly, although still not proportionately, taking their place within it. Those who remain in the lower strata have benefited from improved education and skills, higher wages and higher levels of income redistribution. As the older indigenous companies failed or were taken over, some of the wealthy business families of the earlier period lost ground; others adapted to the new economy and maintained or improved their position, joined by those upwardly mobile from the middle class.[45] A key development has been the emergence of a new, transnational, super-rich class, and of disparities of income and wealth much greater than anything in the preceding

39 J. Ruane, 'Ireland's multiple interface–periphery development model: achievements and limits', in M. Boss (ed.). *The nation-state in transformation: economic globalisation, institutional mediation and political values* (Aarhus, 2010), 220–1.

40 S. O Riain, *The rise and fall of Ireland's Celtic Tiger: liberalism, boom and bust* (Cambridge, 2014), 236–89.

41 D. Donovan and A. Murphy, *The fall of the Celtic Tiger: Ireland and the Euro debt crisis* (Oxford, 2013), 16.

42 Bielenberg and Ryan, *Economic history of Ireland*, 173.

43 See Donovan and Murphy, *Fall of the Celtic Tiger*, 2–3.

44 Breen and Whelan give a figure of 37.7 per cent for males in the combined upper and lower middle class for 1990, and 30.5 per cent for the combined skilled and unskilled manual class. R. Breen and C. T. Whelan, *Social mobility and social class in Ireland* (Dublin, 1996), 17.

45 On patterns of social mobility, see Breen and Whelan, *Social mobility and social class*, 18–45; C. T. Whelan and R. Layte, 'Economic change, social mobility and meritocracy: reflections on the Irish experience', special article in *Quarterly Economic Commentary* Economic and Social Research Institute (Dublin, 2004).

period.[46] The national and social origins of this class are highly varied, as is their visible presence in society and influence on domestic politics.[47] A further development was the growth of a cosmopolitan elite, including both native Irish and foreign high-flying professionals, the latter being attracted to Ireland by high salaries and opportunities of employment in high-tech industries.

From 1921 onwards the view that the Irish middle class have held of their society has closely matched the upward and downward cycles of its economy, with the former characterised by a sense of optimism and self-confidence and the latter by retrenchment and pessimism. The crash of 2008 proved particularly traumatic, intensified by its suddenness and the long period of growth that preceded it. Its immediate economic consequences – lost jobs, reduced incomes, depleted wealth and negative equity – were severe but akin to the impact of crises in the past. This time, however, the crisis also impacted on class culture and confidence. The manner in which the crash came about, the close relationship between leading political figures, bankers and developers, and the belief that those most responsible have escaped its worst consequences, have led the middle class to a painful reassessment of the nature of their society and their place within it.[48]

After 1921 the Irish middle classes were exceptional in the extent of their social and political influence over their society. The class above them was significantly weaker than its equivalent elsewhere and posed little challenge. The political elites came from their ranks and were attentive to their needs, and the economic and social ideologies of the two main political parties in the south – Fianna Fáil and Fine Gael – as much as the long-dominant Ulster Unionist Party (UUP) in the north were largely a reflection of such class domination. If the middle classes sometimes had occasion to question their political leaders' competence or judgement, they did not doubt their support, integrity or sincerity. This began to change in the late 1980s as the close links between key political figures and the new super-rich class became apparent. A succession of tribunals confirmed the depth of the problem without providing a solution.

Today the middle class no longer has the trust or confidence it once had in its political elite, or in its ability to shape its society. Indeed, by a historical irony, it now finds itself in a situation very similar to that of its forebears in the early twentieth century: on the fringes of spatially wide-ranging, multi-levelled, relationships, subject to the decisions of wealthy and powerful transnational elites, and dependent on domestic elites

46 This class features in national and international Rich Lists. The *Sunday Independent*'s list of the Top 300 in 2015 estimated the top fortune at €14.5 billion and the bottom one at €26.5 million. A number have signalled their pre-eminence by acquiring and restoring the great houses of the Anglo-Irish.
47 The extent of their influence is difficult to establish, but in some cases it has been considerable and corrupting; see E. Byrne, *Political corruption in Ireland 1922–2010: a crooked harp* (Manchester, 2012), 143–91.
48 It is evident in the many books and innumerable newspaper columns about the crisis and its aftermath. For an example, see M. Cooper, *Who really runs Ireland?* (Dublin, 2009).

whose motives and competence they no longer trust. Their forebears had the choice of exit, voice or loyalty, and chose exit. This time exit is not an option.

The transformation in Northern Ireland since the 1960s has been equally profound but has taken a radically different direction. The British assumption that there was majority cross-community support for moderate politics was quickly dashed. The Ulster Workers' Council strike of 1974 brought down the first power-sharing executive; it was followed by two decades of political stalemate and violence, and it was 1998 before a settlement (the Good Friday Agreement) was reached.

The period between was one of economic decline, sharply increasing unemployment and class restructuring. Violence dissuaded inward industrial investment, accelerating the structural shift from primary and secondary sectors to service sectors, and within this to public (state) services, much of it based on security.[49] The expansion of the state benefited the relatively affluent middle class, creating a large managerial and professional stratum in the public sector – now more than a quarter of the workforce – and increasing the divide between it and the workless. Increasingly effective fair employment policies meant that the Catholic professional and managerial middle class were particular beneficiaries.[50]

Throughout this period only one party stood for cross-community moderate politics – the Alliance Party of Northern Ireland. Its activists had a stronger professional middle-class profile than did other parties, its support base was disproportionately urban and middle class, and it won only limited support, seldom more than 10 per cent. The largest unionist party through the period, the UUP, had a middle-class leadership, but typically those involved in Orangeism, or those with strong family connections in politics.[51] The Democratic Unionist Party (DUP) began with a strong clerical and Free Presbyterian presence in its leadership, and had a somewhat stronger working-class support base than did the UUP. As it grew in strength and overtook the UUP as the largest unionist party in the 2000s, its elite became less clerical, more Orange, and closer to the class profile of the UUP.[52] The Social Democratic and Labour Party (SDLP) was strongly rooted in the Catholic middle classes, and had a leadership in which teachers

49 See B. Rowthorn and N. Wayne, *Northern Ireland: the political economy of conflict* (Cambridge, 1988).
50 The change took time, and it was not until well into the 2000s that Catholics took a close-to-proportional place in the higher civil service. J. Ruane and J. Todd, 'Beyond inequality: assessing the impact of fair employment, affirmative action and equality measures on Northern Ireland', in G. Brown, A. Langer and F. Stewart (eds.), *Affirmative action in plural societies: international experiences* (Basingstoke, 2012). Gender equality has advanced even less quickly: see R. Miller, 'Social mobility in Northern Ireland', in B. Osborne and I. Shuttleworth (eds.), *Fair employment in Northern Ireland: a generation on* (Belfast, 2004). M. Potter, *Review of gender issues in Northern Ireland*, NIAR 210–14, Northern Ireland Assembly Research Paper, 28 January 2014, available at www .niassembly.gov.uk/globalassets/documents/raise/publications/2014/ofmdfm/1514.pdf, accessed 24 February 2016.
51 D. Hume, *The Ulster Unionist Party 1972–1992* (Lurgan, 1996), 168.
52 J. Tonge, M. Braniff, T. Hennessey, J. W. McAuley and S. Whiting, *The Democratic Unionist Party: from protest to power* (Oxford, 2014), 65–80, 138–9, 149–52.

predominated: after 1974 it refocused its attention not on cross-community but on cross-class and cross-state politics in an attempt to leverage reform and end violence.

As in the first decades of the northern state, many professionals and managers of a Protestant background kept their distance from politics. They retreated from public life, focusing on family, career or business in a society where class now determined not just income, advance and education, but also safety. The tendency to look to Britain for opportunities increased, with students going in ever greater numbers to British universities and then making their careers in Britain. There was a similar, though less pronounced, tendency in the Catholic middle class.

There were times, however, when sections of the middle class had more significant political impact. In response to increasing violence and popular support for republicanism in the early 1980s, moderate nationalists in the SDLP came to exert considerable influence on the Irish government which now aimed to end nationalist 'alienation'. The British and Irish governments negotiated the Anglo-Irish Agreement (1985) that provided new avenues for peaceful influence and new status for nationalists in Northern Ireland. It was soon followed by the Fair Employment Act of 1989 which particularly benefited the Catholic professional and middle class. It also helped convince republicans, and the wider nationalist population, that reform and equality were achievable within Northern Ireland.

The wider business and professional middle class also made a contribution. In the 1980s, business figures argued for the creation of a north–south trade corridor and in the 1990s gave strong support to the peace process and the Good Friday Agreement. In the 1990s, too, a massive British investment in peace and conflict NGOs created a body of articulate and non-aligned professional middle-class activists important in the peace process. There emerged an activist, cross-community, cross-class and professional-led women's movement in the Northern Ireland Women's Coalition.

The past decades have seen the middle class expand and prosper in Northern Ireland and many have distanced themselves from organised unionism and nationalism. However, there is little evidence of a cross-community middle class with sufficient cohesion to sustain a politics of moderation and pragmatic consensus. The Good Friday Agreement of 1998 (and the later St Andrews Agreement of 2006) remains a compact between opposed unionist and nationalist parties, a form of imposed conflict regulation between political elites who hold no shared vision of the society, of the Agreement(s) or of the future trajectory of Northern Ireland.

Sections of business and the middle classes still articulate a shared vision of society, but their political influence is limited. Unlike the relatively cohesive and assertive southern middle class, the northern middle class remains deeply divided in politics, is quick to retreat, and has little influence on the now heavily politicised working classes. This means that while political stability has been (more or less) achieved, its foundations remain fragile and without an internal dynamic at elite or middle-class level that would allow it to cope with future crises or with long-term demographic, economic or geopolitical change.

11.6. Conclusion

The birth of the two, very different, states on the island had a class dimension that was to remain important. We have focused on the contrasting positions of the middle classes, north and south. In the south independence was achieved by a cross-class nationalist movement under middle-class leadership and the middle classes subsequently controlled the state. There had been no pre-independence class bargain with the poorer classes, and the small post-independence wealthy class was unable or unwilling to assert itself. The northern state was achieved by a unionist alliance of upper class (industrial and landowning) and working class; the class bargain was explicit and it underwrote the new state. The Protestant middle class was not part of the bargain and, though comfortable in the new state, kept a certain distance from its politics. The Catholic middle class was on the margins.

For a brief period Terence O'Neill attempted to modernise unionism by challenging the old alliance and bringing the liberal Protestant middle class into the political process. Instead the regime collapsed. The middle class has prospered under direct rule and devolution, but it has continued to maintain its distance from a conflict in whose outcome it has an interest but whose terms and political expression it strongly dislikes.

Over the same period the political elite and middle class of the Republic moderated its earlier nationalism and adopted an economic model based on international trade and foreign direct investment, membership of the EU and – later – globalisation. It brought substantial benefits to all classes. But it brought disproportionately more to the wealthiest strata, and fostered a new transnational, super-rich, class. Since the early 2000s, the middle class has been conscious of a slippage in its position in the social hierarchy, and has been questioning in whose interests the political elite is acting. The crash of 2008, and the possibility of a new level of working-class mobilisation, has given these questions added urgency.

FURTHER READING

Allen, K. *The corporate takeover of Ireland* (Dublin, 2007).

Campbell, F. *The Irish establishment 1879–1914* (Oxford, 2009).

Clancy, P., N. O'Connor and K. Dillon. *Mapping the golden circle* (Dublin, 2010).

Coulter, C. *Contemporary Northern Irish society* (London, 1999).

Crotty, R. *When histories collide: the development and impact of individualistic capitalism* (Cumnor Hill, 2001).

Eipper, C. *The ruling trinity: a community study of church, state and business in Ireland* (Aldershot, 1986).

Gibbon, P. *The origins of Ulster unionism: the formation of popular Protestant politics and ideology in nineteenth century Ireland* (Manchester, 1975).

Heath, A. F., R. Breen and C. T. Whelan (eds.). *Ireland north and south: perspectives from social science* (Oxford, 1999).

Ó Gráda, C. *A rocky road: the Irish economy since the 1920s* (Manchester, 1997).

Osborne, B. and I. Shuttleworth (eds.). *Fair employment in Northern Ireland: a generation on* (Belfast, 2004).

Pašeta, S. *Before the revolution: nationalism and social change and Ireland's Catholic elite, 1879–1922* (Cork, 1999).

Peillon, M. *Contemporary Irish society: an introduction* (Dublin, 2002).

Wright, F. *Two lands on one soil: Ulster politics before Home Rule* (Dublin, 1996).

PART II

People, Culture and Communities

12 Consumption and Living Conditions, 1750–2016

Andy Bielenberg and John O'Hagan

12.1. Introduction

In general, economists and economic historians have focused more on production than on consumption and living conditions, with the latter being of greater interest to social historians.[1] This chapter broadly charts some of the major changes in the patterns of Irish consumption and living conditions across the social spectrum. It is hard to grasp the scale of the change in a little more than 250 years. For example, in rural Ireland in 1750, and even still a hundred years later, much of consumption would have taken place directly through home production of food in particular, for the vast majority of the lower-income classes. For most having shelter from the elements, a place to sleep, water to drink and a basic diet would have constituted the major elements of their daily consumption. The bulk of personal consumption hinged on acquiring the bare necessities, with subsistence and semi-subsistence agriculture co-existing in the economy at large with market-driven transactions.

Living standards and living conditions are clearly closely related. Living standards are usually measured in terms of average income per head of population in a society. It is incomes that allow consumption to take place. As average incomes increase though, basic consumption requirements and living conditions can be greatly extended and for small sections of the Irish population such possibilities existed even in the eighteenth century, with some experiencing lavish living conditions in terms of magnificent houses, fine clothes, personal services provided by others such as tuition for their children and housework, travel for leisure purposes and fine horse-drawn carriages.

1 In this genre, see for example J. Hill and C. Lennon (eds.), *Luxury and austerity* (Dublin, 1999).

Such living conditions, though, were still a distant dream for the vast majority of the pre-Great Famine population. In the century after 1850 rising incomes meant that the consumption possibilities rose significantly across the social spectrum and included better housing, diet, education and health services. Technological innovations impact on the composition of living conditions, such as, for example, the advent of trains, then cars and telephones, and most particularly electricity. Air travel, radio, TV, dramatic changes in medical care and the internet followed later in the twentieth century.

As incomes are the main determinants of consumption it follows that, given that there was huge variation in income per head within Ireland, not just between the north and the south but also between urban and rural areas, and within urban areas, vast differences in living conditions were also evident. Historically the Irish economy, north and south, had been greatly influenced by the economy of its larger neighbour.[2] This influence persists to the present day, although by breaking the link with sterling in 1979 and later joining the Euro the southern economy has decoupled somewhat from the UK. Besides, since the 1970s living standards in the south have caught up with and surpassed those in the UK. Thus, from lagging significantly behind the UK norm for more than two centuries, the south now has one of the highest standards of living in the world.

The first half of this chapter will outline some of the major changes in market transactions and living conditions up to 1922, notably food and drink. The second half of the chapter reflects the extraordinary changes in living standards made possible by both a marked rise in living standards and a range of new technologies, which dramatically altered living conditions.

12.2.   1750–1922

12.2.1.   Precarious Growth of Market Transactions

Most of the population rarely visited shops or trading outlets in the mid-eighteenth century. The diary of a farmer (Mr Lucas) provides a rare window on a fairly narrow range of market transactions carried out in the early 1740s, when his animals, butter or corn were sold at fairs and markets or to merchants or meal women on occasional trips to the town of Ennis (County Clare) and at this point outstanding bills with the principal merchants of the town were partially or entirely paid off.[3] Yet commercial

---

2 See N. Gibson and J. Spencer (eds.), *Economic activity in Ireland: a study of two open economies* (Dublin, 1977). For a more recent discussion of the two different economies, see J. Bradley and M. Best, *Cross-border economic renewal* (Armagh, 2012). For useful comparative statistics for north and south, see *Census 2011: Ireland and Northern Ireland*, CSO and Northern Ireland Statistics and Research Agency (Dublin and Belfast, 2014).
3 B. O Dalaigh, 'The origins, rise and decline of the Ennis fairs and markets', in D. A. Cronin, J. Gilligan and K. Holton (eds.), *Irish fairs and markets* (Dublin, 2001), 54–5.

transactions were greater in urban contexts, notably in the larger ports. Hamilton's drawings of the mid-eighteenth-century cries of Dublin reveal street traders hawking an array of items, from coarse earthenware to turf, or foodstuffs destined for the households of the middling and lower orders, in addition to the provision of other services such as cobblers or chimney sweep; this illustrates the diversity of retailing in Ireland's largest market, which was also served by shopkeepers, rural dealers with products from the countryside and merchants selling imported wares.[4]

Consumption requirements and living conditions were greatly extended for a narrow elite from the second half of the eighteenth century. Barnard's searching assessment of Protestant society has considerably advanced our understanding of the cultural significance of luxury goods and lavish consumption in defining social status at the top. The financial capacity to construct Big Houses expressed in architectural terms the intimidating position of landlords at the apex of Irish society, all of which played a role in defining status. Powell's study of the politics of consumption also focuses largely on the Protestant elite, yet the growing significance of 'the middling sorts' is acknowledged as a core element in the expansion of Irish consumerism in the second half of the eighteenth century, and the tensions arising between the consumption of more fashionable colonial and British goods and the more patriotic patronage of Irish manufactures. Sarah Foster provides a window on the more up-market retailing of goods in Dublin's more fashionable shopping thoroughfares in the late eighteenth century patronised by those with disposable income, where native and imported wares in ornate and fashionable shops were comparable to those in the major cities in Britain and elsewhere in Europe.[5]

Although such goods were still a distant dream for the vast majority of the Irish population, the steady expansion of trade in the towns and ports, in villages, fairs and markets, the expansion of coinage and bank notes in circulation, all indicate a marked advance in commercialisation during the second half of the eighteenth century, albeit with a highly unequal distribution of its benefits. Yet clearly the consumption of goods like tea, flour, bread, whiskey, sugar and tobacco were steadily moving down the social scale. Tea, for example, which had been considered a refined and exclusive drink in the mid-eighteenth century, had become more commonplace for the middling sorts and tradesmen, though it still remained something of a rare luxury for the poor by the 1830s. Yet by the 1880s its widespread diffusion as a primary beverage across all classes was complete.[6] Tobacco was even more widely consumed

4 W. Laffan (ed.), *The cries of Dublin; drawn from the life by Hugh Douglas Hamilton, 1760* (Dublin, 2003).
5 S. Foster, 'Going shopping in 18th century Dublin', *Things*, 4 (Summer 1996), 33–61; S. Foster, '"Ornament and splendour"; shops and shopping in Georgian Dublin', *Irish Architectural and Decorative Studies*, 15 (2012), 12–33.
6 P. Lysaght, '"When I makes tea, I makes tea": innovation in food – the case of tea in Ireland', *Ulster Folklife*, 33 (1987), 44–71.

by the early nineteenth century, with per capita consumption levels close to those in Great Britain.[7]

Yet the evidence from the Poor Law Reports in the mid-1830s reveals substantial impoverished sections of the population whose purchasing power was exceedingly limited. The reports indicate that much land let by farmers on conacre to cottiers and labourers in the mid-1830s was still worked off through labour provided to the farmer as opposed to a rental payment in cash, or labourers could be paid through provisions rather than cash. This reveals that even by the 1830s there were sub-stantial pockets of rural Ireland where the impact of the cash economy remained tenuous at the bottom of the social spectrum.[8] Historical archaeology has pro-vided important new evidence on subaltern material culture for a substantial group located between this substantial impoverished group at the bottom and the elite at the top; evidence from digs at the former Nary household at Ballykilcline in County Roscommon (a 30–50 acre farm family subsequently evicted in 1847–8) revealed an abundance of ceramics indicating extensive purchases of both Irish manufactured coarse earthenware and finer ceramics of English manufacture. These, along with other items recovered, imply that those engaged in commercial farming (while not having security of tenure) were already enjoying some of the benefits of English mass production.

Customs and excise data also reveal some of the broader consumption trends: Irish imported wine and spirit consumption per head declined from the late eighteenth century, displaced by the growth of the native distilling industry; whiskey, along with tea, coffee and sugar, experienced some growth for the duration of the continental/Napoleonic wars, with consumption of these items stagnating from 1815 to the Great Famine. There was a marked rise in tea, tobacco and wine consumption in the post-fam-ine decades. The growth of native spirit consumption from the mid-eighteenth century to the 1840s stands out. Spirits were cheap and their consumption became an endemic feature of pre-famine society across the social spectrum.[9] This gradually stalled with the influence of the temperance movement and the post-famine devotional revolution, combined with increased competition from beer in the second half of the nineteenth century, when the pattern of alcohol consumption in Ireland fell somewhat more into line with the rest of the UK.[10]

7 A. Bielenberg and D. Johnson, 'The production and consumption of tobacco in Ireland', *Irish Economic and Social History*, 25 (1998), 1–21.
8 British Parliamentary Papers, 1836, vol. xxxi, Poor Inquiry, Ireland, Appendix D.
9 Data on the per capita consumption of these commodities between the 1790s and the 1860s can be found in *Thom's Directory* (Dublin, 1871), 930. On illicit distilling, see K. Connell, *Irish peasant society* (Dublin, 1996).
10 E. Malcolm, 'The rise of the pub: a study in the disciplining of popular culture', in J. S. Donnelly and K. A. Miller (eds.), *Irish popular culture* (Dublin, 1998), 50–77; A. Bielenberg, *Ireland and the Industrial Revolution: the impact of the Industrial Revolution on Irish industry* (London, 2009), 77–104.

12.2.2. The Central Significance of Food

Food was by far the most important commodity consumed by the 1830s. Clarkson and Crawford concluded that by the end of the eighteenth century, there was a clear dichotomy in the quality of the diet between the top 40 per cent in Irish society (who broadly conformed to British patterns of consumption) and the impoverished bottom third, with an intermediate group consuming a wider range of foodstuffs than the more monotonous diets of the poor.[11]

The growth of the money supply had dramatically outstripped that of population in the preceding half-century, which points to a general increase in market transactions. Cullen notes that potatoes even for the poor could only be relied upon in the winter and spring, so that harvest fluctuations had a critical influence on both the food supply and the state of the economy.[12] Rising per capita consumption between the mid-eighteenth century and the eve of the famine of potatoes grown on the farm freed up limited cash resources for other market transactions. The bulk of Irish clothing, notably woollens and linens, was still supplied by the Irish market in the late eighteenth century, but British textiles and clothing were becoming increasingly fashionable. Between the 1780s and the 1820s British manufactured exports to Ireland rose far more dramatically than other items.[13] By the mid-1830s, manufactured cottons topped the list of British imported commodities.[14]

The Poor Law Inquiry evidence reveals that the poor spent between 60 and 71 per cent of their household expenditure on food (including the cost of renting potato ground) in the mid-1830s.[15] The stellar growth in food prices between 1845 and 1847 (a signal of the major extent of the famine crisis) pushed survival far beyond their limited means. Solar has made estimates of the calorific shortfall from the deficit in the potato and corn supply, which cruelly hit the substantial potato-dependent population.[16] The famine quickly changed the composition of agricultural output and altered economic and demographic behaviour, not least in terms of consumption patterns, as flour derived from imported wheat increasingly assumed far greater dietary importance,

11 L. Clarkson and E. M. Crawford, *Feast and famine: food and nutrition in Ireland 1500–1920* (Oxford, 2001). For a series of relevant articles see 'Special edition: food and drink in Ireland', in *Proceedings of the Royal Irish Academy*, Section C, 115 (2015).

12 L. M. Cullen, *Anglo-Irish trade 1660–1800* (Manchester, 1968), 52; L. M. Cullen, *An economic history of Ireland since 1660* (London, 1972), 95, 106.

13 C. Ó Gráda, *Ireland: a new economic history, 1780–1939* (Oxford, 1994), 160.

14 British Parliamentary Papers, 1837–8, vol. xxxv, The Report of the Railway Commissioners, Appendix B, no. 11.

15 F. Geary and T. Stark, 'Trends in real wages during the Industrial Revolution: a view from across the Irish Sea', *Economic History Review*, 57, 2 (2004), 365.

16 P. Solar, 'The Great Famine was no ordinary subsistence crisis', in E. M. Crawford (ed.), *Famine: the Irish experience* (Edinburgh, 1989), 113–26. On prices, see L. Kennedy and P. Solar, *Irish agriculture: a price history from the mid-eighteenth century to the eve of the First World War* (Dublin, 2007).

thus intensifying commercialisation. The evidence on living standards suggests there were some gains in the post-famine decades with wages and living standards rising in the 1850s through to the early 1870s. Evidence on wages reveals a process of moderate wage convergence with the British economy from the mid-nineteenth century to the First World War.[17]

12.2.3. Retailing Revolution, 1840–1914, but Continued Dominance of Food

The communications revolution, centred on the rail network and steam navigation, facilitated a retailing revolution from the 1840s. Small shops proliferated in smaller towns and villages selling dry goods, food, drink, hardware and household goods and clothing, etc., and the growing share of the population living in urban centres of more than 1,500 inhabitants (which rose from a sixth to a third of the population) between 1845 and 1914 intensified commercialisation. The railway network was centrally important to the Victorian consumer revolution in Ireland in terms of integrating and expanding markets, transporting British textiles, hardware and pottery across the island's retail networks, in addition to Indian tea and American tobacco. With rising living standards, the urban middle class utilised rail to leave the confines of the city; by the late 1850s already the coastline between Dublin city centre and Bray was brought within commuting distance, leading to middle-class suburban development. The railways reduced transport costs sufficiently for poorer people to travel more often, opening up transport to the masses. Cormac Ó Gráda notes that the number of train journeys per person per annum rose from 1.7 in 1860 to 3.9 in 1885, with a more dramatic hike up to 7.1 by 1913.[18] This reflects a general rise in living standards and mobility and the continued expansion of the network. But it was not only on the movement of people and freight that the railways had a major impact. They also facilitated a far greater diffusion of information throughout Ireland. The mail system was dramatically improved by the use of rail, in addition to the distribution of newspapers (local, national and English). The telegraph system also used the land along the railways, so the whole revolution in communications was intimately connected.

The cities provided larger and more sophisticated specialist retail outlets. Musgrave's, for example, opened its first grocery store in Cork city in 1876, adding more branches subsequently. Findlater's in Dublin developed from its pre-famine position as wine and spirit merchants selling a few dry goods in a few premises, to having a chain of grocery stores all over Dublin and its suburbs. For clothing and apparel there were already four

17 F. Geary and T. Stark, 'Regional GDP in the UK, 1861–1911: new estimates', *Economic History Review*, 68 (2015), 123–44.
18 C. Ó Gráda, *Ireland: a new economic history*, 239.

so-called 'Monster houses' in Dublin by the late 1850s, and by the end of the nineteenth century large department stores like Cleary's in that city or Cannock's in Limerick provided consumers with a huge range of items conveniently located under one roof. A number of British multiples opened in Ireland from the late nineteenth century including Lipton's grocery stores, Burtons the Tailors and Singer Sewing Machines, and on the eve of the First World War, Messrs F. W. Woolworth & Co. opened their first store. More specialist retailers such as Eason's, the newsagent chain, had already been established in the 1880s.

Despite this dramatic transformation, food still dominated consumer expenditure in Ireland (as in the rest of the UK), accounting for 63 per cent of household expenditure in the household budgets of 123 Irish working-class families assessed in 1907. This approximated to that estimated for the 1830s, yet rural households in the 1890s in the relatively poorer Congested Districts spent a somewhat lower share as they were in a position to consume food grown on farm. Evidence from the Baseline Reports of the Congested Districts indicate that the share going on food in the early 1890s in Donegal amounted to roughly 34 per cent (mostly meal and flour) while tea, tobacco, alcohol and snuff collectively accounted for almost 22 per cent. Food grown and consumed on farms remained important.[19]

The continued significance of food in mass consumption is underlined by Solar's trade evidence, which reveals that the value of agricultural goods rose from almost 14 per cent of total Irish imports in 1784–6 to around 27 per cent in 1909–11, as imports increasingly augmented the indigenous food supply. The growing importation of manufactures (mostly British and more than half of which were textiles) rose from less than 18 per cent of the value of total imports in 1784–6 to almost 37 per cent of the total in 1909–11.[20]

The British Industrial Revolution (including those aspects centred on transportation) increased Irish access to British and colonial consumer goods and, although most of the island had not become industrialised, it shared to some degree in the benefits of the United Kingdom consumer revolution. But Ulster, and more particularly east Ulster, appears to have enjoyed this rise in consumption to a greater degree, thanks largely to industrialisation. This is confirmed by the greater share of Irish imports of a range of consumer goods in 1904 entering the port of Belfast.[21] This implies that Ulster households lived somewhat less frugally than those in the rest of the island. Yet cheaper imported colonial stimulants, in contrast, such as tea, sugar and cocoa, were far more

19 C. Breathnach, *The Congested Districts Board 1891–1923* (Dublin, 2005), 114.

20 P. Solar, 'Irish trade in the nineteenth century', in D. Dickson and C. Ó Gráda (eds.), *Refiguring Ireland* (Dublin, 2003), 279.

21 *Report on the trade in imports and exports at Irish ports during the year ended 31st December 1904* (Dublin, 1906). These items included hardware, fruit, matches, boots and shoes, soap, and preserved and canned meats.

evenly dispersed across all the major Irish ports, indicating a wider market base in these more affordable items. But Ulster folk appear to have been more averse to coffee and wine consumption than their southern compatriots, reflecting some regional, cultural and religious differences in consumer preference not always connected to living standards.

Claudia Kinmouth's study of Irish vernacular furniture implies that specialist furniture-making was limited for most of the rural population for much of the nineteenth century. In the pre-famine era, terms such as 'hedge carpenter' speak for themselves, but mass-produced furniture gradually began to make an appearances in the second half of the nineteenth century, by the end of which most of the larger towns had furniture factories.[22] Imports through the port of Belfast in 1904 again imply that Ulster households were importing a higher relative share of total imports of carpets and furniture.[23] If industrialisation had drawbacks in terms of health and life expectancy, the benefits in terms of household consumption appear to be clear-cut.

While some improvements in gentry and middle-class housing in both rural and urban contexts was evident enough in the century before the Great Famine, by 1841 77 per cent of the housing stock recorded was in low quality third- and fourth-class housing. The stellar improvement in quality is apparent from census data between 1841 and 1911, with the share of first- and second-class houses rising from less than 23 per cent just before the Great Famine to more than 77 per cent by the eve of the First World War. While famine and emigration and the resulting fall in population reduced the poorest quality housing, rising living standards undoubtedly contributed to this dramatic improvement.[24] Despite the slum conditions of the larger towns and cities and the persistence of rural poverty more notably in the west, these statistics provide one of the strongest indicators of a general improvement in living standards across the population at large.

12.2.4. Limited Role of the State

The role of the state had remained fairly limited in the eighteenth and much of the nineteenth century when the United Kingdom including Ireland was effectively a fiscal military state. For many decades after the Napoleonic wars a significant share of state expenditure went to either paying off the Irish share of British debt or covering the costs of the garrisons in Ireland.[25] This at least brought some benefits to

22 C. Kinmouth, *Irish country furniture 1700–1950* (New Haven, 1993), 20.
23 *Report on the trade in imports and exports at Irish ports during the year ended 31st December 1904* (Dublin, 1906).
24 *Census of Ireland for the year, 1861; Part v General Report* (Dublin, 1864), xix; *Census of Ireland, 1911: general report* (London, 1913), 66.
25 *Thom's Directory* (Dublin, 1855), 404 and (Dublin, 1865), 835.

the locations where the army and navy had a presence. But up to the 1870s Ireland paid much more in taxes than it received in terms of state expenditure. Expenditure on non-military headings rose somewhat thereafter as education and other government services increased including the establishment of the Congested Districts Board and the Department of Agriculture in the 1890s. The payment of the old age pension from 1908 was particularly beneficial, leading to a situation where state expenditure in Ireland was briefly actually higher than the revenue raised there. This was dramatically reversed during the First World War, owing to the major rise in Irish taxation.[26]

Falling real living standards for the working classes, and a widening gap between farm labourers and farmers (as farmers benefited from rising prices), rapid wartime inflation and the highly regressive increase in taxation of consumer goods such as tea, sugar, tobacco and alcohol, all probably contributed to the success of Sinn Féin in the 1918 election as the status quo fell out of favour and the franchise widened to poorer voters. Despite fiscal retrenchment in the 1920s following the establishment of the Irish Free State, greater state intervention, expenditure and taxation were to become far more pronounced features of the Irish economic landscape both north and south of the border as the twentieth century proceeded.

12.3.   1922–2015

12.3.1.   Public versus Private Consumption/Investment

Consumption takes place in terms of two main categories of goods/services: those provided via the private sector (e.g. food, bicycles, cars, TVs) and those provided largely via the state (e.g. water/sewerage, education, health care, social security). Up to the middle of the twentieth century there were minimal services provided through the state, apart from the police and the army, with only a very basic level of education, health care, water and sewerage provision well into the twentieth century. Since the 1950s, there has been a rapid growth in state provision of education, health and social security services, financed by taxation.

As the century progressed, rising living standards allowed also for the wider consumption of cars, a more varied diet, more holidays, radios, TVs and white goods, and more recently extensive foreign travel, internet services and hugely improved communication networks. Rising living standards also allowed increased taxation which in turn allowed for increased services provided through the state, such as running water

26 P. Travers, 'The financial relations question 1800–1914', in F. B. Smith (ed.), *Ireland, England and Australia* (Cork, 1990), 41–69; C. Ó Gráda, 'The greatest blessing of all: the old age pension in Ireland', *Past and Present*, no. 175 (May 2002); C. H. Oldham, 'The public finances of Ireland', *Economic Journal* (March 1920), 61–73.

to all houses, greatly improved sewerage services, electricity, education and health care, and improved social protection through various state benefits.

One general trend across Europe was the decline in the share of national output devoted to private consumption and investment, as the shares of public consumption and investment increased in the first half of the twentieth century. For example, in the UK as a whole, private consumption dropped from 82 per cent of national output in the 1920s to just 61 per cent in the 1970s. This came about because of the large rise in state expenditure in education and health in particular, but also in infrastructure such as housing, water, sewerage and transport. Thus by the 1970s the state, north and south, had assumed a much bigger role in contributing to living standards than in the 1920s. This share has waned and risen over the decades, but mainly in response to swings in national output as opposed to big changes in public expenditure in these areas.

Much of the population now aged sixty-five and over who lived in rural Ireland will remember, for example, going to a well or handpump for drinking water; using outside dry toilets in summer; gas lamps and candles instead of electricity; using bicycles but not cars; with a dramatic transition subsequently including rural electrification, the advent of TV, increasing purchases of white goods, eating out, foreign holidays, the internet, and so on. But these changes are merely a reflection of the changes throughout Europe in the twentieth century.[27] What drove these consumption changes were both the marked rise in incomes and new technologies. To illustrate this, five major areas relating to living conditions will be considered: housing/electricity/water, motor cars, air travel/leisure, telecommunications, and shopping and eating patterns.

12.3.2. Housing, Electricity and Water

One consequence of the increased role of the state was the huge improvement in housing conditions in Ireland, first in the better-off areas of the country but eventually spreading to almost all areas. Apart from the construction of state housing, the provision of proper water and sewerage facilities for other houses transformed domestic living standards for huge sections of the Irish population.

The quality of housing improved greatly over time, as reflected in changes in floor space, the availability of electricity, running water and a separate bathroom. In the interwar years, the installation of electricity was a priority all over Europe, and in some countries, practically all buildings had electricity by the 1950s. At the same

---

27 B. Tomka, *A social history of twentieth-century Europe* (London, 2013); parts of some of the later sections draw on this.

time, only 15 per cent of homes had electricity in Greece; moreover, in Portugal and in the Balkan countries, only approximately 50 per cent of the households had access to electricity even as late as the 1960s, a situation that applied also in parts of Ireland. The increasing availability of running water and a separate bathroom also reflected the growing comfort level of homes. Plumbing construction had already intensified in the UK in the first half of the twentieth century, and by the mid-century, the availability of running water reached a level of 80–90 per cent. However, even in the UK, bathrooms became a standard feature in homes only after the Second World War.

The pattern in Ireland followed all of this but with a time lag, reflecting different income per capita levels, and varied both between the north and south, and also probably more markedly between rich and poor regions within each. For example, the number of private housing units in the south increased by more than 50 per cent between the 1930s and 1991 and has continued to increase rapidly since. Many city dwellers in Dublin at the beginning of the twentieth century lived in tenement houses, often in just one-room apartments with no water or toilets. In rural Ireland prior to the 1950s living conditions in many houses were also very poor, with no electricity, running water or toilets, and often damp and dark.

Like in the rest of Europe, the advent of electricity made a huge difference to housing standards, first in the cities and later in rural areas, making women's housework somewhat less arduous, but this improvement in living conditions merely freed up more time for other chores, rather than creating more leisure time.[28] Electric lights replaced candles and gas lamps. Electric cookers replaced cooking often over an open fire. Besides, it became possible to pump water to homes and inside toilets and bathrooms became more common. The state built homes to replace the poorer dwellings of small farmers and farm labourers, and in the cities tenement buildings were pulled down and replaced by new housing estates in the suburbs.

Around 61 per cent of the households in 1946 did not have piped water, although more than half of these used either a private well or private pump for their water supply, and in rural Ireland an indoor water supply was a rare luxury.[29] By 1991 the number of households reported as not having a piped water supply had been diminished to less than 2 per cent. Of the households that had piped water in 1946, only around 40 per cent of them (or just 15 per cent of all households at the time) had the use of a fixed bath or shower. This is a stark reminder of the far tougher basic living conditions even within living memory.

28 M. Shiel, *The quiet revolution: the electrification of rural Ireland 1946–1976* (Dublin, 1984).
29 CSO, *This was then, this is now: change in Ireland 1949–1999* (Dublin, 2000). Also see M. Daly "'Turning on the tap": the state, Irish women and running water', in G. Valiulus and M. O'Dowd (eds.), *Women and Irish history* (Dublin, 1997).

12.3.3.   Transport, Communication and Leisure

Prior to the advent of the motor car, walking, horses, bicycles and trains/trams were the major modes of transport across Ireland. Indeed until well into the 1960s most people in Ireland did not possess a car, but that has changed dramatically since. The car made regular medium-distance travel more convenient and affordable, especially in areas without railways. The construction of motorways first in the north and later in the south accelerated the revolution in personal mobility. This impacted not just on travel for leisure purposes but also for work and greatly on shopping patterns.

Improved transportation accelerated the outward growth of cities and towns in Ireland and as elsewhere led to the development of suburbs. Besides, until the advent of the car, workers lived close to work, especially factory workers, and thus the arrival of the motor car had a profound influence on inner-city communities in Belfast and Dublin: people could now move to low-density suburban areas far from the city centres and closely knit inner-city communities. As a result people were able to and did commute much longer distances to work, with that trend accelerating in recent decades. The arrival of the car was of course a boon for the tourist industry in areas such as the south-west and west, plus the north-west and north of the island. Individuals, families and groups were able now to have holidays in distant places where they could experience natural scenery seen prior to this by only a few, have seaside breaks, enjoy more golf and visit heritage sites out of reach for most up to this time.

Road transport was slow to develop in Ireland, but from the 1920s onwards came into its own as more public money was invested in improving and surfacing roads, so that the mileage of surfaced roads rose from 5,000 to 14,000 between 1930 and 1950 and up to 55,000 miles by the 1980s.[30] Expansion was set back briefly by the Second World War, but by the 1960s car ownership in Ireland took off, as rising living standards and low-priced smaller and economical models such as the Volkswagen, Anglia or the Mini made them more affordable; meanwhile Ford brought out the larger Cortina in 1963 which was more suitable for the larger average family size found in Ireland. By 1968 there were 348,000 cars licensed (up from just around 15,000 in the 1940s). By the time Ireland entered the EEC in 1973 48 per cent of households in the Republic of Ireland had a car.

Since the 1970s the car has constituted one of the major items of personal consumption, increasingly displacing other forms of transport. Consumer culture, work, leisure all became more intimately connected with motor access so that public institutions and buildings, sports clubs, pubs, factories, hospitals, shops and supermarkets, etc. simply had to have car parks. The construction of motorways linking the major Irish cities

---

30 G. Quinn and P. Lynch, 'The latest phase in Irish transport', in K. B. Nowlan (ed.), *Travel and transport* (Dublin, 1973), 158; S. Barrett, *Transport policy in Ireland* (Dublin, 1982), 176.

and the staggering growth of car usage in the following decades accelerated particularly from the 1990s, so that by 2015 there were around 2 million cars (or roughly one for every two people), reflecting both the dramatic rise in living standards during the Celtic Tiger and the relative lack of investment in other forms of transport.[31]

There have been dramatic changes in air travel in Ireland, especially since the early 1950s. As an island Ireland was a natural focus for air travel. The first air service to and from the island was launched in 1933, operating a Dublin–Belfast route as well as one from Liverpool to Dublin. Aer Lingus launched the first Irish transatlantic service in 1948. The liberalisation of air transport from the mid-1980s onwards led to a major lowering of prices, with a huge increase in cross-channel traffic following this, as well as greatly increased traffic to the rest of Europe. The Irish airline Ryanair had a major impact on this development, not only in Ireland, but across Europe. One statistic captures the huge change perhaps since the early 1950s: in 1950 106,000 people travelled on the Dublin–London route, whereas by 1998 this had risen to 4,071,000, a fortyfold increase.

All of this facilitated business, but much more important was foreign travel for leisure purposes. In the past, time for leisure was minimal and it really was only in the twentieth century that the concept of leisure time and its use became prominent. This was brought about by the large decrease in annual working hours and the introduction of fixed work schedules. This in turn facilitated the separation of work time and leisure time like never before for the vast majority of the population.

Prior to this, favoured amusements were dancing, singing and chatting, which were largely free. Other venues especially in Ireland such as pubs and dance halls were also popular prior to this, but the advent of the café came much later in Ireland than in many parts of Europe. The invention of the motion picture allowed a large audience to enjoy collectively a common experience: independent cinema buildings were constructed, films became longer, and their quality also improved. The number of cinema-goers increased quite dramatically, across all social classes. Cinemas screened primarily for entertainment but there were also newsreels. They also had a social impact in that they represented often idealised female roles. Couples also frequently watched films together, and thus the appearance of women in public entertainment venues increased and became more accepted, arising in this case simply from increased leisure time.

The first telephone exchange in Ireland was opened in Dublin in 1880. By the end of the First World War there were more than 12,000 subscribers' lines, of which half were in Dublin. Even by 1949 very few households possessed a telephone: there were still

31 A. Horner, 'The Tiger stirring: aspects of commuting in the Republic of Ireland 1981–96', *Irish Geography*, 32 (1999); N. Commins and A. Nolan, 'Car ownership and mode of transport to work in Ireland', *Economic and Social Review*, 41 (2010); L. J. K. Setright, *Drive on: a social history of the motor car* (London, 2002); A Reynolds-Feighan, 'Accessibility, transportation, infrastructure planning and Irish regional policy: issues and dilemmas', in E. O'Leary (ed.), *Irish regional development: a new agenda* (Dublin, 2003).

only fewer than 15,000 residential exchange lines, of which half were in Dublin. Many were manual, requiring operator assistance even for a local call. By 1997 the picture had changed dramatically. There were almost one and a half million exchange lines. Add to this the huge increase in mobile phone usage since then, plus the use of the internet for communication, and one senses the reality of the major communication changes of the past half-century.

Part of this of course was due not just to the telephone and the internet but also radio and TV. One of the biggest stations setting the international standard in radio and TV was the British Broadcasting Corporation (BBC), which was granted a broadcast monopoly in Britain in 1922. Regular radio broadcasting began in Dublin on New Year's Day 1926, and by 1949 about three-quarters of the population had coverage. In 1947 there were only seven hours of broadcasting a day. Today there are multiple Irish radio stations broadcasting around the clock, with access through the internet to thousands of radio stations across the world.

The first experimental television transmissions were launched as early as 1936 in London. Television, like the radio earlier, reached the masses first in Britain, where regular broadcasting was introduced in 1946. Television was seen in the Republic of Ireland for the first time in 1951. During the 1950s the expanding BBC service spread across Northern Ireland, a service that could be picked up in the south on the east coast and in the border counties. Irish TV started transmission on a snowy New Year's Eve in 1961. TV ownership grew rapidly after this and by 1966 more than half of all homes had a black and white TV set, providing more depth to the public sphere in the political domain, extending an important new medium for advertising and offering competing exposure between Anglo-American and indigenous productions. Today of course almost every house has at least one TV set, plus a range of computer devices, many with access to hundreds of TV channels.

There were quite dramatic changes also in shopping and eating patterns over the century, to the extent that shopping in itself has become a major leisure activity. Retailing began to move away from the labour-intensive Victorian model whereby each customer was personally served; the forty-one supermarkets in Ireland by 1966 had at that point cornered less than 7 per cent of total food and drink sales, but this rose rapidly to almost 41 per cent by 1987, leading to a dramatic displacement of traditional grocery stores; by 1998 multiple supermarkets accounted for 56 per cent of all grocery sales and in Dublin the figure rose to 81 per cent.[32] The expansion of supermarkets, department stores and subsequently shopping malls brought greater convenience in terms of access and customer parking and significant economies of scale which kept operational costs low. Concentration reached other sectors as well in the 1980s, such as furniture

32 A. Bielenberg and R. Ryan, *An economic history of Ireland since independence* (London, 2013), 106–10.

and interior decoration, DIY (do-it-yourself) products and construction material, electronic appliances, and stationery. From this point onwards a number of British chains entered the Irish market.

From the mid-1980s, shopping centres, planned in detail, also started to appear on the outskirts of Irish cities, typically, offering other services related to free-time activities, such as cinemas, restaurants and fitness centres. There was also over the past thirty years the internationalisation of business and hence greater consumer choice. Examples of this include IKEA, the Swedish chain, and the German low-budget supermarket chains, Aldi and Lidl, which are steadily increasing their market share.

The range of foods available increased enormously, reflecting rising incomes but also the internationalisation of food production. From very basic diets, people in Ireland now consume a rich and varied diet, with obesity – an almost unheard of problem just forty years ago – now a major health issue. Even sixty years ago few people ate meals out in restaurants and/or hotels, whereas today around 30 per cent of all meals are eaten out.[33] Moreover, much of the food eaten at home is processed and/or ready-made, the advent of the microwave facilitating this development of course. Another explanation for this might be the huge rise in the proportion of women entering the labour force, a trend that was particularly marked in the twenty years up to 2007. It is somewhat ironic that, given the huge prominence of starvation following the Great Famine and the subsequent concern with getting enough food to live even up to fifty years ago, the concern now is with food quality, food safety and excess food intake.

12.4. Conclusion

The marked rise in incomes, new technologies and rising productivity have been the major factors which have improved living conditions in Ireland between the mid-eighteenth century and the present. These improvements were fairly limited for the bulk of the population down to the mid-nineteenth century, but they accelerated somewhat thereafter as average Irish wage levels began to achieve partial convergence with the rest of the UK; basic living conditions such as housing improved dramatically between the 1850s and the First World War and diet became more varied, while a wider choice of clothing and other consumer goods became more readily available to the general population. Despite surviving pockets of poverty in the cities and in rural Ireland, notably in the Congested Districts, living conditions on average experienced a marked improvement between 1850 and 1914, while state and local authority expenditures also began to have some impact in spheres such as education, health and from 1908 the

---

33 See A. Matthews, 'The agri-food sector', in J. O'Hagan and C. Newman (eds.), *The economy of Ireland* (Dublin, 2014).

old age pension. Yet for all these improvements, food still dominated the expenditure profile in most household budgets.

The impact of state intervention on living conditions, both north and south of the border following partition, became increasingly more marked between the 1930s and the 1980s, notably in housing, health, education and transport services. Household consumption accelerated particularly in the 1960s as car usage, white goods and televisions became commonplace, but the general rise of household incomes and consumption was even more marked between the early 1990s and 2007 as the labour force in the Republic of Ireland experienced unprecedented expansion and this led to a transformation of the retail landscape. This rise has shifted consumption patterns for the average household away from a primary focus on the basic necessities, notably food, to a far wider range of consumer items.

If major improvements in the provision of basic necessities such as housing, diet and health provision have increased life expectancy since 1750, the limited geographical horizons for most of the population have also been dramatically widened. A host of new communication technologies have increased and intensified the exchange of goods and services globally, with people now travelling substantial distances to work, to shop and for leisure. All this has not made life necessarily more meaningful than in the mid-eighteenth century, but it has dramatically improved living conditions.

FURTHER READING

Barnard, T. *A guide to the sources for the history of material culture in Ireland 1500–2000* (Dublin, 2005).

Barnard, T. *A new anatomy of Ireland: the Irish Protestants, 1649–1770* (New Haven, 2003).

Bielenberg, A. and D. Johnson. 'The production and consumption of tobacco in Ireland', *Irish Economic and Social History*, 25 (1998).

Clarkson, L. and E. M. Crawford. *Feast and famine: food and nutrition in Ireland 1500–1920* (Oxford, 2001).

Clear, C. *Women of the house: women's household work in Ireland 1922–1961* (Dublin, 2000).

Costello, P. and T. Farmar. *The very heart of the city: the story of Denis Guiney and Cleary's* (Dublin, 1992).

Cronin, D., J. Gilligan and K. Holton (eds.). *Irish fairs and markets* (Dublin, 2001).

Cullen, L. M. *Eason & Son: a history* (Dublin, 1989).

Daly, M. '"Turning on the tap"; the state, Irish women and running water', in G. Valiulus and M. O'Dowd (eds.), *Women and Irish history* (Dublin, 1997).

Findlater, A. *Findlaters: the story of a Dublin merchant family 1774–2001* (Dublin, 2001).

Foster, S. '"Ornament and splendour"; shops and shopping in Georgian Dublin', *Irish Architectural and Decorative Studies*, 15 (2012).

Hill, J. and C. Lennon (eds.). *Luxury and austerity* (Dublin, 1999).

Kinmouth, C. *Irish country furniture 1700–1950* (New Haven, 1993).

Lambe, M. 'At the cross: a shop in rural Ireland, 1880–1911', in D. Cronin, J. Gilligan and K. Holton (eds.), *Irish fairs and markets* (Dublin, 2001).

Lysaght, P. '"When I makes tea, I makes tea": innovation in food – the case of tea in Ireland', *Ulster Folklife*, 33 (1987).

Orser, C.E. *Unearthing hidden Ireland: historical archaeology at Ballykilcline, County Roscommon* (Bray, 2006).

Powell, M. J. *The politics of consumption in eighteenth century Ireland* (Basingstoke, 2005).

Rains, S. *Commodity culture and social class in Dublin 1850–1916* (Dublin, 2010).

Savage, R. J. *A loss of innocence? Television and Irish society 1960–72* (Manchester, 2010).

Shiel, M. *The quiet revolution: the electrification of rural Ireland 1946–1976* (Dublin, 1984).

Tomka, B. *A social history of twentieth-century Europe* (London, 2013).

Walsh, B. *When the shopping was good: Woolworths and the Irish main street* (Dublin, 2010).

13 Housing in Ireland, 1740–2016

Ellen Rowley

13.1. Introduction

Housing could be described as the architecture of ordinary life: 'home' touches all lives in some way, creeping from the personal into officialdom and public discourse. In the period from 1740, the locations, standards and style of housing inevitably changed and this chapter attempts to chart those changes. As a history of housing by its most inclusive definition – that is, social and so-called working-class housing, as well as housing for the middle classes; urban and rural, suburban and exurban housing – this chapter considers the physical frameworks for domestic life in Ireland over 270 years, effectively becoming a history of Ireland's 'middle landscape'.[1] Generally the study takes a formal approach – where built fabric becomes the text – and as such, it brings in research from historical and cultural geography; from architectural history; from folklore studies and archaeology; and from social and material culture history. A key source (and approach) is the Royal Irish Academy's 2011 annual proceedings, where the editors tackled a single theme for the first time, in this case 'the domestic', embracing an interdisciplinary narrative and an extensive chronology (from Neolithic settlements to Celtic Tiger house extensions).[2] The other important single source was the multi-authored volume IV of *Art and architecture of Ireland*, entitled *Architecture 1600–2000* where housing is considered not in opposition to the 'Big House' (see Chapter 10, above), but rather alongside that canon, and often, as its by-product. Volume IV's comprehensive approach, grappling with the built environment in all its

1 The term 'middle landscape' comes from P. Rowe, *Making a middle landscape* (Cambridge, MA, 1991).
2 E. Fitzpatrick and J. Kelly (eds.), *Domestic life in Ireland*, Proceedings of the Royal Irish Academy, Section C, vol. III, 2011 (Dublin: 2012).

complexities, not as a passive backdrop but as an active protagonist in social history, made for a pioneering inclusive architectural history of Ireland across centuries and borders, in which housing plays a central role.[3]

Underpinning our present chapter is the reality that during the period, 1740–2016, housing became an important instrument in public health and social policy. By the 1920s when the Irish Free State and Northern Ireland were established, the provision of labourers' cottages and better housing for city workers were seen as the means of counteracting social agitation and as a key tool in public health reform. In 1950, Taoiseach John Costello stated, 'The best way we can insure [*sic*] that each person is a good citizen is to give everyone a stake in the country and the way in which we can do that is to give him his own home.'[4]

The issue of housing had become entrenched in Irish politics from 1887, when government funding was provided to support the construction of cottages for rural labourers, as part of a wider process of land reform. Legislation providing for slum clearance and working-class housing in cities and larger towns, such as the Artisans' Dwellings Acts and Housing of the Working Classes Acts (1851–94) followed the model of British legislation. The first specific legislation for Irish city housing was the Clancy Act in 1908, the first time that urban working-class housing could be subsidised, though the subsidy was tiny. By 1914 although Dublin Corporation could claim to have provided housing for a higher proportion of citizens than any city in the United Kingdom, conditions in Dublin were much worse than in any British or, indeed, western European city. While a government inquiry blamed the influence of slum landlords over the city council, the appalling housing standards were a reflection of poverty – the poverty of the slum dwellers and of local authorities whose rateable valuation could not support the loans required to build the volume of houses that were needed. [5] Whether they lived in cities or in the countryside, the majority of Ireland's population inhabited insanitary or insubstantial homes during the eighteenth, nineteenth and into the early decades of the twentieth century. The 1841 census revealed that 40 per cent of the country's total housing stock comprised two- to four-roomed dwellings, of which there were 470,000 recorded. Differentiation was made between tenant farmer and landless labourer. The latter's domain, known variously as hut, cabin or hovel, the most modest housing typology in Irish history, accounted for more than one-third of the housing stock. The vernacular farmhouse, of one or two storeys and of more permanent materials such as stone and thatch, has been the singular enduring image on the Irish landscape.

3 R. Loeber, H. Campbell, L. Hurley, J. Montague and E. Rowley (eds.), *Art and architecture of Ireland, vol. IV: Architecture 1600–2000* (Dublin, 2014).
4 Costello speech (1950) cited in M. Daly, *The buffer state: the historical roots of the Department of the Environment* (Dublin, 1997), 348.
5 P. J. Meghen, *Housing in Ireland* (Dublin, 1963), 5–12.

13.2. From Cabins to Philanthropic Estates

The cabin, or *creaght* (in Ulster, meaning timber framework), was usually a windowless single-storey space, erected using mud, turf or wattle walls, depending on location, plastered with cow dung and with a timber structure of sorts. Cabins consisted of one rectangular room; some contained a loft or a space for animals. As Roche's research shows, these were the dwellings of the poorest peasantry and while pervasive, their built fabric barely survives; histories of cabins come from travellers' observations and artists' sketches.[6] It would seem that ribbon developments of cabins occurred along particular roadsides, where labourers built their houses using the sides of a ditch as the home's walls.[7] Many such accounts capture the squalid living conditions which these homes, in many cases underground dens partly excavated out of bog land, presented

Figure 13.1 Roadside cottage, Glencolumbkill, Co. Donegal, nineteenth century. Image courtesy of Deputy Keeper of the Records, Public Record Office of Northern Ireland, D/1403/2/24/A.

6 The most important sketches and descriptions of eighteenth-century rural Ireland come from *Arthur Young's tour in Ireland* (London, 1892).

7 For example, see de Latocnaye's account in *A Frenchman's walk through Ireland, 1796–7* (Belfast, 1984), 42, cited by N. Roche, 'The forgotten building type: examining contemporary notices of the Irish cabin' (unpublished paper, 2003). I am indebted to Roche's exhaustive research in the area of cabin architecture and history; see Roche, 'A contemptible habitation', in T. Reeves-Smith and R. Oram (eds.), *Avenues to the past* (Belfast, 2003), 235–52.

their occupants.[8] With earthen floors, no chimney or window, no separation of accommodation and little furniture, Irish cabins signalled the most rudimentary of dwellings. Fires were lit in the centre of the space with smoke notionally escaping through the entrance doorway. The atmosphere must have been damp and heavy, with no references to personal hygiene or domestic technology applicable.

With the condescension then typical of the 'improving' European metropolitan elite contemplating 'primitive' peasant culture, the Lord Chief Justice Edward Willes revealed an Orientalist attitude to the labourers and their cabins, in his 1760s letters: 'the cabins in the rough part of the mountains I apprehend ... much like the Indian huts, and I presume the inhabitants not much better.'[9] The primal nature of the dwelling clearly lent a primal air to the inhabitant! The poor quality of labourer cabins reflects both the poverty of the dwellers – labourers built their own cabins – and the fact that labourers often moved in search of work, or when the rent of their potato garden was increased. The appearance and disappearance of these cabins reflected the vagaries of Irish agricultural processes: population change, and estate and farm management. With the Great Famine of 1845–9 (see Chapter 3, above), thousands of cabin dwellers died or emigrated. Government loans for the construction of labourers' cottages from the 1880s, and a dedicated programme by the Congested Districts Board, which erected new cottages and provided grants for the construction of outhouses, brought major improvements in rural housing. Nevertheless, as late as 1938, a Limerick labourer applying to the government for a new cottage described his current home as a mud cabin with a roof of sheet iron in which he, his wife and their eight children lived.[10] Clearly, the typology persisted.

Tenant farmers with more than twenty acres lived in more solid structures, the cottage or vernacular farmhouse. The form of vernacular farmhouses has been examined since the earliest studies of Irish rural life, when analysis of built fabric sought to understand lifestyle patterns and standards.[11] Although scholars have highlighted regional differences, certain traits – such as two low-lying entrances with a half-door placed at either end of the long main facade, rectangular and one-room deep plans divided into two to four rooms forming 'long houses', single chimneys (the hearth) placed near one entrance, and a projecting bed pod or 'outshot', thought to be for the married couple – were common to most regions. Stone walls, whitewashed externally

8 See Thomas Reid's description of cabin form in *Travels in Ireland* (1823), cited in A. Hadfield and J. McVeagh (eds.), *Strangers to the land* (Gerrards Cross, 1994).

9 J. Kelly (ed.), *The letters of Lord Chief Baron Edward Willes to the Earl of Warwick, 1757–1762* (Aberystwyth, 1990), 39.

10 John O'Donoghue, 5 March 1938, box 540, DLGPH, NAI, cited in A. M. Walsh, 'Cottage schemes for agricultural labourers', in J. Augusteijn (ed.), *Ireland in the 1930s* (Dublin, 1999), 56.

11 See studies by Ake Campbell, Alan Gailey and Kevin Danagher. For the best recent overview of vernacular houses, see 'Houses' in F. H. A. Aalen, K. Whelan and M. Stout (eds.), *Atlas of the Irish rural landscape* (Cork, 2011).

and mud-plastered (and lime-washed) internally, surmounted by thatched roofs, and punctuated by a small window or two, complete the physical picture of the Irish farmhouse or cottage.

Many larger farmhouses were of one and a half or two storeys, with animal accommodation and hay/grain storage facilitated beyond the dwelling, in ancillary farm buildings. Loeber cites the example of many such houses in County Wexford sporting timber fittings taken from shipwrecks. He outlines how the courtyards, gateways and ancillary structures to these vernacular houses contribute considerably to the Irish landscape, and how over generations, with the replacement of thatch by slate roofs, the two-storey farmhouse became the singular domestic building in Ireland.[12] That prismatic form of rectilinear mass and pitched roof endured through Irish housing history, influencing the geographies and physiognomy of mid-twentieth-century suburbanisation.

Most farmhouses were built by the tenant farmer, though landlords might supply timber, stone and other materials, From 1740 to the 1870s, a so-called 'enlightened' period was marked by research into agriculture and industrial methods, propounding new ideas around the links between productivity, better infrastructure and improved living conditions for the workers. From the 1750s, pattern books of designs for these new housing environments emerged. There were many examples of landlords erecting new houses and redeveloping villages and towns, sometimes in the hope of attracting new enterprises to their estate. Landowners who built substantial tenant housing included the Earls of Lansdowne (Kerry, Laois) and Clancarty (Galway), and the Dukes of Devonshire (Waterford) and Leinster (Kildare). In most cases, landlords sponsored the erection of terraces of one-storey symmetrical houses, predominantly stone with slate roofs. The primary innovation from the dwellers' perspective was newfound domestic comfort derived from dry and relatively smoke-free living spaces, and the separation of accommodation, often through the addition of a second storey which would become sleeping rooms. The other change for inhabitants was increased cost, owing to higher rent or personal investment where landlords encouraged tenants to build their dwelling. The Dwellings for Labouring Classes (Ireland) Act (1860) enabled landlords to obtain public loans for cottage building. As a collective of housing, designed rather than self-built, new repetitive estate cottages were planned, signalling a departure from vernacular building traditions.

Tellingly, studies of ordinary housing from 1740 through the nineteenth century tend to focus on the squalor of slum conditions, or overstate the housing utopias presented by improvement schemes. In truth, the improvement schemes were in the minority, but they were so marked, especially the planned villages of industrial enterprises, that they attracted attention. As Graham and Proudfoot outline, housing within village

12 R. Loeber, 'Vernacular farmhouses', in Loeber *et al., Architecture 1600–2000*, 332–5.

improvement schemes makes up one repetitive part in a triad of landscape artefacts – demesne, Big House, village – which represented the elite's ordered worldview during the eighteenth and early nineteenth century: new housing was a central symbol or talisman through which the landlord constructed his geography.[13]

Waterford's Portlaw, a model village – constructed in two phases (1830s/1860s) – of various workers' housing types, is an important example which was developed from the most successful cotton factory in nineteenth-century Ireland (1820s–1870s) – owned by the Quaker industrialist David Malcomson. Malcomson related workers' housing to both his factory's success and the overall order of Portlaw. The housing was a means of accommodating an industrial workforce, as an extension of the productivity of the factory but according to the healthy and idealised conditions of nineteenth-century reform. Interestingly, the tarmacadam barrel or curved roof form of the single-storey cottages on Portlaw's main street was adopted, probably due to its relative cheapness, in two other instances of philanthropic industrial housing schemes – at Bessbrook, County Armagh (1840s) and at Pim's Cottages, Harold's Cross, Dublin (1864).[14] Examples of estate improvement housing abound. Like the collective of thatched cottages flanking the Earl of Dunraven's main street at Adare, County Limerick (1820–1840s), such housing was part aesthetic – a public relations exercise – and part social infrastructure, at once efficient and nostalgic, folkloric and functional.

From the 1840s with the growing emphasis on environmental causes of fevers and epidemic disease, improvements in housing were associated with advances in public health. With the publication of the report of the Royal Commission on the Housing of the Working Classes in 1885, and various legislative developments from 1866 and 1875 (the Artisans and Labourers Dwellings Improvement (Cross) Act), as well as the establishment of the Dublin Sanitary Association in 1872, a campaign to eradicate insanitary accommodation, rural and urban, began throughout Ireland. Local councils were encouraged to clear squalid housing and to lease those sites to voluntary and joint-stock agencies, which would erect modern housing. From the 1870s, companies like the Thomond Artisans' Dwellings Company in Limerick and the Improved Dwellings Company in Cork emerged, all meeting a demand which the local authorities were financially and initially legally constrained from undertaking. Through their general provision of comfortable and healthy houses, built by good builders, these schemes became precedents for later public housing projects.

Almost as a hybrid of the dwelling company and the model village, industrialist-sponsored urban housing estates developed at the end of the nineteenth century:

---

13 B. Graham and L. Proudfoot, *Urban improvement in provincial Ireland 1700 – 1880*, Irish settlement studies 4 (Athlone, 1994), 36.

14 L. Hurley and K. Whelan, 'Planning of towns and villages from the seventeenth to the nineteenth century', in Loeber *et al.*, *Architecture 1600–2000*, 397.

rent-subsidised homes which were built to the highest technological and accommodation standards and sited close to the centre of employment, for those regular employees or artisans. In Dublin, complexes of cottages or multi-storey blocks were provided by railway and tram companies and by family-run industries such as Pims and the Guinness brewery.[15] Taking the example of American banker George Peabody (Peabody Trust, 1862) in London, Cecil Guinness set up a housing trust in 1890 (Iveagh Trust from 1903). In the 1860s and 1880s, in collaboration with the Dublin Artisan Dwelling Company (DADCo.), the Guinness family built employee housing near its Dublin brewing complex. With the Iveagh Trust, they constructed exemplary flats (c.250 units by 1915, 214 upgraded units by 2016) in eight five-storeyed blocks at Bull Alley, Dublin from 1899, to the designs of London's Smithem and Joseph (with Kaye-Parry and Ross, Dublin). Architecturally sophisticated and inhabited to the present day – albeit the flats have been adapted for bathrooms and more – the Bull Alley project was also sociologically significant. Ancillary services comprising a community centre, swimming pool, market, shop units and homeless hostel created a ready-made urban community, with healthful housing occupying centre-stage. Each flat contained well-lit living and sleeping spaces, with a small scullery; thereafter washing and cooking facilities were communal.

Figure 13.2 Flat interior, Iveagh Trust housing, Bull Alley, 1899–1906. Photograph by Paul Tierney. Credit, Dublin City Council 20th-Century Dublin Architecture project, 2011– ongoing.

15 F. H. A Aalen, *The Iveagh Trust: the first hundred years, 1890–1990* (Dublin, 1990); L. King, 'Progressive housing: the role of two industrial families in the development of philanthropic architecture in Dublin', NCAD, unpublished thesis, 1994.

Ultimately, the housing companies were commercial entities seeking a modest return on capital. The rents charged and company regulations meant that only artisans or labourers in secure jobs were accepted as tenants; families displaced to make way for these houses invariably moved into other slum properties. Despite the best efforts of these housing companies, and employers who provided housing, Irish cities, other than Belfast, remained notorious for insanitary housing. Slum conditions in Cork and Dublin came less from industrialisation and more from a large workforce of irregularly employed and unskilled labourers.[16] While government housing programmes were in place from the 1870s, Dublin and Cork corporations were unable to fund more than piecemeal programmes. In Waterford, despite a high death rate of 42 per 1,000 due in large part to poor housing, the population was too small to qualify for the Cross Act (1875) government loans.[17] Despite this, as Fraser outlines, Waterford was the first authority to build local authority houses.

13.3.   Leitmotifs: Hearth, Parlour, Terrace, Bungalow

Consider the material culture of Irish domestic life. With all traditional Irish housing, the hearth becomes the house's centre, if not physically then symbolically. As a large recessed fireplace under a timber canopy, it was the site for sociability, dominating the main living space. With its crane from which a kettle and pot might hang, the hearth was used for cooking. Hearth and kitchen were bound together. As O'Reilly explains, into the nineteenth century, the kitchen hearth was the space where families not only cooked, washed and heated the house but slept and socialised.[18] The kitchen–hearth conflation led to their unrivalled importance within the traditional house's function-ality, threading through the life of the modern planned house in twentieth-century Ireland; as Gailey summarises, 'a social history of Irish housing might be constructed solely around the kitchen'.[19]

In reaction to rural electrification, a 1956 article in the Irish Countrywomen's Association (ICA) journal called for the preservation of the kitchen hearth as the sanctum of Irish life, warning against the 'danger that these centres of Irish fam-ily life will become replicas of their counterparts in America and England with their glistening gadgets and clinical air'.[20] The ICA commentator lamented the departure of the settle bed and the dresser, both of which were key examples of Irish domestic

---

16 F. Cullen, 'The provision of working and lower middle class housing in urban Ireland', in E. Fitzpatrick and J. Kelly (eds.), *Domestic life in Ireland, special issue of Proceedings of the Royal Irish Academy, Section C*, 111 (2011).
17 Ibid., 243.
18 B. O' Reilly, 'Hearth and home: the vernacular house in Ireland from *c*.1800', in Fitzpatrick and Kelly, *Domestic life in Ireland*.
19 A. Gailey, *Rural houses of the north of Ireland* (Edinburgh, 1984), 211.
20 E. Casey, 'Farm-house kitchens', *ICA, Our Book* (1956), 39.

multi-functionalism. A settle bed was generally pulled out as nightly sleeping quarters and remade into a bench for daytime use. St Brigid crosses, handlooms, wooden butter churns, wooden washtubs, brick bread ovens, along with a table placed against the wall and shelves in recesses, were customarily all the furniture and technology that the traditional Irish household used. As a result of this paucity, the dresser played a major role in the Irish house interior. According to Kinmouth, dressers were popularised during the nineteenth century with the mass production of china, and were used to store kitchen utensils, while also accommodating chickens and geese away from predators in their lower sections.[21] There was never a notable practice of Irish vernacular furniture making, due in part to deforestation and a consequent shortage of timber in Ireland, but also, plainly, as a result of economic poverty. Whitelaw's 1798 account of Dublin describes furniture-less homes where the inhabitants slept on floors 'swarming with vermin, and without any covering'.[22] In Belfast of 1853, Revd O'Hanlon recorded dens 'of darkness and squalor', encountering 'a woman sitting upon a bundle of straw, without a particle of furniture, and amidst a scene of desolation'.[23] Later depictions do not improve: Cooke's chilling photographs of 1913–14 (part of the Dublin Housing Enquiry) portray dark interior after dank room, with little or no furniture,[24] while recent excavations in Dublin's Monto area unearthed samples of 'tenement china' in the form of tin-cans and other sundry items, highlighting the dearth of material from this part of Irish social history.[25] Somewhat less impoverished depictions coming from Sean O'Casey plays/scene notes emphasise the copies of religious paintings ('holy pictures') and statues sitting on mantels, and suggest a more aspirational domestic space.

Cottage interiors contrasted sharply with those of the middle-class professional where two or three reception rooms, a large tiled kitchen (with serving areas of pantry and cloakroom), and four or five upstairs bedrooms were richly furnished. Heavy wallpapers, dark colours and opulent fabrics, lit by oil-fuelled (and from the 1850s, paraffin) lamps, adorned Ireland's middle-class homes through the nineteenth century. Somewhere between the furniture-less spaces of congested tenement areas or rural cabins, and the overstuffed Victorian red-brick domains in new leafy suburbs, sat the artisan dwelling with its signature parlour space. Mostly the artisan dwelling contained four rooms and a backyard, with the parlour occupying the front room,

---

21 C. Kinmouth, *Irish country furniture 1700–1950* (London, 1993).

22 J. Whitelaw, *An essay on the population of Dublin being the result of an actual survey taken in 1798* (Dublin, 1805), 51.

23 W. M. O'Hanlon, *Walks among the poor of Belfast* (Belfast, 1853), 8.

24 John Cooke's photographs, collection of Royal Society of Antiquaries of Ireland, reprinted in C. Corlett (ed.), *Darkest Dublin: the story of the Church Street disaster* (Dublin, 2008).

25 'Digging the Monto', 2011/2012, Heritage Council of Ireland + Dublin City Council Art Office, available at www.heritagecouncil.ie/education/projects-weve-funded/digging-the-monto-the-1913-lockout/, accessed 10 August 2016.

Figure 13.3 Tenement room interior, darkest Dublin. Cooke Collection, 1913. Photograph by John Cooke. Credit, Royal Society of Antiquaries of Ireland.

typically mediated by a small entrance stair hall. This 'parlour type' house plan continued through early twentieth-century housing provision, with the Department of Local
Government's 1925 housing manual describing five house-types from four-roomed
labourers' cottages to three-, four- and five-roomed suburban types, mostly with par-
lours.[26] Considering the extreme shortage of healthful housing (and the dominance of
large families) in nineteenth- and early twentieth-century Ireland, the persistence of the
extravagant parlour space was contentious. In the midst of Dublin's 1940s slum-clear-
ance programme, architect Noel Moffett observed, 'It is interesting to note that our
psychological necessity for luxury expresses itself, in low-cost housing, in the provision
of a best-parlour or holy-of-holies – a small sitting-room used only on Sunday evenings
or for entertaining special guests.'[27]

As the ordinary house in Ireland moved from self-build project to planned scheme,
the terrace became housing's key expression. Unsurprisingly, its origins were economic
where two or more cottages shared partition walls, thus becoming less expensive to
construct. The terrace was adopted for most housing developments in Irish towns and

26 Irish Ministry of Local Government, *House designs, books A–E* (Dublin, Prescribed by the Minister for Local
Government under the Housing (Building Facilities) Act, 1924).
27 N. Moffett, 'Low-cost urban housing', *Architectural Design* (July 1947, Ireland issue), 188.

cities, including suburban neighbourhoods constructed from the mid-nineteenth century until the 1950s, when semi-detached housing and detached bungalows became more common. The model for those first suburban dwellers, signalling the rise of a substantial middle class in Ireland, was the eighteenth-century townhouse. Not only was the terrace reproduced in the Dublin suburban townships, so too were the window and door arrangements of Georgian townhouses. Hickey refers to this quickly spreading type as 'mini-Georgian', where the classical proportions, the one or two storeys over basement and the respectable fanlight-above-doorway represented a miniaturisation of the Georgian terrace.[28]

Terraced housing is also a leitmotif of working-class life in Ireland. As with British industrialisation, Belfast's housing stock emerged from workforce needs: streets of low-rise red-brick terraced houses, termed 'by-law housing', were constructed through the city from 1850 onwards. In Dublin, Limerick and Cork, working-class schemes came later and were mostly constructed by artisan dwelling companies, but again, the model of choice was the low-rise terraced house. By 1910 the DADCo. counted 16,000 tenants inhabiting its 3,500 units – the majority in terraced cottages, two- or one-storeyed. Despite DADCo.'s early foray into flat block construction, the company soon realised that the single-family unit was more popular and profitable.

Figure 13.4 Street view of Dublin Artisan Dwelling Company estate, Stoneybatter, Dublin, 1901–8. Photograph by Paul Tierney. Credit, Dublin City Council 20th-Century Dublin Architecture project, 2011– ongoing.

28 G. Hickey, 'Suburbs and terraces in the nineteenth century', in Loeber *et al., Architecture 1600–2000*, 429.

Its many terraces characterise extensive areas of Dublin and arguably, designs and materials influenced local authorities and other house builders through the twentieth century. Certainly the well-built terrace of modest homes, constructed out of fine local materials, uniform but allowing an element of elevation variation, was an exemplar for T. J. Byrne's Arts-and-Crafts cottages (1910s, South Dublin Rural District Council) at Rathfarnham and Chapelizod, or for Dublin Corporation's Ormond Market scheme of 128 mixed units (1917–21, C. J. MacCarthy). As the mass-housing programme escalated from the 1930s through the 1950s, and local authorities built to aggressive political deadlines, the terrace was the means: economy of repetitive and shared structures, and preference for single-family homes ensured terraced housing's primacy.

In apparent contradiction to the terrace, the bungalow stands as another leitmotif of Irish housing. Where the terrace house reflects the collective, the bungalow represents individual endeavour. Commonly found in rural Ireland or on the outskirts of provincial towns, these are one-off houses whose spread and formulaic design have led to nicknames like 'bungalow blitz' and 'McBungalow'. Typologically, the bungalow is a combination of vernacular cottage and 'Big House'; the latter is a colonial Irish equivalent of the villa, with aspects of its classical form being replicated both in larger farmhouses from the late eighteenth century and in mid-nineteenth-century suburban villas. The bungalow is a disencumbered, residential building, set into its own differentiated landscape, on to which social status was inscribed. The last decades of the twentieth century, following the publication of the Department of Local Government's house plans (1960s) and Jack Fitzsimons's pattern book *Bungalow bliss* (1971 onwards), witnessed increasing numbers of large dormer-bungalow houses, sitting atop rural sites parallel to principal roads and sporting variously decadent porches and large picture windows. With their proliferation in areas of natural rural beauty, they are cited as Ireland's greatest post-1970s planning blight, stimulating journalistic polemics and reactionary architectural research.[29] MacNamara examines how a dissociated urban middle class dismisses bungalows as products of aesthetic impoverishment – as kitsch housing writ large on the Irish landscape.[30]

The bungalow is *the* house form of the Irish countryside and is wrapped up in national narratives of a pre-modern, idealised rural Ireland – signifier of nostalgia, land and landscape ownership. Historically, the bungalow can be read as a form of state-sponsored social housing for the rural context, beginning in the 1930s with grants and subsidies for one-off houses which developed, according to Boyd, as a reconciliation of a 'prevailing mid-century ideology of a bucolic Ireland of small-holdings and "cosy

---

29 See F. McDonald, 'Bungalow blitz', *Irish Times*, 12–14 September 1987; S. O'Toole (ed.), *SubUrban to super rural* (Venice, 2006).

30 A. MacNamara, *Bungalow blitz: another history of Irish architecture* (Alberta, 2006).

homesteads"' with the modernising industrial exigencies of the 1960s.[31] Boyd points to those pattern books in which government ministers wrote forewords, asserting that the bungalow was a state tool in the twentieth-century battle against rural depopulation.

13.4.   Twentieth-Century Housing: Accommodating Two States

Layered over the demographic backdrop of rural depopulation and the discourse of slum clearance is the dichotomous nature of the rural/urban and Northern Ireland/Free State housing histories. The rural/urban dichotomy was overcome by the mid-century with the suburb's ascendancy – as part-rural and part-urban site for ordinary housing. But the trajectories of housing in Northern Ireland and the Free State (the Republic, from 1949) ran pretty distinctly through the century. Where Dublin, Limerick and Cork were full of unmaintained eighteenth-century buildings, housing their populations in dire conditions (1901 census), more than 80 per cent of Belfast's housing was categorised as first and second class. The international success of local industries ensured that most of the housing stock in Ireland's northern cities was new by the 1880s. A Royal Commission (1884–5) reported that Belfast's and Derry's housing was of the highest standard in these islands; Derry's by-laws dictated that new houses in that city were of minimum space standards, incorporating a toilet.[32]

With the surplus of dwellings in the 1900s, municipal housing in the north was not a priority. Following the First World War and partition, with a shortfall in public funding from Westminster, housing provision was somewhat overlooked. With bomb damage afflicting Belfast during the Second World War, the authorities were forced to address housing again, and in 1944, a new Northern Ireland Housing Trust (NIHT) was established. From the outset, coming out of the perceived crisis of wartime bombing, the NIHT used experimental technologies of prefabricated housing, alongside traditional methods. With these innovations, ordinary housing in Northern Ireland contrasted with independent Ireland, where the latter's conservativism and wartime neutrality made for continuity in housing typologies and techniques between pre-and post-war building programmes. In the south, the pebbledash-rendered, concrete-block two-storey suburban cottage reigned supreme. Irish architectural journals published the NIHT's housing schemes as inspiration for the Republic's relatively halting endeavours. Though not as progressive or productive as the British post-war housing project, the NIHT did employ mechanised systems for two-storey concrete houses – 'Orlit', 'Easiform', 'Sectron', 'Secco'. Fleetingly, and in order to accelerate the housing programme of the

---

31 G. Boyd, 'Bungalows and one-off houses' in Loeber *et al.*, *Architecture 1600–2000*, 397.
32 Cullen, 'The provision of working and lower middle class housing', 243; S. Lappin, 'Public housing in Northern Ireland in the twentieth century', in Loeber *et al.*, *Architecture 1600–2000*, 441.

Inter-Party Government (1948–51), Dublin Corporation deployed the Orlit system on the Crumlin Estate (south-west Dublin, 1934–*c*.1960). However, complaints about bad structures and leaking roofs meant that these systems were unpopular and concrete-block construction remained the preferred means.

While flat blocks were built in both Belfast and Dublin, they were consistently undermined by lower rents and more expensive construction, by badly maintained experimental technologies, inhuman scale or unrealised ancillary services. At the end of the 1970s after decades of disappointment, despite Dublin Corporation's quite beautiful flat schemes offering one- to three-bedroomed homes in the city centre, the flat as a place for ordinary living was effectively abandoned. Dublin's and Cork's slum clearance projects following the 1931–2 housing legislation were motivated by Garden Suburb principles to undo high-density urban living, so that flats, most usually placed on brownfield urban sites, became associated with the stigma of city tenements. Flat blocks were confined to Dublin, until the small-scale experiments of Cork and Galway Corporations in the early 1970s (at Togher and Mervue). The apotheosis of flat building was Dublin's edge-city Ballymun Estate: a mix of system-built tower blocks, spine blocks and houses. Overseen by the new National Building Agency from 1965, Ballymun responded to the housing crisis of 1963 when two city-centre houses collapsed, killing four people and motivating the evacuation of 156 houses and the displacement of 520 families from central Dublin. Northern Ireland's version of this was

Figure 13.5 Marrowbone Lane flat scheme, Dublin Corporation Housing Architects, Herbert Simms, 1938–41. Photograph by Paul Tierney. Credit, Dublin City Council 20th-Century Dublin Architecture project, 2011–16.

the Divis Estate in west Belfast, where from 1966 twelve eight-storey blocks and one twenty-storey tower were built, housing Belfast's poorer Catholic population in stream-lined accommodation. At Ballymun and Divis, the concrete architecture was blamed for subsequent anti-social behaviour and both places were largely demolished – Divis in 1993 and Ballymun ongoing since 2004.

Though 50,000 units were built in Northern Ireland between 1919 and 1939, by the late 1960s housing in Northern Ireland was at a crisis juncture. The nineteenth-century housing infrastructure was fast crumbling under the weight of sectarian allocation policies. In 1969, a housing report (the Cameron Commission) led to the replacement of the NIHT with the Northern Ireland Housing Executive (1971). A more impartial approach to housing distribution emerged, as well as a slum clearance project intent upon replacing houses (and their street pattern) with new high-density schemes, set into cul-de-sac and courtyard street frameworks.[33] The primary common feature between the Republic and Northern Ireland was this preference for single-family ter-raced housing over multi-family multi-storey blocks, reinforced through the 1980s in reaction to the Divis and Ballymun high-rise schemes. In Dublin, following a hous-ing competition in 1976 for the City Quay area, a similar low-rise high-density model developed, where each household had its own front door entered from the street. With brick elevations and tiled pitched roofs, these urban terraced houses emulated the arti-san cottages of the 1900s and sought, in however tokenistic a way, to bring family life back into Ireland's cities.

With the New Towns (Northern Ireland) Act of 1965 and the Myles Wright 1967 report *The Dublin region*, the piecemeal adoption of Abercrombie-inspired, ex-urban housing policies was formalised. The right to live in an ordinary house on a plot of one's own land in a fresh-air environment was championed above all other consider-ations. Ultimately, this was an ecologically aggressive policy promoting new building on greenfield sites which persisted through Irish housing peaks in the 1930s, 1950s, 1970s and 1990s. In Northern Ireland, a 'Brave New City' planned for County Armagh, Craigavon (*c*.1965), attempted to demarcate urban and rural housing. In general, the northern housing authority prioritised urban provision, building few rural houses from 1920. Conversely, the Free State concentrated on rural housing in a bid to con-tinue the reform instigated by the 1880s Land legislation which had seen 45,000 rural dwellings constructed across Ireland between 1884 and the outbreak of the First World War.[34] House building by rural agencies like the Land Commission or Bord na Mona (est. 1946) was conflated with that by the Department of Local Government. From the

---

33 NIHE, *Brick by brick: a short history of the Northern Ireland Housing Executive 1971–1991* (Belfast, 1991); C. Brett, *Housing a divided community* (Dublin, 1986).

34 M. McCarthy, 'The provision of rural local-authority housing and domestic space: a comparative north–south study, 1942–60', in Fitzpatrick and Kelly, *Domestic life in Ireland*.

Figure 13.6 Protest against evictions, York Street, Dublin, 1964. The Wiltshire Photographic Collection. Courtesy of the National Library of Ireland.

Department's triumphalist annual *Building Construction Engineering,* we learn that the Land Commission built 3,000 houses between 1940 and 1954, and that national house building reached a new peak in 1952–3 when 13,291 houses were constructed (7,476 local authority, 5,815 private), most being suburban.[35]

Despite modernised materials (concrete, asbestos, cement, plastics), rural houses continued to be cottage-like and disencumbered: three-roomed in plan, hinged around a hearth and with little indoor plumbing for sanitary facilities. Through the Free State's 1930s rural and urban housing programme, such innovations as indoor bathrooms and fitted kitchens were markedly absent. While each of Dublin Corporation's new 1930s–1940s flats contained a cubicle toilet, the bath was under the scullery table. Philanthropic organisations such as the Civics Institute campaigned for better domestic

35 E. Rowley, 'Suburban housing estates', in Loeber *et al., Architecture 1600–2000,* 440.

facilities, holding a housing exhibition (Mansion House, Dublin, 1937), as well as spawning lobby groups like the Citizens' Housing Council and the Irish Countrywomen's Association (ICA), which in an attempt to better the lot of rural women sponsored a rural housing architectural competition, in 1944. But it was not until the late 1950s that municipal housing in the Republic began to commonly incorporate domestic technologies, democratised through national electrification, growing standards of living and the mechanised production of household goods, and it was only in the 1960s that an aggressive campaign was launched – led by the ICA – to bring running water to a majority of rural houses.

13.5. Into the Twenty-First Century

If twentieth-century housing in Ireland was largely a story of moving people from rural and city-centre homes to new suburban housing colonies, that suburbanisation process continued into the twenty-first century. The middle and end decades of the twentieth century were busy for housing, establishing patterns for the next three or more generations. This was an era of White Papers and projections – *Post-war housing* (1944), *Housing – progress and prospects* (1964), *Housing in the seventies* (1969) – ultimately manifesting in legislation such as the Housing (Amendment) Acts of 1950 and 1958, the Housing (Loans and Grants) Act (1962) and the Housing Act (1966). The most tangible shift brought housing production from state-sponsored to private development: by the 1970s, 179,011 private houses were built compared with 60,630 local authority ones;[36] crucially, during the same decade, 60,026 local authority houses were sold to tenants, entrenching the preference for home ownership in Irish society. More than half of Ireland's current (2016) rural housing was built from the 1970s onwards, and from this time an ugly corruption, emerging out of informal associations between politics and certain builders and developers, has been the salient force behind Irish housing.[37] Arguably enabled by the state's increasing disengagement from housing provision, this network operated outside official planning recommendations.[38]

Housing echoed Ireland's economic shift from agriculture to industry, and with urbanisation came unbridled suburbanisation or, by the 2000s, *ex*-urbanisation. Polycentric patterns of living where housing development has absorbed its commuter town, transforming it into an urban centre in its own right, as well as the growth in one-off non-farm houses – in 2011 there were 433,564 one-off houses – have led to the

36 T. Corcoran, 'Government policies towards public housing', *Administration*, 3 (1995), 614.
37 M. Corcoran, K. Keaveney and P. J. Duffy, 'Transformations in housing', in B. Bartley and R. Kitchin, *Understanding contemporary Ireland* (London, 2007), 250.
38 P. Kenna, *Housing law, rights and policy* (Dublin, 2006), 48–9.

term 'rurbanisation' being applied to the landscape of twenty-first-century Ireland.[39] Ireland's ordinary housing is shuddering from the effects of environmental reckless-ness after decades of irresponsible housing-estate construction on floodplains and the build-up of pollution from one-off houses' septic tanks. On the flip side to Ireland's remarkable (in EU terms) *laissez-faire* rural planning, attention was belatedly turned to urban renewal through tax incentives offered by the 1986 Urban Renewal Act. This changed the character of Ireland's recent housing stock through the proliferation of multi-storey apartment blocks. Aside from thoughtful examples in Dublin's Temple Bar (Green Building (Murray O'Laoire, 1991) or Tall Building (De Blacam and Meagher, 2000)), Dublin's docklands and the successful warehouse conversions at Galway's docks, for instance, apartment building during the 1990s and early 2000s in Irish cities produced yet more 'bad' residential architecture. Developer- and investor-led, these apartments were organised like hotel spaces off long windowless corridors; having little storage, bad insulation and small rooms, they never became family homes. However, they did reintroduce significant residential communities into Ireland's urban centres and by 2011, the census recorded 122,587 purpose-built apartments.

Figure 13.7 Speculative apartment building, Dublin City centre, 1990s. Photograph and credit, Paul Tierney 2015.

39 CSO, 'The roof over our heads' (2012), www.cso.ie/en/media/csoie/census/documents/census2011profile4/Profile_4_The_Roof_over_our_Heads_Full_doc_sigamended.pdf, accessed July 2015; P. Collier, 'Ireland's rurban horizon: new identities from home development markets in rural Ireland', *Irish Journal of Sociology*, 13, 1 (2004), 88–108.

While housing was responding to market forces and the role of the state in housing provision was diminishing at the turn of the century, the need for social housing did not disappear; if anything, with the precarious property bubble created by uncontrolled market forces from the mid-1990s to *c.*2008, social housing need increased. In 2007, there were almost 50,000 people waiting for social housing. When record numbers of private houses were completed in 2004, social housing construction fell from 13,000 to 12,145 units.[40] Social housing (i.e. state tenancy) has been considered the inferior option and while the agencies involved have sought new design and tenancy solutions alike from duplex and urban cottage estates to affordable purchase schemes, state housing was always associated with poverty. Mirroring this tendency, the average price of a new house jumped from €72,732 in 1994 to €249,191 in 2004.[41] With such amazing statistics as a 243 per cent increase over ten years (!), the house had become a commodity, to generate wealth through trading. It is not surprising that in 2008 the bubble burst and Irish housing was in crisis. The crisis's physical manifestations were the unfinished and abandoned housing schemes or ghost estates, of which there were 2,846 in 2010. Of those, 180 were identified as completely abandoned by developers (2011), and while most were in hinterlands of major cities, there were many in counties Mayo and Donegal (likely linked to holiday accommodation) and alarmingly, despite its small population, County Leitrim had thirteen abandoned dangerous estates.[42]

Ghost estate inhabitants, with their exposure to open pits and no public lighting, are the latest group to join the list of unsatisfactorily housed people in Ireland: a list traditionally made up of newly weds, elderly and disabled people, TB sufferers, agricultural labourers, Gaeltacht natives and, since the Housing Act (1988), travellers.[43] The consistent problem with Ireland's housing, especially post-independence, has been the conception of a housing system as composed of physical units of housing alone, what Patrick Abercrombie warned Irish architects against in 1922: to put 'a valuable jewel into an ill-designed setting'.[44] The lack of accompanying social infrastructure, coupled with the more intangible condition of the ever-increasing rise in living standards, especially from the 1950s, and falling household size, has undermined both public and private housing development in modern Ireland. However, we do not reflect enough on the material improvements coming with each generation. One

40 *Irish Times*, 12 July 2005, cited in Corcoran *et al.*, 'Transformations in housing', 253.
41 P. J. Drudy and M. Punch, *Out of reach: inequalities in the Irish housing system* (Dublin, 2005), 11.
42 R. McManus, 'Celtic Tiger housing', in Aalen *et al.*, *Atlas of the Irish rural landscape*, 160–1.
43 Kenna, *Housing law, rights and policy*, 52.
44 P. Abercrombie *et al.*, *Dublin of the future* (Dublin, 1922), 27.

Figure 13.8 Ghost estate housing, Co. Tipperary, Photograph and Credit, Paul Tierney 2015

example from the 2011 census reminds us that the average number of persons per room in an Irish dwelling fell from 1.19 in 1926 to 0.51 by 2011.

Physical shifts in the composition of the house's internal spaces (like the gendering of sleeping arrangements and the fitting of domestic technologies) present us with important evidence of social change. Taking a formal approach – where built fabric becomes a text – this overview of Ireland's housing typologies and their lineages touches on histories of poverty, of human settlement, of family formation and of migratory patterns. It is a history of dwelling, primarily concerned with built structure: that which frames and supports everyday living in Ireland from 1740 to the present day.

FURTHER READING

Casey, C. (ed.). *The eighteenth-century Dublin town house* (Dublin, 2010).

Crowley, J. S., R. J. N. Decoy, D. Lineman and P. O'Flanagan (eds.). *Atlas of Cork city* (Cork, 2005).

Danaher, K. (C. Ó Danachair). *Ireland's vernacular architecture* (Dublin, 1975).

Gailey, A. *Rural houses of the north of Ireland* (Edinburgh, 1984).

McCullough, N. *Dublin: an urban history* (Dublin, 2007).

McManus, R. *Dublin, 1910–1940* (Dublin, 2002).

Mullane, F. 'Vernacular architecture', in N. Buttimer, C. Rynne and H. Guerin (eds.), *The heritage of Ireland* (Cork, 2000), 71–9.

O'Riordan, C. 'The Dublin Artisans' Dwellings Company', *IADS*, 8 (2004), 156–83.

Paris, C. (ed.). *Housing in Northern Ireland– a comparison with the Republic of Ireland* (Coventry, 2001).

Prunty, J. *Dublin slums 1800–1925* (Dublin, 1999).

Rowley, E. and E. Conroy. 'Flat blocks, 1930–70', in R. Loeber, H. Campbell, L. Hurley, J. Montague and E. Rowley (eds.), *Art and architecture of Ireland, vol. IV: Architecture 1600–2000* (Dublin, 2014).

14

Food in Ireland since 1740

Juliana Adelman

14.1.   Introduction

In 2010, the average Irish adult consumed less than half a pound of potatoes per day: this was a significant drop from an average of just over one pound per day recorded in the late 1940s, but a huge decline from the estimated ten pounds consumed by the pre-Great Famine labourer. Bread, sugar and meat all form a much larger proportion of the diet in Ireland today than in the past.[1] Yet these dramatic changes took place relatively gradually over the period and they are only one aspect of the relationship between Irish society and food. Food is affected by cultural and technological change and the practices of preparing and sharing meals have significance beyond the provision of basic nutrients. Dietary change, especially in the period 1740 to 1900, has been well studied. However, the broader relationship between Irish society and food is only beginning to be explored. This chapter attempts to synthesise a body of existing research on diet with the emerging scholarship on 'foodways' to offer some new and old insights into food and diet in Ireland.

For convenience, the chapter is divided into five chronological sections that coincide with events that affected food preparation and consumption. The Great Famine marks the division between the first two sections and the transition from an early modern to a modern diet. The disruptions of the First World War, the Irish Revolution and the Second World War suggest a third division because of their impacts on farming and

1 Irish Universities Nutrition Alliance, *National adult nutrition survey*, March 2011, available at www.iuna.net/wp-content/uploads/2010/12/National-Adult-Nutrition-Survey-Summary-Report-March-2011.pdf, accessed 17 August 2016; *National nutrition survey: Part I. Methods of dietary survey and results from Dublin investigation* (Dublin, 1953), 5.

trade. The end of the Second World War was not an immediate end to rationing (relevant especially to Northern Ireland), but agriculture and trade gradually stabilised and further changes through rural electrification and the establishment of a Department of Health in the Republic mark a new departure. A further all-island nutritional survey in 1999 conveniently marks the division between the twentieth and the twenty-first centuries. The division is imperfect, but offers a working scaffold for existing research.

14.2. 1740–1845

For the period between 1740 and the Great Famine there is a sizeable literature on food and diet, much of which has focused on the potato. Throughout the eighteenth century, the potato assumed an ever greater importance in Irish diets. The causes and consequences of the potato diet are still debated. Some historians claim that reliance on the potato emerged as early as the seventeenth century and was a principal cause of population growth.[2] Others argue that the rise of the potato diet cannot be definitively tied to the rise of population. Whatever its relationship with population growth, by 1845 the potato was no longer a seasonal part of the diet but the main food of the poorest class of agricultural labourers. The advantages of the potato as a dietary staple were many: in nutritional terms the potato is a nearly complete food. When supplemented with a little milk, the diet of a labourer was healthy if monotonous. Cheap potatoes also facilitated the fattening of pigs and thus the spread of pig rearing and the increased consumption of pig meat. Travellers described the hearty appearance of the Irish poor despite their ragged clothes and the average stature of Irish men may have been greater than their English counterparts.[3] However, another important consequence of a nationwide monoculture was extreme susceptibility to crop disease. Crop failures were frequent but local before 1845. One exception was the famine of 1740–1, caused by severe weather, which was also widespread.

The potato diet came to be synonymous with poverty, but potatoes were eaten by Irish people of all social classes. Even the Irish upper classes were viewed as having a peculiar appetite for potatoes.[4] This fondness for potatoes is reflected in, for example,

---

2 K. H. Connell, 'The potato in Ireland', *Past and Present*, 23 (1962) is the classic article; L. M. Cullen, 'Irish history without the potato', *Past and Present*, 40 (1968), 72–83 is the classic reply. See also more recent work: N. Nunn and N. Quinn, 'The potato's contribution to population and urbanization: evidence from a historical experiment', *Quarterly Journal of Economics*, 126, 2 (2011), 593–650.

3 J. Mokyr and C. Ó Gráda, 'The height of Irishmen and Englishmen in the 1770s: some evidence from the East India Company Army records', *Eighteenth-Century Ireland*, 4 (1989), 83–92; C. Ó Gráda, 'The heights of Clonmel prisoners, 1845–1849', *Irish Economic and Social History*, 19 (1992), 24–33.

4 L. A. Clarkson and E. M. Crawford, *Feast and famine: a history of food and nutrition in Ireland, 1500–1920* (Oxford, 2001), 47–8.

the number of recipes for sweetened potato puddings to be found in manuscript recipe books from the eighteenth and nineteenth centuries. This period established the potato as a peculiarly Irish food, as well as creating a class of 'potato people' for whom the Great Famine would prove devastating.

In contrast with the potato people, the wealthy of eighteenth- and early nine-teenth-century Ireland enjoyed a varied diet dominated by meat. Clarkson and Crawford's examination of household account books suggests that the better-off may have allocated one-third of their food budget to meat (including poultry and game).[5] Through imports and the use of greenhouses they also had access to a wide range of exotic fruits and vegetables which supplemented the usual fare of potatoes, carrots and cabbages. The growth of the grocery sector in Ireland allowed wider access to imported dry goods including tea, sugar, coffee and spices. Until the later nineteenth century the consumption of these goods was dominated by the wealthy; tea and sugar were the first to move into the labourer's diet.[6] None the less, as early as the 1770s Arthur Young had observed tea drinking among the working classes, particularly those in northern linen towns.[7] Bread and grains were also important, but to a lesser extent than for their European counterparts.

Even the poor made use of a range of foods, but variety was often derived from nature or was limited in season. Information about their diets is available from the observations of travellers and from statistical surveys and thus is likely to be an incomplete picture. Potatoes, skimmed or butter milk, and the occasional meat or fish provided the core of the diet. Porridge or stirabout made from oats was most important in the north-eastern districts. Cabbages and beans joined wild greens such as nettle as seasonal supplements that provided trace nutrients and some variation in flavour as well as the basis for traditional cures. Wild foods were also resorted to in times of dearth. In coastal areas seaweed, fish and shellfish could be obtained. Rivers and lakes might provide access to eels and salmon and fields to wild birds, rabbits and hares. Of course the rights to such foods were often held by landlords and thus hunting brought the risk of prosecution under game laws.

Diets up and down the social scale were affected by the variety of foods one could access but also by the technologies of food preparation available. For most labourers and cottiers, their cooking technologies consisted of an open fire and some kind of pot. Therefore the poor consumed foods that could be prepared by boiling. Potatoes boiled in their skins required almost no utensils to prepare or to consume. The whole family used their hands to retrieve potatoes from the basket or skib which had been used to drain them. A table was formed by resting the skib on the pot used to boil

5 Ibid., 36.

6 Ibid., 50–2.

7 L. M. Cullen, *Economy, trade and Irish merchants* (Dublin, 2014), 109.

the potatoes. A relatively modest eighteenth-century farm household might have added a roasting spit, with dripping tray, and a bread oven to the basic cooking pot.[8]

The upper classes had not only a greater variety of ingredients but also greater exposure to cultural influences and a wider choice of items to cook and serve food with. The Irish gentry followed their English counterparts in their embrace of French food and cookery techniques. According to Nuala Cullen, Hannah Glasse's *The art of cookery made plain and easy*, first published in 1747, was the most influential cookery book in Ireland.[9] Food was central to social obligations in the Big House and a combination of elaborate dishes at an evening meal was an expected component of entertainment. Manuscript recipe books from the period reflect the assimilation of Irish elites into English culinary culture as most dishes have no particular local character.[10] Up until the nineteenth century the open fire dominated food preparation in cottage and Big House alike. From the early 1800s, ranges built into the hearth became more commonplace in the British Isles, but taming their fierce heat was still done through cooking techniques and implements.[11] The eighteenth century also saw an elaborate flourishing of household goods, many of which affected the preparation, presentation and consumption of food. While the 'potato people' were eating with their hands, Sir Thomas Taylor made use of a tea kettle, spoons, plates, an orange strainer, a punch dish, a butter boat and a breadbasket, all of silver.[12]

14.3.   1845–1914

The social and demographic consequences of reliance on the potato were dramatically illustrated in the famine years of 1845–9 when repeated crop failures resulted in devastation. The potato's virtues were also its vices: as the cheapest, most nutritionally complete food available it could not be easily replaced by any single other food. Maize (known at the time as Indian meal) and soups could at best provide temporary respite to the starving masses who soon succumbed to malnutrition, disease and death. The public provision of food relief was slow and irregular, although the public soup kitchens begun in 1847 probably did prevent some from starving. They were the brainchild of the French chef and English celebrity Alexis Soyer who opened the first kitchen

8 N. Cullen, 'Women and the preparation of food in eighteenth-century Ireland', in M. MacCurtain and M. O'Dowd (eds.), *Women in early modern Ireland* (Dublin, 1991), 263–75, at 266.

9 Ibid.

10 M. Shanahan, '"Whipt with a twig rod": Irish manuscript recipe books as sources for the study of culinary material culture, c.1660–1830', *Proceedings of the Royal Irish Academy, Section C*, 115C (2015), 1–22.

11 A. Ravetz, 'The Victorian coal kitchen and its reformers', *Victorian Studies*, 11, 4 (1968), 435–60.

12 T. Barnard, *Making the grand figure: lives and possessions in Ireland, 1641–1770* (New Haven, CT, 2004), 144–5.

in Dublin to much fanfare and critique.[13] The famine also inspired the publication of treatises advising on the preparation of cheap food, including several by Soyer, and broadsides explaining how to prepare Indian meal and rice.[14]

After the famine, the poor returned to the potato but this was supplemented by other staple foods. An increase in diversity was the rule. *Indian meal*, imported from America and turned into stirabout or porridge, remained a cheap and filling staple in the workhouse but also in the home. Meat consumption gradually increased for the poor, often in the form of cheap, imported bacon. Perhaps most significant was the increased use of two other imported products: tea and sugar. White bread, bought rather than made, entered the diet as a special occasion food but replaced wheaten bread when the purchaser had a choice. These changes were not welcomed by reformers who felt that the Irish diet was in a process of decay and degradation that mirrored that of the nation as a whole.[15] Indeed variety may not have been an improvement. Clarkson and Crawford, using evidence from nutritional surveys, have estimated that the diet of labourers in Ireland declined in protein content and in calories between the mid-nineteenth century and the early twentieth century.[16]

As Ian Miller has recently shown, the Irish diet came under intense scrutiny by scientific and medical communities and by those engaged in post-famine reform. Cookery and domestic science entered the National School system with a new intensity and public analysis began to target food producers and sellers for standards of purity. From the late nineteenth century, activists of various stripes focused on the feeding of infants and children and argued that the diets of the poor required substantial reform to improve the nation. They agreed on change but not on how or by whom it should be implemented. For example, some nationalist advocates of school lunch provision claimed that the British government was starving Irish children and thereby reducing the vitality of the nation.[17]

By the early twentieth century, a lower-income labourer in Dublin had a diet dominated by tea and bread rather than potatoes and buttermilk. Food was often the largest item of expenditure in the household budget, but the poor could afford only a limited variety. The largest meal of the day, taken at midday, often contained potatoes, cabbage and a small quantity of boiled meat (often American bacon). Breakfast and tea were mostly bread and butter, sometimes with the addition of fish in the morning or jam in the evening.[18] This diet contrasted with that of the middle-class residents of the

13 I. Miller, *Reforming food in post Famine Ireland: medicine, science and improvement, 1845–1922* (Manchester, 2014), 33–7.

14 For example: A. Soyer, *Soyer's charitable cookery; or The poor man's regenerator* (London, 1846); R. Collins, *Two letters addressed to the Right Hon. Henry Labouchere, chief secretary of Ireland...*(Dublin, 1846).

15 See Miller, *Reforming food*, 85–101.

16 Clarkson and Crawford, *Feast and famine*, 183–5.

17 Miller, *Reforming food*, 164–7.

18 C. A. Cameron, *How the poor live* (Dublin, 1904), 11.

same city who now had access to an even wider variety of imported and manufactured foods, alongside more traditional fare. In 1908 Dublin's first Indian restaurant opened on Sackville Street (now O'Connell Street), although it was short-lived.[19] The restaurant was at the more exotic end of Dublin's flourishing restaurant culture which was dominated by French culinary influences.[20] Advice manuals for housekeepers reflected a more traditional diet for the comfortable classes dominated by meat, milk, bread, butter, sugar and tea.[21] In rural areas there was an increase in the growing of fruits and vegetables and in egg production, all of which tended to increase variety and protein.

In the later part of the period the nature of the rural household was undergoing dramatic change. Efforts to consolidate, industrialise and generally modernise food production tended to push women out of occupations (such as egg and butter production) that they had previously dominated. These women were now, more than ever, engaged in unpaid labour in the home. Much of this labour went into food preparation with an increased investment in more difficult and time-consuming baked goods. The use of a range, for those who could afford it, necessitated yet more time in maintaining and cleaning it. Cooking at an open hearth remained common but the purchase of small kitchen goods like spoons and spatulas increased.

14.4. 1914–1945

The rhetoric of decline which had come to dominate discourse about food in Ireland was only heightened by shortages, both real and anticipated, arising from war. Housewives were exhorted to practise economy and farmers were asked and then required to 'grow more food'. Tillage was targeted because of wartime disruptions to the supply of flour and grains. During the First World War, simmering concerns about the possibility of another food crisis to rival the famine emerged as a topic of public debate and a space for government intervention. The Department of Agriculture and Technical Instruction was joined by voluntary bodies like the Women's National Health Association (known for their involvement in the campaign against TB) in demanding that housewives fend off potential shortages by choosing inexpensive, nourishing foods and reducing waste. Traditional themes continued: tea, white bread and potatoes should be abandoned in favour of dairy and oats.[22]

The Easter Rising created temporary but serious food shortages. Food could not easily pass into Dublin from rural areas nor could imported products easily leave for the

19 M. Kennedy, '"Where's the Taj Mahal?": Indian restaurants in Dublin since 1908', *History Ireland*, 18, 4 (2010), 50–2.

20 M. Mac Con Iomaire, 'Haute cuisine restaurants in nineteenth and twentieth century Ireland', *Proceedings of the Royal Irish Academy, Section C*, 115C (2015), 1–33 [advanced online access].

21 T. Farmar, *Ordinary lives: three generations of Irish middle-class experience* (Dublin, 1991), 26–7.

22 Miller, *Reforming food*, 176–7.

countryside. Milkmen could not leave the city to attend to milch cows. Rising fears and dwindling supplies caused food prices to shoot up.[23] Food and diet in Ireland during the 1920s and 1930s has not been a major area of research and thus little is known about the effects of civil war and then Anglo-Irish trade war on diets. Certainly there was considerable ink spilled on advising women on how to cook economically with few ingredients. The establishment of the Free State in 1922 did not end food shortages. Potato failures continued to plague the Congested Districts of the west. For example, between 1922 and 1925 a particularly severe crop failure in Connemara necessitated food relief and caused embarrassment to the new government.

The neutrality of the Free State could not insulate it from the shortages caused by the Second World War. The conflict led to a dramatic decline in the availability of foods that had become household staples at all levels of society since the famine: tea, sugar and flour. During the war, tea was made from recycled leaves and black bread from whole-grain flour. A Grow More Food campaign pushed farmers towards tillage but could not supply the want of wheat. Cooking was also affected by the shortage of fuel needed for electricity supplies. The novelist and broadcaster Maura Laverty published *Flour economy* to assist housewives in making substitutions for wheaten flour, principally with oats and potatoes. Government publications, radio broadcasts and activities by bodies like the Irish Countrywomen's Association reinforced the message of frugality.[24] People resorted to the black market and smuggling increased, especially between Northern Ireland and the Republic which were under different regimes of rationing: bread and tea passed south while beef and butter passed north.[25] Fear about the loss of food supplies northward contributed to the passing of various Emergency Powers orders but these appear to have had little impact.

The war also accentuated differences between rich and poor. The diet of the poor continued to worsen, with many at risk of malnutrition, while those with money could still buy almost anything. The disparity was particularly evident in Dublin, where hotel dining rooms and restaurants appeared almost unaffected by shortages and rationing. By some contemporary accounts, Dublin of the 1930s and 1940s was full of American GIs gulping down steaks in its many restaurants while restaurateurs smuggled black market meat, butter and bread into their kitchens.[26] Throughout the late nineteenth and early twentieth century dining out, principally in restaurants, had emerged as a more accessible activity for the urban middle classes. Dublin benefited most obviously from this trend as its restaurants and hotel dining rooms adopted French *haute cuisine*.

23 Ibid., 184.

24 C. Wills, *That neutral island: a history of Ireland during the Second World War* (London, 2008), 239–47.

25 B. Evans, '"A pleasant little game of money-making": Ireland and the "new smuggling", 1939–45', *Éire-Ireland*, 49 (2014), 44–68.

26 M. Mac Con Iomaire, 'The emergence, development and influence of French haute cuisine on public dining in Dublin restaurants, 1900–2000', unpublished PhD dissertation, Dublin Institute of Technology, 2009, vol. II, 244.

During and after the Second World War these restaurants provided respite from rationing in the United Kingdom.

The Second World War and the economic problems of the new state probably delayed some aspects of household modernisation. In 1940 most kitchens still contained an open hearth for cooking. Piped water was not widespread, nor was electricity. Thus the cooking technology available to the Irish housewife in 1945 was not enormously different to that which had been in use one hundred years earlier.[27]

14.5. 1945–1999

In the period following the Second World War the modernisation of Ireland included significant changes to the household. Rural electrification, the provision of hot and cold tap water and new ideas of household design all had impacts on food. Lack of electrical infrastructure had had clear consequences for the use of home appliances. The adoption of electrical refrigerators and gas-burning ranges in Ireland was (and is) well behind that of the USA and of many European countries. Throughout the 1940s indoor plumbing was not considered a necessity nor was it included in the form of kitchen sinks or water closets. This pattern continued into the 1960s.[28] Government housing provision, both north and south, was slow to make changes to a house design centred around a kitchen hearth where a large room encompassed cooking, dining and living spaces at once. Through propaganda and with the assistance of local societies and even American foundations, the image of a modern kitchen was promoted to rural Irish women. There was an evident tension between the appeal of convenience and that of tradition: the Electricity Supply Board's (ESB) model farm kitchen design showcased electrical appliances in a cooking space open to a living area with the hearth relegated to providing warmth and atmosphere.[29] As electrification spread, this new model kitchen and its appliances became increasingly accessible. Televisions, however, were taken up more quickly than refrigerators.[30]

The establishment of the Department of Health in 1947 and the publication of a National Nutrition Survey in 1953 suggested that food and diet had won a place in government policy in the south. The opening pages of the report argued not only that food was central to health, but that 'food policy will have important bearings

27 The roll out of piped water and electrification was still underway in the early 1960s. C. Clear, *Women of the house: women's household work in Ireland 1922-1961* (Dublin, 2000), ch. 7.
28 M. McCarthy, 'The provision of rural local-authority housing and domestic space: a comparative north–south study, 1942–60', *Proceedings of the Royal Irish Academy, Section C*, 111C (2011), 287–310.
29 R. R. Kenneally, 'Towards a new domestic architecture: homes, kitchens and food in rural Ireland during the long 1950s', *Proceedings of the Royal Irish Academy, Section C*, 115C (2015), 325–47.
30 Farmar, *Ordinary lives*, 176.

on food production'.[31] The sample was around three thousand families, divided into socio-economic categories including Dublin slum dwellers, residents in Congested Districts, farmers and farm labourers, and residents of towns. The survey also considered differences between the diets of employed and unemployed, widows and pensioners. The survey particularly noted that what it termed 'bread and spread' meals, the mainstay of the poor in rural and urban Ireland, were the cause of nutritional deficiencies.[32]

Almost fifty years later, another nutrition survey conducted by academics from across the island of Ireland gave a rather different picture. Irish people were still drinking tea (91%), eating potatoes (99%), bread (99%) and dairy (99.7%). However, protein consumption was now more than adequate and most consumed adequate nutrients. The researchers instead focused on the emergence of high rates of obesity, excessive alcohol consumption and nutrients linked to particular medical problems.[33] While food consumption has increased, the cost of purchasing food has decreased. Between 1951 and 1995, the percentage of a household budget spent on food decreased from more than 37 per cent to around 21 per cent.[34] This change occurred across all income levels, but was most pronounced among those with lower incomes. An overall improvement in purchasing power has also resulted in a large proportion of those surveyed eating meals outside the home.

14.6. The New Century

Food continues to inform debates about Irish identity and also about health and welfare. Ireland continues to be a food supplier to other economies, exporting more food (in terms of value) than it imports. It continues to import foods that it creates in excess (meat, dairy, eggs) in addition to those where more variety can be supplied by imports (vegetables, fruit, cereals).[35] Recent health concerns have focused on obesity and food poverty rather than dearth. The cultural significance of Irish food is now as a commodity marketed to cookery book readers, international tourists and the Irish themselves. Hasia Diner, examining the Irish emigrant community in particular, has asserted that the Irish never identified nation with food culture. Instead alcohol and the pub became

---

31 *National Nutrition Survey, part I: Methods of dietary survey and results from Dublin investigation* (Dublin, 1953), 5.
32 Ibid., 16.
33 Irish Universities Nutrition Alliance, *North/south Ireland food consumption survey: summary report* (Dublin, 2001), 18–24, available at www.iuna.net/docs/NSIFCSummary.pdf, accessed 17 August 2016.
34 K. McCormack and P. Meany, 'Consumer prices and expenditure', in A. Redmond (ed.), *That was then, this is now: change in Ireland, 1949–1999* (Dublin, 2000), 73–9.
35 H. Tovey, 'Food and rural sustainable development', in S. O'Sullivan (ed.), *Contemporary Ireland: a sociological map* (Dublin, 2007), 283–98.

the place of gathering and of asserting group identity.[36] If this was correct in the past, a number of efforts are now underway to 'correct' this perceived lack and to revitalise the rural economy as a place of artisanal food production and gastro-tourism.

In 2016, Fáilte Ireland has a section of its website devoted to 'food tourism', with pages providing advice on developing food tourism and even a selection of 'food heritage' recipes such as 'Dublin coddle'.[37] The campaign is a recognition that gastronomy is now firmly associated with tourism in Ireland. The potential of Ireland for food tourism was recognised by the chef and entrepreneur Myrtle Allen who, with her farmer husband, opened Ballymaloe House as a restaurant in 1964. A guest house, cookbook and cookery school followed. Now the house is one of many former 'Big Houses' offering 'authentic Irish Country House food'.[38] The genre of Irish country cookery has been the subject of many cookery books by both Irish and international writers. But what is 'authentic' Irish food? A study of Irish cookbooks from the 1940s up to the 2000s has argued that, while older books looked inward to authenticate Irish food as part of a cultural tradition based in a traditional cottage with traditional ingredients, more recent cookbooks have looked outward and incorporated international techniques and ingredients while still considering the result to be 'Irish'.[39] Cookery writers and chefs who identify themselves as Irish do not shy away from using ingredients and techniques borrowed from distant countries and cultures.

In the globalised economy of food the label 'local' has acquired significance. The word, as both Hilary Tovey and Bridin Carroll have argued, is used to mean many different things.[40] For Tovey, attempts to 'relocalise' the chain of food production and consumption have tangible values for civil society in rural areas. Concerns about climate change have also supported those wishing to promote local food. Whether the Irish people will voluntarily return to a diet dominated by locally produced foods, even an expanded variety of them, remains to be seen.

FURTHER READING

Andrews, C. *The country cooking of Ireland* (San Francisco, 2009).

Bielenberg, A. *Ireland and the Industrial Revolution: the impact of the Industrial Revolution on Irish industry, 1800–1922* (London, 2009).

---

36 H. Diner, *Hungering for America: Italian, Irish and Jewish foodways in the age of migration* (Cambridge, MA, 2001), 98–102, 139.

37 See www.failteireland.ie/Supports/Food-Tourism-in-Ireland/Food-heritage.aspx, accessed 17 August 2016.

38 See D. Allen, *30 years at Ballymaloe: a celebration of the world renowned cookery school with over 100 new recipes* (London, 2014).

39 R. R. Kenneally, 'Cooking at the hearth: the "Irish cottage" and women's lived experience', in O. Frawley (ed.), *Memory Ireland, vol. II: Diaspora, memory and practices* (Syracuse, 2012), 224–41.

40 B. E. Carroll, 'Rhetoric of "Buy Irish food" campaigns: speaking to consumer values to valorise the "local" and exclude "others"', *Irish Geography*, 45, 1 (2012), 87–109.

Bourke, J. *Husbandry to housewifery: women, economic change, and housework in Ireland, 1890–1914* (Oxford, 1993).

Bourke, J. 'Working women: the domestic labour market in rural Ireland, 1890–1914', *Journal of Interdisciplinary History*, 21, 3 (1991), 479–99.

Cullen, L. M. *Economy, trade and Irish merchants at home and abroad, 1600–1988* (Dublin, 2012).

Dickson, D. *Arctic Ireland* (Belfast, 1997).

Ó Gráda, C. *Ireland before and after the famine: explorations in economic history, 1800–1925* (Manchester, 1988).

O'Neill, T. P. 'Minor famines and relief in Galway…', in G. Moran (ed.), *Galway: history and society* (Dublin, 1996).

Sexton, R. *A little history of Irish food* (Dublin, 1998).

Shanahan, M. *Manuscript recipe books as archaeological objects: text and food in the early modern world* (Lanham, MD, 2014).

Smyth, W. J., M. Murphy and J. Crowley (eds.). *Atlas of the Great Irish Famine* (Cork, 2012).

15 Literacy and Education

Ciaran O'Neill

15.1. Introduction

The nineteenth century brought with it a new world of readers. It generated a wide and variegated readership that contributed to the public sphere in ways that had not been imagined in previous centuries. Mass literacy had been achieved across Europe, or parts of it at any rate, by the 1860s. Globally this was also true of China and Japan, but nowhere else had literacy reached such heights as in European societies.[1] In this European context Ireland may fairly be ranked alongside France and Belgium in the second tier of developed Europe by the end of the nineteenth century. The change had begun pre-Enlightenment, but the eighteenth century, across Europe, was still a time when advanced reading, elongated schooling and proficient writing were all markers of middle-class to elite status. By the end of the nineteenth century access to formal and informal schooling had deepened and widened, and permeated down to the semi-skilled and labouring classes via the urban middle classes and artisans in town and country.

In addition to this, and as a further complication, we must admit that it is a difficult thing to agree on what precisely constitutes literacy. Is it a reading age of twelve or above, does it require that you can write well (if so, many of our statistical 'literates' are not literate) and if needed, compose in prose? Are we interested in adolescent literacy or adult literacy? Does bilingualism skew our statistics, and can

---

1 Rates in China were lower. Evelyn Rawksi estimates a male literacy rate of 35–40 per cent in the second half of the nineteenth century. E. Rawski, *Education and popular literacy in Ch'ing China* (Michigan, 1979), 140; R. Rubinger, *Popular literacy in early modern Japan* (Honolulu, 2007); H. J. Graff, *The legacies of literacy: continuities and contradictions in western culture and society* (Bloomington, IN, 1987).

we easily separate out orality from literacy? If most work on literacy has tended to depend on state statistics harvested for internal bureaucratic consumption, how seriously should we take them, and how close can they take us to literacy as a component of a lived life, or as something which cannot be neatly captured by decennial survey?

There is, of course, a link between schooling and literacy in Ireland as elsewhere, but not quite the causal link one might expect. Mass schooling in Europe came at a point when most populations were already mostly literate, in the 1880s and 1890s. What separates the Irish experience and makes it somewhat unique is that mass schooling had been available some fifty years previously, right in the middle of this hundred-year revolution in reading. Furthermore, mass literacy was achieved in the same generational cycle as the primary language of use in Ireland shifted from the Irish language to the English. These two features of the Irish experience have understandably dominated the literature on literacy and education, obscuring paths that might otherwise have been well trodden by researchers, such as the relationship between education and social class, multiple literacies, and education as empowerment – to name but a few. Rather than revisit some of these developed debates this chapter will survey the literature in an attempt to move more quickly to speculate on what might prove fruitful grounds for researchers interested in both fields in the future. Literacy was widespread in Ireland, even prior to the nationalisation of elementary education, so the chapter will follow the same sequence, looking at literacy before education.

15.2. Literacy

Though literacy and education may be taken as interlinked social processes, the literatures that have emerged on both topics in Irish historiography do not in fact dovetail in the way that a student might expect. Where international debate has focused on the age of mass literacy as more or less a positive development in human history, Irish scholars interested in literacy from the eighteenth century onwards have typically approached the subject in more negative terms. This is arguably because so much of the interest in the topic comes from a base interest in language shift, or language loss, rather than an interest in literacy as empowerment or indicative of positive social change. Traditionally the expansion of literacy in the nineteenth century had been read as the product of colonially motivated mass schooling. In other words, despite the elementary school system being raised from Irish rates, and built by Irish hands, to school Irish children, it has been read as a colonial imposition aimed at eliminating both a 'real' Irish culture and the Irish language. As mass schooling has been linked (rightly or wrongly) with growing literacy, it has become difficult to separate the literacy debate from the educational and the colonial.

Figure 15.1 Sunday school, 1899. Dillon Collection. Courtesy of the National Library of Ireland.

The process of becoming generally literate accelerated from the late eighteenth century across Europe. In revolutionary France more than half of the population was illiterate, and the same was true across all European polities, with as much as 20 per cent difference between male and female literacy, always favouring the male. The 1860s represent a sort of general turning point for much of the continent, and by the 1890s more than 90 per cent of people in Germany, England and the Netherlands were at least functionally literate and the balance between the genders was almost even. Southern Europe experienced a greater level of economic retardation than the north and west and thus the percentage of literacy in Italy stood at 62 per cent, 50 per cent in Spain, and as low as 25 per cent in Portugal.[2] Though it is often tempting to correlate economic

2 These figures are taken from G. Tortella, 'Patterns of economic retardation and recovery in south-western Europe in the nineteenth and twentieth centuries', *Economic History Review*, 47, 1 (1994), 1–21, at 11.

Figure 15.2 Irish-speaking children, girls' school, Connemara, 1932. In contrast to the children in Figure 15.1, these are barefooted: a mark of class, as much as environment. Image from the Wiltshire Collection. Courtesy of the National Library of Ireland.

retardation with mass illiteracy it is not always a reliable indicator. Ireland, like Finland and Norway, had a poor but well-read population in the 1890s. Portugal was both poor and poorly read. The British had lower rates of literacy for longer than their Irish neighbours – despite being the richer partner in an unequal union and despite helping to fund the impressive state-wide Irish education system.

To date Irish literacy has been investigated through statistical analysis of school registers, censal records and other 'signature' based methodologies. By the 1980s this approach was being vigorously contested by the new book historians, who preferred to think of literacy as emerging within a more socially diffuse and diverse context, through literacy in the home and in the community as well as through formal or informal modes of schooling. Both techniques can be traced in the Irish scholarship relating to literacy, but only John Logan's extensive, but unpublished, analysis (1992) of literacy attempts to provide an overview incorporating both aspects of the debate.[3]

Key texts by Tony Crowley, Niall Ó Ciosáin, Nicholas M. Wolf and Garret FitzGerald have contributed much to our understanding of language shift and changing patterns of language usage in particular, and some innovative work has been done on the history of Irish language literacy in the twentieth century. None the less, the only survey works accessible to students of literacy in relation to population change are those collected by Daly and Dickson (1990) and unpublished studies by John Logan (1978, 1992).

3 J. Logan, 'Schooling and the promotion of literacy in nineteenth century Ireland', PhD thesis, University College Cork, 1992, especially chs. 2, 7 and 8.

FitzGerald's posthumously published work (2013), valuable as it is, represents the more statistical approach, relying heavily on the type of government-generated information so comprehensively problematised by Ó Ciosáin in his work. So too is Cormac Ó Gráda's baronial analysis of literacy very useful to those seeking to enumerate.[4] Taken together their work offers the student of literacy and schooling a neat contrast as well as a complementary analysis.

Part of the problem for historians interested in quantifying literacy in eighteenth-century Ireland is related to source material, or rather the lack of it. Prior to 1841 we have no reliable data from which to extrapolate literacy rates and are instead forced to trace backwards from the census of 1841, by which time Ireland had become an admirably literate society, albeit with vast regional discrepancies corresponding to other economic indices between Ulster (70% males literate, 52% females) and descending through Leinster (65% males, 45% females) Munster (48% males, 24% females), and finally to Connacht (37% males, 15% females). These rates were marginally lower than in either England or Scotland, but were better or the same as those of much of western and central Europe in 1841, a point at which many societies had about 65–70% basic literacy.[5] All available data, problematic though they may be, indicate that Irish literacy had begun to take large strides from the 1780s.

One of the obvious differences in the Irish case is that it is one of the few Catholic countries in Europe to have enjoyed such high levels of literacy, which may in part be explained by the element of denominational competition in schooling (more on that below) and of course, less concretely, a positive by-product of being a minor partner in the United Kingdom. This Catholic illiteracy would appear to fit into a Weberian conception of the world in his *Protestant ethic*, and it is instructive to think that his text was composed more or less at the moment of peak literacy in Britain and Germany, *c.*1904, while most Catholic countries of his acquaintance lagged behind in terms of literacy. In the world as Weber saw it, Catholic countries lagged behind not only economically (his principal focus) but also arguably culturally, and since the self-sufficiency of Bible-reading populations appeared to justify the Protestant emphasis on individual interpretation of holy texts, it is natural that he would have correlated the two variables.

Work on literacy from a statistical point of view has suffered because of a lack of suitable source material, but also because the cliometric turn in Irish history came and went without much attention paid to the topic. The cultural significance of language and literacy, however, has loomed large since independence, and was reignited again by a surge in cultural studies, book history and reception history from the mid-1990s.

4 C. Ó Gráda, 'School attendance and literacy in Ireland before the Great Famine: a simple baronial analysis', in G. FitzGerald, *Irish primary education in the early nineteenth century* (Dublin, 2013), 113–32.
5 For a recent survey of literacy in Europe, see M. Lyons, *A history of reading and writing in the western world* (Basingstoke, 2013).

15.3. Language Acquisition as Loss

The tendency to see literacy as a social practice, or a particular set of social practices, that certain groups value but others may not, is worth considering in Ireland, where the debate has very often become embroiled in the rights and wrongs of English-language acquisition precisely at the moment that European societies became more literate. This is perhaps understandable in light of the progressive decline in usage of the Irish language from the late eighteenth century. The willingness to read Irish language loss within a post-colonial framework has not led to all that much in the way of original research on the process itself, and we are not close to understanding why the Irish language was so quickly dispensed with, or by whom. Revisionist interpretations of Irish language loss emphasised its inevitability, seeing the shedding of the Irish language as natural, but this too is insufficient as an explanation.[6] This remains important. The extent to which we can view English language *acquisition* as enforced, rather than adopted, is perhaps the key aspect of this debate.

The remarkable three-generation transformation of the majority of Irish citizens from monolingual Irish-speaking, to bilingual, to monolingual English-speaking constitutes one of the most compelling features of Irish modernity. This sense of language loss is apparently inextricable from the colonial nature of the relationship between Ireland and the neighbouring island of Britain, which in one form or another had been in control long before and after the generations in which the Irish language was substantively 'lost', forgotten or marginalised by Irish people. As recently noted by Wolf, the tendency in the scholarship on Irish language decline has tended to equate that loss with a parallel loss of an authentic Irish culture and way of life in an interpretive framework that can be traced back at least to Daniel Corkery's *The hidden Ireland* (1924) – a classic post-independence study of language and culture. This interpretation was mercilessly mocked by Brian O'Nolan, better known as Flann O'Brien, in his comic novel *An Béal Bocht* (1941), later reprinted in English in 1973. O'Nolan had little enough time for the literacy-as-loss narrative, highlighting, endorsing and skewering two of the dominant tropes in the hidden Ireland thesis throughout his short text: that Irish was lost through English brutality and that Irish-speakers represented a noble essentialised and authentic 'Irishness'. The first he sends up with the figure of the local schoolmaster, who ritually christens his new arrivals with the generic name 'Jams O'Donnell', followed by a blow to the head, and thus – at a stroke – consigning their Gaelic identity to a hybrid name of their master's making. The second trope is more systematically eviscerated,

---

6 A point made by N. Ó Ciosáin, 'Gaelic culture and language shift', in L. M. Geary and M. Kelleher, *Nineteenth century Ireland: a guide to recent research* (Dublin, 2005), 136–152, at 138; A. Bourke, '"The baby and the bathwater": cultural loss in nineteenth-century Ireland', in T. Foley and S. Ryder (eds.), *Ideology and Ireland in the nineteenth century* (Dublin, 1998), 79–92.

with the author's protagonist, Bónapárt Ó Cúnasa, living out his rural childhood in an exposition of the 'droch-scéal ar an droch-shaol' (a hard story about the hard life) that could be accused of just about anything other than romanticising rural poverty.[7] O'Nolan's distaste for the idea that there was a nobility inherent in living the 'hard life' was obvious and surely aimed at the tourist gaze of what he lampooned as the 'Gaelgóir' in britches, exoticising the Irish-speaking districts they holidayed in. It also reinforced another of the enduring narrative tropes of Irish history: that Irish-speakers made up, by default, the poorest, most vulnerable segment of society that were either killed as a result of the Irish famine of 1846–51, or left Ireland because of it.

Nicholas M. Wolf's work (2014) does much to complicate this story, identifying Irish language usage at all social levels and across the Atlantic archipelago. Broadly speaking, however, it holds true that speaking Irish was often a marker of economic vulnerability. Where Ireland's literacy development seems normal, then it is also partially the result of a dramatic loss of poor, illiterate citizens who were more likely than not to have been native Irish-speakers, and at a key stage of European literacy development.

If Wolf's work shows a willingness to rely on analysis of the reader, speaker and writer as an individual with active agency in their own literacy and language development, we might point to several other directions that may help to continue his valuable widening of scope. In recent years concepts of literacy have moved towards an understanding of their multiplicities. Literacy is socially coded and bourgeois-led, often foisted upon the deserving or undeserving poor with a paternalistic agenda of 'improvement'. Where literacy can empower, it can only empower within a hierarchically ordered social structure that is inherited.[8] To be basically literate is one thing, but to survive or excel in a progressively complex world of symbolic, visual, oral and embodied codes is quite another.[9] More work will need to go into a close reading of the dynamic between formal and informal language acquisition, and its effect (or non-effect) on social structure. It has been noted by others that a rise in literacy may be taken to equate to a rise in the general standard of living, but not amounting to a socially transformative or revolutionary change in and of itself. Complementary studies of orality have emerged over the decades since Walter Ong's seminal work on the 'technologising' of the word in 1982, and these point the way to a more multi-layered understanding of competing and converging print, voice and sound cultures.[10]

Reception history is another area where scholars have been producing new and interesting material. Ó Ciosáin's work on publishing and reading complements emerging

---

7 See J. Leersen, *Hidden Ireland, public sphere* (Galway, 2002). This point is alluded to in D. Kiberd, *Inventing Ireland: the literature of the modern nation* (London, 1996), 503.

8 See É. Ó Ciardha, 'The Irish book in Irish, 1691–1800', *Eighteenth-Century Ireland*, 28 (2014), 13–37.

9 G. Kress. *Literacy in the new media age* (New York, 2003).

10 W. Ong, *Orality and literacy: the technologizing of the word* (London, 1982). For new work in an Irish context see 'Further reading' below.

work on book history and popular reading, recently captured in the monumental five-volume *Oxford history of the Irish book*. Numeracy, aurality and other forms of literacy need further exploration.[11] Outline studies by Clarke on the learning of book-keeping across different social levels, or reading as consumption, allow us a glimpse at what we might learn from a willingness to define literacy more broadly.[12] Arguably we should be following the lead of scholars of 'new literacies', interested in literacy as something constantly shifting and changing in response to new technologies.[13] In this sense, learning to negotiate new work practices, complex or networked systems, opens up new possibilities in how we might approach literacy in the past.

15.4. Education

Bruce Curtis once complained that despite an abundance of contemporary educational ethnography, offering compelling interpretations of the social process of education, 'most studies of the history of education stop at the schoolroom door'.[14] It is certainly true in the Irish case, and the gap between policy, governance and the personal experience of education is a considerable opportunity for researchers of the future. Irish educational historiography has focused for the most part on the struggle for power between the developing centralised 'official' state and the interested religious bodies. It is, in essence, provider-focused. There are very few Bourdieu-influenced studies of the effect of schooling on challenging or reproducing societal structure, and there are equally few studies of the experience of having attended an Irish school. Institutional histories of schools and school providers are of course very useful, but their approach is almost always self-serving and myopic, especially in a country so dominated by religious schooling as Ireland is. Much of Irish educational history has been written by educationalists or the religious orders and the result is unsatisfactory and uneven. Irish historians have generally focused on controversies surrounding elementary and university education to the exclusion of the intermediate stage, and almost no space has been given to the independent sector operating at either end of the economic and social spectrum. In this chapter I will focus briefly on the three customary levels of education,

11 See, for example, T. De Moor and J. Luiten Van Zanden, '"Every woman counts": a gender-analysis of numeracy in the Low Countries during the early modern period', *Journal of Interdisciplinary History*, 41, 2 (2010), 179–208; A. M. Ochoa Gautier, *Aurality: listening and knowledge in nineteenth-century Colombia* (Durham, NC, 2014).
12 P. Clarke, 'The teaching of book-keeping in nineteenth-century Ireland', *Accounting, Business and Financial History*, 18, 1 (2008), 21–33; D. Weiss, 'Maria Edgeworth's infant economics: capitalist culture, good-will networks and "Lazy Lawrence"', *Journal for Eighteenth-Century Studies* (2014), 313–33.
13 V. Coghlan and G. O'Connor, 'The Kildare Place Society: an influential force in 19th century Irish education', in S. Morag and E. Arizpe (eds.), *Acts of reading: teachers, text and childhood* (Stoke-on-Trent, 2009).
14 B. Curtis, 'Patterns of resistance to public education: England, Ireland, and Canada West, 1830–1890', *Comparative Education Review*, 32, 3 (1988), 318–33, at 318. The standard survey work for Irish education remains J. Coolahan, *Irish education: its history and structure* (Dublin, 1981).

before turning to aspects of education that are largely neglected in the literature: teachers themselves, domestic education, adult or vocational education, and the for-profit or independent sector.

15.4.1. Elementary

The focus on elementary education is a tendency common among historians of education everywhere: a propensity to privilege the study of the expansion of education in the nineteenth century to a broader middle and lower middle class to the exclusion of research on those above and below these lines. We have reasonably full coverage of state intervention in education from the 1830s onwards, as well as religious provision of education post-1793, but there are large and significant gaps in our understanding of many of the other elements that made up the educational landscape. We know far too little about the proliferation of free-market providers of education at the other end of the social spectrum (Logan, 1992 has an extended discussion of this). In rural areas, as Cullen and others have noted, the hedge school reigned supreme in the eighteenth century, but in urban areas the commission of 1824 revealed a widespread proliferation of one-room or back-room schooling of variable quality that has, for want of archival footprint, been treated in a highly statistical manner. Studies by Brenan (1935) and FitzGerald (2013) have helped to remedy this, but much more should be done.

The topography of Irish education differs from much of western Europe owing to its persistent denominational division. The broad pattern of mass education across much of Europe was that it became secularised gradually post-Enlightenment, culminating in the almost marginalisation of religiously branded education in western Europe after the *Kulturkampf.* In Ireland no such secularisation was possible owing to the particular influence of the Catholic Church, so that even the state-sponsored expansion of elementary education in Ireland was gradually made more homogeneous, facilitating an apparently natural division of secular schools into 'Protestant' or 'Catholic' schools according to the regional dominance of one sect or the other. In this way state secular schools were harnessed by competing religious groups and instead of breaking down denominational division, they in some sense reinforced it. Recent work by Lougheed (2012) has done much to elucidate the regional distribution of this 'revolution' in elementary education, adding a much-needed full-length study to the foundational work of Akenson (1970) and Mary E. Daly (1979). But the social meaning of the system itself, the transfer of pupils from scattered independent providers to a state system, and the effect of standardised schooling at a societal and classroom level are all aspects of the revolution that are under-studied. Michael Coleman's work points to the value of comparative analysis, and Marilyn Cohen's and Kevin Mc Kenna's historical anthropology of schools in County Galway and County Down point the way to a potentially rich seam of focused case study, as does the rich portrait of Patrick Pearse's school at St Enda's.[15] To date, the only other area with a growing literature relates to institutional child abuse within religious and state providers.[16]

We might argue, as Cohen and Mc Kenna have, that the impulse to educate widely but not deeply was an essentially paternalistic one. For once the British government and the various churches agreed on something, it was important to educate the population so that they might reach a manageable level of civility, but to go beyond that was not a priority for either provider. In this respect there was a clear gap between the ideologies of educated citizens outside church and state, who campaigned for educational reform while their superiors in some cases actively worked against it. This disconnect was captured in a speech by Dennis Caulfield Heron in 1872 on the subject of education as potential empowerment for the lower classes.

> Education tends to level the inequalities of rank and fortune, and offers the prizes of the world to young men who otherwise would remain, in sour discontent, peasants on the farm where they were born. Even now education is relieving the pressure of competition for the land, and education brings the clever young men from the respectable farming classes, and from the country towns of Ireland, into competition for the prizes of the Civil Service of the empire. I speak not merely of the prizes in the home and colonial, the military, the engineering, the medical services, now open to competition. Even the most recent competitive examinations show how shrewdly the young men of Ireland avail themselves of every educational advantage open to them.[17]

In his speech Heron unequivocally identified education as the obvious and vital route to an improvement of social mobility. He also treated of education as if it could transform lowly, but 'clever young men' into the next generation of professionals, relieving the 'pressure on the land' that would result in the land agitation towards the end of the decade. This was in sharp contrast with the views of Cardinal Cullen, who had argued in front of the Powis Commission on Education, that if the poor were to receive 'too high an education', it would leave them discontented and render them 'unfit for following the plough, or using the spade', and that they should rather be educated with 'a view to the place they hold in society'.[18] This view remained current,

---

15 M. C. Coleman, *American Indians, the Irish, and government schooling: a comparative study* (Lincoln, NE, 2007); M. Cohen, 'Paternalism and poverty: contradictions in the schooling of working-class children in Tullylish, County Down, 1825–1914', *History of Education*, 21, 3 (1992), 291–306; K. Mc Kenna, 'Charity, paternalism and power on the Clonbrock Estates, County Galway, 1834–44', in L. M. Geary and O. Walsh (eds.), *Philanthropy in nineteenth-century Ireland* (Dublin, 2014); E. Sisson, *Pearse's patriots: St Enda's and the cult of boyhood* (Cork, 2005).

16 For a useful survey, see P. Garrett, '"It is with deep regret that I find it necessary to tell my story": child abuse in industrial schools in Ireland', *Critical Social Policy*, 30, 2 (2010), 292–306.

17 'The education question', *Freeman's Journal*, 18 January 1872; see also 'The education question: a great Catholic meeting', *Irish Times*, 18 January 1872.

18 Earl Powis, *Royal Commission of Inquiry into Primary Education (Ireland), vol. I: Containing the report of the commissioners, with an appendix* [Powis Commission] HC 1870 [C.6a], XXVIII, Pt.II.1, 506.

enacted and embodied until well into the twentieth century. Irish education was bottom-heavy, with a huge proportion of the population educated to a basic level. To rise into advanced education, however, required – at least until 1878 – considerable social and economic capital. Less than 5 per cent of the population was educated to age seventeen at any point between 1760 and 1922. The 1920s to the 1950s saw a slowly modernising system struggle to ease the transition from elementary to advanced education, and it was not until the late 1960s that successive progressive legislation led to universal and free intermediate education in Ireland. The structural history of the southern primary school has hardly changed at all since independence: 96 per cent of primary schools were religiously controlled in 2015, with only the Educate Together initiative providing any sort of secular alternative in a country where religious observance has casualised to the point that such a system now looks more anachronistic than it did in the 1920s, or even the 1990s. The cosy accommodation of segregated education may no longer be sustainable in a society where more than 15 per cent are 'new Irish' and thus being asked to tolerate a religiously inflected system they were not born into. In the north the decision of the Catholic Church not to engage with the government commission in 1922 facilitated structural segregation north of the border, creating an underfunded voluntary sector in 1923 which persisted until 1968 when denominational and largely independent providers became either controlled or 'maintained' schools.[19] The integrated education movement in the north has been a formalised political goal since the 1980s, but in truth its success in its first thirty-five years or so has been limited.

15.4.2.   Intermediate

The 'intermediate' stage of education has received surprisingly little scholarly attention, especially relative to elementary and university education. In fact, only one survey of secondary education pre-independence exists (McElligott, 1981) and the majority of work done has homed in on the spread of state secondary education in the twentieth century. There are several gaps in the literature.

A progressive nationalisation of secondary or intermediate education was underway across France and Germany in the early nineteenth century, but it did not occur in Ireland and Britain on such a grand scale until the twentieth century. In contrast to elementary education, so pervasive by the mid-nineteenth century, intermediate education was inaccessible to the majority of the population and thus remained the stage at which social stratification was decided or accelerated. The numbers who received a superior or advanced education were shockingly low throughout the nineteenth

---

19 M. McGrath, *The Catholic Church and church schools in Northern Ireland: the price of faith* (Dublin, 2000), 40–8.

century in Ireland and Britain, with no more than 5 per cent of the population receiving anything approaching one.

At elite levels only two studies of the longstanding tradition of large-scale transnational education exist, and only one has been published.[20] Studies of middle-class education in Ireland are largely institutional in character, and tend not to take account of the fact that until independence, Irish education at intermediate level was almost entirely delivered by private-sector providers operating with minimal state interference, and surprisingly little input from bishops. Lastly, the spread of female education from the eighteenth century onwards awaits a definitive history.[21] Across all of the literature there has been an underestimation of the importance of the inherently transnational character of Irish education, both in terms of influences from abroad and also in relation to the thousands of Irish children educated outside Ireland through the eighteenth and nineteenth centuries. Ian D'Alton and Kieran Flanagan have shown that in excess of 1,500 Protestant boys were being educated in Britain throughout the nineteenth century, thus debilitating domestic middle-class education, while an unknown number of their sisters followed suit.[22] This was a tradition that persisted long after 1922. Catholic figures were smaller, but also substantial, with many of the girls opting for a French or Belgian education in preference to an Irish or British one. But the transnational element of Irish education should not be imagined to be outward only. The majority of the prestigious teaching orders entering Ireland from the 1820s to the 1860s were coming from outside Ireland – mostly from France – and were keen on recruiting large numbers of English-speaking postulants ahead of their expansion into the English-speaking New World.

Part of the reason no sustained discussion on intermediate education has taken place is a lack of systematic statistical data and government reports until 1878. A significant number of archives exist, however, especially for those interested in bourgeois education, and are underexploited. Several major commissions sat through the nineteenth century, and some of these have been analysed, but those looking to get past the school door will need first to access a school archive.[23]

After independence education continued to be dominated by the churches, with the Free State making significant concessions to the Protestant minority in the form of

20 K. Flanagan, 'The rise and fall of the Celtic ineligible: competitive examinations for the Irish and Indian civil services in relation to the educational and occupational structure of Ireland 1853–1921', DPhil. thesis, University of Sussex, 1978; C. O'Neill, *Catholics of consequence: transnational education, social mobility, and the Irish Catholic elite 1850–1900* (Oxford, 2014).

21 See a recent survey for a summary of the literature: J. McDermid, *The schooling of girls in Britain and Ireland* (Abingdon, 2012).

22 K. Flanagan, 'The rise and fall of the Celtic ineligible'; I. D'Alton, 'Educating for Ireland? The urban Protestant elite and the early years of Cork Grammar School, 1880–1914', in *Éire-Ireland*, 46, 3–4 (2011), 201–26.

23 See K. Flanagan, 'Commissions of inquiry as ritual: Bourdieu, the marquis and the Endowed Schools of Ireland, 1854–58', *Irish Studies Review*, 19, 3 (2011), 281–306.

preferential grants facilitating subsidised boarding (and de facto denominational seg-regation) that continues to the present. Politically this was likely a compromise sought to stymie any opposition to the cosy relationship between the Catholic Church and state in relation to education. In the north, similar segregation was achieved by differ-ent means. The first secularist state intervention in secondary education in the south was via the vocational sector in the 1930s, part of a long and difficult internal political conversation about what to do about the education of the disadvantaged. The resultant technical and vocation system is understudied, but the social reputation of the 'tech' schools was picked up in the longitudinal studies of the 1980s as highly stigmatised. This has meant that the only secular providers in Irish education have been those with lowest social status, while elite providers have been unfailingly religious in charac-ter, even above what is considered normal in Irish society.[24] The last major structural change in Irish education was the decision to make intermediate education free for all in 1968. This decision opened up new opportunities for the lower middle classes espe-cially, though the decision to bankroll a fee-paying sector by paying teacher salaries at elite boarding schools meant that no social levelling came about as a result of what was, by any standard, a progressive piece of legislation. The decision to fund intermediate education finally raised the south to the level of investment that had been available north of the border for some time, for all the problems of distribution and equity, and meant that both governments were now, effectively, paying a great deal of money for a denominational system of education over which they had very limited classroom-level control, and which was not aiming for social equality for all citizens.

15.4.3. University

By the late nineteenth century an aspirant university student was spoiled for choice in Ireland. For so long at the top of a ladder with one rung, Trinity College Dublin remained the most prestigious of the many options available, and had allowed Catholics and dissenters to attend (albeit with restrictions and never on equal social terms) since 1793. Three regional non-denominational universities had been founded as a result of progressive reform in 1845 at Galway, Belfast and Cork, and the Catholic University in Dublin (originally founded in 1854 by Newman) had gradually begun to resemble a modern university after its move in 1883 to Earlsfort Terrace where it later became University College Dublin. This constituted a credentialist revolution, facilitating a gradual but perceptible rise in the bourgeois professions of law, medicine and divinity as well as a concomitant rise in the new professions, and proxy occupations relating to

---

24 V. Greaney and T. Kellaghan, *Equality of opportunity in Irish schools: a longitudinal study of 500 students* (Dublin, 1984); C. T. Whelan and D. F. Hannan, 'Class inequalities in educational attainment among the adult population in the Republic of Ireland,' *Economic and Social Review*, 30. 3 (July 1999), 302–3.

merchant trade and industry across urban Ireland. Some work has been done on the related university issues of cramming and instrumentality after the opening up of the Indian civil service in 1855, and the domestic civil service in 1870, but more could be done on the 'supply' aspect, with increasing rates of university degree awards.[25] More could also be done to elucidate the experience of attending university, socialisation and hidden curriculum. What we have in abundance are alumni-aimed or academic institutional histories, but a rich history of ideas and people – two of the more interesting aspects of university life – awaits further research.

The university debates of the nineteenth century have arguably the most developed history. All three of the Queen's Colleges (Cork, Belfast and Galway) have a history devoted to them, as does UCD, and Trinity College Dublin has several. Though this institutional element is well served, historians have been less successful in their attempts to show how the university of the eighteenth and nineteenth century connected to the city and the society surrounding it and interacting with it. Likewise, the technical and vocational sector is not as well served, though several useful histories exist. On the various university debates of the 1840s and the 1870s, in particular, new work has emerged from Senia Pašeta, Aidan Enright and others. So too have the networks that linked the university to science and technology received some recent attention.[26] An intellectual history of the nineteenth-century university in Ireland is yet to be written, with much more coverage given to seventeenth- and eighteenth-century thinkers such as John Toland, William Molyneaux and George Berkeley, while the intellectual history of twentieth-century Ireland is also strikingly under-researched. In the twentieth century the opening up of university education was really a feature of the late 1960s and 1970s, when such education became accessible for a much wider base of the population north and south of the border at around the same time as universities across Europe began to take on revolutionary character. This did not translate to long-term social change. A longitudinal study of five hundred Irish students published in 1984 found that students from lower-income backgrounds were less likely to progress to third level and that the bulk were opting out of the school system at second level. The 1960s and 1970s provided a temporary boost to social mobility, much more than the more recent abolition of university fees (1996–2010), which arguably provided a bonus to middle-class parents likely to send their children to university in any case, without notably altering the numbers or success of non-traditional students entering full-time higher education.

25 See M. E. Daly, 'The formation of an Irish nationalist elite? Recruitment to the Irish civil service in the decades prior to independence, 1870–1920', *Paedagogica Historica*, 30, 1 (1994), 281–301; C. Shepard, 'Cramming, instrumentality and the education of Irish imperial elites', in D. Dickson, J. Pyz and C. Shepard (eds.), *Irish classrooms and British empire: imperial contexts in the origins of modern education* (Dublin, 2012), 172–83.
26 J. Adelman, *Communities of science in nineteenth-century Ireland* (London, 2009); D. O'Leary, *Irish Catholicism and science: from godless colleges to the Celtic Tiger* (Cork, 2012).

15.5.   New Directions

By far the most serious gap in Irish educational history is the treatment of female education, a point reiterated in several recent survey articles.[27] Little is understood of the
expansion of convent education in the early to mid-nineteenth century, and even the
treatment of female education in the state system is slight.[28] Historians tend to emphasise a sort of Protestant-led revolution in middle-class education from the 1860s, but
this is outdated, as are hagiographical treatments of pioneers in female education such
as Anne Jellicoe. Much more could and should be done.

Teachers are almost as neglected as their students in Irish educational literature;
although there are some studies of prominent pedagogues, they are mostly of the laud-
atory kind and nearly always biographies of the head teacher – a very different figure. Teachers are vitally important interlocutors, culturally, intellectually and of course
spiritually. Their absence is partly owing to a lack of qualitative sources. However, a
recent article on the Irish-language poet Brian Merriman as a schoolmaster shows what
an imaginative scholar can do with limited source material.[29]

A different sort of teacher – the domestic tutor or governess – is also largely absent
from survey histories of Irish education, another casualty of the focus on large-scale
providers. Notable groundwork by John Logan and Deirdre Raftery aside, little is
known of the daily lives of those educating in the home.[30] We can estimate that their
numbers were in the thousands through much of the nineteenth century, and that they
were a mixture of Irish, British, French and German professionals. Recent work on
French and German governesses points the way for those interested in the Irish governess or tutor, but it is worth remembering that although many of these solo practitioners doing the rounds in Irish homes were foreign, there was a simultaneously rich
tradition of exported Irish governesses working the rounds abroad. The most notable
examples of this are probably the authors Maura Laverty and Kate O'Brien, who were
both working as governesses in Spain in 1922, and Margaret Eager, who left behind a
memoir of her time as governess to the daughters of Tsar Nicholas II, the last emperor
of Russia, in the early 1900s.[31]

---

27 For example, D. Raftery, J. Harford and S. M. Parkes, 'Mapping the terrain of female education in Ireland,
1830–1910', *Gender and Education*, 22, 5 (Nov. 2010), 565–78.

28 Notable exceptions include M. M. Kealy, *Dominican education in Ireland 1820–1930* (Dublin, 2007); J. Logan,
'The dimensions of gender in nineteenth century schooling', in M. Kelleher and J. H. Murphy (eds.), *Gender
perspectives in nineteenth-century Ireland* (Dublin, 1997).

29 L. M. Cullen, 'Merriman in a world of schoolmasters', *Eighteenth-Century Ireland*, 26 (2011), 80–94.

30 J. Logan, 'Governesses, tutors and parents: domestic education in Ireland, 1700–1880', *Irish Educational
Studies*, 7, 2 (1988), 1–18; D. Raftery, 'The nineteenth century governess: image and reality', in B. Whelan (ed.),
Women and paid work in Ireland, 1500–1930 (Dublin, 2000), 57–68.

31 M. Eager, *Six years at the Russian court* (New York, 1906).

Historians of technical, vocational and adult education will find that there is a reasonable amount of work done on the Mechanics' Institutes that peppered the country from the 1820s and served the 'common reader' of the working class, some work also on the Repeal reading rooms of the 1840s, but very little else other than a cluster of work around the Gaelic League and other independent cultural improvement bodies. Adult education itself did not become a state priority until the second half of the nineteenth century, and the various technical teaching colleges slowly gained in status through the twentieth century, always in a lower social bracket as with the 'tech' schools at intermediate level.[32] What we might call 'gentlemanly' adult education – antiquarianism, natural sciences and so on – are better covered, but not collectively. Nuala Johnson's work on botanical gardens provides a model for those scholars interested in taking a wider approach to this.[33]

One final area ripe for further exploration is that of pay schools, hedge schools and other small, for-profit enterprises. From the early nineteenth century the hedge schools (note: these were *not* generally open-air schools held in hedges) and the urban cram school were most important, yet we know next to nothing about them. They usually appear on our radar only if they are unusual – such as Gregor Von Feinaigle's mnemonics school at Aldborough House in Dublin (1813–30) – or if they feature in a biography of a famous individual, such as Bram Stoker's time at Bective House, 15 Rutland Square, in the 1860s.[34] Because these schools rarely outlived their masters, the want of archival collections has meant they have been largely overlooked. Nevertheless, this was a dynamic segment of a dynamic and ever-changing field of education through the eighteenth to the twentieth century.

It seems superfluous to offer a conclusion to a field in progress. A huge amount of new work has emerged on Irish education since the 1970s; less has emerged on literacy. This is, in part, at least, due to a tapering off of cliometric analysis and the social and economic history techniques that rewarded statistical work of this nature. This leaves the scholar of both related areas with a preponderance of perfectly good, if dated, statistic-heavy work, and very little of a case-study or qualitative nature. If we want to burrow down into what Mary Poovey has called 'the social body' of mass culture, then it is precisely this sort of intimate inquiry that we will need.

FURTHER READING

Akenson, D. *The Irish education experiment: the national system of education in the nineteenth century* (London, 1970).

Brenan, M. *The schools of Kildare and Leighlin, AD 1775–1885* (Dublin, 1935).

32 N. MacMillan (ed.), *Prometheus's fire: a history of scientific and technological education in Ireland* (Dublin, 2000).
33 N. C. Johnson, *Nature displaced, nature displayed: order and beauty in botanical gardens* (London, 2011).
34 On Von Feinaigle, see M. Quane, 'The Feinaiglian institution, Dublin,' *Dublin Historical Record*, 19, 2 (1964), 30–44.

Coolahan, J. *Irish education: history and structure* (2nd edn, Dublin, 1987).

Cronin, N., S. Crosson and J. Eastlake (eds.). *Anáil an Bhéil Bheo: orality and modern Irish culture* (Newcastle, 2009).

Crowley, T. *Wars of words: the politics of language in Ireland 1537–2004* (Oxford, 2005).

Daly, M. E. 'The development of the national school system, 1831–40', in A. Cosgrove and D. McCartney (eds.), *Studies in Irish history presented to R. Dudley Edwards* (Dublin, 1979), 150–63.

Daly, M. E., and D. Dickson (eds.). *The origins of popular literacy in Ireland: language change and educational development 1700–1920* (Dublin, 1990).

De Fréine, S. *The great silence: the study of a relationship between language and nationality* (Dublin, 1965).

Doyle, A. *A history of the Irish language from the Norman invasion to independence* (Oxford, 2015).

Logan, J. 'Literacy in Ireland 1741–1931: a preliminary survey', Thomond College of Education, Limerick, 1978.

Logan, J. 'Schooling and the promotion of literacy in nineteenth century Ireland', PhD dissertation, University College Cork, 1992.

Lougheed, K. 'National education and empire: Ireland and the geography of the national education system', in D. Dickson, J. Pyz and C. Shepard (eds.), *Irish classrooms and British empire: imperial contexts in the origins of modern education* (Dublin 2012), 5–17.

McElligott, T. J. *Secondary education in Ireland, 1870–1921* (Dublin, 1981).

Mac Giolla Chríost, D. *The Irish language in Ireland* (London, 2005).

Ó Ciosáin, N. 'Oral culture, literacy and the growth of a popular readership, 1800–1850', 'Pedlars and book distribution' and 'Almanacs in the nineteenth century', in J. H. Murphy (ed.), *The Oxford history of the Irish book, vol. IV* (Oxford, 2011), 173–91, 192–7, 198–220.

Ó Ciosáin, N. 'Publishing and reading in the Celtic languages 1700–1900: an overview', *Cultural and Social History*, 10 (2013), 347–67.

Ó Croidheáin, C. *Language from below: the Irish language, ideology and power in 20th century Ireland* (Oxford, 2006).

Ó Riagáin, P. *Language policy and social reproduction, Ireland 1893–1993* (Oxford, 1997).

Raftery, D. and S. M. Parkes. *Female education in Ireland 1700–1900: Minerva or Madonna* (Dublin, 2007).

Wolf, N. *State, religious community and the linguistic landscape in Ireland, 1770–1870* (Madison, WI, 2014).

16 Health and Welfare, 1750–2000

Catherine Cox

16.1. Introduction

Ireland's history of health and welfare is intimately linked to its history of poverty and charity, and to conflicting intellectual and philosophical outlooks that repeatedly redefined the state's responsibility for the health, welfare and 'well-being' of its population in the modern period. Research into Ireland's social history developed relatively late with most welfare and medical histories privileging governmental policies and institutional histories. This work revealed the main legislative and policy innovations and delineated official and philanthropic conceptualisations of, and attitudes towards, Irish poverty in the nineteenth and twentieth centuries. In Ireland, the institutional model remained central to the delivery of health and welfare supports throughout the modern period. The poor, especially the sick poor, and the institutions established to provide for and manage them have attracted the majority of scholarly inquiry. Histories interrogating the health and welfare of other classes and alternative mechanisms of relief are less familiar to us. Reflecting current scholarship, this chapter is concerned with the development of official policy, the *pursuit* of health and the *avoidance* of poverty, diseases and 'ill health'.

16.2. The Rise of the Institution

In post-Reformation Europe attitudes towards poverty and modes of assisting the poor altered significantly, reflecting a general reluctance to support what was regarded as indiscriminate charity. In England, these changes, coupled with increasing poverty, prompted the introduction of the Elizabethan Poor Law (1601), a parish-based system of relief that divided the poor between the 'deserving' and 'undeserving' and provided indoor relief, through workhouses, alongside outdoor relief. Similar legislation was not introduced to Ireland until the reform period of the nineteenth century. None the less, in its absence, rational, instrumental forms of medical and welfare relief, producing formalised and institutionalised mechanisms, which sought to discourage indiscriminate almsgiving, such as was evident throughout most of Europe since the Reformation, also emerged in Ireland. In the modern period there was an explosion in the number of institutions constructed to tackle the perceived problems of poverty and disease. These included the highly punitive houses of industry opened in Dublin, Limerick, Cork, Clare, Wexford, Waterford, Belfast, Coleraine and Lisburn (from 1772), which, financed under the grand jury system, provided general relief to the destitute and punished beggars; a 'proto' workhouse founded in Dublin in 1703 and later converted in the Dublin Foundling Hospital and Workhouse (1725); and numerous voluntary hospitals (general and specialist), infirmaries, fever hospitals and dispensaries.

Often, the enabling legislation did not compel grand juries and elites to act and consequently development of these institutions was not uniform but dependent on local initiative and resources. When institutions were established, their foundation was prompted by a combination of eighteenth-century philanthropic impulse and anxieties about the spread of contagious diseases, especially among the poor. Their proliferation was also related to urban settlement and expansion: the west of Ireland was badly served. Dublin, with a population of approximately 130,000 in 1750 and 224,000 in 1822, accrued an extensive range of institutions that provided forms of relief to the poor and the sick.[1] In addition to the workhouse and house of industry, waves of philanthropic activities resulted in the foundation of voluntary and specialist hospitals including the Charitable Infirmary (1718), Dr Steeven's Hospital (1733), Mercer's Hospital (1734), the Dublin Hospital for the Poor Lying-in, otherwise known as the Rotunda Hospital (1745), Swift's hospital for the insane poor (1757) and the Cork Street Fever Hospital (1804). As the cities of Belfast, Cork and Limerick developed, similar hospitals were established, though in these cities there was greater emphasis on general hospitals, with maternity and fever hospitals opening slightly later. For example, lying-in hospitals were established in Belfast in 1793 and in Cork in 1798. Philanthropic activities also led to the establishment of numerous private charities, such as the Sick and Indigent Roomkeepers' Society in Dublin (1790), intended to relieve the poverty that pervaded the city at that time.

The historiographical preoccupation with state and philanthropic development in the arena of health and welfare has resulted in the relative neglect of informal forms

---

1 C. Ó Gráda, 'The Rotunda Hospital and the people of Dublin, 1745–1995', *Éire-Ireland*, 30 (1995), 51.

of welfare and health-care services. David Dickson found evidence of an *ad hoc* Irish poor law operating at the level of Church of Ireland parishes in Dublin in the eighteenth century, but acknowledged that the 'overall number of citizens touched by parish charity remained limited'. In his close analysis of Archbishop Whately's 1836 Royal Commission for Inquiring into the Condition of the Poorer Classes in Ireland, Niall Ó Ciosáin uncovered the ubiquity of informal almsgiving in Irish society. His study revealed complex sets of relationships between donors, and vagrants and mendicants based on 'gift exchanges'. Farmers, labourers and, in the urban areas, shopkeepers provided alms more frequently during the 'hungry' summer months, with shopkeepers giving cash and farmers and labourers providing food, usually potatoes. These transactions were gendered: the wives of farmers regularly provided relief to a female representative of a family of beggars in exchange for the 'performance' of blessings or prayers by mendicants of good character. Ó Ciosáin also contends that in their evidence, the witnesses to Royal Commission, in addition to the commissioners, divided the poor into deserving and undeserving, demonstrating the pervasiveness of these categories even in the absence of an Irish poor law. The professional Irish beggar, 'the boccough', was contrasted with the 'honest' beggar whose prayers possessed greater efficacy. While Ó Ciosáin identifies evidence of confessional divisions in testimonies from Roman Catholic and Protestant clergy, they agreed on their opposition to informal mechanisms of relief. This contrasted with members of the laity, in particular the rural laity, who were resistant to a compulsory mechanism of relief funded through taxation on the basis that it would undermine the traditional bonds of charity.[2]

In his examination of patterns of state-funded interventions in matters of welfare relief in the late eighteenth and early nineteenth century, Oliver MacDonagh has argued that such precocious governmental policies in Ireland represent efforts to compensate for the relative absence of a paternalistic landlord elite in specific regions. Likewise, Andrew Sneddon found that the County Infirmary Act (1765) was intended to redress an urban–rural imbalance and provide facilities for the poor outside the major sites of urban development in areas where there was a lack of landlord-led philanthropic initiative.[3] Other state-funded initiatives included the provision of additional financial support to dispensaries in receipt of charitable subscriptions (from 1805), encouraged the opening of fever hospitals (from 1818) and mandated the establishment of a network of district lunatic asylums (from 1817). The fever hospitals were introduced in the context of repeated outbreaks of epidemic diseases in 1816–19.

2 N. Ó Ciosáin, *Ireland in official print culture, 1800–1850* (Oxford, 2014), chapters 4 and 5.
3 O. MacDonagh, *Ireland: the Union and its aftermath* (London, 1977), ch. 2; A. Sneddon, 'State intervention and provincial health care: the county infirmary system in late eighteenth-century Ulster', *Irish Historical Studies*, 38 (2012), 5–21.

Scholars have not considered in any great depth the extent to which these initiatives were implicit or explicit compensations for the absence of the Elizabethan Poor Law in Ireland. Instead, explanations for the state intervention in health and welfare services in Ireland have coalesced around three main themes. While for MacDonagh, publishing in the late 1970s and 1980s, these were evidence of how Ireland under the Union was treated as a form of 'social laboratory', recent work on eighteenth-century Ireland has located traces of the 'fashionable desire to improve Ireland and the Irish', alongside self-interested and altruistic motivations, as propelling philanthropic interventions.[4] There was a consensus among British and Irish politicians, reformers and travel writers, both before the Union and in the decades immediately after, that Ireland was in need of improvement. In numerous parliamentary commissions, in travel literature and commentaries, the Irish were portrayed as, and found to be, a diseased, vagrant, mendicant people, and Ireland was depicted as an unhealthy place. There were repeated food shortages and famines in 1740–1, 1800–1, 1813–14 and 1816–17, and epidemics of various fevers and diseases. A conservative estimate suggests there were 310,000 deaths during the famine of the 1740s (the population was estimated to be 2.4 million) while excess mortality is estimated at 65,000 during the 1816–17 crisis.[5]

The question of the nature and scale of Irish poverty also dovetailed with broader debates on the 'state of Ireland': shorthand for a neglectful landlord class, social and political unrest, and poor economic performance. Virginia Crossman has interpreted state interventions in welfare as attempts to assuage the anxieties of a disaffected Irish population, which needed to be convinced of the efficacy of the Union and bound more firmly to the polity of the United Kingdom of Great Britain and Ireland.[6] The nineteenth century also saw the active, and ostensibly beneficent, state become manifest in enhanced methods of inspection in the arena of health and welfare. The establishment of networks of institutions brought with them separate, dedicated inspectorates including the Irish Poor Law Commissioners (1847) and a lunacy inspectorate (1845), while local and national boards of health were established and collated data on outbreaks of fever.

The intractable nature of Irish poverty was apparently confirmed during the humanitarian crisis of the Great Famine. The famine hit Ireland less than a decade after the introduction of the 1838 Irish Poor Law Act, the most comprehensive intervention thus far in welfare provision – medical and non-medical. It brought to Ireland a network of workhouses, most of which were completed on the eve of the famine, and by

---

4 A. Sneddon, 'Institutional medicine and state intervention', in J. Kelly and F. Clark, *Ireland and medicine in the seventeenth and eighteenth centuries* (Farnham, 2010), 137–62, at 140.

5 D. Dickson, *Arctic Ireland: the extraordinary story of the Great Frost and the forgotten famine of 1740–41* (Dublin, 1997), 72.

6 V. Crossman, *The poor law in Ireland 1838–1948* (Dundalk, 2006), 5.

the end of the nineteenth century, the poor law had become the main organ of public health provision. In contrast to the English poor law, provision for outdoor relief was not included under the 1838 Irish act. As Crossman and Donnacha Seán Lucey have suggested, outdoor relief was deemed particularly unsuitable for Irish conditions and was 'associated with excessive expenditure, dependency and lax administration'. The famine crisis forced a fundamental change in policy and in the face of considerable resistance, an 1847 amending act allowed poor law authorities to extend relief to the destitute outside the workhouses. Resistance to outdoor relief remained entrenched, however, and many poor law guardians reverted to pre-famine practice at the end of the crisis. In the post-famine period, there was significant diversity in the provision of outdoor relief, brought about, as Crossman has shown, by political campaigns and economic crises, and expenditure on it increased after 1880. In response to the near-famine conditions in the west of Ireland in 1879–81, poor law guardians were forced to 'abandon their opposition' and outdoor relief 'became an accepted, and acceptable, method'.[7] Some guardians remained resolutely opposed: this was notable among the pro-Union poor law guardians in the north of Ireland. Among these unions, Olwen Purdue has noted a division between two welfare systems: one among the 'more liberal eastern unions' dominated by Presbyterian, commercial-based guardians, which tended to spend more on outdoor relief, and another overseen by boards in southern and western Ulster, which were landlord-dominated, did not appoint female guardians and favoured indoor over outdoor relief.[8]

In the decades after the Great Famine, the poor law system became responsible for the administration and implementation of a range of public health legislation including child welfare schemes under the boarding-out system. In addition, the workhouses became steadily more 'medicalised' as the century proceeded. In 1862, for example, access to workhouse infirmaries was extended to the non-destitute. In the mid- to late nineteenth century, the proportion of able-bodied workhouse inmates steadily declined while the numbers of sick and infirm poor seeking relief expanded. These included the 'insane, imbeciles and epileptics', who were not always maintained in district lunatic asylums. The post-famine workhouse inmates were often night-lodgers who, through their interaction with boards of guardians, exposed themselves to the threat of prosecution under the 1847 Vagrancy Act.[9]

The famine also prompted a reassessment of the relationship between the poor law and medical services, especially the dispensaries. Almost immediately after the crisis,

7 V. Crossman, *Poverty and the poor law in Ireland, 1850–1914* (Liverpool, 2013), 64.

8 O. Purdue, 'Poor relief in the north of Ireland, 1850–1921', in V. Crossman and P. Grey (eds.), *Poverty and welfare in Ireland, 1838–1948* (Dublin, 2011), 23–36.

9 Crossman, *Poverty and the poor law in Ireland*, 1–12, 198–225.

the dispensary system was enlarged and incorporated into the poor law system under the 1851 Medical Charities Act. Ireland was divided into 723 dispensary districts with 776 dedicated dispensary doctors and 10 midwives.[10] The number of midwives appointed to the service increased but at a very slow pace: there was resistance from dispensary doctors and rates of pay were low. The dispensary service provided outdoor relief for the sick poor – an estimated 650,000 cases in 1909 – at dispensaries and at their homes. The combined impact of the dispensary system and the expansion of out-door relief after 1880, Crossman has argued, resulted in the decline of the number of sick admissions into the workhouses.

The medical dispensary system, local infirmaries and workhouses provided consid-erable employment to Irish doctors. Between 1750 and 1860, medical education had evolved significantly, producing large numbers of qualified doctors many of whom emigrated. By the mid-nineteenth century, changes to the older educational structures alongside the blurring of traditional occupational boundaries of each grouping had facilitated the rise of a more generalist practitioner. This group became the local family doctor, pivotal actors in the delivery of health care and, until the late nineteenth cen-tury, usually male. Their medical education was more likely to include medical and surgical training as well as a qualification in midwifery, allowing them to secure the potentially lucrative if risky business of childbirth. When and where possible they had private practices, seeking out a more affluent clientele and providing medical treatment and care in the domestic environment. Yet, success was dependent on the local econ-omy of an area and there were significant differences in the regional distribution of reg-istered practitioners, with a strong, if predictable, urban bias. For example, according to the 1861 *Medical Directories*, Dublin city had one registered practitioner to 478 people, Cork had one to 904 while the large county of Mayo had one for 14,988.[11] And it was in domestic settings that most of the Irish population received their health care from a range of practitioners – the formally trained doctor and the self-styled healers who were competing for trade in a busy market – and partook of forms of domestic medicine associated with both the English-language public sphere and older, healing traditions.

16.3. Health, Welfare and Morality, 1750–1880

Ireland's health and welfare infrastructure was augmented further in the nine-teenth century through the consolidation and expansion of religious communities' involvement. Eighteenth- and early nineteenth-century philanthropy is associated with

10 R. D. Cassell, *Medical charities, medical politics: the Irish system and the poor law, 1836–1872* (Woodbridge, 1997), 92.
11 C. Cox, 'Access and engagement: the medical dispensary service in post-famine Ireland', in C. Cox and M. Luddy, *Cultures of care in Irish medical history, 1750–1970* (Houndmills, 2010), 57–78.

Protestant, usually Anglican and often female, laity. From the early nineteenth century, however, there was a growth in the involvement of Roman Catholic religious communities, especially female, in health and welfare activities. This is exemplified by the establishment by Margaret Aylward, foundress of the Holy Faith Sisters, of St Brigid's Orphanage in 1829 and by Mary Aikenhead, foundress of the Sisters of Charity in Ireland, of St Vincent's Hospital in 1834. The number of these institutions and the range of their activities expanded over the course of the century and went beyond Dublin. For example, the Sisters of Mercy founded the Mater Infirmorum Hospital in Belfast in 1883. It became a teaching hospital attached to Queen's University Medical School. An increasingly confident and affluent Roman Catholic middle class supported these pursuits, though there was a relative absence of lay Catholic charities until the twentieth century.

Protestant charity work remained an important part of the welfare landscape. It was wide-ranging, involving various forms of rescue work, and contributed to child welfare, notably through the activities of the Protestant Orphan Society. Also, some older medical institutions such as Adelaide, Dr Steeven's and Sir Patrick Dun's hospitals retained a distinctly Protestant 'hue' well into the twentieth century. From the 1870s, there was an intensification of lay, female, Protestant charitable work. Most organisations were managed by all-female committees with male figures involved as honorary members, often acting as treasurers. Oonagh Walsh has estimated that by '1914, there were between 470 and 500 Protestant full time voluntary charity workers in Dublin, whose labours were augmented by over 1,600 women'.[12] In Belfast, philanthropic activities were imbued with a strong Protestant evangelicalism supported by a relatively affluent Protestant middle class. There were disputes between Anglican and Presbyterian as well as between Catholic and Protestant organisations.

The activities of these lay and religious groups entrenched confessional divisions within Irish welfare and hospital facilities, as well as medical education. While accusations of souperism were heightened during the famine, the charge of conversionism was laid at the feet of most state and philanthropic organisations. Sectarian clashes between the clergy of the different religions assigned to the country's workhouses were commonplace and often vitriolic. In these contexts, saving the bodies of the poor and saving their souls – at birth, at death and in between – became a constant source of tension.

The gatekeeping and management of access to health and welfare services in lay and religious institutions exemplified various articulations of health and welfare entitlements, revealing attitudes about class, gender and confessional affiliation. Concepts of

12 O. Walsh, 'Protestant female philanthropy in Dublin in the early 20th century', *History Ireland*, 5 (1997), 27–31.

deserving and undeserving continued to underpin responses to the poor and entitlements to relief under the various welfare and health schemes. Generally, the poor were
divided between those who had fallen into difficulties through no fault of their own
and those whose 'immoral' and disreputable behaviour precipitated their decline. Yet,
these definitions varied according to the ethos of the institutions. Under the poor law,
all categories of the destitute poor were entitled to relief; however, mere poverty, and
not destitution, was the official criterion for entitlement to relief from the dispensary
system. There were, however, repeated claims that the dispensary 'ticket' system was
easily and regularly abused by patients with the means to pay for medical treatment.
As noted above, from 1862 admission to workhouse infirmaries was on medical need
rather than for destitution. None the less, the stigma associated with the poor law system, reinforced by the requirement that the names of recipients of outdoor relief be
posted publicly, remained engrained in Irish popular attitudes. A repeated criticism
of indoor poor law relief, especially among the Catholic clergy, was the perceived failure to impose a 'moral classification of inmates', and in particular the failure to separate the respectable from the 'immoral' poor. Such critics directed their strongest
admonishment at the practice of mixing female 'prostitutes' and single mothers with
'respectable' women.[13] The presence of nursing nuns in the workhouses was intended
to guard against the spread of moral contagion among 'respectable' inmates.[14] Finally,
as other chapters in this volume highlight, there are significant difficulties in differentiating health and welfare mechanisms from the more punitive apparatus of the state and
of charitable and religious bodies. Despite the range of Protestant charitable work, by
the end of the nineteenth century, the extent to which Catholic organisations involved
themselves in welfare and health provision ensured that they operated almost as 'a state
within a state'.

16.4. The Rise of State Medicine, 1880–2000

Many of the nineteenth-century structural and ideological patterns, which typified
health and welfare services, persisted in twentieth-century Ireland. Internationally,
trends in health and welfare provision in the late nineteenth and the first half of the
twentieth century were characterised by increased state responsibility for the general
well-being of populations. In Britain, this culminated in the foundation of the National
Health Service in 1948. Increasingly, the emphasis within governmental policy moved

13 Crossman, *Poverty and the poor law*, 168–97.
14 M. Luddy, *Women and philanthropy in nineteenth-century Ireland* (Cambridge, 1995); Luddy, '"Angels of
mercy": nuns as workhouse nurses, 1861–1898', in G. Jones and E. Malcolm (eds.), *Medicine, disease and the state
in Ireland, 1650–1940* (Cork, 1999), 102–20.

away from individual freedom in matters relating to health and welfare towards a collective responsibility administered and enforced by the state. Key drivers underpinning this change were the ideology of universalism and efforts to de-stigmatise access to health and welfare provision, especially poor law services, ensuring that welfare policies started to reach the middle classes.[15]

In pre-independence Ireland, evidence of the shift in governmental policy towards collective responsibility and coercion can be traced in the public health campaigns to combat communicable infections such as smallpox, diphtheria, typhus, cholera and other epidemic diseases. The provisions of the late nineteenth-century Public Health Acts, though potentially far reaching, were undermined somewhat by the lack of resolve among the local and municipal authorities empowered to clear and clean unhealthy living environments. None the less, nationally the incidence of diseases such as typhus declined by the late 1880s, although the rate of decline was slower in urban centres and was linked to improved housing conditions, in part facilitated by the Labourers' Acts of 1883 and 1885, rather than medical innovation. The incidence of tuberculosis remained stubbornly high in Ireland while declining elsewhere in Europe. Pulmonary tuberculosis was one of the most common causes of death during the

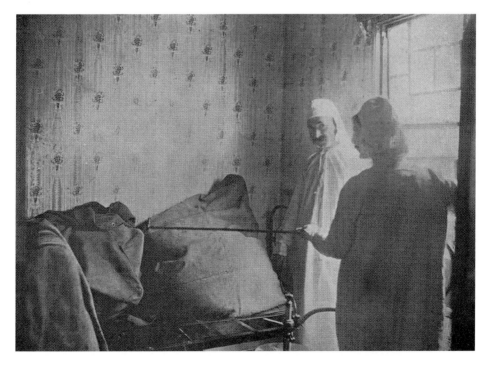

Figure 16.1 Disinfectors at work. Courtesy of the Dublin City Libraries and Archives.

15 D. Porter, *Health, civilization and the state: a history of public health from ancient to modern times* (London, 1999), 196–230.

nineteenth century, but it was the 1890s before it attracted concerted attention from public health officials. Despite accounting for 16 per cent of all deaths in 1904, compulsory notification of the disease was not introduced until the 1940s.

By the end of the nineteenth century, there was a general consensus that the main provider of welfare services, the poor law, was in need of reform, though there was significant debate among British and Irish politicians and social reformers about the shape the restructured service should take. Two separate commissions – the 1906 Viceregal Commission and Arthur Balfour's 1905 Royal Commission on the Poor Law – made a series of recommendations for reform but the new Liberal government in power following the 1906 general election pursued its own agenda. Its welfare reforms marked a shift from the earlier laissez-faire system, associated with mid-nineteenth-century classic liberalism, to a more collectivist and interventionist approach, associated with modern liberalism. In terms of social legislation for Ireland, the most important initiatives were the 1908 Old Age Pensions Act and 1911 National Insurance Act. The Old Age Pensions Act, funded through taxation and means tested, was an important boon to the poor; the 5 shillings payment for those aged over seventy years was a significant sum in Ireland where the weekly wage for unskilled labour ranged from 7s. to 12s. in towns and from 4s. to 7s. for domestic work in the west. Timothy Guinnane has suggested that it increased household co-residence of older people and ensured they were less dependent on indoor and outdoor poor relief. In 1919, it is estimated that 18.9 per cent of the payments in the United Kingdom went to claimants in Ireland. Unemployment insurance and national health insurance were provided under the 1911

Figure 16.2 Dublin sanitary officers, late nineteenth century. Courtesy of the Dublin City Libraries and Archives.

National Health Insurance Act. It provided insurance for all manual and non-manual workers over the age of sixteen and earning up to £250 per annum, but the medical benefits included in the Act were not extended to Ireland and the working of the legislation was gendered. It entitled members to benefits during sickness and disablement only, while women's benefits were restricted on marriage. In 1923, of a workforce of about 1 million, approximately 420,000 people were insured under the Act and 29 per cent of these were women.[16] Until 1933 the national insurance scheme was the only form of unemployment assistance.

Cormac Ó Gráda has concluded that on the eve of the First World War living conditions had improved for much of the Irish population with regional variations and the gap between men and women narrowing, while the population benefited from evolving social legislation. By 1911 there was an increase in small savings held in post offices, a rise in tobacco, tea and sugar consumption, improved housing standards (with the near disappearance of the once ubiquitous single-room cabins), a rise in birth weights, and a rise in wages for skilled but not agricultural workers.[17] In terms of agriculture, the main economic activity, there had been a radical transfer of land away from large landlords and into the ownership of farmers, accompanied by a reduction in the number of labourers and cottiers. While these improvements and the benefits of preventive measures support a meliorist interpretation of Ireland's health and welfare history, it is important not to exaggerate the reach of these advances. On the eve of the First World War, the infamous housing conditions in Dublin lagged behind those in Belfast while the nutritional status of the population, as indicated by the height of prisoners, reveals little improvement among Dubliners between the 1840s and 1900s.[18] With its strong industrial economy, Belfast provided men and women with job opportunities unavailable to their Dublin peers. Most state health and welfare institutions were severely overcrowded with staff and patients inhabiting outdated and decrepit buildings, encouraging the spread of lethal diseases such as dysentery, tuberculosis and influenza among residents and staff. Following the reform of local government in 1898 responsibility for public health and welfare infrastructure and services fell to the new local county councils and monies were raised through local taxation. These councils were often reluctant to authorise increases to expenditure for necessary improvements, or to pursue expensive public health policies likely to alienate local electorates. In addition, the voluntary hospitals were under severe pressure following the First World War. Already heavily dependent on parliamentary grants by 1911, the marked decline in

16 M. Cousins, 'Sickness, gender and national health insurance, 1920s to 1940s', in M. Preston and M. Ó hÓgartaigh (eds.), *Gender and medicine in Ireland 1700–1950* (Syracuse, 2012), 169–88, at 170.
17 C. Ó Gráda, *Ireland: a new economic history 1780–1939* (Oxford, 1994), 236–54, at 250.
18 M. E. Daly, *Dublin: the disposed capital: a social and economic history 1860–1914* (Cork, 1984, 1985, 2011), 55–64; Ó Gráda, *Ireland*, 245.

public subscriptions and the deleterious impact of inflationary wartime conditions on the cost of medical services, temporarily alleviated by the British army's need for hospital beds and willingness to pay for them, threatened their long-term survival.

The partition of Ireland presaged a division in health and welfare systems. The timing of Irish independence (1922) was as important a factor as independence itself. The Irish Free State became independent just as Britain was entering a period of significant change in relation to social policy, marked by an increasing ambivalence towards institutional solutions and founded on the ideology of universalism. Initially, in independent Ireland, social policy stagnated, remaining in many respects based on Victorian values and policies. In 1920 local authorities and poor law guardians loyal to the then 'alternative' Dáil Éireann state broke with the Local Government Board and were faced with a huge gap in funding. This gap remained after independence and a policy of retrenchment in welfare was embarked upon. Steadily, the existing poor law system was replaced by the local authority county schemes. While there were variations at a local level, the schemes replaced the existing workhouses with a reduced number of county homes for the aged and infirm, and county hospitals for maternity, medical and surgical cases. Outdoor relief was expanded in the form of home assistance, while those eligible for relief were defined as any person who was unable to provide 'for himself or his dependents the necessaries of life'. The poor law boards of guardians were abolished and responsibilities were transferred to local authorities: the poor law was formally dismantled in 1925. Local authorities acted as the main organ of public health campaigns, strengthened further from 1926 by the appointment of county medical officers of health. These officers were responsible for local sanitary health, the implementation of infectious diseases acts and schemes to treat venereal diseases, originally introduced in 1917. Throughout the 1920s and into the early 1930s, the policy of what Mel Cousins has described as 'national retrenchment' was continued; there were significant cuts to the old age pension and more stringent means testing. Unemployment increased rapidly in this period, but the new state lacked an employment policy and in spite of the deliberations of numerous departmental committees, support for the unemployed continued to be provided through unemployment insurance, the provision of short-term relief work or support through local authority home assistance schemes. In terms of an underpinning political philosophy, entitlement to welfare provisions continued to be divided between the 'deserving' and 'undeserving', with implementation of means testing and limited movement towards the principle of universalism. There was some change in the 1930s with the new Fianna Fáil government's commitment to a programme of greater spending, which included expenditure in health and welfare. This resulted in the introduction of widows' and orphans' pensions in 1935, unemployment assistance to uninsured workers in 1933 and, later, children's allowances in 1944. With the exception of the widows' and orphans' pensions, access to these forms of relief was usually means tested – in the case of children's allowances this was in the form of a taxation 'clawback' – and payment was made to male heads of households. As Cousins has argued, 'Fianna Fáil's policy saw women as part of the broader family unit and economically dependent on men', while initiatives such as the children's allowance were driven by a concern to relieve family poverty rather than by the pronatalism evident in other European countries.

In Northern Ireland, the poor law and associated welfare provision remained in place until the introduction of the National Health Service in 1948. Until then, social protection retained many of the principles laid out under the nineteenth-century poor law and the subsequent Liberal Party reforms with some modifications. For workers with insurance, the medical benefit system, which had not been extended to Ireland in 1911, was introduced under the 1930 National Insurance Act (Northern Ireland). Closely modelled on the British system, the Act provided the insured with access to a panel of doctors; however, as Peter Martin argues, it did not remove the taint of pauperism from the Northern Irish welfare system. The dispensary system continued to be drawn on by the sick poor without insurance until the introduction of the NHS.

In independent Ireland, state interventions in matters of health and welfare, especially at the intersection between morality and health, frequently encountered deep-felt opposition from proponents of Catholic social teaching, supporters of subsidiarity and voluntarism, and opponents of the form of social welfare policy advocated in William Beveridge's 1942 report which had outlined proposed reforms for Britain and Northern Ireland. The report, adopted by the British Labour government after the Second World War, became the basis of a series of legislative reforms that became known as the National Health Service and were introduced in 1948. The key legislative planks, which also extended to Northern Ireland, were the National Insurance Act, the National Assistance Act and the National Health Service Act. The National Assistance Act abolished the poor law and provided assistance to those who were not covered under earlier National Insurance Acts. The reforms also included the 1945 Family Allowances Act, which provided children's allowances to families. Beveridge was opposed to means testing access to social protection and the underlining principle of the acts was universalism – equality of opportunity and the equitable distribution of wealth – thereby following a European model of welfare, particularly notable in Germany.

At the time of the publication of the Beveridge report there was an agreement within the Department of Local Government and Public Health that health care and social welfare policy in the southern state was in need of reform. In 1944, a Public Health Bill was drawn up which proposed extending state responsibility and powers in the control of infectious diseases, medical inspection of school children, and the extension of maternity and child welfare provisions. The bill was out of step with intellectual currents in the south at the time. Chief among these was the growth in popularity of Catholic social teaching, which attempted to apply the teachings of papal encyclicals, notably *Quadragesimo Anno* (1931) and *Casti Connubii* (1930), to contemporary social and economic problems. These encyclicals advocated the principle of subsidiarity, according to which the role of the state was kept to a minimum; the state's activities should support the work of vocational groups and corporations to further common interest but it should not supersede these groups. Aligned to this was the view that the family was the foundation of moral and social order and the state should protect it in terms of its social and economic policies. These principles had powerful advocates in Irish society, most notably among the Roman Catholic hierarchy and, in particular, the archbishop of Dublin, John Charles McQuaid, but also among Irish doctors and civil servants. Alternative proposals for the reform of services based on these principles were also tabled in the 1940s but the government remained committed to the original set of proposals, in the form of a 1945 Public Health Bill. The measures were strongly bureaucratic and centralised while components, such as the maternity and child health services, contained elements of universalism. The 1945 bill was defeated, but the subsequent 1947 Public Health Bill, which was substantially the same, passed, though some of the controversial proposals had been amended. Despite these concessions, there was significant opposition from political and other vested interests. The campaigns to resist the Act revealed powerful alliances between Catholic doctors, the Irish Medical Association and the hierarchy of the Catholic Church, notably McQuaid, alongside political opposition from the Fine Gael party. Shortly after the passage of the bill, the Fianna Fáil government published a White Paper on further reform, which proposed to provide free access to health services.

A new inter-party government attempted to implement the clauses of the 1947 Health Act between 1948 and 1951, in particular the welfare services for mothers and children, known as the 'Mother and Child scheme'. These were intended to be free of charge and not means tested, though there was no compulsion to use the service. Opposition to the 1947 Act, in particular to the Mother and Child scheme in the 1950s, was based on a suspicion that the provisions were a form of 'socialist' medicine, that they diminished medical professional autonomy and income, and exposed adherents of the Catholic faith to potentially corrupting influences, especially in relation to teaching on family planning. The inter-party government fell as a result of the controversy over the Act, although many of its provisions were carefully renegotiated and eventually implemented in more circumscribed forms during the 1950s. The subsequent 1953 Act and the social welfare reforms of the 1950s consolidated a two-tier, tax-based system of welfare and health provision in Ireland, entitlement to which was based on means testing and through private insurance. The principles underpinning this remained relatively unchanged until the 1970s and differed significantly from Northern Ireland, which benefited from the NHS model.

It is a mistake to interpret the actions of the Roman Catholic hierarchy in the arena of health and welfare as expressions of confessionalism alone; they reflected profound anxieties over international ideologies shaping mid-twentieth-century welfare provision, especially at the intersection between morality and welfare. Catholic lobby groups were not unaware of the very real threats to the health of the Irish population. Irish life expectancy, while improving in the first half of the twentieth century, had not kept pace with that of Britain, the USA and Europe. Alongside the continued threat of tuberculosis, infant mortality rates remained high until the 1940s. The decline in the mortality rates from typhoid, typhus, diphtheria, scarlet fever and puerperal sepsis achieved in the 1930s – the last fell from 687 deaths in 1936 to 273 in 1941 – was reversed in the later stages of the Emergency (the Second World War).[19] In 1953, mortality rates from all forms of tuberculosis were significantly higher in the southern state than in Great Britain and Northern Ireland.

The southern state remained heavily dependent on Catholic welfare and health services. Intrinsic to their activities was protecting the Catholic population from the 'wrong' influences on matters relating to health and welfare, and especially in relation to reproductive health. The Catholic Social Welfare Bureau, established by Archbishop McQuaid in 1942 and operated by the Legion of Mary, was intended to tackle social

Figure 16.3 Destroy House Flies poster. Courtesy of the Dublin City Libraries and Archives.

19 M. E. Daly, 'Death and disease in independent Ireland, 1920–1970', in Cox and Luddy, *Cultures of care*, 229–50, at 234.

problems under a Catholic aegis. The Bureau included a Family Welfare section (1945) that acted as an agency to train hospital almoners and social workers in a Catholic environment. In addition, there were sections of the Bureau concerned with the welfare of emigrants (established in 1942), playgrounds (1943) and welfare in primary schools (1944). In Northern Ireland, 'voluntary action' also had a strong religious character and the dominant organisations were closely aligned to Protestant bodies. A key organisation in the sector was the Belfast Council of Social Welfare established in 1919; its lineage can be located in the Belfast Charity Organisation Society (1906) and Belfast Christian Civic Union (1903). The Council was involved in a range of activities, including financial contributions to voluntary hospitals, providing after-care services for young men discharged from borstals, and child guidance services. The Council acted as an umbrella body for a range of organisations providing relief during the crisis of the 1920s and 1930s, reporting that two thousand working-class families in Belfast were destitute in the 1920s.[20] The organisation continued to be active after the introduction of the NHS.

The 1950s has been characterised as a period of compromise in terms of health and welfare in the Republic of Ireland. An increase in spending on health services improved hospital services, provided routine BCG vaccinations against tuberculosis, and augmented services for mothers and infants. Life expectancy improved, but the Republic lagged behind its neighbours. In 1958, its infant mortality rates were higher than those in Northern Ireland, England and Wales, and Scotland, although rural Ireland continued to be a healthier place to live.[21] As Mary E. Daly argues, the increase in expenditure fell short of the NHS model of welfare, and private insurance remained a significant actor in the health landscape. The dependence on local rather than central taxation to fund medical services was also a significant impediment.

Contemporaries viewed the Republic's admission to the European Economic Community (EEC) in 1973 as an opportunity to increase state expenditure on health and welfare. It appears, however, that in the late 1970s expenditure on social welfare was a declining proportion of overall government spending, a trend continued during the recession of the 1980s. The combined impact of the 1970s women's movement and entry into the EEC improved women's rights in terms of not only equal pay but also entitlements to welfare support. The Commission on the Status of Women, established as part of the 1967 United Nations Commission on the Status of Women directive, reported in 1973, and recommended changes in employment law, pay, pension rights and jury service, alongside welfare rights for women. In terms of welfare policy,

20 N. Acheson, B. Harvey, J. Kearney and A. Williamson, *Two paths, one purpose: voluntary action in Ireland, north and south. A report to the Royal Irish Academy Third Sector Research Programme* (Centre for Voluntary Action Studies, University of Ulster, n.d.), 34–5.

21 Daly, 'Death and disease in independent Ireland', 240; L. Earner-Byrne, *Maternity and child welfare in Dublin, 1922–60* (Manchester, 2007), 40.

the Commission influenced the shape of the 1974 Social Welfare Act, which introduced direct payment to women of children's allowance, while an unmarried mothers' allowance had been introduced in 1973. The principle of gender equality in social and welfare policies was further supported through recourse to the European Court of Human Rights. In 1979, for example, an especially significant case was taken by Mrs Johanna Airey against the Irish state. Airey sought a judicially ordered separation, but was unable to obtain it as, in the absence of legal aid, she lacked the financial means to retain a solicitor. The Court found this was a violation of her right to access a court for determination of her civil rights and obligations. Within European law the finding is interpreted as setting a precedent that states may have positive obligations with respect to civil and political rights. While no longer treating women as dependants, these legislative changes did not alter the overall approach to Irish welfare and health policy which continued to be based on a system that determined access through insurance or means-tested benefits to non-insured workers.

In Northern Ireland, the arrival of the NHS is generally associated with improvements in welfare services and in the health of the population, although there are few critical assessments. Ferriter has noted that its arrival 'prompted a battle of statistics' on the performance of services each side of the border.[22] The figures suggest that the service brought some improvements. The rates of maternal and infant mortality in Northern Ireland, for example, declined in the 1950s and 1960s, falling below rates in the Republic. Politicians and policy-makers in Northern Ireland insisted on the principle of maintaining parity with welfare services in England and Wales but, as demonstrated in the case of provision for children, this was also shaped by local concerns. This is reflected in the history of the Mater Infirmorum in Belfast after 1948. The hospital, which the Sisters of Mercy continued to manage, remained outside the operation of the NHS until 1971 and did not receive grants from the Department of Health. The decision to withhold funds differed from the English practice where voluntary hospitals outside the NHS were given financial support. Moreover, the conservative nature of Northern Ireland society on matters relating to sexual health, in particular women's health, was apparent in the delay in introducing clinics to treat venereal diseases in the interwar period and a family planning service between 1950 and 1974.

16.5.   'Pushing the State Back Out'?

As earlier sections of this chapter suggest, the development of lay and religious philanthropic welfare services is well documented. Other aspects of what has been broadly and rather imprecisely defined as 'voluntarism' remain relatively underexplored. In

---

22 D. Ferriter, *Ambiguous republic: Ireland in the 1970s* (London, 2012), 451.

part, this neglect is a result of the relative weakness of the self-help movement in the nineteenth century. For example, the Friendly Society movement in Ireland was less prominent within, though by no means absent from, the nineteenth-century welfare landscape. Research on voluntary organisations operating in the south indicates they were prominent in campaigns to combat poverty and diseases, and made effective use of the media in communicating their messages. The National Association for the Prevention of Tuberculosis and Consumption and the Women's National Health Association are early and well-known examples of these initiatives, but from the 1950s, for example, voluntary organisations campaigned for improved facilities for survivors of poliomyelitis. The Irish Cancer Society pursued anti-tobacco campaigns during the 1970s while the Gay Health Action group was active during the AIDS/HIV epidemic of the 1980s and 1990s.

Prior to the 1970s, most organisations had to negotiate the influence of McQuaid. Some secured his patronage, while others, such as the Anti-Tuberculosis League, did not. In this instance, McQuaid endorsed the activities of the Anti-Tuberculosis section of the Irish Red Cross, which he believed to be a safer pair of hands. The Society of St Vincent de Paul and the Society for the Prevention of Cruelty to Children were also approved forms of Catholic welfare relief. The Combat Poverty Agency (1986), incorporated into the Department of Social and Family Affairs in 2009, and the Conference of Religious in Ireland (CORI), established in 1981, were at the forefront of campaigns for the elimination of poverty during the employment and economic crises of the 1980s. CORI was part of the change in attitude towards poverty evident from the late 1970s. It advanced a system of support founded on the concept of a basic income for all rather than solely focused on supporting the male, breadwinner, family-based system. In recent decades, central government's financial support for voluntary organisations has grown north and south of the border, enhanced by contributions from European programmes.[23]

In recent decades there has emerged a 'new welfare history' of the Anglophone world which has shifted the focus from inquiries into state structures and elite politicians and technocrats to incorporate 'absent' protagonists, most especially the experiences and attitudes of consumers and recipients – voluntary and involuntary, and often poor – of state and philanthropic services. There are relatively few studies of this kind for Ireland, but the research that has been completed identifies the extent to which the sick and impoverished, and their families, while subject to surveillance and responded to with doubt and suspicion, were not always passive protagonists upon whom specific ideals of class, behaviour and power were inscribed. None the less, since the late 1990s, the 'endless stream of controversies and inquiries involving the abuse' of children and

---

23 Acheson *et.al.*, 'Two paths, one purpose', 195, 240.

vulnerable women in institutional care has revealed the punitive and brutalising nature of many institutions, and of state and religious welfare regimes.[24] Numerous documentaries, official inquiries and investigations have revealed harrowing accounts of sexual and physical abuse and the ways in which people were processed between state and voluntary institutions and systems. The revelations have added significantly to previous, often ignored, survivors' memoirs and testimonies, some of which had circulated for at least a decade.[25]

16.6. Conclusion

In an influential study published in 1990, the Danish sociologist Gøsta Esping-Andersen divided welfare states across the western world into three models; the Social Democratic model based on the principle of universalism; the Christian Democratic model based on the principle of subsidiarity and heavily dependent on social insurance schemes; and the Liberal model based on market dominance and private provision. Esping-Andersen found that the welfare models then in operation in Ireland, both north and south, did not neatly fall into any of these categories.[26] The reasons for this are, in part at least, historical. In the Republic of Ireland dependence on religious-run, and often institutional, solutions to health and welfare problems was enduring, while private insurance and means testing in accessing provision continues to be commonplace. Some of these legacies were also evident in Northern Ireland, in spite of its inclusion within the NHS. The literature reviewed here highlights the complexity of changing responses to poverty and vulnerability, revealing the necessity of understanding the historical roots of contemporary patterns and structures. To tease out what Esping-Andersen observed further work is needed that situates Ireland's history of health and welfare policy in relation to that of other countries.

FURTHER READING

Buckley, S. A. *The cruelty man: child welfare, the NSPCC and the state in Ireland, 1889–1956* (Manchester, 2013).

Cousins, M. *The birth of social welfare in Ireland, 1922–1952* (Dublin, 2003).

Cox, C. *Negotiating insanity in the southeast of Ireland* (Manchester, 2012).

24 H. Ferguson, 'Abused and looked after children as "moral dirt": child abuse and institutional care in historical perspective', *Journal of Social Policy*, 36 (2007), 123.

25 'Early days in Letterfrack: memories of an industrial school by Peter Tyrrell', *Hibernia* (June 1964); P. Doyle, *The God Squad* (Dublin, 1988); M. Raftery and E. O'Sullivan, *Suffer the little children: the inside story of Ireland's industrial schools* (Dublin, 1999).

26 G. Esping-Andersen, *The three worlds of welfare capitalism* (Princeton, 1990), 26–9.

Curtis, M. *Challenge to democracy: militant Catholicism in modern Ireland* (Dublin, 2010).

Daly, M. E. '"An atmosphere of sturdy independence": the state and Dublin hospitals in the 1930s', in Jones and Malcolm, *Medicine, disease and the state in Ireland*, 234–52.

Daly, M. E. '"Oh Kathleen Ni Houlihan, your way's a thorny way": the condition of women in twentieth century Ireland', in A. Bradley and M. G. Valiulis (eds.), *Gender and sexuality in modern Ireland* (Amherst, 1997), 102–26.

Daly, M. E. *The slow failure: population decline and independent Ireland, 1920–1973* (Madison, WI, 2006).

Earner-Byrne, L. *Mother and child: maternity and child welfare in Dublin, 1922–60* (Manchester, 2007).

Geary, L. M. *Medicine and charity in Ireland, 1718–1851* (Dublin, 2004).

Gestrich, A., E. Hurren and S. A. King. 'Narratives of poverty and sickness in Europe 1780–1938: sources, methods and experiences', in A. Gestrich, E. Hurren and S. A. King (eds.), *Poverty and sickness in modern Europe: narratives of the sick poor, 1780–1938* (London, 2012), 1–34.

Gorsky, M. '"Voluntarism" in English health and welfare: visions of history', in D. S. Lucey and V. Crossman (eds.), *Healthcare in Ireland and Britain from 1850: voluntary, regional and comparative perspectives* (London, 2014), 31–60.

Gray, A. M. 'Government and the administration of hospital services in Northern Ireland, 1948–1973: the Northern Ireland Hospitals Authority', PhD thesis, University of Ulster, 1993.

Guinnane, T. W. *The vanishing Irish: households, migration, and the rural economy in Ireland, 1850–1914* (Princeton, 1997).

Jones, G. and E. Malcolm (eds.). *Medicine, disease and the state in Ireland, 1650–1940* (Cork, 1999).

Jordan, A. *Who cared? Charity in Victorian and Edwardian Belfast* (Belfast, 1994).

Kelly, G. and J. Pinkerton. 'The Children (Northern Ireland) Order 1995: prospects for progress?', in M. Hill and J. Aldgate (eds.), *Child welfare services: developments in law, policy, practice and research* (London and Philadelphia, 1996), 40–55.

Kelly, J. and F. Clark. *Ireland and medicine in the seventeenth and eighteenth centuries* (Farnham, 2010).

Kennedy, F. *Cottage to crèche: family change in Ireland* (Dublin, 2001).

McCormick, L. '"The scarlet woman in person": the establishment of a family planning service in Northern Ireland, 1950–1974', *Social History of Medicine*, 21 (2008), 345–60.

McCormick, L. 'Venereal disease in interwar Northern Ireland', in C. Cox and M. Luddy, *Cultures of care in Irish medical history, 1750–1970* (Handmills, 2010), 191–206.

MacDonagh, O. *States of mind: a study of Anglo-Irish conflict, 1780–1980* (London, 1983).

McKee, E. 'Church–state relations and the development of Irish health policy: the Mother and Child scheme, 1944–53', *Irish Historical Studies*, 25 (1986), 159–94.

Martin, P. 'Ending the pauper taint: medical benefit and welfare reform in Northern Ireland, 1921–39', in V. Crossman and P. Grey (eds.), *Poverty and welfare in Ireland, 1838–1938* (Dublin, 2011), 223–36.

Ó Ciosáin, N. *Ireland in official print culture, 1800–1850* (Oxford, 2014).

Ó Gráda, C. '"The greatest blessing of all": the old age pension in Ireland', *Past and Present*, 175 (2002), 124–61.

O'Neill, T.P. 'Fever and public health in pre-famine Ireland', *Journal of the Royal Society of Antiquaries of Ireland*, 103 (1973), 1–34.

Tyrrell, P. *Founded on fear*, ed. D. Whelan (Dublin, 2006).

17 Old Age, Death and Mourning

Patricia Lysaght

17.1. Introduction

In Irish society until relatively recent times, an extensive array of highly formalised traditional protocols for dealing with a deceased person were known to and practised by members of the community, on the occasion of death. An overview study of death ceremonial in Ireland appeared in the 1950s and a regional work on the same topic was published in the 1990s. Both of these publications have dealt fairly extensively with mortuary practices largely in the circumstances of 'good death', that is death from old age in the presence of family and community.[1] The present chapter also treats of 'good death' as the full range of mortuary customs as practised in Ireland, extending from the moment of death onwards, can thereby be brought into play. While Hartmann's 1952 work was essentially a contribution to the study of Indo-Germanic religion, and Tyers's 1992 publication was largely of a descriptive nature, this chapter proposes to examine traditional death ceremonial in Ireland in the nineteenth century, and for much of the twentieth, in the light of Arnold van Gennep's 1909 (translated 1960) theory of passage rites or ceremonial patterns which, in different cultures, mark an individual's transition from one phase of life to the next, or from one social world to another. Van Gennep divided passage rites into three sub-groups in accordance with the order in which they were observed: rites of separation, rites of transition and rites of incorporation. These

---

1 Other studies appearing in the intervening years, some of which are mentioned in this chapter, have focused on different aspects of the wake or vigil for a deceased person, or on the position concerning the wake in circumstances of anomalous death, especially that arising from violence, drowning, stillbirth or the lack of baptism before death.

corresponded to the stages of the transition involved, namely, separation from the first group, the actual transition itself and union with the second group.

According to van Gennep's analytical framework, the passage rites in the case of death can be understood as marking the deceased person's separation from the living social group, his or her transition to, and incorporation into, the community of the dead. As we shall see in this chapter, this symbolic structure can be applied, to a greater or lesser extent, to traditional mortuary practices in Ireland, ranging from the moment of death to the burial process and to the visitation of the grave thirty days after interment.

But before dealing specifically with traditional and contemporary death ceremonial in Ireland, it is of interest to review briefly some of the main works in death studies from a range of scholars and disciplines in Europe and further afield, especially from the 1950s onwards.

17.2. Literature Survey

The second half of the twentieth century witnessed a proliferation of literature on death in the western world. This literature included the publication of English translations of classical early twentieth-century works on aspects of death ritual by a number of eminent scholars. These included the French sociologist Robert Hertz, whose 1907 essay 'Contribution à une étude sur la représentation collective de la mort', dealing with the mortuary practices of the Dayak tribes of Borneo, appeared in translation in 1960. The essay is concerned with the phenomena which the French ethnographer and folklorist Arnold van Gennep generalised as *rites de passage* (1909). This 'rites de passage' approach to the study of death in culture has been of fundamental importance in thanatological analysis since its appearance in translation in 1960. Important interdisciplinary studies of death ritual appeared from the 1950s as well as what might be described as a literature providing instructions or guidelines for the bereaved about how to cope with death in a dignified and rational way. The message of much of the last variety of works was that in the modern, industrialised and urbanised western world of the second half of the twentieth century, death, as a natural process, and as an aspect of everyday life, had become unfamiliar, and that death had, in effect, become a taboo topic in society. In his 1965 work, the English sociologist Geoffrey Gorer strongly argued that not only had the process of dying, and death itself, become an unmentionable topic, even a sort of pornography in modern society, but bereavement also had become privatised, resulting in public grieving being considered unseemly, and being, in effect, socially forbidden.

In the USA, Roul Tunley's rhetorical question 'Can you afford to die?' in the *Saturday Evening Post* (17 June 1961) gave rise to a vigorous public discussion of the cost of funerals, shortly before Jessica Mitford's well-known stark commentary on the excesses of the country's funeral industry appeared (1963). At this time, members of various professions and disciplines in the USA had already begun to contribute to a growing literature on death. The psychologist Herman Feifel is credited with establishing dying and death as subjects worthy of scholarly and scientific study in the USA, thanks to his edited volume *The meaning of death* (1959). The work of the Swiss-American psychiatrist Elisabeth Kübler-Ross is well known, especially in terms of her conceptualisation of the emotional stages of dying (1969), while the sociologist David Sudnow (1967), in considering how dying is socially organised, drew attention to the tendency to isolate, both physically and socially, those at the final stage of life – a circumstance which he termed 'social death' – before actual biological death occurred, as part of hospital management strategies. While works such as these drew attention to the psychosocial needs of the dying, a volume both interdisciplinary and cross-cultural in scope, edited by a Yale University history scholar, David E. Stannard (1974), and including essays by Jack Goody ('Death and the interpretation of culture') and Philippe Ariès ('The reversal of death', a translation of 'La mort inversée ...' (1967)), examined attitudes towards death as a dimension of American cultural history.

In the European context, interest in the subject of death by scholars in a range of disciplines was also becoming evident at this time. Swiss and German academics who published on the topic included the psychotherapist Verena Kast (1988) who dealt with the mourning process, while the sociologist Norbert Elias (1982, 1985) regarded the tacit and early isolation of the aged and the dying, leading to what he termed 'the loneliness of dying', as a failure of western society. Gerhard Schmied (1985), also a sociologist, sought to characterise and explain attitudes to dying, death and mourning in modern society as a guide or form of assistance for modern living. Death and burial as themes in Christian theology is the subject matter of a collection of essays edited by the eminent Catholic theologian Klemens Richter (1990) of Münster, Germany.

Scientific studies on the subject of death by historians such as Philippe Ariès, Michel Vovelle, François Lebrun and others, in France, are well known, as are those relating to England by scholars from a number of disciplines. These include Claire Gittings, Julian Litten, David Cressy, Ralph Houlbrooke, Peter C. Jupp and Glennys Howarth. A collection of essays on the topic of death, dying and bereavement edited by Donna Dickenson and Malcolm Johnson (1994) surveys mainly English material from a variety of perspectives suitable for counselling purposes. In Ireland, Susan Leigh Fry's 1999 study of burial practices references the medieval era, while Clodagh Tait's 2002 work deals with the process of dying, funerals, burials, the commemoration of the dead and ideas about the afterlife in early modern Ireland. A recent volume edited by James Kelly and Mary Ann Lyons (2013) looks at the subject of death and dying in Ireland, Britain and Europe from various thematic, historical and geographical perspectives.

Anthropologists have also been active in the field of death studies in the twentieth century. Peter Metcalf and Richard Huntington's cross-cultural analysis of rituals surrounding death (1979, 1991) – which notes, inter alia, that the culturally prescribed reactions to death 'not only reflect social values but are an important force in shaping them' – has been of significance, not only in anthropological studies, but also in sociological and religious approaches to death and dying. Maurice Bloch and J. P. Parry's 1982 edited volume focusing on the significance of the symbols of sexuality, fertility and rebirth in funeral rituals has also been influential in an interdisciplinary context. Referring to the Mediterranean area, Loring Danforth and Alexander Tsiaras's work pointing to the emotional power of funeral rituals also appeared in 1982. The general overview of literature and perspectives on the anthropology of death – and of work by scholars in related disciplines, including sociology, psychology, psychiatry and psychohistory, who concern themselves with cultural implications of death – provided by Phyllis Palgi and Henry Abramovitch in 1984, clearly indicated the significant growth of a cross-cultural perspective in death studies. Referring to Brittany, Ellen Badone's 1989 work explored the complex web of change and continuity in contemporary Breton death ritual and related folk traditions, in the light of social, cultural, religious and economic change. In his study of death rituals in a County Donegal community, Lawrence J. Taylor's approach (1989) was to view death not only as a problem that requires a solution through church rituals and creative popular responses, but also as an opportunity for furthering social, cultural and political ends.

With regard to studies by folklorists, the second half of the twentieth century saw the publication of major works on death customs, beliefs and rituals by leading scholars, especially in Scandinavia. These included highly influential works by the Finnish scholar of comparative religion, Juha Pentikäinen, who dealt with Nordic dead-child traditions (1968), the Swedish-Finnish folklorist Nils Storå, who published a comprehensive study of the burial customs of the Skolt Lapps in Norway and Finland (1971), and Lauri Honko's study of death laments of the Baltic Finns (1974). As we shall now see, studies of death ritual in Ireland were also undertaken by folklorists, especially from the 1950s.

17.3. Dying, Death and Mourning in Ireland: Folkloric Studies and Perspectives

In Ireland, studies by folklorists of aspects of dying, death, burial and mourning also appeared in the second half of the twentieth century and in the first decade of the twenty-first. Based essentially on folklore archival sources and field research, these studies largely reflect late nineteenth- and twentieth-century Catholic rural standpoints. The 1952 study by the German scholar Hans Hartmann contains overview chapters on deathbed, wake and funeral customs, while Pádraig Tyers's 1992 work ranges from the pre-death to the post-funeral situation as understood and practised in Corca Dhuibhne, West Kerry, in the late nineteenth century and for much of the twentieth. A different perspective is taken by Rosemary Power in her 1994 article, which records some contemporary Northern Ireland funeral practices, including from the Protestant traditions.

Other work by folklorists has largely concentrated on different aspects of the death event. This is evident in the study of Irish wake games in a European context by Seán Ó Súilleabháin (1961, 1967), of the traditional lament for the dead by Rachel Bromwich (1948) and Seán Ó Tuama (1961), and of the banshee, an omen of death connected to specific Gaelic families, by Patricia Lysaght (1986, 1996, 1998). The wake and funerary rites for young children, where held, and particularly nineteenth- and early twentieth-century traditions about the burial practices and places of unbaptised children (stillborn children or children who died naturally before baptism), as collected from oral tradition, have been dealt with by Séan Ó Súilleabháin (1939) and Pádraig Ó Héalaí (2006), with the latter also contrasting children's obsequies in contemporary Ireland with those of a few generations ago. Anne O'Connor's work (1991, 2005) concerns Irish and European folk traditions about the supernatural appearance of the spirits of women who have murdered children and the souls of children who have died without baptism.

A central element of the wake event is the provision of hospitality by the deceased's family. Referring to a number of adjacent townlands in the foothills of the Mourne mountains, Maurna Crozier noted (1987) that irrespective of religious persuasion neighbours were expected to attend a wake, and hospitality was provided for all by the family. Patricia Lysaght (2002, 2003) has also focused on the role of hospitality on the occasion of death from the seventeenth to the twentieth century, commenting on the attitudes of lay and clerical commentators to the often excessive provision of hospitality, especially concerning alcoholic beverages, in the deceased's home, particularly before the interment of the corpse. The contemporary innovation of holding the main hospitality event after the interment of the deceased is also noted.

Revelry and lamentation, as integral parts of the wake ceremony, have also been dealt with – by Gearóid Ó Crualaoich in his structural analysis of the symbolic form of the so-called 'merry wake' (1990, 1998) and by Patricia Lysaght in relation to the traditional lament for the dead (1995, 1997).

As the main purpose of this chapter is to view Irish mortuary practices in the light of van Gennep's theory of passage rites, we will commence with the observances which come into play once the deceased person has passed away.

17.4. Moment of Death and Initial Mortuary Rites in Ireland

After an individual's death, a variety of activities of a ritual nature were engaged in by the deceased's relatives, who represented the living social group, and whose task it was to perform all the practices prescribed by tradition for dealing with a dead person. As soon as death had intervened, the deceased's eyes were closed to the world of the living, by a relative, and the family withdrew from his or her presence for a number of hours. Mirrors were covered, and the windows and doors of the house were opened, in order, it was said, to let the life spirit or soul depart. Clocks in the house, stopped at the time of death, were not restarted until after the burial had taken place – effectively indicating the duration of the separation process for the deceased person, engaged in by the relatives and the community. During the period of withdrawal from the deceased, the family and close neighbours, taking the initiative in the presence of death, began to make preparations for the wake and funeral – by arranging for the provision of wake goods, especially food and drink, mortuary clothes where necessary, and a coffin. Thereafter attention turned again to the deceased who had to be prepared for public viewing during the wake.

The next step in the process of the separation of the deceased from the world of the living consisted of washing, grooming and clothing him or her according to traditional precepts. These procedures, which were conducted in a highly ritualised fashion, were carried out by community members, usually neighbouring women, who were skilled in the preparation of a deceased person for presentation to the living community for the duration of the wake, and for the journey to, and incorporation into, the realm of the dead through funeral and burial. The preparation of the corpse was usually carried out in silence and movement was clockwise around the body. The washing commenced at the head, moving down the body to the feet and back to the head on the left side. Movement across a corpse was avoided, and domestic animals such as the cat and the dog were removed from the house. The water and other items used in the washing of the corpse were carefully disposed of after use, often being committed to the earth, like the corpse would later be at burial. At the conclusion of the preparation process, the deceased, clothed in a white shroud or in later times in the brown habit of the Carmelite Order, was placed supine on a table or on a bed, and a crucifix or a rosary beads, or both, were placed in his or her joined hands. The body was then ready for viewing by relatives and the community during the wake. The deceased's funerary clothes, religious accessories and supine position further set him or her apart from the living community, though still in its presence in a physical sense.

It was at this juncture of the separation process that the family and close relatives first gathered around the corpse to ritually express their grief and to thereby acknowledge the deceased's passing. This event also signalled the commencement of the wake for the dead – a continuous watch kept by the living over a deceased person prior to burial, and a central element of mortuary practice in Ireland, in both urban and rural settings. This highly ritualised ceremony, with its well-known protocols and procedures, can also be regarded as constituting a vital phase in the ongoing process of the separation of the dead person from the world of the living and of transition to the world of the dead. As the wake was generally held in the deceased person's presence, this transition or symbolic journey to the afterlife thus took place in the company of family and community and was facilitated by their engagement in various observances, including revelry to reassert vitality and life, and lamentation to express grief at his or her passing. The duration and elaboration of the wake, especially for a person who died of old age in familiar surroundings, reflected the mode of death of the deceased person, their own social status, and that of their family, in the community of the living. The wake or death vigil was usually held in the deceased person's own home with essentially the same ritual pertaining to both men and women (Lysaght 2001, 472–4). Drama-like in content and performance, the wake consisted of a number of episodes or stages, starting with the presentation of the deceased for viewing by the community, and concluding with their removal from the house, accompanied by family and community members, for burial. As a commemorative occasion for the deceased, it was one in which the community at large participated by, first of all, visiting the house and by paying their respects to the deceased and the family. Strict protocol, which afforded prominence and precedence to the deceased, surrounded a visit to a wake-house. On entering, the visitor, male or female, was expected to go directly to where the deceased was laid out in the presence of the family, and to stay some moments there, usually to say a prayer. Thereafter the wake attendee was expected to approach the dead person's relatives to proffer condolences and to recount (favourable) memories of the deceased, thus honouring his or her life in death. The visitor was then offered refreshment (usually an alcoholic drink), as well as tobacco/cigarettes or snuff, and later a meal, as the wake also included the provision of hospitality by the deceased's relatives (often assisted by neighbours and friends) for those in attendance. Wake visitors were expected to partake of the refreshments and the repast provided in the wake-house, as they were offered in the name of the deceased. At recognised intervals during the wake a collective prayer (usually the Rosary) was said for the benefit of the deceased and the wider community of the dead.

In addition to its commemorative, hospitality and prayerful aspects, the wake occasion, until relatively recent times, and in many urban and rural areas of the country, could also include further activities. These were performed by community members in honour of the deceased and the bereaved family, in the course of the wake event.

Prominent among these were the playing of wake games and the performance of the traditional lament for the dead.

Engaging in forms of entertainment by wake guests was an integral part of wake procedure in many parts of Europe down through the centuries. As Seán Ó Súilleabháin's work on wake amusements (1961, 1967) clearly shows, this was also the case in Ireland in many urban and rural areas, at least until the late nineteenth century or the early decades of the twentieth. When the holding of two-night wakes prior to the burial on the third day after death was common in Ireland, many forms of entertainment, interspersed with times of prayer, formed essential components of the wake. Singing, dancing, music, storytelling, card playing, riddling and rhyming were commonly engaged in, apparently in order to help to pass the time, especially during all-night wakes. These pastimes seem to have more or less escaped the sanction of the Christian churches, which reserved their particular opprobrium for wake games, often referred to as wake abuses in church literature. As Ó Súilleabháin's work shows, these games, performed in a confined space, were usually very robust, often leading to contention and disruption at wakes. Even the corpse could become involved in wake-house pranks by being given a hand of cards, having a pipe placed in the mouth, or by being taken out on to the floor to dance, or even by having the table or bed on which it lay overturned, thus spilling the remains on the floor (Ó Súilleabháin 1967, 66–7). While such behaviour was condemned by church authorities (Ó Súilleabháin 1967, 146–58; Connolly 1982, 159–65), it was not necessarily disapproved of by bereaved families, who probably bowed to tradition and to the weight of community involvement and expectation on the occasion of death. But the games which the clergy particularly objected to were those which were clearly of a sexual nature and those which mocked or imitated various sacraments, such as the sacraments of confession and matrimony (Ó Súilleabháin 1967, 92–9; Connolly 1982, 152–7, 162). In Ireland, games of this kind, and also the well-attested practice of courting at wakes, were repeatedly condemned by the Catholic Church authorities over a period of about four centuries, including by national synods even as late as 1927 and 1956 (Ó Súilleabháin 1967, 154; Corish 1985, 213). These activities eventually petered out due essentially to the passage of time, the requirement that the deceased should repose in the church on the eve of burial (Corish 1985, 213), and because of change in social outlook in the course of the twentieth century.

In addition to the aspects of revelry outlined above, the wake also involved ritual lamentation for the dead. This stylised poetic expression of mourning for a deceased person was performed at intervals during the wake event. The lament or dirge for the dead can be defined as poetry of lamentation performed by improvisation but following traditional verbal expression, stylistic norms and conventions. An ancient cultural inheritance in many parts of the world, it is attested in Ireland from early times and it continued, to some extent, into the early twentieth century, in some parts of the country at least, despite the vigorous opposition of the Christian Church authorities over a number of centuries (Ó Súilleabháin 1967, 130–45; Connolly 1982, 162–64). Its persistence was probably connected with the idea that lamentation was regarded as an obligation to a deceased person, as well as a custom in the context of death. Lamentation in the corpse house took place at certain key moments during the wake.

The lament was usually performed by women. If family members themselves were unable to lament a deceased relative in the traditional fashion, they hired talented keeners to fulfil the obligation to the deceased in their stead. The lament was performed in the presence of the corpse – the lamenters were formally arranged at either side of the deceased, their rhythmical movements and mourning gestures emphasising the ritual character of the performance. The lament rhythm was set by the leading keening woman, who chanted the verses and who also led a choral cry, in which the other lamenters present and the wake audience joined. This communal lamentation is often described as having a cathartic effect on family and community members present at the wake.

Generally sung or chanted in praise of the deceased, the lament was a direct address to the dead person, whose first name was called repeatedly even when the family was represented by a hired mourner. Terms of endearment were used to address the deceased, grieving questions were posed to him or her, and often poignant personal and family details were mentioned, giving rise to an intense sense of loss and mourning. Praise for the dead person's valour, genealogy and hospitality might also be included, as well as the calling for blood revenge, as expressed, for example, in the well-known lament for Art O'Leary, who died violently in 1773 (Ó Tuama 1961, 37, 44, 45). While the dominant cultural model is thus praise of the deceased, mock laments, usually by a widow satirising her deceased husband, are known to have been performed at wakes in Ireland (Lysaght 1997, 79–82).

Revelry and lamentation can thus be regarded as two key elements of the traditional wake for the dead in Ireland, aspects of which correspond to the two universal features of the funeral rites of traditional cultures identified in van Gennep's analysis of passage rites, namely a period of licence and one of public mourning. In this scenario, the games and other activities with sexual overtones performed in the presence of the deceased can be regarded on a symbolic level, as indicated by Bloch and Parry, as a means of reasserting and emphasising the continuing vitality of, and the potential for renewal in, the community, in the face of death. Likewise, the lament, also performed in the presence of the corpse and addressed directly to him or her, both at the wake and funeral, can be understood as a ritual act of reconciliation by the family and the community towards the deceased, in order to effect their separation from the living group and to enable transition to, and incorporation into, the community of the dead to be achieved (Honko 1974, 58 n.137; Ó Crualaoich 1990, 146–7; Lysaght 1997, 68–9).

17.5.   Removal of the Deceased, Funeral and Burial

As the wake drew to a close, physical separation procedures involving the deceased person became more evident. While community members represented by neighbours and friends vacated the corpse house and waited in the open air for the removal of the deceased, the corpse was placed in a coffin, close family members bid a formal farewell, and another bout of lamentation, louder and more emphatic in tone, ensued. When the coffin was carried from the house it was placed briefly on chairs, and at the moment of the final removal, signalled by the departure of the funeral cortège to the cemetery, the ritual lamentation reached a crescendo. The lament was also performed at intervals during the journey to the cemetery, on arrival at the cemetery, and at the lowering of the coffin into the grave. After the grave had been filled in by neighbours and friends of the family, the Rosary was recited, and then the deceased's relatives and community members left the cemetery. The burial, at the conclusion of the funeral process, represented the final physical act of separation of the deceased from the living community.

Thirty days after burial, and corresponding in van Gennep's terms to the last phase of the deceased's transition to and incorporation into the community of the dead, the grave was visited by family members after attending the Month's Mind Mass in the church. It was blessed by the priest, the Rosary was said, and then the family left the cemetery. Thereafter the grave was visited by the family only when members came to the cemetery on the occasion of another local funeral, or when another death occurred in their own family. But the mourning stage for the immediate family of the deceased continued for a further period of time, usually until the first anniversary of the death; signs of this mourning included the wearing of black clothes and the non-participation in entertainment or other festive activities during that time.

17.6.   Contemporary Observances

The traditional wake for the dead as described in outline above went into decline, in some areas more than others, from the late nineteenth century onwards. According to Ó Súilleabháin (1967, 164), 'The more or less continual barrage of episcopal condemnation of abuses slowly, but surely, achieved its purpose.' The parish mission movement from the mid-nineteenth century onwards also contributed to the decline of the so-called wake abuses through sermons and threats to withhold absolution from those engaging in wake amusements (Ó Súilleabháin 1967, 157). In addition, Purgatorial Societies, established by some bishops in their dioceses, called on the laity to assist them in the task of ridding wakes of amusements (Ó Súilleabháin 1967, 164). Of more significance was the obligation to remove the corpse to the church on the evening before burial as this essentially reduced the wake to a one-night event. Some of the wake practices outlined above generally took place in the circumstances of a two-night wake. As news of death spread in the locality, and as family members and relatives arrived home from different parts of the country or from abroad, the second night of the wake usually witnessed the larger attendance, and it was on that occasion, for the most part, that various forms of entertainment, including wake games, the so-called wake abuses, were most vigorously performed. The change to a one-night wake had already been introduced in the ecclesiastical province of Dublin in the 1850s; and the new code of Canon Law (1918) laid down that the funeral liturgy and Mass should henceforth take place in the church (Corish 1985, 213). Despite this requirement, two-night wakes continued in some areas until the 1950s or 1960s, as one-night wakes were considered by some families to be a sign of meanness and to be inappropriate to the memory of the deceased. In The Rosses in north-west Donegal, there was still a reluctance to change to one-night wakes even in the 1970s, as many had relatives working in Scotland and England who wished to attend the wake and could do so only on the second night (Lysaght 2002, 286–7). Nevertheless, one-night wakes did eventually take hold, with the result that the performance of wake games and lamentation, particularly associated with the second night of the wake, lost momentum (Ó Súilleabháin 1971, 157).

It would appear, therefore, that by the late 1960s one-night wakes were more or less the norm throughout most of the country, and that the wakes themselves had become quiet and decorous events, the main purposes of which were to offer prayers for the deceased person and to sympathise with the bereaved family. By the 1970s the wake event itself was evidently in decline, even in many rural areas, as recourse to care homes for the aged became more pronounced. The opportunity of removing a deceased person from a care home directly to a funeral parlour or funeral home for community viewing prior to the funeral, something which was possible from the late 1960s onwards,[2] also contributed to decline of the wake in the deceased's home. The use of such an establishment for the laying out and viewing of the corpse also became somewhat fashionable, and its use was even viewed on occasion as a family tribute to the deceased person. The availability of mortuary areas in hospitals, in which a deceased could also be laid out for viewing by relatives prior to removal, also led many families to remove the corpse directly to the church rather than taking the remains home for waking, something which also contributed to the custom's decline. Nevertheless, the wake for the dead still pertains to some extent, largely in a modernised and truncated form, in both urban and rural Ireland. But it is no longer the recognised or expected way of dealing with a

2 The first funeral home in Ireland was opened by T. Val O'Connor, O'Connor Brothers, undertakers, North Gate Bridge, Cork, in 1967. See www.oconnorfuneralcork.ie/our-history.html, accessed 19 March 2015.

deceased person: for some it is the continuation of an old tradition in new social, religious and cultural circumstances, for others it involves the revitalisation of an erstwhile custom, while for others still it is a matter of the adoption of a 'new' way of dealing with death and loss.

Funeral services have also undergone modernisation and reflect changing attitudes to death and to institutionalised church authority. Such services are no longer necessarily church-based and the demand for non-religious and humanist funeral services is on the increase. The availability of cremation services has also led to change as the traditional burial rites at the graveside no longer pertain when cremation is chosen as the mode of disposal of the corpse.

Attitudes to children's funerals and burials have perhaps changed most significantly over the past three decades or so. Instead of being quiet and quick events, children's funerals today are matters of social significance, usually involving a full funeral service and, in the Catholic tradition, the celebration of a special funeral Mass, and burial in the family grave with officiating clergy present. The revised Code of Canon Law (1983) allowed church burial for children who died without baptism when the parents had intended to have the child baptised. This changed attitude towards the fate of unbaptised children is reflected in the *Order of Christian Funerals* (1991) as its substantial 'Funeral rites for children' (Part II) includes all children, both baptised and unbaptised, within its remit. This is a far cry from the former strict prohibition on church burial for unbaptised children and one which acknowledges and is in accord with present-day views, expectations and sensitivities (Ó Héalaí 2006, 99–102).

17.7. Conclusion

The 'rediscovery of death' in the western world, especially in the second half of the twentieth century, led to the production of a very substantial body of interdisciplinary literature on the subject. In this, the growth of the hospice movement focusing attention on the dying person has been discussed, as have the excesses of modern funerary practices and the position of the bereaved in contemporary society. The loss of traditional practices and protocols for dealing with dying, death and bereavement in much of western society has also been commented on. With regard to Ireland, what is noticeable is that while many of the rituals that once surrounded death in Irish society have been lost, the Catholic Church still retains a vital role at the crisis of death – by public consent. Thus, despite its very substantial loss of standing in recent decades for a variety of reasons, by and large the family will arrange for the holding of a religious service in the local Catholic church with an officiating clergyman, which relatives, neighbours, friends and colleagues will attend as a mark of respect for the deceased and their family.

FURTHER READING

Ariès, P. *L'homme devant la mort* (Paris, 1977).

Ariès, P. *The hour of our death* (London, 1981).

Ariès, P. 'La mort inversée. Le changement des attitudes devant la mort dans les sociétés occidentales', *Archives européennes de sociologie*, 8 (1967), 169–95.

Ariès, P. *Western attitudes toward death: from the Middle Ages to the present* (London, 1974).

Badone, E. *The appointed hour: death, worldview and social change in Brittany* (London, 1989).

Bloch, M. and J. Parry (eds.). *Death and the regeneration of life* (Cambridge, 1982).

Bromwich, R. 'The keen for Art O'Leary, its background and its place in the tradition of Gaelic keening', *Éigse: a Journal of Irish Studies*, 5 (1948), 236–52.

Connolly, S. J. *Priests and people in pre-famine Ireland 1780–1845* (Dublin, 1982).

Connolly, S. J. *Religion and society in nineteenth-century Ireland* (Dundalk, 1987 [1985]).

Corish, P. *The Irish Catholic experience: a historical survey* (Dublin, 1985).

Cressy, D. *Birth, marriage and death: ritual, religion, and the life-cycle in Tudor and Stuart England* (Oxford, 1997).

Crozier, M. '"Powerful wakes": perfect hospitality', in C. Curtin and T. M. Wilson (eds.), *Ireland from below: social change and local communities* (Galway, [1987]), 90–1.

Danforth, L. M. *The death rituals of rural Greece*, with photography by A. Tsiaras (Princeton, NJ, 1982).

Dickenson, D. and M. Johnson. *Death, dying and bereavement* (2nd edn, London and Milton Keynes, 1994).

Elias, N. *The loneliness of dying* (Oxford, 1985).

Elias, N. *Über die Einsamkeit der Sterbenden in unseren Tagen* (Frankfurt am Main, 1982).

Feifel, H. *The meaning of death* (New York, 1959).

Fry, S. L. *Burial in medieval Ireland 900–1500* (Dublin, 1999).

Gittings, C. *Death, burial and the individual in early modern England* (London, 1984).

Gorer, G. *Death, grief and mourning in contemporary Britain* (London, 1965).

Gorer, G. 'The pornography of death', *Encounter* (Oct. 1955), 49–52.

Hartmann, H. *Der Totenkult in Irland* (Heidelberg, 1952).

Hertz, R. 'Contribution à une étude sur la représentation collective de la mort', *Anné sociologique*, 10 (1907), 48–137.

Hertz, R. *Death and the right hand* (London, 1960).

Hertz, R. 'La prééminence de la main droite: étude sur la polarité religieuse', *Revue philosophique*, 68 (1909), 553–80.

Honko, L. 'Balto-Finnic lament poetry', *Studia Fennica*, 17(1974), 9–61.

Houlbrooke, R. *Death, religion and the family in England 1480–1750* (Oxford, 1998).

Houlbrooke, R. (ed.). *Death, ritual and bereavement* (London, 1989).

Jupp, P. C. and G. Howarth (eds.). *The changing face of death: historical accounts of death and disposal* (Basingstoke, 1997).

Kast, V. *A time to mourn: going through the grief process* (translated from the German, Einsiedeln, 1988).

Kast, V. *Trauern. Phasen und Chancen des psychischen Prozesses* (Stuttgart, 1982).

Kelly, J. and M. A. Lyons. *Death and dying in Ireland, Britain and Europe: historical perspectives* (Sallins, 2013).

Kübler-Ross, E. *On death and dying* (London, 1969).

Lebrun, F. *Les hommes et la mort en Anjou aux XVIIe et XVIIIe siècles: essai de démographie et de psychologie historique* (Paris, 1971).

Litten, J. *The English way of death: the common funeral since 1450* (London, 1991).

Lysaght, P. *The banshee: the Irish supernatural death-messenger* (1986; 2nd edn, Dublin, 1996).

Lysaght, P. 'Caoineadh na Marbh: Die Totenklage in Irland', *Rheinisch-westfälische Zeitschrift für Volkskunde*, 40 (1995), 163–213.

Lysaght, P. 'Caoineadh os Cionn Coirp: the lament for the dead in Ireland', *Folklore*, 108 (1997), 65–82.

Lysaght, P. 'Hospitality at wakes and funerals in Ireland from the seventeenth to the nineteenth century: some evidence from the written record', *Folklore*, 113 (2003), 403–26.

Lysaght, P. *A pocket book of the banshee* (Dublin, 1998).

Lysaght, P. 'Wake and funeral hospitality in Ireland in the nineteenth and twentieth centuries: continuity and change', in P. Lysaght (ed.), *Food and celebration* (Ljubljana, 2002), 285–302.

Lysaght, P. 'Wakes', in G. Howarth and O. Leaman (eds.), *Encyclopedia of death and dying* (London and New York, 2001), 472–4.

Metcalf, P. and R. Huntington. *Celebrations of death: the anthropology of mortuary ritual* (New York, 1979, rev. edn 1991).

Mitford, J. *The American way of death* (New York and London, 1963).

Nenola-Kallio, A. *Studies in Ingrian laments*, FFC 234 (Helsinki, 1982).

O'Connor, A. *The blessed and the damned: sinful women and unbaptised children in Irish folklore* (New York, 2005).

O'Connor, A. *Child murderess and dead child traditions. a comparative study*, FFC 249 (Helsinki, 1991).

Ó Crualaoich, G. 'Contest in the cosmology and the ritual of the Irish "merry wake"', *Cosmos: The Yearbook of the Traditional Cosmology Society*, 6 (1990), 145–60.

Ó Crualaoich, G. 'The "merry wake"', in J. S. Donnelly Jr and K. A. Miller (eds.), *Irish popular culture 1650–1850* (Dublin, 1998), 173–200.

Ó Héalaí, P. 'Children's funerary rites in Ireland: a compensatory dimension', in F. Mugnaini, P. Ó Héalaí and T. Thompson (eds.), *The past in the present: a multidisciplinary approach* (Catania, Italy, 2006), 87–106.

Ó Héalaí, P. 'Gnéithe de Bhéaloideas an Linbh ar an mBlascaod', *Leachtaí Cholm Cille*, 22 (1992), 81–122.

Ó Súilleabháin, S. 'Adhlacadh Leanbhaí', *Journal of the Royal Society of Antiquaries of Ireland*, 69 (1939), 143–51.

Ó Súilleabháin, S. *Caitheamh Aimsire ar Thórraimh* (Dublin, 1961).

Ó Súilleabháin, S. *Irish wake amusements* (Cork, 1967).

Ó Tuama, S. *Caoineadh Airt Uí Laoghaire* (Dublin, 1961).

Order of Christian Funerals (Dublin, 1991).

Palgi, P. and H. Abramovitch. 'Death: a cross-cultural perspective', *Annual Review of Anthropology*, 13 (1984), 385–417.

Pentikäinen, J. *The Nordic dead child tradition*, FFC 202 (Helsinki, 1968).

Power, R. 'Death in Ireland: deaths, wakes and funerals in contemporary Irish society', in D. Dickenson and M. Johnson (eds.), *Death, dying and bereavement* (London and Milton Keynes, 1994), 21–5.

Power, R. *The Moravian burial ground at Whitechurch, County Dublin* (London, 2014).

Richter, K. (ed.). *Der Umgang mit den Toten. Tod und Bestattung in der christlichen Gemeinde* (Freiburg im Breisgau, 1990).

Schmied, G. *Sterben und Trauern in der modernen Gesellschaft* (Leverkusen, 1985).

Stannard, D. E. (ed.). *Death in America* (Philadelphia, 1974).

Storå, N. *Burial customs of the Skolt Lapps*, FFC 210 (Helsinki, 1971).

Sudnow, D. *Passing on: the social organization of dying* (Englewood Cliffs, NJ, 1967).

Tait, C. *Death, burial and commemoration in Ireland, 1550–1650* (Basingstoke, 2002).

Taylor, L. J. 'Bás in Éirinn: cultural constructions of death in Ireland', *Anthropological Quarterly*, 62, 4 (1989), 175–87.

Taylor, L. J. 'Introduction: the uses of death in Europe', *Anthropological Quarterly*, 62, 4 (1989), 149–54.

Tyers, P. *Malairt Beatha* (Dún Chaoin, 1992).

van Gennep, A. *The rites of passage* (London, 1960).

Vovelle, M. *Piété baroque et déchristianisation en Provence au XVIIIe siècle. Les attitudes devant la mort d'après les clauses des testaments* (Paris, 1973).

Vovelle, M. and G. Vovelle. *Vision de la mort et de l'au-delà en Provence d'après les autels des âmes du purgatoire. XVe–XXe siècles* (Paris, 1970).

18 Celebrations and the Rituals of Life

Diarmuid Ó Gilláin

18.1.   Introduction

To study the celebrations and rituals of life is to focus on the collective, the 'people', the force of tradition. 'Traditional' cultures hence are often characterised by the notion of the commons – farmers sharing their seeds and storytellers sharing their tales – though traditions are no more likely to be evenly shared than other resources. Often it was only through the legal criterion of delinquency that individual agency in popular culture was identified: the background to a sensational murder trial in 1895, for example, was the 'collective', 'traditional', belief in fairy abduction. The antiquaries, travel writers, and proto-folklorists and proto-anthropologists who in the eighteenth and nineteenth centuries 'discovered' and described popular culture indeed saw a collective phenomenon. As scientific fields, folklore and anthropology were conceptualised in the German-speaking lands in the 1770s and 1780s 'as part of the Enlightenment endeavour to create some order in the growing body of data on peoples, nations or *Völker* in the world of that era'.[1] These data contributed both to the study of the inhabitants of a single polity (*Volkskunde*) and to the comparative study of peoples (*Völkerkunde*). But it is in the Herderian *Volksgeist* and in its Romantic expansion that we find the key notion that is at the core of the later development of these fields.

Herder's location of cultural authenticity in the traditions peculiar to each people – expressed in his anthology of *Volkslieder* (1778–9) – thus was an essential development: the oral artistic genres of folksong and folktale transcended the material conditions of rural life – as 'art'. The word 'folk-lore' dates from 1846 and was coined by William John

1 H. F. Vermeulen, 'Origins and institutionalization of ethnography and ethnology in Europe and the USA, 1771–1845', in H. F. Vermeulen and A. Álvarez Roldán (eds.), *Fieldwork and footnotes: studies in the history of European anthropology* (London and New York, 1995), 39–40.

Thoms who, in a letter to the antiquarian journal *The Athenaeum*, sought the editor's aid 'in garnering the few ears which are remaining, scattered over that field from which our forefathers might have gathered a goodly crop'.[2] Raymond Williams sees the genesis of the 'folk' term and its derivatives in English in the context of the new urban industrial society, contending that it had the effect of 'backdating all elements of popular culture', in contradistinction to modern forms 'either of a radical and working-class or of a commercial kind'. Thoms's 'folk-lore' was understood through a narrative of progress, with later Darwinian nuances especially after the appearance of Tylor's *Primitive Culture* in 1871.

Nineteenth-century popular traditions in Ireland and elsewhere were defined in two ways, aesthetically and socially. From the aesthetic perspective, they were epitomised by their various artistic forms and stood outside and above wider social and historical processes. They were a national inheritance, as with Herder's *Volkslieder*, whose contents included poetic works as different from each other as folksong and Shakespearean verse, each faithful to the national genius.[3] From the 'social' perspective, such traditions consisted of certain cultural products that were proper to the lower classes of a residual agrarian world, and were destined to be replaced by superior ones. They were comprehended through relations of domination and inequality. Definitions of popular culture as much as of folklore hence move between the national and the popular, shaping both what was recorded and how it was interpreted.

Folklore research, which long pre-dated anthropology in the European context, invested above all in the fidelity of tradition and identified the individuals who were the necessary legitimation of the chain of transmission. By the late nineteenth century, numerous individuals were identified as storytellers, singers and narrators of 'myths'. A significant part of what we know about pre-industrial Irish rural ('traditional') culture has been extracted from the testimonies given by such individuals to folklorists, especially those of the Irish Folklore Commission (1935–70), whose collections constitute one of the largest and most important folklore archives in the world. Those interviewed were most often elderly Irish-speakers, born in the decades after the Great Famine, and they gave information from their own experience or acquired through oral transmission. Much of this information can be supported by other, non-oral, sources. The west of Ireland was favoured, though not to the exclusion of other regions, by the 'socially' inclined scholars because its backwardness was more conducive to the maintenance of cultural 'survivals', and by the 'aesthetically' inclined because its remoteness was a guarantee of its cultural authenticity.

---

2 W. Thoms, 'Folklore and the origin of the word' [editor's title], in A. Dundes (ed.), *International folkloristics: classic contributions by the founders of folklore* (Lanham, MD, 1999), 11.
3 Indeed Gramsci (*Letteratura e vita nazionale* (Rome, 1991), 123) noted that 'national' and 'popular' are synonymous in many languages, instancing German and Russian.

18.2. Traditional Rural Worlds

Folklore studies distinguished the rural population, their primary focus, from the more mobile urban proletariat and from the cosmopolitan ruling classes. The former, of course, was not monolithic, and in addition to the distinctions between artisans, labourers and farmers was that between small and big farmers, with cultural distinctions that lasted well into the twentieth century in Ireland.[4] Neither was popular culture itself monolithic. There are traditions specific to peasants, to blacksmiths, to hunters, to women, to men, to children, to healers, to musicians. There are aspects of popular culture that belong to the *longue durée* and that can be discussed in terms of the development of religions, the origins of agriculture and the growth of peasant society. There are regional cultural differences that can be accounted for by both historical and geographical factors: a more archaic north-west and western fringe, and a low-lying and accessible east and south-east more open to incoming influence. There are other phenomena that have their origins in the recent past. Yet the imminent demise of folklore has been an *idée fixe* at least since the time of Herder. Sir William Wilde's observations immediately after the Great Famine graphically illustrate that:

> In this state of things, with depopulation the most terrific which any country ever experienced, on the one hand, and the spread of education, and the introduction of railroads, colleges, industrial and other educational schools, on the other, – together with the rapid decay of the Irish vernacular, in which most of our legends, romantic tales, ballads, and bardic annals, the vestiges of Pagan rites, and the relics of fairy charms were preserved, – can superstition, or if superstitious belief, can superstitious practices continue to exist?[5]

The recording of folklore was always an eleventh-hour mission. Thoms warned of the death of folklore, as did Douglas Hyde and W. B. Yeats. Conservative writers mourned the death of the cultural authenticity both of folklore and of high culture, complaining 'that it was the intermediary that was most alive, urban popular culture and mass culture'.[6] A corollary of that was the idealisation of marginal regions such as the Irish western fringes in which a picturesque agrarian life could be observed until late and where social differences were smaller than elsewhere, 'with no large rural proletariat to disturb the image of a happy village *Gemeinschaft*', as Orvar Löfgren writes of Dalecarlia in Sweden.

For Le Roy Ladurie, rural civilisation brought together certain 'cellular groups' that were incorporated or dominated by external economic and social forces that co-existed with or succeeded one another, among which he lists 'feudalism, towns, states, trade and industry, [and] capitalism'. He points out that the subjection of peasants to a land-owning nobility went back to ancient times and that 'the essential centres of decision

---

4 C. M. Arensberg and S. T. Kimball, *Family and community in Ireland* (3rd edn, Ennis, 2001 [1940]), 264, 272, 285.

5 W. Wilde, *Irish popular superstitions* (Dublin, 1979 [1852]), 10–11.

6 J. J. De Carvalho, 'O lugar da cultura tradicional na sociedade moderna', in C. M. Ferreira (ed.), *Seminário folcolre e cultura popular*, Série encontros e estudos 1 (Rio de Janeiro, 1992), 27.

and of exaction (the state, the church, the town, the landlords) more or less escape from peasant control'.[7] This is congruent with classic anthropological and sociological formulations, such as that of Redfield, who characterised peasant societies as 'part-so-cieties'.[8] Peasants (subsistence agriculturalists) participated both in their own agrarian world and in the wider society symbolised in Ireland by church, Big House and town. The cultural consequences in some ways can be compared to diglossia, the bilingualism of the dialect ('low', informal)/national language ('high', formal) type, with, for example, the Irish language or the holy well corresponding to the former, the English language or the chapel to the latter domain. Folk traditions have sometimes been interpreted as debased versions of elite cultural forms, from Hans Naumann's notion of folklore as *gesunkenes Kulturgut* to Gramsci's description of folklore at around the same time as 'a confused agglomerate of fragments of all the conceptions of the world and of life that have succeeded one another in history'.[9] While cultural circulation is inevitable between social classes, much of culture too is specific to a way of life. There is a historical dimension to the separation of elites from popular culture in western Europe, a process largely ended by the early nineteenth century and which had additional ethno-religious dimensions in Ireland. Corresponding to and following on from elite withdrawal from popular culture was a more general 'civilising mission' aimed at the people by both state and church (partly coinciding in Ireland with the 'devotional revolution').

William Paden uses the notion of 'world' in studying religion on the basis that each religion is unique and conceives, constructs and inhabits its own universe. General cultural differences between social classes or between genders are reflected in the experience of religion and in its institutional forms. 'Where privileged classes use religion to legitimise their own life pattern and place in the world, the particular need of the disprivileged', according to Paden, 'is release from suffering, future compensation, and salvation'.[10] Max Weber's observations on the religion of the 'non-privileged classes' considered the specificity of urban artisans and traders for whom kinship was less important than for peasants, who had much less connection with nature, and among whom 'dependence on magic for influencing the irrational forces of nature cannot play the same role'.[11] Hence the distinction between 'historical religions', with a linear sense of time, and the agrarian 'cosmic religions', associated with seasonal change and fertility. Eliade indeed argued that peasant societies had no real historical consciousness; their history was a recurring sacred history transmitted through myths and rituals.

7 E. Le Roy Ladurie, *La civilisation rurale* (Paris, 2012 [1972]), 36.
8 R. Redfield, 'Peasant society and culture', in Redfield, *The little community and peasant society and culture* (Chicago, 1960), 23–39.
9 A. Gramsci, *Selections from cultural writings*, edited and translated by W. Boelhower, D. Forgacs and G. Nowell Smith (London, 1985), 189.
10 W. E. Paden, *Religious worlds: the comparative study of religion* (2nd edn, Boston, 1994), 55–6.
11 M. Weber, *The sociology of religion*, translated by E. Fischoff (4th edn, Boston, 1993 [1922]), 97.

Festivals and rituals of life were cyclical, paradigms of the phases of the sun, the moon, the tides, the fertility of humans, plants and animals. But the natural cycle had many uncertainties. Babies were still-born or died in infancy, crops failed, there were storms, droughts and floods. But misfortune was not arbitrary; according to Eliade, 'suffering proceeds from the magical action of an enemy, from breaking a taboo, from entering a baneful zone, from the anger of a god, or – when all other hypotheses have proven insufficient – from the will or the wrath of the Supreme Being'. De Martino argued that magic was still such an important part of the worldview of peasants in southern Italy because of the 'immense power of the negative throughout the individual life, with its procession of shocks, defeats, frustrations, and poverty'. In his analysis, peasants denied the 'historicity' of collective and individual crises by projecting an otherwise stable magico-religious order, ruptured by the evil eye, sorcery, the breaking of a prohibition, etc.

18.3. The Agrarian Year

The agrarian year was experienced in terms of an active period beginning in spring and ending in autumn, and a quieter period, marked by fireside gatherings in the evenings for discussion and storytelling. For early modern France, Muchembled emphasises the 'semi-activity' of wintertime, to the extent of a significant fall in the rates of homicide and violence: the liturgy of Advent banning marriages and prescribing fasting and abstinence indicated 'a rupture of biological rhythm'.[12] Festivals helped to reckon time, avow community and invoke protective supernatural power. Certain kinds of work, or work in general, were prohibited during festival, and a social solidarity embracing the family, the community and the dead was asserted in the rituals and celebrations involving food, drink, games, music and dance. Divination was also a feature since festival was 'time out of time', both a suspension and an abolition of time, telescoping past, present and future.

In festive processions, 'youth affirmed their role of collective guarantor of luck, fecundity and fertility',[13] visible in the masked groups that participated in festivals such as St Brigid's Day, Hallowe'en and St Stephen's Day. But the young – as Zemon Davis has shown for early modern France – were also moral arbiters in certain ways, as in 'horning' or 'blowing', a mostly Leinster version of *charivari* in which disapproval of an unsuitable marriage (typically of an elderly widower) was publicly expressed through blowing of horns from surrounding hillsides, or in the threatening behaviour of 'Straw Boys', traditionally masked and uninvited guests, at the wedding. Groups of masked

12 R. Muchembled, *Société, cultures et mentalités dans la la France moderne XVIe–XVIIIe siècle* (Paris, 1990), 95–7.
13 Ibid., 102.

youths on St Brigid's Day ('Biddies'), Hallowe'en and St Stephen's Day ('Wren Boys') as well as the 'Straw Boys' did not so much conceal individual as assert collective identity. In the Straw Boys, the whole community was symbolically present at a wedding. In the welcome they received and in their dance with the bride, a social contract was fulfilled.

The sacred calendar represents the periodic re-enactment of sacred deeds. As Eliade expresses it, '[i]n every periodic festival the same sacred Time is met again that was made evident in the festival of the previous year or in the festival of a hundred years ago'.[14] In the festival people renewed themselves through contact with supernatural power. Dixon Hardy mentioned the belief of the crowds at the midsummer pattern at the Struel wells in County Down that 'as long as [they] remain on sacred ground, they cannot contract new guilt'.[15] Sacred time and the present merged: St Brigid travelled around Ireland on the eve of her feast day and St Conall appeared on 1 June every year during the pattern at the well dedicated to him in Inniskeel Island, County Donegal. Between sunset on May Eve and sunrise on May Day, and again at Hallowe'en, supernatural powers were abroad in unusual proximity to the mortal world.

The ritual masking of Biddies and their like erased individual identity, and the various gatherings of the young, on hilltops and lake sides for Lúnasa celebrations, or dancing around Maypoles and attending May Balls, affirmed solidarity. In a celebrated work Mikhail Bakhtin argued that the people experienced a utopian realm of community in festival.[16] The emphasis on the abundance of food and drink, on convivial interaction between the sexes, on games and on fighting – what he called 'the material bodily principle' – pointed to the constantly renewed biological community that transcended temporal hierarchy and death. Victor Turner used the term 'liminality' to refer to being on the margins of or outside, ordinary life, a condition that is potentially sacred and that characterises pilgrimage. The withdrawal from everyday life and from customary social roles and the ritual humiliations of fasting and mortifications led to a spontaneous and egalitarian sense of community – 'communitas', as Turner called it.[17]

Corresponding to the 'quarter days' – St Brigid's Day, May Day (*Bealtaine*), the harvest festival (*Lúnasa*) and Hallowe'en (*Samhain*) – that divided the year into four 'true quarters', with the solstices or equinoxes in the middle of each, were the four 'crooked quarters' marked by the solstices or equinoxes: the Christian festivals of St John's Day, Michaelmas, Christmas and St Patrick's Day. Traditions associated with these latter four festivals were relatively sparse. St Brigid's Day, which will by way of example be treated at greater length here, was the first day of spring and the festival of the patron saint of cattle and dairying. Rituals stressed fertility, protection, divination and family and community solidarity. The

14 M. Eliade, *Lo sagrado y lo profano*, translated by L. Gil (5th edn, Barcelona, 1983), 64.
15 P. D. Hardy, *The holy wells of Ireland* (Dublin, 1836), 39.
16 M. Bakhtin, *Rabelais and his world*, translated by H. Iswolsky (Bloomington, IN, 1984).
17 V. Turner, *Dramas, fields and metaphors* (Ithaca and London; 1974).

saint travelled the country on the eve of her festival, blessing people and livestock. A ribbon ('*Brat Bríde*') left on the windowsill overnight was used as a cure for headache as well as barrenness, to help with childbirth, to protect against evil, and for divination. Sometimes any work that involved the turning of wheels was forbidden. Commonly a cake or a slice of bread and butter were left on the windowsill, to be shared among the family members in the morning or taken away by a beggar or by the Biddies. The family shared a festive supper, often associated with the making of the crosses of rushes or straw that were hung in the dwelling house and outhouses as protection for the year ahead.

The Biddies, sometimes only girls, sometimes only boys, went from house to house on the eve of the festival carrying a symbol or effigy of the saint, the *Brídeog* or 'Biddy', and they were rewarded with a gift. In west Galway the *crios Bríde*, 'St Brigid's Girdle', a long straw rope, was brought to each house by the Biddies, the occupants being passed through it to ensure the saint's protection as well as freedom from illness during the year ahead. Elsewhere seed grain was hung up in a cloth beside the St Brigid's cross until sowing time, when it was mixed with the rest of the grain, or a potato was pinned to the roof and added to the seed potatoes at the time of planting. The residue of the crosses was added to the bedding of horses and cattle, and used for making spancels for various animals to protect them in the year to come.

May Day heralded the beginning of summer. Various rituals were intended to safeguard the essential interests of the community. Magical butter-stealing was especially feared, a common phenomenon throughout Europe. Wells were guarded on May Eve and May Morn. 'In different parts of the country', according to Danaher, 'it was held that one should not dig, whitewash, bathe or sail on May Day.'[18] Fairy forts were believed to be open on May Eve, and people were afraid to be out late. The early nineteenth-century diarist Amhlaoibh Ó Súilleabháin tells of a wisp of straw lit at each side of a gap and cattle driven through. He describes May Balls, for which young men played hurling matches and around which the young danced. There is much evidence for violence on May Eve. In Dublin, where, according to Sir William Wilde, '[t]he preparations for the May Day sports and ceremonial … commenced about the middle of April, and even earlier', violence between opposing groups was to do with 'which street or district would exhibit the best dressed and handsomest May bush, or could boast the largest and hottest bonfire'.[19] Stealing the May bush meant taking the luck of the coming year from its rightful owners; a well-known incident in Dublin, where the weavers cut down and stole the bush of the butchers, was recorded in the nineteenth century in the form of a song.

Customs associated with *Lúnasa*, the harvest festival, are found from St Mary Magdalene's Day on 22 July to the Feast of the Assumption on 15 August, in part Christian attempts to replace the pagan feast that bears the name of the god Lugh. This

18 K. Danaher, *The year in Ireland* (Cork, 1972), 87–8.
19 Wilde, *Irish popular superstitions*, 47.

festival was characterised by young people assembling by lakes and rivers, at holy wells and on hilltops where they picked flowers and berries, the first fruits of the harvest. In a few cases, the hilltop assemblies were in the form of pilgrimages, most famously that of Croagh Patrick. Fairs were also held, of which the best known are Puck Fair in County Kerry and the Auld Lammas Fair in County Antrim. Hugh Dorian in his memoir of Donegal life, covering the years 1830 to 1890, refers to the festival as 'the termination of a long, perhaps hard summer, and the season of enjoyment and plentiness is supposed to set in for the weary hardworking husbandman himself and the labourer after many months of hope and toil'.[20]

As *Bealtaine*, May Eve, seems to have represented the beginning of the summer half of the Celtic year, so the winter half began with *Samhain* (Hallowe'en), a festival corresponding to an ancient feast of the dead (and with certain overlaps with the Christian festivals of All Saints and All Souls). It was replete with rituals and beliefs associated with the dead and the spirit world in general, from the belief that fairies were about, to laying out food for the visit of deceased relatives. Of the festival, Hugh Dorian wrote: 'At this time the farmer can calculate almost to a certainty his returns and is satisfied or discontented as the case may be. In any case, the feast of *Samhain* cannot be forgotten, though some might be in grief and many might rejoice or the contrary'.[21]

Festivals in agrarian communities tended to cluster around the high points of the agricultural year. Most 'patterns', for example, were held in summer or autumn and especially in the month of July: anxiety about the harvest was a crucial dimension. Máire Mac Neill investigated the traditions of some eighty *Lúnasa* patterns where she found faction fighting to have been a common feature. She found the richest information from patterns on mountain tops or mountain passes – Mám Éan between the Joyce Country and Connemara, Arderin on Slieve Bloom between Laois and Offaly, and Caher Roe's Den on the Blackstairs between Carlow and Wexford – where the fighting took place between groups from opposite sides of the mountain range. She interpreted it as a ritual battle 'between parties representing the forces of fertility and blight, or perhaps from a real rivalry inspired by the concept that the prosperity of the year might go to the victorious side'.[22] The same applied to the pattern in Gougane Barra on St Johns' Eve. Accounts in other countries of symbolic contests at spring or summer festivals are comparable. The great Breton midsummer *pardon* of Saint-Servais in the nineteenth century culminated in a stick fight between pilgrims from Cornouaille and from Vannetais for possession of the banner and statue of the saint. The rivalry expressed in fighting at key points in the agricultural year seems to have been based

20 H. Dorian, *The outer edge of Ulster: a memoir of social life in nineteenth-century Donegal*, edited by Breandán Mac Suibhne and David Dixon (Dublin, 2000), 261.
21 Ibid., 262.
22 M. Mac Neill, *The festival of Lughnasa* (Oxford, 1962), 380.

on a notion of 'limited good', that the abundance of one was only made possible by the scarcity of another.[23]

18.4. Pilgrimages

Among the phenomena of popular culture most often described by travellers and anti-quaries from the late eighteenth century was the 'pattern' ('patron'). It was a pilgrimage to a sacred place associated with a saint, usually on the feast day. The patronage of the saint was assured by submission to certain rituals, by feasting and observing the day as a holiday – legends tell of misfortune befalling those who neglected to do so. The pattern was usually focused on a holy well, but the site often included a tree, mounds of stones, ancient ecclesiastical buildings and other 'stations'. There were holy wells on mountain or hill tops (the rituals of the Croagh Patrick pilgrimage formerly involved visiting a holy well at the foot of the mountain), on mountain passes, on the seashore, on offshore islands or on islands in lakes. The association with a specific place is very important, but there were also wells that moved because they were profaned. A figure of some three thousand holy wells for the whole country is often cited, most dedicated to Irish saints (with Brigid and Patrick the most common). Many wells are known from their curative reputation, with names such as Tobar na Súl ('of the eyes') very common, though such wells often have a parallel designation from a saint's name. The proper time for the pattern included the saint's feast day, at Christian festivals such as Easter Sunday, at the summer solstice (or St John's Eve) or, in many cases, at any time between certain dates.

A key function of the holy well was healing. The well's water was most efficacious at special times: on the saint's day, or at midnight between 23 and 24 June in the case of wells dedicated to St John the Baptist. The well's power cured mental illness, eye diseases, toothache and barrenness, ensured the safe delivery of children and kept away plagues and epidemics. Sacred power was never easily accessed: sometimes the well had to be visited before sunrise, or between sunrise and sunset; sometimes on three successive days, or on Sunday, Friday and Sunday. A specific number of 'rounds' of each of the site's various stations had to be undertaken. The ritual included Mass, prayers, circum-ambulations, adding stones to cairns and leaving a token of some kind. Patterns drew pilgrims from the local parish or from further afield, sometimes from a wide hinterland. Thousands often were in attendance. Earlier accounts of rounds undertaken barefoot or on the knees as well as fasting from daybreak suggest severe mortifications – Thackeray, at the foot of Croagh Patrick during his Irish tour of 1842, referred to this 'frightful exhi-bition' with pilgrims 'suffering severe pain, wounded and bleeding in the knees and feet, and some of the women shrieking with the pain of their wounds'.[24] Dixon Hardy gave an

---

23 G. M. Foster, 'Peasant society and the image of limited good', *American Anthropologist* 67, 2 (1965), 293–315.
24 W. M. Thackeray, *The Irish sketchbook, 1842* (Dublin, 1990 [1843]), 236.

account of a pilgrim who had come from County Galway to Struel, begging, and who could not leave the pattern, where he had already spent ten days, because his feet and knees were bruised and ulcerated. Beggars were famously numerous at patterns.

The simple devotion and the boisterous revelry at the pattern usually made a strong impression on outsiders. The prayers and rounds finished, pilgrims repaired to crowded tents selling food and alcohol. At Gougane Barra, Crofton Croker noted heavy drinking, the singing of rebellious songs and dancing, with the women choosing their partner. By evening 'drunken men and the most depraved women mingled with those whose ideas of piety brought them to this spot; and a confused uproar of prayers and oaths, of sanctity and blasphemy sounded in the same instant on the ear'. He made no distinction between those present, remarking '[a]ll become actors – none spectators'.[25] Faction fighting too, as we have seen, was common at patterns. The perception of the pattern as a barbarous custom played a large part in its suppression: Dixon Hardy referred to 'superstitious and degrading practices' and saw them as 'the prolific sources of much of the IRRELIGION, IMMORALITY, and VICE [sic] which at present prevail to such an awful extent through so many portions of our highly favoured land'.[26] Gradually becoming moribund in the course of the nineteenth century, patterns were sometimes revived under the influence of the cultural revival, but in a more orthodox Catholic form.

18.5. Rites of Passage

Van Gennep's identification of the three stages of rites of passage – separation, transition and incorporation – remains the classic formulation. He argued that in the move to a new social status, one leaves one's old status for a transitional period, before being incorporated into the new one. The separation, transition and incorporation have an essential social dimension. The community lost members through death and gained them through birth. Yet the ritual process neither ended with biological death nor began with birth. Rites of passage dealt with processes rather than events. We will briefly look at some of the customs and beliefs associated with birth and marriage.

For married women, fertility was an expectation and there were many rituals to encourage and facilitate childbirth and to protect the unborn child. At the same time, pregnancy was a period fraught with risk. In order to avoid the danger of the child having a club foot or a harelip, a pregnant woman should not enter a graveyard or encounter a hare. Fairy abduction was seen as a threat both to newly born children and to

---

25 T. Crofton Croker, *Researches in the south of Ireland. Illustrative of the scenery, architectural remains and the manners and superstitions of the peasantry with an appendix containing a private narrative of the rebellion of 1798* (Dublin, 1981 [1824]), 281. Indeed Bakhtin argued that 'carnival … does not acknowledge any distinction between actors and spectators' (*Rabelais*, 55).
26 Hardy, *Holy wells*, iii.

nursing mothers. Birth alone did not admit a child to the community: through baptism it was ritually incorporated into the family and the community. The proverb advised 'pós ar an gcarn aoiligh agus faigh cairdeas Críost i bhfad ó bhaile' (marry on the dung-hill – i.e. nearby – and find a godparent far from home). The status of children who died before being baptised was ambiguous: they were buried in liminal places such as disused graveyards, the north-west corner of the local graveyard or beneath boundaries.

Shrovetide was the traditional time for marrying and it was assumed that the person who did not marry by then would not marry for the rest of the year. Customs emphasised disapproval of those who did not marry: sprinkling ashes on the clothing of elderly women and men on Ash Wednesday, smearing chalk on them on the first Sunday of Lent ('Chalk Sunday'), throwing salt on them (to 'preserve' them until next Shrove) or the circulation of mocking verses, the so-called 'Skellig Lists' (from the idea that Lent began later on Skellig Michael). Other customs – such as 'horning' mentioned above – were occasioned by marriages that breached social solidarity. Widespread was the custom of the affluent – strong farmers, merchants and their social equivalents – throwing money after their wedding to the crowd outside, usually beggars, though sometimes children. It was common, especially in the north, to light bonfires on the occasion of a wedding; elsewhere, the bonfire was an indication of social status. A race home by the young male guests after the wedding was known all over Ireland, on foot or on horseback or with carriages; according to one explanation, if the winner was from the bride's side, the husband would die first. Known only from parts of the south-west was the custom of boys or young men drawing a rope across the road to stop the wedding party on its way home from the church; the party could proceed only by making a payment (in the case of young men, sufficient for a round of drinks). Straw Boys as uninvited visitors to weddings were known over most of the country and were generally well treated, though they could also be a nuisance, especially if more than one group appeared.

18.6.   Plus Ça Change …?

'"Cultural change"', according to Stuart Hall, 'is a polite euphemism for the process by which some cultural forms and practices are driven out of the centre of popular life, actively marginalised.'[27] Amhlaoibh Ó Súilleabháin made many references to the celebration of popular festivals in his diary. An entry from 1830 mentions 'a specially blessed St Patrick's Day, for I do not see a single person, man, woman or boy, drunk', for which he thanked a priest's sermons. His references to St John's Eve tell of young people dancing at bonfires and enjoying themselves at the fair on St John's Day until late in the

---

27 S. Hall, 'Notes on deconstructing "the popular"', in R. Samuel (ed.), *People's history and socialist theory* (Abingdon, 2016), 227–8.

evening. For 1834, 'I saw no respectable bonfires, for the law is against them … This day was always a holiday of obligation till today, but it has been suppressed by the Church; for it was a great day for drinking, after bonfire night.'[28] Sir William Wilde writing in the middle of the nineteenth century referred to the earlier loss of May Day traditions in Dublin: 'our Finglas sports were interdicted by a special act of the Privy Council – fairy lore has given place to a newspaper political religion – the new police banished the bonfires'.[29] Hugh Dorian often commented on cultural change, for example, with regard to the custom of the May Tree or Maypole: 'although the practice is not entirely forgotten and is carried out in most places, no one can assign any reason for such foolish observances further than that when one person sees his neighbour do so, he also thinks it is right, or in other words, he does not wish himself to be odd'.[30]

Modernisation, cultural nationalism, commercialisation and tourism are among the factors that have influenced the practice and the meaning of the celebrations and the rituals of life in the nineteenth and twentieth centuries. The influence of the Marian cult was grafted on to the patterns and, most recently, followers of New Age religions ('Celtic' or neo-pagan) have shown an interest in certain patterns. A regional pilgrimage such as that of Croagh Patrick became a national one, now very much on the tourist calendar as well, as are the Puck and Auld Lammas fairs. Hallowe'en has become commercialised, from the sale of American-style masks to the bakery production of the traditional specked loaf (*bairín breac*), but it remains an important festival. The Wren Boys now often go from public house to public house, collecting for charity. According to Néstor García Canclini, if '[f]olk or traditional cultural facts are today the multidetermined product of actors that are popular and hegemonic, peasant and urban, local, national, and transnational',[31] the logic of this broader dimension was always present insofar as folklore and popular culture, as much as any other part of culture, were always part of wider social, economic and historical processes.

FURTHER READING

Arensberg, C. M. and S. T. Kimball. *Family and community in Ireland* (3rd edn, Ennis, 2001 [1940]).

Bakhtin, M. *Rabelais and his world*, translated by H. Iswolsky (Bloomington, IN, 1984).

---

28 A. Ó Suilleabháin, *Cinnlae Amhlaoibh Uí Shúileabháin: the diary of Humphrey O'Sullivan*, edited and translated by Revd M. McGrath, S.J., 4 vols. (London, 1928, 1929, 1930, 1931), IV, 41.
29 Wilde, *Irish popular superstitions*, 34.
30 Dorian, *Outer edge of Ulster*, 259.
31 N. García Canclini, *Hybrid cultures: strategies for entering and leaving modernity*, translated by C. L. Chiappari and S. L. López (Minneapolis and London, 1995), 157.

Bourke, A. *The burning of Bridget Cleary: a true story* (London, 1999).

Brenneman, W. L. Jr. and M. G. Brenneman. *Crossing the circle at the holy wells of Ireland* (Charlottesville and London, 1995).

Briody, M. *The Irish Folklore Commission 1935–1970: history, ideology, methodology*, Studia Fennica, Folkloristica 17 (Helsinki, 2007).

Bunzl, M. 'Franz Boas and the Humboldtian tradition: from Volksgeist and Nationalcharakter to an anthropological concept of culture', in G. W. Stocking, Jr., *Volksgeist as method and ethic: essays on Boasian ethnography and the German anthropological tradition* (Madison, WI, 1996), 17–78.

Burke, P. *Popular culture in early modern Europe* (rev. edn, Aldershot, 1994).

Cirese, A. M. *Dislivelli di culture e altri discorsi inattuali* (Rome, 2006 [1997]).

Crofton Croker, T. *Researches in the south of Ireland. Illustrative of the scenery, architectural remains and the manners and superstitions of the peasantry with an appendix containing a private narrative of the rebellion of 1798* (Dublin, 1981 [1824]).

Danaher, K. *The year in Ireland* (Cork, 1972).

De Carvalho, J. J. 'O lugar da cultura tradicional na sociedade moderna', in C. M. Ferreira (ed.), *Seminário folclore e cultura popular*, Série encontros e estudos 1 (Rio de Janeiro, 1992), 23–39.

De Martino, E. *Sud e magia* (Milan, 1981 [1959]).

Dorian, H. *The outer edge of Ulster: a memoir of social life in nineteenth-century Donegal*, edited by Breandán Mac Suibhne and David Dixon (Dublin, 2000).

Dow, J. R. 'Hans Naumann's gesunkenes Kulturgut and primitive Gemeinschaftskultur', *Journal of Folklore Research* 51, 1 (2014), 49–100.

Eliade, M. *The myth of the eternal return, or cosmos and history*, translated by W. R. Trask (New York and Princeton, 1971).

Eliade, M. *Lo sagrado y lo profano*, translated by L. Gil (5th edn, Barcelona, 1983).

Fabre, D. 'D'une ethnologie romantique', in D. Fabre and J.-M. Privat (eds.), *Savoirs romantiques: une naissance de l'ethnologie* (Nancy, 2010), 5–75.

Ferguson, C. A. 'Diglossia', in P. P. Giglioli (ed.), *Language and social context* (Harmondsworth, 1972).

Foster, G. M. 'Peasant society and the image of limited good', *American Anthropologist* 67, 2 (1965), 293–315.

García Canclini, N. *Hybrid cultures: strategies for entering and leaving modernity*, translated by C. L. Chiappari and S. L. López (Minneapolis and London, 1995).

Gramsci, A. *Letteratura e vita nazionale* (Rome, 1991).

Gramsci, A. *Selections from cultural writings*, edited and translated by W. Boelhower, D. Forgacs and G. Nowell Smith (London, 1985).

Grignon, C. and J.-C. Passeron. *Le savant et le populaire. Misérabilisme et populisme en sociologie et en littérature* (Paris, 1989).

Hall, S. 'Notes on deconstructing "the popular"', in R. Samuel (ed.), *People's history and socialist theory* (Abingdon, 2016), 227–40.

Hardy, P. D. *The holy wells of Ireland* (Dublin, 1836).

Jenkins, R. M. 'Witches and fairies: supernatural aggression and deviance among the Irish peasantry', *Ulster Folklife*, 23 (1977), 33–56.

Lagrée, M. *Religions et cultures en Bretagne, 1850–1950* (Paris, 1992).

Le Roy Ladurie, E. *La civilisation rurale* (Paris, 2012 [1972]).

Löfgren, O. 'Rational and sensitive', in J. Frykman and O. Löfgren (eds.), *Culture builders: a historical anthropology of middle-class life*, translated by A. Crozier (New Brunswick and London, 1987).

Mac Cana, P. *Celtic mythology* (London, 1970).

Mac Néill, M. *The festival of Lughnasa* (Oxford, 1962).

Muchembled, R. *Culture populaire et culture des élites dans la France moderne (XVe–XVIIIe siècle)* (2nd edn, Paris, 1991).

Muchembled, R. *Société, cultures et mentalités dans la France moderne XVIe–XVIIIe siècle* (Paris, 1990).

O'Connor, A. *The blessed and the damned: sinful women and unbaptised children in Irish folklore* (Bern, 2005).

Ó Danachair, C. 'Some marriage customs and their regional distribution', *Béaloideas*, 42–4 (1974–6), 136–75.

Ó Duilearga, S. *Leabhar Sheáin Í Chonaill. Sgéalta agus Seanchas ó Íbh Ráthach* (3rd edn, Dublin, 1977).

Ó Giolláin, D. *Locating Irish folklore: tradition, modernity, identity* (Cork, 2000).

Ó Giolláin, D. 'Revisiting the holy well', *Éire-Ireland*, 40, 1–2 (2005), 11–41.

Ó Giolláin, D. 'Who owns folklore? From collective creation to collective ownership', *Béaloideas*, 79 (2011), 44–59.

Ó Muimhneacháin, A. (ed.). *Seanchas an Táilliúra* (Dublin, 1978).

Ó Muirgheasa, É. 'The holy wells of Donegal', *Béaloideas*, 6, 2 (1936), 143–62.

Ó Súilleabháin, A. *Cinnlae Amhlaoibh Uí Shúileabháin: the diary of Humphrey O'Sullivan*, edited and translated by Revd M. McGrath, S.J., 4 vols. (London, 1928, 1929, 1930, 1931).

Paden, W.E. *Religious worlds: the comparative study of religion* (2nd edn, Boston, 1994).

Redfield, R. 'Peasant society and culture', in Redfield, *The little community and peasant society and culture* (Chicago, 1960).

Thackeray, W. M. *The Irish sketchbook, 1842* (Dublin, 1990 [1843]).

Thoms, W. 'Folklore and the origin of the word' [editor's title], in A. Dundes (ed.), *International folkloristics: classic contributions by the founders of folklore* (Lanham, MD, 1999).

Turner, V. *Dramas, fields and metaphors* (Ithaca and London, 1974).

Turner, V. and E. Turner. *Image and pilgrimage in Christian culture* (New York, 1978).

Van Gennep, A. *The rites of passage*, translated by M. B. Vizedom and G. L. Caffee (London and Henley, 1960 [1908]).

Vermeulen, H. F. 'Origins and institutionalization of ethnography and ethnology in Europe and the USA, 1771–1845', in H. F. Vermeulen and A. Álvarez Roldán (eds.), *Fieldwork and footnotes: studies in the history of European anthropology* (London and New York, 1995), 39–59.

Weber, M. *The sociology of religion,* translated by E. Fischoff (4th edn, Boston, 1993 [1922]).

Wilde, W. *Irish popular superstitions* (Dublin, 1979 [1852]).

Williams, R. *Keywords: a vocabulary of culture and society* (London, 1988).

19 Gender Roles in Ireland since 1740

Lindsey Earner-Byrne and Diane Urquhart

19.1. Introduction

Life has never been lived 'without distinction of sex'.[1] The social, cultural and political dynamics that shaped the relationship between sex and gender evolved in complex ways during the period from 1740 to the beginning of the twenty-first century. Central to the definition of these roles were notions of male and female arenas of operation which served to idealise, regulate and confine behaviour. This process was at various points one of negotiation, imposition, compromise and command. It was enforced by collective will, communal pressure, legal restraint, economic and social structures, overseen and rationalised by culture. This chapter explores some of these processes and the consequent meaning of marriage, work and sexuality for the genders across two and a half centuries.

19.2. Gender and Place

The most powerful force of gender conditioning throughout this period was undoubtedly the family. While itself an institution that changed significantly, the role men and women played therein as respective providers and nurturers was always central to its purpose. The emergence of the gendered family was complex, but intertwined with notions of male and female roles were issues of economics, inheritance and social status. Although the reality often did not conform to the tidy equation of separate spheres, the ideal became increasingly important in social and cultural terms and for political and

1 Article 3, Constitution of the Irish Free State (Saorstát Éireann), 1922.

legal status. Patriarchy was seen as the organising principle of civilised capitalism: much hinged on its success, transgressing its norms carried significant penalties for either sex, but with little economic power women ultimately paid the social price of non-conformance. The interests of the family were also tethered to collective compliance: if a daughter 'misbehaved', it had implications for the marriage prospects of other daughters. Social disgrace was a powerful tool in enforcing gender behaviour. Furthermore, matrifocality, the control of kin networks, did not necessarily equate to power within families. Indeed, women often had little control over some of its key tenets such as the number and spacing of births. Economic necessity as well as desire also led many women to work outside the home whilst men often faced economic displacement. Both sexes also struggled to establish families of their own and, as marriage rates declined and negative stereotyping of spinsters and bachelors grew, migration provided salvation for many.

Religion was second only to the family as a transmitter of gender norms. There was much common ground between the churches' notions of gender roles: women were the purveyors of moral and religious instruction within the home and men the authoritarian breadwinners. The message Revd John Gregg gave his Church of Ireland audience in 1856 would have been warmly received by almost any other congregation in Ireland at the time: 'The large portion of the labours of life – of public life – fall almost exclusively to the lot of men; but a most important portion of the duties of life, especially private life, falls to the share of women. God has adapted our sex to the peculiar duties to which we are especially called'.[2] This was a relatively static view expressed in pastorals, sermons, encyclicals, devotional literature and religious education. It extended beyond the hierarchy and clerics, to the huge numbers of Irish men and women who entered religious life from the nineteenth century onwards and to the lay population of all denominations who helped embed gender ideals through the mediums of philanthropy, censure and class missionising.

Closely associated with faith and family, education formed an important part of the socialisation of both boys and girls, hence the sustained struggle by the various religions to control it. For much of the eighteenth century education either was for the elite or operated at an informal local level, often run by churches, charities or carried out entirely within the home. The nineteenth century witnessed the beginning of formalised external education available, in theory at least, to all Irish children from the 1830s. Research indicates that girls were more likely to attend and stay longer in school, reflecting a confluence of factors, from their relative lack of importance in the economy (particularly in rural areas) to their increasing prominence in emigration trends.[3] The

---

2 Revd J. Gregg, 'Women: a lecture delivered in Trinity College' (Dublin, 1856), cited in M. Luddy, *Women in Ireland, 1800–1918: a documentary history* (Cork, 1995), 13–14.

3 D. Fitzpatrick, '"A share of the honeycomb": education, emigration and Irishwomen', in M. E. Daly and D. Dickson (eds.), *The origins of popular literacy in Ireland: language, change and educational development 1700–1920* (Dublin, 1990), 167–87.

school curriculum was highly gendered, particularly in the practical work expected of boys and girls, for example, needlework, knitting and lace-making for girls.[4] Almost all adults in Ireland claimed to be literate in the 1911 census, and this was a particular achievement for women as at the outset of the nineteenth century men were three times as likely as women to be literate.[5] While the sexes were often taught together, by the end of the nineteenth century the tendency was increasingly to either divide the room along gender lines, or have separate schools. This effectively prepared both boys and girls for their allotted 'place' in life. However, it should be remembered that the genders exerted their own, however limited, agency; many Irish girls employed a strategy of 'female escapology' by exploiting the education system to secure a life abroad.[6]

As literacy rates rose, the press became an ever-increasingly powerful purveyor of gender rhetoric. Women's columns were a feature of the Irish secular and religious press, with, for example, the *Freeman's Journal's* 'The Irishwoman: maid, wife and mother', the *Irish Independent's* 'In women's realm' and the *Catholic Bulletin's* 'For mothers and daughters' encapsulating traditionalist gender roles and reinforcing the idea of appropriate gender behaviour as proof of respectability, particularly important for those aspiring to middle-class status.[7] While few of the women's columns of the nineteenth and twentieth centuries questioned that the domestic sphere was feminine, it was through the women's pages in the early 1970s that a significant social revolt against such gendered prescription began.[8]

19.3. Gender and Work

Ireland fitted into a broader western European pattern in relation to gender and work that witnessed a consistent, if uneven, move from a peasant family economy to a wage economy, which facilitated greater and more visible gender stratification. While the division of roles based on sex has a long history, from the mid-nineteenth century an increasing economic, social, cultural and legal framework developed to support the idea of men and women occupying different spaces. This shift was epitomised by the concept of the public and private sphere, which was used to externalise 'work' and men's influence, while internalising women's nurturing domain. This cultural rationalisation of gendered spaces reflected the changes in agricultural practices and the impact

---

4 A. M. Ireland, 'Records of pupils in national schools: samples from the records of the National Archives of Ireland', *Irish Archives: Journal of the Irish Society for Archives* (2013), 16–26.
5 Fitzpatrick, 'A share of the honeycomb', 168.
6 Ibid.
7 See C. Clear, 'No feminine mystique: popular advice to women of the house in Ireland, 1922–1954', in M. Gialanella Valiulis and M. O'Dowd (eds.), *Women and Irish history* (Dublin, 1997), 189–204.
8 J. Levine, *Sisters* (Dublin, 2009 [1982]); A. Stopper, *Mondays at Gaj's: the story of the Irish women's liberation movement* (Dublin, 2006).

of industrialisation in which the male breadwinner ideal became 'an article of faith'.[9] Yet, poverty often made a mockery of these ideals. A substantial percentage of working-class men and rural labourers were unable to fulfil their financial obligations in relation to their families. The majority of working-class wives, mothers and widows supplemented the family income through cleaning, mending, dressmaking, piecework, washing and taking in boarders.[10] In rural Ireland, the family economy continued in conjunction with the wage economy until at least the 1960s, as evidenced by the many women working on the family farm. There is also substantial evidence to suggest that until at least the 1970s families functioned as a unit and family need was the key driver in deciding issues like employment rather than any individual notion of personal fulfilment.

For many men and women the story was one of declining overall employment during the nineteenth and twentieth centuries, resulting in rising unemployment, underemployment, celibacy and emigration. The second half of the nineteenth century saw the virtual disappearance of the cottier and labourer population, the decline of

Figure 19.1 Carding and wool spinning in Donegal. Image courtesy of Deputy Keeper of the Records, Public Record Office Northern Ireland, D1403/2/27/A.

9 P. Mandler, 'Poverty and charity in the nineteenth century metropolis: an introduction', in P. Mandler (ed.), *The uses of charity: the poor on relief in the nineteenth-century metropolis* (Philadelphia, 1990), 1–37, 25.
10 F. Kennedy, *Cottage to crèche: family change in Ireland* (Dublin, 2001), 72–5.

subsistence-sized farm holdings, and the collapse of the linen industry outside Ulster.[11] While the demand remained for domestic servants, Irish women appeared increasingly reluctant to take up this work in Ireland. Men's work also changed significantly during this period: while Ireland remained a predominantly agricultural economy, the nature of that agriculture changed, as did the reality of landownership. The labourer found himself increasingly on the seasonal migration rota, while the middling farmer asserted himself and his values on rural Ireland.

The debate surrounding the issue of women and work outside the home originates in the changing economic climate of the mid-nineteenth century and endured throughout the twentieth century in various guises. At any given time it reflected contemporary proprieties *and* anxieties: it was argued, for example, that women's rights were being protected by an insistence upon her role in the home because women in the workplace were a threat to the family and the interests of *both* men and women. In 1936, the Roman Catholic priest and professor of philosophy and political theory Cornelius Lucey claimed: 'women are not competing with men on anything like equal terms … Both sexes are suffering as a consequence. Women find themselves wretchedly paid for their work. Men find themselves either ousted altogether from work, or compelled to accept a lower wage than the family wage.'[12] This was a view shared far beyond the conservative confines of the Catholic Church; for example, Louie Bennett, feminist and union organiser, argued 'where the financial burden of keeping home lies upon the male wage-earner … it would be madness for women workers to attempt to disturb fundamentally the present distribution of industrial work'.[13] Rejecting the fatalistic attitude that accepted the 'system', fellow feminist and trade unionist Helena Moloney averred, 'the mere prohibition of women in certain industries is no remedy for the urgent modern problem of unemployment which affects men and women equally'.[14] The writer and journalist Alice Curtayne also claimed that the idea of equality in the workplace would result in woman's 'own undoing', as it would lead to the death of appropriate gender behaviour (motherhood and chivalry), an increase in unemployment and, ultimately, the end of the long history of men and women's 'communion in endurance' and thus the 'depreciation of the home'.[15] Significantly, for the first half of the twentieth century 'feminists, church leaders, political leaders and the general public shared the view that motherhood

11 M. E. Daly, 'Women in the Irish Free State, 1922–39: the interaction between economics and ideology', *Journal of Women's History*, 6–7, 41 (1995), 98–115.
12 Revd C. Lucey, 'The problem of the woman worker', *Irish Ecclesiastical Record*, 48 (July–December 1936), 449–67, at 463. Lucey held the Chair of Philosophy and Political Theory at Maynooth College between 1929 and 1950 and was ordained bishop of Cork in 1950.
13 *Irish Citizen*, November 1919.
14 'Women's status in Ireland', *Model Housekeeping*, 7, 9 (August 1935), 558–9.
15 Ibid.

was the ultimate calling of woman', while the ideal man was to be a conscientious breadwinner.[16]

Contemporary debates on the evils of female workers also reflected real concerns about the international rise of male unemployment and a fear that modernity was incompatible with 'family life' and morality. The tendency to associate women working with a perversion of the 'natural order' and the destruction of the family conflated these issues in the minds of many contemporaries. The introduction of the marriage bar in 1933 and the Conditions of Employment Act of 1936 confirmed much of this logic in Irish Free State legislation: the latter, while improving workers' conditions in general, allowed the government to prohibit women's employment in certain industries and fix a quota in others. While it had little practical impact on women's working lives, it nonetheless contributed to an environment that was hostile to female workers.[17] Much of the rhetoric validating domestic motherhood was not supported by concrete legislation in the southern Irish state, despite the promise in the Constitution of Éire (1937) to 'endeavour to ensure that mothers shall not be obliged by economic necessity to engage in labour to the neglect of their duties in the home'. When children's allowances were introduced in 1944 (the only payment that might have been construed as fulfilling this endeavour), the payment was made to the father, because society should 'regard the father as the head of the family, and responsible for the proper utilisation of the family income'.[18] Nothing was done to support unemployed single women; the Unemployment Assistance Act (1933) specified that single women could only qualify if they had a previous record of insurable employment.[19] Similarly, the 1951 'family man's budget' reorganised the tax system to give preference to 'the man with children to support'.[20] Northern Ireland tended to follow Westminster reform with the 1940s in particular heralding significant reforms such as family allowances in 1945, free health care under the National Health Service Act of 1948 and benefits for anyone in need under the National Assistance Act of the same year.

The continued high marital fertility rate in Ireland was another contributory factor in the low employment rates for women. Birth control was made illegal in the Irish Free State in 1935 and remained so until 1979, and, while it was not illegal in Northern Ireland, it remained difficult to access and socially unacceptable until the 1970s. It was often too difficult for mothers of large families to arrange childcare and in many cases it would have negated the financial gains of working. Exceptionally large families also necessitated many single women to become 'wee mammies', staying at home to help mind

16 Kennedy, *Cottage to crèche*, 92.
17 Daly, 'Women in the Irish Free State'.
18 *Dail Debates*, 24 November 1943, vol. 92, col. 224.
19 M. Cousins, *The birth of social welfare in Ireland* (Dublin, 2003), 60.
20 'Family man's budget,' *Irish Times*, 16 April 1947.

siblings.[21] The proportion of married women in the workforce had always been higher in Northern Ireland, but during the 1970s the rate rose rapidly; thus in 1981 Northern Ireland's rate was double that of the Republic. Much of this increase in married women's employment was as a result of an increase in part-time work, presumably deemed more family-friendly, whereas the rate of part-time female workers in the Republic remained the lowest in the European Economic Community (EEC).[22] Indeed, it is significant that the sharp decline in the Republic's fertility rate in the 1980s was accompanied by a rise in the proportion of married women in the workforce.[23]

The 1970s witnessed the first major shift in gender and work in modern Ireland with the beginning of a move towards the double-income family.[24] This was aided by an international re-examination of the status of women and the emergence of the so-called Second Wave Women's Movement. This process was reflected in the reversal of legislation based on the male breadwinner norm: for example, the marriage bar was ended, unmarried mothers were paid an allowance and women could serve on juries on the same basis as men. However, the confluence of other economic and political issues, such as the Republic's entry into the EEC in 1973, the entrance of the first cohort of beneficiaries of free second-level education into the workforce from 1972, and rising male unemployment in the 1980s, probably had as significant an impact in eroding the idealised notion of men's place. Significantly, it was argued in 2001 that it was not the increased participation of women per se in the labour market that fuelled the 'Celtic Tiger' (Ireland's economic boom of 1997–2008), but the increased rate of working mothers with young children.[25] While this implies a significant shift in what men and women deemed appropriate and necessary for family life, numerous studies also show that women continued to do the vast majority of caring and household duties, even when working outside the home.[26] Furthermore, despite the introduction of the Employment Equality Act (1977), women continued to earn less than men. In 2015, the Republic of Ireland had a 14 per cent pay gap between men's and women's wages; this disparity is even less favourable the higher the pay scale, and furthermore, 23.6 per cent of women as opposed to 17.6 per cent of men remain in low-paid jobs.[27] This is in contrast to

21 J. Hamill, 'Childcare arrangements within the Belfast linen community', in B. Whelan (ed.), *Women and paid work in Ireland 1500–1930* (Dublin, 2000), 120–32.

22 M. Hill, *Women in Ireland: a century of change* (Belfast, 2003), 141.

23 B. Walsh, 'Labour force participation and the growth of women's employment, Ireland 1971–1991', *Economic and Social Review*, 24, 4 (July 1993), 369–400.

24 Kennedy, *Cottage to crèche*, 92, 95–6.

25 G. Collins and J. Wickham, *What childcare crisis? Irish mothers entering the labour force* (Dublin, 2001), cited in L. Connolly, 'Locating "the Irish family": towards a plurality of family forms?', in L. Connolly (ed.), *The 'Irish' family* (London and New York, 2014), 10–38, at 32.

26 Connolly, 'Locating "the Irish family"', 32.

27 S. Pentony, '20% of Irish workers are low paid', *Village*, 9 March 2015, available at www.villagemagazine.ie, accessed 9 March 2015.

Northern Ireland where full-time female workers now earn on average 3.3 per cent more than men, a significant shift in less than a decade.[28]

19.4. Gender and Relationships

If gender is to a large extent about 'thinking in relations'[29] and the household was men and women's greatest 'theatre of collaboration',[30] then dating and mating are essential to any gender analysis of Irish society. Although marriage was the presumed destiny of most Irish men and women, it was an increasingly unattainable ideal. Census material from 1841, although not without problems of accuracy, comparability and inclusion, reveals long-lived changes in marital patterns. Single women in the permanent celibacy category, comprising those aged 46 to 55 years, outnumber unmarried men from 1841 to 1901. At times this female numerical superiority was considerable: in 1841, for example, 37,934 women were recorded as permanently celibate compared with 29,176 men.[31]

After 1851 no one under the age of 15 was recorded as married. This was at the extreme end of a trend which saw the average age at marriage for both sexes increase: for women this rose from 24–25 years in 1841 to 28 years in 1911 with a corresponding increase in the average age of male marriage, as longer life expectancy meant that men waited longer to inherit the farms required to attract a spouse and primogeniture and dowry payments took hold across the classes.[32] This also heightened male authority; an inheriting, usually elder, son would arrange his own match and those of his dowered sisters. As ever, there were exceptions: if there were no male heirs, daughters might inherit and a piecemeal reform of married women's property rights gradually increased female control over wages, inheritance and property from the nineteenth century.

It was not only later marriages which emerged as a characteristic Irish trait: the total number of the population which was married fell consistently, declining 51.6 per cent from 1841 to 1911. Munster's proportion of married population fell most steeply from the post-famine period onwards, declining from 33.4 per cent in 1841 to 26.4 per cent in 1911. This was at least partially determined by sustained rates of migration. Ulster

28 In 1997 full-time male workers in Northern Ireland earned 16.5 per cent more than full-time female workers. The change is due to the high number of female public sector employees in Northern Ireland. *Independent*, 20 March 2015.

29 G. Bock, 'Women's history and gender history: aspects of an international debate', *Gender and History*, 1, 1 (March 1988), 7–30.

30 D. Fitzpatrick, 'Review article: women, gender and the writing of Irish history', *Irish Historical Studies*, 27, 107 (1991), 267–73.

31 W. E. Vaughan and A. J. Fitzpatrick, *Irish historical statistics: population, 1821–1971* (Dublin, 1978), 87, 90.

32 M. E. Daly, *A social and economic history of Ireland since 1800* (Dublin, 1981), 92. See chapter 21 in this volume for further discussion of dowries.

was the only province to experience an increase in its married population: by 1911 27.9 per cent were married, representing a 0.8 per cent increase from the 1901 census, a comment on its more-developed economy, rapid urbanisation and industrialisation.[33] By the mid-twentieth century marriage rates outside Ulster recovered, and at times exceeded, their mid-nineteenth-century position; by 1971 34.8 per cent of Munster's population was married. Rates of marriage were even higher in Leinster: its married population increased to 35.4 per cent by 1971. A complex picture emerges as to the impact of this gender history: for example, despite rising marriage rates, 1950s contemporaries were diagnosing 'a crisis in masculinity among bachelor farmers' in rural Ireland.[34] Irish women were portrayed as particularly proactive in rejecting these bachelors as husbands by migrating to the nearest town or leaving Ireland altogether. Bachelors, spinsters, the widowed, deserted, separated and divorced all deviated from the stereotypical marital 'norm'. Whilst the first two groups often fed into the ever-increasing migrant stream, those who were unable to leave Ireland in consequence of financial constraints or because they were the designated carer of ageing relatives were often depicted, and sometimes ridiculed, as a socially redundant and surplus population.

As to life behind closed doors, a survey of Dublin families in the 1950s revealed a nuanced understanding of marriage and gender negotiations within the home and a sense that the sexes were closer than in previous generations. One young wife explained: 'Everybody in the family is much more closely knit now than they used to be. And that is especially true about husbands and wives … [I]n my parents' day … the women were the slaves to men.'[35] However, Dorine Rohan's pioneering 1969 study, *Marriage Irish style,* based on hundreds of interviews, emphasised high levels of marital discontent caused by poor communication and a lack of sensitivity and of emotional maturity.[36] Remaining in an unhappy marriage was often due to the lack of a means to escape. Separation precluded remarriage and divorce entailed a costly private parliamentary act until 1922 in the Irish Free State and 1939 in Northern Ireland. The latter then moved to a court-based process, but divorce was banned from 1937 to 1996 in independent Ireland.[37] By the 1970s the Committee of Catholic Bishops' Council for Social Welfare admitted that desertion was one solution and 'a particularly Irish' form of separation.[38]

There was also an expectation that marriage would bring children; 'barren' women were often returned to their family with their dowries intact. Such a practice underscores

---

33 Vaughan and Fitzpatrick, *Irish historical statistics*, 90, 114, 145, 159, 160.
34 Connolly, 'Locating "the Irish family"', 10–38, 17.
35 A. J. Humphreys, *New Dubliners: urbanization and the Irish family* (London, 1966), 122.
36 D. Rohan, *Marriage Irish style* (Cork, 1969).
37 The grounds for divorce also varied between the sexes until the 1920s. See D. Urquhart, 'Ireland and the Divorce and Matrimonial Causes Act of 1857', *Journal of Family History*, 38, 3 (July 2013), 301–20. In the south it was reintroduced in 1997, after the 1996 referendum.
38 *Irish Times*, 20 August 1974. See chapter 21 in this volume for a further discussion of divorce.

the sexual double standard in relation to the allocation of blame for infertility; a man might remarry by annulling the marriage, yet all in the local community would be aware of the woman's situation, making her an unattractive match. Akin to marriage rates, birth rates are hard to determine: with no civil registration in Ireland until 1864, census commissioners conservatively estimated the number of births. In the 1830s annual birth rates averaged 198,039 per annum, but declined sharply due to fertility being affected by malnutrition in the 1840s and the continued migrant outflow. By 1920 the annual number of births was below 100,000, with 22.2 births recorded per 1,000 population. Birth rates in the immediate post-independence period were fairly level, declining in the late 1920s before increasing in the 1940s: by 1971 there were 22.7 births per 1,000 population. Births in Northern Ireland were slightly higher, reaching a high of 24.2 births per 1,000 of the population in 1942 before declining to 20.7 in 1971.[39]

Bearing children was, however, high risk. Maternal and infant mortality was experienced by many, but the onus was again gendered: it was a mother's role to preserve infant life.[40] As Belfast's Medical Superintendent Officer of Health emphasised, 'the lowering of the infant mortality rate depends upon educated motherhood, upon mothercraft.'[41] Yet, mortality rates, especially for illegitimate children, were slow to improve. Mortality was higher in the Irish Free State than in Northern Ireland, though the latter's rate was often three times that of England and Wales: Belfast's infant mortality rate was 'abnormally high' in 1942 and 3,292 infant deaths were recorded in the Irish Free State in 1947.[42] The rate of infant deaths gradually fell in the 1950s due to the increased use of drugs, especially penicillin: the solution thus lay in medicine rather than mothercraft.[43]

19.5. Gender and Sexuality

A matter which appears more intimately to our common human nature than any temporary madness is the attitude of the Celt towards women who have fallen from virtue … Whether it has really anything to do with an exceptional love of virtue or horror of vice one must doubt, seeing that it exists side by side with the extraordinarily loveless marriages which still obtain over a great part of Ireland. This savage idea of virtue which perverts even the heart of parenthood is surely rather a distorted form of pride.[44]

39 Vaughan and Fitzpatrick, *Irish historical statistics*, 87, 102, 241, 244–5, 249–50, 254–5.

40 Maternal mortality refers to the death of a mother from any cause during pregnancy, labour or within six weeks of the birth of a child. Infant mortality refers to death within the first year of life.

41 Minute book of Belfast Corporation Maternity and Child Welfare Committee, 11 January 1933 (Public Record Office of Northern Ireland, LA/10/9/AD).

42 Registrar-General, Annual Report, 1928 (National Archives, Dublin, s 8587), xlii–xliii and *Irish Press*, 14 May 1948. The 1918 Midwives Act made unofficial midwifery illegal, but the practice continued.

43 Memorandum from the Department of Health, 26 October 1953 (National Archives, Dublin, s 13444L).

44 K. Tynan, 'A new Irish novelist', review of Grace Rhys' Land League novel, *Mary Dominic* in *The Bookman* (January 1899), 118. We are grateful to Anna Pilz for drawing this passage to our attention.

Katharine Tynan's late nineteenth-century words epitomise the complexity of Irish gender roles and their impact on sexuality, morality and gender relations. Gender expectations meant that women straying from the confines of purity were stigmatised as 'fallen' at best and 'deviant' at worst, and homosexuality remained long-hidden, illegal and penalised either by violence or by imprisonment. Ideas of moral contagion were rife in the Victorian era and explain why the contagious diseases acts, applying to specified garrison towns and ports from 1864 to 1886, only identified women as the carriers of venereal disease.[45] Similarly it was prostitutes who were arrested rather than the men who purchased their services. Women bearing children outside of marriage were often outcast, hidden from the public gaze in Magdalen asylums and mother and baby homes and travelling from Ireland to accessible ports like Liverpool to procure abortions.[46] Abortion was also seen as a female 'crime' even though it, and the purchase of abortifacients, was frequently financed by men.[47]

Infanticide and the concealment of birth leading to an infant's death were further believed to be almost exclusively carried out by female perpetrators with the legal frame clearly aligning these acts to mental disturbances associated with childbirth.[48] However, shame and fear were also causal factors in infant killings. At trial in 1895 Mary O'Connor averred: 'I was out of my mind from my shame. God forgive me, I am suffering the torments of the d[amne]d since it happened. I don't care what will become of me', while Ellen Gill claimed her child was still-born in 1898: 'I was in a hurry to throw it away as I was afraid my brother would come in and kill me.'[49] Yet, court records also reveal culpable male and female parties. Rural women and those residing in small towns were removed from the networks of non-familial support which grew up in more urban areas from the late eighteenth century onwards and levels of infanticide and child abandonment were consequently higher in these areas.[50]

As reflected in the infant mortality rate, infanticide was also closely associated to illegitimacy. This was similarly apparent in the legal framework which regarded infant murder as a capital offence (although no Irish woman was executed, for example, in the 1850 to 1900 period), yet from 1803 a lesser charge of concealment of birth was introduced for hiding the birth of an illegitimate child who was subsequently found dead, with a maximum term of two years' imprisonment with hard labour. Although

45 In Ireland the acts applied to the Curragh in County Kildare, Cork and Queenstown (now Cobh) in County Cork.

46 The last Irish Magdalen asylum closed in 1996.

47 C. Rattigan, '"Crimes of passion of the worst character": abortion and gender in Ireland, 1925–50', in M. Gialanella Valiulis (ed.), *Gender and power in Irish history* (Dublin, 2009), 115–39.

48 A charge of concealment of birth was brought where it could not be proved that a child had been born alive. An estimated one in fifty infanticide cases was brought to trial. A. Guilbride, 'Infanticide: the crime of motherhood', in P. Kennedy (ed.), *Motherhood in Ireland: creation and context* (Cork, 2004).

49 E. Farrell (ed.), *Infanticide in the Irish crown files at assizes, 1883–1900* (Dublin, 2012), 291, 443–4.

50 See chapter 21 in this volume for a detailed discussion of unmarried mothers, infanticide and Irish morality.

this was later extended to legitimate children, it raises serious questions regarding the value attached to illegitimate life. Like women who were deemed sexually deviant, those found guilty of infanticide or concealment of birth were detained. Given the clear association of this crime with post-natal illness, mental hospitals might be expected to be the lone destination for these women. However, a range of institutions held their fate: prisons, Magdalen asylums as well as familial care. From the 1950s more women were transferred to mental hospitals, but institutional care did not guarantee recovery, support or safety.

The history of domestic abuse and violence is also highly gendered. Spousal murder, for instance, was an overwhelmingly male act and a sense of female endurance prevailed. Belfast feminist L. A. M. Priestley McCracken referred to the longstanding notion that women who provoked their husbands 'did not deserve anything but harshness'.[51] Maggie Murray in Dublin's tenements recalled her mother's lifetime of domestic abuse: 'All her life beaten. Me mother had black eyes … She'd have run or she'd be dead … Oh, God, the sadness in her face.' Many abused women were told by parents, the churches and the state to persevere: 'he was your husband and when you married him you had to do what he told you. Like it or lump it. Or you'd get a few punches.'[52] The *Love is for life* pastoral issued by the Irish Catholic hierarchy in 1985 similarly saw marital breakdown and divorce as posing more significant threats to family life than violence.[53]

Until 1970 a deserted wife was not entitled to state benefits. Even with that reform, state support would end when a woman co-habited with another man so her dependence was transferred. The Family Home Protection Act (1976) and the Family Law (Protection of Spouses and Children) Act (1981) enabled violent spouses to be barred from the marital home, with twenty thousand banning orders made from 1984 to 1994.[54] The recognition of rape within marriage in 1990 was also groundbreaking, coming two years ahead of the UK reform, highlighting the need for protection within the familial unit that the state held as a stabilising influence. More recently violence against men has become recognised with the establishment of the Amen organisation in 2000. Nonetheless, research on domestic abuse, which indicates that in 2014 one in four women experienced physical and sexual violence at the hands of a male partner, is a sobering reminder of women's particular vulnerability within many intimate relationships.[55]

---

51 *Irish Citizen*, September 1919.
52 K. C. Kearns, *Dublin tenement life: an oral history* (Dublin, 1994), 51, 63.
53 T. Ó Fiach, K. McNamara, J. Cunnane and T. Morris, *Love is for life: a pastoral letter issued on behalf of the Irish hierarchy* (Dublin, 1985).
54 T. Fahey, *Irish Times*, 16 January 1996.
55 Safe Ireland, *National domestic violence service statistic report, 2014* (Athlone, 2015), 3.

19.6.   Gender and Social Change

As the state became more involved in welfare, education became more widely available and new secularising influences filtered through to Irish society from the EEC, the media and the USA, there was a shift in the meanings and perceptions of gender. The Guardianship of Infants Act (1964), the Succession Act (1965) and the Unmarried Mothers Allowance (1973) are examples of the state's acknowledgement that the actuality of family life could fall short of the idealisation of the family. The 1987 Status of Children Act also made very important moves in legitimising those born outside marriage and in so doing challenged the constitutional premise that the family was determined by marriage. Laws on contraception, homosexuality, censorship and, after two spikey referendums, divorce followed, but this was not an easy transition. Gender was repoliticised in the 1970s and reforms were hard won: 'It is understandable that many people should grieve at the passing of traditional certainties. But there is a growing recognition that … those certainties exacted an unconscionable price from the minorities, the marginalised and the disadvantaged.'[56] This traditionalism inspired a backlash in the 1980s; some women expressed a sense of having been devalued by the feminist movement of the 1970s: '[T]hey make housewives feel they're inadequate.'[57] The divisive abortion referendum of 1983 has also been interpreted as part of this backlash 'against the feminism inherent in some of the legislative initiatives of the 1970s'.[58] In that referendum the people of the Republic voted to include an eighth amendment in the Irish constitution in which the 'state acknowledges the right to life of the unborn and, with due regard to the equal right to life of the mother, guarantees in its laws to respect, and as far as practicable by its laws to defend and vindicate that right'.[59]

The debate surrounding this referendum exposed deep faultlines in Irish society between those who wished to protect, preserve, and even reassert, conservative traditional values and those who sought to liberalise and modernise Ireland's social and legal attitude to sexuality and morality. The 1983 debate was followed by two highly publicised cases: the death of a fifteen-year-old school girl, Ann Lovett, from exposure along with her newborn infant, and the discovery of two infant corpses in County Kerry leading to the arrest of one woman and a subsequent inquiry into police handling of the case.[60] Both cases involved unmarried motherhood, the life and value of illegitimate infants, and the status of women in Ireland. Interestingly, neither of these

56 *Irish Times*, 26 September 1996.
57 Irish Consumer Research, *The Irish Housewife: A Portrait* (Dublin, 1986), 79.
58 M. J. Maguire, 'The changing face of Catholic Ireland: conservatism and liberalism in the Ann Lovett and Kerry babies scandals', *Feminist Studies*, 27, 2 (Summer 2001), 335–58.
59 Constitution of Ireland, Article 8.
60 *Report of the Tribunal of Inquiry into 'the Kerry babies case'* (Dublin, 1985).

stories was unique – both had been played out numerous times in Irish history – but Irish society was ready to see these stories as part of a wider narrative of hypocrisy and, for some, misogyny. The feminist Nell McCafferty summarised the sense that 'woman-hood was on trial' in Ireland and, for many, these cases proved the need for a renego-tiation of the impact of gender roles on sexual morality and, in particular, on women's personal lives.[61]

Northern Ireland experienced a similar period of social turbulence in relation to the perception of sexuality and morality, a process complicated by the outbreak of the 'Troubles' in 1969. While a women's movement emerged in Northern Ireland, it was compromised by the deeply contested campaign for social justice for Roman Catholics. Some women involved in the Northern Irish 'Troubles', for example female IRA volun-teers, argued that there was little gender equality within that 'struggle'.[62] Furthermore, deep political tensions cut across any gendered alliance northern women may have hoped to forge: for example, for working-class Catholic women housing was the pri-mary issue, for middle-class Protestant women law and order was the main concern.[63] In fact, Northern Ireland lagged behind the rest of the UK in terms of legislation and attitudinal change; for example, Britain liberalised the law on homosexuality in 1967, but when this was mooted for the north, Ian Paisley's Democratic Unionist Party responded with the 'Save Ulster from Sodomy' campaign. Similarly, abortion, which was legalised in Britain in 1967, was not introduced into Northern Ireland and contin-ues to be governed by strict medical criteria. However, homosexuality was decriminal-ised in Northern Ireland in 1982 and in the Republic in 1993, and civil partnerships for same-sex couples have been possible in Northern Ireland since 2005 and in the Republic since 2010. On 22 May 2015, the Republic of Ireland became the first country to mandate its government by popular vote to legalise same-sex marriage.

19.7.   Conclusion

Class, region and religion have always intersected and competed with the ideals and realities of gender in Ireland. Gender provided a defining concept of identity, yet it was often divisive and many men and women lived beyond its idealised strictures. Poverty, pay and violence continue to point to deep gender-based discrimination in both the Republic of Ireland and Northern Ireland. The majority of women cluster in low to mid-workforce ranks and domestic violence remains a crushing reality in

61 N. McCafferty, *A woman to blame: the Kerry babies case* (Dublin, 1985). See chapter 21 in this volume for discussion of the Lovett case.
62 E. Fairweather, R. McDonough and M. McFadyean, *Only the rivers run free. Northern Ireland: the women's war* (London, 1984).
63 Hill, *Women in Ireland*, 138, 178–80.

many homes. In the 2000s Ireland ranked 51st out of 58 in global gender gap indices, based on economic opportunities, maternity benefits, discrimination and state provision of childcare.[64] Irish young men are five times more likely than Irish women to take their own lives.[65] Although support for the nuclear family remains, nearly a quarter of Irish children live in one-parent families, considerably above the EU average of 13.6 per cent; 86 per cent of those families are headed by women. Men and women in the Republic of Ireland continue to have the highest fertility rate in the EU, but they also wait the longest in their lifecycle to start having those babies.[66] While co-habitation is the norm for most Irish couples, it is usually a prelude before marriage which continues to appeal to both sexes and is now legally available to those of the same sex in the Republic. The history of twenty-first-century Ireland may well prove to be one lived 'without distinction of sex', but in 2016 distinct ideas of gender continue to shape legislation, social mores, expectation and opportunity and, most crucially, the lives of men and women.

FURTHER READING

Bourke, J. *Husbandry and housewifery: women, economic change and housework in Ireland 1890–1914* (Oxford, 1993).

Clear, C. *Women of the house: women's household work in Ireland, 1926–1961: discourses, experiences, memories* (Dublin, 2000).

Cullen Owens, R. *A social history of women in Ireland* (Dublin, 2004).

Earner-Byrne, L. *Mother and child: maternity and child welfare in Dublin, 1922–60* (Manchester, 2007, 2013).

Hayes, A. and D. Urquhart (eds.). *The Irish women's history reader* (London and New York, 2000).

Hill, M. *Women in Ireland: a century of change* (Belfast, 2003).

McCormick, L. *Regulating sexuality: women in twentieth-century Northern Ireland* (Manchester, 2009).

MacCurtain, M. and M. O'Dowd (eds.). *Women in early modern Ireland* (Edinburgh, 1991).

McLaughlin, E. 'Women and the family in Northern Ireland: a review', *Women's Studies International Forum*, 16, 6 (1993).

Redmond, J., S. Tiernan, S. McAvoy and M. McAuliffe (eds.). *Sexual politics in modern Ireland* (Sallins, 2015).

64 P. O'Connor, 'Still changing places: women's paid employment and gender roles', *Irish Review*, 35 (Summer 2007), 64–5. Bangladesh was in 53rd place.

65 E. J. Hade, 'Suicide rates hit an all-time high as 554 take own lives', *Irish Independent*, 20 March 2014.

66 Connolly, 'Locating "the Irish family"', 27.

20 Childhood since 1740

Sarah-Anne Buckley and Susannah Riordan

20.1.   Introduction

The origins of historical research into childhood are usually traced to the publication of Philippe Ariès's 1960 study, translated into English as *Centuries of childhood*. Here, Ariès argued that while there have always been children, the concept of 'childhood' – the recognition, celebration and, frequently, idealisation of an intermediate stage of life between infancy and adulthood – only developed in the seventeenth century and then primarily among the wealthier middle classes. Later scholars have dismissed Ariès's portrayal of the Middle Ages as a period in which parents had a largely unemotional relationship with their children. However, there has been a general consensus that by the middle of the eighteenth century, certainly in elite families, the child was increasingly being recognised as an individual with needs which differed from those of adults. This chapter, therefore, charts a period of enormous change beginning with the 'discovery of childhood' and ending with the insertion of 'the rights of the child' into the Irish constitution in 2012.

Ariès inspired the development of a new field of scholarship, employing age – like gender, race or class – as a tool of historical enquiry. Methodologically, this poses challenges for historians as even within a limited region and timeframe, the definition and experience of 'childhood' is not universal. Furthermore, children are less likely than adults to have created records that have been preserved and, where they are extant, these sources may elude analysis by the modern adult. Historians are usually dependent on sources written or recorded by adults and, in consequence, Harry Hendrick has asked 'can the history of children/childhood ever be more than that of what adults have done to children and how they conceptualised childhood?'[1] This question is not merely rhetorical. Internationally, the historiography of childhood has evolved from concentration on the changing ways in which adults – whether parents, philosophers, philanthropists or politicians – represented and thought about children, to studies of the increasing intervention by states into the lives of poor, 'criminal', illegitimate and other vulnerable children, to attempts through the use of such sources as oral histories, memoirs, folklore collections and children's literature to discover the authentic voices, and the agency, of children in the past.

The history of children and childhood in Ireland has largely followed this trajectory, not least because it was late to develop and influenced in part by the intense social concerns about the historical abuse of children in institutions which emerged in the 1990s. Irish children's history is now flourishing: 2014 witnessed the publication of Maria Luddy and James M. Smith's edited volume, *Children, childhood and Irish society: 1500 to the present*, and the first major interdisciplinary conference on the history of childhood in Ireland. However, this history remains dominated by those aspects of childhood accessible through organised collections of records: education, institutions, the welfare system and the penal system. There are many questions remaining to be answered about the history of the Irish child and of Irish childhood – or rather *childhoods*, since in Ireland as elsewhere childhood experience was marked by diversity of experience according to age, class, gender, geography, religion and ethnicity.

20.2.   Family Life

By 1750 in Ireland, the evidence of representational art, material culture, and the correspondence and reading habits of the upper and middle classes suggest that childhood was viewed as a distinct period of life. Children were cherished as individuals with their own personalities, characterised by an innocence untainted by the temptations and vicissitudes of life, and not merely as imperfect adults, economic units or a means of ensuring the survival of families. Parents understood that their offspring had the potential to mature into good and useful citizens, or, if inadequately nurtured and guided, the opposite. Ariès associated this development with improving survival rates for infants and children in the early modern period. Though childhood mortality figures are difficult to estimate for Ireland before the advent of regular censuses, it has been suggested that between a quarter and a third died before their fifteenth birthday in the early eighteenth century.[2] This statistic improved incrementally over the course of

---

1 H. Hendrick, handout circulated at Conference on the History of Childhood, Boston College, Ireland, April 2008.

2 S. Connolly, 'Family, love and marriage: some evidence from the early eighteenth century', in M. MacCurtain and M. O'Dowd (eds.), *Women in early modern Ireland* (Edinburgh, 1991), 285.

the next two hundred years, with the exception of the Great Famine during which the death rate of the under-nines, and particularly the under-fives, was disproportionate to their total numbers.[3] Despite the general improvement in infant and child mortality, by the end of the nineteenth century Irish rates were noticeably higher than those in Britain and remained high by western European standards until the 1940s. For the most part, this reflected the poverty, overcrowding and poor diet of those in urban areas, particularly Dublin's tenements.

Sources, from the diaries and correspondence of eighteenth-century aristocrats to oral testimonies about tenement life in the first decades of the twentieth century,[4] bear witness to the constant anxiety of parents about the health of their children, particularly in the first year of life. While the death of infants was often attributed to 'convulsions', epidemic diseases were the main cause of concern for the mothers and fathers of older children, ranging from smallpox – prior to the introduction of a relatively safe method of inoculation in 1768 – to gastroenteritis and tuberculosis. Parents often expressed their grief on the death of children in terms of resignation to the will of God and gratitude for the child's translation to a better world. Historians have warned against mistaking conventional expressions of piety for indifference. As Steven Ozment has observed, 'surely the hubris of an age reaches a certain peak when it accuses another age of being incapable of loving its children properly'.[5] None the less, Irish fatalism about the country's abnormally high levels of infant and child mortality into the twentieth century – among policy-makers as well as parents – appears to have been exceptional and debilitating.

Survival was, therefore, the main challenge posed to the Irish child. Thereafter, its upbringing was – certainly until after the Second World War – determined by its parents' understanding of its future role in society. Increasing survival rates meant larger families: more sons to be provided with land, a career or a trade; more daughters to be dowered or provided with a means of making a livelihood. This challenge existed in every class and was not peculiar to Ireland: where Ireland was remarkable was in the lack of alternative opportunities for non-inheriting children, the continued dominance of the pre-industrial family economy well into the twentieth century, and reliance on the emigration of excess children as a family survival strategy. In these circumstances, the destiny of the Irish child, including decisions about inheritance, marriage, emigration and – towards these ends – education and employment, was under the near-total control of parents, principally fathers.

---

3 P. P. Boyle and C. Ó Gráda, 'Fertility trends, excess mortality, and the Great Irish Famine', *Demography*, 23, 4 (1986), 555.

4 For example, K. C. Kearns, *Dublin tenement life: an oral history* (Dublin, 1996).

5 S. Ozment, *When fathers ruled: family life in Reformation Europe* (Cambridge, MA, 1983), 162.

Gabrielle Ashford has suggested that the eighteenth-century nobility and gentry experienced the 'discovery' of their own children in terms of the enjoyment of their company as well as the care of their health and education and were more comfortable with family intimacy than their English peers.[6] However, although the international history of childhood has been dominated by middle-class childhoods in the nineteenth century, the domestic lives of middle-class children in general and of children of all classes in the nineteenth century are yet to be assessed by historians of Ireland. Whether the isolated and eccentric childhoods that were the staples of 'Big House' literature at the beginning of the twentieth century were more than the tropes of an elegiac genre and whether Irish children of the middle classes experienced a 'Victorian' upbringing are questions that remain to be answered.

Family life in the pre-famine tenant-farming and labouring classes is also largely unexplored and, given the absence of sources, may remain so. But the Irish farming family in the hundred years after the famine has – because it differed significantly from western norms – attracted considerable scholarly attention. Most children in this period grew up on small family farms or over small-scale family businesses with close ties to the agricultural community. Irish demographic anomalies, such as late marriage, large families and endemic emigration, as well as the close relationship between land, shop and family, gave these childhoods some distinctive characteristics, frequently shared by the urban working classes. The age gap between parents, particularly fathers, and children was such that being orphaned in childhood was commonplace. Often there was also a sizeable age gap between older and younger siblings, with the latter scarcely knowing brothers or sisters who had left home or emigrated while they themselves were still in infancy. Older and younger children within the same family could experience radically different childhoods as the fortunes of the family altered – for example, the earnings of older children might be used to facilitate the education of younger ones.

Within the family economy, particularly on the farm, life and work were strictly segregated by gender and age. Young children remained in close proximity to their mother as she worked, though in both rural and urban families older siblings, particularly sisters, were often actively involved in the care of younger children to the extent that the term 'little mammies' was in widespread use to describe such girls. The stem three-generation household was in decline by the late nineteenth century but was still more common in Ireland than in other western countries. Where a grandmother was in residence, she frequently took charge of childcare, and the care of a frail or sick grandparent in turn commonly became the special responsibility of an older child. At the age of six or seven boys began to associate to a greater extent with their father and

6 G. M. Ashford, 'Childhood: studies in the history of children in eighteenth-century Ireland', unpublished PhD thesis, St Patrick's College Drumcondra, 2012, 56.

older brothers, running errands and undertaking simple jobs. After the age of about ten or eleven boys could expect to be brought home from school when some crucial task such as hay-making required their labour. At about fourteen children left school, either to work alongside their mother or father or to find live-in work with another farmer.

Such patterns of working and living were usual in pre-industrial western Europe, but the rigid age-structuring of society in late nineteenth- and twentieth-century Ireland struck anthropologist Conrad Arensberg as anomalous.[7] Irish children and adolescents had less autonomy than their counterparts and idiosyncratic relationships with parents and siblings. Arensberg considered relationships between fathers and children (sons in particular) to be distant and potentially antagonistic. This is also characteristic of Irish childhood memoirs and oral histories in which the cold, brutal, feckless or drunken father is a stock character, matched by the saintly – and frequently prematurely deceased – mother. These accounts must be regarded with caution but their ubiquity is noteworthy, as is Caitriona Clear's observation that a generational shift occurred during the 1940s when it became more usual for fathers to involve themselves in childcare.[8] The post-war period, and particularly the 1960s, brought gradual changes to family relationships as both the age of marriage and the size of families gradually decreased and the comparative economic value of children's labour declined. Combined with improved educational and, ultimately, employment opportunities for young people, these factors resulted in a longer, and more autonomous, childhood and adolescence and – conceivably – more companionate relationships between parents and children, and between siblings.

20.3. Learning, Working, Playing

Prior to the establishment of the national school system in 1831, education was an irregular experience for most children. A variety of voluntary schools had been established, mainly with a view to promoting the Protestant faith, but they accounted for a small minority. Private academies also offered merchants' sons and daughters an education suited to their expectations. For all classes in rural areas, education depended on the availability of an appropriate and affordable teacher. Governesses were few in number and, until the 1860s, unlikely to have had an academic education. Tutors were even scarcer and appear often to have been shared between several households. The reform of the public school system in England made this an increasingly attractive option for

7 C. M. Arensberg and S. T. Kimball, *Family and community in Ireland* (3rd edn, Ennis, 2001 [1940]), 45–65.
8 C. Clear, *Women of the house: women's household work in Ireland 1921–61: experiences, memories, discourses* (Dublin, 2000), 200.

Anglo-Irish parents.[9] The enthusiasm of the poorer classes for educating their children was regularly remarked upon by travellers to Ireland at the end of the eighteenth century. 'Hedge schools' were found in most parishes, usually conducted by a single teacher who charged a modest fee for each child to be taught reading and writing (in English) and arithmetic. In 1821 some 44 per cent of boys and 26 per cent of girls aged six to thirteen were attending a school.[10] Under the national school system, education became more standardised, although the frequency and duration of attendance usually depended on family circumstances. It was not until 1892 that school attendance began to be compelled, and then only in urban areas as the availability of children for occasional farm work continued to take priority.

The first day at national school features significantly in memoirs of rural childhood and was an occasion of wonder for children from isolated farms, particularly for Irish-speaking children introduced into this English-speaking environment. For some, exposure to books, kind teachers and the company of other children were unalloyed pleasures, but for others schooldays were marked by a brutality that was both traumatic and unconducive to learning. School was also a stage for the enactment of class. In towns, where possible, commercial and professional families preferred to send their children to fee-paying religious primary schools, and where national schools brought together children of different social backgrounds they tended not to associate.

Education in national schools depended on rote-learning with an emphasis on obedience and conformity, and Irish independence brought little change other than the extension of compulsory attendance in 1926 and the determination of successive governments to use the national schools as the main instrument for reviving the Irish language. From the 1960s campaigning by parents, previously excluded from involvement in educational discourse, together with educational reforms and developments in teacher training, began to revolutionise the primary school system. Gradually, and not without opposition, more child-centred educational values were introduced. For the vast majority of Irish children until the 1960s, leaving primary school, usually at fourteen, meant the end of formal education. For those who could afford it, fee-paying Catholic secondary schools run by religious orders began to be established from the 1780s and received indirect funding on a payment-by-results basis from the state from 1878. Less research has been undertaken into the childhood experience in secondary schools – or the 'vocational' or continuation schools established in the Irish Free State from 1930 – than into the national schools. However, historians of education have drawn attention

9 J. Logan, 'Governesses, tutors and parents: domestic education in Ireland, 1700–1880', *Irish Educational Studies*, 7, 2 (1988), 1–19.
10 G. FitzGerald, 'Irish primary education in 1824', unpublished typescript (2010), cited in C. Ó Gráda, 'School attendance and literacy before the famine: a simple baronial analysis', www.thehealthwell.info/node/662098, accessed 22 August 2016.

to the social consequences of an education which was heavily exam-oriented and in which young people were segregated by gender, religion and class, distinctions that were also reflected in the curriculum until the process of reform began in the 1960s. In 1967, the introduction of free secondary education in the Irish Republic contributed significantly to the extension, and consequently the transformation, of childhood and the development of adolescence as a central stage of development.

In Northern Ireland, where the control of education was highly contentious, the Education (Northern Ireland) Act (1947) made education for all children compulsory to age fifteen with an exam taken at age eleven, known as the 'eleven plus', determining whether the child would proceed to a technical, secondary modern or grammar school. Originally intended to match children by aptitude to the most appropriate continuation education, the 'eleven plus' quickly became regarded as an excessively arduous and class-biased competition for admission into the prestigious grammar schools. None the less, it was retained in Northern Ireland after it was discontinued in most of England and Wales.

With comparatively low levels both of industrialisation and of adult wages, child labour in mills and factories was not extensive in Ireland, and legislation reducing the hours of labour and increasing the hours of education for factory and mill children in the 1830s and 1840s resulted in a significant decline. In 1878, the Factory and Workshops Act imposed restrictions on the employment of children in smaller workshops also and by 1920 the employment of under-fifteens in factories and workshops was effectively eliminated.[11] By the beginning of the twentieth century, in Ireland as in Britain, concerns about child labour were largely focused on street trading, the extent of which had been revealed by a series of reports, including that of the Street Trading Children Committee (Ireland) in 1902. Most children engaged in street trading did so in addition to attending school and there were few objections to their working in principle. Rather, the Employment of Children Act (1903) was prompted by moral anxieties about these very visible street children. It permitted, but did not compel, local authorities to regulate working hours and the age at which it became legal for children to be employed and to prohibit children from certain occupations.[12]

Gillian McIntosh's 2014 study of this Act and of public attitudes to street children was one of the first directly to address the question of child labour in Ireland.[13] This is a subject that remains under-researched and there is no sustained treatment to compare with Marjatta Rahikainen's *Centuries of child labour* or Peter Kirby's *Child labour in*

11 D. Greer and J. W. Nicolson, *The Factory Acts in Ireland, 1802–1914* (Dublin, 2003).

12 H. Hendrick, 'Child labour, medical capital and the school medical service, c. 1890–1918', in R. Cooter (ed.), *In the name of the child: health and welfare, 1880–1940* (Oxford, 1992).

13 G. McIntosh, 'Children, street trading and the representation of public space in Edwardian Ireland', in M. Luddy and J. M. Smith (eds.), *Children, childhood and Irish society: 1500 to the present* (Dublin, 2014).

Britain.[14] Insights into child labour have most frequently emerged from contemporary literature[15] or as a by-product of historians' discussions of the adult workforce.[16] One reason for this has been the degree to which child labour was an aspect of the domestic or hidden economies.

John Cunningham has pointed out that while 'according to the 1891 census, 1,278 young people under the age of 15 were employed in County Galway', it is probable that this is an underestimate of the number of children actually working. Firstly, it did not take into account the number of 'dependent' children who worked with their parents on the farm or in the family business; secondly, details of children in employment may have been withheld from census officials.[17] If there was a tendency to conceal child labourers in 1891, this is likely to have increased by the census of 1901: while the majority of Galway children aged eleven to fourteen years were returned as 'Scholar', 'Pupil' or 'Attending School', this may reflect a perceived necessity to appear compliant with the compulsory education measures introduced in 1892. If the figures are unreliable, however, census data do provide an indication of the kinds of work undertaken by children in Galway and other rural areas. Most were employed as servants, agricultural labourers or messengers while others worked with their parents at tailoring and dressmaking, brush-making or bag-making outwork. In Dublin, Belfast and other urban areas the increase in children working as street traders, as well as newsboys and messengers, outside school hours reflected both the decline in less flexible forms of employment such as factory work and domestic service – which declined sharply for girls under fifteen from 1901 – and the introduction and enforcement of compulsory schooling. From 1926, this would see a further decline as all children were required to attend school until the age of fourteen. From the 1960s, while many more teenagers were attending school to the age of sixteen years, they also benefited from increased employment opportunities and were holding on to some, if not all, of their wages.[18] This contributed to the growth in a material youth culture, especially in regard to music, fashion, recreation and travel. By the late twentieth century, with the advent of free third-level education, adolescence was further extended, creating a protracted

---

14 M. Rahikainen, *Centuries of child labour: European experiences from the seventeenth to the twentieth century* (Aldershot, 2004); P. Kirby, *Child labour in Britain, 1750–1870* (Houndmills, 2003).

15 Notably, P. McGill's autobiographical novel *Children of the dead end: the autobiography of a navvy* (London, 1914).

16 For example, A. O'Dowd, *Spalpeens and tattie hokers: history and folklore of the Irish migratory agricultural worker in Ireland and Britain* (Dublin, 1991); J. Bourke, *Husbandry to housewifery: women, economic change, and housework in Ireland, 1890–1914* (Oxford, 1993); Greer and Nicolson, *The Factory Acts in Ireland*.

17 *City Tribune*, 29 April 1988.

18 See C. Holohan, 'Challenges to social order and Irish identity? Youth culture in the sixties', *Irish Historical Studies*, 38, 151 (2013), 389–405.

period of dependence on parents or guardians for some teenagers and young adults and on precarious part-time employment for others.

Patterns of play among Irish children also require further study, though memoirs suggest that, here as elsewhere, whether urban or rural, middle or working class, children derived the most entertainment from playfully imitating the work of adults. Dolls – bought or home-made – were nursed, the machinery of agriculture, transport and construction lovingly recreated, and juvenile priests dispensed 'communion' to their siblings. In wealthier homes, such as that of novelist Elizabeth Bowen, such play was facilitated by a range of toys.[19] Two factors appear to distinguish the poorer Irish child at play in the second half of the nineteenth and first half of the twentieth century: an apparent obsession with the gathering and cooking of food and the centrality of the cinema to both family and, more particularly, autonomous child leisure, financed – for those without pocket-money – by running errands or doing chores for pennies or by collecting the refundable glass bottles which were accepted as the price of admission by some cinema owners.

With comparatively high rates of child literacy from the early nineteenth century, the publication of books and, later, comics, for children was a flourishing industry and an aspect of childhood that has been of great interest to historians, though more often concentrating on the literary, didactic and political aspects of this literature rather than on the child as consumer. Certainly, by the beginning of the twentieth century, children's leisure had become highly politicised. The comic a boy (in particular) read, like the sport he played and the youth movement he joined, defined him as a nationalist or an imperialist – a dichotomy which was replicated in Northern Ireland during the 'Troubles'. However, the extent to which this reflected the politics of his parents rather than his own agency, is open to question. Similarly, children's play, however autonomous, was broadly subject to adult sanction. Howard P. Chudacoff has suggested that American children's play went 'underground' in the 1950s as adult supervision of children's play increased and children in turn sought to avoid this oversight.[20] While the Irish post-war boom dates from the 1960s rather than the 1950s, the emergence of the teenager, and adult concerns about the increasing precocity of younger children, marked the last decades of the twentieth century.

20.4.   The State and the Child: *c.1740–c.1920*

Mary O'Dowd has demonstrated that the relationship between the state and the Irish child in the Tudor and Stuart periods was almost the direct opposite of that between

19 P. W. Moran, 'Elizabeth Bowen's toys and the imperatives of play', *Éire–Ireland*, 46, 1–2 (2011), 152–76.
20 H. P. Chudacoff, *Children at play: an American history* (New York, 2007), 182–213.

the state and the English or Welsh child. While the sons of elite Gaelic families were seen as suitable means of transmitting English language and customs as well as pledges for the loyalty of their fathers, there was little state provision for the welfare of poor or abandoned children who – in the absence of an Irish poor law – were left in the reluctant hands of parish authorities.[21] However, by the early eighteenth century the abandonment of children, particularly illegitimate children, had become a significant public concern. These children were regarded as both a potential public nuisance and a civic and religious opportunity.

Established in 1703, the Dublin workhouse was empowered to receive children aged between five and sixteen years, educate them in the Protestant faith and apprentice them to Protestant masters. By 1725 the workhouse was overwhelmed with children. It was reconstituted as the Dublin Foundling Hospital and Workhouse and in 1730 permitted to admit children of all ages, with infants usually being sent out to nurse. This was intended to help prevent infanticide and the deaths of illegitimate children through abandonment and neglect. The hospital's record of preserving life, however, was dismal. Parliamentary enquiries in 1737 and 1743 suggested that 75 per cent of the infants admitted had died while inmates.[22] Conditions in the hospital improved over time but until it closed in the early nineteenth century the Dublin Foundling Hospital, like a smaller Cork institution, was associated with corrupt administration, poor diet, disease, infestation and cruelty.

Similarly, the workhouses established under the Poor Relief (Ireland) Act (1838) were not initially intended for the reception of orphaned or abandoned children but became the main source of provision for them both before, and particularly during, the Great Famine. In the first quarter of 1844, the number of children in workhouses was 22,585, representing about half the total workhouse population. By 1850 this had grown to an estimated number of 120,000. In the fifty years after the famine, the number of children in workhouses declined to less than 14 per cent in 1900.[23] The Irish poor law system was designed to be workhouse-based under conditions which discouraged paupers from seeking relief, including the separation of families and the removal of children over two years of age from their parents. Officially, only orphaned or deserted children were permitted to enter the workhouse unaccompanied, though parents frequently 'abandoned' their children, hoping to reclaim them later.

Childhood experiences of workhouse life were diverse but some general observations may be made. Children were usually allowed three meals a day – of milk and

21 M. O'Dowd, 'Early modern Ireland and the history of the child', in Luddy and Smith, *Children, childhood and Irish society*, 42.

22 J. Robins, *The lost children: a study of charity children in Ireland, 1700–1900* (Dublin, 1980), 17.

23 V. Crossman, 'Cribbed, contained and confined? The care of children under the Irish poor law, 1850–1920', in Luddy and Smith (eds.), *Children, childhood and Irish society*, 82.

oatmeal, potatoes or bread – compared with the two permitted to adults. Poor diet and overcrowding contributed to the spread of infectious diseases with workhouses in the post-famine period being particularly associated with childhood ophthalmia. Mortality rates were high, especially in the larger urban unions. Children were supposed to attend school for a minimum of three hours per day but this generally amounted to little more than mass supervision in cold and dirty surroundings. Like adults, children were expected to engage in labour and in some workhouses they were trained in trades or in agricultural or domestic work or hired out as farm labourers. In many, children spent their days without any occupation. Unruly or violent behaviour and absconding were frequent. Improvements in dress, diet and educational and training standards occurred as numbers reduced after the famine and with the amalgamation of poor law unions for educational purposes, which was permitted from 1855. However, the prospect of their children being sent away to school became a deterrent to relief for some parents.

By mid-century concerns were being raised about the welfare of children in institutions. Internationally, this debate is associated with a mid-Victorian fascination with the innocence and moral malleability of children, with the idealisation of domesticity, and with fears about the corrupting influences of urbanisation and industrialisation. Despite a comparative lack of industrialisation in Ireland, the numbers orphaned or abandoned during and after the famine meant that such children were highly visible in towns and cities. This resulted in an intense, cross-sectarian, public debate about instituting a boarding-out system for orphaned and abandoned children, which revolved around whether or not children's physical and moral welfare would be better preserved in foster homes than in workhouses.[24] In 1862 boarding out of orphaned or abandoned legitimate children under five was permitted, later increased incrementally to fifteen. However, Irish Poor Law Guardians did not adopt the boarding-out option enthusiastically and children in workhouses always outnumbered those boarded out. In part, this was due to a difficulty in identifying suitable foster-parents. While many must have offered caring homes, others were interested primarily in the payment they received and in the child's potential as an unpaid labourer.

The mid-century combination of humanitarianism and fear of childhood criminality also resulted in the growth of voluntary agencies intended to care for destitute children. Concerns about proselytism also played a significant role in the establishment of orphanages, children's homes and 'ragged schools' for street children, and Cardinal Paul Cullen actively promoted the involvement of Catholic orders of religious sisters in the institutional care of children. Debates about child criminality also influenced the establishment of reformatories and industrial schools, though it is noteworthy that, regardless of religion, Irish commentators, unlike their British counterparts, considered

24 Ibid., 85–8.

youth offending to be a by-product of poverty and the conditions in the workhouses in which many such youths had been raised, rather than as evidence of the existence of a criminal sub-class.[25]

Legislation to establish reformatories for young offenders aged between twelve and sixteen was passed in 1858 and to establish industrial schools a decade later. Drawing on British models – which in turn reflected continental European developments – both were built and managed through voluntary (which in Ireland usually meant religious) effort, with the state certifying and inspecting the institutions and, together with local authorities, providing capitation grants for inmates. Both were denominational, segregated by gender, and provided moral and literary education and occupational training. Under the Industrial Schools (Ireland) Act (1868), children under fourteen could be committed to an industrial school if found to have been begging, without a home or proper guardianship, destitute, or 'frequent[ing] the company of reputed thieves'.[26] Children under twelve convicted of a misdemeanour could also be sentenced to detention in an industrial school. The great majority of children were committed on the grounds of begging and from the outset industrial schools were more closely associated with poor, destitute or abandoned, rather than 'criminal' children, gradually replacing the workhouse in this capacity.

Schools varied in size from institutions with tens of inmates to St Joseph's in the Dublin suburb of Artane, which could accommodate 800. An average occupancy of 100–150 children who ate, slept, worked and learned in large groups, undermined the schools' insistence that they, unlike workhouses, provided an approximation of family life and were, indeed, superior to the 'unsatisfactory' home. Where parents were living, family ties were deliberately cut and committal was generally for the maximum period, to the age of sixteen. As with other institutions, infectious diseases were commonplace, though the death rate does not appear to have exceeded that in the general child population and compared favourably with that in workhouses. From their inception, industrial schools, like reformatories, paid considerable attention to diet, seen as an essential component in the moral as well as the physical development of children. The diet was initially far superior to that in workhouses, though standards declined by the end of the century.

Industrial school regimes promoted obedience and conformity through silence, order and discipline. 'Industrial education' occupied most of the day with schooling typically taking place before 9 a.m. The quality of training varied widely in the nineteenth century. Some girls' schools specialised in crafts such as lace-making and embroidery while in Artane, for example, a range of trades were taught to boys. Often, however, 'industrial education' amounted to no more than the employment of children's labour for

25 J. Barnes, *Irish industrial schools, 1868–1908* (Dublin, 1989), 15.
26 Ibid., 42.

the maintenance of the institution. In theory, and by repute, corporal punishment was administered rarely in boys' schools and never in girls'. In reality, nineteenth-century records indicate high levels of corporal punishment, including severe beatings. The Commission to Inquire into Child Abuse (2009) found that in the twentieth century '[p]hysical and emotional abuse and neglect were features of the [industrial schools]. Sexual abuse occurred in many of them, particularly boys' institutions. Schools were run in a severe, regimented manner that imposed unreasonable and oppressive discipline on children and even on staff.'[27]

During the eighteenth century, and for most of the nineteenth, the state's responsibility for children was largely restricted to those without parents, not least because of the emphasis placed on the obligation to maintain one's own offspring. By the late 1880s, however, the dangers posed to children *by* their parents had become matters of public and official concern, resulting in the passage, over the next twenty years, of fifty-two Acts relating to child welfare and child protection. The most significant of these were the Prevention of Cruelty to, and Protection of, Children Act (1889) and the consolidating Children Act (1908). The latter remained the main statutory instrument dealing with child protection in the Republic of Ireland until the passage of the Child Care Act (1991).

Throughout western Europe, the beginning of the twentieth century was marked by concerns about national deterioration and by state initiatives to improve the health of children through, for example, the provision of school meals, the medical inspection of school children and measures to improve the nutrition of nursing mothers and infants. Such legislation was delayed in the case of Ireland, often due to concerns expressed by Catholic clergy and others about state interference with the family. Official reluctance to confront this attitude prompted voluntary efforts but some nationalists accused the Westminster Parliament of deliberate neglect. Infant welfare became a political battleground in the first decades of the twentieth century – though with little impact on the survival rates of infants.

20.5. Child Welfare and the State since 1920

Despite the abolition of the poor law system in the Irish Free State, the establishment of the Commission on the Relief of the Sick and Destitute Poor in 1925, and the recognition by the state of 'the Family as the natural primary and fundamental unit group of Society, and as a moral institution possessing inalienable and imprescriptible rights, antecedent and superior to all positive law', many scholars have argued that the first decades of Irish independence were typified by an erosion of the rights of parents as carers

---

27 S. Ryan, *Final Report of the Commission to Inquire into Child Abuse* vol. IV (Dublin, 2009), 451.

and educators. In legislation relating to compulsory education, institutional provision, welfare and illegitimacy, parents and children in poverty were the focus of measures that regularly led to the removal of children from the home. Working-class families suffered most from church and state action, as the sanctity of the family espoused in Catholic doctrine and political rhetoric was often far from the reality. Integral to this discussion is the state's lack of planning and initiative in reducing poverty. These issues would all culminate in increasing attention to child welfare from the 1970s. Ireland was not unique in its treatment of families in poverty and children in care, but in many respects nineteenth-century systems and structures continued longer in Ireland than elsewhere in western Europe.

In 1924 the Courts of Justice Act provided for the establishment of children's courts in the four larger cities and responsibility for reformatory and industrial schools was transferred from the prison service to the Department of Education. However, as the Commission of Inquiry into the Reformatory and Industrial School System (or Cussen Commission) reported in 1936, this had resulted in little change in the standards of care: the schools were over-crowded and under-funded, there was a lack of recreational facilities, teachers were underqualified and nourishment was questionable.[28] The Cussen report had little impact and the question of childcare in reformatory and industrial schools was not addressed again until the publication in 1966 of the report 'Some of our children' by the London branch of the Tuairim discussion group. This was a contributing factor in the setting up of the Committee on Reformatory and Industrial Schools under Eileen Kennedy. Although Kennedy's 1970 report did not address questions of sexual and emotional abuse, it is widely seen as turning the tide of the relationship between children and the state. The report recommended an end to the industrial and reformatory school system and the establishment of group homes.[29] However, the last industrial school did not close its doors until 1984.

The post-war period was also marked by increased attention to aspects of child welfare which had previously been regarded as outside the remit of the state. Provision for legal adoption was made in 1952, after vigorous campaigning, and despite political concerns that it would be opposed by the Catholic hierarchy. The increased visibility of adolescents and concerns about juvenile delinquency meanwhile gave rise to both the establishment of a Commission on Youth Unemployment in 1943 and the establishment of a Juvenile Liaison Officer Scheme in 1962.

In Northern Ireland, child welfare services were determined by the retention of the British legislative framework and the extension of the welfare state in the post-war period, together with the adoption of a policy of parity in welfare provision. However,

---

28 *Commission of Inquiry into the Reformatory and Industrial School System Report, 1936* (Dublin, 1936).
29 E. Kennedy, *Reformatory and industrial schools system report, 1970* (Dublin, 1970), 6.

they were limited by the ambivalence of the unionist government, by the outbreak of the Troubles, and by the imposition of direct rule. While the rest of the UK was moving towards a home-based child welfare system, the Northern Ireland government, influenced by the significance of the religious voluntary sector, was unenthusiastic. Greg Kelly and John Pinkerton argue that the Children and Young Persons Act (NI) (1968) – based on English and Welsh legislation dating from 1963 – represented an attempt to forestall further changes rather than an eagerness for the statutory provision of child welfare services.[30] During the period of direct rule, it was recognised that Northern Irish children and young people, growing up in an atmosphere of violence, were in particular need of welfare services but that these should be removed from party politics and placed in the hands of the National Health Service. This allowed the development of a highly professionalised child welfare service in the 1970s and 1980s, but one that was distanced from local communities.[31]

In Northern Ireland, as in the Republic, the 1990s were marked by concerns about child sexual abuse and debates about child protection were strongly influenced by the difficulties of ensuring disclosure. The passage of the (UK) Children Act (1989), which obliged courts, local authorities and parents to regard the welfare of children as paramount, made provision for the wishes of children to be taken into account during contested hearings, and emphasised the desirability of caring for children in their own homes, was followed by Children (NI) Orders (1993, 1995) to bring Northern Ireland practices into line. The Northern Ireland Act (1998) both devolved powers relating to child protection to the Northern Ireland Assembly and directed that all measures passed by the Assembly be compatible with the European Convention on Human Rights. Consequently, according to Alice Diver, the aims underlying the United Nations Convention on the Rights of the Child (1992) 'have also gradually begun to inform thinking in this area, especially in relation to the child welfare "paramountcy" principle and in relation to the "participation rights" of the child'.[32]

In the Republic of Ireland, the 1990s also witnessed a significant reform of child welfare with the passage of the Child Care Act (1991), the major provisions of which were implemented in 1995. The first substantial piece of legislation in this area since 1908, this Act was primarily concerned with the treatment of children in the care of the state but it also established principles similar to those embodied in the British legislation. It obliged courts to take account of the wishes of both parents and children in decision-making, but established the welfare of the child as the most important

30 G. Kelly and J. Pinkerton, 'The Children (Northern Ireland) Order 1995: prospects for progress?', in M. Hill and J. Aldgate (eds.), *Child welfare services: developments in law, policy, practice and research* (London, 1996), 43.
31 Ibid., 45.
32 A. Diver, *Report on the enforcement of family law judgments in Northern Ireland* (The Hague, 2007), available at http://ec.europa.eu/civiljustice/publications/docs/family_rights/united_kingdom_northern_ireland_en.pdf, accessed 22 August 2016.

guiding principle. However, debates about child welfare during this decade were deeply coloured by revelations about contemporary and historical child abuse, including child sexual abuse, associated in particular with religious-run institutions and calling into question the state's traditional reliance on an ill-regulated voluntary sector. The broadcast, in 1999, of the documentary series *States of fear*, produced by Mary Raftery, which detailed the abuse of children principally in reformatory and industrial schools, prompted both an apology on behalf of the state by Taoiseach Bertie Ahern 'to the victims of childhood abuse for our collective failure to intervene, to detect their pain, to come to their rescue'[33] and the establishment of a Commission to Inquire into Child Abuse which reported in 2009. Meanwhile, 2004 witnessed the publication of 'Children first', a policy document intended to provide national guidelines for the protection and welfare of children, in line with the United Nations Convention on the Rights of the Child and paying special attention to the reporting of abuse and the identification and protection of children at risk of abuse.

These developments drew national attention to the emergence of the rights-based approach to child welfare which had been driven by the United Nations since 1992. In 2012, following a referendum, the Irish constitution was amended to affirm 'the natural and imprescriptible rights of all children' and 'in exceptional cases' to provide for the care by the state or the adoption of children whose parents had failed in their duty of care to their children to the extent that the child's safety and welfare had been jeopardised. Notable for removing a distinction in law between children whose parents were and were not married, this amendment was viewed by some as an act of reparation for the historical mistreatment of children but by others as a means of transferring rights from families to a state which had proved itself incapable of protecting its children.

20.6. Conclusion

Beginning with the 'discovery of childhood' and concluding with the enshrinement of the 'rights of the child' into the Irish constitution, this chapter may appear, overall, to be a story of progress. Over the course of two and a half centuries childhood has emerged in Irish society, as elsewhere, as a stage of life with its own requirements and the vulnerability and potential of children have been recognised as having particular claims on parents, society and the state. Yet some of the consequences of this evolution have proved disastrous as benign intentions fell victim to political and religious ideology, indifference, corruption, parsimony and neglect. However, it is crucial to recognise that research into childhood in Ireland remains dominated by the experience of the 'public child'. The centuries that witnessed the increasing institutionalisation and,

---

33 *Irish Times*, 12 May 1999.

frequently, the abuse of some children were also marked by advances in the lives of the majority of children through improving health, diet, education and standards of living. While this is a topic that requires further research, it is clear that Irish childhoods have both reflected international developments and been moulded by the country's socio-economic, constitutional and religious heritages. The current enthusiasm among scholars for the history of children suggests that the coming years will see a revolution in the understanding of how childhood was experienced in Ireland's past.

FURTHER READING

Barnes, J. *Irish industrial schools, 1868–1908* (Dublin, 1989).

Buckley, S. *The cruelty man: child welfare, the NSPCC and the state in Ireland, 1889–1956* (Manchester, 2013).

Countryman, J. and K. Matthews (eds.). *The country of the young: interpretations of youth and childhood in Irish culture* (Dublin, 2013).

Cox, C. and S. Riordan (eds.). *Adolescence in modern Irish history* (Houndmills, 2015).

Fischer, K. and D. Raftery (eds.). *Educating Ireland: schooling and social change 1700–2000* (Dublin, 2014).

Luddy, M. and J. M. Smith (eds.). *Children, childhood and Irish society: 1500 to the present* (Dublin, 2014).

MacLellan, A. and A. Mauger (eds.). *Growing pains: childhood illness in Ireland 1750–1950* (Dublin, 2013).

Maguire, M. J. *Precarious childhood in post-independence Ireland* (Manchester, 2009).

Reidy, C. *Ireland's 'moral hospital': the Irish borstal system, 1906–1956* (Dublin, 2009).

Robins, J. *The lost children: a study of charity children in Ireland, 1700–1900* (Dublin, 1980).

Shine Thompson, M. *Young Irelands: studies in children's literature* (Dublin, 2011).

21 Marriage, Sexuality and the Law in Ireland

Maria Luddy

A referendum held in Ireland on 22 May 2015 saw an overwhelming majority of Irish voters vote for same-sex marriage. Ireland became the first country in the world where a popular vote supported such marriages. While the strategies of the 'yes' and 'no' campaigners will no doubt be analysed in coming years, the vote does reflect how Irish attitudes to marriage, family and sexuality have changed over the past two centuries. The purpose of this chapter is to look at some of the ways in which marriage, concepts of the family, and the understandings and practices of sexuality have evolved in Ireland.

21.1. Marriage

That families were important in Ireland can be revealed in the fact that few people lived alone, only one in twelve of the population in 1926 compared with more than one in five by 1996.[1] The complexities of family formations and relationships are shaped by social, economic and religious concerns. Within all families there are shifting relationships of dependence, physical, emotional, economic and social, that occur along with changing roles of individuals within families that happen as the lifecycle progresses. Little historical work has been conducted into how Irish families were formed and operated in the eighteenth and nineteenth centuries. Sociologists and other scholars have given some attention to Irish families from the mid- to late twentieth century.

---

1 F. Kennedy, *Cottage to crèche: family change in Ireland* (Dublin, 2001), 240.

There were many routes to marriage from the eighteenth to the twentieth century in Ireland. Women were abducted, couples fell in love, families arranged marriages; where couples did not accept arrangements they ran away or eloped together. Couples lived together without getting married, there were bigamists, and those who broke promises to marry. People killed in fits of jealousy, or if they thought they were being replaced by a more 'suitable' partner; they killed when they thought their partner was adulterous, and over how material items might be utilised in a household. Marriage was of significance to women and men for social, emotional and economic reasons. Society considered women's natural place to be in the home, tending to the needs of husband and children. Married women had greater status than unmarried women, the most acceptable way to form families was through marriage and, as in all time periods, both men and women desired children. Economic stability, though not necessarily guaranteed by marriage, was an inducement to marriage for many women, especially in a society where paid employment opportunities for them were limited.

In 1807 one commentator observed that in Ireland 'an unmarried man … or a woman … is rarely to be met in the country parts'.[2] Before the Great Famine only a small proportion of the population did not marry, 8–12 per cent of men over fifty-five and 12–15 per cent of women of the same age.[3] A County Clare labourer who gave evidence before the poor law inquiry commissioners of the 1830s stated:

> it is always the poorest man marries first, because he knows he cannot be worse off by it; it is better for him to marry early than to seduce the girls, who are so poor and wretched that this would often happen. Besides, we poor people have a strange idea that it is a good thing to have children as soon as possible, in order to help and support us when we begin to grow old.[4]

The landed classes were careful about marriage and sought stability and security for their property. Marriages were carefully arranged. Heiresses were protected from fortune-hunting husbands by a variety of legal devices but like all other married women, aristocratic wives were disadvantaged by legal disabilities that saw separation and divorce as the prerogatives of men.[5]

The catastrophe of the Great Famine ushered in considerable changes in Irish demography. Marriage patterns changed and emigration became commonplace. The proportion of 45–54-year-old men who had never married rose from 12 per cent in 1851 to 27 per cent in 1911; among women in the same age group the rise was from 13 to 25 per cent.[6] In the post-famine period the need for a man to earn a reasonable

2 T. J. Rawson, *Statistical survey of the County of Kildare* (Dublin, 1807), 23.

3 T. W. Freeman, 'Land and people, c.1841', in W. E. Vaughan (ed.), *A new history of Ireland: Ireland under the Union, 1801–70* (Oxford, 1989), 260.

4 *Selection of parochial examinations relative to the destitute classes in Ireland* (Dublin, 1835), 233–6.

5 A. P. W. Malcomson, *The pursuit of the heiress: aristocratic marriage in Ireland, 1740–1840* (Belfast, 2006). D. Wilson, *Women, marriage and property in wealthy landed families in Ireland, 1750–1850* (Manchester, 2009).

6 C. Ó Gráda, *Ireland: a new economic history 1780–1939* (Oxford, 1994), 249.

wage or to be in possession of a farm before he could marry would have inhibited his marital opportunities, just as the lack of a dowry or 'fortune' would have impeded women's opportunity to marry.

The usual pattern for strong farmers, both in pre-and post-famine Ireland, was to consolidate their land holdings. This in turn supported individual inheritance, where the farm was left often, but not always, to the eldest son; sometimes a middle or younger son could inherit. Less frequently a daughter might inherit, though in that case it was often dependent on some suitable man marrying into the farm. Parents decided when to give up the farm and sometimes the wait to inherit could be a long one. Late marriage patterns in farming families may be explained to some extent by the hold that fathers, and widows, had on a farm, unwilling to relinquish that control for a considerable time. In 1871, 43 per cent of all women aged 15–45 were married. In 1911 only 36 per cent of women in this age range were married. By 1911, the average age of marriage for women was 29 while that of men was 33 years. In 2014 the average age of brides was 33, while the average age of grooms was 35, reflecting the fact that couples often decide to live together for a number of years before marrying. The marriage rate was 4.8 per 1,000 of population in 1864, the first year for which records exist. Marriage rates were at their lowest in Ireland in the 1930s. There were 22,045 marriages registered in Ireland in 2014.[7] Marriage was and remains an important rite of passage for Irish couples. The actual legalities of marriage in Ireland over the past two hundred years or so have changed considerably. Given Ireland's denominational structure, from the sixteenth century the Church of Ireland was the state church, and the legal disabilities under which Roman Catholics and dissenters laboured, meant that the legal situation was complex.[8]

Various laws, known as the penal laws, had been put in place from 1697 to ensure that property in Ireland remained in Protestant hands. It was a capital offence for a Catholic clergyman to officiate at the marriage of a Catholic and a Protestant. It was not until 1833 that the death penalty, for treason, for any Catholic priest who celebrated a mixed marriage was removed from the statute books.[9] A marriage performed by a Catholic priest where either or both parties were Protestant was null and void until 1871.[10] During the eighteenth century the validity of marriages conducted by Presbyterian ministers was a

---

7 In 1932, 13,029 marriages were recorded in the Irish state; in 1974 the number was 22,833; the numbers fell to fewer than 16,000 in 1995. The latest figures, for 2014, show that there were 22,045 marriages registered, 6,167 civil marriage ceremonies, that is non-religious ceremonies, and 392 civil partnerships. Of couples married in 2014 12 per cent intended to reside outside Ireland. In 1964 the average age of the groom was 29.8 years; it was 26.2 in 1977. For brides the average age in 1964 was 26.3 and 24 in 1977. Data available on the Central Statistics Office website: www.cso.ie/en/releasesandpublications/er/mcp/marriagesandcivilpartnerships2014/#.VWcGvOfBeWU, accessed 22 August 2016.
8 After disestablishment in 1869 the Church of Ireland was no longer the state church.
9 3 & 4 Wm IV, c.103. See P. Corish, *The Irish Catholic experience: a historical survey* (Dublin, 1985), 220.
10 19 Geo. II, c.13.

controversial subject. In 1782 marriages between Presbyterians were legalised though a marriage between a member of the Church of Ireland and a Presbyterian was recognised as valid only from 1845. The marriage of two Catholics before a Catholic priest had always been regarded as complying with the requirements of the common law; there was little government interference with Catholic marriage practices in Ireland and it was not until 1863 that Catholics were obliged to register their marriages with the civil registrar.[11]

Up to the 1840s 'irregular' or clandestine marriages were common amongst the poorer levels of Irish society. These marriages were often conducted by a 'couple beggar', a suspended clergyman or a minister or cleric without a parish or community to serve, usually of the Catholic or the established church. Such marriages were nearly always valid, as the person conducting the proceedings was often a cleric who had been ordained by a bishop. There were a number of couple beggars operating throughout Ireland up to the 1840s and they offered an attractive option to many who wished to wed; they were cheap, they offered secrecy, and couples who did not have their parents' consent found couple beggars amenable. All of the churches opposed these clandestine marriages but struggled to enforce their regulations in relation to marriage. The main concerns of the Catholic hierarchy were 'irregular marriages', issues of consanguinity and affinity, and mixed marriages. One way around these last two problems was to grant dispensations, and that this was done on numerous occasions is evident in the various diocesan archives. A case from 1851 shows a number of issues at play. A cleric wrote to Cardinal Cullen about one of his parishioners, Edward Duffy, who

> did not tell me the truth about sending his pretended wife away. He has her concealed in some of his neighbour's houses every day and they go together every night. When I can get them to live separately every night, I will inform your Grace of it. Duffy's now pretended wife and his first wife were first cousins. To avoid scandal it might be desirable to grant them a dispensation in the above impediment in the second degree of affinity, if they separate for some time.[12]

Not only does the case show a couple engaging in extra-marital sex and unwilling to follow church regulations, but also that neighbours are ready to collude with the couple to keep the priest at bay.

The fear for the Catholic clergy was that making difficulties for Catholics in the area of marriage might drive them to be married within a Protestant church. But over the nineteenth century the Catholic Church gained much more control over the marriage of Catholics and the controversial papal decree of *Ne Temere*, in 1908, symbolised that control. Under this decree all children of a mixed marriage had to be raised as Catholics and the marriage had to be conducted by a priest, in front of two witnesses.

---

11 Corish, *Irish Catholic experience*, 219–21.
12 Thomas Dunleer to Cardinal Cullen, 21 March 1851. Cullen Papers 39/2 File IV: Armagh Priests, 1851. Dublin Diocesan Archives, Dublin.

21.2. Marriage Breakdown

It is much easier to uncover information about marriages that went wrong than to read about happy marriages. Husbands deserted wives, and wives deserted husbands. A number of individuals engaged in bigamous marriages. Between 1805 and 1918, for example, there were 1,027 individuals committed to trial for bigamous offences.[13] Irish men made up more than 90 per cent of defendants in these cases, attesting perhaps to the greater level of social freedom and mobility available to men. Women, burdened with children, were least likely to engage in bigamy. A number of defendants claimed that they believed their first marriage to be illegal because it had not been conducted by a Church of Ireland clergyman, or it had been conducted by a 'couple beggar'. The criminalisation of bigamy dates back to an Act of 1604 which decreed the death penalty for those convicted, the exception being in those cases where a first spouse had been absent for seven years, or some form of divorce or annulment had been secured.[14] In 1830, for instance, Michael Audlin was convicted of bigamy at Macroom, and was sentenced to seven years' transportation.[15] After further legal changes in 1861 the maximum sentence was reduced from possible transportation to penal servitude of not less than three years and not more than seven. Bigamy was a form of desertion and was one of the ways in which couples, or attached individuals, who no longer wished to live together, could separate.

Desertion of a spouse or family was another strategy used by the poor in particular to escape an unhappy marriage or burdensome responsibilities. In 1698 a woman named Jenat Collbeart refused to live with her husband and noted that 'she can't have a life with him [as he] will not labour to get them bread, but she is willing to dwell with him if he will make any provision for his family'.[16] In 1823 Daniel Barry was imprisoned on suspicion of killing his wife and child. However, Barry stated that the family had to leave Ennis where he could not find any work. His wife and he separated, placing their child 'on the publick'. This left the wife free to engage in dealing and he to roam the country looking for work. It was their intention to meet up again when their circumstances improved.[17] In the period between about 1828 and 1920 there were about 2,538 men awaiting trial or imprisoned for short periods for deserting their wives and families.[18]

13 This excludes the years 1815–20 and 1918, for which no figures appear to be available. Prison committal reports, 1805–1815 and Judicial and Criminal Statistics, 1865–1921.
14 B. Capp, 'Bigamous marriage in early modern England', *Historical Journal*, 52, 3 (2009), 539.
15 *Freeman's Journal*, 1 April 1830.
16 J. M. Barkley, 'History of the ruling eldership in Irish Presbyterianism', 2 vols., unpublished MA Thesis, Queen's University Belfast, 1952, II, 77–8.
17 Prisoners Petitions and Cases, 1778–1836, 18 Sept. 1823, VI/21/1/1812, National Archives of Ireland, Dublin, [hereafter NAI].
18 Irish Prison Registers, 1790–1924.

These cases come to light because poor law authorities were willing to prosecute men and women who deserted their spouses or children and left them a burden on the work-house. Such prosecutions underestimate the true level of desertion; during the period of the Great Famine few poor law unions had the ability or desire to prosecute in cases of the many thousands of husbands, wives and children who were deserted during this crisis.[19] Poorer women did not necessarily depend on their husbands for support in the same way that middle-class wives did. Many poor women could look after themselves but found themselves in difficulties when pregnant and unable to work, or when they were burdened by numbers of children. These women often ended up in workhouses, established in 1838 around the country. Workhouse officials were sometimes fearful of 'being overrun by such cases' and a number advertised rewards for information on the whereabouts of deserting husbands. Workhouse officials attempted to prosecute such individuals, but many pauper women refused to provide information about deserting husbands, suggesting that the desertion was not actual and that the stay in the work-house might be a survival or subsistence strategy on the part of the family.[20] Women in poorer or labouring families did not expect their husbands to be the sole support of the family. The secretary of the County Wexford Labour League noted to a commission in 1893 that 'women were half the support' in labouring families.[21] Desertion remained a problem for Irish couples and the 1991 census returns reveal 23,685 desertions. This level probably reflects the inability of couples to divorce in Ireland.[22]

Couples also agreed to separate. Formally this could be done under the Matrimonial Causes (Ireland) Act of 1870, which allowed the High Court to issue judicial separations. Such separations did not allow remarriage. Cases reported in the newspapers suggest middle-class husbands were sometimes sued for non-payment of maintenance granted under these legal separations. A more formal divorce was available to those who could afford it. Prior to changes in the laws on divorce from the mid-nineteenth century a husband, but not a wife, could petition the House of Lords for a dissolution of marriage. Under this process he was obliged to initiate law suits in both the ecclesiastical and civil courts and then participate in a parliamentary investigation into the marriage. Divorce was very expensive and available only to the rich. The process could cost between £200 and £5,000. Eleven private divorce Acts were passed by the Irish Parliament between 1730 and 1800.[23] Between 1840 and 1843 there were 57 actions for

---

19 Evidence of these desertions is to be found in workhouse admission registers throughout the country.

20 See, for instance, the Minutes of the Galway Union, 25 February 1854; Minutes of the Ballymoney Union, 24 June 1848.

21 *Royal Commission on Labour: Agricultural Labourer*, vol. IV, part II, (C.6894), HC 1893–4, xxxvii, pt. i. 207. 75.

22 Figures available from the Central Statistics Office, www.cso.ie/en/census/index.html, accessed 22 August 2016.

23 J. Bergin, 'Irish private divorce bills and Acts of the eighteenth century', in J. Kelly, J. McCafferty and C. McGrath (eds.), *People, politics and power: essays on Irish history 1660–1850 in honour of James I.McGuire* (Dublin, 2009), 94.

divorce, 203 between 1901 and 1909, and 357 between 1970 and 1979.[24] The grounds for divorce were strongly gendered: a wife's proven adultery was sufficient for a husband to gain a divorce. The transmission of property and the paternity of those inheriting clearly shaped the understanding of adultery. For a wife to gain a divorce proving adultery on the husband's part was not enough; it had to be combined with other failings, such as bigamy, rape or unnatural practices such as sodomy, incest or considerable cruelty. So divorce was available in Ireland and could be obtained as a private bill in the Westminster Parliament. In 1925 the Irish Free State government made it impossible for private bills to be introduced in the future. The parliament in Northern Ireland granted sixty-three divorces between 1925 and 1939, before moving to a court-based system.[25]

As an issue divorce began to be debated in Ireland from the 1980s. The 1986 census returns showed that more than 37,000 individuals were returned as separated; by 1991 that figure had increased to 55,000 persons. Divorce was finally introduced into Ireland in 1997 after a very divisive campaign, much of the opposition to divorce arising from a fear of what would happen to property and farms in divorce situations. The number of divorced persons increased from 35,100 to 59,500 between 2002 and 2006, an increase of 70 per cent, revealing a backlog of cases that required resolution. The number of divorces granted in 2013 was 2,949.[26]

21.3.   Marriage and Relationships

A newspaper article published in 1830 lamented the force with which money shaped marriages. 'Although the bright blaze of beauty may sometimes be the torch which leads our beaux to the … altar, yet I fear the dazzling glare of money – filthy money – is often the loadster that attracts them. If you hear now a days a man about to enter the holy state, the first question asked is, not to whom he is to be united; but, to how much?'[27] Property and money were important features of marriage. While we know that dowries were very much part of the marriage system in post-famine Ireland, and to a lesser extent in pre-famine Ireland, we still do not have a comprehensive understanding of how dowries were used, or the value of dowries over time in different parts of Ireland and in relation to different classes. What is clear from looking at the available archival sources is that a dowry, or fortune, was expected in marriages after the 1850s: lack of a dowry, or what was believed to be an insufficient dowry, was used, for instance, by

---

24 D. Fitzpatrick, 'Divorce and separation in modern Irish history', *Past and Present*, 114 (Feb. 1987), 175.

25 D. Urquhart, 'Irish divorce and domestic violence, 1857–1922', *Women's History Review*, 22, 5 (2013), 821.

26 Data available on the Central Statistics Office website: www.cso.ie/en/releasesandpublications/er/mcp/marriag esandcivilpartnerships2014/#.VWcGvOfBeWU, accessed 22 August 2016.

27 *Connaught Journal*, 17 May 1830.

defendants in breach of promise cases as a reason to break off a proposal of marriage. The actual amount given in dowries varied with the status and means of those involved but it could in some cases be quite substantial.

One landlord in County Cork in the 1820s claimed that he knew a tenant who had given his daughter, one of five or six children, £1,000. A parish priest in the same county presented what he called 'rich farmers' as giving their daughters between £100 and £300.[28] The need to provide a dowry influenced the marriage age in post-famine Ireland, and also ensured that class became a more significant feature of marriage. In one of William Carleton's stories a man who has the temerity to show interest in a girl of higher social status than his own is told by her mother to go to look for a girl he might 'have a right to expect', and not one that 'could lay down guineas where you could hardly find shillings.'[29]

Match-making saw an individual, who had a reputation for bringing couples together or was a family member who sought to bring about a good match, secure a marriage that was considered beneficial to both parties (meaning the families involved and not the individuals). In farming communities the match appears to have been very rigid with little room for individual choice, particularly for women. A man (or a man's family) who wished to marry would ask a match-maker to find a suitable girl, which usually implied a woman with a certain amount of money, and the families would get together and negotiate a financial settlement. These were very formal, unromantic bargains, and when they appear in court cases, such as in breach of promise cases, the judge and juries, who were members of elite society and for whom love is a central part of courtship, often remarked that the deal could have been that of a sale of a cow or pig. How extensive match-making actually was around the country is still unclear and is a subject that requires further investigation. An article on the Ballinasloe fair in 1924 noted that on the Saturday all the young folks dressed up and came with their parents to the fair to partake in amusements. 'A good deal of "matchmaking" takes place and the young people court and the old people discuss their fortunes. Many betrothed people meet for the first time at the fair and the marriages which follow are usually happy. The country woman's dress nowadays is as up to date as her town bred sister.'[30]

Looking specifically at match-making and dowries tells us a great deal about how families were constructed in this period, about the use of material resources in a household, about status, about the place of women and men in households, about power relationships and, of course, about the importance and value of land in Irish farming families. Dowries were so common by the 1860s that in one breach of promise to marry case the judge admonished the defendant for not inquiring about a woman's fortune,

---

28 S. Connolly, *Priests and people in pre-famine Ireland, 1780–1845* (Dublin, 1982), 206.
29 W. Carleton, 'Shane Fadh's wedding', in *Traits and stories of the Irish peasantry* (London, 1890).
30 *Irish Times*, 10 October 1924.

and other 'particulars' before he proposed to her and had discussions with her father. It was too late, he stated, to do so after the event and discover that such matters were unsatisfactory.[31] Dowries were still being sought in some marriages even into the 1950s and 1960s.

21.4. Marriage and the Law

Marriage had a significant legal effect on women; it was also the institution that most shaped women's adult lives. In the words of the eminent eighteenth-century jurist Sir William Blackstone, 'by marriage, the husband and wife are one person in law: that is, the very being or legal existence of the woman is suspended during the marriage, or at least is incorporated and consolidated into that of the husband: under whose wing, protection and cover she performs everything'.[32] This was a state that made the wife completely subordinate to the husband. The legal assumption that husband and wife were one person and that that one person was the husband informed social beliefs and values for centuries. What is to be noted here is that it is with marriage that women lost their legal rights; single women could exercise legal rights such as owning property, bequeathing or buying property. The property of wealthy women could be protected by a system of trusts developed by the courts of equity to circumvent the common law. This allowed trustees to 'protect' a woman's property against her husband, but did not necessarily give control of the property to the woman.

A married woman could not dispose of real or personal property without the consent of her husband,[33] and any income that she earned was subject to his control. A husband had an obligation to maintain his wife and any children of the marriage; he also became responsible for his wife's debts.[34] The relationship between husband and wife could never be equal and the well-being of the family could very well depend on the character and temperament of the husband. Various laws passed from the 1870s relating particularly to married women's property gradually changed the financial reliance of women on their husbands. However, the incremental granting of rights relating to property did not change how society viewed the marriage relationship, where men were seen as the family breadwinners and where their authority was deemed absolute. It was not until the mid-twentieth century that legal changes had a significant impact on women's legal rights in marriage in the Republic. The Married Women Status Act (1957) gave a woman separate rights to property and allowed her a formal contractual capacity.

31 *Belfast Newsletter*, 6 December 1860.
32 Sir William Blackstone, *Commentaries on the laws of England: in four books* (14th edn, London, 1803), I, 442.
33 R. S. Roper, *A treatise on the law of property arising from the relation between husband and wife*, 2 vols. (London, 1820), II, 235.
34 Blackstone, *Commentaries on the laws of England*, I.

The Guardianship of Infants Act (1964) gave a woman legal rights to her own children by giving parents the right to joint guardianship. In 1974 separated, deserted and single mothers qualified for a social welfare allowance. The Family Home Protection Act (1976) protected the family home and required prior written consent of both spouses for the sale of the family home or chattels. In other words the family home, its furniture and fittings could not be sold without the wife's consent.[35]

21.5. Fertility and Illegitimacy

Accurate fertility rates for Ireland before the mid-nineteenth century are difficult to ascertain. The Great Famine of the 1840s, which saw the deaths of about a million people and the emigration of more than two million between 1846 and 1855, had a profound impact on marriage, fertility and indeed sexual behaviour in Ireland. The 1911 census noted that Irish women who had been married for between twenty and twenty-four years gave birth to an average of 5.87 live children. In 1960, Irish women were on average having 2.4 children over the life-course, compared with the European average of 1.8. The Total Fertility Rate (TFR) halved between 1960 and 1999; in the latter year the TFR stood at 1.89 compared with a European average of 1.45. In addition, the proportion of births occurring outside marriage increased dramatically in Ireland. In 1970, only 3 per cent of births were reported to occur outside marriage, while by 2000 almost a third were. Changing fertility patterns reflect access to and availability of contraceptives, the reduced social stigma of illegitimate births, the inclination for couples not to marry and the availability of state support in the form of benefits and allowances for unmarried mothers. Illegitimacy rates remained fairly constant in Ireland in the period between the 1920s and the 1970s, with an average of about 1,900 illegitimate births being registered each year. During the period of the 'Emergency' (1940–5) such rates went up, due, in no small part, to the travel restrictions placed on Irish women during the war years; reduced again by the 1950s, they were to rise again in the 1960s, and by 1971 had reached 1,871.[36] Infant mortality rates were high. It has been estimated that 154 infants from every 1,000 live births in Ireland in the 1820s and 1830s died. In 1915, the rural infant death rate was 69.9 per 1,000 live births, with an urban rate of 134.4.[37] Improved medical assistance, diet and living standards have had an impact on infant mortality, which in 2010 was recorded as 3.6 per 1,000 births.[38]

35 A. J. Shatter, *Family law in the Republic of Ireland* (Dublin, 1977); Kennedy, *Cottage to crèche*, ch. 9.
36 Kennedy, *Cottage to crèche*, 30–2.
37 L. Kennedy and L. Clarkson, 'Birth, death and exile: Irish population history, 1700–1921', in B. J. Graham and L. J. Proudfoot (eds.), *An historical geography of Ireland* (London, 1993), 170–1.
38 Data available on the Central Statistics Office website: www.cso.ie/en/census/index.html.

Cormac Ó Gráda argues that by 1911 many Irish couples, urban and rural, were practising some form of family planning. Those most likely to do so were the larger farmers, those in non-agricultural occupations and Protestants.[39] That information on family planning was available to some extent is evidenced in the archives. An American doctor, Robert Swift Bruce, advertised his 'Pessarie Preventive' in 1872 using testimony from a Belfast mill worker to show the strains on women of having large families.[40] Thomas Haslam produced a pamphlet on the 'safe' period. Irish men and women were in contact with Marie Stopes in the early 1920s seeking advice on contraception. A Northern Ireland Society for Constructive Birth Control existed in Belfast in 1930. A Marie Stopes' mothers' clinic also operated in Belfast from 1936, but closed in 1947, having advised up to four thousand women.[41] A family planning clinic was available to medically referred patients at the Royal Maternity Hospital in Belfast from 1940.[42] In all of these endeavours religion was noted to be the greatest obstacle in providing information on family planning. In the Free State, Sections 16 and 17 of the Censorship of Publications Act (1929) banned the printing, publishing, distribution and sale of publications advocating contraception or abortion as a means of birth control. Section 17 of the Criminal Law Amendment Act (1935) banned the importation and sale of contraceptives. Mail order catalogues from the 1920s reveal that contraceptives may have been accessible to some individuals in Ireland.[43] The bookseller and distributor Charles Eason noted to the Evil Literature Committee in May 1926 that contraceptives were sold freely in England and Ireland.[44] Of all the books banned in Ireland between 1930 and 1945 just over 12 per cent were prohibited because they advocated contraception or abortion.[45] While officially contraceptives were unavailable, it is likely that some were smuggled into the country or sent through the post, or those returning from England brought some with them. People also improvised. Dr Michael Solomons, writing of his experiences as a young doctor in 1940s Dublin, noted that 'desperation bred ingenuity. As no mechanical means of contraception were available, people improvised. While attending one birth, a colleague came across the strange phenomenon of a baby

39 C. Ó Gráda, *Ireland before and after the famine* (Manchester, 1993), 152–97.

40 See D. Urquhart, 'Gender, family and sexuality, 1800–2000', in L. Kennedy and P. Ollerenshaw (eds.), *Ulster since 1600: politics, economy, and society* (Oxford, 2013), 254–5.

41 G. Jones, 'Marie Stopes in Ireland: the mothers' clinic in Belfast, 1936–47', *Social History of Medicine*, 5 (1992), 247.

42 Urquhart, 'Gender, family and sexuality', 255.

43 See the 'Seymour's catalogue and price list' in Evil Literature Committee, Department of Justice File 7/2/17, NAI. Seymour operated from London and advertised condoms from 5d. to 9d. each, reusable condoms of 'stout sheet rubber' cost between half-a-crown and 10s. 6d.

44 Oral evidence provided by Charles Eason, 26 May 1926. Evil Literature Committee, Department of Justice File 7/1/2, NAI.

45 M. Adams, *Censorship: the Irish experience* (Tuscaloosa, AL, 1968), appendix 2, 242–3.

born with the top of a Guinness bottle stuck on its head. The mother had hoped it would act as a contraceptive.[46]

The Northern Ireland Family Planning Association was formed in 1965. In March 1969 the Fertility Guidance Company (later renamed the Irish Family Planning Association) opened in Dublin. The organisation provided free contraception for clients, who then made a donation, and thus sidestepped the law. In 1973 the Supreme Court ruled in McGee v. Attorney General and the Revenue Commissioners that when Customs, following the Criminal Law Amendment Act (1935), seized spermicidal jelly that Mrs McGee had ordered from England, her constitutional right to privacy in marital affairs had been violated. In 1979 the Health (Family Planning) Act legalised contraception but contraceptives, including condoms, were only available on prescription from a doctor. This was seen at the time as an 'Irish solution to an Irish problem'.[47] While further legislation in 1985 extended the legal availability of nonmedical contraceptives, it was not until 1993 that condoms could be sold freely in Ireland, and in May of that year the Irish Department of Health began advocating the use of condoms as a defence against HIV infection. The clash between morality and health became an issue during the 'AIDS' crisis, revealing tensions between a conservative attitude to sexual morality and the imperative of governments to protect the health of its citizens.

The ability of women to control their fertility is hugely advantageous in allowing choices in their lives. Unwanted pregnancies have blighted the lives of innumerable women over the centuries. For many women, particularly poorer women, an illegitimate child could ruin their lives and prospects. In the eighteenth, nineteenth, and even for much of the twentieth century it was believed that women who had illegitimate children were likely to end up as prostitutes. For the myriad numbers of Irish women who worked as servants, overtures from the male members of the household, seduction or even rape which resulted in pregnancy could ruin any opportunity that woman had of keeping her post and maintaining independence, and could drive her into poverty. A large number of women in such situations committed infanticide. Between 1850 and 1900 there were at least 4,645 individual cases of suspected infanticide in Ireland.[48] In the period between 1900 and 1950 hundreds more women also committed infanticide.[49] The levels of infanticide reveal a society that was intolerant of unmarried motherhood.

The ideal of the Virgin Mary held out to Irish Catholic school girls in the twentieth century suggested the impossibility of perfection and the tensions girls could and did face around unmarried pregnancy. Many Irish towns have a grotto built around the statue of Mary, the Virgin Mother of God. In January 1984, Ann Lovett, a young

---

46 M. Solomons, *Pro life? The Irish question* (Dublin, 1993), 6.
47 This was the response of Charles Haughey, the Minister for Health, to the legislation.
48 E. Farrell, 'A most diabolical act': infanticide and Irish society, 1850–1900 (Manchester, 2013).
49 C. Rattigan, 'What else could I do?' Single mothers and infanticide, Ireland 1900–1950 (Dublin, 2012).

unmarried fifteen-year–old, died, along with her baby, while giving birth alone in such a grotto. The case received intense publicity in Ireland, many women especially linking Lovett's plight to the silence imposed on all Irish women who became pregnant outside marriage. In the political context of an Ireland that had just witnessed an acrimonious debate on abortion, Lovett's unacknowledged pregnancy and lonely death echoed the plight of thousands of Irish women, who for decades had been forced to hide their pregnancies, abandon their babies or emigrate to hide their 'shame'.[50]

Unmarried motherhood has proved as problematic in Ireland as it has in most other European countries. Reflecting badly on the 'moral character' of the woman, unmarried motherhood carried a stigma that was almost impossible to shake. An unmarried mother's child was more likely than a legitimate child to die in infancy; the mother, once her status was known, found it difficult, if not impossible, to find respectable employment and was often shunned by her family. As an issue unmarried motherhood had become firmly problematised in Ireland by the end of the nineteenth century. Representing possible immorality, a drain on public finances and someone in need not only of rescue, but also of institutionalisation, the unmarried mother had become, by the foundation of the Irish Free State in 1922, a symbol of unacceptable sexual activity and a problem that had the potential to blight the reputation not only of the family but of the nation.

In practical terms, a number of charitable institutions assisted unmarried, expectant mothers in the nineteenth and early twentieth century. Many rescue homes excluded girls who were pregnant outside marriage for a second time. Indeed, repeated pregnancy outside marriage came to be identified with mental deficiency. From 1922 religious communities of nuns established and staffed homes specifically targeted at unmarried mothers.[51] Conditions in these mother and baby homes were often very difficult and many women were forced to have their babies adopted. Infant mortality rates were also very high. The discovery of a grave in the grounds of one of these homes in Tuam led to public outrage in 2013 and has led to the establishment of a public inquiry, looking at the period between 1922 and 1998, into the management, organisation and treatment of infants and mothers in these homes. It is believed that about 35,000 women used these institutions during the period.[52]

The fate of unmarried mothers was generally to be shamed and disgraced. From the foundation of the state unmarried mothers, while they generally enjoyed the benefits of

---

50 See A. Bourke, S. Kilfeather, M. Luddy, M. MacCurtain, G. Meaney, M. Ni Dhonnchadha, M. O'Dowd and C. Wills (eds.), *The Field Day anthology of Irish writing: vols. IV and V, Irish women's writing and traditions* (Cork, 2002), IV, 637–8; V, 1435–9.

51 *Annual reports of the Department of Local Government and Public Health* (Dublin, 1933–4, 1934–5).

52 For further details see www.dcya.gov.ie/viewdoc.asp?fn=%2Fdocuments%2FMotherandBabyInfoPage.htm, accessed 22 August 2016.

citizenship as women, had, ironically in a state that applauded motherhood, no rights as mothers. The opprobrium shown to unmarried mothers and illegitimate children preserved the sanctity of marriage. Like other 'undesirable elements' within Irish society unmarried mothers were expected to be hidden away from public view. There was little support for greater levels of tolerance towards unmarried mothers in Ireland until the 1960s and 1970s.

Abortion, another means of fertility control, had been criminalised in Ireland under the 1861 Offences against the Person Act. Given the subject matter it is very difficult to assess the level of abortions or their availability in Ireland over the centuries. During a trial in 1943 a detective was asked about the prevalence of back-street abortions and in his response noted, 'We know very little about it but we understand it is fairly prevalent. It is done in secrecy.'[53] A number of individuals were prosecuted for offences relating to abortion between the 1930s and 1950s. The most infamous case was probably that of Mary Ann Cadden, a disqualified midwife. In November 1956 she was found guilty of murder following an abortion death.[54] While abortion laws in England were liberalised in 1967, the law was not extended to Northern Ireland. A right-to-life movement emerged in Ireland in the 1980s. Within the context of the 1979 papal visit to Ireland and the emergence of a 'Women's Right to Choose' group, a Pro-Life Amendment Campaign successfully lobbied for a referendum to re-insert a pro-life clause into the Irish Constitution. Irish women who seek an abortion, however, continue to have to do so in Britain where the procedure has been legal since 1967. It is estimated that about five thousand women travel each year to England for abortions. Further changes in legislation regarding abortion were shaped by campaigns to provide information on abortion services, and particularly the 'X' case when in 1992 the Attorney General secured a High Court injunction preventing a fourteen-year old girl, who had been raped, from travelling to England for a termination.[55] Abortion in Ireland is legal only when a pregnant woman's life is at risk, including the risk of suicide; access to abortions in such cases is governed by the Protection of Life during Pregnancy Act (2013). In Northern Ireland the legal situation is confused. In 2001 the Family Planning Association prosecuted the Northern Ireland government for not publishing clear guidelines on abortion. The judgment, offered in 2003, recommended that this happen. However, to date this issue has not been resolved.

21.6. Prostitution

It was noted in 1784 that there were swarms of prostitutes operating in the Essex Street area of Dublin and it was claimed that there were about three hundred brothels in

53 Summary of case prepared for the Appeal Court. State File, Court of Criminal Appeal, number 53, 1943, NAI.
54 K. Deale, *Beyond any reasonable doubt* (Dublin, 1990), 132–52.
55 L. Connolly and T. O'Toole (eds.), *Documenting Irish feminisms* (Dublin, 2005), 63–75.

the city.[56] In the late 1790s it was claimed that Dame Street had more streetwalkers than London's Strand.[57] Prostitutes were evident in the streets of Irish towns, especially those where soldiers were stationed. They were feared because it was believed that not only did they carry contagious diseases which might infect the entire population but also that their very presence might induce young women to follow in their footsteps.[58] Prostitutes were considered sinners and rescue workers attempted to persuade them to leave their occupation. They did this through opening rescue homes, or Magdalen asylums. The first Magdalen asylum in Ireland was founded in Dublin in 1765 by Lady Arabella Denny. By the twentieth century the majority of Magdalen asylums in Ireland were managed by nuns. In the eighteenth and nineteenth centuries these asylums were flexible institutions where women made a choice to enter, leave or remain in the institution. Life was difficult for the women and the work done, mostly laundry work, was hard labour. By the late nineteenth century women who were not prostitutes were also making their way into the Magdalen asylums; some were destitute, some were unable to secure employment having had illegitimate children, some were sent to the asylums by the court system.

One of the most interesting features of the uncovering of Ireland's sexual pasts is the role played by the media. This has been significant in bringing the mother and baby homes into the general public domain. Likewise the abuse scandals of the industrial and reformatory schools was first brought to light in a television documentary aired on Irish television in 1999.[59] Magdalen asylums entered Irish public consciousness suddenly in September 1993. At that time about a hundred bodies buried within the grounds of the Convent of Our Lady of Charity of Refuge at High Park in Drumcondra, Dublin were exhumed and later reburied, having been cremated, in Glasnevin cemetery.[60] Further programmes such as the 1993 BBC documentary entitled 'Washing away the stain' engaged public opinion. Through interviews with women who had been inmates, this told the history of these asylums in Scotland and Ireland from the mid-twentieth century.[61] The public's interest in Magdalen asylums again surfaced in 1998 with the broadcast of a Channel Four documentary entitled 'Sex in a cold climate' which relied on the evidence of a number of women who had been incarcerated in the Magdalen asylums in Ireland in the 1940s and 1950s. Since 1993 there have been television documentaries, a film, television dramas, plays, songs and poetry, art installations,

---

56 *Hibernian Journal*, 9–11 February 1784; 7 October 1783.
57 *Freeman's Journal*, 21 February 1797.
58 M. Luddy, *Prostitution and Irish society, 1800–1940* (Cambridge, 2007).
59 Mary Raftery's series *States of fear*.
60 See *Irish Times*, 4, 8, 13, 21 September 1993; *Sunday Tribune*, 5 September 1993, *Sunday Press*, 12 September 1993.
61 'Washing away the stain', BBC Scotland, broadcast 16 August 1993.

and historical works created around the subject of Magdalen asylums.[62] Magdalen asylums have emerged as a key cultural construct within Ireland.

The perception of Magdalen asylums in twentieth-century Ireland is extremely negative. Undoubtedly, women were institutionalised and harshly treated. While they might have been places of welfare in the nineteenth century this may not have been the case in the twentieth century. From some of the documentary evidence of government files, and the oral testimonies of women who were in these institutions, women were held against their will, engaged in unpaid labour and lost whatever rights both the law and the constitution granted to them as Irish citizens. From the late nineteenth century it is evident that the asylums were beginning to be used by Catholic parents to hide the 'shame' visited on their families by wayward or pregnant daughters. The abuses that took place in these institutions led to an inquiry, chaired by Senator Martin McAleese, which reported in 2013. It was noted that about ten thousand women entered these Magdalen asylums between 1922 and 1996.[63]

Reading through the historical records available in numerous archives around Ireland it is clear that many Irish people enjoyed pre-marital sex, engaged in adultery, and did not always much care what their neighbours or priests thought of their actions. Levels of infanticide, the appearance of men and women before their local church sessions to account for their extra-marital affairs or pre-marital fornication, prostitution, the comments of clerics on the sexual habits of their flocks, the numbers of desertions, bigamy cases, breach of promise to marry cases and seduction cases attest to a society where the expression of sexuality was less inhibited than historians believed. It was really, for instance, only in the late nineteenth century that unmarried motherhood came to be viewed as a serious moral problem.

After independence there is ample evidence to show that there was considerable discussion on sexuality in Ireland in the 1920s and 1930s. Within the sphere of government the printed, but unpublished, 'Report of the Interdepartmental Committee of Inquiry Regarding Venereal Disease' (1926) and the 'Report of the Committee on the Criminal Law Amendment Acts (1880–85) and Juvenile Prostitution (1931)', known as the Carrigan Committee report, offer extensive and complex accounts of perceived sexual activity throughout the country and the fears raised by that activity. Other publications include *The Report of the Committee on Evil Literature* (1927) and the *Report of the Commission on the Relief of the Sick and Destitute Poor* (1927). The 'Inter-Departmental

---

62 'Les Blanchisseuses de Magdalen', a film by Nicolas Glimois and Christophe Weber (1998), available as 'Convents of shame', Marathon International Video; 'Sex in a cold climate', Testimony Films Documentary for Channel Four, broadcast 16 March 1998; 'Sinners', Parallel Productions/BBC Northern Ireland, drama, broadcast 26 March 2002; 'The Magdalene sisters', written and directed by Peter Mullan, Dublin, A PFP Films Production in association with Temple Film, 2002.

63 'Report of the inter-departmental Committee to establish the facts of state involvement with the Magdalen Laundries' can be found at www.justice.ie/en/JELR/Pages/MagdalenRpt2013, accessed 22 August 2016.

Ad-Hoc Committee on the Suppression of Prostitution' (1947–8), which was again unpublished, provides much information on the 1920s and 1930s.[64] Through these reports and investigative committees concerns were raised about illegitimacy, unmarried mothers, the apparent spread of venereal diseases, prostitution, levels of sexual crime, deviancy, and the dangers of sociability, particularly reflected in dance halls and the motor car, which appeared to offer possibilities for unrestricted mixing of the sexes. Throughout the period earthy newspaper accounts of sexual crime, the extensive publication of clerical sermons and pamphlets about immorality and about the dangers of sex, reinforced public concern about sexual morality. Both the state and the church emphatically presented women's place as being in the home and the ideal role of the Irish woman was as mother. The idealisation of motherhood was a significant feature of the rhetoric of politicians in the new Irish state; the female body and the maternal body, particularly in its unmarried condition, became a central focus of concern to the state and the Catholic Church.

While the politicisation of sexual behaviour had been a feature of Irish nationalism from the late nineteenth century, evident most strongly in the equation of the British garrison as a source of moral and physical contagion for Irish women, problems were to arise when the British garrison was gone, but levels of sexual immorality appeared to rise rather than decrease in the new state. Regarding one form of vice, prostitution, Richard S. Devane, S.J., evangelical in his concern with sexual immorality, observed in 1924 that as long as the British garrison was 'in Dublin it was impossible to deal with prostitution effectively. Now a new order has opened up, and things can be done with comparative ease, quite impossible before.'[65] However, what was to emerge from the early 1920s was a belief, strongly evident in the various reports mentioned above, and in clerical and public discussion of sexuality, that the real threat to chastity and sexual morality resided in the bodies of women. Thus moral regulation, by church and state, attempted to impose, particularly on women, standards of idealised conduct that would return the nation to purity.

While much more can be said about all of these reports, and the nature of sexuality in the first decades of the Free State, it is enough to note at present that making these reports public would have made evident a suggestion that sexual chaos and sexual immorality were rife in the state. It is clear that unmarried mothers, venereal disease and prostitution formed a significant focus of concern in these various enquiries and

---

64 *The Report of the Committee on Evil Literature* (Dublin, 1927); *The Report of the Commission on the Relief of the Sick and Destitute Poor, Including the Insane Poor* (Dublin, 1928). The 'Report of the Committee on the Criminal Law Amendment Acts (1880–85) and Juvenile Prostitution (1931)' can be found in Department of the Taoiseach File, S 5998, NAI; 'Suppression of Prostitution Inquiry' can be found in Department of Justice File DJ 72/94A, NAI; the unpublished Report of the Inter-Departmental Committee of Inquiry Regarding Venereal Disease can be found in the file 'VD in the Irish Free State', Department of the Taoiseach File, S4183, NAI.
65 Evidence of R. S. Devane in 'VD in the Irish Free State', Department of the Taoiseach File, S4183, 30, NAI.

reports. The need to control venereal disease was used as a rationale for moral regulation. Unmarried mothers and prostitutes were particularly targeted as sites of contagion. Women were central to understanding how both disease and immorality became so evident in society. Much of the moral legislation imposed, such as the Criminal Law Act of 1935, reveals an attempt by the state and church to curtail sexual autonomy, particularly that of women. Clear also is an attempt to curtail any expression of sexuality, and to curb, for instance through censorship and the regulation of dance halls, the consumption of sexuality. Moral judgement had social power in Ireland, seen particularly in the condemnation of unmarried motherhood. Intervention into the lives of unmarried mothers saw the state and the church concur in creating a system that kept these women incarcerated, at best, in mother and baby homes and, at worse, in Magdalen asylums. The policing of sexual activities was to become a feature of Irish life for much of the twentieth century. This, allied with familial and community surveillance, exerted its greatest force on women.

It was only from the 1970s that Irish people were willing to challenge the status quo in relation to attitudes to sexuality. Factors such as urbanisation, feminism, higher levels of education, returned migration, access to changing forms of media have all assisted in broadening attitudes to how individuals in Ireland might live their lives. Ireland's entry into the European Economic Community in 1973 was also influential as it allowed considerable growth in the economy, and various development programmes contributed to the prosperity of the 1990s. The campaign for the decriminalisation of homosexuality, which had begun in the 1970s, was finally successful in 1993 when decriminalisation occurred. The considerable reduction in the power of the Catholic Church to shape attitudes to social and moral issues is also evident. The various scandals relating to child abuse, and the church's inability to deal with this issue over the decades, have eroded its moral authority. Given these changes it is not difficult to understand why people, and particularly young people, voted in favour of same-sex marriage.

FURTHER READING

Bourke, A., S. Kilfeather, M. Luddy, M. MacCurtain, G. Meaney, M. Ni Dhonnchadha, M. O'Dowd, and C. Wills (eds.). *The Field Day anthology of Irish writing, vols. IV and V: Irish women's writings and traditions* (Cork and New York, 2002).

Connolly, S. J. *Priests and people in pre-famine Ireland, 1780–1845* (Dublin, 1982).

Cronin, M. G. *Impure thoughts: sexuality, Catholicism and literature in twentieth-century Ireland* (Manchester, 2012).

Farrell, E. *'A most diabolical deed': infanticide and Irish society, 1850–1900* (Manchester, 2013).

Ferriter, D. *Occasions of sin: sex and society in modern Ireland* (London, 2009).

Hug, C. *The politics of sexual morality in Ireland* (Basingstoke, 1999).

Kennedy, F. *Cottage to crèche: family change in Ireland* (Dublin, 2001).

Luddy, M. *Prostitution and Irish society, 1800–1940* (Cambridge, 2007).

McCormick, L. *Regulating sexuality: women in twentieth-century Northern Ireland* (Manchester, 2009).

Rattigan, C. *'What else could I do?': Single mothers and infanticide, Ireland 1900–1950* (Dublin, 2012).

Redmond, J., S. Tiernan, S. McAvoy and M. McAuliffe (eds.). *Sexual politics in modern Ireland* (Sallins, 2015).

Rose, K. *Diverse communities: the evolution of lesbian and gay politics in Ireland* (Cork, 1994).

Smith, J. M. *Ireland's Magdalen laundries and the nation's architecture of containment* (Notre Dame, IN, 2007).

Urquhart, D. 'Gender, family and sexuality in Ulster, 1800–2000', in L. Kennedy and P. Ollerenshaw (eds.), *Ulster since 1600* (Oxford, 2012), 245–59.

Urquhart, D. 'Ireland and the Divorce and Matrimonial Causes Act of 1857', *Journal of Family History*, 38, 3 (July 2013), 301–20.

Urquhart, D. 'Ireland's criminal conversations', 37, 2 (Autumn/Winter 2012), 65–77.

Urquhart, D. 'Irish divorce and domestic violence, 1886–1922', *Women's History Review*, 22, 5 (Oct. 2013), 820–37.

22 Crime and Punishment

Mark Finnane and Ian O'Donnell

22.1. Introduction

Crime and punishment are two dimensions of Ireland's political as much as social history since throughout the period under consideration in the present volume. In government circles, disorder was frequently taken to be characteristic of Irish life, capable of remedy only through ever more inventive techniques for disciplining the unruly Irish. Behind the stereotypes, however, lie the paradoxes – long periods of evident tranquillity, and a capacity to reshape policing and repression along lines that make possible the restoration of civil order. And every perspective we take on these dimensions reveals rich social and institutional histories, whose significance reaches out beyond the borders of the island. In this chapter we consider the changing contours of crime and the responses to it, embodied not only in the history of the Irish constabulary and its successors, but also in punishment, capital and carceral.

22.2. Crime and Responses

Our knowledge of historical crime is tied to the conditions that make it known. For the pre-Great Famine period the sources are newspaper reports and a scanty record of court prosecutions (for the most part destroyed in 1922). The mid-Victorian consolidation of government through information found one expression in the publication, from 1863, of *Judicial statistics*, a wide-ranging record of police arrest, prosecutions and punishment outcomes, aggregated and also by county or smaller districts. Earlier counts were published, including the *Return of Outrages Reported to the Constabulary Office* and the *Statistical returns of the Dublin Metropolitan Police*, but even in combination these do not allow a reliable longitudinal measure of the pattern of crime prior to the late 1830s. How far official statistics reflect the incidence of crime is a perennial question of criminology and policy. And so it becomes necessary at any point in time to consider the context from which crime figures arise, and the possible factors shaping reporting and official attention.

With these qualifications we can paint in broad strokes the patterns of crime after 1740 and through the long nineteenth century. Throughout this period there is apparent continuity – evidence of relatively low criminality in everyday life qualified by intense outbreaks of violence exercised against people and property at periods of acute economic and political stress. The point is not uncontroversial. On the one hand, many commentators within and outside Ireland, then and since, have highlighted the country's disturbed condition and evidence of high levels of criminality and, of course, associated repression. On the other hand, the closer they have looked at the patterns, the more historians have found reason to emphasise the qualifications to any portrait of an unambiguously violent society, even to highlight the relative quietude of Ireland. That said, even the revisionists have also entered their own qualifications, noting important and possibly telling exceptions to their general conclusions.[1]

Eighteenth-century Ireland was a troubled and divided country, with a political system excluding the Catholic majority, and an economic system, largely agricultural, characterised by deep divisions in wealth and power. Throughout the century its convicted criminals might be executed publicly in spectacles that attracted large crowds, or else transported to the American and later Australian colonies.[2] Yet there is good reason to observe the evidence for relatively low levels of criminality, at least of the kind that attracted prosecution and severe punishment. Notably Ireland was, relative to its population, a much smaller contributor of convicts to the American colonies, and its rates of execution were also lower than in eighteenth-century England.[3]

But in themselves such comparisons beg questions about factors shaping prosecution and punishment. As Connolly notes, strong vertical ties of mutual dependence united the interests of local landed proprietors with the classes below them, perhaps contributing to high rates of jury acquittal known already in eighteenth-century Ireland as a challenge to criminal prosecutors. Significant outbreaks of violence associated with the Whiteboys (agrarian rebels) in the 1760s and above all with the 1798 rising unsettled Ireland profoundly. At the same time, to the extent that such outbreaks constitute a contrast with a more peaceable social life, they draw attention to the instrumental character of Irish criminal acts. The purposeful and even quasi-legal character of collective

1 S. J. Connolly, *Religion, law, and power: the making of Protestant Ireland, 1660–1760* (Oxford, 1992), C. Conley, *Melancholy accidents: the meaning of violence in post-famine Ireland* (Lanham, MD, 1999).

2 B. Henry, *Dublin hanged: crime, law enforcement, and punishment in late eighteenth-century Dublin* (Blackrock, 1994).

3 N. Garnham, *The courts, crime and the criminal law in Ireland, 1692–1760* (Dublin, 1996).

violence is evident also in the moral economy that informed the behaviour of bread riot crowds in eighteenth-century Dublin, a phenomenon repeated in the early hungry decades of the nineteenth century.[4]

The increasing strains on Irish society in the pre-famine decades aggravated the conditions that produced crimes against both property and people. Between 1790 and 1840 more than 26,000 convicts were transported to Australia directly from Irish ports, mainly from Cork, and mainly to New South Wales. Compared with the British and Scottish cohorts, Irish convicts were more likely to be first offenders, to be women and to be rural in origin, even if they were tried in cities. Although there was no absence among Irish-born convicts of serious offenders, detailed studies of convict origins have highlighted the banality of the crimes committed by the majority, which were over-whelmingly against property.[5] Stereotypical views of homicide as especially prevalent in the pre-famine decades have been challenged by more recent studies.[6] We must dis-tinguish in the nineteenth century between the experience of everyday life and that in times of acute stress. One such period that highlights the importance of extreme violence during times of hardship was the 'Captain Rock' agrarian rebellion of 1821–4, concentrated in its most dramatic episodes in Limerick and north Cork. The murders of even entire families of middlemen as well as individual landlords and agents were met with fierce repression, exemplary public hangings and forced marches of rebels sentenced to transportation to their embarkation port at Cork.[7]

The stress of the famine was reflected in the enormous growth in numbers convicted of property crime in particular by the early 1850s. But the *Judicial statistics* suggest that most kinds of interpersonal crime declined in the later nineteenth century, with a consequent drop in the numbers in convict prisons. The level of homicide declined too, though less so until the end of the century if we exclude infanticide, which was still prosecuted as a capital offence but the incidence of which declined rapidly in the decades after the famine (see Figure 22.1).[8] The crime decline may be explained in part by increased policing, its legitimacy possibly measured by the declining rate of assaults on police; in part also by the changing demographics, with large numbers of young people (almost equally men and women) leaving Ireland. The post-famine devotional revolution as well as the extension of general education may also have played their part, moralising and civilising in the way that has been considered influential in the longer term in modern European history. There are, however, exceptions to the downward

4 V. Crossman, *Politics, law and order in nineteenth-century Ireland* (New York, 1996).
5 D. Oxley, *Convict maids: the forced migration of women to Australia* (Cambridge, 1996).
6 R. McMahon, *Homicide in pre-famine and famine Ireland* (Liverpool, 2013).
7 J. S. Donnelly, *Captain Rock: the Irish agrarian rebellion of 1821–1824* (Madison, WI, 2009).
8 I. O'Donnell, 'Lethal violence in Ireland, 1841 to 2003: famine, celibacy and parental pacification', *British Journal of Criminology*, 45 (2005), 671–95.

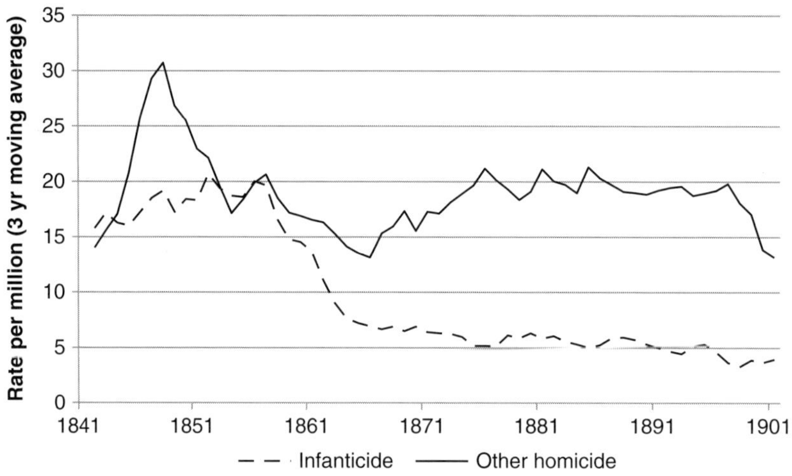

Figure 22.1 Unlawful killing: infanticide and other homicide rates, 1841–1901. Note: Rates calculated from Return of Outrages Reported to Constabulary Office, Statistical Returns of Dublin Metropolitan Police and Judicial Statistics.

trend in policing and prosecution of serious crime, especially for sexual offences such as rape.[9] How far such exceptions reflect an increased rate of sexual violence in the later nineteenth century remains difficult to tell: the removal of rape from the list of capital offences may have played a role in increasing prosecutions, and it is also clear that a rape conviction resulted in serious punishment.[10] Comparing Irish violence rates with those in Britain suggests a lag in the Irish decline, or alternatively a convergence by the early decades of the twentieth century.[11]

This brief overview of patterns of criminality suggests a vital condition for understanding their contours and colours, namely the response of public authority in the shape of courts and policing. If there are grounds for suggesting that Ireland was not so exceptional in its criminality, the position is arguably somewhat different when we turn to policing.

22.3. Policing and Punishment

An influential study of Ireland under the Union highlighted the phenomenon of Ireland as a social laboratory for the development of new institutions and policies.[12] Policing was one of the chief exemplars. From the creation of a professional police

9 M. Finnane, 'A decline of violence in Ireland? Crime, policing and social relations, 1860–1914', *Crime, History and Societies*, 1, 1 (1997), 51–70.

10 C. Conley, 'No pedestals: women and violence in late nineteenth-century Ireland', *Journal of Social History*, 28 (1995), 801–18.

11 S. J. Connolly, 'Unnatural death in four nations: contrasts and comparisons', in S. J. Connolly (ed.), *Kingdoms united? Great Britain and Ireland since 1500* (Dublin, 1999).

12 O. MacDonagh, *Ireland: the Union and its aftermath* (London, 1977).

force for the Dublin metropolitan area to the demise of the Royal Irish Constabulary (RIC) (in 1922 in the twenty-six counties, although it continued until 2001 as the Royal Ulster Constabulary in Northern Ireland), a public police played a controversial role in the government of Ireland. Yet the new police forces of the nineteenth century were designed as something other than a blunt instrument of government, and this is as true of Ireland as of its contemporaries.[13]

Breaking from the local government tradition of parish constables and night watch-men as the guardians of order, the Dublin Police Act of 1786 reflected a determination of Dublin Castle to assert control over an increasingly troubled city, violent and rebel-lious. A Parisian model of armed and centralised police may have influenced the design of the Dublin police, and an ideology of civic government helped shape the scope of its functions for improving the amenity of the city, facilitating mobility through its crowded streets and regulating its markets.[14] Although disarmed within the decade, and so becoming through subsequent reformations a more familiar modern civilian police, the Dublin police continued as an independent urban force until the creation of An Garda Síochána in 1925. A separate urban police was also created in Belfast in 1800, a last legacy of pre-Union government, though it was to be absorbed in the gen-eral police in 1865.[15]

Urban policing proved less dominant in Ireland than an alternative model that also shared a good deal with the French approach. Recurring agrarian disorder and threat-ening rebellion, especially in the south and west of the country, prompted from 1814 a series of radical interventions by Dublin Castle. Critical of the inadequacy of local magistrates to respond effectively to crime and disorder, the Irish government under Chief Secretary Robert Peel and his successors initiated the proclamation of districts that would be policed (and taxed for this purpose) by armed constabularies. When this piecemeal approach proved unable to contain violence, the government responded with a Peace Preservation Act. This not only bolstered emergency law to facilitate pros-ecution of violent offenders, but established throughout the country a constabulary that would be responsible for maintaining order. In its centralised governance and comprehensive coverage of the country the Peace Preservation Force proved a momen-tous innovation, unprecedented in the United Kingdom. Only slowly, however, could it displace the tradition of police at the beck and call of local magistrates.

The centralised police was transformed in 1836 into the Irish Constabulary (named Royal after its major service in suppressing the Fenian rebellion in 1867) through

13 E. Malcolm, *The Irish policeman, 1822–1922: a life* (Dublin, 2006).
14 S. H. Palmer *Police and protest in England and Ireland, 1780–1850* (Cambridge, 1988).
15 B. Griffin, *The bulkies: police and crime in Belfast, 1800–1865* (Dublin, 1997).

Figure 22.2 David O'Shea after his arrest for the murder of Ellen O'Sullivan, Cork/Kerry border, 13 June 1931. The Independent Newspapers (Ireland) Collection. Courtesy of the National Library of Ireland.

legislation that laid the way for a peace-keeping role intended to be freer of sectarian and local influence than the earlier police forces. One result was that the Irish police developed a much more civic role than might be imagined from its origins and the controversy that surrounded its coercive function during times of trouble. Central government might find it too weak in the face of serious outbreaks of political violence, while local magistrates and communities might consider it too ineffective as a general police to respond to crime. As one of the largest employers in post-famine Ireland the constabulary was always as much part of the society as apart from it. While there may have been a greater 'domestication' of the constabulary by the Edwardian years, aspects of civil policing preceded even the famine, especially as collectors of information for government and processors of the disorderly for families and communities; one result may have been the high rate of institutionalisation of non-criminal populations by the later nineteenth century.[16] Throughout the period of the Union, however, the civic potential of policing was threatened every generation by the recurrence of political rebellion and social unrest, making the legitimacy of the

16 W. J. Lowe and E. Malcolm, 'The domestication of the Royal Irish Constabulary, 1836–1922', *Irish Economic and Social History*, 19 (1992), 27–48; M. Finnane, *Insanity and the insane in post-famine Ireland* (London, 1981).

Figure 22.3 Royal Irish Constabulary, 1897. Poole Photographic Collection. Courtesy of the National Library of Ireland.

Irish police a perennial question, reaching into the late twentieth century in Northern Ireland. The outbreak of the First World War and then nationalist rebellion rendered the RIC into a target of political violence, and made inevitable the force's eventual disbandment.

Irish policing reform was centralised because local political forces proved so fragile from the late eighteenth century. An ineffectual magistracy of local landowners and the propertied class was gradually displaced by Dublin Castle's appointees, magistrates on a stipend from the government. The work of the stipendiaries played a critical role in developing a more responsive justice system, and one perhaps a little less in the service of local politics. The weakness of local government and the fears attending private prosecutors during times of trouble aided another innovation of nineteenth-century government in Ireland, the crown prosecutor.[17] Juries too were a continuing challenge, their role perhaps contributing to lower conviction rates and certainly shaping the choices of governments about the scope of exceptional law in times of trouble.[18]

17 J. F. McEldowney, 'Crown prosecutions in 19th century Ireland', in D. Hay and F. Snyder (eds.), *Policing and prosecution in Britain 1750–1850* (Oxford, 1989).
18 N. Howlin, 'Nineteenth century criminal justice: uniquely Irish or simply not English?', *Irish Journal of Legal Studies*, 3, 1 (2013), 67–89.

Policing was not the only criminal justice innovation in nineteenth-century Ireland. While the country was largely a borrower in the development of the prison, the bureaucratic leaning of government helped shape some important changes. The options were largely those shared with the other parts of the United Kingdom: capital punishment (declining through the nineteenth century), transportation (revived to Australia in the 1780s and playing a major role from 1791 to 1853) and, increasingly, imprisonment. Ireland adopted the penitentiary, rather than led the way, though it was ahead of time in the establishment, more than a decade before Broadmoor, of the first criminal lunatic asylum at Dundrum in 1850.[19]

There was some distinction in prisons administration, in particular the oversight of conditions, notoriously poor in the eighteenth century, through the role of an inspector-general. In this regard, the first incumbent, Sir Jeremiah Fitzpatrick (appointed in 1786), was to the fore, advocating an approach to the penitentiary that would reform the prisoner.[20] Alongside the convict prisons such as Mountjoy (Dublin, completed 1850), developed along nineteenth-century penitentiary lines for the discipline and reformation of long-sentence prisoners, Irish prisons were run locally under the authority of county grand juries and funded on the rates. A large number of bridewells, for short-term detention of minor offenders or those on remand awaiting trial, were also maintained until the 1880s. But their ineffectiveness and poor conditions prompted the closure of most of them after the establishment of the General Prisons Board in 1878, when prisons administration was consolidated and effectively nationalised.[21] By this time population decline combined with a fall in serious crime enabled a wide-scale consolidation of prisons. Committals to bridewells fell from 88,899 in 1850 to 4,830 in 1878; those resident in county gaols from about 10,000 to 2,817 in the same period; while the numbers of long-sentence prisoners declined from 3,427 at the beginning of 1855 to 1,114 in 1878.[22] Of great influence on the design of prison systems and prison discipline was the administration and advocacy of Walter Crofton, first chairman of the Convict Prisons Board (1854). Crofton's four-stage progressive system of prison discipline was designed to reform prisoners by first quarantining them from adverse associations and influences, then allowing them more freedom, with opportunities for training and work as they progressed through their sentence, before release on licence. This system involved the establishment of open prisons to supplement the harsh discipline of the conventional penitentiary. The Crofton system could not free the prison system of all its risks to government. As the agitation of the Land War filled the prisons

19 P. Prior, *Madness and murder: gender, crime and mental disorder in nineteenth-century Ireland* (Dublin, 2008).
20 O. MacDonagh, *The inspector general: Sir Jeremiah Fitzpatrick and the politics of social reform, 1783–1802* (London, 1981).
21 P. Carroll-Burke, *Colonial discipline: the making of the Irish convict system* (Dublin, 2000).
22 First Report of the General Prisons Board Ireland [Cd 2447], HCPP, 1878–9, 14–18.

with not just political prisoners but indeed elected politicians, the conditions of nine-teenth-century punishment were exposed for all to see in a new light.[23]

22.4.   Exports

Both crime and policing may be counted among Irish exports in a variety of ways dur-ing the period of the Union, and even before and after it. While some aspects of this legacy may be best approached through the framework of political violence, there are vital stories to be told about Irish convicts and Irish police and policing abroad that repay brief attention here.

When Jeremy Bentham asked whether convicted criminals were best sent to the pen-itentiary or Botany Bay he raised a question much debated in his own day and after. The tens of thousands of Irish convicts sent to the American and later Australian colonies formed only a minority of those so transported from the British Isles. Not all of them left Irish ports – many instead had been convicted of crimes in the British cities to which they migrated. But the cultures they took with them helped shape their desti-nations significantly. The high proportion of female Irish convicts in New South Wales (nearly 60 per cent) meant that nearly two-thirds of the first generation of convict ori-gin had at least one Irish parent.[24] In Australia especially, the opportunity afforded by access to land helped turn many into landholders of domains they could never have dreamt of in Ireland. These were a minority, as in their country of origin; the resent-ments of those denied good land or the resources to prosper could boil over into later outrage, iconically so in the career of Ned Kelly, son of a male convict. Those who sur-vived the voyage and the often difficult conditions of colonial convict-dom for the most part lived menial lives, if with a greater degree of comfort than many had left behind.[25]

It was not people alone that Ireland exported. The half-century of innovation in policing that was represented by the Dublin police, the Peace Preservation Force and then the Irish Constabulary proved immensely fruitful in the service of empire. The model of a centralised armed civilian police, under the direction of executive govern-ment, was transferred into colonial domains as well as adopted by the self-governing settler colonies. Techniques of training, organisation and discipline forged in Dublin were widely dispersed. In the process they were adapted and transformed, in some cases merged with those of the London Metropolitan Police.[26] Late in the Victorian

23 S. McConville, *Irish political prisoners, 1848–1922: theatres of war* (Oxford, 2003).

24 S. Nicholas and P. R. Shergold, 'The convict period,' in J. Jupp (ed.), *The Australian people: an encyclopedia of the nation, its people and their origins* (Cambridge, 2001), 16–25.

25 R. Reece, *Irish convict lives* (Sydney, 1993).

26 G. Marquis, 'The "Irish model" and nineteenth-century Canadian policing,' *Journal of Imperial and Commonwealth History*, 25 (1997), 193–218.

period another innovation of Dublin Castle, the Special Branch, emerged as a specialised force for the surveillance and containment of political violence. Its legacy would be found in the British Security Service (also known as MI5) and in a host of Special Branches throughout the police forces of the British empire.

The Irish police model was transferred not merely as an idea or blueprint but as an attribute of the Irish police migrant. Both officers and constables who had served in the various Irish police forces found permanent opportunities abroad. In one case, their onward destinations were promoted as a matter of policy: hundreds of ex-RIC men were posted in 1922 to the British mandated territory of Palestine, where some of them forged long-lasting careers.[27]

22.5. The Colonial Inheritance and the Shrinking Criminal Justice State

When Saorstát Éireann came into existence, criminal justice arrangements were largely undisturbed. The common law legal tradition was maintained, the process remained adversarial, and British laws, policies and practices were allowed to continue. Barristers still wore wigs, robes and bands and deferred to their 'worships' and their 'lordships' on the bench (although the personnel to whom they deferred changed with the abolition of the resident magistracy). An experiment with an alternative judicial model, involving so-called Republican or Dáil courts, was abandoned. The organisation that took the place of the RIC and the Dublin Metropolitan Police was named An Garda Síochána and it was unarmed virtually from its inception. The rationale for this decision was expressed by the first Garda commissioner, Michael Staines, as a desire for his men to 'succeed not by force of arms, or numbers, but on their moral authority as servants of the people'. The new policemen occupied the same barracks and patrolled the same beats as their predecessors. In the north, there was also continuity of organisation, but a change of name as the Royal Ulster Constabulary replaced its predecessor in May 1922. North and south of the border, the reconstituted police forces came to replicate the confessional character of the regimes they served.[28]

When the constitution for the new Irish state was being drafted in 1922, consideration was given to removing the option of capital punishment, which was seen as a bitter reminder of British imperialism. It was believed that the public would have supported such a move. But the ultimate sanction was retained on the basis that it was required as a deterrent to politically motivated killing. Predictably, the crimes of the great majority

---

27 K. Fedorowich, 'The problems of disbandment: the Royal Irish Constabulary and imperial migration, 1919–29', *Irish Historical Studies*, 30, 117 (1996), 88–110.
28 D. Fitzpatrick, *The two Irelands, 1912–1939* (Oxford, 1998).

of those executed had no conceivable political dimension.[29] The same buildings were used to hold men and women sentenced to imprisonment or penal servitude but the numbers so confined fell steeply, reflecting a low level of recorded crime. During the first decades of independence the pattern was of dwindling prisoner numbers and prison closures. A low point was reached in 1958 when there were only 369 prisoners in the country, held in Limerick, Portlaoise and Mountjoy prisons and St Patrick's Institution (which had replaced the Borstal). Most were repeat offenders serving short sentences, described by Peadar Cowan, a former army officer, solicitor and TD, who served time in Mountjoy in the late 1950s, as a collection of 'moochers and whiners'.[30]

The low rates of crime and imprisonment were matched by a low level of interest in criminal justice affairs. While there were occasional criticisms of the operation of the prison system, in general this was seen as a marginal area of public policy and treated accordingly.

22.6.   Halcyon Days?

By the middle of the twentieth century the rate of serious crime was so low that Ireland could be described as 'a policeman's paradise'.[31] In the decade before the renewed outbreak of political conflict, it was already noted that the rate of violent death in Northern Ireland was lowest of eighteen western nations, equalled only by the rate in the Republic.[32] It was estimated that in the 1950s up to 40 per cent of Garda time was spent carrying out administrative duties such as collecting agricultural statistics, delivering old age pension books and acting as census enumerators.[33] But what might appear on the surface to have been a pacific and non-punitive society was a place of intense social control, where a range of institutions outside the criminal justice system was called upon to incarcerate those deemed to be difficult, deviant or distressed. O'Sullivan and O'Donnell coined the term 'coercive confinement' to describe involuntary detention in psychiatric hospitals, reformatory and industrial schools, mother and baby homes and Magdalen asylums as well as in prisons. When these sites are considered as part of an interlocking apparatus of control, a far less benign picture emerges.[34]

---

29 D. Doyle and I. O'Donnell, 'The death penalty in post-independence Ireland', *Journal of Legal History*, 33 (2012), 65–91.

30 P. Cowan, *Dungeons deep: a monograph on prisons, borstals, reformatories and industrial schools in the Republic of Ireland and some reflections on crime and punishment and matters relating thereto* (Dublin, 1960), 5.

31 C. Brady, *Guardians of the peace* (Dublin, 1974), 240.

32 R. Rose, *Governing without consensus: an Irish perspective* (London, 1971), 429.

33 S. Kilcommins, I. O'Donnell, E. O'Sullivan and B. Vaughan, *Crime, punishment and the search for order in Ireland* (Dublin, 2004), 205.

34 The term was introduced in an article in *Punishment and Society*, 9 (2007), 27–48 and later received a book-length treatment in *Coercive confinement in Ireland: patients, prisoners and penitents* (Manchester, 2012).

As the prison population fell, the number of psychiatric inpatients grew. A review of the relationship between mental illness and crime in Europe in the 1930s found that the Irish Free State had the highest rate of institutionalisation for the 'insane or the mentally defective', but the lowest imprisonment rate.[35] The Commission of Inquiry on Mental Illness noted that the number of patients detained involuntarily in psychiatric hospitals appeared to be 'the highest in the world'.[36] As well as involuntary psychiatric inpatients living miserable lives in dreary institutions, large numbers of children were held in reformatory or industrial schools, and unmarried mothers and their babies were detained in county homes. Other women ended up in Magdalen asylums (some sent by the courts on remand or after a conviction for infanticide, others by families who feared that their daughters might be a cause of shame if left at liberty). While these institutions were ostensibly concerned with treatment or welfare, there is little doubt that they felt punitive to those subjected to their strictures. The smallest cohort of the coercively confined, by far, was the prisoners.

Persons incarcerated for reasons unrelated to crime often spent much longer under detention than those in the formal criminal justice system. The average prison term served by those sentenced to death whose sentences were commuted to penal servitude for life was around six years. This was less than the time spent by many destitute children in industrial schools or by the forgotten thousands involuntarily detained in psychiatric hospitals. Indeed, some unmarried mothers spent as long coercively confined as some murderers. A country with a low and declining prison population was a fiercely controlling place for citizens who were perceived to be troubled or troublesome. Without the safety valve of emigration, the level of coercive confinement would have been higher again.

The 1950s marked a watershed with more than one in every hundred men, women and children coercively confined on a given day; in numerical terms this equated to around 31,500 people. After this time a steady decline is evident. By 1971, the number coercively confined had shrunk to 20,000 and by the end of the first decade of the twenty-first century it had dropped to 8,000 against a background of a rising national population. The only institution that bucked the trend was the prison which moved centre-stage, accounting for one in two of those coercively confined in the early twenty-first century compared with one in forty in the 1920s. One of the great untold stories of twentieth-century Ireland is the massive downsizing in coercive confinement, a trend which accrued primarily to the benefit of women and children.

---

35 L. S. Penrose, 'Mental disease and crime: outline of a comparative study of European statistics', *British Journal of Medical Psychology*, 18 (1939), 1–15.
36 Commission of Inquiry on Mental Illness, *Report* (Dublin, 1966), 25.

22.7.   The Legacy of Partition

Republicans who refused to accept the legitimacy of the Free State or Northern Ireland posed a threat to the authorities south of the border. In response, the Offences against the State Act (1939) created a (juryless) Special Criminal Court to be deployed when the government was satisfied that the threat of juror intimidation was such that the ordinary courts were inadequate to the task. It was reinforced by internment, judicial execution and, in 1940, the establishment of a Military Court. From its inception the Special Criminal Court dealt with more than just subversion. While its jurisdiction was restricted to offences that could not be dealt with by the ordinary courts, what was deemed to satisfy this standard was elastic. For example, in the early years most of the matters dealt with were economic, such as black market trading that exploited the rationing arrangements put in place during the Emergency.

The Special Criminal Court stopped sitting in December 1946 and was not reactivated during the IRA border campaign of the 1950s; at this juncture the government opted for internment to deal with the threat to the state. The internees always put in place, and followed, a military command structure. They were seen as different from other prisoners, a reality that was grudgingly acknowledged even by those who vehemently objected to their aims and methods. Republicans were prepared to withstand poor conditions and even to exacerbate them through hunger and strip strikes; by refusing to don the convict's uniform they invited a harsh response which, if taken, served to confirm to supporters the legitimacy of their position. They attempted to escape, recognising the propaganda value that such actions presented, and believing that it was their duty to frustrate their captors using any available methods. Perhaps the most spectacular break-out in the Republic of Ireland occurred in 1973 when a helicopter landed in the exercise yard at Mountjoy prison and whisked three prominent IRA men away to freedom. Similar events had taken place north of the border where, two years earlier, nine IRA men had clambered over the walls of Crumlin Road jail in Belfast and, the previous year, seven internees had swum to freedom from the prison ship HMS *Maidstone*. In terms of scale and propaganda value, nothing compared with the mass escape (thirty-eight men) in 1983 from the H-Blocks at HMP Maze, one of the most secure prisons in Europe.

The Special Criminal Court came back into operation for a few months in 1961 and 1962, when it convicted thirty people (most of whom were released shortly afterwards under the terms of an amnesty). In October 1962 it was formally disestablished only to be reinstated in May 1972 in response to mounting violence in Northern Ireland. It has been continuously in existence ever since. The resuscitated Special Criminal Court differs from its predecessor in that its members are drawn exclusively from the judiciary, with no military personnel involved. It is similar in the extent to which it has become a vehicle for dealing with criminals who are not associated with unlawful organisations, thereby 'normalising' what were intended (or, at least, propounded) as emergency measures. As well as impacting on the courts, the Northern Ireland conflict influenced (in an upward direction) the maximum detention periods allowed for police interrogation, facilitated new procedures for seizing criminal assets, and altered the perceived acceptability of using testimony from known offenders to convict their peers. What were supposed to be extraordinary measures soon spilled over into the ordinary criminal justice realm.

• The Troubles continued to have sporadic repercussions for citizens of the Republic, most catastrophically in 1974 when car bombs in Dublin and Monaghan resulted in the loss of thirty-three lives. Other deaths that may have been related to the political situation occasionally resulted from armed robberies, vigilante activities and the punishment of informers.

The crime rate in Northern Ireland, especially insofar as the most serious offences are concerned, was distorted by the conflict to which the authorities responded with a variety of measures including internment and non-jury courts. The violence was furious at times – there were 470 deaths in 1972 – but when terrorist offences are omitted from the analysis, the level of criminal victimisation was low and the public felt relatively safe.[37] The prison population in Northern Ireland was bloated by an influx of prisoners serving long sentences who posed a qualitatively different set of challenges to the 'ordinary decent criminals' who were present in comparatively small numbers.[38]

After an IRA ceasefire was declared in 1994, and the Good Friday Agreement was ratified in 1998, military fortifications along the border were removed and the number of British soldiers stationed in Northern Ireland was scaled down. The criminal justice system was comprehensively reviewed, paramilitary prisoners who accepted the legitimacy of the peace process were released, the infamous H-Blocks were closed, and the system of policing, including its culture, ethos and symbols, was comprehensively overhauled with the Police Service of Northern Ireland created to replace the Royal Ulster Constabulary.[39] Although militant groups remained in existence (justifying the retention of heavily fortified police stations in some areas) the ceasefire held firm.

22.8. Diversification

The volume of lethal violence grew between 1932 and 2012, albeit from a low base, and the rate of recorded property crime increased by a large multiple (see Table 22.1), although the upward drift was reversed (temporarily) for several years during the 1980s

---

37 J. D. Brewer, B. Lockhart and P. Rodgers, *Crime in Ireland 1945–1995: here be dragons* (Oxford, 1997).

38 K. McEvoy, *Paramilitary imprisonment in Northern Ireland: resistance, management and release* (Oxford, 2001).

39 A. Mulcahy, *Policing Northern Ireland: conflict, legitimacy and reform* (Cullompton, 2006). The 447-page report *Review of the Criminal Justice System in Northern Ireland* was published in 2000 and is underpinned by eighteen separate research reports.

Table 22.1. Rates of recorded crime in Free State/Republic of Ireland

	Homicide (per million)	Robbery	Burglary	Theft and related offences
			(per 100,000)	
1922	–	–	–	–
1932	5.4	1.9	29.9	145.7
1942	4.7	1.5	84.3	460.6
1952	4.4	0.6	87.7	382.7
1962	4.2	1.4	116.2	376.9
1972	9.3	16.1	346.1	845.4
1982	7.8	49.6	938.5	1,678.4
1992	11.8	69.6	1,005.3	1,463.7
2002	15.1	75.0	653.6	1,485.2
2012	13.1	58.4	613.5	1,666.2

NOTE: Homicide comprises murder, infanticide and manslaughter (excluding traffic fatalities and dangerous driving causing death).
SOURCE: Calculated from I. O'Donnell *et al., Crime and punishment in Ireland 1922–2003: a statistical sourcebook* (Dublin, 2005), table 1.1; and Central Statistics Office, Recorded Crime 2012. Data unavailable for 1922.

and each of the following decades. The rise in lethal violence occurred despite the disappearance of infanticide, which had accounted for a significant proportion of homicides in the early decades of independence. These trends can be related to Ireland's changing economic fortunes, the wider availability of drug treatment, fluctuating levels of alcohol consumption, demographic shifts and changing attitudes to unmarried motherhood. There has also been a change in the mix of crimes committed with the emergence of a lucrative trade in drugs, an increase in gang-related violence and the appearance of new criminal opportunities, such as those created by information technology (e.g. online fraud, internet child pornography). White-collar and corporate wrongdoing have had devastating social consequences, although the reckless behaviour that resulted in Ireland's economic collapse at the end of the first decade of the twenty-first century led to few arrests. It is a historical constant that those appearing before the courts are drawn from the lower socio-economic groupings.

Just as the mixture of crime became more variegated, so too did the response it evoked. The closing decades of the twentieth century saw a major expansion of probation and the introduction of a new sanction, the Community Service Order. Each of these developments hearkened back to the country's colonial past. The expanded probation service continued to operate under the Probation of Offenders Act (1907) which defined its role as to 'advise, assist and befriend' and the community service legislation was imported almost verbatim from England and Wales, leading one politician to note

Table 22.2. Imprisonment in Free State/Republic of Ireland

| | Daily average prisoner numbers | | | | | Fine defaulters | 3 yrs and |
	Male	Female	Total	Rate	Total	No. (%)	above No. (%)
1922	607	67	674	22.7	1,981	678 (34.2)	62 (3.1)
1932	537	90	627	21.3	2,524	1037 (41.1)	32 (1.3)
1942	695	77	772	26.0	2,597	287 (11.1)	58 (2.2)
1952	438	42	480	16.2	1,927	314 (16.3)	22 (1.1)
1962	482	8	490	17.3	1,591	294 (18.5)	24 (1.5)
1972	1,009	26	1,035	34.2	2,914	401 (13.8)	59 (2.0)
1982	1,204	32	1,236	35.5	2,557	456 (17.8)	277 (10.8)
1992	2,146	39	2,185	61.5	4,756	1,404 (29.5)	262 (5.5)
2002	3,061	104	3,165	80.8	5,036	–	440 (8.7)
2012	4,166	152	4,318	94.2	13,526	8,304 (61.4)	774 (5.7)

NOTE: Imprisonment rate is per 100,000 population.
SOURCE: Calculated from O'Donnell *et al.*, tables 3.1, 3.5 and 3.6; and *Crime and punishment in Ireland Irish Prison Service Annual Report for 2012*.

that 'this is simply one more example in the ignominious parade of legislation masquerading under an Irish title … which is a British legislative idea taken over here and given a green outfit with silver buttons to make it look native.'[40] Probation supervision consists primarily of individual casework, and it remains in the shadow of the prison which continues to dominate thinking about sentencing and punishment.

The growth in the criminal justice system was not accompanied by an increase in research. There were major data deficits, independent scrutiny was not welcomed and understanding remained poor. Little is known about the prisoner experience and while the police constable has attracted the attention of historians, the prison warder remains largely invisible. Criminology as a discipline did not penetrate the universities in the Republic of Ireland during the twentieth century, with the first Institute of Criminology coming into existence at University College Dublin in 2000 (a similar entity was established at Queen's University Belfast several years earlier). Against this backdrop, sentence lengths increased and the prison population grew, largely comprising young urban men convicted of property offences. The jailing of petty offenders who could not, or would not, pay fines was a stubborn problem (see Table 22.2).

By the beginning of the twenty-first century, Ireland had morphed from a failing economy with a high level of emigration (the 'basket case of Europe') into a desirable destination for people seeking a better life (the 'Celtic Tiger' economy). Illustrating the scale of this change, the monthly number of applications for refugee status rose from

40 John Kelly, Dáil Debates, 3 May 1983, vol. 342, col.169.

an average of three in 1992 to almost a thousand by 2002 (falling back to eighty in 2012, reflecting the country's economic downturn). This indicated that the country had become internationally recognised as both stable and prosperous, a potential haven for those fleeing persecution and financial adversity.

Not unsurprisingly given the changed nature of the resident population, reports of immigrant involvement in criminal activity began to appear in the late 1990s. Translators were required to attend courthouses to ensure that justice was done, and heard to be done, whether in Swahili, Romanian or Yoruba. Previously the infrequent use of Irish was the only breach of English-language dominance. Reflecting wider demographic changes the prison population became much more diverse. The annual reports of the Irish Prison Service show that in 2012, almost one in five committals to prison was foreign born. This contrasts with the situation in 1996 when a survey of 108 prisoners revealed that only three had addresses outside Ireland, two in England (both of whom had been raised in Ireland) and one in Jamaica.[41]

Another striking trend during the middle of the twentieth century was the almost complete decarceration of women, with the daily average in custody falling as low as eight in 1962 (although this trend was not sustained: by 2012, the female prison population had reached new heights (see Table 22.2)). At the same time as they became less prominent as offenders, women began to occupy important leadership roles. At the time of writing (December 2016) the Minister for Justice and Equality, Chief Justice, Director of Public Prosecutions, Attorney General, Chief State Solicitor, President of the District Court and Garda Commissioner were all women. Things have moved some distance since the time that Deputy Frank Sherwin remarked during a parliamentary debate on proposed policing legislation that it would be contrary to the public interest if female Garda recruits were too attractive. As an example of the kind of casual misogyny that ruffled few feathers at the time, it would be difficult to surpass his exhortation to the Minister for Justice that: 'while recruits should not be actually horsefaced, they should not be too good-looking; they should be just plain women and not targets for marriage'.[42]

22.9. Notable Shifts

Anxiety about crime reached a crisis point in June 1996 with the shooting dead of a journalist (Veronica Guerin) and a Garda detective (Jerry McCabe). The killing of the former, who wrote about crime for the *Sunday Independent,* was thought to have been arranged by a gangland figure about whom she was planning an exposé. The latter was shot by an IRA unit that was carrying out an unauthorised 'fundraising' operation. The Guerin and McCabe murders were defining moments in the debate about law and order

41 P. O'Mahony, *Mountjoy prisoners* (Dublin, 1997), 39.
42 Dáil Debates, 22 May 1958, vol. 168, cols. 624–5.

and gave rise to a hardening in political attitudes; no longer could Ireland be considered a 'policeman's paradise'. A raft of legal and policy changes was set in motion to clamp down on organised crime. Minimum sentences of ten years' imprisonment were introduced for certain drug crimes. Temporary release was granted less often and the time served prior to release on parole increased substantially. The prison population grew more rapidly than in other European countries, and overcrowding became endemic.[43]

International surveys and comparative criminal justice statistics revealed comparatively high levels of delinquency, victimisation and serious crime. According to the EU Survey of Crime and Safety, Ireland was 'a high crime country' where robberies were particularly common.[44] In another study, Ireland scored highest for total delinquency across thirty-one countries and rates of self-reported violence and property crime were 'unusually high'.[45] The 2010 edition of the *European sourcebook of crime and criminal justice statistics* confirmed the view that there was no room for complacency, showing that the overall rate of recorded crime in Ireland exceeded the European median as did the rates of more serious crimes such as homicide and rape. Leaving to one side the usual caveats around the cross-national comparability of crime data, the consistency of the picture drawn from several sources suggests that the level of criminal activity in Ireland is no longer peculiarly low. Similarly, the rate of increase in Ireland's prison population has been unusually rapid, albeit from a modest base.

For the first forty years after independence Ireland was distinguished by low rates of crime and imprisonment, co-existing with a high level of coercive confinement. During the subsequent fifty years, it reached and, in some respects surpassed, European norms. The prison moved emphatically to centre stage and the other sites of coercive confinement disappeared or dwindled in significance.

22.10.   Conclusion: Continuities

To understand crime and punishment necessitates understanding migration patterns. One consequence of the outward movement of people was to depress the crime rate at home and to elevate it in host countries. For example, during the 1960s more than twice as many Irish-born men (but fewer women) were committed to prison in England and Wales than in Ireland.[46] In 2015 the Irish still constituted one of the largest groups of

43 I. O'Donnell and E. O'Sullivan, *Crime control in Ireland: the politics of intolerance* (Cork, 2001).
44 J. van Dijk, R. Manchin, J. Van Kesteren, S. Nevala and G. Hideg, *The burden of crime in the EU*. Research Report for the European Commission (Brussels, 2005), 94.
45 D. Enzmann, I. Haen Marshall, M. Killias, J. Junger-Tas, M. Steketee and B. Gruszczynska, 'Self -reported youth delinquency in Europe and beyond', *European Journal of Criminology*, 7 (2010), 179.
46 Calculated from L. Ryan, 'Irish emigration to Britain since World War II', in R. Kearney (ed.), *Migrations: the Irish at home and abroad* (Dublin, 1990), 65; I. O'Donnell, E. O'Sullivan and D. Healy, *Crime and punishment in Ireland 1922–2003: a statistical sourcebook* (Dublin, 2005), 166.

foreign nationals in the prison system of England and Wales. In the 1970s and 1990s, which were characterised by net inward migration (together with rises in prosperity and alcohol consumption) there were spikes in lethal violence. During the former period many of the migrants were Irish-born workers returning home, often with their families, to take advantage of new employment opportunities. More recently the trend has been for the immigrant population to be much more mixed, comprising job seekers from across the EU and asylum seekers from further afield. This has begun to impact on policing, prosecuting and punishing, but not yet in any obvious way on recruitment to An Garda Síochána, which retains its Irish (and rural) bias.

While the past is occasionally acknowledged in debates about crime and punishment, the historical context is seldom fully articulated. Issues are seen in isolation and as disconnected from prior developments. This is illustrated by the controversy that accompanied the decision to build a monument to survivors of childhood abuse in Dublin's Garden of Remembrance. Some felt that locating the memorial beside a monument to the 1916 Rising would detract from the contribution made by those who fought for Irish independence. But it could be argued that the form of independence won by the men and women of 1916, and their successors, created the conditions for large-scale coercive confinement and the outward movement of Irish citizens that came to define the fledgling state. These developments in turn shaped the pattern of crime and the state's response to law breakers.

FURTHER READING

Brewer, J. D., B. Lockhart and P. Rodgers. *Crime in Ireland, 1945–95: 'here be dragons'* (Oxford, 1997).

Conley, C. *Melancholy accidents: the meaning of violence in post-famine Ireland* (Lanham, MD, 1999).

Crossman, V. *Politics, law and order in nineteenth-century Ireland* (New York, 1996).

Donnelly, J. S. *Captain Rock: the Irish agrarian rebellion of 1821–1824* (Madison, WI, 2009).

Finnane, M. *Insanity and the insane in post-famine Ireland* (London, 1981).

Garnham, N. *The courts, crime and the criminal law in Ireland, 1692–1760* (Dublin, 1996).

Griffin, B. *The bulkies: police and crime in Belfast, 1800–1865* (Dublin, 1997).

Henry, B. *Dublin hanged: crime, law enforcement, and punishment in late eighteenth-century Dublin* (Blackrock, 1994).

Kilcommins, S., I. O'Donnell, E. O'Sullivan and B. Vaughan. *Crime, punishment and the search for order in Ireland* (Dublin, 2004).

McConville, S. *Irish political prisoners, 1848–1922: theatres of war* (New York, 2003).

McEvoy, K. *Paramilitary imprisonment in Northern Ireland: resistance, management and release* (Oxford, 2001).

McMahon, R. *Homicide in pre-famine and famine Ireland* (Liverpool, 2013).

McNiffe, L. *A history of the Garda Síochána* (Dublin, 1997).

Malcolm, E. *The Irish policeman, 1822–1922: a life* (Dublin, 2006).

Mulcahy, A. *Policing Northern Ireland: conflict, legitimacy and reform* (Cullompton, 2006).

Ó Longaigh, S. *Emergency law in independent Ireland, 1922–1948* (Dublin, 2006).

O'Sullivan, E. and I. O'Donnell. *Coercive confinement in Ireland: patients, prisoners and penitents* (Manchester, 2012).

Palmer, S. H. *Police and protest in England and Ireland, 1780–1850* (Cambridge, 1988).

Prior, P. *Madness and murder: gender, crime and mental disorder in nineteenth-century Ireland* (Dublin, 2008).

Townshend, C. *Political violence in Ireland: government and resistance since 1848* (Oxford, 1983).

Vaughan, W. E. *Murder trials in Ireland, 1836–1914* (Dublin, 2009).

23 Associational Life, Leisure and Identity since 1740

William Murphy

23.1. Introduction

At the end of April 1739 the trial began of Lord Santry, a leading member of Dublin's Hellfire Club. Nine months earlier when drunk at Palmerstown Fair, he had stabbed an unfortunate porter named Laughlin Murphy. Murphy died of his wounds: Santry was sentenced to death but received a reprieve from George II. Santry's actions and the publicity these attracted confirmed the notorious image and 'hastened the demise' of the club with which he was so closely associated. During its brief existence, the elite Dublin Hellfire Club had acquired a reputation that was irredeemable.[1]

While participation in associational life for the purposes of leisure would rarely result in such scandal again, it has remained vital. Writing of Britain during the modern period, R. J. Morris asserted that the establishment of voluntary associations – clubs and societies with defined rules and typically charging a membership fee – has been 'one major response to the problems posed by change and complexity'.[2] This is also true of Ireland, and in recent years it has been the subject of increased scholarly attention. As yet, however, this scholarship has scarcely scratched the surface of the range of clubs and societies or of the variety of their roles,[3] but we know enough about the subject of this chapter – associational forms of leisure, with an emphasis on sport – to state with

1 D. Ryan, 'The Dublin Hellfire Club', in J. Kelly and M. J. Powell (eds.), *Clubs and societies in eighteenth-century Ireland* (Dublin, 2010), 332–52.
2 R. J. Morris, 'Clubs, societies and associations', in F. M. L. Thompson, *The Cambridge social history of Britain 1750–1950* (Cambridge, 1990), 395.
3 J. Kelly and R. V. Comerford, 'Introduction', in Kelly and Comerford (eds.), *Associational culture in Ireland and abroad* (Dublin, 2010), 2.

certainty that between 1740 and the present day this phenomenon has consistently constituted a vibrant aspect of Irish life, reflecting and affecting the dynamics of identity formation and reformation across the period.

23.2.   1740–1840

In his influential study of clubs and societies, Peter Clark contended that by 1800 'British voluntary associations' had come of age' and that the English and Scottish, particularly urban-dwellers, lived in 'An Associational World'. In Ireland, on the other hand, he suggested, there existed a 'lower incidence of societies', a state of affairs he ascribed to 'lower levels of urbanization, the problematic state of the Irish economy in the later eighteenth century, the small size of the Protestant elite, and the importance of traditional forms of socializing and solidarity', including those associated with the Catholic Church.[4] In an edited collection, which was both inspired by and marks a response to Clark, James Kelly and Martyn Powell have marshalled an impressive overview of Irish associational life during the eighteenth century. They acknowledge that, when compared with England, 'the emergence of an associational life in Ireland was slow', but argue convincingly that associational life 'took off in the middle decades of the eighteenth century and matured speedily during the two decades 1780–1800'.[5]

Though there are no reliable statistics, it seems clear that a significant share (although certainly a minority) of the new clubs and societies established between 1740 and 1800 had a leisure activity as their primary purpose. These functions included dining, drinking, sporting, gambling, reading, debating, theatrics and music. It was not unusual that such clubs would have a secondary purpose, for example political or charitable. For a further and considerable proportion of these new associations, leisure activities (especially drinking and dining) appear to have taken up the greater part of members' time, even if their expressed purpose lay elsewhere: Powell has characterised these clubs as getting 'the business end of their proceedings over quickly to allow them time to concentrate on more sybaritic matters'.[6] Clark's observation that 'the drink interest' was the 'leading patron of societies'[7] provides one crucial reason why it can sometimes be difficult to distinguish clearly between those clubs and societies established for the purpose of promoting particular forms of leisure and those that used leisure as a means of attracting, maintaining and bonding their membership, though ultimately for other objectives. Toasting, a key activity for many clubs with drinking and dining at their

4 P. Clark, *British clubs and societies 1580–1800: the origins of an associational world* (Oxford, 2000), 138–9.

5 J. Kelly and M. J. Powell, 'Introduction', in Kelly and Powell, *Clubs and societies*, 17–35.

6 M. J. Powell, '"Beef, claret and communication": convivial clubs in the public sphere, 1750–1880', in Kelly and Powell, *Clubs and societies*, 353.

7 Clark, *British clubs and societies*, 225.

core, was often both intrinsically political and convivial, just as the concerts organised by a range of performing societies tended to be both philanthropic and entertaining in character.[8]

It is even more difficult to discern the place of conviviality amidst the hierarchy of motivations that underpinned the decisions of ordinary members (overwhelmingly men of means) to join particular clubs or societies. As each individual made his choice, he placed, consciously or subconsciously, the opportunity to eat well, consume alcohol and talk on the scales with other attractions – the lure of politics, the desire for intellectual development or other improvement, a punkish aspiration to reject convention or a Bullingdonesque confidence in flouting it, philanthropic visions, the aspiration to access a vocational or professional network, or the need for insurance in times of illness. Late in the century, certainly in Dublin and Belfast, his choices had multiplied. For example, he could join a range of dining clubs (sedate, somewhat rowdy or outrageously boisterous) depending on his tastes and nerve. In another manifestation of this tendency towards specialisation, dining clubs became places where lawyers or merchants or 'literati' gathered in exclusive groups to network, discuss shared interests, and engender or affirm a group identity.[9]

For Powell, the key motors of the growth in 'convivial' clubs and societies after 1750 were an increased 'number and range' of newspapers through which associations were promoted, a rise in the numbers of coffee houses, taverns and public houses at which associations met, and 'the intellectual justification provided by the Enlightenment' for indulging in pleasure.[10] Given that these were the optimum conditions, it is not surprising that such clubs were centred disproportionately and earlier in cities. Later in the century, larger provincial towns embraced the craze for joining but never to the same degree. In these places, individuals were attracted to association for the same mix of reasons as city dwellers, while they often desired, as David Fleming puts it, to 'demonstrate their gentility by aping current fashions emanating from the capital and elsewhere'.[11] In this way, 'clubs contributed to the dissemination of polite, anglicized modes of conduct throughout Ireland's provinces'.[12]

The boom of the late eighteenth century saw associational life involve the very elite of Irish society, but also a cohort of the professional, business and artisanal classes. The associational expression that achieved widest and deepest penetration in Ireland at that

8 M. J. Powell, 'The Society of Free Citizens and other popular political clubs, 1749–89', in Kelly and Powell, *Clubs and societies*, 248–55; D. Dickson, *Dublin: the making of a capital* (London, 2014), 157.
9 J. Kelly, 'Annuity societies in eighteenth-century Ireland', J. Kelly, 'The Bar Club, 1787–1793: a dining club case study' and E. Magennis, 'Clubs and societies in eighteenth-century Belfast', in Kelly and Powell, *Clubs and societies*, 126–37, 373–91, 466–83.
10 Powell, 'Beef, claret and communication', 353.
11 D. A. Fleming, 'Clubs and societies in eighteenth century Munster', in Kelly and Powell, *Clubs and societies*, 446.
12 Powell, 'Beef, claret and communication', 365.

time was freemasonry, with Petri Mirala estimating that there were at least 30,000 freemasons in the country by 1800. Joining a lodge, or indeed any other club, and participating in its activities did require money, however, ensuring that many – even in urban centres – could not partake. Though comparatively democratic, membership of the freemasons was 'indicative of economic position and respectability'. Membership was seen as a mechanism and marker of social advancement, yet not all freemasons were equal: 'lodges tended to cater for particular social classes or groups'.[13] This was true of the associational world in general: as David Dickson noted, 'there was always a hierar chy in the fluid world of masculine sociability, whether in dining club, masonic lodge, charitable society or gambling den'.[14] The point about a club, of course, is that who is out matters every bit as much as who is in, and the determining factor was likely to be a subtle shade of status, class or respectability. As pubs and taverns became the home to a greater number of more democratic associations towards the end of the eighteenth century, the elite, it seems, began to retreat into more private spaces by acquiring clubhouses. The very durable Kildare Street Club, which was established in Dublin in 1782, is an example of this, while so too is the less enduring Newtown Pery Club which survived a matter of months in Limerick as 1788 became 1789. This trend would continue into the nineteenth century with St Stephen's Green becoming the Dublin locus of such gentlemen's clubs between 1839 and 1850.[15]

This eighteenth-century clubbable world was very male, encouraging homosocial leisure. The presence of women at certain social events might be welcome (even necessary), but their opportunities to join or lead clubs and societies were severely restricted. Some did exist. A convivial society with a charitable rationale was more likely to be open to women, as were some of the more staid dining clubs. For thirty years or so after 1760, a fashion for oyster clubs took hold in many of Ireland's urban centres and these do seem to have welcomed both men and women.[16] During the eighteenth century this would also remain a disproportionately Protestant world. Kelly and Powell observe that 'urban-dwelling Protestants' dominated and benefited most from associations, but they also caution that these were not 'a solely Protestant' phenomenon. Several chapters in their collection discuss the substantial though minority Catholic element in the freemasons, at least until the 1810s, while acknowledging that Catholics and Protestants were often to be found in separate lodges.[17]

---

13 P. Mirala, 'Masonic sociability and its limitations: the case of Ireland', in Kelly and Powell, *Clubs and societies*, 323.
14 Dickson, *Dublin*, 155.
15 Powell, 'Beef, claret and communication', 371; Fleming, 'Munster', 444; D. McCabe, *St Stephen's Green, Dublin 1660–1875* (Dublin, 2011), 301–2.
16 Powell, 'Beef, claret and communication', 368–70; Fleming, 'Munster', 438.
17 Mirala, 'Masonic sociability and its limitations', 325–30; Fleming, 'Munster', 436.

The second half of the eighteenth century also saw associational forms begin to give structures to some elite sport. Hunt clubs – concerned primarily with fox hunting – began to emerge from as early as the 1730s and 'achieved a national distribution' during the 1770s. Through the pooling of resources, these clubs facilitated the expansion of what was an expensive leisure activity that taxed the means of even the very well-to-do. Hunt clubs were conspicuous displays of privilege, and in response 'stopping the hunt' entered the vernacular of Irish rural protest during the second half of the nineteenth century.[18] The Jockey Club (from the 1750s), followed by the Turf Club (from the 1780s), promoted horse racing, again an elite pursuit, although spectators often formed large crowds of diverse social backgrounds. From 1790 the Turf Club aspired to being the national regulator of horse racing, a status it would achieve over time.[19] Paul Rouse has noted the existence of other elite sports clubs prior to 1800 – including a racket club in Cork and a shooting club in Dublin founded in the 1770s – prompting him to speculate that 'most likely there were other clubs in other sports that flowered briefly only to disappear and are now lost to history'.[20]

If clubs made an irrefutable contribution to the development of hunting and horse racing, then much sport remained outside the associational realm. Further, it is tempting to speculate that one of the factors influencing a decline in support among the respectable classes for the sport of cockfighting was the counter-attraction that clubs and societies constituted. It is noticeable that the pattern of cockfighting's apparent retreat towards the status of thoroughly proletarian pastime, as identified by James Kelly – a retreat that he suggests began in Dublin in the 1760s and sped up rapidly in the 1780s – is mirrored by the rise of clubs and societies. Leisure time is not fixed but it is finite, and the rise of one form of leisure, or a particular sporting craze, very often takes place at the expense of a previously popular activity. Of course, as Kelly has pointed out, cockfighting faced other challenges in this period, including attacks from those who characterised it as disreputable because of the gambling that surrounded it and, increasingly, from those who insisted that it was cruel. Notwithstanding these developments, and the introduction from 1837 of laws banning the activity, cockfighting proved remarkably resilient.[21]

---

18 J. Kelly, *Sport in Ireland 1600–1840* (Dublin, 2014), 124–56; M. J. Powell, 'Hunting clubs and societies', in Kelly and Powell, *Clubs and societies*, 392–408; L. P. Curtis Jr, 'Stopping the hunt, 1881–1882: an aspect of the Irish Land War', in C. E. Philpin (ed.), *Nationalism and popular protest in Ireland* (Cambridge, 1987), 349–402.
19 F. D'Arcy, *Horses, lords and racing men* (Kildare, 1991); Kelly, *Sport in Ireland*, 29–123.
20 P. Rouse, *Sport and Ireland: a history* (Oxford, 2015), 68. This is a key work, combining original research and synthesis.
21 Kelly, *Sport in Ireland*, 157–206; N. Garnham, 'The survival of popular blood sports in Victorian Ulster', *Proceedings of the Royal Irish Academy. Section C*, 107 (2007), 107–26.

23.3.   1840–1910

Despite the advance of associations during the eighteenth century, in 1800 the over-whelming preponderance of leisure continued to take place outside that context. In the century that followed, however, more and more of the population's leisure lives would be channelled into and given shape by clubs and societies. Perhaps no aspect of leisure illustrates this so clearly as sport. It is in the sport of cricket that the remarkable trans-formation that is sometimes referred to as 'the sporting revolution' first became evident in Ireland. In the twenty years prior to the Great Famine, cricket clubs were formed in Dublin, Belfast and a few provincial towns, among them Carlow, Kilkenny, Ballinasloe, Lisburn and Carrick-on-Suir. From the late 1850s, however, and for about two dec-ades, cricket grew and extended its social base until it became the most popular sport in Ireland. A remarkable boom in club formation underpinned this. A correspondent to the *Nenagh Guardian* had become only a little carried away when he wrote in July 1873 that cricket 'may well be called a Republican game for it is a great leveller of rank. We have seen, and see, every day farmers' sons invited to form a team and they con-stitute the true element of the club.'[22] Many of the clubs did not last long, and cricket's pre-eminence passed, but the growth of team sports associated with clubs had firmly taken hold.

It would be 1923 before cricket in Ireland established a national governing body. In contrast, the promoters of the football codes of rugby and soccer were much quicker to take that developmental leap. The story of rugby in Ireland begins in Trinity College Dublin in the mid-1850s. Clubs began to accumulate from the mid-1860s and by January 1875 there were sufficient to form rival governing bodies: the Irish Football Union, based in Dublin, and the Northern Football Union of Ireland, centred on Belfast. This very precocious split ended with the formation of the Irish Rugby Football Union in 1879. In 1885 twenty-six clubs affiliated to that body, climbing to seventy-six by 1910. This increase represented a rise not simply in the number of active clubs but also in the number of those that acknowledged the advantages of being bound into a national structure: most obviously access to regional and national competitions held under shared rules. The roots of organised association football in Ireland lie in Belfast. There Cliftonville FC was founded in 1879. The establishment of the Irish Football Association followed quite quickly in November 1880 and seven clubs affiliated to that body in 1881. In 1900 the number of such clubs was 110 and in 1910 it was 420. As Rouse has emphasised, although the social and economic conditions on the islands differed, the development of Irish football was intimately related to the 'football revolu-tion' in England and Scotland, and borrowed its model of development from England

---

22 P. Bracken, *"Foreign and fantastic field sports": cricket in County Tipperary* (Thurles, 2004), 56.

where the Football Association was formed in 1863 and the Rugby Football Union followed in 1871.[23]

A primary function of the new national governing bodies, in both sports, was the selection of teams for international competition. In rugby Ireland's first international opposition was England in 1875, while in soccer it was England again, in 1882. Such competition helped to nurture national identity but, as the great majority of matches were against England, Scotland or Wales, it did so while fostering bonds within the United Kingdom. Neal Garnham has further suggested that tours by Canadian, South African and New Zealand rugby sides during the first decade of the twentieth century were viewed, at least in the Belfast press, as 'fostering imperial cohesion'.[24]

For a significant body of its promoters, the Gaelic Athletic Association (GAA) (established in 1884) was a bulwark against these 'foreign' sports and the imperial contagion they were alleged to carry. As T. F. O'Sullivan, an active GAA official, early historian of the association and ardent nationalist, wrote, 'It [the GAA] has helped not only to develop Irish bone and muscle, but to foster a spirit of earnest nationality in the hearts of the rising generation, and it has been a means of saving thousands of young Irishmen from becoming mere West Britons.'[25] This informing ideology certainly brought some members to the 875 clubs that Marcus de Búrca estimated were affiliated to the association by 1890.[26] Further, nationalism remained intrinsic to the association's identity during a collapse and recovery that followed over the succeeding decades. None the less, the GAA's attractions were not confined to facilitating a collective impulse to assert an Irish-Ireland identity. The association's clubs offered their members a range of sports, including athletics, hurling and Gaelic football. They held these sports on a day that was convenient for the Catholic population, Sunday: most other sports organisations, influenced by sabbatarianism, held their games on Saturday. By facilitating Sunday travel the GAA legitimated Sunday drinking, while joining a GAA club was, it seems, cheaper than most of the sporting alternatives.[27]

Crucially, in its first year the GAA had to win a battle for the control of Irish athletics with the Irish Amateur Athletic Association (IAAA), which was aligned to the Amateur Athletics Association (AAA) in England and used its rules. As part of that struggle the GAA identified itself as an association for the labouring man as distinct

23 L. O'Callaghan, *Rugby in Munster: a social and cultural history* (Cork, 2011), 13–28; N. Garnham, *Association football and society in pre-partition Ireland* (Belfast, 2004), 43; Rouse, *Sport and Ireland*, 123–33.

24 N. Garnham, 'Rugby's imperial connections: domestic politics and colonial tours to Ireland before 1914', in A. Bairner (ed.), *Sport and the Irish: histories, identities, issues* (Dublin, 2005), 44–52.

25 T. F. O'Sullivan, *The story of the GAA* (Dublin, 1916), 1.

26 M. de Búrca, *The GAA: a history* (2nd edn, Dublin, 2000), 41–2.

27 M. Cronin, 'Enshrined in blood: the naming of Gaelic athletic grounds and clubs', *The Sports Historian*, 18, 1 (1998), 90–104; N. Garnham, 'Accounting for the early success of the Gaelic Athletic Association', *Irish Historical Studies*, 34, 133 (2004), 65–78.

from the IAAA, which confined its welcome to the gentleman amateur.[28] As Tom Hunt has demonstrated, one should be careful not to be too credulous of the GAA's claims in this regard,[29] but it did succeed in positioning itself as the association of the common man in a sporting world that remained remarkably middle class in 1910.

The first evidence in associational form of a fashion for archery amongst the elites of Ireland's landed estates is the Meath Archers, instituted sometime around 1833. Archery reached a peak of popularity in the 1850s and 1860s when at least thirty-two clubs were in existence. Tennis displaced it from the Big House lawn during the 1870s. That game slowly extended its reach beyond the demesne walls between 1875 and 1889. During that time forty-five tennis clubs were founded, and then in five remarkable years (1890–4) fifty-five more were established. In these spaces, members from the business and professional elites of provincial towns and city suburbs (and their wives and children) joined men and women of the landed class. Growing in parallel, golf, like tennis, 'provided a social space for the expression of the values and interests of the ascendant middle classes'. Seven clubs, including Belfast Golf Club, which was the first, were established during the 1880s. During the 1890s, 116 more followed, and all of these, through the charging of fees and insistence upon defined social and sporting codes, reinforced for their members a 'sense of privilege and respectability'. This informed the attitudes of land activists, suffragists and nationalists all of whom vandalised golf clubs during the late nineteenth and early twentieth century. The growing middle classes were also quick to transform new technologies into forms of associational leisure. Beginning in 1869, cycling clubs began to appear in Ireland. Their membership was drawn from the professional middle class and they were proud of it. The *Irish Cyclist* boasted in 1890 that cycling in Ireland was 'fashionable' as it was the pastime of academics, doctors, barristers, solicitors and clergymen. The even more elite Irish Automobile Club was founded in 1901.[30]

The emergence of very distinct – sometimes mutually antagonistic – rugby cultures in two key centres of the game is at the heart of Liam O'Callaghan's analysis of *Rugby in Munster*. Cork's rugby – with its predominantly clubbable, suburban and middle-class atmosphere rooted in privileged education and professional networks – was quite typical of the sport in Ireland. In Limerick, on the other hand, rugby developed along a very different trajectory. From the 1880s, Garryowen FC

28 Rouse, *Sport and Ireland*, 168–71, 176–7.

29 T. Hunt, 'The GAA: social structure and associated clubs', in M. Cronin, W. Murphy and P. Rouse (eds.), *The Gaelic Athletic Association 1884–2009* (Dublin, 2009), 183–203.

30 B. Griffin, 'The Big House at play: archery as an elite pursuit from the 1830s to the 1870s', in C. O'Neill (ed.), *Irish elites in the nineteenth century* (Dublin, 2013), 153–71; R. Higgins, '"The hallmark of pluperfect respectability": the early development of golf in Irish society', *Éire-Ireland*, 48, 1–2 (2013), 15–31; B. Griffin, *Cycling in Victorian Ireland* (Stroud, 2006), 55; C. F. Smith, *The history of the Royal Irish Automobile Club 1901–91* (Dublin, 1994), 24; T. Hunt, *Sport and society in Victorian Ireland: the case of Westmeath* (Cork, 2007), 75–92.

Figure 23.1 Waterford Bicycle Club, 1901.
Image from the Wiltshire Collection. Courtesy of the National Library of Ireland.

became the standard bearers of that city's civic pride at senior club level, while fostering a popular and vigorous brand of the game centred on inner-city communities and organised through independent junior clubs, which competed fiercely for the pride of their place in Sunday matches that were contested in front of comparatively large and partisan crowds. Eventually, some of these junior clubs – most famously Shannon and Young Munster – outgrew the patronage of Garryowen, which was both benevolent and parasitic, and Sunday rugby became less important, but that structure, O'Callaghan convincingly argues, was the motor that generated the distinct populist character of Limerick rugby.[31] The first promoters and players of association football in Ireland were middle class, but by 1900, 'perhaps with some justification, the press in both Dublin and Belfast could refer to it as the "game of the masses and not the classes"', while football clubs in Belfast quickly divided along confessional lines.[32]

31 O'Callaghan, *Rugby in Munster*, 65–110.
32 Garnham, *Association football*, 66–8.

The rapid, albeit belated, maturing of Irish sport history has ensured that we can construct a reasonably nuanced picture of sport's development. Other aspects of leisure and the connected associational outcomes have been less well served by historians of nineteenth-century Ireland. If the study of the changing face of leisure was an important aspect of British historians' response to the new social history during the 1970s, this proved markedly less so in the case of Ireland. The comparative lack of urbanisation and industrialisation ensured, it seems, that writing a history of the construction of class identities through leisure was a less pressing matter for historians of Ireland, although there have been those, like R. V. Comerford and, later, Maura Cronin, who have recognised the challenge. In 1994, Cronin wrote that, 'one can hardly stress too much the importance of … popular social activity as a shaper of popular political identities'.[33]

Cronin highlighted the importance of brass bands as an expression of urban working-class culture in Cork from the middle of the nineteenth century. Other scholars of the same city, as well as students of Limerick and Belfast, have demonstrated that bands were expressions not just of class and political identities for their male membership, but also of territoriality.[34] Catch and glee clubs had been a significant element of the new middle-class associational culture of the second half of the eighteenth century.[35] During the second half of the nineteenth century, with rising levels of education, 'music literacy' became 'commonplace in middle-class homes'[36] and this was reflected in a proliferation of musical societies in the cities. These facilitated middle-class access to the practice and performance of classical music and opera while being forums for the self-conscious display of taste. Aloys Fleischmann has pointed out that in Dublin, no fewer than 'twenty-two different music societies, chiefly choral groups, came into existence between 1841 and 1867' and Ita Beausang states that the records of 'approximately sixty musical societies' exist for the city in the second half of the century. The emergence of such societies responded to international fashions in music. Sometimes this occurred with great speed and sometimes following a delay, as in the case of Belfast's embrace of operetta in the 1890s with the formation of the Belfast Amateur Operatic

---

33 R. V. Comerford, 'Patriotism as pastime: the appeal of Fenianism in the mid-1860s', *Irish Historical Studies*, 22, 87 (1981), 241, 246; M. Cronin, *Country, class or craft? The politicisation of the skilled artisan in nineteenth-century Cork* (Cork, 1994), 148.

34 F. Lane, 'Music and violence in working class Cork: the "Band nuisance", 1879–1882', *Saothar*, 24 (1999), 17–31; J. Borgonovo, 'Politics as leisure: brass bands in Cork, 1845–1918', in L. Lane and W. Murphy (eds.), *Leisure and the Irish in the nineteenth century* (Liverpool, 2016), 23–40; J. McGrath, 'An urban community: St Mary's parish, Limerick, and the social role of sporting and musical clubs, 1885–1905', in Kelly and Comerford, *Associational culture*, 127–39; G. Ramsey, 'Band practice: class, taste and identity in Ulster loyalist flute bands', *Ethnomusicology Ireland*, 1 (2011), 1–19.

35 E. Murphy, 'Catch and glee clubs', in H. White and B. Boydell (eds.), *The encyclopedia of music in Ireland, vol. I: A–J* (Dublin, 2013), 171.

36 Dickson, *Dublin*, 403.

Society (1892) and the Ulster Amateur Operatic Society (1894). The effects of cultural nationalism are also to be seen with, for instance, the establishment of clubs in Dublin, Limerick and Cork between 1900 and 1904.[37]

Similarly, the late eighteenth century had seen the beginnings of book clubs and reading societies, especially in north-east Ulster where literacy was at its highest. These had education and improvement as explicit rationales but the opportunities for leisure and sociability also attracted members.[38] Reading rooms were the nineteenth-century descendants of these, providing both a suitable space and reading materials for many of the newly literate who would otherwise not have had the means to pursue the pleasures of the books, periodicals and newspapers which were then being published in ever greater quantities. Nineteenth-century nationalists proved particularly adept at using print culture, and reading rooms and literary societies, to promote their ideas. The Repeal Reading Rooms of the 1840s are perhaps the most famous example of this.[39]

After 1838 the popular temperance movement, led by Fr Theobald Mathew, made extensive use of reading rooms, brass bands and choral groups to promote its cause.[40] Temperance societies are just one example of a range of associational movements that emerged with the aim of improving or policing the leisure of others. Bands and reading rooms provided the movement with a means of promoting the cause, an associational focus for members, and alternative 'rational' forms of entertainment to the public house. Examining Britain in the 1890s, R. J. Morris wrote of 'the bustle and activity of dozens of clubs, societies, associations and fellowships which gathered in the penumbra of churches and chapels … as the middle classes turned one more time to the compulsive leisure activity, bringing the working classes to church'.[41] Founded in 1883 and arriving in Ireland in 1888, the Boys' Brigade was a notable manifestation of this tendency. Influenced by the ideology of athleticism, the leadership of the Boys' Brigade in Ireland pursued their aim of 'the advancement of Christ's kingdom among boys' by enabling and encouraging working-class Protestant adolescents to play football with a

37 A. Fleischmann, 'Music and society, 1850–1921', in W. E. Vaughan (ed.), *A new history of Ireland, vol. VI: Ireland under the Union 1870–1921* (Oxford, 1989), 500–22; I. Beausang, 'Dublin musical societies 1850–1900' and M. McCarthy, 'The transmission of music and the formation of national identity in early-twentieth-century Ireland', in P. F. Devine and H. White (eds.), *Irish musical studies V* (Dublin, 1996), 156–7, 169–78.

38 J. Archbold, 'Book clubs and reading societies in the late eighteenth century', in Kelly and Powell, *Clubs and societies*, 138–62.

39 P. Townend, '"Academies of nationality": the reading room and Irish national movements, 1838–1905', in L. W. McBride (ed.), *Reading Irish histories* (Dublin, 2003), 19–39; M. Legg, 'Libraries' and R. Higgins, 'The Nation Reading Rooms', in J. H. Murphy (ed.), *The Oxford history of the Irish book, vol. IV: The Irish book in English, 1800–1891* (Oxford, 2011), 243–61, 262–73.

40 P. Townend, *Father Mathew, temperance and Irish identity* (Dublin, 2002), 124–6; M. McHale, 'Singing and sobriety: music and the temperance movement in Ireland, 1838–43', in M. Murphy and J. Smaczny (eds.), *Irish musical studies IX: Music in nineteenth-century Ireland* (Dublin, 2007), 166–86.

41 Morris, 'Clubs, societies and associations', 420.

moral purpose. At the same time vigilance and social purity associations were becoming active in Irish cities.[42] From the 1890s, the Gaelic League stimulated enthusiasm for its language revival project using leisure: 'the staples of branch meetings were relatively innocuous, simple pastimes'. Further, a constituency within the Gaelic League was determined to fill a social vacuum that had too often, in their view, been occupied by alcohol, and through this they hoped to foster a 'respectable' Irish population that was demonstrably capable of self-governance.[43]

23.4. 1910–2000

The years 1910 to 1945 were ones of state creation and consolidation. They were also years of devastating international conflict. These contexts had profound implications for associational leisure on the island. There is little doubt that a sporting scene that was already inflected by the politics of nationality and religion became more so during these years. During the Irish Revolution, crowd violence erupted at soccer grounds in Belfast when Linfield played Belfast Celtic. The GAA had introduced, removed and reintroduced politically motivated prohibitions (banning members playing 'foreign' games and excluding particular groups associated with the British state in Ireland) since the late 1880s. These rules were augmented and the commitment to them hardened during the revolution as separatists sought to impose stark choices upon a society and sporting scene that was sometimes too fluid for their tastes.[44] The early months of 1919 saw the return of 'stopping the hunt' as a phenomenon. Then, separatists across rural Ireland used the tactic to define and target their enemies: the British army, magistrates, the '"English" Irishmen' of the Ascendancy and shoneen classes, and the Irish Party. Yet, in this case it was also evident that a gap existed between the complicated reality and the rhetoric of cultural politics: for instance, that most confounding of individuals – a Sinn Féin MP who rode with the hunt – existed.[45]

The partitioning of the island saw the governing association or union of several sports – including cycling, athletics and soccer – split and then descend into decades

42 B. Power, 'The functions of association football in the Boys' Brigade in Ireland, 1888–1914', in Lane and Murphy, *Leisure and the Irish*, 41–60; K. Mullin, 'Irish chastity? British social purity associations and the Irish Free State', in Kelly and Comerford, *Associational culture*, 141–54.
43 T. G. MacMahon, *Grand opportunity: the Gaelic revival and Irish society, 1893–1910* (Syracuse, 2008), 127, 132–40.
44 Garnham, *Association football*, 125–7; P. Rouse, 'The politics of culture and sport in Ireland: a history of the GAA ban on foreign games 1884–1971, part 1: 1884–1921', *International Journal of the History of Sport*, 10, 3 (1993), 333–60; R. McElligott, '1916 and the radicalization of the Gaelic Athletic Association', *Éire-Ireland*, 48, 1–2 (2013), 95–111.
45 W. Murphy, 'Sport in a time of revolution: Sinn Féin and the hunt in Ireland, 1919', *Éire-Ireland*, 48, 1–2 (2013), 112–47.

of wrangling about recognition, nomenclature and jurisdiction.[46] This did not prevent competition at a local level between clubs, for instance in east Donegal and west
Derry,[47] while the GAA and the IRFU remained intact. As the GAA served a nationalist
polity north and south of the border there was never any likelihood that a constituency
demanding a split would emerge. The IRFU, on the other hand, decided to respond to
the new dispensation by variously trying (not always with success) to accommodate
and elide the political differences that existed within its playing ranks. In this regard,
as O'Callaghan has pointed out, these differences were far less marked among senior
officials within the IRFU: at that level, on both sides of the border, 'a Protestant privileged minority' still held sway. Their fellow feeling and perhaps, as Rouse has suggested,
a shared memory amongst the rugby communities north and south of the devastation
wrought upon their membership by the First World War may have discouraged a split.[48]

In the Irish Free State, 'the ban', as the GAA's prohibitions were collectively known,
remained in place and came 'to epitomize the introspective homogeneity of culture and
society' in the years after independence. They constituted a crude attempt by influential ideologues within the association to insist that separate 'Gaelic' and 'West British'
sporting spheres existed, a powerful and influential fantasy that did affect behaviour
but never accurately represented the memberships of the GAA or the targeted sports
of rugby, soccer, hockey and cricket. Further, the GAA sought to foster a hierarchy of
associational leisure by seeking a privileged relationship with the new state. With this
purpose in mind, the association retrospectively exaggerated its role in the creation
of the new state, and the political elites responded. For example, unlike other sports,
the GAA was exempted from income tax in 1927 and from entertainment tax in 1932,
while a GAA record earned a candidate for the Garda Síochána extra points. This state
of affairs was, unsurprisingly, resented by sportspeople not affiliated to the GAA, but
the extent to which it affected the growth of other sports is not at all clear. Further, the
pursuit of 'the ban' ideology could both divide the GAA and bring it into conflict with
the state, as when the association removed the then president of Ireland, Douglas Hyde,
as a patron in December 1938 because he had attended an international soccer match
at Dalymount Park in November.

In 1967, in a book called *The steadfast rule*, Brendan Mac Lua set out to defend
the ban on GAA members playing or attending 'foreign' games from the attacks of
an increasingly vocal group within the association. Breandán Ó hEithir described the

46 P. Griffin, *The politics of Irish athletics 1850–1990* (Ballinamore, 1990); K. Howard, 'Competitive sports: the territorial politics of Irish cycling', in J. Coakley and L. O'Dowd (eds.), *Crossing the border: new relationships between
Northern Ireland and the Republic of Ireland* (Dublin, 2007), 227–44; C. Moore, *The Irish soccer split* (Cork, 2015).
47 C. Curran, *The development of sport in Donegal, 1880–1935* (Cork, 2015), 49.
48 L. O'Callaghan, 'Rugby football and identity politics in Free State Ireland', *Éire-Ireland*, 48, 1–2 (2013), 158–62;
Rouse, *Sport and Ireland*, 269.

experience of reading it as 'rather like entering the caves at Mitchelstown to find men dressed in bearskins painting little pictures on the walls' and, despite Mac Lua's efforts, the GAA removed those bans in 1971. By then the ban, which had always met with a degree of quiet defiance, had been rendered ridiculous in the eyes of the great majority of GAA members who, since the arrival of television, had with pleasure watched soccer and rugby in the privacy of their own living rooms. In addition, the rhetoric that once sustained the ban had come to sound insupportably insular and old-fashioned.[49] As such, the removal of the ban had a parallel in the relaxation in 1967 of the Republic's censorship laws: laws which had been promoted by various Catholic Action and vigilance societies in the years immediately preceding and succeeding Irish independence.

The removal of the ban did not result in the destruction of the GAA, as some of its defenders had feared, but it does mark the moment (in the Republic of Ireland) when associational identities in the arena of sport became more openly fluid. By the end of the century, although each of the major team sports continued to compete for loyalty, to have exclusive adherents and to retain particular (often class-inflected) identities, it was commonplace that individuals would, without a thought, hold memberships in two or more. Indeed, sport has come to be seen as one of the more effective facilitators of integration rather than as a bulwark of division. In recent years, in the context of considerable inward migration, the Office for the Promotion of Migrant Integration has identified sport clubs as key mechanisms for the promotion of inclusion, and the sports organisations, notably the GAA, FAI and Irish Amateur Boxing Association, appear to have embraced this role.[50]

Membership of sports clubs in the Republic had grown steadily in the middle of the twentieth century. Although the size of the overall population of Ireland was stagnant and worse during this period, the steady urbanisation and suburbanisation of the population contributed to this development as new clubs emerged to serve growing and new population centres.[51] This growth was not restricted to sports clubs. Since the nineteenth century children and youth had been a focus for associational activity and this gathered pace during the twentieth century. The Boy Scout and Girl Guide movements arrived in Ireland in 1911, followed by the establishment of the Catholic Boy Scouts and Catholic Girl Guides in 1927. In 1931 the new youth hostel association, An Óige, had two hostels and 250 members. By 1981 these figures had steadily

---

49 Rouse, 'The politics of culture and sport', 359; O'Callaghan, *Rugby in Munster*, 141–77; O'Callaghan, 'Rugby football and identity politics', 153–6; C. McCabe, 'Football Sports Weekly and Irish soccer, 1925–1928', *Media History*, 17, 2 (2011), 147–58; C. Moore, *The GAA v. Douglas Hyde: the removal of Ireland's first president as GAA patron* (Cork, 2012); D. Toms, *Soccer in Munster: a social history, 1877–1937* (Cork, 2015).

50 See www.integration.ie/website/omi/omiwebv6.nsf/page/aboutus-2012update-national-en, accessed 16 June 2015.

51 Rouse, *Sport and Ireland*, 280–7; W. Nolan (ed.), *The Gaelic Athletic Association in Dublin 1884–2000, vol. II: 1960–2000* (Dublin, 2005), 522–3.

Figure 23.2 Boy Scouts, Strabane, 1911.
Courtesy of the Deputy Keeper of the Records, Public Record Office Northern Ireland, D1403/2/24/A.

climbed to more than 28,000 members and fifty hostels.[52] 'Youth' clubs had existed since the mid-nineteenth century as rational recreationists attempted to provide alternatives to the perceived dangers of urban leisure. For example, the establishment of the Young Men's Christian Association (YMCA) in 1844 was followed by the founding, in Limerick in 1848, of the Catholic Young Men's Society.[53] And again during the 1960s, as Carole Holohan has shown, 'growing concerns about how Irish youth spent their leisure time' – in particular young urban males – created a renewed focus on youth clubs, albeit sometimes with limited success.[54]

Club membership in the Republic of Ireland remained high at the beginning of the new millennium. Research conducted in 2003 suggested that 40 per cent of adult men were then members of sports clubs. Those who were wealthier and had higher educational attainments remained, however, much more likely to be a member of a club.

52 M. Curtis, *A challenge to democracy: militant Catholicism in modern Ireland* (Dublin, 2010), 65; T. Trench, *Fifty years young: the story of An Óige* (Dublin, 1981), 132.
53 J. H. Murphy, 'Richard Baptist O'Brien', in J. McGuire and J. Quinn (eds.), *Dictionary of Irish biography* (Cambridge, 2009).
54 C. Holohan, 'A powerful antidote? Catholic youth clubs in the sixties', in C. Cox and S. Riordan (eds.), *Adolescence in modern Irish history* (Houndmills, 2015), 176–98.

Notably, only 20 per cent of adult women were members of a sports club.[55] Women remain under-represented not only as members but as 'coaches, officials and decision makers'.[56] The progress they have made in this regard has been slow and often in the teeth of resistance informed by prevailing ideas as to what was appropriate behaviour and conceptions of the female body. Again class mattered. The sight of women riding with the hunt club became more common in the second half of the nineteenth century. Then, in the final years of that century and the early years of the twentieth, middle-class women achieved some access to clubs that promoted genteel suburban pursuits, for example tennis and croquet clubs. In the mid-1880s cycling clubs began to accept female members and the Nenagh Ladies' Cycling Club became the first all-female such club in 1888. The Irish Ladies' Hockey Union followed in 1894 and An Cumann Camógaíochta in 1905. Women also achieved access to golf. The Irish Ladies' Golf Union was established in 1893, although deep into the twentieth century women were denied membership or had access to a restricted form of membership at many golf clubs. Female participation in athletics became more common during the middle of the twentieth century, and the final decades witnessed further change with growing participation rates, club numbers and public profiles for sports such as women's Gaelic football, soccer and rugby.[57]

Writing in 1993, John Sugden and Alan Bairner came to the 'pessimistic conclusion that sport and leisure in Northern Ireland are deeply implicated in the politics of sectarian division'.[58] The outbreak of 'the Troubles' in Northern Ireland coincided with growing liberalism in the southern state, petrifying sporting choices north of the border even as they became more fluid in the south. There is some evidence that since the mid-1990s sport may have become a less divided sphere in Northern Ireland and that sports clubs have begun to facilitate to a greater extent cross-community interaction, but this should not be overstated.

If the GAA occupied a privileged position within the culture of the southern state, then in the aftermath of partition it was regarded with suspicion by the authorities in Northern Ireland as a sporting association supported exclusively by the 'disloyal' Catholic minority and one which retained (until 2001) a ban on members of the RUC and the British army.[59] The fact that the GAA continued to carry such weight in the matter of national identity politics for many of its northern members also tended to

55 The Irish Sports Council, *Ballpark figures: key research for Irish sports policy* (Dublin, 2008), 18.

56 K. Liston, 'Some reflections on women's sports in Ireland', in Bairner, *Sport and the Irish*, 223.

57 B. Griffin, 'Cycling and gender in Victorian Ireland', *Éire-Ireland*, 41, 1–2 (2006), 213–41; R. Nic Congáil, '"Looking on for centuries from the sideline": Gaelic feminism and the rise of camogie', *Éire-Ireland*, 48, 1–2 (2013), 168–90; M. Ó hÓgartaigh, 'Internal tamponage, hockey parturition and mixed athletics in Ireland in the 1930s, '40s and '50s', *Ríocht na Midhe*, 19 (2008), 215–22; Rouse, *Ireland and Sport*, 198–205.

58 J. Sugden and A. Bairner (eds.), *Sport, sectarianism and society in a divided Ireland* (London, 1993), 129.

59 D. Hassan, 'The GAA in Ulster', in Cronin *et al.*, *The Gaelic Athletic Association*, 77–91.

open up divisions between the GAA in Northern Ireland and the GAA elsewhere on the island over the past forty years. This was true in general, but particularly at times of crisis such as the hunger strikes of 1980 and 1981 when northern members used the GAA to express their sympathy or support for the hunger strikers while the majority of the southern leadership and membership of the organisation attempted to keep the GAA outside political controversy. Since the peace process of the mid-1990s, partly as a consequence of the relaxation of the ban on the Police Service of Northern Ireland (PSNI) and British army, perceptions of the GAA amongst unionist elites, and probably within the unionist community more broadly, have shifted. In October 2013, Peter Robinson, the First Minister of the Northern Ireland Assembly, gave a speech at an event celebrating the GAA's role in the peace process. During it he acknowledged, 'Not so many years ago, it would have been unimaginable that I would have been invited to speak at an event of this kind – or that I would have accepted.'[60] None the less, joining a GAA club remains unimaginable for the overwhelming majority of northern unionists or loyalists.

For much of the post-partition period, rugby clubs within Northern Ireland were a predominantly, if never an exclusively, Protestant terrain. This has been changing during recent decades, in part as a consequence of the peace process, but just as importantly as a result of the growing popularity of rugby with the success of Irish provinces (including Ulster) in the aftermath of the sport's professionalisation and also the growth of the Catholic middle class in Northern Ireland. This shift has probably been eased by the fact that an all-island team competes at international level. None the less, 'Protestant' schools remain the key nurseries of rugby club members in Northern Ireland. For many of those club members the existence of the all-island union and team has facilitated the playing out of quite complex identity politics, providing a space where the identities of Ulsterman, unionist, British and Irish can co-exist, at least some of the time.[61]

Association football clubs in Northern Ireland have drawn and still draw adherents from both sides of the confessional divide, but, as had been the case prior to partition, Catholics typically supported identifiably 'Catholic' clubs and Protestants supported 'Protestant' clubs. Indeed, Bairner is correct when he notes that while 'soccer has brought members of the two communities together on the field and the terraces', it has frequently 'exacerbated rather than improved intercommunity relations'. In the semi-professional Irish League, Catholics do play for 'Protestant' clubs and vice versa, but this has not, in general, shifted the sectarian identities of the clubs. For some

---

60 See www.thejournal.ie/northern-ireland-peace-1135347-Oct2013/, accessed 14 March 2016.
61 A. Bairner, 'Political unionism and sporting nationalism: an examination of the relationship between sport and national identity within the Ulster unionist tradition', *Identities*, 10, 4 (2003), 528–30; J. Tuck, 'Rugby union and national identity politics', in Bairner, *Sport and the Irish*, 105–22.

considerable years, and related to the heightened tensions generated by the Troubles, northern Catholics have tended to support the Republic of Ireland soccer team, while the support of the Northern Ireland team has become increasingly associated with loyalism. The comparative success of the Republic of Ireland team was almost certainly also a factor, but the marking out of many of Northern Ireland's football grounds, in particular Windsor Park, the home of both Linfield and Northern Ireland, as loyalist territory has contributed to this.[62] The qualification of Northern Ireland for the 2016 European championships may increase Catholic support for the team, though this will likely be offset by the simultaneous qualification of the Republic of Ireland.

In 1998, Mike Cronin and David Mayall emphasised that 'sport is a vehicle, in many ways, for the construction of individual, group, and national identities'.[63] This is true of leisure more generally and in particular when it takes associational form. It also remains a reality, despite frequent comment, that in the study of Irish sport and leisure, as in Irish historiography in general, the formation of national identity has received greatest attention. As the work surveyed in this chapter illustrates, however, the study of associational leisure offers considerable scope for nuanced engagement with the construction of confessional, gender, ethnic and class identities. Indeed, it is striking that two of the articles in a recent special number of *Éire-Ireland*, which took as its theme 'Ireland and sport', explored contemporary expressions of gay identity within the worlds of Irish rugby and Gaelic games.[64] As Peter Borsay has reminded us, one of the pleasures of leisure is that it 'appears' to operate 'at one remove from life', yet 'leisure matters' and 'it cannot be separated from the forces that drive the "real" world'.[65]

FURTHER READING

Cronin, M. *Sport and nationalism in Ireland: Gaelic games, soccer and Irish identity since 1884* (Dublin, 1999).

Curran, C. 'Sport and cultural nationalism: the conflict between association and Gaelic football in Donegal, 1905–34', *Éire-Ireland*, 48, 1–2 (2013), 158–62.

62 A. Bairner, 'Soccer, masculinity and violence in Northern Ireland: between hooliganism and terrorism', *Men and Masculinities*, 1, 3 (1999), 284–301; D. Hassan, 'A people apart: soccer, identity and Irish nationalists in Northern Ireland', *Soccer and Society*, 3, 3 (2002), 65–83; G. Fulton, 'Northern Catholic fans of the Republic of Ireland soccer team', in Bairner, *Sport and the Irish*, 140–56.

63 M. Cronin and D. Mayall, 'Sport and ethnicity: some introductory remarks', in Cronin and Mayall (eds.), *Sporting nationalisms: identity, ethnicity, immigration, and assimilation* (London, 1998), 1–2.

64 E. Madden, 'Get your kit on: gender, sexuality and gay rugby in Ireland' and A. Mulhall, '"What's eating Victor Cusack?" Come what may, queer embodiment, and the regulation of hetero-masculinity', *Éire-Ireland*, 48, 1–2 (2013), 246–81, 282–308.

65 P. Borsay, *A history of leisure* (Houndmills, 2006), 217.

Fleming, D. A. 'Diversions of the people: sociability among the orders of early eighteenth century Ireland', *Eighteenth-Century Ireland/Iris an dá chultúr*, 17 (2002), 99–111.

McAnallen, D. 'The radicalisation of the Gaelic Athletic Association in Ulster: the role of Owen O'Duffy', *International Journal of the History of Sport*, 31, 7 (2014), 704–23.

McElligott, R. *Forging a kingdom: the GAA in Kerry, 1884–1934* (Cork, 2013).

McElligott, R. 'Quenching the prairie fire: the collapse of the GAA in 1890s Ireland', *Irish Economic and Social History*, 41 (2014), 54–73.

McElligott, R. and D. Hassan. 'Sport in society: social and historical perspectives', Special issue of *Sport in society*, 19, 1 (2016).

Malcolm, E. *'Ireland sober, Ireland free': drink and temperance in nineteenth-century Ireland* (Dublin, 1986).

Mandle, W. F. *The Gaelic Athletic Association and Irish nationalist politics 1884–1924* (Dublin, 1987).

Mirala, P. *Freemasonry in Ulster, 1733–1813: a social and political history of the masonic brotherhood in the north of Ireland* (Dublin, 2007).

Ó Tuathaigh, G. *The GAA and revolution in Ireland* (Cork, 2015).

Rouse, P. 'Empires of sport: Enniscorthy, 1880–1920', in C. Tóibín (ed.), *Enniscorthy: a history* (Wexford, 2010), 333–68.

Ryan, D. *Blasphemers and blackguards: the Irish Hellfire Clubs* (Dublin, 2012).

Siggins, G. *Green days: cricket in Ireland, 1792–2005* (Stroud, 2005).

PART III

Emigration, Immigration and the Wider Irish World

24 Irish Emigrations in a Comparative Perspective

Kevin Kenny

24.1. Introduction

The scale of Irish emigration is extraordinary. Since 1700 about 10 million men, women and children have emigrated from Ireland. That number is more than twice the current population of the Republic of Ireland (4.6 million), it exceeds the population of the island of Ireland (6.5 million), and it is greater than the population of Ireland at its historical peak on the eve of the Great Famine (8.5 million). An estimated 70 million people worldwide claim some degree of Irish descent, including about 40 million Americans who list 'Irish' as their primary ethnicity. In approaching Irish emigration from a comparative perspective, three principal frameworks suggest themselves: comparisons by period, comparisons with other European countries and comparisons by country of destination.[1] The first approach has the virtue of breaking down a long and complex history into distinct chronological periods, revealing the distinctive characteristics of each period and thereby countering a pervasive tendency to approach Irish emigration as an undifferentiated whole. The second approach reveals that, although the Irish famine was unique and the late nineteenth century highly distinctive, earlier and later periods of Irish emigration had much in common with their European counterparts. The third approach uncovers the nationally specific conditions that shaped the histories of Irish emigrants in their various countries of settlement abroad, once again serving as a corrective against a tendency to homogenise. This chapter will begin by considering the first two approaches together, examining the origins and processes

1 One might also compare the experience of the Irish abroad with that of other immigrant groups in the countries of settlement, but this subject lies beyond the scope of the current chapter.

of Irish emigration by chronological period and drawing some comparisons with other European emigrations. A brief analysis of the main patterns in the social history of the Irish abroad will follow.[2]

24.2. Comparisons by Period and by Country of Destination

The history of Irish emigration falls naturally into six distinct periods: the long eighteenth century (to 1815), the pre-Great Famine generation (1815–45), the famine decade (1846–55), the post-famine era (1856–1921), the twentieth century after 1921, and the early twenty-first century. Emigration in these periods varied by origin, social composition, religion and destination. Relative to the size of its population, Ireland had the highest emigration rate in Europe for most of the nineteenth and twentieth centuries. Yet, although the broad demographic patterns are clear, detailed cross-country comparisons on the origins and character of Irish emigration are lacking. The analysis that follows therefore points to areas in need of comparative analysis as well as discussing the comparative work that has already been conducted.

Between 1700 and the American Revolution, some 60,000–100,000 Irish settled in the mainland American colonies. The migration resumed after the Peace of Paris in 1783, with as many as 100,000–150,000 Irish arriving by 1815. An estimated three-quarters of those who went to America before 1815 were Presbyterians from the province of Ulster.[3] The origins of this first phase of Irish emigration were religious as well as economic. Presbyterians no longer faced imprisonment or torture for their beliefs, as they had in the seventeenth century, but they continued to endure religious disabilities and they could not be sure that persecution would not return. As dissenters from the established church, they were subject to a Sacramental Test Act passed in 1704, which effectively excluded them from municipal office and the military by requiring them to take communion according to Anglican rites. They had to pay tithes to support the Anglican Church, their marriages could be challenged in ecclesiastical courts, and they could not graduate from Trinity College Dublin, Oxford or Cambridge. Ulster Presbyterians were guaranteed religious toleration by an Act passed in 1719, but freedom of worship did not mean full civil or political equality. The test acts, though sporadically enforced,

---

2 As the intention of this chapter is to highlight patterns in emigration considered as a collective movement, the focus is on mass emigration to North America, Britain and, to a lesser extent, Australia, rather than the migration of individuals (soldiers, priests, merchants and others) to continental Europe, India or Africa, subjects worthy of investigation on their own terms.

3 K. A. Miller, *Emigrants and exiles: Ireland and the Irish exodus to North America* (New York, 1985), 137; R. J. Dickson, *Ulster emigration to colonial America, 1718–1775* (London, 1966); L. M. Cullen, 'The Irish diaspora of the seventeenth and eighteenth centuries', in N. Canny (ed.), *Europeans on the move: studies in European migration, 1500–1800* (New York, 1994), 113–49.

were not fully abolished until 1871. The American colonies, especially Pennsylvania, held the prospect of religious toleration.[4]

Economic motives were fundamental, however, as is true of most mass emigrations. The origins of emigration from eighteenth-century Ulster are to be found primarily in problems in the landholding system and the domestic linen industry. Most Presbyterians rented land rather than owning it outright. The linen industry provided sustenance at every level of the rural hierarchy. At one end of the scale were the cottiers who grew flax, spun yarn or wove cloth in return for access to land and a roof over their heads; at the other was a merchant elite that bleached and marketed the finished cloth. Between these two groups was a large class of rural craftsmen who supplemented their income as weavers. By the local 'Ulster Custom', tenants had security of tenure so long as they paid their rents, along with the freedom to sell their right of occupancy to incoming tenants (approved by the landlord) when they vacated their holdings. But landlords arbitrarily reduced the length of leases and raised the rents (known as 'rack-renting'), auctioned off leases to the highest bidder (known as 'canting') or charged tenants exorbitant fees to renew their leases. These problems, on top of local taxes, parish fees, tithes owed to the Anglican Church and bad harvests, accounted for a steady rise in emigration in the eighteenth century. But periodic downturns in the linen industry proved decisive, disrupting the fragile equilibrium of the rural economy. The near collapse of the industry during the recession of the 1770s, triggered by a sudden decline in foreign demand, brought emigration to a peak. The poor left Ireland because they faced destitution, the marginal and relatively comfortable because their position was deteriorating. Whole families, and sometimes congregations, left together when they could. Payments to outgoing tenants under the 'Ulster Custom' often financed the transatlantic passage, but about half of Ulster's transatlantic emigrants in the middle decades of the eighteenth century left as indentured servants. Emigration was interrupted by the American revolutionary war but resumed on a larger scale after the Peace of Paris, with perhaps 150,000 Irish settling in North America between 1783 and 1815, an estimated two-thirds of whom were Ulster Presbyterians.[5]

The first phase of Irish transatlantic emigration, prior to 1815, can usefully be compared with the English, Scottish and German cases. In the seventeenth century, the great age of English migration, an estimated 530,000 people had left England to settle overseas – about 180,000 in Ireland, 190,000 in the Caribbean and 160,000 on the North American mainland (though some of the emigrants counted as English were undoubtedly of Irish birth). In the eighteenth century, by contrast, the Irish dominated

---

4 Catholics were subject to the same religious disabilities, enforced more stringently, but for complex economic and cultural reasons they were much less likely to emigrate in the eighteenth century. See Miller, *Emigrants and exiles*, 3–192.

5 Miller, *Emigrants and exiles*, 137–69; Dickson, *Ulster emigration to colonial America*.

the transatlantic outflow: only about 50,000 English emigrants moved to the mainland American colonies (plus 20,000 to the Caribbean), compared with 75,000 Scots, more than 100,000 Germans, and as many as 200,000 Irish. While the Germans came from a variety of principalities, spoke different dialects and belonged to multiple religious sects, the Ulster Irish were united by their common Scottish origin and Presbyterian religion. Even though their settlements were widely scattered, therefore, the Ulster Irish in America constituted a distinct subculture, whereas the Germans were diffuse and disparate by comparison.[6]

The second phase of Irish emigration, from 1815 to 1845, differed markedly from the first. Between 800,000 and 1 million Irish people emigrated to North America in this thirty-year period. Protestants, most of them Presbyterians from Ulster, continued to dominate until the 1830s but Catholics dominated thereafter, making up more than 80 per cent of the transatlantic flow for the remainder of the nineteenth century. The age of mass Irish Catholic migration was underway. A general rule of migration history is that the poorest of the poor do not leave, as they cannot afford to. Pre-famine Ireland was no exception. Those who did leave had the resources to pay the fare for a transatlantic passage or for a passage across the Irish Sea to Britain, where some 400,000 Irish-born people were domiciled by 1841. As is typical of most mass emigrations in their initial stages, men outnumbered women among those who left pre-famine Ireland (by a ratio of about two to one). Most of these men were young, single and unskilled, and they found work as manual labourers abroad.[7]

The pre-famine emigration resulted from a combination of forces: population growth, lack of diversification in the economy, the mechanisation of the textile industry and a shift in agriculture from tillage to pasture. The number of people living in Ireland doubled from 1 million to 2 million in the first half of the eighteenth century, doubled again by the end of the century, and doubled again to 8 million by 1841. The population was overwhelmingly rural: according to the census of 1841, less than 14 per cent of Irish people lived in towns of 2,000 or more inhabitants and more than 75 per cent of occupied males worked the land. Outside the north-east and Dublin, Ireland lacked large factories or cities. When people left the countryside, therefore, they tended to leave Ireland altogether for Britain or North America. The rise of commercial dairy farming in eastern counties reduced demand for work and the amount of land available for rent. Cultivating the soil required labour but raising animals entailed the eviction of small tenants and the enclosure of their holdings with walls and fences. Sheep and cows, in other words, replaced people on the land. The mechanisation of spinning and

6 N. Canny, 'English migration into and across the Atlantic during the seventeenth and eighteenth centuries', in Canny (ed.), *Europeans on the move*, 39–75.
7 Miller, *Emigrants and exiles*, 193–8; D. H. Akenson, *Ireland, Sweden and the great European migration, 1815–1914* (Montreal and Kingston, Ont., 2011), 94.

weaving and the contraction of the textiles industry into the triangle linking Belfast, Dungannon and Armagh, meanwhile, converted large parts of the north-central region into what one historian has described as 'rural slums'. Regionally, the highest rates of emigration in the pre-famine era were from counties in north Leinster and south Ulster. Departures from the Atlantic seaboard were comparatively low, with potato cultivation facilitating the ongoing subdivision of landholdings and acting as a check on emigration. Mass departure did not become common in the west until the crisis of the Great Famine.[8]

Cross-country comparisons for the pre-famine era are lacking but would be especially helpful in evaluating the origins and scale of Irish emigration. The almost one million Irish emigrants who crossed the Atlantic between 1815 and 1845 left a country whose population stood at only about 6 million at the beginning of this period. The impact of such a heavy outflow was masked by the fact that Ireland's population was still growing rapidly during this period, even if the growth rate was tailing off by the 1830s. Comparisons with English, Scottish and German emigration would once again be instructive. England produced about the same number of transatlantic emigrants as Ireland over the course of the nineteenth century. But just as the presumed affinity of the English with the dominant culture of the American hostland rendered them 'invisible immigrants' in the United States, historians have not systematically studied the English as 'emigrants' either. Emigration in England and Ireland arose from different patterns of rural depopulation, industrialisation and urbanisation, and the English population base was obviously significantly larger. Yet that is all the more reason to study the two cases comparatively, as one of the two main purposes of comparative history is to highlight differences and to reveal unique or distinctive characteristics. The other purpose is to discover similarities and patterns, and in this respect the transformation of Irish agriculture could profitably be studied in conjunction with the Highland clearances in Scotland. Historians seeking to understand the origins and mechanisms of European migration in the 1830s and early 1840s could also usefully compare the Irish case with the mass emigration from the German principalities at this time, which was propelled by a complex mix of economic and religious motives.[9]

The catastrophe that struck Ireland in the 1840s unleashed a wave of emigration on an unprecedented scale. Between 1846 and 1855 (when emigration rates returned to pre-famine levels), more than a million Irish people died of starvation and

8 Miller, *Emigrants and exiles*, 198–227 (quote, 208).
9 C. Erickson, *Invisible immigrants: the adaptation of English and Scottish immigrants in nineteenth-century America* (London, 1972); K. J. Bade, 'German transatlantic emigration in the nineteenth and twentieth centuries', in P. C. Emmer and M. Mörner (eds.), *European expansion and migration: essays on the international migration from Africa, Asia, and Europe* (New York, 1992), 121–55; K. J. Bade and J. Oltmer, 'Germany', in K. J. Bade, P. C. Emmer, L. Lucassen and J. Oltmer (eds.), *The encyclopedia of migration and minorities in Europe from the 17th century to the present* (New York, 2011), 68–9.

famine-related diseases and another 2.1 million people left the country – more than in the previous two and a half centuries combined. About 1.5 million went to the United States, more than 300,000 to Canada (many of whom later moved southward), another 315,000 to Great Britain, and tens of thousands to Australia and New Zealand. Those who were most heavily dependent on the potato, along the Atlantic seaboard of the west and south, were the least likely to emigrate and the most likely to die of starvation or disease. Rates of both mortality and emigration were unusually high, however, in south Ulster (Cavan, Monaghan and Fermanagh). Emigration from the province of Ulster as a whole remained numerically heavy in the famine era, as in earlier periods, even if the proportionate impact was less than in Munster and Connacht, whose western counties experienced very high levels of emigration for the first time. Almost two-thirds of the famine emigrants were between the ages of twenty and forty-five, in part because famine mortality was disproportionately high among the old and young. Although men still outnumbered women, sex ratios were closer to parity than in the pre-famine era.[10]

Irish emigration in the famine era was highly distinctive. In Europe, the blight affected Flanders, southern France, Switzerland, eastern Germany, southern Scandinavia and Scotland, as well as Ireland. But in Ireland an abnormally high proportion of the population depended on the potato. Owing to the combined effects of famine mortality and emigration, Ireland's population declined by one-third between 1846 and 1855, an event without parallel in nineteenth-century European history. The Irish were the single largest immigrant group in the United States in the 1840s, accounting for 45 per cent of the total number of immigrants. The Irish and the Germans each accounted for about 35 per cent of the immigrant inflow in the 1850s, with the Germans exceeding the Irish by the end of the decade and for the rest of the century. One in every two New Yorkers and Bostonians in 1860 was foreign-born and half of these foreigners were Irish-born.

Given Ireland's small geographical area, and the small size of its population, these figures are remarkable. Ireland is about the same size as Indiana, Maine or South Carolina. The other countries that sent comparable numbers of immigrants to North America – England, Germany and later Italy – were much bigger than Ireland geographically and, more importantly, their populations were much larger. In 1861, for example, the German Customs Union (*Zollverein*) had a population of about 35 million, the Italian states had 22 million, and England and Wales had 20 million, compared with 5.8 million in Ireland. For every Irish-born person in the United States that year, only five remained at home. The corresponding figure for Germany was about one in thirty. From the 1840s

10 O. MacDonagh, 'Irish famine emigration to the United States,' *Perspectives in American History*, 10 (1976), 357–446; Miller, *Emigrants and exiles*, 280–344; Akenson, *Ireland, Sweden and the great European migration*, 155–8; J. S. Donnelly, *The great Irish potato famine* (Stroud, 2001), 184–5.

to the end of the century, Ireland had the highest emigration rate in Europe. By 1891, just under 40 per cent of Irish-born people were living in the United States, Britain, Canada or Australia.[11]

The post-famine phase of Irish emigration, from 1856 to 1921, was massive and sustained. The dates serve as convenient bookends, marking the conclusion of the famine decade at one end and, at the other, both the Anglo-Irish Treaty and the passage of comprehensive immigration restriction laws in the United States. Defining the chronological boundaries in these political terms is somewhat misleading, as the post-1921 era was defined not by state policies on either side of the Atlantic but by the decision of Irish emigrants to go to Britain instead of America. The dates 1856–1921 do, however, demarcate a discrete period during which, as one historian puts it, 'Emigration had become a massive, relentless, and efficiently managed national enterprise.' Some 3.5 million Irish emigrants crossed the Atlantic in the post-famine era, just over 3 million of whom went to the United States and 200,000 to Canada. About 300,000 Irish emigrants went to Australia and New Zealand in this period. In addition, as many 1 million Irish settled in Britain, for a total

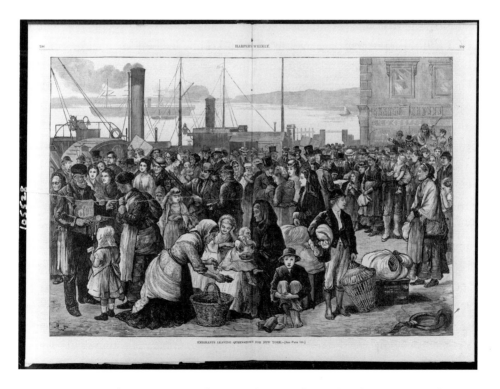

Figure 24.1 Emigrants leaving Queenstown for New York in 1874. *Illustrated London News*, 5 September 1874 and *Harper's Weekly*, 26 September 1874, pp. 796–7.

11 Akenson, *Ireland, Sweden and the great European migration*, 8, 172.

departure level of about 4.5 million. Remarkably, this figure exceeded the number of people living in Ireland in 1900. Emigration had the heaviest proportionate impact in Munster and Connacht, which provided 51 per cent of the emigrants but contained only 41 per cent of Ireland's mean population in the period 1856–1910. Only about 16 per cent of the post-famine emigrants came from Leinster, which made up one-quarter of Ireland's population. Ulster, which made up one-third of the Irish population in the post-famine era, accounted for one-third of the transatlantic flow. Although Catholics left Ulster at a higher rate, perhaps half of those who left the province for North America were Protestants, mostly Presbyterians who went to Canada.[12]

The origins of the post-famine emigration lay in a combination of forces, most of them present in the pre-famine era but accelerated by the upheaval of the 1840s. These included the ongoing shift from tillage to pasture, with a corresponding decline in the demand for labour; the resulting eviction of smallholders and the consolidation of landholdings; and the emergence of commercial farmers as the backbone of the Irish economy. Impartible inheritance and primogeniture became much more common after the famine. Marriage without access to adequate land was seen as reckless. Whereas the pre-famine Irish had resembled other Europeans in marrying young, post-famine Ireland had the latest marriage ages in western Europe for both men and women, as well as the highest rates of non-marriage. The bulk of the population in post-famine Ireland remained dependent on agriculture in an economy that could not provide an adequate supply of either land or work. In the absence of urban or industrial employment, long-distance emigration was often the best option, though labourers from north-west Ireland continued a longstanding pattern of seasonal migration to England and Scotland as well.[13]

For young women, in particular, emigration could offer a welcome escape from restricted opportunity. Virtually alone among their European counterparts in the late nineteenth century, Irish women emigrated to the United States in the same numbers as men. Remarkably, most of these women were single and they crossed the Atlantic unaccompanied. By comparison, only about 20 per cent of southern Italian immigrants were female, and they rarely if ever crossed the Atlantic alone. The sex ratios of Jewish emigrants from eastern Europe and Russia were comparable to those of the Irish, but most of these Jewish women were married or travelled with their families. Only Swedish women resembled the Irish, with large numbers of young single women from both countries emigrating to America and finding work as domestic servants.[14]

12 Miller, *Emigrants and exiles*, 346; D. Fitzpatrick, 'Emigration, 1871–1921', in W. E. Vaughan (ed.), *A new history of Ireland, vol. VI: Ireland under the Union, 1 (1870–1921)* (Oxford, 1996), 607 (quote).
13 Miller, *Emigrants and exiles*, 346–426.
14 Akenson, *Ireland, Sweden and the great European migration*, 239–40.

Figure 24.2 Emigrants on board *The Empress of Britain*, en route to North America, late nineteenth century. Credit: PH-RCS-FISHER-0009-02001-F-00-CROP-001, Cambridge University Library.

No other European country lost nearly so high a proportion of its population to emigration in this period as Ireland. Norway and Sweden had comparable levels, and certain regions within countries – for example, Sicily in the opening decade of the twentieth century – had even higher rates of departure than Ireland. But, taken as a whole, the Irish case was anomalous. In western Europe and the United States, the second half of the nineteenth century was a period of massive population growth, industrialisation and urbanisation. Yet Ireland's population was cut in half, most of the country continued to lack industry, and Irish towns and cities stagnated or even declined in size. These attributes in combination made for a highly distinctive society and a unique pattern of emigration. Especially important in the Irish case was the transmission from America of massive amounts of emigrant remittances, which funded further departures and sustained families at home. This strategy can usefully be contrasted with that of south-ern and eastern European migrants, who also sent back remittances but were much more likely than the Irish to spend time in America as sojourners ('birds of passage') rather than as permanent immigrants. In the early twentieth century, rates of return for southern and eastern European migrants to the United States exceeded 50 per cent, whereas those for the Irish were well below 10 per cent.[15]

In the twentieth century, the underlying cause of emigration remained constant – lack of work in a predominantly agricultural economy – but the destinations of Ireland's emigrants changed markedly. The US Immigration Acts of the 1920s reduced admis-sions from all countries, gave preference to immigrants from north-west Europe and excluded Asians altogether. The 1924 Act set an annual quota of 28,567 for the Irish Free State, which was reduced to 17,853 in 1929. Between 1901 and 1910, some 339,065 Irish immigrants had arrived in the United States, an annual average almost twice that of the 1929 quota. Yet, with only 220,591 immigrants in the 1920s, the Free State did not meet its quota. The shortfall can be explained in part by bureaucratic obstacles and expenses: passports first became common during and after the First World War, and after 1924 all US immigrants were required to obtain a visa from the American consu-late in their country of origin. But the main cause of the decline was the diversion of the emigrant stream to Britain in the 1920s, a process accelerated thereafter by the unavail-ability of work in the United States during the Great Depression and by the disruption of transatlantic shipping during the Second World War. Three-quarters of all Irish emi-grants from the 1920s onward went to Britain. Only 13,167 immigrants arrived in the United States from the Irish Free State in the 1930s and 26,967 in the 1940s. Although 57,332 entered in the 1950s, they accounted for only about 10 per cent of the outflow from Ireland in that decade.[16]

Irish emigration in the twentieth century remained highly distinctive in several respects while resembling broader European patterns in others. Because of its remark-ably high emigration rate, Ireland was unique in the extent of its demographic decline, with the population of the Republic falling to only 2.8 million by the early 1960s. It has been estimated that one in every three people under the age of thirty in independent Ireland in 1946 had left the country by 1971. Fully half a million people left the Republic in the 1950s, the highest rates of departure since the famine era. In a period character-ised by passport and visa controls and the numerical restriction of immigration in the

---

15 T. J. Hatton, and J. G. Williamson, *The age of mass migration: causes and economic impact* (New York, 1998), 33, 75; Akenson, *Ireland, Sweden and the great European migration*, 8; A. Schrier, *Ireland and the American migration, 1850–1900* (Minneapolis, 1958), 15, 104–9; Miller, *Emigrants and exiles*, 357.

16 P. J. Drudy, 'Irish population change and emigration since independence', in P. J. Drudy (ed.), *The Irish in America: emigration, assimilation, impact* (Cambridge, 1985), 73–5; P. Blessing, 'Irish', in S. Thernstrom (ed.), *The Harvard encyclopedia of ethnic groups* (Cambridge, MA, 1980), 528; E. Delaney, *Irish emigration since 1921* (Dundalk, 2002), 7.

traditional receiving countries (the United States, Canada, Australia and New Zealand), Irish emigrants were distinctive in having unrestricted access to their main destination, Britain (except for a brief period between the outbreak of the Second World War and the early 1950s). Yet Irish emigration in the post-war era shared some essential features with Greek, Portuguese, Spanish and Italian migration to Germany, France and the Netherlands. National governments in all these cases were active in facilitating the movement of migrants from the agricultural periphery to core industrial areas. In this respect, Irish emigration was not unique, though the rate of emigration was certainly highest in Ireland.[17]

A strong case can be made that emigration on both sides of the Irish border has operated as a social and political safety valve throughout the period since the famine. Without mass emigration, unemployment in twentieth-century Ireland would have been much higher, generating greater discontent and potential class conflict. Mass emigration may have inhibited economic development by reducing the demand for goods and services, but higher unemployment in the absence of emigration would have had the same effect. By reducing competition for resources, boosting wage levels and attracting remittances from abroad, emigration increased the living standards of those who remained behind. In Northern Ireland, meanwhile, disproportionately high emigration by Catholics served both to reduce unemployment and to maintain the demographic balance on which the province's constitutional balance depended. Faced with discrimination in employment and housing, Northern Ireland's Catholics emigrated at a considerably higher rate than Protestants in the mid-twentieth century. In the period 1939–61, for example, when Catholics made up about one-third of the population of the province, they accounted for just under 60 per cent of the emigrants.[18]

The number of emigrants from Ireland to all destinations in the second half of the twentieth century waxed and waned in line with fluctuations in the economy. Emigration from the Republic of Ireland declined significantly in the 1960s and 1970s. There was a net inflow of 104,000 people into the Republic in the 1970s, including many married couples who had emigrated to Britain when single and now returned with children. As a result, the population of the Republic rose by 9 per cent between 1962 and 1971 and by 15 per cent between 1972 and 1981, the first time since the Great

17 K. O'Rourke, 'Emigration and living standards in Ireland since the famine', *Journal of Population Economics*, 8 (1995), 410; C. Ó Gráda and B. M. Walsh, 'Fertility and population in Ireland, north and south', *Population Studies*, 49, 2 (1995), 259–79; D. Garvey, 'The history of migration flows in the Republic of Ireland', *Population Trends*, 39 (1985), 25; Delaney, *Irish emigration since 1921*, 3, 37; E. Delaney, 'Placing postwar Irish migration in a comparative European perspective, 1945–81', in A. Bielenberg (ed.), *The Irish diaspora* (London, 2000), 331–56.
18 Delaney, *Irish emigration since 1921*, 36, 39, 43; O'Rourke, 'Emigration and living standards in Ireland since the famine', 407–21; D. P. Barritt and C. F. Carter, *The Northern Ireland problem: a study in group relations* (2nd edn, London, 1962), 107–8.

Famine that emigration did not equal or exceed the natural increase in the population. The numbers leaving Northern Ireland rose in the 1970s, by contrast, with the outflow almost negating the natural increase in population. High unemployment led to high emigration from both parts of the island in the 1980s, with a net outflow of 216,000 from the Republic. Significantly, the rate of emigration among Protestants in Northern Ireland from the 1970s onwards has exceeded that among Catholics, reversing the pattern of the previous fifty years.[19]

The great majority of Irish emigrants in the late twentieth century continued to go to Britain rather than the United States. Under the new system of US immigration control introduced in 1965, which abolished the race-based national origins system, Ireland's numerical quota increased slightly from 17,853 to 20,000, the figure now assigned to every nation in the Western Hemisphere. Immediate relatives of US citizens (non-adult children, spouses and parents) were not subject to numerical restrictions. Within the quota system, preference was given firstly to those who had close family ties to US citizens (e.g. siblings or married children of citizens, or the immediate family of resident aliens) and secondly to those with desirable skills in short supply. Most Irish people lacked the required characteristics, but they benefited from special schemes introduced in 1986 and 1990 (known as the Donnelly and Morrison visas), targeted partly or exclusively at prospective Irish emigrants, which awarded non-quota visas by random selection or lottery. Irish emigrants to the United States in the 1980s featured a mix of well-educated youth in search of opportunity abroad, beneficiaries of the special visa schemes, and poor and unskilled workers who entered the country on tourist visas, decided to stay, and joined the ranks of the undocumented. By this time, however, the United States was allocating more than 90 per cent of its visas to non-Europeans.[20]

In the mid-1990s, Ireland entered the intoxicating, but ultimately evanescent, period of economic prosperity known as the 'Celtic Tiger'. With a highly educated young population, massive subsidies from the European Union and low corporate tax rates attracting multinational pharmaceutical and information technology companies, the Irish economy attained annual growth rates as high as 7 per cent. Most middle- and upper-middle-class Irish people enjoyed levels of prosperity undreamed of before, although crime and unemployment continued to plague inner-city areas. Skilled and unskilled Irish workers who had fled Ireland in the 1980s returned. For the first time

19 M. Kelly and A. S. Fotheringham, 'The online atlas of Irish population change 1841–2002: a new resource for analysing national trends and local variations in Irish population dynamics', *Irish Geography*, 44 (2011), 2–3, 215–44; Drudy, 'Irish population change', 65–8, 78; Delaney, *Irish emigration since 1921*, 6, 17; Ó Gráda and Walsh, 'Fertility and population in Ireland, north and south', 264–79; L. Kennedy, *People and population change: a comparative study of population change in Northern Ireland and the Republic of Ireland* (Dublin and Belfast, 1994), 21.

20 M. Corcoran, 'Emigrants, *Eirepreneurs*, and opportunists: a social profile of recent Irish immigration in New York City', in R. H. Bayor and T. J. Meagher (eds.), *The New York Irish* (Baltimore, MD, 1996), 461–80.

in Irish history, large numbers of foreign-born immigrants entered the country, mostly service workers from central and eastern Europe, but also economic migrants and political asylum seekers from Africa. By the late 1990s, it looked as though Ireland's historical tradition as a nation of emigrants had come to an end; just as in Italy, Spain and Germany, a new nation of immigrants was emerging. During the severe recession that followed the dramatic collapse of 2008, however, many of the recent immigrants left Ireland. The Irish-born began leaving their country in large numbers once again, with Britain and Australia rather than the United States being the favoured destinations. And so, after a brief interruption, the long history of Irish emigration resumed.

24.3. Comparisons and Connections by Country of Destination

What were the principal similarities and differences in Irish emigration history in the various places of settlement? As the United States was the largest single destination for Irish emigrants until the 1920s, historians until quite recently focused their attention on the American Irish. Over the past two generations, however, historians have conducted systematic investigations of Irish settlements elsewhere, including Britain, Canada, Australia, New Zealand, Latin America and South Africa – the parts of the world which, in order, received the largest numbers of Irish immigrants after the United States. These studies implicitly, and often explicitly, call into question the extent to which the American Irish set the template for Irish overseas history as a whole. During the century of mass emigration that began in the 1820s, for example, the number of Irish people in the United States was always greater than anywhere else. Yet the Irish-born made up a higher percentage of the populations of Scotland, Ontario, New Zealand and the Australian provinces in 1870 than they did in the United States. The brief comparative survey of Irish overseas history that follows examines three central themes in social history: religious background, the corresponding patterns of social mobility and questions concerning labour.[21]

Like Irish history as a whole, the social history of the Irish overseas had important religious dimensions. Whereas Catholics dominated the flow to the United States after the 1830s, about two-thirds of Irish emigrants to British North America in the nineteenth century were Protestants, the great majority of them from Ulster. Branches of the Orange Order proliferated in the leading centres of Irish settlement abroad, with sectarian tensions leading to violent clashes in Liverpool, Glasgow, Toronto and New York City. At least sixty mainly Catholic protestors were killed by the New York militia in the 'Orange and Green' riots of 1871. Eager to distinguish themselves

---

21 D. Fitzpatrick, *Irish emigration, 1801–1921* (Dundalk, 1984), 5.

Figure 24.3 New York City's 'Orange and Green' riot of 12 July 1871. *Frank Leslie's Illustrated Newspaper*, 29 July 1871.

from the incoming Irish Catholics in the nineteenth century, Irish Protestants in the United States adopted the once pejorative term 'Scots-Irish' as a badge of pride and often formed the vanguard of American nativist movements. Scots-Irishmen, for example, dominated the most powerful anti-Catholic organisation in the United States in the late nineteenth century, the American Protective Association. Catholic Irish Americans since the 1830s have been concentrated in the Northeast, the Midwest and California. But the predominantly Protestant migrants of the previous century, along with their descendants, lived mostly in Pennsylvania, the backcountry of Virginia, the Carolinas and Georgia, and the neighbouring states of Kentucky and Tennessee, where a strong sense of Scots-Irish identity survives today.[22]

Given the nature of Irish history, one might expect the social disparity between Protestants and Catholics to have persisted in America. Yet, although most Irish emigrants were initially very poor by American standards, especially in the famine era, by the turn of the twentieth century Catholic Irish Americans were approaching national averages on income, education and housing. And they tended to be better off

22 K. Kenny, *The American Irish: a history* (New York, 2000), 1–3, 81–2, 129, 158–9.

the further west they settled. The Irish in Boston and New York City lagged behind national measures of social mobility, but in Butte, Montana (the American city with the highest proportion of Irish-born residents in 1900) they dominated not only the labour force but also the employer class. Protestant Irish Americans in the twentieth century, meanwhile, were poorer on average than their Catholic counterparts, in part because they were concentrated in the South, the poorest region in the country. In Canada and Australia various studies have revealed at best 'small differences' between Irish Catholic and Protestant immigrants, challenging prevailing assumptions that Catholics were culturally ill-equipped to do well economically in their new locations overseas.[23]

These findings raise the central debate in the historiography of the overseas Irish. Kerby Miller argued that the Catholic Irish on both sides of the Atlantic were predisposed to see their emigration as a matter of exile and banishment rather than opportunity and self-improvement. He traced the origins of this exile motif not simply to the poverty and alienation of Irish-American urban life but, more controversially, to the culture of pre-migration Ireland. Donald Harman Akenson and Malcolm Campbell, among other historians, questioned the applicability of the exile motif to the Irish globally. By demonstrating that Irish emigrants were not hampered by any such culture in Canada, South Africa, Australia and (to a lesser extent) the western United States, they undermined Miller's negative conception of Irish rural history. Yet these studies, it should be noted, have only an indirect bearing on the culture of Irish emigrants in the towns and cities of the American Northeast and Midwest, where the majority of Irish emigrants settled. These regions were the focus of Miller's book, and to overturn his thesis historians would need to re-examine this region in detail.[24]

The global approach to Irish emigration, none the less, opens up new possibilities for comparative social history, for example on questions of labour. More than half a century ago, E. P. Thompson noted how the Irish in nineteenth-century England constituted 'a supplementary labour force unmolded by the industrial work-discipline' which had 'escaped the imprint of Baxter and Wesley'.[25] This insight could be extended to the wider transatlantic economy, but as yet no sustained comparative work has been

---

23 D. M. Emmons, *The Butte Irish: class and ethnicity in an American mining town, 1875–1925* (Urbana, IL, 1989); R. A. Burchell, *The San Francisco Irish, 1848–1880* (Manchester, 1979); A. Greeley, 'The success and assimilation of Irish Protestants and Irish Catholics in the United States', *Sociology and Social Research*, 72 (July 1988), 231–2; Akenson, *The Irish diaspora*, 243–4; D. H. Akenson, *Small differences: Irish Catholics and Irish Protestants, 1815–1922: an international perspective* (Montreal and Kingston, Ont., 1988); M. Campbell, *Ireland's new worlds: immigrants, politics, and society in the United States and Australia, 1815–1922* (Madison, WI, 2008).

24 Miller, *Emigrants and exiles*; K. A. Miller with B. Boling and D. N. Doyle, '"Emigrants and Exiles": Irish cultures and Irish emigration to North America, 1790–1922', *Irish Historical Studies*, 22 (September 1980), 97–125; Akenson, *Irish diaspora*, 10–11, 217–74; Campbell, *Ireland's new worlds*, vii–ix.

25 E. P. Thompson, *The making of the English working class* (New York, 1966), 432, 433.

done. Irish emigrant workers in both Britain and the United States – on the public works, canals and railways, and in the coal mines – reproduced elements of the collective violent protest endemic in the Irish countryside. These forms of protest ranged from faction fights between gangs of 'Corkonians' and 'Fardowners' to more coherently organised secret societies like the 'Ribbonmen' and the 'Molly Maguires'. This kind of protest gradually gave way to participation in formal trade unionism, with the Irish assuming a leading role on both sides of the Atlantic.[26] As for women's labour, the Irish made up three-quarters of the domestic servants in some American cities at the turn of the twentieth century. In Britain, by contrast, the availability of English and Scottish working-class labour in England meant that the Irish did not enter service as frequently. Once again, no sustained comparative analysis has been conducted on this point.[27]

Approaching the social history of the Irish overseas from a comparative perspective, however, has certain limitations as well as strengths. A transnational perspective is also required. As the radical Irish-American editor and activist Patrick Ford once put it, 'The cause of the poor in Donegal, is the cause of the factory slave in Fall River.'[28] (See Figure 24.4.) As editor of the leading Irish-American newspaper, the *Irish World* (which added the words 'and American Industrial Liberator' to its title in 1879), Ford supported the right of workers to organise unions and go on strike, called for women's rights, an income tax, and an eight-hour workday, and supported Irish land reform and nationalism. With the American land reformer Henry George and the Irish radical Michael Davitt, Ford was part of a transnational working-class movement connecting Ireland with Britain and North America. The syndicalist James Larkin and the republican socialist James Connolly, who both spent considerable time in the United States in the early twentieth century, were also active in a movement spanning both sides of the Atlantic. Labour movements of this kind are best studied as a transnational whole rather than solely in a comparative perspective.

Although a comparative perspective on emigration history can produce many important insights, it cannot on its own capture the complexity of the Irish experience abroad. The comparative method excels at revealing similarities and differences, but historians also need to discover patterns and connections. For the latter, a dynamic

26 P. Way, *Common labour: workers and the digging of the North American canals, 1780–1860* (Cambridge, 1993); K. Kenny, *Making sense of the Molly Maguires* (New York, 1998); D. Fitzpatrick, 'Irish in Britain, 1871–1921', in Vaughan, *New history of Ireland, vol. VI*, 683; D. Montgomery, 'The Irish and the American labor movement', in D. N. Doyle and O. D. Edwards (eds.), *America and Ireland, 1776–1976: the American identity and the Irish connection* (Westport, CT, 1980), 206.

27 M. Lynch-Brennan, *The Irish Bridget: Irish immigrant women in domestic service in America, 1840–1930* (Syracuse, NY, 2009).

28 Quoted in T. N. Brown, *Irish-American nationalism, 1870–1890* (Philadelphia, 1966), 108.

Figure 24.4 Portrait of the radical newspaper editor, Patrick Ford. Library of Congress, Washington, DC.

transnational perspective is needed. The transnational and the cross-national, however, are by no means mutually exclusive. They come together in the concept of diaspora, understood both as a category of practice through which migrants make sense of their world and as a category of analysis through which historians interpret the past. As a category of analysis, diaspora reveals transnational connections not only between emigrants and their homelands, but also between emigrants of common origin in globally scattered communities. When this approach is combined with the comparative method, the result is a powerful conceptual framework for explaining the history of emigration.[29]

29 K. Kenny, 'Diaspora and comparison: the American Irish as a case study', *Journal of American History*, 90 (June 2003), 134–62.

FURTHER READING

Akenson, D. H. *Ireland, Sweden, and the great European migration, 1815–1914* (Montreal and Kingston, Ont., 2011).

Akenson, D. H. *The Irish diaspora: a primer* (Toronto, 1996).

Bielenberg, A. (ed.). *The Irish diaspora* (London, 2000).

Campbell, M. *Ireland's new worlds: immigrants, politics, and society in the United States and Australia, 1815–1922* (Madison, WI, 2008).

Delaney, E. *Demography, state and society: Irish migration to Britain, 1921–1971* (Montreal and Kingston, Ont., 2000).

Delaney, E. *Irish emigration since 1921* (Dundalk, 2002).

Delaney, E. *The Irish in post-war Britain* (Oxford, 2007).

Dickson, R. J. *Ulster emigration to colonial America, 1718–1775* (London, 1966).

Fitzpatrick, D. *Irish emigration, 1801–1921* (Dundalk, 1984).

Kenny, K. *The American Irish: a history* (New York, 2000).

Kenny, K. 'Diaspora and comparison: the American Irish as a case study', *Journal of American History*, 90 (June 2003), 134–62.

Lynch-Brennan, M. *The Irish Bridget: Irish immigrant women in domestic service in America, 1840–1930* (Syracuse, NY, 2009).

MacRaild, D. M. *The Irish diaspora in Britain, 1750–1939* (2nd edn, New York, 2010).

Miller, K. A. *Emigrants and exiles: Ireland and the Irish exodus to North America* (New York, 1985).

O'Farrell, P. *The Irish in Australia* (Kensington, NSW, 1987).

Wilson, D. *The Irish in Canada* (Ottawa, 1989).

25 The Diaspora in Comparative and Multi-generational Perspective

Bronwen Walter

25.1.   Introduction

In 1990 the newly elected president of Ireland, Mary Robinson, recognised an estimated total of more than 70 million people as belonging the diasporic Irish 'family'. The
precise size of the multi-generational diaspora is unknowable but this figure highlights
the very large numbers involved and provides a telling contrast with the present-day
'home' population of around 6.5 million. It reflects the long time period of substantial
emigration, especially in the nineteenth and twentieth centuries, the greatest ratio of
the two populations being in 1891 when 38.8 per cent of those born in Ireland were
living outside.

This decisive move to de-territorialise the nation signalled a remarkable change: as
Richard Kearney put it 'the Irish sense of belonging is no longer pre-determined by
the map-lines of our island'.[1] The struggle to achieve independence, unfinished in the
six northern counties, has given a special resonance to the territorial claim. It was thus
particularly symbolic that the clause stating 'Furthermore, the Irish nation cherishes its
special affinity with people of Irish ancestry living abroad who share its cultural identity and heritage' should be substituted in the rewritten article 2 of the Irish constitution
ratified in 1998 for the sixty-year old assertion of unity with the north. A different and
much more diverse set of people was included in the Irish nation for the first time,
bringing into view 'Ireland's other history'.[2]

1 R. Kearney, 'The fifth province: between the global and the local', in R. Kearney (ed.), *Migrations: the Irish at
home and abroad* (Dublin, 1990), 109.
2 D. N. Doyle, 'The Irish in Australia and the United States: some comparisons, 1800–1939', *Irish Economic and
Social History*, 16 (1989), 78.

Official reluctance to accept this change was illustrated by the distaste expressed in the Dáil in 1995 when Mary Robinson called on the home-based nation to 'cherish the diaspora'. But realignment advanced rapidly over the next twenty years, reflected in an enthusiastic welcome for 'The Gathering' in 2013, especially in business quarters, and followed in 2014 by the appointment of a Minister for the Diaspora. For different reasons historians have not unanimously welcomed an extension of the 'Irish' story to include the diaspora. In 2005 Joe Lee fiercely attacked Don Akenson for the lack of precision in his definition, insisting that, without criteria for measurement, boundaries could not be drawn around this expanded Irish population.[3] Describing diaspora as a 'slippery concept', he argued that indeterminacy about what constituted Irish identities, especially because of outmarriage and the role of personal choice, invalidated the academic use of the term. However, an alternative view sees the blurring of lines over time as both inevitable and of central importance because it demonstrates the huge contribution made by the Irish diaspora to societies of settlement. Hybridity is not a statistical inconvenience but key to ongoing connections between the 'home' population and its increasingly mobile genealogical descendants, as well as a growing facet of the settled population of the island itself.

The large size of emigration flows from Ireland during the modern period means that potentially many generations may claim Irish descent in a very wide range of global locations. Their experiences in different societies over time vary nationally, regionally and locally, according to both their initial family 'baggage', including religion and class, and the contexts encountered. As Catherine Nash points out: 'The result of this geographical analytical lens is a map of locally specific versions of being of Irish descent that reflect the particular place of Irishness in those countries' histories of migration and contemporary configurations of categories of ethnicity, race, indigeneity, nationhood and belonging that can intersect, collide and cross-fertilise as they are set in motion and mobilised.'[4] The importance of spatial context points to the value of a comparative approach which can identify common features and local specificities in the construction of Irish identities outside Ireland.

Three types of comparison are used here to highlight a central aspect of Irish diasporic experiences, the longstanding role of British–Irish relationships. The first, placing the comparative approach in a broader context, is a brief discussion of the significant binary of the USA and Britain as the two largest destinations of Irish migrants. The Irish-American experience is often regarded as the paradigmatic case of the Irish diaspora and is by far the most fully researched. It is included here because the USA has functioned as 'not-Britain' since 1776, a status which has added to its attraction as a

---

3 J. J. Lee, 'The Irish diaspora in the nineteenth century', in L. Geary and M. Kelleher (eds.), *Nineteenth century Ireland: a guide to recent research* (Dublin, 2005), 182–222, at 183–7.
4 C. Nash, *Of Irish descent: origin stories, genealogy and the politics of belonging* (New York, 2008), 265.

destination especially in the eighteenth and nineteenth centuries. The second case study is Britain itself, the three constituent nations of which are rarely placed in comparative tension with one another. As Lee points out, Britain is a 'jumbled' label which usually simply means England. There are very few accounts which distinguish the different experiences of Irish diasporic populations in England, Scotland and Wales, but these each throw light on the submerged roles of competing religions and centre–periphery conditions of power. The long histories of immigration have produced further variations at regional and urban scales with different multi-generational mixes.

Finally, a set of comparisons which illuminate British–Irish relationships outside Ireland is that between overseas Dominions of the British empire with their subsequent Commonwealth status. To what extent have longstanding attitudes been transplanted and transformed under a continuing British political umbrella? How does distance from the centre modify colonial positionings? Two locations where the Irish have been the largest non-British settlers living alongside substantially English populations over many generations have been chosen as case studies. Both are relatively small societies to reduce the analytical complexities of internal diversity and focus on differences of generational spread and backgrounds in Ireland. The first is Newfoundland, one of the oldest destinations of the diaspora, its major period of settlement dating from the early eighteenth century, giving a present-day composition of at least seven or eight generations. Catholics from south-east Ireland and Protestants from south-west England settled in fishing communities along the coast, sharing a primarily working-class positioning, but increasingly separated by religion. Irish 'ways of life' have continued in patterns very close to those of Ireland, and awareness of Irish cultural heritages has remained strong over time. The second example is New Zealand where Irish identities are characterised by a much shorter timeline of three or four generations and include a greater Protestant component. Although 'British' has been the label given to the apparent melding of Anglo-Celtic cultures in New Zealand, Irish Catholics have retained a distinct culture mainly because of the de facto segregated education system.

As in the island of Ireland itself, the key factor in the experiences of Irish populations in the major destinations of the New World, Australasia and Great Britain is the underlying relationship over many centuries with England. To a very large extent this has determined routes taken by migrants, shadowing if not participating equally in dispersions to all parts of the empire. However, a dramatic change took place in 1776 when the North American colonies won their independence. Henceforward Irish immigrants entered a foreign territory rather than one ruled from London. Yet there continued a long legacy of the dominant position of the charter group of English settlers in the form of Anglo-Saxon ethnic superiority, sometimes expressed as 'Yankee'. Virulent anti-Catholic attitudes associated with Anglo-Saxon Protestantism persisted well into the twentieth century. In many ways therefore the very large flow of Irish migrants into the USA in the nineteenth century, especially after the Great Famine of the 1840s, avoided direct clashes with British authorities but was still subject to categorisation as an inferior Celtic 'race'.

It is calculated that more than 80 per cent of the very large famine-related outflow settled in the USA, though the precise number entering another large destination, Britain, cannot be known. It was followed by a very substantial second generation which expanded in the later nineteenth century to become 'Irish America', still strongly conscious of its ethnic origins, especially because of clear Catholic allegiances. For many reasons this population has illustrated most openly the multi-generational nature of the diaspora. The label 'Irish-American' has been readily adopted, and indeed sought after, by ever-expanding numbers of third-, fourth- and later generation descendants. Thus the size and visibility of Irish descent identities is greatest in the USA and most easily accepted in Ireland, albeit often derisively in terms such as 'returned Yank'. But regional and local differences complicate this widely recognised grouping. It relates much more forcefully to city populations in the north-east where Boston, for example, retains a strongly Irish character. Tensions between the English-descended charter group and the Irish Catholic minority were never so prominent further west.

25.2. Multi-generational Identities in Britain

The contrast with multi-generational Irish identities in Britain is striking. A key finding of the *Irish 2* research project completed in 2000–2, which explored second-generation Irish lives in Britain, was the hiddenness of these identities.[5] They were ignored or denied both by 'mainstream' populations who refused to recognise the cultural difference of 'white' people from the 'British Isles' speaking with English (or Scottish and Welsh) accents and by people living in Ireland who challenged the authenticity of those born in Britain. There was no label of 'Irish-British', but instead many of the second generation described themselves by much more local attachments such as 'London Irish' or 'Manchester Irish'. Although the total size of the multi-generational diasporic population is much smaller than that accumulating in the USA over several centuries, numbers in the pivotal second generation, which retains very close ties through Irish-born parents, are far higher in Britain in the twentieth century because of continuing large-scale immigration from Ireland. It is calculated that around 6 million people in Britain had at least an Irish-born grandparent in 1971, when the census recorded parents' birthplace.

---

5 *The second-generation Irish in Britain: a hidden population in multi-ethnic Britain*, ESRC Research Grant R000238367; full report at http://researchcatalogue.esrc.ac.uk/grants/R000238367/outputs/read/f51448f2-6d20-40a4-91da-1b62d84e0713 (accessed 28 September 2016).

The inclusion of a 'White Irish' ethnic category in the censuses of 2001 and 2011 introduced for the first time the possibility for people of Irish descent to record this as their 'cultural background'. However, the take-up was very low, reflecting failure to understand the rubric, the ambiguity of requiring rejection of the category 'British' (a national identity relating to citizenship), puzzlement at the novelty of being offered such a category for the first time, and, for many, feelings of both/and identifications rather than the either/or choice demanded. Again this signalled a very different official attitude to ethnic identities from that in the USA where multiple preferences were available instead of the either/or choice of British census forms.

Only a few generalisations can be made about multi-generational Irish experiences in Britain as a whole, because of the wide variations in experiences of settlement related to factors such as class, gender, cohort and religion. A useful starting point is identification of some of the contrasts between the three principal nations. England has been the often unacknowledged focus of most research published in studies of the 'Irish in Britain'. Academic work on Scotland and Wales has largely remained in smaller, nationally specific monographs and collections. Yet the different periods of arrival and characteristics, and attitudes of the majority populations, give contrasting meanings to Irish heritage in the three nations. There is now a body of qualitative work relating to second, and occasionally to more distant, identities of Irish descent in England. This shows that, in contrast to the low quantitative returns of the censuses, the majority of English-born people of Irish parentage identify themselves to a greater or lesser extent as Irish in some form. However, there is considerable geographical variation.

London Irish is a strong identity reflecting continuous replenishment of Irish-born migrants throughout the twentieth century, with especially large cohorts in the 1950s and 1980s. This has been associated with higher degrees of intermarriage than elsewhere in England so that second and third generations may have grown up in strongly Irish households and neighbourhoods. A robust system of Catholic schooling has reinforced clustering of people from Irish backgrounds and the development, especially from the 1980s, of secular community and welfare organisations. The increasingly multicultural composition of London's population has also provided a context for the recognition of Irish difference as well as intersections, and solidarities, with ethnic populations outside the 'White British' mainstream.

The example of London offers an opportunity to explore a much longer timeline of multi-generational Irish identities. Whilst the earliest records of recognisably Irish neighbourhoods show a clustering in the St Giles area of central London from the seventeenth century, demand for manual labour in the East End docks led to an eastward shift in the early nineteenth century. By 1851 the census was already recording second generations in the East End and by the end of the century third and fourth generations were still being labelled 'Irish' in reports and memoirs.

Very little fresh immigration took place before the Second World War, but the background of the Catholic Irish in the East End remained visible, for example in reports of support for the Jewish population threatened by Oswald Mosley's black-shirts in the Battle of Cable Street in 1936. In the post-war period the Irish-descent population, now well into the fifth generation, was renamed the 'white working class', understood to be English by social researchers. However, traces of East End Irishness continue to emerge, for example in the backgrounds of fourth-generation local councillors.[6] But the redesignation of Irish descent over time in class rather than ethnic terms indicates a key difference between multi-generational identities in the USA and Britain.

In other parts of England the multi-generational recognition of Irish descent has varied with numbers and periods of settlement of migrants. In Liverpool, for example, 'Scouse' identities are clearly of third, fourth and fifth Irish generation but are now claimed as local rather than ethnic senses of belonging. The *Irish 2* project used discussion groups and interviews in three locations outside London: Manchester, Coventry and Banbury. Unlike Liverpool, in Manchester Irish identities were readily claimed and accepted in the second and third generations, reflecting a long history of settlement leading to a well-established Catholic school system and strong musical traditions. The more recently settled Coventry, where large-scale immigration dates only from the post-war period, has had more restricted opportunities for the public expression of Irish identities and greater challenges to employment mobility from local English 'Coventry kids'. Finally, Banbury offers an unusual case study of a largely 'English' town where Irish descent remains a private matter, without wider community support. Elsewhere the longitudinal effect of Irish migration into English cities is only beginning to be recovered, even where it has been substantial, and the experiences of later generations remain unclear. For example, Birmingham also has a long history of Irish settlement from the early nineteenth century and a period of marked growth in the post-war period. However, expressions of Irish identities were abruptly 'driven underground' by the backlash following the Birmingham pub bombings of 1974 and proclaimed again only in the 1990s.

The story of Irish settlement in Scotland is very different, mainly reflecting the context of Presbyterianism, which is deeply embedded in constructions of the Scottish nation. Again there is a strong spatial clustering in the Strathclyde region where demand for labour in the mines, heavy engineering and shipyards was met by immigration from Ireland. Antagonism towards the Catholic Irish led to segregation into specific localities and much sharper hostile attitudes than in England, able to flourish with official

---

6 B. Walter, '"England people very nice": multigenerational Irish identities in the multi-cultural East End', *Socialist History*, 45 (2014), 78–102.

sanction. One consequence has been the retention of family-based Irish identities through several generations. When participants of the *Irish 2* project in Strathclyde were asked to complete a family tree schedule over three generations, of parents, selves and children, they insisted on including grandparents. They argued that second-generation identities were indistinguishable from third-generation ones, because of the longer timeline of family encapsulation within Irish Catholic households, which had already loosened in England.

Although the virulent hostility of the earlier twentieth century had largely subsided, *Irish 2* participants explained that there were still risks attached to giving children Irish first names which could lead to discrimination in employment situations. Almost all had stories of anti-Irish incidents in their lives, labelled 'sectarian', which diminished the underlying ethnic basis of racist attitudes. The serious violence associated with clashes between supporters of Celtic and Rangers football teams could be seen as the 'tip of the iceberg' of otherwise submerged Scottish antagonism towards those of Irish descent. That such attitudes continue to permeate Scottish society, although officially denied, is illustrated by confrontation between academics. In 2005 the journal *Ethnic and Racial Studies* carried an article reporting on qualitative research showing discrimination against Irish Catholics in the workforce.[7] This was subject to a vitriolic attack by academics from a different background who accused the researchers of academic weakness in the methodology and selective bias in the presentation, concluding that 'it is a mistake to treat ordinary people as expert on social realities beyond their immediate experience'. They claimed that statistics showed no evidence at all of discrimination.[8] After allowing a robust rebuttal from the initial authors, the editors quickly closed the debate, but its existence clearly illustrated the entrenchment of Scottish–Irish divisions in many walks of life, now being acknowledged more openly by the Scottish parliament.

A divergent pattern has emerged in Wales, which is rarely mentioned in studies of the Irish in Britain. Paul O'Leary argues that the nineteenth-century hostility towards Irish miners and dockworkers, which was expressed both as anti-Catholicism and in labelling them as strikebreakers and undercutters of wages, softened from the 1880s.[9] Welsh political leaders recognised solidarities in Irish land reform demands and Irish migrants and their families saw the value in representing themselves as 'respectable' members of Welsh society, into which they were accepted. This was symbolised by the

7 P. Walls and R. Williams, 'Sectarianism at work: accounts of employment discrimination against Irish Catholics in Scotland', *Ethnic and Racial Studies*, 26, 4 (2003), 632–61.
8 S. Bruce, T. Glendinning, I. Paterson and M. Rosie, 'Religious discrimination in Scotland: fact or myth?', *Ethnic and Racial Studies*, 28, 1 (2005), 151–68.
9 P. O'Leary, 'The cult of respectability and the Irish in mid-nineteenth-century Wales', in O'Leary (ed.), *Irish migrants in modern Wales* (Liverpool, 2004), 119–38.

annual Corpus Christi procession in Cardiff from the mid-1870s, described by the *Western Mail* in 1891 as 'the event of the year in the town'. Solidarity was also achieved through trade union membership and sporting success, for example in boxing. Separate schooling still produced Catholic–Protestant rivalries, but these were small-scale compared with those in Liverpool and Glasgow. People of Irish descent continued to claim Irish identities, still present, for example, in Irish friendly societies in mining communities such as Mountain Ash in Glamorgan, but this was a cultural choice not the beleaguered resistance to discrimination which characterised Irish community groups in the west of Scotland.

Overall in Britain expressions of Irish identities over multiple generations vary significantly between destinations. At the national level this is strongly related to different constructions of the nation in England, Scotland and Wales. In England the political need to control and suppress Irish difference has been strongest. Mary Hickman argues that an agreement was struck with the Catholic hierarchy after emancipation in 1829 that separate schooling could be permitted on condition that it denationalised the second generation, replacing children's Irish national allegiance with a religious identification.[10] In Scotland the major concern was religious difference, especially the clash with Presbyterianism, which defined Scottishness as a national entity against English domination. The much lower profile of the multi-generational Irish population in Wales reflects both, from above, the more complete incorporation of Wales into an England-and-Wales political unit, and, from below, shared resistances to English attempts to impose their hegemony.

However, there are also similar elements in the positioning of the multi-generation Irish populations in all three nations. Of overriding importance is the ongoing influence of Catholic education. This has continued to hold the allegiance in families of Irish descent, even where these have become 'mixed' and parents no longer express religiosity in other ways. Although Catholic schools, especially in England and Wales, have usually avoided making explicit connections with the Irish backgrounds of pupils, they provide the meeting place where people form lifetime friendships and find marriage partners amongst those with whom they have spent many hours of childhood. Those from families where a stronger Irish heritage has been passed on may reinforce their contemporaries' interest in Irish cultural traditions, especially music. Irish-descent populations in all locations have also been directly affected by British responses to the Northern Ireland Troubles, especially where these 'spilled over' into England. Having an Irish surname could be enough to receive the backlash of hostility anywhere.

10 M. J. Hickman, *Religion, class and identity: the state, the Catholic Church and the education of the Irish in Britain* (Aldershot, 1995).

25.3. Multi-generational Irish Identities in the British Empire and Commonwealth

Relationships between Irish and British settlers within the British empire retained some of the colonial hierarchy experienced in the two 'home' nations. However, new conditions reordered the respective statuses both initially and increasingly over subsequent generations. The most striking continuities were in the political order, where the British retained governing power, and in ongoing antagonisms between the dominant religions in each case. Just as anti-Catholicism persisted in the USA well into the twentieth century, so it became the major context for discrimination against people of Irish descent in the British empire. Moreover Catholicism played a key part in consolidating the persistence of Irish identities in later generations as families were distinguished from their neighbours and children were educated alongside people with similar backgrounds.

These commonalities account for some similarities in the development of multi-generational Irish identities in Newfoundland and New Zealand, which are otherwise very different societies. However, there are also other shared features. In both cases the period of migrant settlement was largely completed before the end of the nineteenth century, in strong contrast to Britain which continued to receive very high numbers during the twentieth century. Very little settlement took place in Newfoundland after the end of the 1830s whilst a third of Irish arrivals in New Zealand were in the Vogel era 1870–85 and 1886 marked the year in which the second generation began to outnumber the first. Both therefore have largely multi-generational Irish populations with a very small migrant component, until the recent post-Celtic Tiger outflow added young people in New Zealand. Again in strong contrast to Britain, in both cases the majority of the Irish settled in rural areas, although a number later moved into towns, so that the two largest settlements in each state, St John's and Auckland, had significant concentrations.

But the different economic and social contexts of settlement have produced contrasting experiences amongst the multi-generational Irish populations. Newfoundland has had a very distinctive history, largely based on the single resource of cod. The fishery industry was organised from the West Country of England, initially run by Bristol merchants in the late sixteenth and early seventeenth century, and later by smaller ports on the south coast of Devon and Dorset. At the height of the trade, in the 1730s to 1760s, around sixty ships left these ports each spring for the Grand Banks fishing grounds which were then accessed by smaller boats from harbours in Newfoundland. The coast was divided into stretches under the control of particular merchants. Seamen were recruited from underemployed agricultural workers in Somerset, Devon, Dorset and Hampshire. When the trade expanded, there was a need for greater numbers which were provided by similar surplus rural populations in south-east Ireland. Irish fishermen were taken on board the English ships when they called in to Waterford to load supplies, mainly of food for the voyage and to supplement fish diets in Newfoundland. Irish women were also recruited to work as servants in the preparation of salt cod for export and became central players in community formation and the economic life of the island.

Irish–English relationships between agricultural labourers-turned-seamen thus began on board ships and were initially continued in the small seasonal settlements in Newfoundland. Marriages and partnerships were formed after a while, when women also arrived, though there were strenuous attempts to limit permanent settlement by the British government, which saw the trade as performing the additional role of training individuals for the navy: fishermen were press-ganged when they returned to English ports. In the case of mixed marriages, the Catholic Church made higher demands so that, unusually, English partners were drawn into Irish families whose descendants believed themselves to be thoroughly Irish. However, the arrival of much more militant priests set up a stronger network of Catholic churches and schools in the later eighteenth and early nineteenth century, separating out subsequent generations both socially and geographically. Distinct sections of the Newfoundland coast became 'English', for example those in the east, such as Trinity and Conception Bays, whilst the southern coast became, and remains, 'the Irish Shore'.

Small settlements thus developed in relative isolation, connected by sea rather than by the rocky inhospitable inland routes. Families intermarried within religious communities and localities so that shared Irish heritages were the norm. Traditions, including music and storytelling, as well as accents, were handed down to children with minimal outside contributions to dilute behaviour and beliefs brought from rural Ireland. From time to time disputes flared up with English neighbouring settlements, for example the Harbour Grace Affray in 1883. Whilst the governorship rotated between men with English and Irish backgrounds, there was no doubt that Newfoundland was an English dominion in which anti-Catholic attitudes were endemic. In 1949 the referendum on whether to join Canada or become a separate state was very narrowly won by those supporting federation, a position rejected by many of Irish descent who saw this as accepting membership of an English Protestant state within the British Commonwealth. Although most willingly adopted the identity of Newfoundlander, reminders of the longstanding Irish–English political division can re-emerge. In 2003 the construction of The Rooms, an opulent provincial museum and art gallery, was interpreted by some of Irish descent as a symbolic reminder of British Protestant dominance. It overshadowed the huge Catholic Basilica which had occupied a prime position on the skyline since its completion in 1855.[11]

11 J. Devlin Trew, 'The forgotten Irish? Contested sites and narratives of nation in Newfoundland', *Ethnologies*, 27, 2 (2005), 43–7.

During the Celtic Tiger years of prosperity the government of Ireland established close links with Newfoundland, strongly supporting the local Irish culture by facilitating exchanges 'from an island to an island'. Annual 'Festival of the Sea' visits were organised to link Irish Newfoundlanders with ancestral families in southeast Ireland, with return trips for Irish families to connect genealogically or out of interest with Newfoundland. Joint expertise and projects in marine research and engineering were developed, including academic exchanges between institutions of higher education. In many ways, therefore, links were reinvented between Ireland and the extended multi-generational Irish community in Newfoundland. What had simply been taken for granted as the 'normal' ethnicity of around half the population of Newfoundland was much more explicitly labelled 'Irish', illustrating the contingent nature of Irish identities and the possibility that they can become more, not less, significant over time.

The story of Irish-descent populations in New Zealand contrasts in many ways with that of Newfoundland. Whereas movement to Newfoundland began in the late seventeenth century and came direct from Ireland, that to New Zealand was started in the 1840s and more than half came indirectly by way of Australia and, to a lesser extent, California. Irish immigration of the 1840s and 1850s was mainly connected to the gold rush and most moved on when the resource was exhausted. More permanent settlement followed planned immigration from Ulster, notably the Vesey Stuart settlements of Katikati in the 1870s and 1880s. Whilst the Irish in Newfoundland struggled with subsistence at the hands of merchants, many of those entering New Zealand at this time had sufficient funds to buy land or establish themselves in trades and professions. Compared with high levels of working-class solidarity in Newfoundland associated with strong communitarian attitudes, there was thus a much greater social class range in New Zealand. Another major difference was the larger proportion of Protestants amongst the Irish in New Zealand, approximately one-quarter of the total, as opposed to the almost exclusively Irish Catholic population in Newfoundland.

Irish immigration to New Zealand dropped sharply when assistance schemes closed after the Vogel era of 1870–85, because of the expense of the long journey. After 1891 Ulster was the main source of migrants and Northern Ireland contributed around half of all new migrants throughout the twentieth century. By 1920 the number of new arrivals was very small and thereafter Irish-descent populations predominated. Expressions of nationalism diminished after the civil war as the Irish placed links to the New Zealand Labour Party higher on their political agenda as they saw themselves as settled members of society.[12]

---

12 S. Brosnahan, 'Parties or politics? Wellington's IRA, 1922–1928', in B. Patterson (ed.), *The Irish in New Zealand: historical contexts and perspectives* (Wellington, 2002).

The relationship to Britishness in the two destinations was very different. In Newfoundland two distinct communities were defined by religion and often geographical location, only coming together more recently as Newfoundlanders who jointly assert their distinct identity within confederated Canada. In New Zealand, on the other hand, the label 'British' appears to have melded English, Scottish and Irish identities into a single category, a very different situation from that within Britain itself where national identities remain separate and clearly defined. For this reason the 'British' culture which developed in New Zealand has been given the technical term 'Anglo-Celtic' by historians and social scientists.[13] The Catholic Irish are usually included unquestioningly in the Anglo-Celtic ethnic category; indeed 'Celtic' appears to signify 'Irish'. However, a more nuanced analysis reveals that this apparently inclusive grouping fails to recognise the distinct Catholic culture nurtured by the segregated religious education system, leaving Irish Catholics 'just slightly a people apart'.[14] But the emphasis on bi-culturalism between European-origin Pakeha and Pacific-origin Maori populations has hidden differences within the 'white' population under a 'powerful glue of Anglo-conformity'.[15]

The overlooking reflects a Protestant hegemony cemented in the nominally secular state education system, which in turn has reinforced Catholic determination to retain a segregated status. The enclosure of Irish-descent children within the Catholic school system over several generations rose from 58 per cent in 1926 to 70–80 per cent in 1950.[16] In addition, children's activities such as Scouts and sports, including basketball, were organised on denominational lines to restrict socialising among young people and encourage endogamy. Akenson argues that ironically the Protestant Irish represented most clearly the values and culture of this 'British' or Anglo-Celtic merger, which later became the core of the Pakeha identity.[17] Because of greater relative numbers and higher social status, the Protestant Irish-descent population thus played a far more important role in the construction of the national identity in New Zealand than in Britain itself, where they have largely been subsumed into mainstream populations without leaving distinctive traces.

These two case studies illustrate the diversity of experiences in the Irish diaspora in different parts of the British colonial world. What they shared was taken-for-granted anti-Catholic attitudes which were embedded in childhood in communities of English descent. Name-calling is often remembered in present-day memoirs, indicating that

13 Following C. Price, 'Ethnic composition of the Australian population', in C. Price (ed.), *Australian immigration: a bibliography and digest* 4 (Canberra, 1979), A68–9.

14 D. Akenson, *Half the world from home: perspectives on the Irish in New Zealand 1860–1950* (Wellington, 1990), 158.

15 D. Pearson, *The politics of ethnicity in settler societies* (Basingstoke, 2001), 76.

16 Akenson, *Half the world*, 171.

17 Akenson, *Half the world*, 158.

these attitudes continued at least into living memory. But analyses of the English diaspora, which might reveal the processes continuing to reproduce these submerged relationships, remain to be written.

25.4. Conclusion

There is a striking persistence in multi-generational Irish identities in the diaspora. In all locations this is strongly related to the determination of the Catholic Church to retain the allegiance of families. This became much more marked in the second half of the nineteenth century when the twin processes of separate Catholic schooling and prohibition of mixed marriages strengthened the boundaries around Irish-descent communities and ensured their survival across generations. Irish musical traditions also continued strongly in some communities in recognisable hybridised forms. Although the religious practices of Irish Protestants were distinctive, they were also divided and could be absorbed into British versions within one or two generations.

However, this persistence was often unacknowledged by dominant groups in areas of settlement, and ignored at home in Ireland. It is only recently that visibility has increased for two important reasons. One, from the inside, is recognition by the Irish state of the economic benefits of harnessing investment from successful overseas entrepreneurs with an Irish heritage.[18] The other is from the outside, through the pursuit of genealogical connections by descendants of earlier migrants, facilitated by the technology of the Internet. Both have led to strengthening physical as well as emotional ties between the 'home' and diasporic populations, through flows of money and 'return' visits by tourists.

A comparative approach shows that the impact has been unevenly spread in the destinations, depending on the place of Irishness in each society. The Irish-American diaspora has been especially targeted by Irish state organisations such as Fáilte Ireland and Tourism Ireland, and has responded most enthusiastically at the personal level. Rains argues that later-generation Irish Americans are unusually 'heritage hungry' as a result of the trauma of the Great Famine, which many believe caused a rupture in their family stability.[19] That this is felt much more strongly in the USA than in other diasporic locations may reflect the importance attached to 'roots' in a history of large-scale and diverse immigrant settlement co-existing with the legacy of slavery. In Britain the pressure to assimilate to a mainstream norm has been dominant so that Irish descent

18 Estimated tourism income of 170 million euros from *The Gathering* in 2013: see www.thegatheringireland .com, accessed 31 March 2015.

19 S. Rains, 'Irish roots: genealogy and the performance of Irishness', in D. Negra (ed.), *The Irish in Us: Irishness, performativity, and popular culture* (Durham, NC, 2006), 130–60.

is remembered privately or lost within a few generations. Although New Zealand is also a 'settler society', Irish-descent identities are similarly submerged as an apparently homogenous 'white' European racial/regional identity melds ethnic differences against a Maori 'other'. By contrast Newfoundland has embraced the resurgence of Irish heritage less problematically, reflecting its far higher proportion of Irish-descended people as well as internal community ties.

Demographic issues are inevitably difficult to resolve as intermarriage leads rapidly to fractional identities, which are claimed by individuals on the basis of preference and partial knowledge. This complexity is reflected at the macro-level by national statistical records which increasingly allow citizens to claim an ethnic affiliation using a great variety of instruments. These reveal state attitudes to the heritages of their citizens so that, for example, an expansive list is offered in the USA allowing multiple backgrounds to be recorded. The Canadian census gave encouragement and the clearest instructions in the last comprehensive questionnaire in 2006, asking: 'What were the ethnic or cultural origins of this person's ancestors? An ancestor is usually more distant than a grandparent', then 'Specify as many origins as applicable'. In the British censuses, by contrast, only one option may be selected from a limited list, offered for the first time in 1991 and extended to include 'White Irish' in 2001 after strong representations from community and welfare groups. The New Zealand questionnaire used in 2013 simply asks: 'What ethnic group do you belong to?' with a single box labelled 'New Zealand European'.

Very rarely have academics sought to retrieve statistical evidence at the micro-level, where this remains in the hands of amateur genealogists. Such evidence, though prolific and potentially rich, is inevitably randomly located and lacks context. Exceptions include John Mannion's detailed reconstruction of the Careen family tree from 1825 in Point Lance on the 'Irish Shore' in Newfoundland, tellingly the only diasporic location in the *Atlas of the Irish rural landscape*,[20] and Alison Light's *Common people: the history of an English family*, which not surprisingly includes two small, previously unknown, Irish branches.[21] The impossibility of garnering precise and representative demographic evidence on a large scale means that other forms of evidence need to be brought into play, including memoirs, biographies and fictionalised accounts by authors with an Irish heritage.

Underlying these complexities is the question of intermarriage. The cohesion of the Irish diaspora has undoubtedly been reinforced by strenuous efforts on the part of the Catholic hierarchy to retain children and their descendants within the church.

---

20 J. Mannion, 'Point Lance: a Newfoundland outport', in F. Aalen, K. Whelan and M. Stout (eds.), *Atlas of the Irish rural landscape* (2nd edn, Cork, 2011), 387–409.
21 A. Light, *Common people: the history of an English family* (London, 2014), 192–3.

Thus 'Catholic' may well be a surrogate measure of majority Irishness, especially where endogamy has been marked, as in Scotland.[22] Nevertheless ethnic and religious inter-mixture has become commonplace over the long history of the diaspora, only recently being exhumed by genealogists. The role of gender is clearly at the forefront of issues of intermixing: although women are most likely to retain family links and pass on knowl-edge to later generations, their own family names are quickly lost. A contentious issue which often involves Irish women more than men is 'mixed-race' partnerships, not uncommon given the class positioning and geographical clustering of minority ethnic groups.

The contribution of Irish descendants to global populations is thus on a huge scale. It is often deeply buried in what are now claimed as the national identities of other states. The electoral value of acknowledging such an identity is illustrated by the efforts of US presidential candidates to excavate an Irish heritage, as for example President Obama's identification in 2007 as the fifth-generation descendant of a migrant originating in County Offaly. In an unattributed and deeply embedded way, it could be argued that the film-maker Danny Boyle drew on his Irish parentage in devising the celebration of Britishness for the opening ceremony of the Olympic Games in London in 2012. The imagery was warmly received throughout Britain as representing positive aspects of national culture, but was shot through with signs of inclusiveness and morality which bore the hallmarks of an Irish Catholic upbringing and non-metropolitan sensitivity.

Low visibility in the public sphere has been paralleled by academic treatment of the diaspora. Stephanie Rains argues that the majority of emigrants and their descend-ants are doubly excluded by historians, on the one hand by their predominantly work-ing-class status, until recently a low priority of traditional historical investigation, and on the other, by overriding concern with bounded 'national histories'. This is especially the case of Ireland and the USA, which both place strong emphasis on constructing inside views of the nation and downplay the significance of outside interests. Even when recognition is given to the diaspora, a fundamental issue is the background of academ-ics, as the acrimonious current dispute about the experience of the Irish in Scotland illustrates. Interestingly Lee concluded his critical appraisal of nineteenth-century Irish diaspora scholarship with a call for self-reflection by academics, asking 'How far are late twentieth-century scholars "distanced" by one or more of the values of national-ity, ethnicity, religion, class, gender and language from their subjects?' He continues: 'Deconstructing the observer begins with ourselves', and concludes: 'There is no more important continuing task for diaspora scholarship.'[23]

22 R. Williams, 'Can data on Scottish Catholics tell us about descendants of the Irish in Scotland?', *New Community*, 19, 2 (1993), 296–309.
23 Lee, 'The Irish diaspora', 222.

FURTHER READING

Akenson, D. *Half the world from home: perspectives on the Irish in New Zealand 1860–1950* (Wellington, 1990).

Bielenberg, A. (ed.). *The Irish diaspora* (Harlow, 2000).

Bradley, J.M. *Ethnic and religious identity in modern Scotland: culture, politics and football* (Aldershot, 1995).

Hickman, M.J. *Religion, class and identity: the state, the Catholic Church and the education of the Irish in Britain* (Aldershot, 1995).

Kenny, K. *The American Irish: a history* (Harlow, 2000).

Keogh, W. *The slender thread: Irish women on the southern Avalon, 1750–1860* (New York, 2008).

Lee, J.J. 'The Irish diaspora in the nineteenth century', in L. Geary and M. Kelleher (eds.), *Nineteenth century Ireland: a guide to recent research* (Dublin, 2005), 182–222.

Mannion, J. (ed.). *The peopling of Newfoundland: essays in historical geography* (St John's, 1977).

Meagher, T. *Inventing Irish America; generation, class and ethnic identity in a New England city, 1880–1928* (Notre Dame, 2001).

Nash, C. *Of Irish descent: origin stories, genealogy and the politics of belonging* (New York, 2008).

O'Leary, P. *Irish migrants in modern Wales* (Liverpool, 2004).

Patterson, B. (ed.). *The Irish in New Zealand: historical contexts and perspectives* (Wellington, 2002).

Walter, B. *Outsiders inside: whiteness, place and Irish women* (London, 2001).

26 Minorities

Eugenio F. Biagini

26.1.   Introduction

Daniel O'Connell and the Gaelic revival helped to embed the myth that Ireland was a religiously and ethnically homogenous society with a monocultural and unchanging identity. As in other countries, this process involved social exclusion, 'the marking out of some groups of people and places as marginal in relation to the nation's core groups and places'.[1] When accompanied by poverty, marginality was explicitly associated with subalternity; when associated with privilege, it encouraged social envy. So, minorities are deeply intertwined with questions of class and national identity.

Ironically, while such issues were not uniquely Irish, some Irish minorities were actually 'imported' as a consequence of other countries adopting even more rigorous exclusionary policies at various stages in their history. This is the case with the religious refugees who arrived from the end of the seventeenth century. Likewise, the stimulus for the liberalisation of Irish attitudes often came from abroad, particularly through the international organisations of which Ireland was part. Thus, Jewish toleration was decided by London in 1656. Three hundred years later the Republic was a proud member of the United Nations and ratified the Convention on the Status of Refugees. However, this had little effect on the monoculturalism which inspired both government practice and social responses. The emphasis remained on control, containment and assimilation, as the Hungarian refugees from the 1956 USSR invasion discovered to their cost.[2] Further change came later, when, under EEC/EU law, new standards began to be incorporated into Irish law.

1 D. Forgacs, *Italy's margins: social exclusion and nation formation since 1861* (Cambridge, 2014), 1.
2 E. Ward, '"A big show-off to show what we could do": Ireland and the Hungarian refugee crisis of 1956', *Irish Studies in International Affairs*, 8 (1996), 131–41.

26.2. The Protestant Refugees

Derisively called Huguenots – a term of uncertain etymology – by their persecutors, after the revocation of the Edict of Nantes (1685), French Protestants had to choose between submission and exile. About half a million opted for the latter, seeking sanctuary in other European countries. Denmark, Poland, Prussia, the Netherlands and England received substantial numbers. They comprised a cross-section of French society, from the nobility and the clergy to merchants and artisans. About five thousand eventually moved to Ireland, settling in Birr, Carlow, Cork, Dublin, Kilkenny, Portarlington, Waterford and Youghal.

They arrived with a complex cultural baggage, including the memory of recent persecution with its accompanying sense of precariousness, compounded by an awareness that in Ireland they were, at the same time, a religious and an ethnic minority. In such a context, it is not surprising that at first their community looked up to leaders often drawn from the military *noblesse d'épée*: the most famous of these was Henri Massue, Marquis de Ruvigny, who became Earl of Galway in 1697. He and other aristocrats were soon assimilated and joined the established church. Although the latter was uncomfortably hierarchical by Huguenot standards, there was much theological common ground between the two traditions. In fact, the community's Calvinist reputation proved a distinct advantage in securing preferment for those who conformed and felt called to the priesthood. Within two generations several Huguenots had risen to deanships and even the episcopacy (such as Richard Chevenix, bishop of Killaloe in 1745 and of Waterford and Lismore in 1746).

Many others, however, remained resolutely Huguenot, even retaining the French tongue in worship. Their language and denominational distinctiveness were part of their collective identity and self-respect. They 'lived' simultaneously in two distinct mental realities – one defined by their own cultural traditions and religious rites, the other by the economic and political environment of the host country. As a diaspora, they cherished links with French exiles in other parts of the world, empowered by an awareness of having originated from a country which had set standards for the rest of the world, and by the accompanying sense that they need not assimilate to the citizens of their countries of refuge, 'but hope[d] to serve them as a model'.[3]

Despite such cultural hauteur, they were still ready to make the most of the opportunities offered by their host countries. The great hope of English social reformers was to lift Ireland to 'continental standards of industry and prosperity',[4] and this was why

---

3 J. P. Erman and P. C. F. Reclam, *Les Mémoires pour servir à l'histoire des réfugiés français dans les États du Roi de Prusse*, 9 vols. (Berlin, 1782–99), I, 302, cited in S. Lachenicht, *Hugenotten in Europa und Nordamerika: Migration und Integration in der Frühen Neuzeit* (Frankfurt, 2010), 322.

4 T. Barnard, *A new anatomy of Ireland: the Irish Protestants, 1649–1770* (London, 2003), 3.

the Huguenots were there. As W. E. H. Lecky noted in his *History of Ireland in the eighteenth century* (1892, p. 353), they 'threw themselves very actively in every form of industry, and identified … thoroughly with Irish interests', establishing, among other things, the first literary journal and the first florists' society. In the first half of the eighteenth century, with the growth of political stability, the community saw the emergence of 'middle ranks' comprising entrepreneurs, innkeepers, haberdashers and medics, together with a mercantile bourgeoisie. As is well known, their most distinctive contribution was in the textile industry, particularly silk, which employed about five thousand people in Dublin around 1760. Such industry, as well as the manufacturing of linen and wool, was important to Huguenot settlements at Lisburn, Kilkenny and Cork, while at Limerick they established lace and glove trades.

Their best-known champion was Daniel Defoe. Though the proponent of a multi-ethnic definition of national identity (as illustrated by his 1701 satirical poem 'The true born Englishman'), his main motivation was a hope that the refugees would improve native trade and industry. Similar anticipations governed and qualified feelings in Ireland, both then and since. That attitudes to immigrants depended on their perceived economic usefulness is further confirmed by the half-hearted welcome reserved to the three thousand German Palatine refugees, who arrived from 1709. This lack of generosity affected even the way historians memorialised them: for example, Lecky – so full of praise for the Huguenots – wrote laconically of the Palatines that 'there [was] not much to be said' (p. 351). They were farmers who belonged 'chiefly to the humblest classes' and settled in poor areas such as Kerry and Limerick. Not only were they less economically useful than the French, but also they could not rely on the network of charitable societies and schools which the Huguenots enjoyed thanks to the patronage of their aristocratic leaders. With limited skills and local support, many Palatines soon emigrated further to the American colonies (in this, at least, conforming to a distinctively Irish pattern of social behaviour).[5] By 1720 only about a thousand of them remained. They were provided with tiny plots: on the Southwell estate (Limerick) these consisted of eight acres of mixed-quality land per family, for which the landlord doubled the rent within two years of the settlement. They were an exploited rural working group and were treated with contempt, which they greatly resented, especially because it came with ethnic prejudice.[6] They were not easily assimilated, as illustrated by the survival of negative stereotypes in both literature and folklore. More than a century after their arrival, Gerald Griffin (1803–40) described them as 'wicked, stupid, ugly, conniving or ridiculous' – stereotypes material inspired

---

5 A. Olson, 'The English reception of the Huguenots, Palatines and Salzburgers 1680–1734: a comparative analysis', in R. Vigne and C. Littleton (eds.), *From strangers to citizens: The integration of immigrant communities in Britain, Ireland and colonial America, 1550–1750* (Brighton, 2001), 482–91.

6 V. Hicks, 'Images of Palatines from folk tradition, novels and travellers', *Béaloideas*, 64/65 (1996/7), 4.

by racial prejudice. And in the 1930s the Irish Folklore Commission (IFC) collected evidence which showed that the descendants of the Palatines (now predominantly Methodist in religion) were sometimes suspected of witchcraft and generally regarded as outsiders, 'strange' people.

On the other hand, the IFC also found evidence of a grudging admiration for Palatine workmanship and tidiness. This went with the myth that the community was rarely molested by their Catholic neighbours. The situation was, however, more complex. The Palatines had a strong sense of loyalty to the Hanoverian monarchy – even many of those who had emigrated to America fled to Canada when the Thirteen Colonies declared independence. In Ireland, both before and after 1798, the Palatines supported the authorities. Not surprisingly, they found themselves at the receiving end of Whiteboy violence, which intensified in the first half of the nineteenth century. In 1821, as Limerick and Kerry descended into 'a virtual state of war', Palatine emigration resumed, this time to Canada and Australia.[7] Some of those who stayed moved out of farming into business. The most famous example is John W. Switzer, who established a tailor's business in Grafton Street, Dublin, in the second half of the 1840s – eventually becoming the landmark Switzer & Co. Even at the time, its founder was described as a 'gentleman', but he began his working life as a pedlar in the Liberties, like many Jews were to do from the 1890s.

26.3. Jews

In some respects, the experience of Jewish people combines some of the features which we have already observed in the case of the Huguenots and Palatines – including both marginality and also social and political achievement, with several eminent politicians, including lord mayors of both Cork and Dublin, TDs, senators and government ministers. Their presence in Ireland goes back to the Middle Ages, but they became a visible community only from 1660, when they established a synagogue near Dublin Castle. Four years earlier Oliver Cromwell had decreed their readmission to what was then the Commonwealth of England, Scotland and Ireland. As in the case of the Huguenots, part of what motivated their Protestant advocates was economic opportunism, most famously articulated by James Harrington in *The Commonwealth of Oceana* (1656). Nothing came of his plan to settle large numbers of highly skilled Jews in Ireland, though the community did grow, if only slowly, with more arriving after 1690. In the religiously pluralist early eighteenth-century Dublin, Jews were unremarkable, being included in the general category of 'merchants and foreign Protestants'. They settled in

---

7 V. Hicks, 'The Palatines: 1798 and its aftermath', *Journal of the Royal Society of Antiquaries of Ireland*, 126 (1996), 16.

Ballybough – previously a Huguenot and Quaker area – where they acquired a burial place in 1718.

Soon Jews started to mix with the intellectual elite, at least in certain specialist areas: in 1737 the teacher of Hebrew at Trinity College Dublin was one Abraham Judah and in 1740 *Reilly's Dublin News Letter* advertised the services of a Jewish tutor in both arithmetic and languages (including French, German and Italian). The first rabbi about whom details have survived was Aron Sophair, originally from Novrogoden (Minsk). His successors were soon dignified with the title of 'Reverend', an appellation at the time denied to Baptist and other dissenting pastors. Over time, the community became well established and influential beyond its size, branching out into manufacturing and the professions, particularly law and medicine (from the eighteenth century the Rotunda Hospital made even the position of Master open to doctors of all religious confessions: the first Jewish physician of note was practising in Dublin in the 1860s).

In 1714 the Irish philosopher John Toland advocated Jewish naturalisation. Several Bills to this effect were unsuccessfully introduced in both the Irish and British parliaments between 1743 and 1747. In 1753 an Act was finally adopted, only to be repealed in 1754, in response to popular opposition. By now associated with the liberal elite, Jewish community leaders articulated their views through that quintessential institution of Enlightenment Europe, the Freemasons. By the 1770s there were Jews in the Dublin Freemasons Lodge, which provided a further venue for contacts between leading members of both Jewish and Christian communities.[8] It may not be without significance that Daniel O'Connell – the most notable nineteenth-century nationalist to express sympathy for the Jewish people – at one stage had been himself a Freemason.

In the late 1840s Jews gave generously to famine relief, but this did not prevent Archbishop Paul Cullen from claiming that 'the Jews of London' were behind the starvation of Ireland through the exploitation of impoverished landlords and graziers.[9] It was nothing more than a standard expression of anti-Semitic prejudice, strengthened by the perception that Jews could not be fully assimilated, because their mental world stretched beyond the shore of Ireland, not only through their ancestral language and religion, but also through their diasporic link with foreign financial centres (as it was indeed illustrated by some eminent families: on securing full political rights, in 1858, their first MP was Lionel de Rothschild). Most of the rest of the Victorian age was uneventful for this small, but solid and respectable community, which saw one of its members – Sir Otto Jaffe – become mayor of Belfast in 1874. (Wolff, of the celebrated Harland and Wolff shipyards, was also of Jewish origin, but a Protestant convert.) They were representative of a successful and well-integrated minority.

8 L. Hyman, *The Jews of Ireland from earliest times to the year 1910* (London, 1972), 59.
9 E. J. Larkin, *The consolidation of the Catholic Church in Ireland, 1860–1870* (Chapel Hill, NC, 1987), 286.

Figure 26.1 Jewish wedding group of Miss Levin, John Street, Waterford, 1901. Credit: Image courtesy of the National Library of Ireland.

Things started to change from the 1880s, with the beginning of the pogroms in the Russian empire, which forced hundreds of thousands of Lithuanian and Polish Jews to leave their homelands. Like their counterparts in England, Ireland's Jewish community felt threatened by the arrival of such large numbers of eastern European refugees. As an 1890 synagogue circular stated, 'of the original congregation only twelve or thirteen families [remain], while the number of foreign Jews amounts to between 600 and 700 souls'.[10] The situation was similar in some other cities: Cork, which had only 26 Jews in 1881, had as many as 217 in 1891 and 447 in 1901. By then the 'new' Jews formed what one source described as 'a Lithuanian village inserted in the midst of a very parochial people'. In Belfast numbers shot from 11 in 1871, to 205 in 1891, and 1,139 in 1911. Dublin was by far the largest Jewish centre in the country, its community expanding from 335 in 1871 to 2,965 in 1911.

The social chasm between the 'Irish' Jews and the Litvaks involved not only income and class, but also lifestyle, education, language, attire, self-presentation and religious

10 Cited in B. Shillman, *A short history of the Jews in Ireland* (Dublin, 1945), 97.

belief. The new arrivals made a living as pedlars and money-lenders, 'disreputable' trades which attracted censorious comments from members of the native community. The mindset of the two groups was also different: the long-established 'Irish' Jews had a history of toleration and bourgeois respectability, while the new refugees were familiar with social oppression and brutal persecution in the countries which they had fled. They were also more orthodox and conservative and were perplexed by Anglo-Jewish practices: to the present day, stories are told of how the Litvaks – when first attending established synagogues such as the one of Adelaide Road – were puzzled by the local tradition of concluding the Sabbath service by singing 'God Save the King'. The unease between the two groups was compounded by class divides, the 'native' Jews being solidly middle class, in contrast to the economically precarious and socially marginal immigrants. All of this contributed to the tendency of the newly arrived to worship in their own, separate prayer rooms, avoiding the synagogues, which were, for them, culturally, socially and politically alien. Yet, from the start the new immigrants fared better than the poorest sections of the host community, particularly in terms of housing, social mobility, health and life expectancy. The last two may have been positively affected by Jewish religious and cultural mores, including a concern for personal cleanliness and basic hygiene.[11]

The community's visibility at a time of international anti-Semitism provided the opportunity for episodes of intolerance, the most infamous of which was the 1904 Limerick Boycott, which devastated the local Jewish businesses. The town had one of the largest and fastest-growing Jewish communities outside Dublin, with numbers rising from 93 in 1891, to 171 in 1901, but also one of the poorest – with all its members bar four entering their occupation in the census as 'pedlars'. The boycott was provoked by the inflammatory rhetoric of one Father John Creagh, member of an order (the Redemptorists) which had acquired an anti-Semitic reputation in France in conjunction with the Dreyfus Affair. Creagh, however, was not isolated: as Dermot Keogh has written, anti-Semitism was at the time articulated by other Irish Catholic priests, who kept alive popular animosity against 'the killers of Christ' and rekindled social prejudice against them.

Operating under such pressures, and with family affiliations which stretched across Europe, the Jewish people had the clear sense of belonging to a diaspora, something that qualified their desire to identify with Ireland and, by reaction, was reflected in Gentile attitudes to them. This was immortalised in James Joyce's *Ulysses*, when 'the Citizen' dismissively states that Jews dreamt of a 'new Jerusalem'. As Leopold Bloom noted, such a view was based on a narrow ethnic definition of Irishness. It was also grossly unfair: following ancient rabbinical injunction to honour the host country, Irish Jews were patriotically attached to their country of adoption and its government,

11 C. Ó Gráda, *Jewish Ireland in the age of Joyce: a socioeconomic history* (Princeton, 2006), 146–52.

Figure 26.2 Scout group, Adelaide Road synagogue, 1959. Credit: Dublin Jewish Museum.

but this could take different shapes. From 1916 the community produced a number of high-profile republicans, including Robert Briscoe, a Zionist who enjoyed a close relationship with de Valera.[12] However, on the whole, like the Palatines, they tended to be loyalist, feeling that the crown was their protector.

In the field of education, from as early as the eighteenth century Irish Jews had benefited from the intrinsic pluralism of Protestant schools. They patronised schools as diverse as the elite St Andrew's College (Presbyterian) and the much smaller Damer School, which met in the basement of the Unitarian Chapel on St Stephen's Green. The revolution did not change this elective affinity: Chaim Herzog, the Irishman who became Israel's first president, hailed from a family which supported the republican cause in the civil war, but was educated in solidly Protestant schools: 'I was sent first to Alexandra College, a girls' school with a kindergarten for both girls and boys. It was quite fashionable and not Catholic, which was probably why my parents sent me there … From Alexandra I moved to Wesley College, an English-style Protestant school, whose most famous alumnus was George Bernard Shaw.'[13] And in Iris Murdoch's *Something special* (written in the early 1950s), a 'no-longer so young' lower middle-class Protestant woman, encouraged by her family, decides to marry a Jewish tailor: there is 'nothing special' about him, but each finds the other utterly non-threatening (by contrast, they both perceive Catholic men as both vulgar and aggressive).

12 K. McCarthy, 'Éamon de Valera's relationship with Robert Briscoe: a reappraisal', *Irish Studies in International Affairs*, 25 (2014), 165–86.
13 C. Herzog, *Living history* (1997), 13–14.

As Herzog's story suggests, over the years, the social profile of the Litvak community changed. By 1926 adult male Jews were primarily occupied as 'repairers' (27%), 'commerce, finance, insurance' (52%) and 'professional' (11%). By 1946 these proportions changed to 35%, 40% and 16.6% respectively. The number of pedlars declined steadily throughout the period, while there was a dramatic increase in the number of merchants, jewellers, manufacturers, dentists, doctors and lawyers.[14] This change was further encouraged by the arrival – from the late 1930s – of refugees from Nazism. The government imposed restrictive limits on 'non-Aryan' immigration (only sixty people were accepted between 1933 and 1947), but a few additional Jewish industrialists were allowed to settle in the country on condition they came with their factories. Three of these – producing hats and ribbons – were transplanted from France, Austria, Czechoslovakia and Belgium to Galway, Mayo and Longford. Meanwhile, tariffs began to shape consumer choices: with the trade war with Britain limiting the importation of fashion items, there was growing demand for Irish-made substitutes, which, in turn, helped to consolidate the position of the refugees, whose work became of unquestionable utility to the public. Thus, unwittingly, protectionism saved lives.

Though there may have been more 'hidden refugees' than we know – that is, people below the authorities' radar working in small factories – tragically, the government refused to continue the imported factories experiment. Even the manufacturers and workers who had been allowed in were on short-term visas, with their children sometimes receiving even shorter-terms permits. The message was clear: their presence was accepted only for as long as they served the nation. It did not help that the factories were seen as the footprint of Fianna Fáil's power, thus conflating the refugee issue with domestic party strife. However, once they were in the country, in practice it became difficult to deport them.

This does not mean that conditions were conducive to integration. The idea that the national identity required cultural homogeneity contributed to the perpetuation of 'racialised constructions of minority groups and exclusionary ideologies of social belonging'.[15] This percolated down into the popular culture, surfacing in various contexts including children's jingles, in which sometimes abusive remarks about Protestants, Jews and Catholics were mixed, expressing old stereotypes and assumptions about 'the other':

> 'Von Shilly! Von Shilly!', the Jewman did cry,
> When a big red-nosed Bobby just then did pass by,
> 'What's the row here, what's the row here? D'ye think ye are in shul?'
> 'If I don't get my shilly, I must get my wool!'

14 Ó Gráda, *Jewish Ireland*, 78–83.
15 B. Fanning, *Racism and social change in the Republic of Ireland* (Manchester, 2002), 4.

> Next Monday morning the Jewman called round
> He knocked at the door but he heard no sound,
> 'Are you in, Missus Murphy?', he cried with a shout,
> 'If I don't get my shilly, you won't get your stout!'[16]

Anti-Semitism was deeply embedded in both state practice and popular attitudes, in which religion provided the idiom to conceptualise the 'acceptable' immigrant. The vetting of the latter was in itself based on religious criteria, as well as distanced from state responsibilities, through the creation of the significantly named Irish Co-ordinating Committee for the Relief of Christian Refugees. While this was a code word for Jewish Catholic converts, even the latter were racialised as 'hybrids'. Thus, despite the 1937 constitutional endorsement of Judaism as one of the religions belonging to Ireland, far fewer Jewish families were allowed into the country than Huguenots and Palatines had been in former centuries.

Not much luckier were five hundred Jewish children whom de Valera tried to let into the country in 1943. Worried about popular hostility to Jews and harassed by anti-Semitic TDs, the Taoiseach never admitted that these asylum seekers were Jewish. Eventually the operation was delayed until it was too late. By contrast, a number of Jewish children were received in Northern Ireland, though they only accounted for a small part of the ten thousand who reached the UK under the *Kindertransport* scheme, which Jewish and Quaker leaders had persuaded the British Prime Minister Neville Chamberlain to introduce (November 1938).[17] In Belfast they experienced the oddities of a host community which was not anti-Semitic, but often altogether unable to grasp a reality beyond the familiar sectarian divides. This is illustrated in Marilyn Taylor's novel *Faraway home*, where one friendly Orangeman inquires: 'D'you mind me asking, what church do you all go to?' On being told that they went to the synagogue, he continued: 'I have never heard of one of those – at least not in the Shankill', and, assuming they were Protestant (because they were not Catholic), he offers to 'come up one night and teach you to play the flute … D'you know the song, "The Auld Orange Flute"?'[18] Whatever the embarrassment of putative Protestantism, well into the twenty-first century the Jewish community in Northern Ireland remembered that in their time of need, they had been allowed to settle in the province and were received by people who were themselves suffering under the Blitz and were fighting to defeat Hitler. This made Belfast Jews 'proud to be British', or at least inclined to support unionism and sceptical about nationalism.[19]

---

16 L. Daiken, 'Religious war songs', from *Out goes she* (1957), 18. Sung to 'The tune of the Aul orange flute'.

17 M. Taylor, 'Millisle, County Down – haven from Nazi terror', *History Ireland*, 4 (2001), 9.

18 M. Taylor, *Faraway home* (Dublin, 1999), 93–4. Cf. C. Hezser, 'Are you Protestant Jews or Roman Catholic Jews?', *Modern Judaism*, 25, 2 (May 2005), 159–88.

19 A. E. Thompson, 'The Belfast Jewish community during the Troubles and their aftermath', unpublished MPhil. dissertation, Cambridge, 2010, 31–3.

In both south and north, the foundation of the state of Israel and the resulting Middle East crises transformed perceptions of Jews. In the country over which Archbishop McQuaid ruled with all the certainties of pre-Vatican II militant Catholicism, Dublin's policy remained primarily influenced by unquestioning loyalty to the Holy See. Despite Briscoe's republican enthusiasm, this atmosphere must have been profoundly destabilising for the community. In David Marcus's *To next year in Jerusalem* (1954) a leading character puts it very clearly when he says, 'I feel as if my soul is perpetually in exile. I feel as if I have no roots, no home, nothing to rely on, nothing I can be sure of. I am always wary, on the qui vive, as it were. In a sense, I am always afraid' (140). Though in 1963 the government formally recognised Israel, for many Jews 'making Aliya' – returning to the Promised Land – became an attractive option. In the north, a bizarre new development took shape from the turn of the century, when republicans started to display the Palestinian flag to show their support for the PLO's struggle against imperialism. This prompted militant unionists to adopt the Star of David, feeling that Netanyahu and Sharon set the example in the best way to deal with IRA-like terrorists. One positive outcome of these developments was that Belfast Jews became bolder in asserting their autonomy and distinctiveness from both Gentile warring factions, particularly through the 'Jews Schmooze' initiative (2009).

The community had reached its demographic peak around 1946 (with about four thousand members in the Republic and some two thousand in Northern Ireland), but numbers declined steadily thereafter, though the trend has been reversed recently. By 2011 there were 1,984 Jewish people in the Republic, mainly concentrated in Dublin, while 335 lived in Northern Ireland. As Ray Revlin notes, 'so steep a rate of decline … in a land free from overt anti-Semitism gives rise to some speculation regarding the catalyst'.[20] There is no simple explanation, but we must consider the 'pull' factor represented by the Irish-Jewish diaspora which had developed in America, England and especially in Israel, and the desire to find suitable marriage partners, which Ireland's small and ageing Jewish community could not supply. On the other hand, this happened while the Republic *attracted* immigrants from all over the world, resulting in the development of new religious minorities, including Muslims and Russian Orthodox, while even the number of Protestants started to increase, reversing a downward trend which had long seemed unstoppable. Only the Jewish community did not benefit from such developments. The extent to which 'lack of *overt* anti-Semitism' disguised the persistence of older attitudes is a question, and in any case hostility to Jews was sometimes open. Thus in 1970 it was the only Independent member of the council of Limerick who called a meeting to dissociate himself and the city from the anti-Semitic remarks made by the city mayor, demanding an apology to the Chief Rabbi, and expressed his

20 R. Rivlin, *Jewish Ireland: a social history* (Dublin, 2011), 236.

regret that none of the clergy had spoken up on this occasion. Certainly, figures indicate that many in the south continue to regards Jews as more alien than other groups, including British migrants, though less undesirable than the Travellers, who form the subject of the next section.

26.4. Travellers

While refugees were sometimes regarded as potential economic assets, despite being ethnically different, the Travellers were often regarded as a social liability, though their Irishness was never questioned. Indeed, from as early as the eighteenth century they were romanticised as the last representatives of the original, 'primitive Irish'. In the Victorian recovery of a heroic Irish past, they were sometimes represented as 'trans-European, Oriental' people, perhaps descendants of pre-Celtic tribes. They captivated amateur anthropologists and linguists looking for unspoiled *Ur*-Irishness. Like the Claddagh – a fishing community of allegedly 'fierce and independent', 'peculiar and primitive' habits – the Travellers seem to fit the bill as 'exemplary indigenous exotic'. This was helped by their fascinating culture: for, '[a]lthough unlettered … [they] were deeply literate … [and] commanded a sprawling corpus of verbal and musical literature that served the communal purposes of cultural continuity, order, and entertainment'.[21] Excitement about the community further increased from 1880, when an American journalist, Charles Leland, claimed to have identified the Travellers' cryptolect as a Celtic language, which he called Shelta. In 1891 the first dictionaries of this 'fifth' Celtic language started to appear.

Moreover, some found the Traveller lifestyle intriguing: free from local allegiances, the Tinkers escaped institutionalisation and evaded state controls. Their allegedly bohemian disregard of rules and conventions was a further reason why they featured positively in the works of Lady Gregory and John M. Synge, authors who were themselves members of a minority. As Lanters notes, 'in addition to a love of horses, disrespect for respectability, and a love of travel, they share with the Anglo-Irish aristocracy an ability to "survive in their habitat" even though they are pushed aside by the "Progress" of the upwardly mobile'.[22]

For many ordinary Irish, interest in the Travellers was more pragmatic, and arose from the economic functions performed by these itinerant multi-taskers, who were expert entertainers at village fairs, supplied farmers with a versatile labour force, including seasonal farm workers, and doubled up as horse-traders, salespeople and tinsmiths. However, as land reform made the peasants more prosperous, 'respectable'

21 A. Cort, *Puck of the Droms: the lives and literature of the Irish Tinkers* (Berkeley, 1985), 6.
22 J. Lanters, *The 'Tinkers' in Irish literature* (Dublin, 2008), 143.

Figure 26.3 Travellers at caravan doorway, Buttevant, Co. Cork, 1954. The Wiltshire Collection. Courtesy of the National Library of Ireland.

and bourgeois, Travellers became increasingly marginal figures, while their subalternity acquired racialised connotations.[23]

The writing was on the wall, or so it seemed: in an age which believed in 'Progress', the Travellers were an implausible group, a doomed anachronism, whose habits allegedly defied modern notions of personal hygiene and market rationality. Therefore, studying them was about 'discovering and recording [their] language and culture … *before they disappeared*'.[24] That they *would* disappear was taken for granted, because they would be crushed 'under the pressure of modern law', as the *Journal of Gypsy Lore* put it in 1889.

23 J. Maclaughlin, 'Nation-building, social closure and anti-traveller racism in Ireland', *Sociology*, 33, 1 (1999), 129–51.
24 B. Taylor, *A minority and the state: Travellers in Britain in the twentieth century* (Manchester, 2008), 6.

It was almost a self-fulfilling prophecy. In the 1930s the evidence collected by the IFC illustrated the cultural and social gap between them and the settled population. Soon legislation on planning and welfare relegated the Travellers to the bottom of the social ladder, well below the urban working class. By 1936 schooling became mandatory for all children aged between six and fourteen, thus depriving Travellers of the income that this age group used to produce, and in 1942 the Department of Education proposed stricter regulation and enforcement, with a measure which, if applied, might have ended the nomadic lifestyle. The Bill was passed by the Oireachtas (Parliament), but declared unconstitutional by the Supreme Court in 1943. There was no indication that these moves were inspired by an increased concern for the social needs of travelling families. Their health, for example, attracted public attention only when it was feared to represent a public hazard, such as in the 1940 County Donegal outbreak of typhus, which was blamed on local Travellers. Across the border the situation was similar. There Travellers were unwelcome also because they were predominantly Catholic, and ratepayers were fiercely hostile to their camps: one confidential report noted in 1953 that 'the general opinion seemed to be that gypsies should be excluded altogether'.[25] While legislation in this sense could not be contemplated, Stormont's weakness gave more weight to local authorities and certain lobbies within their electorate.

Such negative attitudes were influential in deterring the creation of publicly funded camp sites and were reflected even in the lack of precise statistics, with the Garda submitting incomplete returns (though on the whole indicating – in the 1950s – a population varying from six to seven thousand individuals). Governments tended to move the Travellers on when the settled people complained – and did so often, as tighter control of land usage and the widening social and cultural disparities meant that tension between the two communities increased. Meanwhile, the growth in motor car traffic required an expansion in police duties and powers, which affected all road users, especially when their activities might be construed as creating obstruction to the traffic. This was indeed the case with the Travellers.

In 1960 Dublin appointed a commission on 'Itinerants', which, besides responding to concerns from representatives of the public, reflected the need to act on a range of social welfare issues, including mental health. It provided the opportunity to investigate the social composition of the community. While from a 'settled' point of view the community appeared undifferentiated in its peculiarities, actually it was divided by occupational specialisms and significant internal social distinctions based on income and lifestyle. In 1963 an *Economic classification of itinerant families* distinguished between three groups: 'the motor-trailer group of 40–60 families who were

25 Control of Gypsies, in Government of Northern Ireland, Parliamentary Question, Tuesday, 8 December 1953, PRONI, HA/23/1/212.

the affluent dealers; the horse dealers who still used the horse-drawn caravan comprising 300–400 families and a third group of 350–450 families who had horse-drawn caravans or tents', and was the only one to retain the tinsmith affiliation. In contrast to popular stereotypes about Traveller sexual promiscuity, the Commission uncovered a rigid enforcement of morality, which appeared to be well above contemporary settled people's standards. Although the Commission encouraged co-operation between state and charitable organisations in providing services and opportunities for Travellers, the Irish Itinerant Settlement Committee recommended absorption and assimilation, policies which the government endorsed. This resulted in a large movement of Irish Travellers into Britain in 1963–70.

The following period saw the beginning of the politicisation of the Travellers and the internationalisation of their issues, with the advice of bodies such as the Communauté Mondiale Gitane and the International Evangelical Gypsy Mission. Very much like the contemporary civil rights campaign in the north, the struggle for Traveller rights relied upon voluntary organisations, whose number increased with several new bodies being established particularly in the 1980s, including the Travellers' Rights Committee (1981), Minceir Misli (1983), Travellers' Education and Development Group (1984) and the Irish Travellers' Movement (1990). By then, they had found a champion in the Senator of Trinity College, who was elected president of the Republic in that year – Mary Robinson.

26.5.   Towards Pluralism, 1990–2016

In a now famous address to the joint Houses of the Oireachtas (2 February 1995), President Robinson stressed the extent to which the question of minorities is at the centre of the island's history. Though at the time she was criticised by legislators and party leaders, she was actually interpreting the mood of an Ireland which was then becoming a multicultural society, with the Celtic Tiger attracting economic immigrants from all over the world. In 2001 the Refugee Applications Commissioner received 10,325 applications from countries ranging from Nigeria to Russia and Ukraine, and issued more than 36,000 temporary work visas to non-EEA/EU applicants, of which more than 29,000 were new permits. In 1996–2000 *The Economist* ranked Ireland fourth among EU countries in terms of asylum seekers in proportion to the population. The country had come a long way from the xenophobic Eire of 1938–56.

Yet, old practices and attitudes survived. The state remained reluctant to be involved and the reception of refugees was largely left to charities until the 1990s, and from 1991 a state agency co-ordinated the resettlement of the Bosnian refugees (there were 1,089 of them by 1999). The 1996 Refugee Act was not implemented until the end of the decade, when for Bryan Fanning 'the marginalisation of asylum seekers resembled the treatment of refugees prior to 1956'.[26] Again, behind such marginalisation economic pragmatism came first, followed by ethnic prejudice, as illustrated by a 2002 survey: top of the list in terms of economic desirability were English immigrants and Irish Protestants, followed by Spaniards and Jews. The least desirable were Nigerians, Muslims and Arabs, with the Travellers at the very bottom.[27] However, official discourse had long been much more liberal and proactive than popular opinion. In 1995 the *Report of the task force on travelling people* had adopted the concept of 'interculturalism', which rejected assimilationism and acknowledged the reality of power and status inequalities. Within two years in Northern Ireland the Travellers, benefiting from the overhaul of local authorities' power under London's direct rule, became legally recognised as an ethnic minority. In the Republic, they were denied this status, though in 2014 – after a long campaign by Traveller and human rights pressure groups – the government indicated that a change of the law was forthcoming.

Meanwhile, arrivals from Catholic countries made up for part of the long-term decline in the number of native Irish churchgoers. In 2011 there were 36,000 Lithuanians, 20,000 Latvians and 10,000 Slovakians in the Republic. The Polish minority numbered about 122,000 (comparable to the whole of the Church of Ireland population in the Republic, which was then 129,000). Polish became one of the languages which can be taken as part of the Irish Leaving Certificate, and in 2006 the Polish government announced its intention to open a Polish school in Dublin, offering the opportunity for pupils to follow the Polish National Curriculum, while a number of media outlets catering to Irish Poles multiplied, including newspapers in the national language, a section in Dublin's *Evening Herald* and a television channel.

That the real turning point took place in the first decade of the twenty-first century is confirmed by the experience of another group: the Jehovah's Witnesses. They became a visible presence in both Northern Ireland and the Republic from the second half of the 1940s. Though they had faced discrimination and widespread suspicion and persecution around the world – and indeed had been outlawed in some advanced democracies, such as New Zealand – in Ireland they encountered less opposition than one might expect. Even the American analyst of Catholic power, Paul Blanshard – though critical of religious freedom in Ireland – admitted that they 'were permitted to hawk their inflammatory magazines on the streets of Dublin without let or hindrance'.[28] This does not mean that Jehovah's Witnesses enjoyed full respect: in the 1950s there were episodes of popular intolerance, while both Catholic and Protestant clergy denounced

26 Fanning, *Racism*, 108.

27 M. Ó hAodha, *'Insubordinate Irish': Travellers in the text* (Manchester, 2011), 102; J. Garry, N. Hardiman and D. Payne (eds.), *Irish social and political attitudes* (Liverpool, 2006), 9–12.

28 *Irish Times*, 9 Oct. 1954, 4; P. Blanshard, *The Irish and Catholic power: an American interpretation* (London, 1954), 73.

them from the pulpit. Concerned about freedom of speech, in 1960 the group sought the advice of the Irish Association of Civil Liberty.

The majority's perception of, and attitude to, this group can be reconstructed from sources in the public domain. It is interesting, in particular, to map the way they were perceived and reported by the *Irish Times*, which had a historical stake in minority rights. By the mid-1950s the newspaper advertised their Sunday services in the week-end columns, under the heading 'Other Churches and Halls', together with a range of other non-Catholic organisations, including Unitarians, Quakers and Baptists. The Witnesses received a surprising level of positive news coverage. By contrast, their refusal to allow blood transfusion was the single most important source of negative attitudes towards the denomination. This tolerant – if not sympathetic – reporting continued over the years: in 1996, Kevin Myers, surveying Hubert Butler's 1940s campaigns on behalf of minorities in communist Europe, described the Jehovah's Witnesses as 'surely the most innocent and blamelessly apolitical religious sects of all on trial'.[29]

By 1991 the group counted 3,393 members – fewer than the Muslims (then 3,875), but well ahead of the smaller Protestant denominations, including the Baptists, as well as other, more recent religious minorities, such as Hindus and Buddhists (then less than a thousand each). By 1999 Rosin Ingle reported the gathering of as many as five thousand Witnesses in Dublin: quoting the words of several members who referred to the faith as 'a way of life rather than a religion' and commented on the 100 per cent membership growth in thirty years, she focused on the 32-county nature of the crowd and the social function of the convention, where romance blossomed between young community members.[30] And in 2000 the Revd Patrick Comerford placed the group 'On Christianity's margins', on a spectrum that ranged from the (strictly Trinitarian and Evangelical) Plymouth Brethren, to the Mormons and the Christian Scientists.[31]

By then there were more than a hundred 'minor religions' operating in the Republic. Within a few years the government adopted a proactive approach to integration and recognition, starting a series of 'structured talks between the state and various faith groups', including also Eastern Orthodox communities and Muslims: diversity had become a badge of honour. Particularly significant was the growth of the Muslim pop-ulation. According to the 1991 Irish census it numbered fewer than 4,000 in that year. From then on the community grew rapidly through immigration, at first through the arrival of waves of refugees (Bosnians in 1992, then Somalis and Albanians). By 2002, the Muslim community numbered more than 19,000 and by 2011 about 40,000. They

29 *Irish Times*, 29 May 1996.
30 *Irish Times*, 17 July 1999.
31 *Irish Times*, 30 Oct. 2000.

did not form a homogeneous community, but rather a microcosm of the nationalities and diversities which constitute worldwide Islam, encompassing a collection of different economic, ethnic and cultural groups from as many as forty different countries. They included some of the more independent voices within Islam in Europe, with some leaders ready to speak up against extremism and criticise their own community for not doing more to facilitate integration.[32]

The Republic was actively embracing diversity and among community leaders there was a real willingness to work together, on the assumption 'that there is no need to eliminate differences in order to construct a good society', emphasising 'the need to respect and understand the beliefs of others'.[33] Interfaith workshops in various locations around the country identified a widespread lack of understanding and indeed ignorance – compounded by apathy – about members of different religious groups.

This does not mean that old attitudes among the older Irish disappeared. For example, in the spring of 2015 the question of the refugees from the conflict in Syria – a classical case, comparable to those of the Huguenots and the Palatines with which this chapter started – elicited contrasting public responses. An *Irish Times*/Ipsos MRBI poll in May suggested that 'the country [was] pretty evenly split between those who favour[ed] opening our doors to these refugees – 48 per cent – to those opposed – 52 per cent', with the divide overlapping with class (the better-off social groups were massively in favour of resettlement, unlike the poorer sections of society). As in previous examples, hostility to minority groups emanated from class tensions and social deprivation within the majority. Thus, by 2016 the Immigrant Council of Ireland reported that racist incidents were on the rise – reflecting a wider European trend at this time.

Equally important was the extent to which the government's good will was frustrated by lack of understanding of the reality on the ground: thus, while Muslims have risen to become the third largest religious group in Ireland, after Catholics and Protestants, their integration is hampered by the limited extent to which the authorities know and understand the realities of the Irish Islamic communities – and indeed other religious groups, such as the Hindus. In other cases, Catholic morality is entrenched in legislation to an extent that makes real pluralism difficult. One difficult area was attitudes towards abortion: in 2012 the death of Savita Halappanavar from septicaemia after the authorities refused to terminate her pregnancy on the grounds that the foetus was still showing a heartbeat was enormously controversial. There are other, less delicate, areas where multiculturalism can be measured and tested not by grand declarations

32 'Prominent Muslim criticizes other leaders for being soft on extremism', *Irish Times*, 1 Aug. 2016.
33 Shaykh Umar Al-Qadri (President and Imam Al-Mustafa Islamic Educational Cultural Centre Ireland), in G. Forde, *A journey together: Muslims and Christians in Ireland: building mutual respect, understanding and cooperation* (Cork, 2013), 2.

of principle, but by pragmatic decisions that affect everyday practice, as well as by the way existing laws are interpreted or amended and new ones are drafted (see Chapter 33 below). Like most other western democracies, Ireland was becoming a society of minorities, but the process was laborious and complex.

BIBLIOGRAPHY

Bhreatnach, A. *Becoming conspicuous: Irish Travellers and the state 1922–70* (Dublin, 2006).

Burke, M. *Tinkers: Synge and the cultural history of Irish Travellers* (Oxford, 2009).

Butler, D. J. '"A most difficult assignment": mapping the emergence of Jehovah's Witnesses in Ireland', in S. D. Brunn (ed.). *The changing world religion map: sacred places, identities, practices and politics* (Dordrecht, 2015), 1615–34.

Caldicott, C. E. J., H. Gough and J.-P. Pittion (eds.) *The Huguenots and Ireland: anatomy of an emigration* (Dublin, 1987).

Court, A. *Puck of the Droms: the lives and literature of the Irish Tinkers* (Berkeley, 1985).

Daniel, G. *Transforming post-Catholic Ireland: religious practice in late modernity* (Oxford, 2016).

Endelman, T. *The Jews of Britain 1656–2000* (Berkeley, 2002).

Fanning, B. *New guests of the Irish nation* (Dublin, 2009).

Fanning, B. *Racism and social change in the Republic of Ireland* (Manchester, 2002).

Faughnan, P. *Refugees and asylum seekers in Ireland* (Dublin, 1999).

Katsuta, S. 'German Palatine immigration of 1709: an aspect of transition from Ireland of immigration to Ireland of Parliament', in K. Kondo (ed.), *State and empire in British history* (Kyoto, 2003), 67–80.

Keogh, D. *Jews in twentieth-century Ireland* (Cork, 1998).

Keogh, D. '"Making Aliya": Irish Jews, the Irish state and Israel', in D. Keogh, F. O'Shea and C. Quinlan (eds.), *Ireland in the 1950s: the lost decade* (Cork, 2004), 252–72.

Knittle, W. A. *The early eighteenth-century Palatine emigration: a British government redemptioner project to manufacture naval stores* (Philadelphia, 1936).

Lawson, R. and R. T. Cragun. 'Comparing the geographic distributions and growth of Mormons, Adventists, and Witnesses', *Journal for the Scientific Study of Religion*, 51, 2 (June 2012), 220–40.

MacÉinrí, P. and A. White. 'Immigration into the Republic of Ireland: a bibliography of recent research', *Irish Geography*, 41, 2 (2008), 151–79.

Mullane, M. F. 'Distorted views of the people and their houses in the Claddagh in the nineteenth century', *Journal of the Galway Archaeological and Historical Society*, 61 (2009), 170–200.

O'Brien, E. 'From the waters of Sion to Liffeyside: the Jewish contribution', *Medical and Cultural Journal of the Irish Colleges of Physicians and Surgeons*, 10, 3 (January 1981).

Ó Gráda, C. *Jewish Ireland in the age of Joyce: a socioeconomic history* (Princeton, 2006).

Scharbrodt, O. 'Islam in Ireland: organising a migrant religion', in O. Cosgrove, L. Cox, C. Kuhling and P. Mulholland (eds.), *Ireland's new religious movements* (Newcastle upon Tyne, 2010), 318–36.

Taylor, B. *A minority and the state: Travellers in Britain in the twentieth century* (Manchester, 2008).

Ugba, A. 'African Pentecostals in twenty-first century Ireland: identity and integration', in B. Fanning (ed.), *Immigration and social change in the Republic of Ireland* (Manchester, 2007), 168–84.

Wheelan, R. 'Writing the self: Huguenot autobiography and the process of assimilation', in R. Vigne and C. Littleton (eds.), *From strangers to citizens: the integration of immigrant communities in Britain, Ireland and colonial America, 1550–1750* (Brighton, 2001), 472.

Woods, M. and N. Humphries. *Seeking asylum in Ireland: comparative figures for asylum seekers in Ireland and Europe in 2000 and 2001* (Dublin, 2001).

27 Political Violence and the Irish Diaspora

Caoimhe Nic Dháibhéid

27.1. Introduction

The apparent dangers of transnational terrorism have dominated public discourse in the early decades of the twenty-first century. Since 9/11, the spectre of foreign militants crossing national boundaries to launch deadly attacks on civilian populations or, latterly, the threat posed by second- and third-generation 'home-grown' militants, radicalised by observing, supporting or participating in far-off conflicts in their ancestral homelands, occupy places of particular dread in contemporary affairs. The social processes by which this political radicalisation has been reached have been the subject of intense policy efforts, particularly amongst Muslim immigrant communities in the United Kingdom. Yet the history of the Irish diaspora in the previous two and a half centuries, especially in the Anglophone world, provides an illuminating historical example of the social causes, effects and patterns of political violence amongst a diverse immigrant community in a broad chronological framework. Of particular importance in understanding the experience of political violence within the Irish diaspora are the global connections between the Irish homeland and the host society. In recent years, the 'transnational turn' in Irish historiography has fruitfully been applied to both the history of the Irish diaspora and the history of Irish nationalism.[1] There is much of value in such an approach, and the impact of political violence in Ireland upon diaspora communities will be explored in this chapter. Yet, this chapter will also emphasise the specificities of migration in understanding the disaggregated nature of diasporic

1 E. Delaney, 'Our island story? Towards a transnational history of late modern Ireland', *Irish Historical Studies*, 37, 148 (2011), 83–105.

involvement in and experience of political violence across the periods in question. It will argue that the host society, not ancestral animus, provides the critical framework to adequately explain the nature and experience of political violence within the Irish diaspora.

The history of Irish migration since 1740 is deeply complex, and the pace, dynamics and composition of migration varied considerably across the period. The effect of these variations on political violence will be sketched below, but it will suffice here to indicate the broad contours of the migration narrative. By the seventeenth century, as Enda Delaney has noted, the diverse pre-existing patterns of Irish migration were crystallising in a series of overlapping circles radiating outwards from 'old' Europe towards the New Worlds of British imperial expansion.[2] Within the period under survey, a number of principal spikes in migration from Ireland occurred, in each century: the 1770s, the 1780s, the 1840s, the 1880s and the 1950s. The effect of specific instances of political turbulence in Ireland on patterns of migration is perhaps worth further reflection. Certainly, something of a republican exodus seems to have followed the civil war of 1922–3, and had important implications for the subsequent development of Irish-American nationalism in the early years of the Northern Irish Troubles. But these peaks are, it should be emphasised, driven primarily by social and economic developments, catastrophes and opportunities; solely political events, even seismic ones, do not appear to have had a decisive numerical effect upon migration trends. The waxing and waning of levels of migration did, of course, present differing levels of pressure on the host societies, and help to explain varieties of tensions which emerged at different moments. Some of these tensions, as will be argued below, can be understood as typologies of a broad conceptualisation of political violence. The destinations of these waves of migration also varied, although the enormous preponderance of migration to the United States, particularly in the eighteenth and nineteenth centuries, should not be overlooked. Here, the predominantly Protestant (and specifically Presbyterian) character of migration in the 1700s was almost entirely reversed over the course of the nineteenth century, when Catholic Irish moved to the forefront after the 1830s. But the scale of Irish migration to Britain – Protestant and Catholic – particularly after the First World War has at times been overlooked. As Kevin Kenny has pointed out, Britain was the second most popular destination for Irish migrants in the modern era, ahead of Canada, Australia and New Zealand.[3] Other, less popular destinations include South Africa, Latin America and the Asian subcontinent. Such was the scale of the exodus that by 1890 40 per cent of those born in Ireland were living outside the country.[4] Yet the effect of Irish migration on these

2 E. Delaney, 'Migration and diaspora', in A. Jackson (ed.), *The Oxford handbook of Irish history* (Oxford, 2013), 10.
3 K. Kenny, 'Diaspora and comparison: the global Irish as case study', *Journal of American History*, 90, 1 (June 2003), 136.
4 D. Fitzpatrick, *Irish emigration, 1801–1922* (Dublin, 1984), 5.

different destinations varied considerably, not least on a proportional basis: Canada, New Zealand, Scotland and Australia had higher numbers of Irish migrants per capita than the United States by the 1870s.[5] Further variables include age, sex, region of origin and class, and distinct patterns emerge which, it will be argued, fundamentally shaped the development of political violence amongst the migrant community.

Of course, the immediate issue presented when considering the question of political violence and its adherents, victims and effects among the Irish diaspora is the thorny question of definition. What counts as political violence? Clearly, at a basic level, it encompasses the use of violence in order to bring about political change. Under such a rubric can be included the activities of revolutionary movements, as well as more obviously 'terrorist' organisations. Yet such a narrow instrumental definition of political violence implies a degree of intentionality and presupposes a strategic logic of some sort. It also hinges on a rigid definition of 'political change' as distinct from, for example, social, labour or agrarian reform. However, more useful definitions exist. In a landmark study, Charles Townshend identified three principal categories of political violence in the Irish context: 'spontaneous collective violence (or social violence) which may have no explicit political intention but has political implications; systematic covert intimidation or terrorism; and organized open insurrection'.[6] Each of these categories has immediate resonance for understanding the dynamics of political violence in the Irish diaspora. Under the first heading might be grouped three distinct kinds of violence or violent activism: sectarian violence, proto-revolutionary secret societies and, to a lesser extent, labour agitation. The second category, of classic 'terrorism', can immediately be traced in the support for and participation in militant republican campaigns in the late nineteenth and the twentieth century, all of which had significant input from diasporas on both sides of the Atlantic. The third typology, open insurrection, is also evident in the history of diasporic political violence – the Fenian invasion of Canada, for instance – as well as more indirectly in the patterns of diasporic support and financing of a number of insurrectionary moments in Ireland. However, a further analytical category can be introduced, moving away from the inherently statist character of much work on political violence and terrorism. If we broaden the contours of political violence to include pro-state violence, then a more expansive view of the dynamics of violence amongst the Irish diaspora can be delineated. Not least, it widens the analytical framework beyond the confines of Irish nationalism, which has understandably dominated interpretations of political violence. But reflections on, for instance, the diversity of Irish participation in the American Civil War or the frequently violent interactions of Scots-Irish settlers with Native Americans in frontier societies might permit a more

5 Kenny, 'Diaspora and comparison', 136.
6 C. Townshend, *Political violence in Ireland: government and resistance since 1848* (Oxford, 1983), 407–8.

nuanced picture of the diverse ways in which violence shaped the experience of the diaspora across the past three centuries. Finally, this chapter will consider the effects of (as distinct from participation in) political violence for Irish diasporic communities.

27.2.   Secret Societies and Sectarian Violence

Although there is some evidence of 'lone actor' style attacks – Henry O'Farrell's attempted assassination of the Duke of Edinburgh in Sydney in 1868 is the most famous example – political violence and the Irish diaspora was invariably conceived as spiralling out of an ominous subterranean and diabolical network.[7] In some ways, this contemporary perception is accurate: as two recent edited collections demonstrate, an intricate and vibrant associational culture was an integral component of Irish diasporic history from the 1750s. This took a number of forms, some formally linked to religious institutions, some fraternal organisations, and some more explicitly in the vein of mutual aid societies.[8] Of course, that (diasporic) Irish nationalisms similarly operated in overlapping networks of sociability and fraternity has long been part of R. V. Comerford's argument, most notably with his 'patriotism as pastime' thesis.[9] The diasporic engagement with political violence, either directly or indirectly, was for the most part mediated through a dizzying range of voluntary organisations: the Ancient Order of Hibernians, the Orange Order, the Clan-na-Gael, the Irish National Association, the United Irishmen, Irish Confederate Clubs, the Patriotic Association of the Shamrock, Emmet Clubs of varying affiliations, and many more. In a meaningful sense, the structure and practice of political violence by the Irish diaspora can be understood as a history of sociability as much as a history of politics *tout court*.

However, this associational aspect of much Irish diasporic culture has also led to rather loose interpretive boundaries between different forms of diasporic violence, both contemporaneously and in subsequent literature. Fluid progressions between one organisation and another, as well as overlapping memberships and recurrent nominative imprecision, have meant that it is often futile to attempt to draw rigid lines between different outbreaks of violence which frequently have been moulded and inflected by a diverse associational and sectional inheritance. These overlaps present a distinct challenge to any synthesis of political violence, and this challenge is particularly acute when considering the first of Townshend's categories, social or collective violence with

---

7 R. Davis, 'The prince and the Fenians, Australasia, 1868–9: republican conspiracy or Orange opportunity', in F. McGarry and J. McConnel (eds.), *The black hand of republicanism: Fenianism in modern Ireland* (Dublin, 2009), 121–34.

8 J. Kelly and R. V. Comerford (eds.), *Associational culture in Ireland and abroad* (Dublin, 2010); E. Delaney and D. M. MacRaild, *Irish migration, networks and ethnic identities since 1750* (New York, 2007).

9 R. V. Comerford, *The Fenians in context: Irish politics and society, 1848–82* (Dublin, 1998 [1985]).

political implications. I have argued that three kinds of diasporic violence fall under this heading: oath-bound secret societies, sectarian violence and labour agitation. The three of these, while at times distinct, frequently overlap in the histories of violence in the Irish diaspora since the mid-eighteenth century, particularly in the contexts of rapid urbanisation and industrialisation in the New World. This is especially evident in the history of Ribbonism. Don MacRaild and Kyle Hughes have recently traced the Ribbonmen across the diaspora, and have argued that transnationalism, particularly in relation to Britain, was a 'key operating principle of the Ribbon societies'.[10] This builds on the pioneering work of John Belchem, who contended that Ribbonism was a crucial stepping stone to the development of a distinct 'sectarian *national* identity amongst the Liverpool Irish' and, by extension, the Catholic Irish in Britain.[11] However, the nebulous, secretive political agenda of Ribbonism, as well as its fertile coupling with other forms of diasporic associational culture, has meant that it is difficult to definitively trace the movement's political agenda, still less the motivations of its adherents. Moreover, Ribbonism most frequently came to the surface in the form of sectarian clashes with Orange organisations; of course, the propensity of British, Canadian, Australian or American authorities to conflate 'Ribbonism' with Hibernianism (and later Fenianism) makes distinguishing between the two even more difficult.[12] The hazy boundaries between Ribbonism and other Irish organisations in the diaspora reflect the multifaceted nature of the Ribbon movement in Ireland itself. Ribbonism has been interpreted variously as an outcrop of traditional agrarian protest, as a proto-labour union, or as a politicised movement operating as a median point between the Defenders of the 1790s and the more recognisably republican organisations of the later nineteenth century. Certainly, it is possible to trace broad regional variations in the character of Ribbonism in different parts of Ireland: in Ulster it served as a Catholic fraternal society against Protestant Orangeism, in Munster as an anti-tithe league (reflecting middling rural class interests), in Connacht as a more hard-line anti-landlord association, and in Leinster as an embryonic trade union.[13] In each of these broad areas (and with considerable overlap in between), Ribbonism drew its compositional strength from different social strata, and the faint imprint of these distinctions can be traced in the political activity of Ribbon-esque societies among immigrant communities. These regional specificities form the crux of Kevin Kenny's compelling treatment of Ribbonism as it mutated

10 D. M. MacRaild and K. Hughes, 'Irish politics and labour: transnational and comparative perspectives, 1798–1914', in N. Whelehan (ed.), *Transnational perspectives on modern Irish history* (New York, 2014), 52.
11 J. Belchem, '"Freedom and friendship to Ireland": Ribbonism in early nineteenth century Liverpool', *International Review of Social History*, 39 (1994), 50.
12 MacRaild and Hughes, 'Irish politics and labour', 55.
13 T. Garvin, 'Defenders, Ribbonmen and others: underground political networks in pre-famine Ireland', in C. H. E. Philpin (ed.), *Nationalism and popular protest in Ireland* (Cambridge, 1987), 222.

across the Atlantic, combining with the brutalising modernity of the Pennsylvanian mines to emerge as the 'Molly Maguires'.[14]

The violence of the Molly Maguires has recently been described as America's 'first labour war'; yet what is clear is that the events in the Pennsylvania mines, redolent as they were of Thompsonian collective violence and incipient class warfare, were far from unique in the history of Irish labour in the diaspora.[15] The history of the Irish workers on the canals and railroads as North America was opened up is one of faction-alism and rival collective interests. This frequently took the form of localised struggles, with regional identities transported from Ireland grafted on to class interests. Thus the Corkonians, Connachtmen and Fardowners clashed violently along the emerging American canals in the 1820s and 1830s, forcing a violent response in turn by local militia and, eventually, federal troops.[16] In the following decades, Irish immigrants vio-lently displaced slave and freed labour along the waterfronts in the American South.[17] Much of the fuel for these clashes stemmed from the precarious economic position of unskilled Irish migrants and, possibly, from their transience: David Emmons's impor-tant work on the Irish community in the Butte copper mines has suggested that perma-nence (of employment, of residence, of community) bred peaceability.[18] In the interim, access to employment was fiercely contested and zealously guarded by these older asso-ciational networks, and the weapons and tactics adopted were a blend of Irish faction-alism and Irish secret societies. As Irish migrants upskilled, they gravitated towards more mainstream labour activism and, by the latter decades of the nineteenth century, emerged as the dominant group in many American trade unions.[19] However, although American labour radicalised sharply with the injection of anarchist ideology after the 1880s, Irish workers remained largely aloof from attempts to mobilise along class (as opposed to ethnic) lines.[20] There were, of course, exceptions. Two of the most infamous instances of labour violence in the twentieth century – the *Los Angeles Times* bombing in 1911 and the Preparedness Day Parade bombing in San Francisco in 1917 – were

14 K. Kenny, *Making sense of the Molly Maguires* (Oxford, 1998).

15 M. Bulik, *The sons of Molly Maguire: the Irish roots of America's first labour war* (Oxford, 2015).

16 P. Way, 'Shovels and shamrock: Irish workers and labour violence in the digging of the Chesapeake and Ohio Canal', *Labor History*, 30, 4 (1989), 489–517.

17 M. D. Thompson, '"The unacclimated stranger should be positively prohibited from joining the party": Irish immigrants, black laborers and yellow fever on Charleston's waterfront', in D. Gleeson (ed.), *The Irish in the Atlantic world* (Charleston, 2012), 275–306.

18 D. M. Emmons, *The Butte Irish: class and ethnicity in an American mining town, 1875–1925* (Chicago, 1990), 80.

19 K. A. Miller, *Ireland and Irish-America: class, culture and transatlantic migration* (Dublin, 2008), 277; G. Foster, *The Irish civil war and society: politics, class and conflict* (New York, 2015), 203.

20 E. L. Hirsch, *Urban revolt: ethnic politics in the nineteenth-century Chicago labor movement* (Berkeley, 1990), 129–43.

both attributed to second-generation Irish-American labour activists, the McNamara brothers and Thomas Mooney respectively. This broader pattern, of unskilled manual Irish labour occasioning violence in the host societies, was replicated across the diaspora. Tensions revolved in Britain around Irish migrants acting as blackleg workers or undercutting existing labour, although in this instance most historiographical attention has been devoted to exploring the violence provoked by imported Irish labour.[21] Labour violence was frequently expressed via associational culture and, especially, in the form of sectarian violence. For Irish Catholics, the principal vehicles of these were the Ribbon societies already delineated, succeeded in the mid-nineteenth century by the Ancient Order of Hibernians; for Irish Protestants, the Orange Order. As already noted, the sectarian violence between Catholic and Protestant Irish which sporadically erupted across the diaspora was intimately linked with the secret or oath-bound societies of Ribbonmen and Orangemen. It unquestionably had social roots, in competition over access to employment, but in some instances was the vehicle of political or electoral agitation, especially in Canada. This fusion of religious and politico-national identities by rival groups of Irish migrants led to riots right across the host countries: in Britain, particularly Scotland and northern England, in Canada, and in Australia. These episodes speak to a burgeoning political consciousness – certainly it is possible to view Ribbonism as a precursor of Fenianism – but also reinforced nativist and Protestant prejudices about the 'violent' Irish, given to subterfuge and sedition.

27.3. Pro-State Political Violence and the American Revolution

A further aspect of political violence connected to the early experiences of the Irish diaspora in North America is the question of pro-state violence. Pro-state political violence has traditionally been vastly understudied, and the valuable work of the Critical Terrorism Studies school has only begun to redress that balance. Martin Miller's recent critical survey of the history of terrorism has very much proceeded from this vantage point, and includes a crucial central chapter on what he views as the most significant form of terrorism in the United States between the eighteenth century and the present day: the violence waged against indigenous peoples and African-Americans. It is the first of these that concerns us here. Certainly the violence visited upon and by native tribes along the expanding frontier in the eighteenth and nineteenth centuries had political effects: it shaped and reflected shifting geo-political fortunes of rival European colonists in North America, and it fundamentally altered the position of indigenous

---

21 See for instance D. M. MacRaild, *The Irish diaspora in Britain, 1750–1939* (2nd edn, Basingstoke, 2011), 170–3.

groups as the American colonies rushed towards independence. Miller has conceptualised pro-state terrorism as 'violence carried out by legally armed citizens either in the name of the law, or by "taking the law into their own hands" with the tacit or overt consent of the political and judicial authorities'.[22] From this perspective, the participation of Scots-Irish settlers in violent campaigns against Native Americans can be interpreted as something of the latter. This interpretation serves to broaden our understanding of how political violence functioned among the Irish diaspora.

The broad chronology of the violence waged on and by indigenous people has been well established: sporadic outbreaks in the colonial period, significant indigenous participation in the Franco-British wars in the later eighteenth century, the 'Indian War' of the western theatre of the American Revolution, and later 'Indian Wars' in the nineteenth century west of the Mississippi. It is the first of these that saw the most noteworthy participation by Irish migrants, especially the brutal encounters in the Pennsylvania region in the 1750s and 1760s. There, savagery was meted out on both sides: massacres, scalpings, mutilations pepper this grim chapter. Certainly, there appears to be a distinct social profile to these events: the migrants concerned were predominantly Ulster Presbyterians, and the most notorious of these – the Paxton Boys – almost entirely American-born.[23] The 'savagery' of the native attacks on settlers was salaciously reported in Ulster, as Benjamin Bankhurst has detailed, and the effect of this publicity seems to have slightly dampened emigration fever amongst northern Presbyterians.[24] In a later context, David Emmons has posited provocatively that 'the Irish were the Indians of Europe', and has suggested that a mutual recognition characterised Irish immigrant encounters with Native Americans, as both groups suffered the depredations of Anglo-Saxon colonialism.[25] Certainly, reports of the 'Indian' attacks on frontiersmen were likened in Ulster print culture to the 'savagery' of Catholic violence in 1641, and it is possible that this cultural memory was also present among successive generations of Ulster Presbyterian immigrants to colonial America. Yet the association of Scots-Irish migrants with the violence against native peoples must be at least partly driven by the very timing of their migration and their region of settlement. When the bulk of Irish Catholic migration reached American shores the following century, native tribes had been driven back from the eastern seaboard; perhaps more pertinently, Irish Catholics settled overwhelmingly in urban centres, far away from the possibility of encounters, whether of mutual recognition or not. Besides, Irish

22 M. M. Miller, *The foundations of modern terrorism: state, society and the dynamics of political violence* (Cambridge, 2012), 137–62.

23 K. Kenny, *Peaceable kingdom lost: the Paxton Boys and the destruction of William Penn's holy experiment* (Oxford, 2009).

24 B. Bankhurst, *Ulster Presbyterians and the Scots Irish diaspora, 1750–1764* (London, 2013), 77–109.

25 D. M. Emmons, *Beyond the American Pale: the Irish in the West, 1845–1910* (Norman, OK, 2010), 138–72.

Catholic migrants were well represented in the Union army of the 1860s and 1870s, and euphemistically 'encountered' native peoples as the federal state pushed west. In other contexts, we know less about the encounters of Irish migrants with indigenous groups, although recent work on 'Shamrock Aborigines' (the descendants of Irish–Aboriginal unions) confirms Patrick O'Farrell's observations that civility and intimacy were more characteristic of Irish–Aboriginal encounters in Australia than violence and brutality.[26]

Perhaps the most challenging interpretation of the violence of Ulster Presbyterian settlers in the 1760s has been that advanced by Patrick Griffin. He has traced a direct line between these episodes and Ulster Presbyterian participation in the American Revolution, arguing that the Scots-Irish experience of the Indian Wars 'revealed as never before their marginal status in Pennsylvania and their impotent voice in an empire they believed they had a significant hand in fashioning and defending'.[27] This violence, partly racial, partly settler-colonial, partly pro- (the nascent new) state, served thus to politicise successive generations of Scots-Irish and resulted in perhaps the most important episode of political violence in which the Irish diaspora participated. The role of the Scots-Irish in the American War of Independence has been delineated effectively by David N. Doyle, and the centrality of the Pennsylvanian Scots-Irish is evident in forming a strident opposition to the suspected pro-British Quaker colonial elite. Region of settlement appears to have initially been a decisive factor in shaping patterns of participation: Pennsylvania was the vanguard of proto-revolutionary activism for Ulster Presbyterians, while similar mobilisation occurred in Virginia, Delaware and New Jersey. Conversely, the Carolinas were initially more cautious, reflecting a different set of communal experiences from those on the seaboard.[28] Overall, though, Scots-Irish participation in the American Revolution heralded the political maturing of the migrant community, as 'full civic participation and political action' swiftly followed.[29] Into the infant republic arrived a further wave of Presbyterian migration, that of United Irishmen refugees from the 1790s onwards. This development has frequently been identified as the beginnings of Irish nationalism in the United States, but as Timothy Meagher has pointed out, we know very little beyond the political manoeuvrings, controversial as they were, of the United Irishmen elite.[30] Certainly, the arrival of the

26 A. McGrath, 'Shamrock Aborigines: the Irish, the Aboriginal Australians and their children', in G. Morton and D. A. Wilson (eds.), *Irish and Scottish encounters with indigenous peoples* (Montreal and Kingston, Ont., 2013), 108–43.

27 P. Griffin, *The people with no name: Ireland's Ulster Scots, America's Scots Irish and the creation of a British Atlantic world, 1689–1764* (Princeton, 2001), 169.

28 D. N. Doyle, 'Scots Irish or Scotch Irish', in J. J. Lee and M. R. Casey (eds.), *Making the Irish American: history and heritage of the Irish in the United States* (New York, 2006), 166–7.

29 Ibid., 167.

30 T. J. Meagher, *The Columbia guide to Irish American history* (New York, 2005), 201–2.

United Irishmen refugees did not electrify the Irish diaspora in a way which might have been anticipated; much the same point can be made of the Young Ireland exiles in Australia, Canada and the United States after 1848. By then, O'Connellite nationalism had penetrated the diaspora, as it had the Irish at home, and constitutionalism was, for the following sixty years, the dominant vein of political culture.

27.4. Irish Republicanism and the Diaspora

The most straightforward category of political violence in which the diaspora participated is the form of Irish republicanism that emerged in the 1850s: the Irish Republican, or Fenian, Brotherhood. This organisation constituted the first real mass engagement of the Irish diaspora with militant nationalism; indeed, the diaspora was an integral part of the organisation from the outset, with twin hubs in Dublin and New York. Through episodes like the *Catalpa* rescue or the abortive Fenian invasions of Canada in 1866 and 1870 (including many Fenian veterans of the US Civil War), diasporic Fenians engaged in the closest thing to insurrection outside Ireland. In spite of this, we know very little of the early Fenian movement in the United States, although the work of Damien Shiels is going some way to redress this, along with that of David Gleeson for the Confederate army.[31] After Comerford's important early work, there has recently been a flowering of renewed scholarly interest in the Fenians, with significant studies by Matthew Kelly, Owen McGee and Marta Ramon, among others.[32] Of particular importance for this chapter is Niall Whelehan's study of transnational Fenianism, which has reoriented the lens back across the Atlantic and, most valuably, broadened the scope to consider those who conducted, financed and supported the dynamiting campaign of 1881–5.[33] Whelehan has thus begun to provide answers to some of Timothy Meagher's questions posed in a recent survey: 'Were they the upwardly mobile Irish in their communities, local elites yearning for some form of American acceptance? Or were they poorer men, perhaps alienated by their American experience and still yearning for Ireland?'[34] Through a careful examination of subscribers to the *United Irishman*, the newspaper set up by Jeremiah O'Donovan Rossa to publicise and agitate for the dynamite campaign, and the Skirmishing Fund, set up to finance it, Whelehan has added significantly to our understanding of the social profile of Irish-American advanced nationalism in

---

31 D. Shiels, *The Irish in the US Civil War* (Dublin, 2014); D. Gleeson, *The green and the gray: the Irish in the Confederate states of America* (Charleston, 2013).

32 M. J. Kelly, *The Fenian ideal and Irish nationalism, 1882–1916* (Woodbridge, 2006); O. McGee, *The IRB: the Irish Republican Brotherhood, from the Land League to Sinn Féin* (Dublin, 2007); M. Ramon, *A provisional dictator: James Stephens and the Fenian movement* (Dublin, 2007).

33 N. Whelehan, *The dynamiters: Irish nationalism and political violence in the wider world* (Cambridge, 2012).

34 Meagher, *Columbia guide to Irish American history*, 204.

the last decades of the nineteenth century.[35] What emerges is, perhaps, surprising. Rather than a marginalised, impoverished, transient group, supporters of skirmishing were predominantly men in their late thirties and early forties, mostly Irish-born (especially in the south-west of Ireland), who arrived in America in early adulthood, indicating a degree of stability heightened by the lack of internal movement within the USA across the cohort. Moreover, many were married with large families. Unlike the high representation of artisans and skilled workers in similar profiles of Fenians in Ireland, Irish-American Fenians were mostly in secure if low-paid employment. Similar to John Belchem's findings in his innovative work on the role of the pub in Ribbonism, saloons and saloon-keepers seem to have played an important role in providing the social space in which Irish-American Fenianism functioned.[36] This picture of relative stability thus challenges the traditional interpretations of radical nationalism correlating to economic deprivation. Rather Whelehan has suggested that political marginalisation – from the centres of Irish-American political influence and middle-class respectable nationalism – was as important a driver as economic alienation in explaining the growth of militant Fenianism in the 1880s.[37]

Such a rounded profile of the Fenian cohort or their supportive community is, unfortunately, lacking in other contexts. We know very little, for instance, of Fenianism in Australia in the latter part of the nineteenth century, still less of Britain, especially England. The overwhelming identification of the dynamite campaign of the 1880s with Irish-American bombers has contributed to this; as David Fitzpatrick noted in 1989, it seemed that 'physical force was no longer a popular strategy for Irish nationalists in Britain, either in reality or in the imagination of their neighbours'.[38] However, recent work by Máirtín Ó Catháin on Fenians in Scotland has begun to fill in the gaps. The Scottish Fenians who participated in the bombing campaign were, Ó Catháin has argued, also mostly Irish-born, and their occupational profile was similarly clustered around semi- or unskilled backgrounds. This is in contrast even to their Scottish IRB brethren who did not participate in the dynamite campaign, who tended to be from artisanal or even lower-middle-class backgrounds.[39] Conversely to Whelehan, Ó Catháin has interpreted these data as suggestive of a definitive link between economic deprivation and political radicalism. The question of *relative* deprivation – whether economic or in terms of access to political power – is perhaps a way to reconcile the gap between the two positions: it was not the poorest of the poor or

---

35 What follows is derived from Whelehan, *The dynamiters*, 189–217.

36 J. Belchem, *Merseypride: essays in Liverpool exceptionalism* (Liverpool, 2000), 67–100.

37 Whelehan, *The dynamiters*, 197.

38 D. Fitzpatrick, 'A curious middle place: the Irish in Britain, 1871–1921', in R. Swift and S. Gilley (eds.), *The Irish in Britain* (London, 1989), 34.

39 M. Ó Catháin, *Irish republicanism in Scotland, 1858–1916* (Dublin, 2007), 134–5.

those who were entirely politically disenfranchised who turned to radical nationalist solutions, but those who felt unjustly excluded from economic or political prosperity. This pattern can also be seen in what little we know of the social profile of Fenians across the British world, in Canada, Australia, New Zealand and South Africa. In Canada, the movement struggled to recover from the dent to its reputation following the botched invasion and faced significant obstacles. Firstly, as in the rest of the British world, Fenianism was technically a seditious activity, and thus Fenian movements within the empire simply could not organise as openly as in the United States. Secondly, there were demographic challenges. Whelehan has shown that Fenianism flourished in the large American cities on the eastern seaboard; urban centres were far fewer in Canada, and the Irish population (both Catholic and Protestant) overwhelmingly rural-dwellers. In spite of this, and perhaps because of the Orange ascendency which allowed an overtly oppositional culture to develop, Fenianism in Canada survived fluctuations in strength and influence from the 1870s to the late 1880s.[40] Yet, it is clear that Fenianism there drew on earlier Ribbon societies as an organisational base, which had a distinctly working-class complexion, particularly in Montreal and Quebec. In Australia, Patrick O'Farrell has observed that the strength of the IRB lay in the gold-fields, while in South Africa, the work of Donal McCracken has identified a hub of advanced nationalist activity around the Rand mining settlements, culminating in the pro-Boer Irish Brigade led by John MacBride.[41] In all of these contexts, within the British world and without, there were two competitors to the active and militant nationalism represented by the Devoy-led Clan na Gael. The first was the overwhelming popularity of constitutional nationalism, given an additional fillip by the successful fusion of political and agrarian agitation after the New Departure. Throughout the late nineteenth century, the most popular organisations among the Irish diaspora were the Land League, the National League and the United Irish League. The second competitor was mainstream advanced nationalism, which in many places (not least in Ireland) retrenched into commemorative activity or literary societies as a means to build the broad support base necessary for future campaigns.

The next phase in militant nationalism came, of course, with the Irish Revolution of 1916–23. As we know, the Easter Rising was primarily financed by Clan na Gael money and gold, much of which ended up buried in Kathleen Clarke's garden. An important cohort amongst the rebels themselves were the 'Kimmage garrison', mostly from Liverpool or London, who had returned to Ireland in late 1915 and early 1916, possibly to avoid conscription, and were taken in by Joseph Plunkett in his rambling

40 D. C. Lyne and P. Toner, 'Fenianism in Canada, 1874–84', *Studia Hibernica*, 12 (1972), 27–76.
41 P. O'Farrell, *The Irish in Australia* (Sydney, 1992), 214; D. P. McCracken, 'Irish settlement and identity in South Africa before 1910', *Irish Historical Studies*, 28 (1992–3), 134–49.

house south-west of Dublin. But much as the Irish public were taken by surprise by the rebellion and radicalised sharply *afterwards*, so the diaspora overseas struggled to keep up to date with rapidly changing political contexts. As in Ireland, this radicalisation was reflected initially in the pattern of donations to relief agencies providing for the welfare of prisoners and their dependants. The Irish National Aid Association and Volunteer Dependants Fund (INAVDF) received money from across the Irish diaspora, and its records offer an important glimpse into the shifting allegiances of Irish communities abroad, as constitutional nationalism was eclipsed in favour of a radical alternative.[42] Of course, support for prisoner welfare had long been a feature of Irish nationalism, at home and abroad, and in this sense the INAVDF was merely the most recent in a long line of prisoner welfare and amnesty associations. It is, moreover, important to distinguish between retrospective support for prisoners and support for current or future violent campaigns. But as I have argued elsewhere, these relief organisations provided Irish people with stepping stones towards more overt republican groups, at home and abroad. These organisations – the Friends of Irish Freedom in the United States, the Irish Self-Determination League in Britain, and the Irish National Association in Australia – formed the principal vehicles through which the Irish diaspora engaged with the War of Independence after 1919. This rich seam of associational culture has begun to be unpicked, especially in the British context, with important works by Mo Moulton and Darragh Gannon mapping the nexus of cultural and political organisations which 'bound the minority community together'.[43] The United States was, of course, the target of an extensive propaganda and fundraising campaign by Irish republicans during the War of Independence, with regular visits from prominent figures culminating in Eamon de Valera's controversial tour which divided the Irish-American community.[44] Yet broad-based support for the republican project is not the only entry under the heading 'diaspora' for the Irish Revolution: physical force was also evident. In 1918, seven members of the Australian Irish National Association were arrested after being caught drilling in the Blue Mountains; more pertinently, the Irish Republican Army (IRA) had a significant presence in England, principally in London and the northern industrial cities.[45] Their operational activities have been sketched by Peter Hart and, recently, Gerard Noonan; the campaign included extensive gun-running endeavours as well as sabotage campaigns. Apart from the assassination

42 C. Nic Dháibhéid, 'The Irish National Aid Association and the radicalization of public opinion in Ireland, 1916–1918', *Historical Journal*, 55, 3 (2012), 705–29.

43 M. Moulton, *Ireland and the Irish in interwar England* (Cambridge, 2013), 102–34; D. Gannon, 'The rise of the rainbow chasers: advanced Irish political nationalism in Britain, 1916–1922', *Éire-Ireland*, 49 (2014), 112–42.

44 J. Eichacker, *Irish republican women in America: lecture tours, 1916–1925* (Dublin, 2005); T. Davis, 'Eamon de Valera's political education: the American tour of 1919–1920', *New Hibernia Review*, 10, 1 (2006), 65–78.

45 O'Farrell, *The Irish in Australia*, 274–8.

of Henry Wilson by two IRA members in London and the discarded notion of targeting the British cabinet, violence against the person was relatively rare. Noonan has also begun to compile a profile of the IRA cohort in England: high turnover, socialised into republicanism through cultural nationalist organisations, relatively young (like their counterparts in Ireland), and possibly with family connections to previous republican movements (although this is a common trope in the self-construction of Irish revolutionaries).[46]

One of the most interesting results of the revolution for scholars of the Irish diaspora is the mini-exodus of republicans following the catastrophic civil war. Pioneering works by Gavin Foster and Brian Hanley have suggested a geographical profile which mirrors broader emigration patterns in the twentieth century – overwhelmingly drawn from the western seaboard. Economic factors were similarly the principal driver for the migration, but in this instance these factors had a distinctly political edge: republicans were excluded from much state employment or self-excluded in refusing to take the hated oath of allegiance to the Free State. As Foster has noted, the 'Wild Geese' of the 1920s were simultaneously political refugees and economic migrants.[47] These migrants provided a shot in the arm for the declining Irish-American organisations which principally revolved around Joseph McGarrity and his Clan, with another fillip coming after the Wall Street Crash. Gavin Wilk has traced the fortunes of these organisations in the interwar period: although the American side was in regular contact with the IRA in Ireland, sending money and, at times, unsolicited advice, its most striking function in retrospect was as a social outlet for Irish emigrants, mapping on to and sometimes duplicating the vibrant county organisations which peopled Irish New York, in particular.[48] The performances of the 'IRA Radio Orchestra' on board specially chartered cruises on the Hudson offer an intriguing glimpse of the gentrification (and sanitising) of Irish republicanism in America. Money, rather than personnel, remained the main contribution of the interwar Irish-American community, and they donated in large quantities to the S-Plan or bombing campaign in England between 1939 and 1940. Although strategically sophisticated, the campaign was a military failure, but it did have significant consequences for the Irish community in England. The British government passed emergency legislation to allow for 156 deportations of republican suspects and sympathisers, and there was an outbreak of older tropes of sectarian and anti-Irish sentiment: one note passed to the Home Secretary gave the text of a supposed 'Hiberian

---

46 P. Hart, *The IRA at war, 1916–1923* (Oxford, 2005), 141–77; G. Noonan, *The IRA in Britain, 1919–1923: 'in the heart of enemy lines'* (Liverpool, 2014).

47 G. Foster, '"No wild geese this time": IRA emigration after the Irish civil war', *Éire-Ireland*, 47, 1–2 (2012), 94–122; B. Hanley, 'Irish republicans in interwar New York', *Irish Journal of American Studies*, 1 (2009), available at http://ijas.iaas.ie/index.php/irish-republicans-in-interwar-new-york/, accessed 5 September 2016.

48 G. Wilk, *Transatlantic defiance: the militant Irish republican movement in America, 1923–45* (Manchester, 2014).

[*sic*] oath founded by Rory O'Moore in 1565'.[49] Although it appears certain that those carrying out the bombings almost uniformly travelled from Ireland to do so, a network of support and sympathy was provided by a broader section of the republican community in England, many of whom left the country in 1939 before deportation orders could be served. We know little of the profiles of these deportees, their ages, origins or occupations: their files are closed at The National Archives. Their release, scheduled for 2039, may cast light on the demographic and social make-up of republicanism in the diaspora as the Second World War loomed.

While the abortive border campaign of the 1950s caused minor ripples among the Irish diaspora, the crisis of the northern Troubles was a major event and has been the subject of much scholarship. This has principally centred on the political manoeuvrings of Provisional republican support organisations like Noraid (Irish Northern Aid Committee) and the attempts to counter this by constitutional nationalists such as John Hume. In addition, much attention has been focused on high-level Irish-American politics, culminating in official American intervention in the peace process. But Brian Hanley's important study of the internal politics of Noraid has revealed a fundamental shift in the pattern of diasporic involvement in Irish nationalist campaigns. In the early years of the Troubles, Noraid was dominated by a combination of civil war veterans and recent Irish immigrants, but the period of the hunger strikes attracted increasing numbers of the second- and third-generation Irish Americans, as the concept of ethnic identity blossomed in the United States. However, much like Ribbon and Fenian movements, Noraid appealed directly to the Irish-American working classes, building close relationships with trade unions with a high Irish membership and developing a critique of 'Lace Curtain' Irish Americans too preoccupied with respectability to defend their Irish kin.[50] Noraid was, however, very much a minority taste, and much work remains to be done to effectively chart the response of the 'new' Irish diaspora of the 1980s and 1990s to the violence in the north.

With the Provisional IRA bombing English cities regularly from the 1970s onwards, the experience of the Irish diaspora in Britain was acutely more complex. Something of this experience has begun to be excavated by sociologists like Johanne Devlin Trew and Mary Hickman, suggesting a complex negotiation of Irish identity in Britain deepened (but not necessarily triggered) by responses to the violence in Northern Ireland as well as the rapid modernisation of Irish society from the 1970s onwards.[51] However, this is

---

49 Quoted in T. Craig, 'Sabotage! The origins, development and impact of the IRA's infrastructural bombing campaigns, 1939–1997', *Intelligence and National Security*, 25, 3 (2010), 316.

50 B. Hanley, 'The politics of Noraid', *Irish Political Studies*, 19, 1 (2004), 1–17.

51 See, for example, J. Devlin Trew, *Leaving the north: migration and memory in Northern Ireland, 1921–2011* (Liverpool, 2013); M. Hickman, '"Binary opposites" or "unique neighbours": the Irish in multi-ethnic Britain', *Political Quarterly*, 7, 1 (2000), 50–8.

an area which requires further work, not least in uncovering the experiences of Irish Protestants in Britain, from north and south, who in the twentieth century have perhaps suffered most from the 'ethnic fade' assumed in much historiography: perceived as 'British' in Ireland and 'Irish' in Britain, their histories were perhaps the most complex of all. Other gaps revolve around unionism and loyalism and their mobilisation of supportive diasporas. Work by Stuart Ross and Andrew Sanders will begin to fill in the gap for the Canadian context, yet the social contours of these political (re-)engagements have yet to be uncovered.[52]

27.5. Conclusion

As argued above, a more expansive definition of political violence is essential to a broader understanding of the different ways in which diasporic communities engaged with political violence. Social violence with a political edge, such as the sectarian riots which peppered British, American, Canadian and Australian cities during the nineteenth century, ought to be included in any consideration of the political development of the Irish diaspora, both Catholic and Protestant. Even more pointedly, the frontier violence waged and experienced by Ulster Presbyterian migrants forged a revolutionary consciousness among one of the most important constituent groups of the American War for Independence. This survey of the engagement of the Irish diaspora with political violence has revealed a complex story, with variation emerging across period, place, ideology and extent of the political mobilisation in question. It has also revealed that, sectarian violence aside, the furnace for diasporic political violence, in terms of both participation and support, was the United States. Other destinations were, broadly speaking, remarkably quiescent; this might be explained by the dominant 'British' culture in the empire, or by the more assimilationist tendencies of the Irish outside North America, as argued by Patrick O'Farrell. Another possible explanation might lie in the timing and pattern of settlement. While the origin of migrants seems to have mattered in the early period of Catholic Irish migration, when county identities were paramount in navigating the frequently bewildering American modernity, this seems to have dissipated somewhat after the Great Famine watershed, when region of origin does not appear to have affected propensity to violence in any meaningful way. Most striking, however, is the overwhelmingly urban nature of diasporic nationalism, especially in its militant form. Of course, this is unsurprising in the context of the broader patterns of terrorism and political violence in the nineteenth century: migration, the experience of urban life and the brutalising effects of industrial modernity were similarly instrumental in the emergence of the other wave of political violence which beset

52 S. Ross and A. Sanders, 'The Canadian dimension to the Northern Irish peace process', *Working Paper* (2015).

Europe, America and Russia, in the form of transnational anarchism. Another broad pattern which emerges, particularly from the late nineteenth century onwards, is the prevalence of diasporic support for rather than participation in militant nationalism. Of course, there were important distinctions – not least the Irish-American dynamiting campaign of the 1880s – but the emergent trend is of the diaspora facilitating rather than driving militancy at home.

What were the effects of these experiences, not merely for the participants in political violence, but for the broader diasporic community? In America, the embrace of Irish nationalism – both the advanced and constitutional variants – helped to create a rigid ethnic identity for Catholic Irish migrants, deepening their sense of social and cultural distinctiveness from other Americans. On the other hand, in Britain the rush on the part of many Irish communities to dissociate themselves from the violence of Irish republican campaigns, in the twentieth century as in the nineteenth, testifies not so much to the ethnic fade which has characterised earlier interpretations of migration across the Irish Sea but to the complexities surrounding Irish identity as it evolved over the past two hundred years.

There were, of course, more serious effects: the earlier instances of more 'social' violence delineated above reinforced official attitudes about Irish bellicosity across the diaspora. Suspicions of sedition instituted a culture of official surveillance, which in turn reinforced antagonisms amongst the most militant sections of the diaspora. But perhaps the most potent effect of political violence across the diaspora, regardless of the level of participation therein, was to forge a vibrant commemorative culture. Patrick O'Farrell has commented pithily that the 'colonial Irish were used to identifying their cause with martyrs, not [contemporaneously active] revolutionaries'; this observation might be extended to diasporas outside the British world.[53] Commemorations, if understood as part of a broader cultural sphere, served to socialise diasporic communities into advanced nationalism, just as in Ireland. We can trace a long history of such processes, culminating in the fevered commemorative campaigns after the Easter Rising. On the other hand, if such activities served to gradually broaden the palate towards a more militant position, in the short term they also functioned as 'safe spaces' in which to indulge in 'armchair' militancy, and in this regard clearly attracted significantly greater numbers than advanced nationalism could legitimately claim.

But this discussion has also revealed significant historiographical gaps. Perhaps the most glaring of these is the question of gender, and especially female engagement with political violence. While the role of the Irish 'Bridget' has been the subject of some valuable work, not least in the story of how immigrant Irish women supported the Land League in the United States, we know much less about how migrant women engaged

---

53 O'Farrell, *The Irish in Australia*, 287.

with militant nationalism, beyond the handful of biographical treatments of famous 'rebel women'.[54] Given the overwhelming male dominance of diasporic Irish nationalism, the theme of masculinity might offer a further fruitful lens through which to explore the appeal of organisations such as the Fenian Brotherhood or the Ribbon and Orange societies. The accelerating release of records relating to the Irish Revolution might also broaden our understanding of how that conflict intersected with migration to and from Ireland. Not least, the imaginative work of Damien Shiels in constructing a social history of Irish migration from the pension files of Irish US Civil War veterans is an example of what might be achieved via the Military Service Pension records.[55] A preliminary survey of the countries represented in the Military Service Pensions files reveals applications from the USA, Australia, Canada, the West Indies, British West Africa, Switzerland, Spain, Zimbabwe, Germany and New Zealand, as well as Britain and Ireland. Much can be done with this rich seam. Finally, historians have yet to turn their attention *en masse* to the effects of the Northern Irish Troubles amongst Irish people at home and abroad; while the political contours of the Troubles have been well established, much more work remains to be done in establishing the social dynamics shaping and resulting from that lengthy conflict. The diaspora, especially the Irish diaspora in Britain, is an essential part of understanding both, just as it remains a key feature of Irish engagement with political violence since 1740.

FURTHER READING

Akenson, D. H. *The Irish in Ontario: a study in rural history* (Kingston, Ont., 1984).

Belchem, J. '"Freedom and friendship to Ireland": Ribbonism in early nineteenth century Liverpool', *International Review of Social History*, 39 (1994), 33–56.

Bielenberg, A. (ed.). *The Irish diaspora* (Abingdon, 2000).

Bulik, M. *The sons of Molly Maguire: the Irish roots of America's first labour war* (Oxford, 2015).

Campbell, M. *Ireland's new worlds: immigrants, politics and society in the United States and Australia, 1815–1922* (Madison, WI, 2008).

Delaney, E. and D. M. MacRaild. *Irish migration, networks and ethnic identities since 1750* (New York, 2007).

Diner, H. R. *Erin's daughters in America: Irish immigrant women in the nineteenth century* (Baltimore, 1983).

---

54 E. M. Janis, *A greater Ireland: the Land League and transatlantic nationalism in gilded age America* (Madison, WI, 2015), 137–57.

55 See, for example, 'The Madigans: famine survival, emigration and obligation in 19th century Ireland and America', available at http://irishamericancivilwar.com/2015/04/01/the-madigans-famine-survival-emigration-obligation-in-19th-century-ireland-america/, accessed 20 April 2015.

Fitzpatrick, D. 'Exporting brotherhood: Orangeism in South Australia', *Immigrants and Minorities*, 23, 2–3 (2005), 277–310.

Fitzpatrick, D. *Irish emigration, 1801–1921* (Dublin, 1984).

Fitzpatrick, D. *Oceans of consolation: personal accounts of Irish migration to Australia* (Ithaca, 1994).

Foster, G. '"No wild geese this time": IRA emigration after the Irish Civil War', *Éire-Ireland*, 47, 1–2 (2012), 94–122.

Gannon, D. 'The rise of the rainbow chasers: advanced Irish political nationalism in Britain, 1916–1922', *Éire-Ireland*, 49 (2014), 112–42.

Gleeson, D. *The green and the gray: the Irish in the Confederate states of America* (Charleston, 2013).

Gleeson, D. (ed.). *The Irish in the Atlantic world* (Charleston, 2012).

Gordon, M. A. *The Orange riots: Irish political violence in New York City, 1870 and 1871* (Ithaca, 1993).

Griffin, P. *The people with no name: Ireland's Ulster Scots, America's Scots Irish and the creation of a British Atlantic world, 1689–1764* (Princeton, 2001).

Hanley, B. 'Irish republicans in interwar New York', *Irish Journal of American Studies*, 1 (2009).

Hanley, B. 'The politics of Noraid', *Irish Political Studies*, 19, 1 (2004), 1–17.

Hazley, B. 'Re/negotiating suspicion: exploring the construction of the Irish self in Irish migrants' memories of the 1996 Manchester Bomb', *Irish Studies Review*, 21, 3 (2013), 326–41.

Janis, E. M. *A greater Ireland: the Land League and transatlantic nationalism in gilded age America* (Madison, WI, 2015).

Kenny, K. *Making sense of the Molly Maguires* (Oxford, 1998).

Kenny, K. *Peaceable kingdom lost: the Paxton Boys and the destruction of William Penn's holy experiment* (Oxford, 2009).

Lee, J. and M. R. Casey (eds.). *Making the Irish American: history and heritage of the Irish in the United States* (New York, 2006).

McGarry, F. and J. McConnel (eds.). *The black hand of republicanism: Fenianism in modern Ireland* (Dublin, 2009).

MacRaild, D. M. *Faith, fraternity and fighting: the Orange Order and Irish migrants in northern England, c. 1850–1920* (Liverpool, 2006).

Miller, K. *Emigrants and exiles: Ireland and the Irish exodus to North America* (Oxford, 1988).

Moulton, M. *Ireland and the Irish in interwar England* (Cambridge, 2013).

Ó Catháin, M. *Irish republicanism in Scotland, 1858–1916* (Dublin, 2007).

O'Farrell, P. *The Irish in Australia* (Sydney, 1992).

Whelehan, N. *The dynamiters: Irish nationalism and political violence in the wider world* (Cambridge, 2012).

Whelehan, N. (ed.). *Transnational perspectives on modern Irish history* (New York, 2014).

Wilk, G. *Transatlantic defiance: the militant Irish republican movement in America, 1923–45* (Manchester, 2014).

Wilson, D. A. *The Orange Order in Canada* (Dublin, 2007).

28 The Irish in Australia and New Zealand

Angela McCarthy

28.1. Introduction

Ireland's diaspora over the past two hundred years or so has several distinctive features, including the changing destinations for this migrant stream and its earlier incarnations. Continental Europe and North America loomed large as destinations until 1800, while North America, Britain and Australasia proved attractive in the nineteenth century, with Britain becoming the destination of choice for many decades after 1930. The outflow to Australia and New Zealand was always smaller by comparison with mobility to Britain and North America, but still considerable. Between 1825 and 1935, for instance, almost 400,000 Irish moved to Australasia (most to Australia), though not all remained.[1] Before turning to consider some key themes relating to the social aspects of this movement in a comparative context, a broad summary of the differing demographic issues and settlement patterns in both destinations is required.

28.2. Demographic Overview

Compared with migration to North America, the timing and scale of the Irish outflow to the antipodes differed substantially. Whereas the Irish moved across the Atlantic from the seventeenth century, the earliest arrivals into Australia took place between 1788 and 1868 with convict transportation. Around 40,000 were shipped direct from Ireland to Australia and formed about 30 per cent of the entire convict flow, which

---

1 D. Fitzpatrick, 'Irish immigration 1840–1914', in J. Jupp (ed.), *The Australian people: an encyclopedia of the nation, its people and their origins* (North Ryde, 1988), 560.

Table 28.1. Irish-born (including those from Northern Ireland) in Australia as percentage of total population and non-Australian born population, 1891–1981

Census year	Number	% of foreign born	% of total population
1891	226,949	22.6	7.1
1901	184,085	21.5	4.9
1911	139,434	18.4	3.1
1921	105,033	12.3	1.9
1933	78,652	8.7	1.2
1947	44,813	6.0	0.6
1954	47,673	3.7	0.5
1961	50,215	2.8	0.5
1966	55,176	2.6	0.5
1971	63,790	2.5	0.5
1976	67,363	2.5	0.5
1981	67,738	2.3	0.5

SOURCE: Figures calculated from *Australian immigration: consolidated statistics,* no. 4 (Canberra, 1970), 12–13, and *Australian immigration: consolidated statistics,* no. 13 (Canberra, 1983), 12–13. I am grateful to Professor Eric Richards for providing me with copies of this information.

approximated to their proportion of the population in Britain and Ireland.[2] Free migrants journeyed to the new colonies at the same time, usually as wives and children of convicts. As the century progressed, their numbers increased as a result of assisted migration so that between 1840 and 1914 around a third of a million Irish moved to Australia.[3] Census figures indicate, however, that Australia received only about 1 in 12 of the total outflow from Ireland during the period.[4] In 1891, for instance, the Irish population of Australia was 227,000 while it was 2 million in the USA. Australia, then, was not a major destination for the Irish. But as David Fitzpatrick has aptly put it, 'If Australia was a minor destination for the Irish, Ireland was a major source for the Australians.'[5] This is evident from census figures for Australia in which the Irish-born were second only to those from England for much of the nineteenth century.[6] During the twentieth century, migrants from both the north and south of Ireland continued to settle in Australia (see Table 28.1). Table 28.2, meanwhile, charts the changing proportions of the Irish-born (including those from Northern Ireland) found in census data.

2 D. H. Akenson, *The Irish diaspora: a primer* (Toronto and Belfast, 1996), 56.
3 For a statistical overview of Irish assisted migration to Australia, see R. E. Reid, *Farewell my children: Irish assisted emigration to Australia 1848–1870* (Spit Junction, NSW, 2011).
4 D. Fitzpatrick, *Oceans of consolation: personal accounts of Irish migration to Australia* (Cork, 1995), 6.
5 Ibid., 7.
6 Census figures are complicated before 1891 with states conducting their own returns. Compiling the numbers of Irish-born across the various states reveals that the total numbers in Australia were 160,220 (1861), 202,207

Table 28.2. Irish-born in Australia, 1947–71

Census year	Ireland Republic	Ireland undefined	Northern Ireland	Total
1947	4,664	34,610	5,539	44,813
1954	5,992	32,178	9,503	47,673
1961	7,628	29,429	13,158	50,215
1966	8,340	29,776	17,060	55,176
1971	8,308	33,546	21,936	63,790

SOURCE: As for Table 28.1.

Early Irish migration to New Zealand, meanwhile, encompassed the arrival around coastal ports of sealers, whalers and some convicts from Australia.[7] Despite a small flow of Fencibles (retired soldiers) and the efforts of the New Zealand Company during the 1840s to facilitate migration, it was not until the 1850s onwards that movement increased substantially, especially during the gold fever years of the 1860s. Both Australia and New Zealand then, compared with other regions of the diaspora, had relatively few Great Famine migrants. Until 1870 around 250,000 people moved to New Zealand from Britain, Ireland and Australia, though 100,000 left.[8] But it was the prime period of assisted and nominated migration from 1871 to 1891 that propelled many Irish to New Zealand. They formed around one-third of the more than 115,000 assisted during these decades.[9] As that period came to a close, the Irish-born supplied almost 50,000 of the total New Zealand population. Thereafter their numbers generally declined (see Table 28.3; for details of those from both the north and the south, see Table 28.4).

The origins of the outflow from the island of Ireland to Australia and New Zealand also differed from settlement elsewhere in the world and from each other. New Zealand attracted strong cohorts from Munster and Ulster during the nineteenth and early twentieth century, many of the latter of a Protestant persuasion.[10] Indeed, various studies have estimated that New Zealand's Protestant Irish-born component during the nineteenth century ranged from at least one-quarter to one-third.[11] By contrast, Australia received its Irish migrants predominantly from the southern midlands and Ulster border, and Catholics dominated, comprising around four-fifths of Australia's Irish-born

---

(1871) and 212,633 (1881). See Australian Historical Population Statistics, 2006, Australian Bureau of Statistics, available at www.abs.gov.au/AUSSTATS/abs@.nsf/DetailsPage/3105.0.65.0012006?OpenDocument, last accessed 9 April 2015.

7 See J. Phillips and T. Hearn, *Settlers: New Zealand immigrants from England, Ireland and Scotland, 1800–1945* (Auckland, 2008), for a summary of the flows to New Zealand.

8 Ibid., 34–5.

9 A. McCarthy, *Irish migrants to New Zealand, 1840–1937: 'the desired haven'* (Woodbridge, 2005), 54.

10 Ibid., Table 1.1, 56.

11 Ibid., 60–1.

Table 28.3. Irish-born (including those from Northern Ireland) in New Zealand as percentage of total population and non-New Zealand born population, 1858–1971

Census year	Number	% of foreign born	% of total population
1858	4,554	11.19	7.66
1861	8,831	12.37	8.92
1864	20,317	15.52	11.80
1867	27,955	18.11	12.80
1871	29,733	18.25	11.60
1874	30,255	17.10	10.10
1878	43,758	18.21	10.56
1881	49,363	18.52	10.08
1886	51,408	18.47	8.89
1891	47,634	18.32	7.60
1896	46,037	17.59	6.55
1901	43,524	16.96	5.63
1906	42,460	15.04	4.78
1911	40,958	13.40	4.06
1916	37,380	12.24	3.40
1921	34,419	11.01	2.82
1936	25,865	8.80	1.60
1945	18,615	14.30	1.10
1951	17,172	6.40	0.90
1956	17,508	5.60	0.80
1961	17,793	6.40	0.80
1966	17,603	5.40	0.70
1971	16,165	3.90	0.60

SOURCE: *Figures calculated from New Zealand Population Census.*

Table 28.4. Irish-born in New Zealand, 1936–71

Census year	Ireland Republic	Ireland undefined	Northern Ireland	Total
1936	24,077[a]		1,788	25,865
1945	9,591[a]		9,024	18,615
1951	6,423	1,932	8,817	17,172
1956	6,566	1,857	9,085	17,508
1961	6,784	2,026	8,983	17,793
1966	6,539	1,909	9,155	17,603
1971	5,922	1,534	8,709	16,165

NOTE: [a] includes Ireland undefined.
SOURCE: Figures calculated from *New Zealand Population Census* (Wellington, 1945, 1952, 1959, 1965, 1969, 1975).

population.[12] Despite Irish Protestants being less prevalent in Australia than in New Zealand or Canada, their numbers were larger than in Britain or the United States. Such regional differentiations in respect of origins can also be seen in the migration of Scots to New Zealand, with most emanating from the eastern or western Lowlands.[13] Similar regional characteristics feature among the English-born, with substantial numbers moving from London and Middlesex, the south-east and the south-west.[14]

A further contrast between the Irish in Australia and New Zealand relates to their proportion among the total population. Until just after the First World War the Irish were second only to the English among Australia's population which contributed to perceptions of Australian society as anti-authoritarian. And when the Irish-born peaked at 230,000 in 1891, they accounted for one-quarter of the foreign-born in Australia. This differed significantly from the United States where they were numerically strong but not striking as a portion of the total population. In New Zealand, by contrast, the Irish-born lagged behind both the English and the Scots, the latter's presence and influence prompting claims that New Zealand was 'the neo-Scotland'.[15] Throughout the twentieth century the numbers leaving the north and south of Ireland for Australia declined, although potential migrants still benefited from the White Australia policy which desired ongoing migration from Britain and Ireland. Only after the 1970s did Australia's immigration policies begin to move away from racial discrimination.

Settlement patterns also varied. Unlike in the United States and Britain where the Irish were an urban population, the Irish settled the length and breadth of Australia and New Zealand. Malcolm Campbell has explained this contrast by emphasising the different societies that the Irish were entering. Whereas the United States was characterised by earlier industrial development and urbanisation, Australia was more rural.[16] Fitzpatrick notes too that the Irish in Australia were not inclined to cluster as did their counterparts in the United States and they were willing to settle in agricultural districts. They did, however, often settle in areas where the British chose not to.[17] The Irish in New Zealand, meanwhile, were strongly represented among the foreign-born populations at Westland and Auckland, though significant settlement also occurred at Canterbury, Marlborough and Nelson. Such patterns can be explained by both the economic activity and opportunities prevailing in certain regions, but also the schemes

12 D. Fitzpatrick, 'Irish emigration in the later nineteenth century', *Irish Historical Studies*, 22, 86 (1980), 133; Fitzpatrick, *Oceans*, 14–16.

13 Phillips and Hearn, *Settlers*, 108.

14 Ibid., 68–9.

15 P. O'Farrell, *The Irish in Australia* (rev. edn, Kensington, 1993), ch. 1; J. Belich, *Paradise reforged: a history of the New Zealanders* (Auckland, 2001), 221.

16 M. Campbell, *Ireland's new worlds: immigrants, politics, and society in the United States and Australia, 1815–1922* (Madison, WI, 2008), xi.

17 Fitzpatrick, 'Irish emigration', 135–6.

of assisted and nominated migration enacted by the distinct provinces which meant the Irish followed in the footsteps of their predecessors.[18] Again, similar gravitations to certain regions are discernible among the Scots and the English. The former were predominant at Otago and Southland while the latter dominated at Canterbury.[19] As with Australia, however, migration from the island of Ireland to New Zealand declined throughout the twentieth century.

28.3. Themes and Issues

One of the key themes to preoccupy historians of the Irish diaspora is motives for migration. Broad overviews of Irish migration point to the interaction of social, economic and cultural causes, with subsistence crises and the allure of foreign countries characterising the nineteenth century while the failure of the Irish economy emerges as the overarching explanation for Irish emigration since 1921.[20] For those who moved to Australasia, shipping improvements, the availability of an assisted passage and the operation of networks of family and friends were among the key facilitating factors. Propaganda could also play a part, though negative publicity must also have been influential. Yet as studies of migrant letters and individual migrants attest, a range of personal factors could spur the decision to leave home. Efforts to improve one's health, a desire for independence or expulsion from home all featured in letters from New Zealand.[21] As Agnes Lambert rued in 1877, sixteen years after her banishment from Ireland while pregnant, 'I have Been an outcaste from you all But I forgive him that was the cause of it all as my father ought to have forgiven me.'[22] Similar factors operated for the twentieth century where oral interviews, among other sources, reveal the influence of unfavourable economic conditions but also political violence and religious prejudice. In some cases, including that of George Nicholson who moved from County Down to New Zealand in 1952, such factors combined: 'Could see sectarian trouble brewing and economy declining.'[23] Examination of contemporary migration experiences have, however, been less prevalent in the Australasian context compared with elsewhere in Ireland's diaspora.[24] Accounts of the mobility of other migrant groups likewise suggest that key aspects relating to motivation (including economic improvement and lifestyle

18 McCarthy, *Irish migrants*, 64.
19 Ibid., 63.
20 D. Fitzpatrick, *Irish emigration, 1801–1921* (Dublin, 1984), 29; Delaney, *Irish emigration since 1921*, 32.
21 McCarthy, *Irish migrants*, ch. 1.
22 Ibid., 73.
23 A. McCarthy, *Personal narratives of Irish and Scottish migration, 1921–65: 'for spirit and adventure'* (Manchester, 2007), 49.
24 See, for instance, L. D. Almeida, *Irish immigrants in New York City, 1945–1995* (Bloomington and Indianapolis, 2001); L. Ryan, "'I'm going to England": women's narratives of leaving Ireland in the 1930s', *Oral*

enhancement) were shared during the nineteenth century. After the Second World War, however, divergence deepened, with migration from Ireland continuing to follow in established migrant routes compared with newcomers from Europe and Asia.

Beyond motives for migration, a focus on migrant letters by scholars such as David Fitzpatrick, Patrick O'Farrell and Angela McCarthy has illuminated a range of key pre-occupations of those corresponding with home: organising migration, kin ties, recollections of Ireland, identity, experiences in the new land, money, comfort, companionship, faith and well-being.[25] Providing us with a rich insight of the everyday social concerns of individual migrant lives, these studies demonstrate the strong operation of networks and transnational ties. Despite expressions of loneliness and homesickness, the overall impression to emerge is of largely successful settlement. Such findings stand in stark contrast with Kerby Miller's deployment of migrant letters to examine the Irish experience in North America. Here, by contrast, the Irish are depicted 'not as voluntary, ambitious emigrants but as involuntary, non-responsible "exiles," compelled to leave home by forces beyond individual control'. According to Miller, this abdication of responsibility arose from a 'distinctive Irish Catholic worldview' that compelled migrants to perceive emigration as exile, due to 'overt British oppression'. As such, Miller claims these migrants adapted 'to American life in ways which were often alienating and sometimes dysfunctional'.[26] But if their cultural background is so influential, we need to ask why there has been a more positive interpretation of their settlement in New Zealand and Australia? As Miller's key critic, Don Akenson, puts it: 'If one New World history sees the Irish homeland as producing economically handicapped, lachrymose exiles and another one depicts the same homeland as producing aggressive and at least competent pioneers, something is wildly out of kilter'.[27] Akenson suggests that the answer may lie with each destination within the diaspora receiving a 'markedly different sort of person'.[28] Certainly David Fitzpatrick points to key migrant destinations being linked to particular counties in Ireland, with the United States receiving a strong contingent of Irish-speakers, few Protestants and a large agricultural population. It was a population, he says, that could be termed 'backward'. But no research has identified whether such divergent backgrounds influenced adjustment and experience.[29] Moreover, studies of migrant letters for other ethnic groups, particularly in the United States, suggest that

History, 30 (2002), 42–53; J. D. Trew, *Leaving the north: migration and memory, Northern Ireland 1921–2011* (Liverpool, 2013), 67, 85.

25 Fitzpatrick, *Oceans*; P. O'Farrell, *Letters from Irish Australia, 1825–1929* (Kensington, NSW, 1984); McCarthy, *Irish migrants to New Zealand*.

26 K. A. Miller, *Emigrants and exiles: Ireland and the Irish exodus to North America* (Oxford, 1985), 4, 7, 556.

27 D. H. Akenson, 'Reading the texts of rural immigrants: letters from the Irish in Australia, New Zealand, and North America', *Canadian Papers in Rural History*, 7 (1990), 390.

28 Ibid., 389.

29 Fitzpatrick, 'Irish emigration', 126–43.

they were likewise preoccupied with similar concerns surrounding migration and settlement.[30] Yet whether Irish correspondents in the antipodes differed in their concerns
from other ethnicities is unknown given the absence of such studies.

Some tantalising avenues of difference, however, do emerge, including claims that
Scottish women were less inclined to want to leave their homeland.[31] Irish migration,
by contrast, is known for its gender parity and the willingness of Irish women to move.
Indeed, women formed around half the Irish flow to Australia.[32] In New Zealand, by
contrast, they were outnumbered by Irish men.[33] We might ask if such differentiations
explain marriage patterns. On the west coast of New Zealand almost 93 per cent of
Irish women had married, a figure paralleling that for Victoria, Australia, and Irish
Catholic women were more likely to choose Irish-born husbands and marry men of the
same denominational persuasion.[34] Marriage patterns in Australia show that approximately 50 per cent of Irish wives had Irish-born husbands, while those who married
Australian-born men were likely to be marrying within the multi-generational Irish
descent group.[35] This throws light on debates as to whether Irish women moved in
search of employment or marriage.[36] Some scholars have linked both explanations
by suggesting that Irish women in the nineteenth century pursued economic gains in
order to enhance their marriage prospects.[37] The work women undertook included
domestic service, factory work and hotel-keeping, among other occupations, but in
Australasia we lack the fine-grained studies of such activities as evident in other areas
of the diaspora, and for other ethnicities.[38] Systematic scrutiny of Irish men's working
and marital lives is similarly scant in the historiography of the Irish down under. How
these Irish women and men participated in courtship practices, chose their partners,

30 See, for instance, B. S. Elliott, D. A. Gerber and S. M. Sinke (eds.), *Letters across borders: the epistolary practices of international migrants* (New York, 2006); C. Erickson, *Invisible immigrants: the adaptation of English and
Scottish immigrants in nineteenth-century America* (London, 1972).

31 R. McClean, 'Reluctant leavers? Scottish women and emigration in the mid-nineteenth century', in T.
Brooking and J. Coleman (eds.), *The heather and the fern: Scottish migration and New Zealand settlement*
(Dunedin, 2003), 103–16.

32 Fitzpatrick, *Oceans*, 13.

33 McCarthy, *Irish migrants*, 62.

34 L. Fraser, *Castles of gold: a history of New Zealand's west coast Irish* (Dunedin, 2007), 87, 95.

35 Fitzpatrick, 'Irish immigration', 563.

36 The key works are H. Diner, *Erin's daughters in America: Irish immigrant women in the nineteenth century*
(Baltimore, 1983); B. Gray, *Women and the Irish diaspora* (London and New York, 2003); J. Nolan, *Ourselves
alone: women's emigration from Ireland, 1885–1920* (Lexington, 1989); B. Walter, *Outsiders inside: whiteness, place
and Irish women* (London and New York, 2001).

37 K. A. Miller, D. N. Doyle and P. Kelleher, '"For love and liberty": Irish women, migration and domesticity in
Ireland and America, 1815–1920', in P. O'Sullivan (ed.), *Irish women and Irish migration* (London, 1995), 41–65.

38 See, for instance, M. Lynch-Brennan, *The Irish Bridget: Irish immigrant women in domestic service in America,
1840–1930* (Syracuse, 2009), and W. M. Gordon, *Mill girls and strangers: single women's independent migration in
England, Scotland, and the United States, 1850–1881* (Albany, NY, 2002).

raised their children and lived their lives similarly requires examination. As a critique of gender and the Irish diaspora concluded, 'the gendering of the Irish diaspora still has a long way to go.'[39]

Nevertheless extant work does provide insights into the diverse aspects of Irish women's experiences. In Australia, this has encompassed, among other investigations, consideration of convicts, orphan girls, criminals and the insane. Engaging with their experiences and representations, these accounts document the diversity of women's lives.[40] Examination of individuals such as Eliza Davis, who was transported to Van Diemen's Land for child murder, shows the importance of researching convict lives after emancipation. Eliza, for instance, subsequently married twice, raised a family and continued to move around Australia.[41] A focus on Irish women in New Zealand, meanwhile, has included assessment of attitudes to the arrival of groups of single women, networks and personal experiences of migration as documented in migrant letters.[42] Similar concerns have preoccupied studies of Irish women in other destinations of the diaspora, but we require more research on the female experiences of diverse migrant groups in Australia and New Zealand to make comparative judgements.[43]

Case studies of the Irish in specific communities have, like studies of migrant letters, enriched our understanding of the migrant experience in Australia and New Zealand, encompassing motives, identities and adjustment. Passenger lists, vital events records and wills have been among key sources deployed in these microhistories. Such studies, however, differ from the dominant theme of transience that characterises Irish settlement in Britain. Former Whiteboy Edward Ryan, for instance, transitioned to a 'transplanted Tipperary' in New South Wales and Malcolm Campbell examined two generations of the rural community that Ryan established. Recognising the influence of cultural background, Campbell also argued for the crucial importance of local conditions on adjustment.[44] The experiences of New Zealand's Irish

39 D. Hall and E. Malcolm, 'Diaspora, gender and the Irish', *Australasian Journal of Irish Studies*, 8 (2008/9), 22.

40 T. McClaughlin (ed.), *Irish women in colonial Australia* (St Leonards, NSW, 1998).

41 J. Kavanagh and D. Snowden, 'From Cronelea to Emu Bay, to Timaru and back: uncovering the convict story', in A. McCarthy (ed.), *Ireland in the world: comparative, transnational, and personal perspectives* (London and New York, 2015), 34–60.

42 C. Breathnach, 'Even "wilder workhouse girls": the problem of institutionalisation among Irish immigrants to New Zealand 1874', *Journal of Imperial and Commonwealth History*, 39, 5 (2011), 771–94; L. Fraser, 'Irish women's networks on the west coast of New Zealand's South Island, 1864–1922', *Women's History Review*, 15, 3 (2006), 459–75; A. McCarthy, '"In prospect of a happier future": private letters and Irish women's migration to New Zealand, 1840–1925', in L. Fraser (ed.), *A distant shore: Irish migration and New Zealand settlement* (Dunedin, 2000), 105–16.

43 Two works which do consider female migration to New Zealand are: C. Macdonald, *A woman of good character: single women as immigrant settlers in nineteenth-century New Zealand* (Wellington, 1990); L. Fraser and K. Pickles (eds.), *Shifting centres: women and migration in New Zealand history* (Dunedin, 2002).

44 M. Campbell, *The kingdom of the Ryans: the Irish in southwest New South Wales, 1816–1890* (Sydney, 1997).

have similarly been captured in community studies. Ethnic networks and religion were key to Irish Catholic adjustment in Christchurch where English Anglicans were dominant. On the west coast, where the Irish were on a par and in some cases in a majority over the English-born, family, locality and class were more vital than ethnicity in shaping migrant adjustment.[45] Such studies therefore provide deep insight into the thoughts and actions of the Irish as they settled, worked, married, bred, prayed and voted. Case studies of the Scots in particular communities, by contrast, show the continuity of Scottish cultural heritage. At Waipu in New Zealand, Highland Scots displayed ethnic attachments through their Gaelic language and naming patterns, while at the same time possessing strong loyalties to family and religion, in this case Presbyterianism.[46] Meanwhile, in the Swan River colony of Western Australia manifestations of Scottishness were discerned in their everyday practices including naming patterns, dress, songs and networks.[47] Comparative studies of the erosion or endurance of ethnic practices are required before firm conclusions can be made.

If family provided a key informal network for the Irish abroad, some migrants drew on more formal associations, including the Orange Order and Ancient Order of Hibernians, among other societies. These institutions not only facilitated ongoing hostility between Catholic and Protestant, but their sociable and charitable ethos assisted migrants to cope with social or economic strains. The Orange Order has attracted considerable attention within studies of Ireland and its diaspora, often with a focus on issues of sectarianism, parades and riots, material culture and the role of Irish women. Jim MacPherson surveys the organisation in more detail (see Chapter 32, below), but a few points are worth noting in relation to Australia and New Zealand. By contrast with areas like Canada, the Orange Order was relatively weak in Australia and New Zealand. Explanations for this include general Australian antipathy to extremism in all its guises and the low proportion of Irish Protestants in Australia.[48] Events such as the attempted assassination of the Duke of Edinburgh at Sydney in 1868, however, bolstered Orange membership numbers, though as the Order continued to grow, membership was no longer solely Irish. Rioting was also less prevalent in Australia compared with other destinations in the diaspora, and New Zealand can be characterised similarly, despite Irish Catholic attacks on Orange parades in Timaru and Christchurch on Boxing Day 1879.[49] If older works sought to examine sectarian issues and political tensions, recent

45 L. Fraser, *To Tara via Holyhead: Irish Catholic immigrants in nineteenth-century Christchurch* (Auckland, 1997); Fraser, *Castles of gold*.

46 M. Molloy, *Those who speak to the heart: the Nova Scotian Scots at Waipu, 1854–1920* (Palmerston North, 1991).

47 L. S. L. Straw, *A semblance of Scotland: Scottish identity in colonial Western Australia* (Glasgow, 2006).

48 O'Farrell, *The Irish in Australia*, 102–5.

49 S. Brosnahan, 'The "battle of the borough" and the "saige O Timaru": sectarian riot in colonial Canterbury', *New Zealand Journal of History*, 28, 1 (1994), 41–59.

Figure 28.1 Women's, men's and junior lodges at an Orange parade in Christchurch, New Zealand, 1950s. Reproduced with the kind permission of Colin Buist and Patrick Coleman.

investigations consider reasons for Orangeism's longevity including its appeal among the broader non-Irish Protestant community, especially the working class.[50]

The main ethnic association of Catholics throughout the diaspora was the Hibernians, a friendly society which sought to provide financial relief to male members for funerals, and in times of sickness or as a result of accidents. It was not a nationalist organisation but one strongly oriented to the Catholic religion. Like the Orange Order, however, it began as an agrarian secret society, but then became a friendly society. The society's symbolism, however, indicated that the memory of Ireland was strong. Among its symbols were the Irish Celtic cross, the Harp of Erin, shamrocks, a wolfhound and a round tower. Hibernians also came together to celebrate St Patrick's Day which combined an emphasis on their Irish heritage and Catholic religion. In Australia and

---

50 R. P. Davis, *Irish issues in New Zealand politics 1868–1922* (Dunedin, 1974); P. Coleman, 'Orange parading traditions in New Zealand, 1880–1914', *Australasian Journal of Irish Studies*, 10 (2010), 81–104; G. Horn, 'The Orange Order in Wellington 1874–1930: class, ethnicity and politics', *Australasian Journal of Irish Studies*, 10 (2010), 55–80.

Table 28.5. Comparisons between the Orange Order and Hibernians

Orange Order	Hibernians
Progressively a benefit society	Primarily established as a benefit society
Secret society	Rituals and laws but not secret
Overt political aims	Indirect political involvement
Loyalty to Protestantism	Loyalty to Catholic Church, and then Irish nationalism
From various denominations	From one denomination
Overtly anti-Catholic	Not overtly anti-Protestant
Came directly from Ireland	Originated in Ireland but came via Australia

SOURCE: P. J. Coleman, 'Transplanted Irish institutions: Orangeism and Hibernianism in New Zealand, 1877–1910', MA thesis, University of Canterbury, 1993.

New Zealand the organisation's origins have been explained by the hostility directed towards Catholics and a wish to establish a society conducive to their faith. Religion rather than ethnicity was the key membership criterion. New Zealand's Hibernianism crossed the sea from Australia and branches were established from 1869.[51] Usefully, Patrick Coleman has provided a chart (see Table 28.5) to outline the differences between the two associations in New Zealand.

A comparative approach with Scottish associations, identified as more culturally than politically or religiously inclined as with Irish clubs, is also beneficial. Several explanations can be offered for such contrasts. Firstly, some Irish migrants maintained an interest in political issues in the island of Ireland. The timing of increased Irish migration to the antipodes in the 1860s also coincided with the rise of Irish nationalism as a mass force which took place from the 1860s through to the 1920s and beyond. Also important is the occupational difference of the Irish who, unlike the Scots, found it harder to achieve upward social mobility which then reflected itself in political angst. Scots, by contrast, were mainly uninterested in Scottish political issues, a trend which some argue largely continues to the present day among Scottish diasporic communities. A number of reasons explain this. Firstly, unlike Ireland, Scotland was never subjected to English conquest. Instead, nineteenth-century Scottish political conventional wisdom stressed the partnership nature of the Treaty of Union of 1707. Secondly, for all of the period between the end of the eighteenth century after the Jacobite defeat at Culloden until the First World War, Scotland gained enormously in economic terms from imperial markets and Scots benefited from related career opportunities to a much greater extent than the Irish. Thirdly, it is vital to recognise that the Scots were never discriminated against on religious grounds within the empire,

51 See R. Sweetman, *Faith and fraternalism: a history of the Hibernian Society in New Zealand, 1869–2000* (Dunedin, 2002), 2–4.

unlike Irish Catholics. The Treaty of Union of 1707 incorporated the pro-union Act of Security and as a result Westminster accepted that Scottish Presbyterianism was as legitimate as Anglicanism.

Consideration of these associations raises the question of religion, an aspect of the migrant experience more readily examined for the Irish in Australia than for their counterparts across the Tasman Sea. Although much of the literature focuses on the clergy – and the Catholic clergy at that – glimpses emerge of the way faith featured in the social lives of the Irish abroad. Faith was similarly part of the cultural baggage of Scottish Presbyterians and English Anglicans, but differences are identifiable. Passengers at sea, for instance, commented on the manner in which Catholics conducted their worship, presumably arising from the consequences of the Devotional Revolution (see above, pp. 69–70). As Scotswoman Jane Findlayson commented from her ship in 1876, 'There are a lot of Roman Catholics besides us. We are amused and astonished at their mode of prayers. They are on their knees for nearly an hour saying their rosary and counting their beads they are truly like the Pharasies of old making much ado about their prayers.'[52] Whether faith for the Irish in New Zealand was 'the most common context for affirmation of cultural continuity in a menacing environment', as Fitzpatrick has claimed of the Irish in Australia, remains to be seen. Indeed, more research is required in respect of migrants' belief systems and the ways they resembled or diverged from practices at home and elsewhere in the diaspora and from other ethnicities.

The experiences of Catholics in Ireland, primarily their encounters with colonialism, have been posited as a key reason for alleged empathy and affinity between Irish Catholics and indigenous peoples. According to one commentator: 'Perhaps because they share a history of oppression and land loss, and have both been the butt of racist jokes, the Maori and Irish in New Zealand have long identified with one another.'[53] And, as analysis of Maori-language newspapers reveals, Maori linked struggles in Ireland with their own move for self-determination.[54] Yet, key from the New Zealand situation is that Scottish migrants also drew parallels and affinities with Maori.[55] The other argument – that of 'Irish emigrants choosing to do unto others what others had already done unto them'[56] – can also be seen among Highland Scots encounters with the Kurnai people of Gippsland: 'The heart of the tragedy is that these previously dispossessed Scots should come to inflict dispossession on others.'[57] Despite the reality of these more

---

52 Shipboard diary of Jane Findlayson, 1876, Alexander Turnbull Library, MS-Papers-1678.
53 A. Rogers, *A lucky landing: the story of the Irish in New Zealand* (Auckland, 1996), 92.
54 L. Paterson, 'Pākehā or English? Māori understandings of Englishness in the colonial period', in L. Fraser and A. McCarthy (eds.), *Far from 'home': the English in New Zealand* (Dunedin, 2012), 133.
55 A. McCarthy, *Scottishness and Irishness in New Zealand since 1840* (Manchester, 2011), ch. 7.
56 D. H. Akenson, *If the Irish ran the world: Montserrat, 1630–1730* (Liverpool, 1997), 175.
57 R. Hall, 'Preface', in D. Watson, *Caledonia Australis: Scottish Highlanders on the frontier of Australia* (Sydney, 1990 [1984]), xii.

unsavoury encounters, the apparent absence of evidence for English migrants drawing parallels with indigenous peoples does highlight this as a key area for future comparative enquiry. Affinities between the Irish and Aboriginal people, for instance, point to the descendants of Irish–Aboriginal descent publicly engaging with their Irish ancestry, compared with those whose Aboriginal forebears intermarried with other ethnic groups. Part of the reason, according to Ann McGrath, lies with Irishness being utilised in opposition to English superiority to enable Australia's indigenous history of oppression to be linked with a history – that of the Irish – which was longer and 'internationally known'.[58]

Both harmonious engagements and the less savoury side of such encounters, however, have yet to be examined at length. Another question is whether the destination rather than migrant origins was more pertinent in determining migrant attitudes towards indigenous peoples. This is possible, but in any case it is critical to consider the importance of a migrant's occupation and the time period when they wrote in shaping their impressions.[59] Future research must also move beyond this focus on indigenous encounters and consider the cross-cultural encounters between the Irish and other migrant and ethnic groups. This includes not only 'exotic' groups like the Chinese, but Irish interactions with the English and Scottish-born. As Louise Ryan notes, drawing on her research into Irish, Polish and Muslim migration in Britain, findings are often interpreted as being related to Irishness rather than the migration process more broadly.[60] The importance of historical approaches is likewise endorsed, with Ryan ruing the 'historical myopia of much migration research' among social scientists because 'patterns being hailed as new and innovative were being exhibited by the Irish decades ago'.[61]

Irish nationalism has generated extensive investigation in Australia, particularly in relation to convicts, nationalists and rebels. While few early convicts were political rebels, being mainly petty criminals and prostitutes instead, many of those convicted for political crimes landed on Australian shores in the 1840s including the transported Young Irelanders and the Fenians in the 1860s. The historiographical focus, however, has largely centred on the changing character of nationalism in Australia, including the activities of Fenians, the Home Rule movement (and opposition to it) as a means of integration into Australia, and the involvement of prominent individuals, including

---

58 A. McGrath, 'Shamrock Aborigines: the Irish, the Aboriginal Australians, and their children', in G. Morton and D. A. Wilson (eds.), *Irish and Scottish encounters with indigenous peoples: Canada, the United States, New Zealand, and Australia* (Montreal and Kingston, Ont., 2013), 109, 129–31.
59 McCarthy, *Scottishness and Irishness*, 199.
60 L. Ryan, 'Compare and contrast: understanding Irish migration to Britain in a wider context', *Irish Studies Review*, 21, 1 (2013), 12.
61 Ibid., 9.

the Catholic clergy, in the nationalist cause. This was seen particularly around the events of Easter week 1916, with Archbishop Mannix speaking out against conscription and Bishop Liston at Auckland being accused of sedition for his comments on the Easter Rising.[62] Irish nationalism, however, was never strong in Australia and even less so in New Zealand, where studies of nationalists and rebels are thin on the ground, though Seán Brosnahan has examined rebels from 1916–28.[63] Both O'Farrell and Campbell have provided a number of explanations to account for this situation in Australia, most of which apply to New Zealand. For O'Farrell the key factors included Ireland's remoteness and the 'time lag' in reporting events, members being mainly well-to-do, suspicion among the clergy and internal divisions.[64] Campbell, meanwhile, cites local, rather than national, attachments, the absence of nationalist feeling among English Benedictines controlling the Catholic Church in Australia, distance, the imperial connection, estrangement, and a focus on Australian concerns as precluding strong nationalist attachment. Such factors reinforce Campbell's overarching conclusion that Irish nationalism throughout the diaspora should be seen as a product of their new homelands.[65]

If nationalist divides could sometimes disrupt settlement experiences, so too could mental health issues which often led to admission to a lunatic asylum. In a wide-ranging and informative overview, Elizabeth Malcolm has surveyed a number of theories seeking to explain the disproportionate representation of Irish migrants in asylums both in Ireland and throughout the diaspora. In Australia, the key reasons proffered include the deliberate shipment from Ireland of the insane, poverty, absence of will power, demonstrativeness, and the stress of migration.[66] We must remember, however, that people were institutionalised for reasons other than insanity. As Akenson reminds us in relation to prison confinements, not only could the Irish be discriminated against but young men and women could behave boisterously.[67]

A recent study of madness at Seacliff asylum in Dunedin, New Zealand, includes consideration of the Irish among other migrant groups and suggests that the provision of and access to asylums also played a role in confinement. But that study moves

---

62 R. Sweetman, *Bishop in the dock: the sedition trial of James Liston* (Auckland, 1997).

63 S. Brosnahan, '"Shaming the shoneens": the Green Ray and the Maoriland Irish Society in Dunedin, 1916–22', in Fraser, *A distant shore*, 117–34; S. Brosnahan, 'Parties or politics? Wellington's IRA, 1922–1928', in B. Patterson (ed.), *The Irish in New Zealand: historical contexts and perspectives* (Wellington, 2002), 67–87.

64 O'Farrell, *Irish in Australia*, 198–200, 202, 209, 212.

65 M. Campbell, 'Irish nationalism and immigrant assimilation: comparing the United States and Australia', *Australasian Journal of American Studies*, 16 (1996), 24–43.

66 E. Malcolm, 'Mental health and migration: the case of the Irish, 1850s–1990s', in A. McCarthy and C. Coleborne (eds.), *Migration, ethnicity, and mental health: international perspectives, 1840–2010* (New York, 2012), 30–2.

67 Akenson, *The Irish diaspora*, 119.

Figure 28.2 Bridget N., 'an Irish woman by birth, which may account for her quick temper'. Seacliff Hospital Medical Casebook, Archives New Zealand Dunedin Regional Office, DAHI/D264/19956/58, case 4037.

beyond a focus on reasons for admission and looks at the patients themselves, albeit often refracted through the eyes of asylum doctors. Here we find descriptions of patients including 'A very garrulous rambling and incoherent Irishman' and a 'very voluble and communicative – a quick tongued jerky little Irishwoman of low class'. Housewife Bridget N. was said to be 'an Irish woman by birth, which may account for her quick temper'. Other Irish patients included 'a fairly intelligent old Irishman but is incoherent' and 'a white haired old woman 68 years of age, a native of Ireland … She is a nice spoken respectful woman, inclined to the humorous side'.[68] Their language was also noted, with one Irish woman's 'English imperfect. Speaks Irish Gaelic'. A striking example exists in relation to James A. who allegedly reported in 1876 that 'he was sent into here for the word "care" which he says "is an Irish word"'.[69] The patient probably meant the Irish-language word 'cearr' which means a wrong or injury and is

68 A. McCarthy, *Migration, ethnicity, and madness: New Zealand, 1860–1910* (Liverpool, 2015), 180, 137.
69 Ibid., 186.

sometimes used to refer to someone who is 'wrong in the head'. Possibly the patient was attempting to tell the doctor his problem.

Yet comparative analysis reveals that the Irish-born were not alone in being identified in this way; all ethnicities except the English-born received comments about their physiognomy and language, but the Irish and the Chinese were targeted more than other groups. A comparative agenda also reveals that few examples of racial or ethnic remarks appear in scholarly studies of the Irish in Lancashire asylums in Britain. In Elizabeth Malcolm's work on Manchester and Liverpool asylums, she argues that case notes 'contain on occasion stereotyped and derogatory comments' but what these derogatory comments were is unknown.[70] Did they, for instance, link the Irish to prognathism (a pronounced jaw) and simianisation (ape-like), thus replicating broader depictions in British society in which the Irish were portrayed as threatening and animalistic during periods of rebellion or political unrest?[71] A more recent study of the Irish in Lancashire asylums cites only one case where an Irish patient was equated with a monkey, while other examples noted patients as being 'old' but without any associated comment about 'race' or ethnicity as found in the Seacliff records.[72] Greater comparison across the diaspora will inevitably reveal more in this regard. The struggles of these patients within as well as outside asylum walls will also expand our understanding of the social lives of Ireland's diaspora.

28.4. Conclusion

In adopting a comparative assessment of Irish migration to the antipodes, this chapter is situated within a broader framework of comparative studies, of which two main approaches dominate Ireland's diaspora. The first centres on contrasts between the Irish and other migrant groups, especially the Scots, and emerged from a history of comparison between the domestic histories of these societies which began from the late 1970s with a series of edited collections. T. M. Devine, in his comparison of the Catholic Irish and the Scots experiences in the USA in the nineteenth century, concludes that 'divergence rather than convergence was often the norm'.[73] He identifies several key differences to explain the more positive reception of the Scots: their Protestantism, dispersed settlement and skill base. By contrast, the Irish were negatively typecast for

---

70 E. Malcolm, '"A most miserable looking object": the Irish in English asylums, 1851–1901: migration, poverty and prejudice', in J. Belchem and K. Tenfelde (eds.), *Irish and Polish migration in comparative perspective* (Essen, 2003), 37.

71 S. Pearl, *About faces: physiognomy in nineteenth-century Britain* (Cambridge, MA, 2010), 108–9, 120; see also L. P. Curtis Jr, *Apes and angels: the Irishman in Victorian caricature* (rev. edn, Washington, DC, 1977).

72 C. Cox, H. Marland and S. York, 'Emaciated, exhausted, and excited: the bodies and minds of the Irish in late nineteenth-century Lancashire asylums', *Journal of Social History*, 46, 2 (2012), 515, 506.

73 T. M. Devine, *To the ends of the earth: Scotland's global diaspora, 1750–2010* (London, 2011), 126.

their Catholic faith, poverty, the scale of their migration and their unskilled occupa-tions.[74] Meanwhile, the key variable contributing to 'differentiation in the immigration experience' derives, Devine reckons, from the 'contrasting paths of development of the countries from which they had come after the 1850s'. Scotland, more industrial than Ireland's rural agricultural economy, supplied a more skilled workforce.[75]

Apart from comparing Ireland with other ethnic groups and nation states such as India and Sweden, the second key comparative framework to have developed in the wider migration historiography is between the Irish in different destinations. Australia and the United States figure in David Doyle's comparative agenda with a focus on sim-ilarities rather than difference.[76] Malcolm Campbell, meanwhile, deploys case studies of Minnesota and New South Wales, and California and eastern Australia, concluding that the economic and political factors that Irish migrants encountered abroad were more influential in shaping their adjustment to new lands than their prior experiences or cultural attributes.[77] In this way, then, he differs from scholars such as Devine and Kerby Miller, who prioritise origins and prior experience to explain migrant adjust-ment and experience.[78]

Comparative history has, however, come under attack in recent years, with schol-ars influenced by the 'transnational turn' and the quest to find reciprocal connections beyond the nation state. Certainly a focus on the consequences of transfers, exchanges and connections across borders, especially reciprocal contact, can, as Enda Delaney has recently and persuasively demonstrated, move the country's past from 'an older island-centric history to a more inclusive global one' which charts the connections and entanglements of 'people, ideas and objects over time'.[79] Both Delaney and Kevin Kenny have recommended several avenues for such investigation which transcend the nation state, including popular politics, labour, class and power dynamics, settlement patterns, labour, race and nationalism.[80] Yet, as Kenny has convincingly argued, a transnational approach benefits most by merging with a comparative methodology: 'Nation-based comparisons cannot capture the fluid and interactive processes at the heart of migration

74 Ibid., 142–3.

75 Ibid., 143–4.

76 D. N. Doyle, 'The Irish in Australia and the United States: some comparisons, 1800–1939', *Irish Economic and Social History*, 16 (1989), 78–80.

77 Campbell, *Ireland's new worlds*, 183; see also B. Walter, *Outsiders inside: whiteness, place and Irish women* (London and New York, 2001); J. M. Gallman, *Receiving Erin's children: Philadelphia, Liverpool, and the Irish famine migration, 1845–1855* (Chapel Hill and London, 2000). Though not strictly comparative, some interesting similarities and differences between destinations are made in Akenson, *The Irish diaspora*.

78 Miller, *Emigrants and exiles*.

79 E. Delaney, 'Our island story? Towards a transnational history of late modern Ireland', *Irish Historical Studies*, 37 (2011), 85, 104.

80 Delaney, 'Our island story?'; K. Kenny, 'Diaspora and comparison: the global Irish as a case study', *Journal of American History* (2003), 135.

history … But a strictly transnational approach can underestimate the enduring power of nation-states and the emergence within them of nationally specific ethnicities.'[81] The social history themes outlined in this chapter offer additional avenues for such exploration from a comparative and transnational perspective including cross-cultural encounters and histories of insanity. Yet it is crucial to remember that in undertaking such approaches we cannot ignore the local and regional in our accounts, for people lived their lives in specific communities. How they did so still requires investigation in a range of diaspora destinations.

FURTHER READING

Akenson, D. H. *Half the world from home: perspectives on the Irish in New Zealand* (Wellington, 1990).

Campbell, M. *Ireland's new worlds: immigrants, politics, and society in the United States and Australia, 1815–1922* (Madison, WI, 2008).

Campbell, M. *The kingdom of the Ryans: the Irish in southwest New South Wales, 1816–1890* (Sydney, 1997).

Davis, R. P. *Irish issues in New Zealand politics 1868–1922* (Dunedin, 1974).

Fitzpatrick, D. *Oceans of consolation: personal accounts of Irish migration to Australia* (Cork, 1995).

Fraser, L. *Castles of gold: a history of New Zealand's west coast Irish* (Dunedin, 2007).

Fraser, L. (ed.). *A distant shore: Irish migration and New Zealand settlement* (Dunedin, 2000).

Fraser, L. *To Tara via Holyhead: Irish Catholic immigrants in nineteenth-century Christchurch* (Auckland, 1997).

McCarthy, A. *Irish migrants to New Zealand, 1840–1937: 'the desired haven'* (Woodbridge, 2005).

McCarthy, A. *Scottishness and Irishness in New Zealand since 1840* (Manchester, 2011).

McClaughlin, T. (ed.). *Irish women in colonial Australia* (St Leonards, NSW, 1998).

O'Farrell, P. *The Irish in Australia* (rev. edn, Kensington, NSW, 1993).

O'Farrell, P. *Letters from Irish Australia, 1825–1929* (Kensington, NSW, 1984).

81 Kenny, 'Diaspora and comparison', 135.

29 Irish America

Timothy Meagher

29.1. Introduction

Ethnic groups are made in history and Irish Americans have been no exception. Irish Americans changed over time because people came to America from an Ireland which kept changing, because new generations of American-born Irish grew to maturity, and because the United States too kept changing. The American economy soared or crashed; the nation fought new wars; political parties rose and fell; and perhaps as important as anything else, new groups arrived in America and old ones were themselves remade, and thus whom Irish Americans could count as friends and whom they might suspect as enemies continued to change too. While Ireland would remain significant for most Irish Americans over the four centuries of their history, it would be an Ireland of their own imagining, an Ireland that they constructed to meet their own needs and carry their own hopes, and not necessarily an Ireland that the Irish themselves would recognise. That is because in response to changes within their own people as well as outside them in the American environment, they were, in fact, constantly constructing and reconstructing – inventing and reinventing – themselves over time too.

29.2. The Colonial and Revolutionary Eras

The first Irish came to North America in the mid-1580s as part of Walter Ralegh's colony planted on the Outer Banks of what is now North Carolina, but they and the colony were gone within a few years, and over the next century or more, few Irish would follow. Perhaps 3,300 Irish-born went to North America in the seventeenth century, a tiny number compared with the 147,000 English and Welsh who went there, or even the

50,000 Irish who went to the West Indies. The majority of these Irish in North America were indentured servants. Some of them had been shanghaied and shipped west after Cromwell's wars, but others, like most of the nearly 90,000 migrants who were servants from England, came of their own accord to seek new opportunities.

Immigration from Ireland to North America would be far larger in the eighteenth century. Because records of people leaving Ireland or arriving in the colonies are so fragmentary and inconsistent, we do not know exactly how much larger that migration actually was. Some historians say as few as 100,000 people left Ireland for North America in the eighteenth century before the American Revolution, but others insist that it must have been more than 200,000. Even though historians do not know the exact size of the Irish migration, they all agree that Ulster Presbyterians constituted a majority of those migrants, double or more the numbers of Church of Ireland members or even Catholics.

Why Presbyterians came in such huge numbers and Catholics, so much more numerous in Ireland, did not, puzzled observers then and remains a historical debate now. Some suggested then, and many still do now, that Irish Catholic culture inhibited initiative and risk taking and rooted Catholics in their homeland, while the individualistic and 'modern' Presbyterians were quick to recognise opportunities in America and seized them. Undoubtedly, the cultures of the two groups played a role in the difference in numbers between the two, but there were other reasons for that difference as well.

Perhaps the most important was the Presbyterians' heavy involvement in Ireland's burgeoning linen industry. That industry's occasional severe crashes often provoked Presbyterians to leave. More important was the linen industry's strong trade ties with the North American colonies. These ties provided immigrants easy access to ships going to America and information about the 'New World', and helped Ulster's Presbyterians to easily develop the kind of networks of kin and friends that constituted 'a migration machine', which kept pumping out migrants going west. Ireland's Catholics in Ulster did not participate in the linen industry to nearly the same extent in the eighteenth century, and in most of southern Ireland they did not possess such network trade links. When Catholics did have similar kinds of connections, such as in the shipping of food and emigrants from Waterford and its hinterland to Newfoundland, Catholics were willing to leave their homes and cross the Atlantic.

Though linen often provoked their migration and made it possible, the largely Ulster immigrants did not come to America to make linen. Instead, often they took a path into the wilderness that would make them very different from the people they had left behind in Ireland. They wanted land, which would be their economic anchor, a 'competency' as they called it, so that neither they nor their children would be reduced to the kind of dependency on landlords that they had left behind in Ireland. Most landed at Philadelphia or other Delaware river ports but kept moving through Pennsylvania over the Susquehanna river and the Allegheny mountains or south through Virginia and the Carolinas. They did so not so much from a culturally inbred restlessness or a desire to shake off the Old World's civilisation, but because they had to do so to get enough land for themselves and/or their children. If land was abundant in America, it was almost never free, and as the American economy grew and markets expanded west, land prices in older eastern areas kept rising, so Irish immigrants had to keep moving. In this constant push to the edges of American colonial settlement, they also became caught up in ferocious battles with native peoples beginning largely with the world-wide clash of empires in the 1750s. Though older settlers among Ulster Presbyterian or Catholic immigrants might have remembered the Williamite Wars, the bulk of both probably did not. The havoc wreaked by Native Americans and Irish on each other in these encounters thus left a new kind of habit or expectation of violence among the American Irish that profoundly affected their society and culture. Much has been made by some scholars of the survivals of Ulster or even Lowland Scottish culture in America, particularly in the Carolinas. It is the difference, however, between the Ulster Scots in America and the people back home in the northern Irish Province, who were already passing through a stage of proto-industrialisation and lived through the relative quiet of eighteenth-century Ireland, that seems striking.

The experiences of Irish immigrants in America, however, also differed from colony to colony, suggesting further the critical importance of the American environment, or perhaps better put, environments, upon them. In Pennsylvania and Virginia, Presbyterianism, which had been the religion of most of them, would survive, though severely ruptured by a split over belief and practice into 'Old Side' and 'New Side'. In the Carolinas, however, Ulster Scot Presbyterianism would begin to disintegrate. Both Old and New Side Presbyterians believed in educated ministers, but the Presbyterian Church could never provide enough such clergy for their adherents south of Virginia and barely enough south of Pennsylvania. Baptists had no such educational requirements for their preachers, and deploying a multitude of ministers in the southern colonies, they found hundreds, even thousands, of converts among former Presbyterians of Ulster Scot ancestry.

Irish political experiences also varied from colony to colony. In Pennsylvania, Ulster Scots had become enraged with the Quaker-dominated legislature for its failure to protect their western settlements during the Indian Wars of the 1750s and 1760s. After the war they formed a Presbyterian party uniting members of that denomination in both the city and the country and then combining them with German Evangelical allies to challenge Quaker control of the province. In both North and South Carolina rebellions called 'regulations' (an old English term for out-of-door political action) broke out in the 1760s. Neither Carolina regulation was fought out in religious or ethnic terms as in Pennsylvania, however; rather, what happened in these regions were regional uprisings by westerners of all faiths and ethnic backgrounds against eastern elites.

These differences carried into the American Revolution. In Pennsylvania, the Irish, mostly Ulster Scots, virtually took over the revolutionary movement and the new state government. Together with their revolutionary allies they created the most radical state constitution in the new United States. Elsewhere the Irish role would be less visible or decisive. In western North Carolina, many Ulster Scots sat out a revolution led by the easterners who had put down their regulation, and in South Carolina, the struggle became a bewildering regional and familial mêlée of brutal violence with Irish fighting on both sides.

The loyalties of Church of Ireland and Catholic immigrants or their children in colonial and revolutionary America are harder to follow. The Church of Ireland Irish are difficult to detect because as members of the established church they blended easily into an English mainstream in this outpost of the empire. Catholic immigrants are hard to trace too, but for different reasons. They were poor and came as indentured servants or even as convicts transported to America. They were also almost all men who could not find Catholic brides in America, and most colonies prohibited Catholics from establishing churches or even worshipping openly. It appears, however, that many settled among the Ulster Scots and merged easily into Ulster Scot and Presbyterian (or Baptist or unchurched) life on the American frontier.

Between the end of the American Revolution in 1783 and the close of the Napoleonic Wars in 1815, more than 150,000 Irish would come to the new United States. The great majority, as before, were from Ulster, as the province's 'migration machine' seemed to crank up and begin running immediately at the end of the war – almost as if there had been no war at all. The vast majority would also be Protestants, and the majority of those, as before the Revolution, Presbyterians. If there was continuity in this migration, however, there was also change. There would be no transported convicts to the United States, now an independent nation, and few indentured servants, since in the new republic there could be no ranks of free and unfree among whites. Most important, many of the immigrants would be political exiles fleeing a failed republican uprising in Ireland. The exiles included scores of United Irish leaders, newspapermen and agitators, and hundreds (perhaps thousands) of the United Irish rank and file. They brought a fierce Irish nationalism to the United States as well as republican zeal but, importantly, a definition of Irish and Irish America that was non-sectarian.

It was not just the political exiles who made this new era different for Irish Americans, however, for the American Revolution had changed the country, and older Irish immigrants and their descendants already living there as well. Religious tolerance had become broadly pervasive in the new America of the revolutionary era, and Catholics, so long reviled and outlawed in most colonies, now emerged from the shadows to practise their religion and find respect from their Protestant neighbours. They, in turn, redefined rules of governance for their church and even Catholic liturgies and church architecture to harmonise with the republican mores of the new nation.

Furthermore, even before the arrival of the United Irish exiles, immigrants from Ireland and their descendants in Pennsylvania had already begun to call themselves Irish or Irish American. Enemies of the Ulster Scots in America in the colonial era had derided them as wild Irish papists – 'O'Briens' – but these Ulster Presbyterians had vehemently denied their 'Irishness'. In 1771, however, Presbyterians, Anglicans and Catholics from Ireland had formed the Friendly Sons of St Patrick in Philadelphia, and in the ensuing decades numerous social, benevolent and political organisations began to call themselves Irish or Hibernians or Sons of Erin or, as in New York, more Friendly Sons of St Patrick. What was notable was that almost all these societies, like the Philadelphia Friendly Sons, were non-sectarian.

Political developments after the American Revolution also helped define this new Irish-American identity. In the 1790s, both Irish Protestants and, over a longer time, Irish Catholics, encouraged by United Irish exile journalists and political leaders, found their way into the same party, the Democratic Republicans, thus reinforcing their ethnic bond with common political interests and boundaries. Through the political warfare between the Democratic Republicans and their Federalist enemies, the Irish also emerged as the iconic image of the white common man and white men's democracy in America, the archetypal 'new men' of the republic. To Federalist opponents they were unlettered, crude and unqualified nobodies, who exploited the new democracy to shove aside the well-bred in the pursuit of power and riches; to Democratic Republicans, they were model yeomen of rustic virtue or artisan pride. To all, however, they were rapidly becoming symbols of white egalitarianism. The new iconic status of the Irish, however, also seemed to set a precedent for pitting the interests of Irish Americans, representing white common men, against African Americans in Democratic Republican and later Democratic Party rhetoric.

29.3. The Pre-Famine Migration

In 1815, an American army led by Andrew Jackson, the child of Ulster immigrants, defeated a British expeditionary force outside New Orleans, capping the second American war with Britain and reaffirming the new republic's independence. More important, for Ireland, and probably in the long run for Irish America as well, British and Prussian armies crushed Napoleon's last gasp at Waterloo in the same year and ended for good the twenty-five years of war set off by the French Revolution. Ireland's economy then crashed and over the next thirty years the island's people would suffer as a bloated population scrambled to adjust to more straitened times. Perhaps as many as a million people would leave Ireland for North America over those three decades, far more than had gone since the beginnings of Britain's colonies on the continent, but given the hardships in Ireland, some historians wondered why there were not many more.

For the first fifteen or more years, from 1815 to the early 1830s, Irish Protestants, most of them from Ulster and the bulk Presbyterians, dominated this migration as they had previous ones. Indeed, this was an extension of older migrations, provoked by troubles in the linen industry and facilitated by the linen trade's networks. This Protestant migration may have been larger than the pre- and post-revolutionary ones, but it seemed almost invisible at the time and has been largely ignored by historians since. That may have been because the Protestant Irish arriving after 1815 did not think of themselves as Irish as so many of the '98 exiles had so noisily done at the turn of the nineteenth century. It must also have been because few Americans thought of them as foreign now, as they had even as recently as the battles between Federalists and Democratic Republicans in the 1790s. Who could really consider Irish Protestants aliens now, as two sons of Ulster immigrants, Andrew Jackson and John C. Calhoun, served as president and vice president, and legions more Irish-American Protestants achieved political prominence?

It is thus hard to trace these Irish Protestant newcomers to America. What evidence of them exists suggests that they no longer went to the South as Ulster Scots and other Irish immigrants had done before and after the Revolution. The development of a thriving slave economy there severely limited opportunities for prospective small farmers or artisans like them. Instead, large numbers of Ulster Presbyterians – it is impossible to say how many – seemed to make their way into the Midwest, where fertile lands were being sold off by the federal government at affordable prices, while others, such as former linen workers displaced by a changing Irish economy, found jobs in burgeoning textile manufactures in or around Philadelphia and New York.

As a huge Protestant Irish immigrant population seemed to dissolve into thin air in this era, Irish Catholics, long a small minority, became more numerous and noticeable. Historians estimate that the number of Catholics in the United States may have grown from 200,000 in 1820 to more than 600,000 by 1840. Not all of them were Irish, of course, but probably the bulk of them were. Irish Catholic construction labourers ranged widely throughout this period and became Catholic pioneers in the new towns of the Midwest or upstate New York created by the canals and roads that they themselves had built. Irish Catholics also began to appear in New England in significant numbers for the first time, taking advantage of cheap ship fares, which took them to nearby ports in Canada, as well as the region's demand for labourers to build the infrastructure of its blossoming industrial revolution or for domestic servants to serve the newly prosperous in its growing cities. Irish Catholics made their way to the mid-Atlantic states as well, to familiar haunts like Philadelphia, but increasingly to New York City, where their numbers reached an estimated 60,000 or more by 1845.

There was evidence in pre-famine America of the kind of Orange–Green battles that were becoming commonplace in Ireland during this era, but relations between Irish Catholics and Irish Protestants were more complicated in the United States.

Most members of both religions would remain within the same Democratic Party until the early 1840s. Nevertheless, if most Irish Protestants were not open enemies of Irish Catholics now, they were not friends either, and they had little interest in celebrating a non-sectarian Irish-American identity, or maintaining the organisational structure that had embodied it.

Irish Catholics, for their part, were eager to carve out their own communities in America, but found it difficult to determine where they fitted in a tumultuous Jacksonian America transformed by the reopening of issues of slavery and race, an economic 'market revolution' and a Second Great Awakening, a nationwide Protestant religious revival was called. In the first instance, Irish Catholics would quickly look upon African Americans as economic competitors, but, just as rapidly, they imbibed American notions of white supremacy which made them bridle at any black manifestations of aspirations for self-improvement. They also, however, resented African Americans' white allies, the abolitionists, angry at their taking up black people's cause, but also suspecting the abolitionists' evangelical religion. Irish Catholics therefore sought out powerful allies of their own as a counter to these Northern evangelical whites and their black clients, and found them in Southern Democrats, who shared the Irish immigrants' disdain for both. Becoming white, however, hardly solved Irish Catholics' problem of where they fitted in early nineteenth-century America. Though largely unskilled, they joined in the powerful, artisan-led labour revolts in New York and Philadelphia in the 1830s, but those uprisings collapsed in the depression of 1837 and the emergence of new waves of anti-Catholic nativism that followed it. That nativism would become immensely stronger in America in the early nineteenth century than it had been in the revolutionary era, but before the Great Famine it would grow only in fits and starts and its power and persistence varied widely across the country. It would be strongest in New England, where Massachusetts began deporting Irish immigrants back to Ireland in the 1830s and Rhode Island started to restrict their suffrage in the early 1840s. Nevertheless, even there, as well as in other regions, Irish Catholics and local native-stock Protestants in many growing small towns managed to feel their way to temporary, fragile social and political accommodations. These towns were so new and growing so fast that local elites were emerging even as Irish Catholic immigrants arrived, and thus the relation-ships between the two were fresh experiments. Where they had such good relations, Irish Catholics often supplied a cheap and dependable labour supply to local leaders. It would be different in older, bigger cities, however, no matter what the region. There Irish Catholics could not forge such ties to elites, even with French Catholic creoles in New Orleans. In big cities, too, their numbers would also be large enough to seem a threat but still too small even to provide very useful allies in coalitions. Thus nativism gained footholds in the big cities earlier than in small towns and grew faster in them, forcing Irish Catholics to adjust to the relentless, bitter antagonism of religious prejudice.

Irish Catholics' problems in building communities were not just with outsiders, however. In most towns and cities their efforts to create communities were fraught with internal conflict. Violent rivalries based on Irish county or provincial origins were endemic in canal workers' camps but also in troubled small towns like Worcester or Lowell in Massachusetts, Providence in Rhode Island and neighbourhoods in cities like Boston. Class divisions erupting over temperance overlay some of these battles in Lowell, Providence and Boston and also fragmented the Catholic community in Philadelphia. Moreover, even in a city like New York, with the largest Irish Catholic population in the nation, the Irish Catholic institutional infrastructure was debt-ridden, rickety and fragile. The weakness of Irish Catholic communities was evident in their response to Daniel O'Connell's Repeal Association. The American Repeal movement clearly revealed Irish Catholics' dependence on native-stock Democratic allies, some of them slaveholders and most of them slavery supporters, to give their movement the status and clout that the Irish Catholics themselves could not.

29.4.   Famine, Civil War and Reconstruction

Even as O'Connell's movement flagged, the blight which would destroy Ireland's potato crop was crossing the North Atlantic from America to Europe, virtually unnoticed, in the holds of merchant ships. The famine it caused would prompt a huge migration, which has become a kind of origin myth for Irish Catholics in America. A really close look at the period might raise questions about whether it was not only not the origin of the Irish in America, but scarcely a decisive moment in their history at all. Some of the critical trends remaking Irish America – mass migration, the shift from Protestants to Catholics among migrants, and from artisans and sons of middling farmers to poorer men and women – had started by the mid-1830s or earlier and were well under way by the early 1840s before the catastrophe.

And yet the significance of the famine migration to Irish America is not to be under-estimated. The famine migration dwarfed all previous waves of Irish immigrants to the United States. One and a half million Irish arrived in the United States between 1845 and 1855. That was almost one-tenth of what the total white population of the United States had been in 1840. In 1850, the number of Irish-born in the United States only equalled the number living in Canada and Great Britain; by 1870 the number of Irish living in the American republic was nearly twice as many as the number in Canada and Britain combined. The famine thus established the United States as the principal destination for Irish immigrants in the diaspora and it would remain so for the next seventy-five years. Famine immigrants also decisively reshaped the Irish origins of Irish America from a northern Ireland people to a southern and western Ireland one, with all that that meant in terms of different kinds of experiences with religion and nationalism in the old country.

Finally, it was during the famine migration years that the definition of Irish America as Catholic, Democratic and nationalist hardened and would be set for decades to come.

The majority of the famine Irish immigrants landed in the lowest ranks of the American economy and most of them would find it hard to secure much better work over their lifetime. About one-third of Irish-born working men across the country called themselves simply 'labourers' in 1860, and there was little variation in that percentage among the regions east of the Rockies. This did not mean they were passive or 'scattered debris', as one of their spokesmen, Archbishop John Hughes of New York, would suggest. In Midwestern cities like Chicago, where working men's cottages spread out across the prairies, as many as 22 per cent of Irish household heads would own their own homes by 1860, and in the east, Irish households would prove to be avid and careful savers. As suggested above, however, this impressive accumulation of wealth by people so poor was not usually the product of upward occupational mobility, but rather the fruits of long years of domestic service by women or wandering labour by men before marriage and/or the products of stuffing crowded households with paying boarders and putting children to work.[1]

Compounding the troubles of the famine Irish immigrants was the emergence of a new powerful, national anti-Catholic nativist movement in the 1850s called the Order of the Star Spangled Banner or, more often, the 'Know Nothings'. By the autumn of 1854, the Know Nothings had a million members and they were powerful players in the politics of several states, particularly in New England, and nativist riots, church burnings and murders occurred in towns and cities from Manchester, New Hampshire to New Orleans, and Newark, New Jersey to St Louis, Missouri, or even further west to San Francisco.

However, Catholic pastors and bishops in Irish Catholic communities quickly found the Know Nothing assaults useful in presenting a common enemy to their divided communities, and they discovered powerful resources among the migrants and in the developing 'Devotional Revolution' within the church to bring competing Irish Catholic factions together to meet the threat. There were more women, for example, among these famine Irish immigrants than among earlier inflows, and immigrant women would prove not only more dutiful communicants than the men but extraordinarily helpful in raising money for their parishes. The famine migration would also include substantial numbers of laity from the Catholic heartland in Leinster and east Munster, where regular Mass attendance was relatively high, as well as increasing numbers of Irish clerics and religious women. Meanwhile, the rising 'Devotional Revolution', prompted by Rome, provided priests and bishops with arrays of new tools,

1 T. Conley and D. Galenson, 'Nativity and wealth in mid nineteenth century cities', *Journal of Economic History*, 58, 2 (June 1998), 468–93.

such as devotions and parish mission revivals, to bind the new immigrants to the church. Drawing on those resources and making the best of the Know Nothing crisis, a number of pastors – not all of them Irish – managed to squash county rivalry factionalism and, indeed, any internal dissent, within Irish-American communities, unite their congregations, and even finally put their institutions on a sound financial basis.

The Know Nothings had emerged out of the chaos of an American political rupture over the issue of slavery in the 1850s and the same rupture tore up the Democratic Party. Irish Protestants in the North would now leave it and, appalled by the advent of so many bedraggled Irish Catholics, would merge into an American Protestant mainstream or insist on distinguishing themselves from the newcomers as Scotch Irish. Reduced to a husk of its former self in the North by this and other defections, the Democratic Party became increasingly reliant on Irish Catholics as an essential element in its political base. Yet the Irish needed the Democrats as much as the Democrats needed the Irish, for Irish Catholics saw the Democrats as their only shield against not just the Know Nothings, who, in the North, were also often anti-slavery, but the new anti-slavery Republicans, who had inherited many of the nativist movement's suspicions of Catholics.

Irish-American Catholics in the North would none the less rally to the Union when the fight over slavery finally erupted into the Civil War. Most would not fight for the abolition of slavery. Indeed, after Lincoln's Emancipation Proclamation became official in 1863 and the introduction of a military draft later that year, riots, opposing the government and sometimes viciously racist, broke out among Irish Catholic immigrants not only in New York City but in Boston, Detroit, Vermont quarry works and the Pennsylvania coal-mining country. Some Irish soldiers fought in the war simply because they had no better prospects in civilian life and reaped some benefits from bounties offered for new recruits as well as regular paycheques. Yet a disproportionate number of skilled or even white-collar Irish men enlisted in the Union army, particularly in the 'Irish' regiments like the 69th New York, the 23rd Illinois and the 9th Massachusetts. These men were committed to the United States and the notion of it as a safe, republican haven for people like themselves who had to flee unbearable conditions at home.[2]

This did not, however, signal Irish Catholic eagerness to abandon ethnic loyalties and disappear into an American mainstream. Indeed, the war would create the first, mass-based nationalist movement in Irish-American history: the Fenians. Some Irish-American Fenians had signed up for the Civil War armies to be trained to fight to free Ireland, but the Civil War was no sideshow for the bulk of America's Fenians. Most men joined the Fenians not at the beginning of the war but in its last two years, and many were thoroughly committed to preserving the American Union. Fenianism for

2 J. Zibro, research in progress for dissertation, 'Paddy Yank,' Catholic University of America.

them was as much about creating a new Irish-American ethnicity as about helping to free Ireland. That ethnicity fused Irish and American republicanism with a new, self-confident Irish-American masculinity, forged, as they sang, in the 'Irish-American army's' service in the war to defeat the Southern rebellion.

In the aftermath of the Civil War Irish Americans began to reconsider their opinions of African Americans. In the Reconstruction era, the two most important newspapers in Irish America, the *Boston Pilot*, edited by John Boyle O'Reilly, and the *Irish World*, edited by Patrick Ford, would both become strong backers of African-American rights. Even Tammany Hall would shelve its racist appeals and go looking for black votes. Still, Irish-American Catholics continued to guard their neighbourhoods and jobs against black entry. Moreover, the measured, fragile support Irish Americans gave to African-American rights did not include other non-whites, for Irish-American Catholics in California would be at the forefront of the movement to exclude the Chinese from the United States in the 1870s.

29.5. The Turn of the Twentieth Century

Though the future world of Irish Americans had been largely set in the famine era, Irish Americans would none the less continue to change in important ways over the turn of the century. In the 1880s and 1890s, some Protestant Irish would try to give the long-time but vague separate identity of 'Scotch Irish' some organisational substance in a new Scotch Irish Society. It would, however, muster more support in the North than it did in the South, where descendants of old Ulster Scot colonial immigrants were most numerous, and even in the North it was not lasting or substantial. The South had remained more open to a broadly conceived non-sectarian Irish identity through much of the nineteenth century but that began to change in the early twentieth century. Then, most in the region joined opponents of rising immigration from southern and eastern Europe and took up the new broader racism rooted in Social Darwinism which inspired that opposition. By the 1910s, most white Southerners, descendants of Ulster Scots and others, began to identify themselves as Anglo-Saxons, and, by then, the South had also become the new national stronghold of anti-Catholicism.

In the North, Irish-American Catholic communities were changing too. Though heavy immigration from Ireland would continue, the American-born children of famine immigrants would dominate those local communities through the turn of the century era. Members of the new generation were proud of their American birth, avidly participated in American popular culture pastimes like vaudeville and base-ball, and were more economically and geographically mobile than their parents or recently arrived immigrant cousins. 'We're all young fellows bran' new', crowed the American-born Irish boys in a song written by the third-generation Irish Ned Harrigan and second-generation Irish Tony Hart, kings of American popular theatre in the 1880s and 1890s. [3] Yet the economic success of the second-generation Irish was limited, even if clearly better in the Midwest or the far west than on the east coast, and as they dispersed throughout cities, in places like Boston, New York or Chicago, the second-generation Irish still often settled in working- or lower middle-class neighbourhoods. Intriguingly, they married later than their parents and more did not marry than among their parents' generation: their marriage ages and celibacy rates were, in fact, more like those of the Irish in Ireland than their parents. Finally, most were as fiercely Catholic as they were fervently American, finding in Catholicism a strict sexual morality to help them delay or avoid marriage and, for many, a path to respectability. That religious commitment produced a torrent of clerical vocations among the second generation, particularly in the eastern United States. By the early twentieth century, most understood themselves as American Catholics – patriotically American but militantly Catholic – reflected in the spectacular rise of the fraternal society, the Knights of Columbus, which embodied and promoted that ideal.

As much as cultural change between the generations, it was America's unique balance of ethnic power relations, however, that helped forge such an identity and locked it into place. A revival of anti-Catholic nativist movements and the ongoing discrimination of a Protestant establishment combined with the Vatican's retreat from a brief flirtation with liberalism into reaction to kill any opportunity for accommodations with the American white, Protestant mainstream. The advent of millions of new immigrants, most of them Catholic Italians, Poles and others, at the same time, however, gave Irish Catholics a way out of ethnic isolation and permitted them to emerge as leaders of a motley collection of 'outs' not only in the Catholic Church, but also in the Democratic Party and the American labour movement. They held this coalition together by representing themselves as opponents of a hostile WASP (white, Anglo-Saxon Protestant) oppression, providing political machine favours and services, advocating a new 'urban liberalism' of government welfare and favourable labour laws, and by alternately praising and bullying the new immigrants. In not only politics, unions and the church, but also in popular culture and on the streets, Irish-American Catholics were not only leaders, but exemplars, of an 'Irish way', a path for white ethnics in most north-eastern or Midwest cities to follow to become American. No other part of the diaspora, in neither Australia, Canada nor Britain, had the same mix of such groups in the same configuration of power at this time.

The Irish-led 'outs', however, left several groups 'out', or only partially or strategically 'in'. The San Francisco Irish, who had played such an important role in excluding the

---

3 From the play 'The Mulligan Guard Ball', in D. Braham and E. Harrigan, *Collected Songs: Part I, 1873–1882*, edited by J. Finson (Middleton, WI, 1997), 83–5.

Chinese, were as aggressive in campaigning against Japanese immigration. Moreover, if Irish-American politicians were now sometimes more attentive to African-American political interests (the attention measured out according to black people's voting power and partisan loyalty), as we have already noted, most Irish Catholics continued to jealously guard their neighbourhoods and jobs against racial integration.

The importance of Ireland to Irish Americans during the turn of the century period rose and fell in topsy-turvy fashion. At the very beginning of the era in the early 1880s, the Land League had been broadly popular in the United States. In the 1890s, provoked by an America riven with ethnic and religious conflict and nourished by the cultural revival in in Ireland, Irish-American Catholics, led by the Ancient Order of Hibernians, displayed considerable interest in Irish language, sports and history. Yet, unable to attract sufficient American-born Irish, the Ancient Order of Hibernians began to stagnate by the 1910s, and thus so did the popular interest in reviving Irish culture.

When the First World War broke out in Europe, Irish-American nationalists quickly turned on John Redmond's Home Rule Party, vigorously agitated against American entry on behalf of Britain, and a small cadre took an active part in funding the rebellion of 1916 and negotiating German support for it. It is not clear, however, how many Irish Americans actively backed these nationalist efforts. When the United States entered the war in 1917 the American Catholic community, led by second-generation Irish Americans, mobilised swiftly to support the American war effort. Some American-born Irish did so to dispel any suggestion that Irish nationalism might make Irish-American Catholics disloyal to the United States. Most American-born Irish were not opposed to Irish nationalism, however, but simply valued American allegiances over Irish ones. After the war, Irish-American Catholics of all generations found in Woodrow Wilson's rhetoric of self-determination for small nations a means to harmonise their Irish and American loyalties and embraced Ireland's War for Independence.

29.6. The First Half of the Twentieth Century

This broadly based Irish-American enthusiasm for Ireland's political destiny would never be repeated again. Indeed, it declined almost immediately after the peace treaty of 1921 and over the next forty years virtually disappeared. In part, this was because most Irish Americans believed the War of Independence had resolved Ireland's fate and were confused and disappointed by the ensuing Irish Civil War. Irish-American Catholics were also not sympathetic when Ireland later remained neutral during the Scond World War. Interest in Ireland declined, too, simply because the number of Irish immigrants in the United States began to fall drastically. The influx of new immigrants from Ireland virtually stopped by the 1930s and only weakly revived in the late 1940s and early 1950s.

If it became, then, an 'Irish America without Ireland', it was an Irish America that none the less flourished. From the 1920s to the late 1950s the American institutions which Irish Catholics dominated became more powerful than they had ever been. On the whole, Irish-American Democrats enjoyed extraordinary political success in Franklin Roosevelt's New Deal and did even better during the Fair Deal of his less patrician successor, Harry Truman. As they profited from the Democratic Party's rise in the 1930s and the 1940s, so Irish-American Catholics also rode the stunning revival of American labour in the same decades.

Irish-American Catholic success in the Democratic Party or in the labour movement was contingent on their positioning in between the WASP establishment and the newer white ethnic Italians, Poles and others. That positioning continued to afford them the opportunity – though now with higher stakes – to wheel and deal, include and exclude. Their success lay not only in their positioning, however, but, in this age of the New Deal's Democratic Party revival and labour uprising, in their skill in representing themselves as the 'people'. Hollywood helped them to do so by frequently presenting them in the same way as 'regular guys', twentieth-century urban versions of the white American common man.

They, none the less, remained a distinct people, and what distinguished them more than anything from others, perhaps, was their ongoing role in the Catholic Church, not just as leaders but as models of American Catholicism. A higher proportion of them went to Mass or confession, sent their children to Catholic schools or had large families than any other Catholic ethnic group. This was not simply a continuation of older traditions or a reflection of Irish Americans' economic immobility. It was middle-class Irish Americans, the college educated, who led in these categories: college-educated Irish-American women, for example, expected to have larger families than any other significant demographic group in America in the late 1950s and early 1960s. Now well educated, often in Catholic schools and colleges, they knew church teaching on family limitation and other moral choices much better than their predecessors had. Yet they were also attentive to those teachings because they still identified strongly as Catholics. That derived, in part, from frustration over the paradox of their improving economic status but continued social exclusion. The intensity of their Catholicism also drew more specifically, however, from the infusion of a messianic, religious anti-communism insistently promoted by Rome but abetted by the Cold War, which suffused almost every aspect of American Catholic life in the 1940s and 1950s.

29.7.   The 1960s and After

There were whispers of subtle dissent from this American Catholic version of Irish Americanism even as it flourished in the 1950s, but it would have been hard to predict its rapid breakup in the very next decade. Long-term trends of upward occupational mobility and movement to the suburbs undoubtedly played a role in its downfall, but, as noted, upward mobility in the 1950s had seemed to foster Catholic zeal not sap it. Rather a series of events and broad trends running through American life seemed to combine with these internal changes. They included John F. Kennedy's election as president; the Catholic Church's Vatican Council; the civil rights movement; the feminist and gay rights movements; and the Vietnam War – or more accurately the controversy that erupted over it.

Rocked by these changes, the institutions at the centre of the Irish-American Catholic community began to crumble. Kennedy's election, the Vatican Council and the civil rights movement all undermined the Catholic–Protestant opposition, which had stoked Catholic militancy for so long. Irish Catholic marriages across not only ethnic but now religious grounds soared. Religious militancy would endure among a substantial minority of Irish-American Catholics, though the enemy would now be 'liberals,' including Catholic ones, and not Protestants. Nevertheless the drastic decline of the Catholic Church was clear. Today, about one-twelfth of the nation's entire population are *former* Catholics – a higher proportion than any Protestant denomination except the Baptists.

The Democratic Party also suffered in the 1960s and succeeding decades and emerged as a very different political organisation from the one in which Irish-American Catholics had once played such a critically important role. Here again long-term trends of white, including Irish-American Catholic, upward mobility and suburbanisation undoubtedly had a significant effect. Democratic defections were not only among the middle class, however. The paradox of measured political backing of black interests with defence of Irish and white territory and job niches had been Irish-American Catholics' position on race since Reconstruction. It now unravelled. African Americans were no longer willing to tolerate its inequities and many working- and middle-class Irish-American Catholics and other whites left the Democratic Party to them. The party did not break up only over race, however. There had long been fault-lines within it dividing 'regulars' and 'reformers': Irish Americans, especially working-class Irish Americans, had much preferred the regular Democrat Harry Truman in 1948, over the Democratic reformer Adlai Stevenson in 1952 and 1956, for example. The issues, which regulars and reformers fought over in the 1960s and thereafter, included the Vietnam War and foreign policy, but also cultural questions revolving around sexuality and gender: women's roles, abortion and gay rights. The battles between reformers and regulars, however, were also about power: who would rule in the Democratic Party. Most Irish Catholics probably sided with the regulars but not all – a small but notable number of gay activists of Irish Catholic background, like Anne Maguire or Sean O'Brien Stub, for example, have battled for gay rights from the 1960s and 1970s to the present day.

Through all of this there were important regional distinctions in Irish-American Catholic responses. Race appears to have been more powerful in influencing Irish Americans and other white ethnics' flight from the Democratic Party in the Midwest or

Philadelphia, which had long traditions of Irish–black conflict as well as high home-ownership rates. In New York, on the other hand, a battle between Irish-American Catholic regulars and Jewish, WASP and liberal Catholic reformers over control of the Democratic Party had already led to significant Irish-American Catholic defections to the Republicans by the 1950s. Massachusetts Irish Catholics were not more 'liberal' in their values than their fellows in New York or the Midwest – indeed, they had been particularly virulent McCarthyites in the 1950s and Irish-American Boston neighbourhoods became notorious for resistance to racial integration of schools in the 1970s – but most of them (and the Irish and other Catholics in neighbouring Rhode Island) remained in the Democratic Party. Reformers were not as numerous in Massachusetts as they were in New York, where they were strong enough to push Catholic regulars out at the party's lower levels. Conversely, Irish-American Catholics in New England continued to resent Yankee Protestants and, therefore, never saw the Yankee-run, Liberal Republican Party as a welcoming haven for them as the New York Irish perceived the more conservative Republican Party or even the Irish-founded Conservative Party in their state.

The convulsions of the 1960s and after left no consensus among Irish Americans on who they were. The issue was more pointed now because the circumstances that had locked them in and determined that identity as a Catholic one had melted away. Their ethnic identification now became optional. If some persisted in the old militant American Catholicism it was clear that they held no monopoly on the definition of Irish or Irish America anymore. St Patrick's Day parades became battlegrounds over whether gay people might be Irish Americans. While representatives of older Irish organisations close to the Catholic Church insisted that they could not, gay Irish Americans, like Irish immigrant Brendan Fay, contended that they could. Moreover, if Irish American no longer automatically meant Catholic, then people of Irish ancestry of any religion could be Irish American now. Celebrations of Irish, or more broadly Celtic, roots thus began to bloom in the South as well as the North among people of all (or no) religions, but of Irish ancestry.

Though no longer trapped in an Irish-American identity, many Irish Americans, like white ethnics of all ancestries, wanted one. They became caught up in a broader 'white-ethnic revival' in the 1960s and 1970s that reflected that era's passion for personal and cultural authenticity and roots. Irish Americans began to define their Irish-American identity now in terms of Irish music and dance traditions as well as searches for their own family histories and not religion. Inevitably the quest for an authentic 'Irish Americanness' led back to Ireland itself, so long ignored by Irish Americans for much of the twentieth century. With the advent of jet travel, American tourism in Ireland boomed, as Irish Americans flooded the island looking for cultural and personal origins.

The same search for authenticity also seemed to play an important role in Irish-American responses to the emerging conflicts in Northern Ireland. It is still not clear which or how many Irish Americans were interested enough in that struggle to follow it closely or give money to the combatants. If there may have been a vague broader interest in Northern Ireland's 'Troubles' among Irish-American Catholics, the number of Irish-American activists backing the IRA seems to have been actually quite small – though large enough to be vital to its endurance. Noraid, 'recognized from an early stage as the sole representative of the Provisional IRA in the United States', for example, 'was never a mass organization'. Brian Hanley argues persuasively that participants in the struggles saw their support for Noraid as a mark of being authentically Irish and standing up for their people just as members of other groups did in a multi-ethnic, multi-racial America. Noraid's spokesmen thus routinely hammered at upwardly mobile Irish Americans who, they insisted, had sacrificed their Irishness for success. Noraid members also mocked the green beer, 'Paddywhackery' of once-a-year, Patrick's Day Irish Americans.[4]

29.8. Conclusion

It is hard to say what Irish America is or where it is going today. The quieting of the north has made Ireland less prominent in American public consciousness. Irish-American relations with the people of the Republic of Ireland grew closer with the attack on the World Trade Center on 11 September 2001, but widened again as many in Ireland, as in most of western Europe, recoiled at the American invasion of Iraq. In the recent depression, the Irish government made an effort to cultivate the diaspora, and particularly Irish America, with mixed success. Meanwhile, in the United States, the steam has seemed to finally go out of the 'white ethnic revival' that began more than fifty years ago. Yet, Irishness and even Irish Americanness still retain powerful symbolic meanings in the English-speaking, and, perhaps, even the broader world. For a moment at least during the recent depression, for example, Irish Americans emerged as representatives of the white American working class on movie screens, a couple of centuries after such images had first become popular at the turn of the nineteenth century. Perhaps identifying as Irish American or Irish will always have appeal or meaning for Americans of Irish descent, no matter how distant or threadbare their ties to the island.

FURTHER READING

Adams, W. *Ireland and Irish emigration to the New World: from 1815 to the famine* (Baltimore, 1980 [1932]).

Anbinder, T. 'Moving beyond rags to riches: New York's famine Irish immigrants and their surprising savings accounts,' *Journal of American History* (December 2012), 741–70.

4 B. Hanley, 'The politics of Noraid', *Irish Political Studies*, 19, 1 (2004), 10.

Barrett, J. *The Irish way: becoming American in the multiethnic city* (New York, 2012).

Bric, M. *Ireland, Philadelphia and the re-invention of America* (Dublin, 2008).

Fanning, C. *The Irish voice in America: Irish American fiction from the 1760s to the 1980s* (Lexington, 1990).

Ferrie, J. *Yankeys now: immigrants in the antebellum United States, 1840–1860* (New York, 1999).

Fogleman, A. 'From slaves, convicts and servants to free passengers: the transformation of immigration in the era of the American Revolution', *Journal of American History*, 85, 1 (June 1998), 43–76.

Gleeson, P. 'Smaller differences: "Scotch Irish" and "real Irish" in the nineteenth century American South' *New Hibernia Review*, 10, 2 (Summer 2006).

Griffin, P. *The people with no name: Ireland's Ulster Scots, America's Scots Irish and the creation of the British Atlantic world, 1689–1764* (Princeton, NJ, 2001).

Guinnane, T. and M. C. Foley. 'Did Irish marriage patterns survive the emigrant voyage? Irish American nuptiality, 1880–1920,' *Irish Economic and Social History*, 26 (1999).

Hale, G. *A nation of outsiders: how the white middle class fell in love with rebellion in post-war America* (New York, 2011).

Hanley, B. 'The politics of Noraid', *Irish Political Studies*, 19, 1 (2004), 1–17.

Miller, K. *Emigrants and exiles* (New York, 1985).

Miller, K., A. Schrier, B. D. Boling and D. N. Doyle. *Irish immigrants in the land of Canaan: letters and memoirs from colonial and revolutionary America, 1675–1815* (New York, 2003).

Mitchell, B. *The Paddy camps: the Irish of Lowell, 1821–1861* (Urbana, IL, 1988).

Tentler, L. *Catholics and contraception: an American history* (Ithaca, NY, 2004).

Way, P. 'Evil humors and ardent spirits: the rough culture of canal construction labourers', *Journal of American History*, 79, 4 (March 1993).

Whelan, B. *United States foreign policy and Ireland: from empire to independence, 1913 to 1929* (Dublin, 2006).

Wilson, A. *Irish America and the Ulster conflict, 1968–1995* (Washington, DC, 1995).

Wilson, D. *United Irishmen, United States: immigrant radicals in the early republic* (Ithaca, NY, 1998).

30 The Irish in Britain

Roger Swift and Sean Campbell

30.1 1750–1914 Roger Swift

30.1.1 Introduction

The Irish who migrated to Britain during the long nineteenth century were by no means a homogeneous group, for their ranks contained both rich and poor, middle class and working class, skilled and unskilled, Catholics and Protestants (and unbelievers), nationalists and loyalists, and men and women from a variety of distinctive provincial rural and urban cultures in Ireland. Nevertheless, the vast majority were poor Roman Catholics, and it was their experience, often presented in monochrome as a heroic struggle against poverty and prejudice, particularly during the early Victorian years, which dominated early historical studies of the Irish in Britain. More recently, however, within a burgeoning historiography of national, regional and local studies, the reductionism of earlier studies has been challenged, and there is now a greater awareness that Irish migration and settlement during the period was a multi-generational phenomenon and that the experiences of the Irish-born and their descendants were more complex and variable in both time and place than earlier studies suggested.

30.1.2 Migration and Settlement

The nature and pattern of Irish migration to Britain, prompted as it was by the interaction of a combination of influences, some 'pushing' the Irish out of Ireland, others 'pulling' them from Ireland, lacked the permanence of Irish migration to North America and Australasia owing to the short distances involved and the social, economic, political and cultural links between Britain and Ireland.[1] There was a longstanding tradition of seasonal migration from Ireland to Britain which can be traced back to the Middle Ages, and by the early eighteenth century Irish harvesters were a familiar feature of the British rural landscape, variously reaping corn, digging potatoes, collecting turnips, picking hops and draining land in order to supplement the family income and support their domestic holdings in Ireland. This tradition was to continue well into the twentieth century, although as mechanisation advanced the number of Irish harvesters progressively declined. However, with the onset of the Industrial Revolution, employment opportunities for sojourning migrants were extended by the demand for casual work in mines, docks and construction industries, and these itinerant labourers and their families put down roots in ports such as London, Bristol, Liverpool and Glasgow and, more generally, in the emerging industrial towns of south Lancashire and the central lowlands of Scotland. Smaller Irish communities also emerged in garrison towns such as York and Chester, where some Irish soldiers took up permanent residence following their discharge from military duties in the British army, notably after the conclusion of the Napoleonic Wars in 1815.[2]

Thereafter, the continuing expansion of the British industrial economy witnessed a corresponding increase in the pace and scale of Irish migration. Census returns indicate that the Irish-born population of England, Scotland and Wales rose from 182,000 to 419,000 between 1821 and 1841, when the largest Irish-born urban populations were to be found in London (108,548), Liverpool (83,813), Glasgow (59,801) and Manchester (52,504), and, in addition to Clydeside and south Lancashire, Irish-born migrants were also present in significant numbers in the industrial districts of the West Riding, the West Midlands and south Wales. The Great Irish Famine of 1845–52 served as a catalyst for these processes and by 1851, the number of Irish-born in Britain had virtually doubled, having risen to 727,000, and peaked at 806,000 in 1861, when Irish migrants were even more dispersed geographically and were present in significant numbers in Cumbria and County Durham, and on Tyneside, Wearside and Teesside. However, as migration from Ireland to Britain slowed down during the late nineteenth century, the number of Irish-born migrants also declined to 550,000 in 1911, reviving only later in the twentieth century. These statistics exclude the second-generation Irish – the children born in Britain of Irish parents – who were variously classified as English, Scottish or Welsh; hence by 1914, when Irish-born migrants and their descendants were present in every county in England, Scotland and Wales, the actual size of the ethnic Irish community in Britain was undoubtedly far higher than census returns suggested.[3]

1 D. Fitzpatrick, *Irish emigration, 1801–1921* (Dublin, 1984), 226–9.
2 A. Redford, *Labour migration in England, 1800–1850* (London, 1926; rev. edn Manchester, 1964), 132–64.
3 R. Swift, *Irish migrants in Britain, 1815–1914: a documentary history* (Cork, 2002), 27–35.

The Irish urban experience differed from one settlement to another. Much contemporary qualitative evidence, which referred specifically to 'the lowest Irish' (the very poorest and largely Catholic Irish), suggested that by mid-century the newcomers were concentrated in so-called 'Little Irelands', isolated from the surrounding populations in particular streets and courts. The tendency of the Irish poor to cluster in such districts was influenced by the availability of cheap accommodation, including lodging houses, the existence of familial and kinship networks, proximity to available employment, and the development of Irish social, cultural and religious organisations. Yet even where Irish migrants dominated particular streets, courts and squares, they were seldom shut off from the native population. In short, the poor Irish lived largely among the English poor, although further residential segregation sometimes operated at the micro-neighbourhood level in districts populated by both Irish Catholics and Protestants. Moreover, where 'Little Irelands' did exist, they were far from being static communities, for they were inhabited by a notoriously transient populace and experienced continual in- and out-migration, with only relatively small numbers of migrants establishing permanent settlements. Victorian slum zones and their occupants were themselves also constantly shifting and by the 1880s many of the Irish slums depicted during the early Victorian years, including Manchester's 'Little Ireland' and Wolverhampton's Caribee Island, had disappeared in the wake of slum clearance legislation and their populations had been dispersed elsewhere. In other towns the Irish population was dispersed and districts once inhabited by the Irish were populated by later migrants, as in London, where Stepney became a focus for eastern European settlement by the end of the century.

30.1.3 Employment and Social Mobility

Overall, among the country immigrants to British towns and cities, the Irish were generally the least prepared to succeed in their new environment and in 1836, in 'The report on the state of the Irish poor in Great Britain', George Cornewall Lewis observed that Irish immigration was 'an example of a less civilized population spreading themselves, as a kind of substratum, beneath a more civilized community, and, without excelling in any branch of industry, obtaining possession of all the lowest departments of manual labour'.[4] Nevertheless, whilst noting contemporary perceptions that the Irish lowered wages and thereby reduced the standard of living of non-Irish labourers, the report recognised the value of Irish labour.

The great majority of Irish-born males entered the lowliest and least healthy of urban occupations and were overwhelmingly concentrated in unskilled labour in mines, ironworks, textile mills, manufactories, building works and railway construction. These

---

4 'Report on the state of the Irish poor in Great Britain', *Parliamentary Papers*, 34, xxxiv, (1836), 456–7.

were occupations for which a sophisticated city like London held very few rewards and although some skilled workers entered sweated industries like cobbling and tailoring, casual dock work and street-selling were, as Henry Mayhew observed in the 1840s and 1850s, the most common occupations among the Irish in London's East End.[5] By contrast, the occupational profile of Irish women – still the 'great unknown' of Irish diaspora studies, and whose experiences warrant further study – also varied by town and region but was in general characterised by a range of poorly paid occupations. In the textile districts of England and Scotland women found employment as spinners, weavers and factory workers, and in London and the Home Counties there was a demand for Irish domestic servants in well-to-do Protestant households, but elsewhere their general role in supplementing the family economy lay in taking in work at home or in employment as washerwomen, charwomen, hawkers, seamstresses, servants or farm labourers. Overall, most Irish migrants provided a mobile pool of unskilled and semi-skilled labour, moving within and between towns according to the availability of work and, as such, their occupational patterns served as a barometer of the structural and regional changes in the British economy, as Hugh Heinrick observed in his survey of the Irish in England prepared for *The Nation* in 1872. [6] Moreover, by the end of the century, although upward economic and social mobility was difficult for the Irish to obtain, a small proportion of second-generation Irish men were securing skilled employment in most industrial districts as mechanics, boilermakers, smiths, platers and fitters, whilst Irish women were beginning to enter a range of low-paid professional occupations, including social work and nursing. The late Victorian period also witnessed the emergence of a small Irish middle class of professional men – doctors, lawyers, teachers, merchants, journalists, businessmen, retailers, publicans and shopkeepers – many of whom served the major Irish centres, as John Denvir noted in his survey of 1892, *The Irish in Britain*.[7] Historians have only recently begun to explore this middle-class world and there is some evidence to suggest that, as in Liverpool, these 'Micks on the make' served as important culture-brokers, developing forms of collective mutuality which reinforced a sense of Irish distinctiveness, creating and sustaining positions of leadership among their fellow Irish, and winning respectability, fame and fortune for themselves.[8] By contrast, London, especially, became a focus for Irish writers, journalists, artists and parliamentarians.[9]

5 H. Mayhew, *London labour and the London poor*, 4 vols (London, 1861–2), I, 104–5.

6 H. Heinrick, *A survey of the Irish in England* (1872), edited, with an introduction by A. O'Day (London, 1990), Letters XII–XIV, 87–114.

7 J. Denvir, *The Irish in Britain* (1892), ch. XLI, 'The Irish in various districts of Great Britain', 389–458.

8 J. Belchem, 'Class, creed and country: the Irish middle class in Victorian Liverpool', in R. Swift and S. Gilley (eds.), *The Irish in Victorian Britain: the local dimension* (Dublin, 1999), 190–211.

9 R. F. Foster, '"An Irish power in London": making it in the Victorian metropolis', in F. Cullen and R. F. Foster, *Conquering England: Ireland in Victorian London* (London, 2005), 12–25.

30.1.4 Communal Culture

The overwhelming majority of Irish migrants were Roman Catholics and the cultural development of Irish communities in Britain was crucially bound up with the survival of Catholicism, for the Roman Catholic Church in England, Scotland and Wales was the only native institution with a fundamental claim on Irish loyalties. Initially, the Catholic clergy sought to re-evangelise the Irish Catholic faithful by the creation of missions for the urban Irish poor and were almost overwhelmed by this task during the 1840s and 1850s, the heroic age of missionary Catholicism. Thereafter, the development of the parochial system and the increased recruitment of priests was accompanied by a boom in church building which transformed the austere and simple Catholic chapels of the past into people's palaces, awash with the new iconography of altars, statues and pictures, which were the expression of Irish Catholic communal pride and self-assertiveness. The Catholic Church helped Irish migrants to adapt to urban life by providing a social and cultural world based on the parish church. Catholic welfare and recreational provisions included schools, social clubs, charities, lectures, dinners, bazaars, temperance groups, festivals, church suppers, choral societies, bands and excursions. Initiatives such as these, which exercised a particular influence over Irish women and children, were designed in part to counter the process of 'leakage' (the failure of some Catholics to pass on their faith to a generation born in England, Scotland and Wales). Nevertheless, Irish migrants found both a national and a religious identity within the Roman Catholic Church, a distinctiveness which was developed and maintained through networks within the Irish diaspora at home and abroad. This identity, itself a reflection of Irish 'Otherness', was reinforced by manifestations of anti-Catholicism, even though Victorian 'No Popery' was much more than simply anti-Irishness, and Irish Catholics formed a viable and distinct culture which was intrinsically dynamic in that being Irish, Catholic and working class forced individuals to reconcile different demands and particular identities.[10]

Yet Irish migrant communities also included Irish Protestants, largely of Ulster extraction, whose migration, settlement and cultural experience has only recently been explored by historians. Early studies of the Irish in Britain presented these migrants as little more than the ancillaries of animosity, unionist politics and sectarianism, which continued well into the twentieth century in Liverpool and Glasgow, where the Orange Order had strong roots, and whose activities were compounded by mid-Victorian 'No Popery' scares and the Home Rule crises of 1886–1914. However, there is now evidence that Orangeism also adapted to the needs of Irish Protestant migrants in working-class

---

10 S. Gilley, 'Roman Catholicism and the Irish in England', in D. MacRaild (ed.), *The Great Famine and beyond* (2000), 147–67.

districts in northern England and Scotland by gradually becoming less a political movement and more a way of life, offering mutualistic associational opportunities for its members and their families, and prospects for enhanced economic mobility and social status, even if these initiatives were not always successful.[11]

30.1.5 Attitudes towards Irish Migrants

Nevertheless, the Irish presence in nineteenth-century Britain was generally unpopular. Even before the famine exodus, some social commentators, including James Phillips Kay, Thomas Carlyle and Frederick Engels, regarded Irish immigration as little short of a social disaster which, it was held, would demoralise the native population. Recent scholarship has established that while these fears were real, they were often unfounded, as, for example, in the popular belief that Irish migrants were the harbingers of crime and disorder.[12] Such negative perceptions of the Irish need in part to be understood in the context of the many contemporary issues – urban squalor, disease, disorder, vagrancy and unemployment – with which they became entangled, yet it was a tragic coincidence that the growing awareness of acute urban problems during the 1830s and 1840s, reflected in the 'Condition of England' question, occurred at the same time as the rising tide of Irish immigration, and for which Irish migrants became convenient scapegoats and appeared isolated and outcast from mainstream society.

This was reflected in manifestations of anti-Irish prejudice which punctuated the period and which ranged from antipathy and psychological abuse in the workplace to more violent public disorders, whose causes were complex and whose incidence varied in time and place. These included serious anti-Irish riots at Stockport (1852), Oldham (1861), London (1862) and Tredegar (1882), and the more widespread Murphy riots in the industrial districts of the Midlands and north-west between 1867 and 1871. Of course, anti-Irish attitudes in British society had a long and complex history, and Irish Catholics had widely been regarded with suspicion by the British Protestant establishment on the grounds of their Catholicism (and their allegiances to the Pope in Rome) and their sympathy for Irish nationalism (and perceived disloyalty to the crown and the Union). However, some historians have argued that this prejudice was based fundamentally on the British assumption that the Irish were racially inferior,[13] as reflected in contemporary descriptions, visual representations in magazines like *Punch*, or in advertisements stating 'No Irish Need Apply'. Others have rejected this view, arguing

11 D. MacRaild, *Faith, fraternity and fighting: the Orange Order and Irish migrants in northern England, c.1850–1920* (Liverpool, 2005), 200–41.
12 R. Swift, 'Heroes or villains?: The Irish, crime and disorder in Victorian England', *Albion*, 29, 3 (1997), 399–421.
13 L. P. Curtis, *Apes and angels: the Irishman in Victorian caricature* (Newton Abbot, 1971; rev. edn Washington and London, 1997), 109–47.

that the British stereotype of 'Paddy' had a benign as well as a malign face and that anti-Irish prejudice is best explained in terms of contemporary class attitudes and a range of specific social, economic, religious and political factors.[14]

30.1.6   Accommodation and Integration

In the long term, however, manifestations of anti-Irish sentiment did not militate against co-operation between Irish migrants and their English, Scottish and Welsh working-class neighbours, as witnessed by Irish participation in radical and labour movements in nineteenth-century Britain. There was, for example, an important Irish presence in Chartism which provided the movement with an additional cutting edge in its final distinctive phase in 1848, when Chartists and Irish Confederates came together with a joint programme of reform and repeal. Moreover, and contrary to their popular image as strike-breakers and blacklegs, Irish migrants also made important contributions to the development of embryonic trade unions in the cotton textile districts of south Lancashire and in Scotland, where Irish cotton spinners, handloom weavers and miners participated in trade unions and strikes, despite opposition from the Catholic Church and the Orange Order, which suggests that sectarianism was not always a barrier to class co-operation during a period that witnessed the shifting identities of class, religion and politics. Later, during the 1880s and 1890s, first- and second-generation Irish migrants, including Will Thorne, Ben Tillett, P. J. King and Albert Kenny, played prominent leadership roles in the 'New Unionism' of unskilled workers in England, Scotland and Wales, whilst James Connolly and James Larkin, brought up in Irish communities in Edinburgh and Liverpool respectively, were also influential figures in trade unionism in both Britain and Ireland.

Broader influences in late Victorian and Edwardian society also assisted the accommodation of the Irish in Britain. The development of more organised procedures for the expression of working-class social, economic and political grievances and improvements in the means of maintaining public order were accompanied by a general decline in the incidence of popular disorders, including anti-Irish riots, despite periodic outbreaks of sectarian violence. Changes in British popular culture also encouraged Irish interaction with mainstream society, as evidenced in the field of popular recreation and mass spectator sport. In Scotland, for example, association football clubs were established in Irish Catholic communities in Glasgow (Celtic), Edinburgh (Hibernian) and Dundee (Dundee United), whilst in south Wales, Irish Catholic participation in, and support for, rugby football and boxing also served to reduce ethnic tensions,

14 S. Gilley, 'English attitudes to the Irish in England, 1780–1900', in C. Holmes (ed.), *Immigrants and minorities in British society* (London, 1978), 81–110.

although Irish participation in these and other cultural forms, including music, theatre and the arts, still awaits detailed investigation. The impact of Catholic educational provision was also double-edged, for whilst on the one hand it signified difference, it also prepared Irish migrants for life in the world beyond Irish Catholic neighbourhoods. Moreover, the extension of the franchise to most adult Irish males through the Reform Acts of 1867 and 1884 brought Irish migrants, who were generally politically apathetic, more fully into British political democracy. Indeed, with the failure of the Fenian campaign of the 1860s, which occasioned British public outrage and was largely disavowed within Irish Catholic communities, Irish nationalist activity in Britain was increasingly expressed through legitimate organisations and Irishmen were elected to borough councils in many towns, including Manchester, Liverpool and Glasgow. However, Irish voters were rarely sufficiently numerous in parliamentary constituencies to return an Irish nationalist MP, the sole exception being T. P. O'Connor, who served the Scotland division of Liverpool from 1885 to 1929. Liverpool, indeed, whilst the most Irish of British cities, was itself exceptional, a Conservative stronghold dominated by a militant Tory political culture, influenced by Orangeism, anti-nationalism and anti-Catholicism, as a majestic study of the Liverpool Irish has recently shown.[15] Arguably, the greatest successes of Irish political activity came in the 1880s, when the Irish Parliamentary Party created a mass organisation which gained a measure of respectability through Gladstone's conversion to Home Rule in 1886. Thereafter, most Irish Catholics supported the Liberal Party, whilst Irish Protestants saw their natural home in the Conservative (and Unionist) Party, although during the twentieth century it was the emerging Labour Party which became a major recipient of the Irish Catholic working-class vote in Britain.

30.1.7　Conclusion

By 1914, with the sharp decline in migration from Ireland to Britain, Irish immigration and its consequences were no longer matters of great public concern, although the 'Irish Question' continued to loom large in British politics. Ironically, the perceived threat to British society now came not from the Irish 'Other' but from the thousands of poor Jewish migrants fleeing from persecution in eastern Europe during the 1880s and 1890s, who received a reception in Britain that was almost as hostile as that accorded to Irish migrants forty years earlier. By this time, however, Irish migrants and their descendants had been largely integrated into British society. For many, this had been a long, gradual and at times painful process over successive generations, and in order to harmonise better with the English, Welsh and Scottish populations with whom they

15 J. Belchem, *Irish, Catholic and Scouse: the history of the Liverpool-Irish, 1800–1939* (Liverpool, 2007).

co-existed, the Irish had to some extent moderated their sense of Irishness in order to preserve it, as recent studies of the complex and shifting concept of Irish identity illustrate.[16] Indeed, some Protestants and Catholics gradually eschewed their Irish roots and merged into British working-class society, adopting local and regional mores and identities and becoming much like others of their social class. But most Irish Catholics were also able to retain and maintain a sense of distinctiveness and to define themselves, if they wished, not only as British but also as Irish (which itself concealed a variety of identities, both in Ireland and Britain) and Catholic, and this distinctiveness was subsequently maintained through familial and communal relationships and associational networks, both formal and informal, religious and secular, in Britain, Ireland and the Irish diaspora well into the twentieth century and beyond.

30.2   Since 1914   Sean Campbell

30.2.1   Introduction

While the period spanning the late nineteenth and early twentieth century saw a marked decline in the number of Irish migrants arriving in Britain,[17] in the mid- to late twentieth century this group would swell in size to become the country's largest migrant minority.[18] The most significant period of Irish migration to Britain in this century occurred between the 1930s and the 1960s, and this part therefore focuses on this historic 'second wave'.

30.2.2   Locating the Second Wave

In the context of poor economic conditions and low employment prospects in Ireland, and in light of new restrictions on immigration to the United States, the second wave of large-scale Irish migration to Britain would begin in the mid-1930s.[19] This eastward movement would continue for many decades, with Britain remaining the key destination for Irish migrants throughout the twentieth century. This gravitational pull was especially marked in the period during and after the Second World War, when Britain faced a major labour shortage.[20] By 1951, then, there were more than half a million

16 See especially M. Busteed, 'Resistance and respectability: dilemmas of Irish migrant politics in Victorian Britain', and A. O'Day, 'A conundrum of Irish diasporic identity: mutative ethnicity', in R. Swift and S. Gilley, *Irish identities in Victorian Britain* (London, 2011), 50–65, 189–211.

17 D. Fitzpatrick, 'The Irish in Britain, 1871–1921', in W. E. Vaughan (ed.), *A new history of Ireland, vol. VI: Ireland under the Union, 2 (1870–1921)* (Oxford, 1996), 654.

18 E. Delaney, *The Irish in post-war Britain* (Oxford, 2007), 2.

19 E. Delaney, *Demography, state and society: Irish migration to Britain, 1921–71* (Liverpool, 2000), 45.

20 M. E. Daly, *The slow failure: population decline and independent Ireland, 1920–1973* (Madison, WI, 2006), 140–1.

Irish resident in Britain, marking a population increase of 65 per cent in two decades.[21] In Scotland alone there were approximately 90,000 Irish-born people by the middle of the century, with around half from independent Ireland and half from Northern Ireland.[22] By 1971, the size of Britain's Irish-born populace would reach a historical peak of approximately one million.

While this second wave was marked by a slight gender imbalance (with women outnumbering men),[23] it was quite homogeneous in certain other respects. The vast bulk of migrants hailed from lower-class, Catholic backgrounds in rural parts of independent Ireland, and had been educated to only primary level.[24] They settled in mostly urban areas, congregating in the English cities of London (the principal destination), Birmingham (the second most popular destination) and Manchester, locales in which British industry had become increasingly concentrated. A few towns not hitherto associated with Irish migrants, such as Luton and Coventry, attracted large numbers of Irish at this time, with the latter's Irish populace increasing from 1,079 in 1921 to 9,983 in 1951 (largely in response to the emergent car industry in that locale).[25] At the same time, locations with longstanding Irish communities, such as Merseyside and Scotland, saw a decrease in Irish migrants after the 1920s.[26] In this context, Mo Moulton notes that, in the 1930s, migrants would eschew 'the depressed industrial north' for 'the new light industries in the Midlands'.[27] Scotland was particularly affected by this shift, with the number of Irish halving between the early and mid-century.[28] In common with earlier migrant waves, this cohort settled in less affluent districts, and found work in low-skilled professions. While the key sites of employment for Irish men comprised construction, factories and industry,[29] Irish women (many of whom had found work in the earlier period as domestic servants and parlour maids)[30] gravitated towards the hotel and catering industry, as well as nursing. The concentration of low-skilled Irish workers in poor urban areas engendered certain negative views of this group. In particular, the stereotype of the 'navvy', 'a hard-working and heavy-drinking "rough" and unpredictable character, prone to violence', came to dominate British perceptions of the 'Paddy'.[31]

21 Delaney, *The Irish in post-war Britain*, 17.

22 Ibid., 17.

23 Ibid., 3, 4.

24 L. Ryan, 'Assimilation of Irish immigrants in Britain', Ph.D. thesis, St Louis University, 1973, 137; D. Hannan, 'Irish emigration since the war', unpublished RTE Thomas Davis Lecture (1973), 6.

25 R. King, A. Strachan and I. Shuttleworth, 'The Irish in Coventry: the social geography of a relic community', *Irish Geography*, 22 (1989), 68.

26 Delaney, *The Irish in post-war Britain*, 95–6.

27 M. Moulton, *The Irish in interwar England* (Cambridge, 2014), 271.

28 Delaney, *The Irish in post-war Britain*, 17.

29 Ibid., 105, 113.

30 Moulton, *The Irish in interwar England*, 271, 274.

31 Delaney, *The Irish in post-war Britain*, 114.

While such caricatures were clearly pernicious, there was, says Lambert, 'a greater propensity for crime among Irish immigrants than among other immigrants and than among the native English population'.[32] A number of factors, including '[s]ocial deprivation, poor housing, a transitory population, and limited economic opportunities', might explain this trend.[33] This aspect of migrant life did not go unobserved in Ireland. As Liam Ryan explains:

> To the unskilled and unemployed [in Ireland] England [and by extension Britain] seemed a land of opportunity, but to the fifty-acre farmers and the petty bourgeoisie of the towns and villages [in Ireland] it seemed a kind of ghetto for Irish people, a kind of huge Irish slum, a place where none of the better class of people ever went … And the threat of a son or daughter to take the boat train was a threat that the family name might be tainted with the mark of the emigrant and coupled with the labourers and others who somehow weren't talented enough to get employment at home.[34]

Such views were, however, at odds with the advantages that these immigrants had afforded Ireland's economy. The departure of large numbers of people not only relieved pressure on a state that was not yet able to provide for its populace, but this migration would yield – in the form of remittances – a significant boost to the Irish economy, with individuals dispatching (in the period 1939–69) approximately £3 billion through telegrams and money orders.[35]

30.2.3 Being Irish in Britain

These migrants often saw life in Britain as a short-term sojourn in a strange and foreign place.[36] Having been educated in the schoolrooms of newly independent Ireland, where Anglo-Irish relations were viewed through the lens of the emergent state,[37] many migrants would arrive in Britain with antagonistic attitudes towards that state.[38] In turn, migrants often met anti-Irish sentiments from the host society. Such prejudices had echoes of the earlier period, but were exacerbated by contemporary tensions, not least IRA bombing campaigns. In this context, the 1939 attacks on London, Manchester, Birmingham and Coventry not only increased anti-Irish sentiments but led to the introduction of the Prevention of Violence Act, which gave the Home Secretary the power 'to deport, exclude, and detain any persons who he was satisfied were engaged

32 J. Lambert, *Crime, police and race relations: a study in Birmingham* (Oxford, 1970), 126.
33 Delaney, *The Irish in post-war Britain*, 185.
34 Ryan, 'Assimilation of Irish immigrants in Britain', 114.
35 U. Cowley, *The men who built Britain: a history of the Irish navvy* (Dublin, 2001), 29.
36 Delaney, *The Irish in post-war Britain*, 8, 32, 63, 124, 128.
37 D. Fitzpatrick, 'The futility of history: a failed experiment in Irish education', in C. Brady (ed.), *Ideology and the historians* (Dublin, 1991), 176–7.
38 S. Lambert, *Irish women in Lancashire, 1922–1960: their story* (Lancaster, 2001), 88.

in the IRA campaign', requiring 'all Irish citizens on the mainland [*sic*]' to register with the police.[39]

Such tensions only intensified the alienation of migrants who had been reared in largely rural and highly religious locales but had found themselves in rather secular, urbanised spaces. Perhaps inevitably, then, a certain wish for 'return' was often nurtured among such migrants. While this remained (largely) unrealised, this wave of migrants would (in contrast to their predecessors) benefit from the ease and accessibility of affordable travel across the Irish Sea.[40] This was augmented by the increasing availability, in the late twentieth century, of low-cost air travel. Throughout this period, then, Irish migrants maintained a strong connection with Ireland by regularly visiting home.

This affective investment was underpinned, while in Britain, by involvement in myriad social, cultural and religious activities that enhanced attachments to home. In London, for instance (where a third of the Irish-born population of England and Wales were residing by the mid-twentieth century),[41] a range of venues emerged to service the needs of the Irish community. These included dance halls (such as the Galtymore), pubs (for instance the Crown in Cricklewood) and community venues (such as the London Irish Centre). For the smaller numbers of middle-class Irish, the Irish Club on Eaton Square, or the National University Club on Grosvenor Place,[42] offered a forum for socialising. More generally, the Gaelic Athletic Association, which had been active in Britain since the late nineteenth century, could count nearly sixty affiliated clubs in London alone by the 1960s.[43] A range of other initiatives emerged in the post-war years, often under the umbrella of the Federation of Irish Societies (1964–), which served to promote, says Breda Gray, 'the interests of the Irish community in Britain through community care, education, culture, arts, youth welfare and information provision'.[44] These efforts were underpinned by the emergence of community media, not least the launch of the *Irish Post*, a newspaper specifically for the Irish in Britain, in 1970.

Another key institution, of course (for a cohort that was largely Catholic), was the church, which remained a 'central institution', notes John Jackson, for Britain's Irish populace.[45] Through its parishes, schools and social clubs, the church supplied a forum in which Irish migrants could convene. It is worth noting, though, that the church,

---

39 J. Bailkin, 'Leaving home: the politics of deportation in postwar Britain', *Journal of British Studies*, 47, 4 (2008), 873.
40 Delaney, *The Irish in post-war Britain*, 39, 67.
41 Ibid., 89.
42 Ibid., 92–3.
43 F. Whooley, *Irish Londoners: photographs from the Paddy Fahey Collection* (Stroud, 1997), 34.
44 B. Gray, 'From "ethnicity" to "diaspora": 1980s emigration and "multicultural" London', in A. Bielenberg (ed.), *The Irish diaspora* (London, 2000), 71.
45 J. Jackson, *The Irish in Britain* (London, 1963), 135.

throughout this century, pursued what Moulton calls a 'quietist doctrine of accom-modation' towards Britain,[46] encouraging a collective Catholicity over forms of Irish difference. Thus, the church sought, says Hickman, to 'transform the Irish into useful citizens, loyal subjects, respectable members of the working class and good Catholics'.[47] Whether or not the church was successful in this regard, religious attendance would decline among Irish migrants in the late twentieth century.[48]

30.2.4 Difference, Diversity and Discrimination

The religious make-up of this wave was, of course, not exclusively Catholic. However, relatively little research has been conducted on the non-Catholic constituents of this migrant group, with Irish Protestants being 'seriously under examined', notes Donald MacRaild.[49] This elision is symptomatic of the fact that Irish Protestants were, in the words of MacRaild, 'largely considered to lack visibility',[50] and were thus assumed to have assimilated with ease into the host culture,[51] with the effect that they 'disappeared', as Delaney relates, 'with little a trace'.[52] The presence of Orange lodges across Britain, particularly in Scotland, Tyneside and Merseyside, appears to complicate this. The social function of such institutions exceeded simple sectarianism, with the Orange Order acting as 'a unifying and galvanizing social organism' for Irish Protestants.[53] More broadly, it is clear that non-Catholic migrants were a significant component of this migrant wave, constituting approximately one-quarter of the Irish-born populace in Britain in the twentieth century.[54] Further research on the experience, identities and outlook of the non-Catholic Irish is required if we are to gain a fuller (and more nuanced) sense of migrant life.

If Irish Protestants did 'disappear' into the host populace, it was often assumed that Irish Catholics did the same. Sociologists such as Liam Ryan, for instance, claimed that assimilation, for the Irish in Britain, was 'practically complete in a single generation'.[55] Similarly, John Rex argued that 'the incorporation of the Irish into the [indigenous]

46 Moulton, *The Irish in interwar England*, 271.
47 M. J. Hickman, *Religion, class and identity: the state, the Catholic Church, and the education of the Irish in Britain* (Aldershot, 1995), 274.
48 Delaney, *The Irish in post-war Britain*, 162.
49 D. M. MacRaild, *The Irish diaspora in Britain 1750–1939* (Basingstoke, 2010), 90.
50 Ibid., 91.
51 Delaney, *Demography, state and society*, 95; Belchem, *Irish, Catholic and Scouse*, xii.
52 Delaney, *Demography, state and society*, 95.
53 D. M. MacRaild, *Irish migrants in modern Britain* (Basingstoke, 1999), 122.
54 MacRaild, *The Irish diaspora in Britain*, 92–7.
55 L. Ryan, 'Irish emigration to Britain since World War II', in R. Kearney (ed.), *Migrations: the Irish at home and abroad* (Dublin, 1990), 60.

working-class [was] relatively easy'.[56] However, while class was an important aspect of Irish life in Britain, ethnicity (as observed above) also played a crucial role.[57] Indeed, it is worth noting, in this context, that assimilation was often erroneously inferred from the (relative) invisibility of Irish migrants, a point to which certain historians, not least Eric Hobsbawm, have been alert. 'To say that [Irish] immigration has been assimilated would be misleading,' said Hobsbawm in the 1960s. 'However, it has increasingly become accepted, because invisible – at any rate compared to the much more obviously recognisable new migrants of the 1950s.'[58] Clearly the Irish became less conspicuous in the context of increasing African-Caribbean and South Asian migration in the mid-century.[59] Reflecting on this point, Richard Weight relates that the 'hostility towards black Britons benefited the Irish because much of the public animus directed at them was diverted towards the new arrivals'.[60] Antipathies towards the Irish were unarguably eclipsed by the state's needs for Irish labour. The British government was, as Mary Daly explains, 'keen to retain the links between the two labour markets',[61] irrespective of anti-Irish prejudices or IRA actions, and thus government policies would enable Irish immigration.

Neither fully visible nor wholly assimilated, this wave would come to inhabit what Delaney calls 'an intermediate position, between that of white British workers and Caribbean and South Asian immigrants'.[62] This inbetweenness was enshrined, at state level, in the 1948 British Nationality Act, which contrived a unique legal status for Irish migrants as 'neither subjects nor aliens'. Thus, the Irish 'were to be regarded as neither British subjects nor aliens but as Irish citizens with all the rights of British subjecthood', a stipulation that was 'without precedent in legislation dealing with nationality'.[63] The anomalousness this afforded to Britain's Irish (which continued despite Ireland's withdrawal from the Commonwealth and its attainment of republic status in 1949) was not extended to African-Caribbean or South Asian migrants, many of whom were British subjects.[64] Instead, post-war immigration from the West Indies, India and Pakistan (despite being numerically exceeded by concurrent immigration from Ireland) was policed by a series of Nationality and Immigration Acts (1948, 1962, 1968, 1971, 1981), despite official recognition that 'the problems allegedly caused by immigration

---

56 J. Rex, 'Immigrants and British labour: the sociological context', in K. Lunn (ed.), *Hosts, immigrants and minorities: historical responses to newcomers in British society 1870–1914* (Folkestone, 1980), 26.

57 Moulton, *The Irish in interwar England*, 271.

58 E. Hobsbawm, *Industry and empire: from 1750 to the present day* (London, 1969), 312.

59 M. Mac an Ghaill, 'The Irish in Britain: the invisibility of ethnicity and anti-Irish racism', *Journal of Ethnic and Migration Studies*, 26, 1 (2000), 137–47; P. M. Garrett, '"No Irish need apply": social work in Britain and the history and politics of exclusionary paradigms and practices', *British Journal of Social Work*, 32, 4 (2002), 477–94.

60 R. Weight, *Patriots: national identity in Britain, 1940–2000* (London, 2002), 145.

61 Daly, *The slow failure*, 143.

62 Delaney, *The Irish in post-war Britain*, 125.

63 K. Paul, *Whitewashing Britain: race and citizenship in the postwar era* (Ithaca, 1997), 90.

64 Ibid., 90–110.

– overcrowding, strain on social services, and dangers to public health – were the same for both [i.e. New Commonwealth and Irish] groups'. This privileging of white Irish migrants over black British subjects belied a conflation of 'race' and nation in British immigration policy. Thus, while 'officials made few references to Irish migrants' skin colour, the lengths to which they went to preserve the labor supply … suggest that the Irish passed an unwritten test of potential Britishness measured according to a racialized concept of the world's population'.[65]

If the Irish came to be seen as a less alien populace, this was in part enabled by their inclination, in the post-independence period, to eschew ideological forms of Irishness for more individualised or cultural/ethnic identifications.[66] In this context, a more 'leisure-oriented, aesthetically informed version of Irish minority culture' would replace the 'older networks of republican activism'.[67] Thus, second-wave voting patterns were shaped more by the day-to-day concerns of life in Britain than by the political situation at home, with the vast majority gravitating towards the Labour Party. However, even if migrants were impelled less by Irish political concerns, the post-1969 Troubles, and especially the IRA's bombing campaign, would cast a dark shadow on Irish life in Britain. In particular, events such as the Birmingham pub bombings of 1974 profoundly changed the way Irish people were seen. As K. I. Ziesler explains, in the days following the bombings:

> Irish organizations and individuals became the targets for abuse and obscene phone calls; stones and a petrol bomb were thrown through the windows of the Irish Centre; an Irish pub … was badly damaged by another petrol bomb; two lorries belonging to an Irish construction firm were damaged; and a Roman Catholic junior school and a church, the Holy Family in Small Heath, were attacked. At the British Leyland works in Longbridge, where some 3,000 Irish were employed, there was a walk-out by car assembly workers.[68]

Meanwhile, six Birmingham-based Irishmen were arrested and wrongly convicted of planting the bomb, before being imprisoned for sixteen years in what became one of the most notorious miscarriages of justice in English legal history.[69] The hastily introduced Prevention of Terrorism Act (PTA) bestowed upon the Secretary of State 'considerable new powers to control the movement of people between Ireland and Great Britain', including 'extensive powers to establish a comprehensive system of port controls' as well as 'the power to remove people who are already living in Great Britain to either Northern Ireland or the Republic of Ireland'.[70] While the PTA lacked the powers of the Nationality and Immigration Acts to which other migrant groups were subjected

---

65 Ibid., 90, 107.
66 Moulton, *The Irish in interwar England*, 274.
67 Ibid., 306.
68 K. I. Ziesler, 'The Irish in Birmingham, 1830–1970', Ph.D. thesis, University of Birmingham, 1989, 341.
69 J. Moran, *Irish Birmingham* (Liverpool, 2010), 204–10.
70 P. Hillyard, *Suspect community: people's experience of the Prevention of Terrorism Acts in Britain* (London, 1993), 5, 13.

in the post-war period (British–Irish land, sea and air borders were conceived as a 'common travel area'),[71] the Act – which was renewed in 1976, 1984 and 1989 – was seen as 'a discriminatory piece of law'.[72] As Paddy Hillyard observed in the 1990s, the PTA 'is directed primarily at one section of the travelling public. In effect it means that Irish people in general have a more restrictive set of rights than other travellers. In this sense, the Irish community as a whole is a "suspect community"'.[73]

30.2.5 Conclusion

In the face of increasing anti-Irish prejudices in the 1970s and 1980s, public bodies began to address the experience of the migrant Irish. Most significantly, the Greater London Council (GLC) – under the leadership of Ken Livingstone – issued a series of reports on the Irish, one of which offered, as Gray explains, 'the first public institutional acknowledgement of anti-Irish racism'.[74] If such initiatives served to increase the visibility of Irishness in Britain,[75] they would eventually inform the inclusion of an Irish ethnic category in the 2001 UK census. By this time, there were more than 600,000 Irish-born people living in England and Wales, the largest concentration of Irish-born people outside Ireland anywhere in the world. This number included an additional wave of migrants who had arrived in the 1980s. Impelled by Ireland's economic downturn in that decade, the social character of this wave was quite distinct from earlier waves in that the bulk of these migrants were middle-class university graduates who found work in professional occupations.[76] This demographic distinction engendered certain tensions within the now multi-generational migrant group, not least between the new wave of aspirant Irish-born professionals and the often less well-off British-born offspring of the second wave.[77]

What these different constituencies of Irish arguably shared in common, though, was a certain hybrid subjectivity that crossed strict ethno-national affiliations; for Britain's Irish populace accrued 'a curious dual status',[78] maintaining affective (as well as material) investments in both the homeland and the host space.[79] This ability to identify

---

71 E. Meehan, 'Free movement between Ireland and the UK: from the "common travel area" to The Common Travel Area', *Studies in Public Policy*, 4 (2000), 26–30.

72 Hillyard, *Suspect community*, 5, 13.

73 Ibid.

74 Gray, 'From "Ethnicity" to "Diaspora"', 72.

75 Ibid., 71.

76 Delaney, *The Irish in post-war Britain*, 115.

77 S. Campbell, 'Beyond "Plastic Paddy": a re-examination of the second-generation Irish in England', *Immigrants and Minorities*, 18, 2–3 (1999), 266–88.

78 D. Fitzpatrick, *The two Irelands 1912–1939* (Oxford, 1998), 215.

79 M. J. Hickman, S. Morgan, B. Walter and J. Bradley, 'The limitations of whiteness and the boundaries of Englishness: second-generation Irish identifications and positionings in multiethnic Britain', *Ethnicities*, 5, 2 (2005), 178.

with, and belong to, more than one nation state was undoubtedly eased in the years towards the century's end, with the post-1995 ceasefires in Northern Ireland (and, in turn, the unfolding peace process) affording a less fractious Anglo-Irish dynamic. The historic state visit of the president of Ireland, Michael D. Higgins, to Britain in 2014 served to underline this crucial shift as well as highlight the place of Britain's Irish in the country's complex multi-ethnic matrix.

FURTHER READING

Aspinwall, B. and J. McCaffrey. 'A comparative view of the Irish in Edinburgh in the nineteenth century', in R. Swift and S. Gilley (eds.), *The Irish in the Victorian city* (London, 1985), 130–57.

Bailkin, J. 'Leaving home: the politics of deportation in postwar Britain', *Journal of British Studies*, 47, 4 (2008), 852–82.

Belchem. J. *Irish, Catholic and Scouse: the history of the Liverpool-Irish, 1800–1939* (Liverpool, 2007).

Busteed, M. 'Identities in transition: Irish migrant outlooks in mid-Victorian Manchester', in D. G. Boyce and R. Swift (eds.), *Problems and perspectives in Irish history since 1800* (Dublin, 2004), 80–94.

Campbell, S. *'Irish blood, English heart': second-generation Irish musicians in England* (Cork, 2011).

Chinn, C. '"Sturdy Catholic emigrants": the Irish in early Victorian Birmingham', in R. Swift and S. Gilley (eds.), *The Irish in Victorian Britain: the local dimension* (Dublin, 1999), 52–74.

Collins, B. 'Irish emigration to Dundee and Paisley during the first half of the nineteenth century', in J. M. Goldstrom and L. A. Clarkson (eds.), *Irish population, economy and society* (Oxford, 1981), 195–212.

Cowley, U. *The men who built Britain: a history of the Irish navvy* (Dublin, 2001).

Cullen, F. and R. F. Foster. *Conquering England: Ireland in Victorian London* (London, 2005).

Curtis, L. *Nothing but the same old story: the roots of anti-Irish racism* (London, 1984).

Daly, M. E. *The slow failure: population decline and independent Ireland, 1920–1973* (Madison, WI, 2006).

Davis, G. *The Irish in Britain, 1815–1914* (Dublin, 1991).

Delaney, E. *Demography, state and society: Irish migration to Britain, 1921–71* (Liverpool, 2000).

Delaney, E. *The Irish in post-war Britain* (Oxford, 2007).

Farrell, J. 'The Irish in Hammersmith and Fulham in 1851', *The Local Historian*, 29, 2 (May 1999), 66–95.

Fielding, S. *Class and ethnicity: Irish Catholics in England, 1880–1939* (Buckingham, 1993).

Finnegan, F. *Poverty and prejudice: Irish immigrants in York, 1840–75* (Cork, 1982).

Fitzpatrick, D. 'The futility of history: a failed experiment in Irish education', in C. Brady (ed.), *Ideology and the historians* (Dublin, 1991).

Foster, R. F. *Paddy and Mr Punch: connections in Irish and English history* (London, 1993).

Garrett, P. M. '"No Irish need apply": social work in Britain and the history and politics of exclusionary paradigms and practices', *British Journal of Social Work*, 32, 4 (2002), 477–94.

GLC *Ethnic minorities and the abolition of the GLC* (London, 1984).

GLC *Irish youth: who cares?* (London, 1986).

GLC *Policy report on the Irish community* (London, 1984).

GLC *Report on the consultative conference on the effects of the workings of the Prevention of Terrorism Act upon London's Irish community* (London, 1984).

GLC *Report of the second London Irish women's conference* (London, 1985).

Gray, B. 'From "ethnicity" to "diaspora": 1980s emigration and "multicultural" London', in A. Bielenberg (ed.), *The Irish diaspora* (London, 2000), 65–88.

Handley, J. E. *The Irish in modern Scotland* (Cork, 1947).

Handley, J. E. *The Irish in Scotland, 1789–1845* (Cork, 1943).

Hannan, D. 'Irish emigration since the war', unpublished RTE Thomas Davis Lecture (1973).

Herson, J. 'Migration, "community" or integration?: Irish families in Victorian Stafford', in R. Swift and S. Gilley (eds.), *The Irish in Victorian Britain: the local dimension* (Dublin, 1999), 156–89.

Hickman, M. *Religion, class and identity: the state, the Catholic Church, and the education of the Irish in Britain* (Aldershot, 1995).

Hickman, M. and B. Walter. *Discrimination and the Irish community in Britain* (London, 1997).

Hobsbawm, E. *Industry and empire: from 1750 to the present day* (London, 1969).

Howard, K. 'Constructing the Irish of Britain: ethnic recognition and the 2001 UK censuses', *Ethnic and Racial Studies*, 21, 1 (2006), 104–23.

Jackson, J. A. *The Irish in Britain* (London, 1963).

Jeffes, K. 'The Irish in early Victorian Chester: an outcast community?', in R. Swift (ed.), *Victorian Chester: essays in social history, 1830–1900* (Liverpool, 1996), 85–118.

Kanya-Forstner, M. 'Defining womanhood: Irish women and the Catholic Church in Victorian Liverpool', in D. MacRaild (ed.), *The Great Famine and beyond* (Dublin, 2000), 168–88.

King, R., A. Strachan and I. Shuttleworth. 'The Irish in Coventry: the social geography of a relic community', *Irish Geography*, 22 (1989), 64–78.

Lambert, J. *Crime, police and race relations: a study in Birmingham* (Oxford, 1970).

Lambert, S. *Irish women in Lancashire, 1922–1960: their story* (Lancaster, 2001).

Lees, L. *Exiles of Erin: Irish migrants in Victorian London* (Manchester, 1979).

Mac an Ghaill, M. 'The Irish in Britain: the invisibility of ethnicity and anti-Irish racism', *Journal of Ethnic and Migration Studies*, 26, 1 (2000), 137–47.

McFarland, E. *Protestants first: Orangeism in nineteenth-century Scotland* (Edinburgh, 1990).

MacRaild, D. *The Irish diaspora in Britain 1750–1939* (London, 2010).

MacRaild, D. 'Irish immigration and the 'Condition of England' question: the roots of an historiographical tradition', *Immigrants and Minorities*, 14, 1 (March 1995), 67–85.

Meehan, E. 'Free movement between Ireland and the UK: from the "common travel area" to The Common Travel Area', *Studies in Public Policy*, 4 (2000), 1–112.

Mitchell, M. (ed.). *New perspectives on the Irish in Scotland* (Edinburgh, 2008).

Moran, J. *Irish Birmingham* (Liverpool, 2010).

Moulton, M. *The Irish in interwar England* (Cambridge, 2014).

Neal, F. 'The foundations of Irish settlement in Newcastle upon Tyne: the evidence in the 1851 census', in D. MacRaild (ed.), *The Great Famine and beyond: Irish migrants in britain in the nineteenth and twentieth centuries* (Dublin, 2000), 71–93.

O'Day, A. 'Varieties of anti-Irish behaviour in Britain, 1846–1922', in P. Panayi (ed.), *Racial violence in Britain, 1840–1950* (Leicester, 1993), 26–43.

O'Dowd, A. *Spalpeens and tattie hokers: history and folklore of the Irish migratory agricultural worker in Ireland and Britain* (Dublin, 1991).

O'Leary, P. (ed.). *Irish migrants in modern Wales* (Liverpool, 2004).

Peavitt, H. 'The Irish, crime and disorder in Chester, 1841–1871', Ph.D. thesis, University of Liverpool (2000).

Pooley, C. 'Segregation or integration?: The residential experience of the Irish in mid-Victorian Britain', in R. Swift and S. Gilley (eds.), *The Irish in Britain, 1815–1939* (London, 1989), 71–110.

Rex, J. 'Immigrants and British labour: the sociological context', in K. Lunn (ed.), *Hosts, immigrants and minorities: historical responses to newcomers in British society 1870–1914* (Folkestone, 1980), 22–38.

Ryan, L. 'Assimilation of Irish immigrants in Britain', Ph.D. thesis, St Louis University (1973).

Ryan, L. 'Irish emigration to Britain since World War II', in R. Kearney (ed.), *Migrations: the Irish at home and abroad* (Dublin, 1990), 45–67.

Swift, R. *Behaving badly?: Irish migrants and crime in the Victorian city* (Chester, 2006).

Swift, R. and S. Gilley (eds.). *Irish identities in Victorian Britain* (London, 2011).

Swift, R. and S. Gilley (eds.). *The Irish in the Victorian city* (London, 1985).

Thompson, D. 'Ireland and the Irish in English radicalism before 1850', in J. Epstein and D. Thompson (eds.), *The Chartist experience: studies in working-class radicalism and culture, 1830–1860* (London, 1982), 120–51.

Turton, J. 'Mayhew's Irish: the Irish poor in mid-nineteenth century London', in R. Swift and S. Gilley (eds.), *The Irish in Victorian Britain: the local dimension* (Dublin, 1999), 122–55.

Walter, B. 'The Irish community in Britain – diversity, disadvantage and discrimination', paper presented to the Commission on the Future of Multi-Ethnic Britain, 18 June 1999.

Walter, B. 'Strangers on the inside: Irish women servants in England, 1881', in Swift and Gilley, *Irish identities in Victorian Britain*, 151–71.

Weight, R. *Patriots: national identity in Britain, 1940–2000* (London, 2002).

Weindling, D. and M. Collins. 'The Irish in Kilburn: myth and reality', *The Local Historian*, 32, 2 (May 2002), 118–31.

Whooley, F. *Irish Londoners: photographs from the Paddy Fahey Collection* (Stroud, 1997).

Ziesler, K. I. 'The Irish in Birmingham, 1830–1970', Ph.D. thesis, University of Birmingham (1989).

31 Missionary Empires and the Worlds They Made

Sarah Roddy

31.1. Introduction

Stretching back more than two hundred years, modern Irish Christian missionary endeavour has involved dozens of organisations across all denominations, each with its own separate structures and histories and each peopled by hundreds of individual missionaries, both male and female. These orders, societies and missions have reached over the entire world, criss-crossing rising and falling empires and perhaps even creating 'spiritual empires' of their own in the process. In that time they each encountered millions of men, women and children of all classes and races and of many established and emerging ethnic and national identities, impacting upon myriad lives, for better or worse, as they went. Thus, there is a need to map, insofar as possible, the field of Irish missionary history as it stands, but, equally importantly, to point to ways in which it might develop and grow from here. The chapter will therefore present an overview of Irish Anglican, Presbyterian and Catholic missionary structures and geographical scope based on existing scholarship. It will then draw out some significant themes surrounding the missionary work itself, something that ought to be done at least partly in conversation with the historiographies of Christian missionary endeavour originating from elsewhere in the western world. Finally, it will attempt to locate Irish missions within the broader sweep of Irish social history and suggest some possibilities for how that history might be taken forward in the future.

31.2. Who were Irish Missionaries?

Before establishing who Irish missionaries were in detail, it is necessary to determine who they were in abstract. Who counted as a missionary? This question is more complicated than it might appear, and is an especially knotty one in relation to Ireland.

Although in most modern contexts 'missionary' has come to denote a person engaged in the conversion of 'heathens' on so-called 'foreign' missions, it has historically been a much more elastic term. Essentially, anybody who left his or her home area on defined religious business for an extended period could be seen to be engaging in mission. Thus, Protestant and Catholic clergy fundraising among their respective diasporas, newly ordained priests temporarily joining an English Catholic parish (which were known as 'missions' until the early twentieth century) or even priests bringing spiritual renewal to other Irish parishes could all claim the title of missionary. Because of their inherently temporary nature, we can reasonably exclude these categories from the analysis that follows. More problematic is whether to include not only those 'foreign' missionaries who went abroad with the aim of reaping new converts to Christianity but also those who went to serve migrant Irish communities of existing, though perhaps faltering, Christians. For entirely understandable reasons of limited space and time, few studies do both. None the less, while accepting here that there are some key theological, practical and theoretical distinctions between what Andrew Porter has deftly termed 'missions of discovery' and 'missions of recovery', this chapter will address both these forms of overseas mission.[1]

Our key term thus defined, a certain amount of periodisation ought to follow. It is certainly the case that all Irish churches had some individuals who engaged in missionary activity abroad from at least the eighteenth century, and that many of them achieved a pioneer status, particularly in North America, that served as motivation for their Irish successors working around the world. These prominent Irishmen were of course joined by several other individual clergy at lower levels of their churches, who found themselves called abroad for reasons that could include lack of career opportunities at home as much as a sudden outpouring of evangelising zeal. However, the emergence of what might be termed formal missionary movements in each church does not necessarily map on to the careers of such men, and, to use a hackneyed and value-laden term, the 'golden ages' of each church's missionary endeavour certainly came later. Thus this chapter will focus, for the most part, on the mid-nineteenth to mid-twentieth century.

31.2.1. Anglicans

Perhaps unsurprisingly, given its many advantages as the established church, the Church of Ireland was earliest in the field of formal missionary enterprise. The Society for the Propagation of the Gospel in Foreign Parts (SPG), created in England in 1701, had an

---

1 A. Porter, *Religion versus empire? British Protestant missionaries and overseas expansion, 1700–1914* (Manchester, 2004), 160.

active Irish auxiliary by 1714. 'Active' in the overseas missionary context generally meant two things. It denoted, in the sending country, a formal structure, or web of structures, dedicated to peopling, funding and otherwise supporting missions, and, in the mission field, a network of missionaries dedicated to spreading their church and engaged in frequent contact with those at home. At points Ireland's SPG certainly had both, although its activity was never fully autonomous from its parent organisation. Despite the Dublin auxiliary committee, there was nothing to stop Irish clergy working through the auspices of the London SPG, and long after the Irish auxiliary's advent, there were hints that the Irish church did not pull its financial weight when it came to supporting 'its' missionaries. Much like its parent, the Irish SPG also went through peaks and troughs. Despite continued recruitment of Irish Anglican missionaries, it proved difficult to sustain popular enthusiasm for the SPG into the nineteenth century. It was only in the 1840s, in response to challenges both within and without the Church of Ireland, that a network of district committees was finally established in Irish dioceses. Even then, its growth was limited, and financial and rhetorical support still relatively weak.

As Hilary Carey has noted, the overarching purpose of the SPG was always at least notionally twofold, its founding charter referring to both missions aimed at colonial settlers and 'foreign' missions. However, by the nineteenth century, a gradual shift towards the latter was in train.[2] Irish SPG missionaries thus served not only in the settler colonies in North America, Australasia and southern Africa, but also, increasingly, in areas with few white settlers, including India, China and other parts of Africa. The reason for this shift in focus, and part of the reason for the 1840s reboot of the Irish SPG, had to do with the emergence of another missionary organisation. The SPG's evangelical rival, the Church Missionary Society (CMS), founded by Clapham Sect Anglicans in 1799, was a Low Church response to the perception that the older, High Church organisation had concentrated too much on ministering to colonial settlers and not enough on preaching to non-Christians. The CMS, too, was joined by an Irish auxiliary, the Hibernian Church Missionary Society, or HCMS, in 1814. As Joseph Hardwick has argued, the HCMS experienced much brighter fortunes than the Irish SPG, partly because of the popular contemporary impulse to so-called 'home missions', or attempts to convert the Irish Catholic population, which gained traction from the 1820s onward. Often the same personnel, and even more often, the same guiding principles, were involved in organising both forms of evangelical work.[3]

The presence of two rival organisations competing for the patronage of a relatively small Irish Anglican population may have been problematic, threatening to divide

2 H. M. Carey, *God's empire: religion and colonialism in the British world, c.1801–1908* (Cambridge, 2011), 87.
3 J. Hardwick, *An Anglican British world: the Church of England and the expansion of the settler empire, c.1790–1860* (Manchester, 2014), 157–61.

already scant resources. Yet the two organisations were at loggerheads in Ireland less often than one might expect, and it may be that over the longer term whatever mild controversy the competition between them created drew more lay attention to overseas missions than would otherwise have been the case. Indeed, despite the divergent philosophies and some quite bitter conflict at an elite level within the wider Anglican Church, instances of joint parish branches of the SPG and HCMS were not unknown.[4] None the less, it was the latter society which truly captured lay imaginations, having more branches, holding what were, at least for Ireland, innovative promotional and sponsorship events, and attracting, according to one estimate, 'in excess of £1 million' at the height of the foreign missionary tide from 1870 to 1930.[5] Yet these two organisations were not the only elements of the Irish Anglican missionary movement. With relatively limited success, branches of the CMS's own colonial mission offshoot, the Colonial Church and School Society (CCSS), appeared in the 1850s around Dublin and in Ulster. Moreover, they were not the only Irish Anglican organisation to send missionaries to China and India. Trinity College's Dublin University Fukien Mission (DUFM), founded in 1885, had forty students at its foundation, and five years later, that mission was joined by the Dublin University Mission to Chota Nagpur.[6]

31.2.2. Presbyterians

Although Irish Presbyterians could justly make a claim to have been the first of their compatriots in the overseas missionary field, recent work suggests that it was only in the 1790s that a true missionary 'awakening' occurred. To this point can be traced, as in the Church of Ireland, a gradually increasing awareness of and enthusiasm for participation in existing structures across the Irish Sea. Auxiliaries to the voluntary, cross-denominational Protestant body the London Missionary Society (LMS), founded in 1795, sprang up in Ulster, Dublin and Cork in the early decades of the new century. Coterminously, the two main Presbyterian synods' previous reluctance to officially encourage overseas missions gradually dissipated.[7] The Scottish Missionary Society,

4 Revd J. W. Stokes to Hawkins, 4 September 1839, USPG Archives, Administration and Finance, H94, f.88 [thanks to Joseph Hardwick for this reference]. See also A. Acheson, *A history of the Church of Ireland 1691–1996* (Dublin, 1997), 221.
5 T. G. McMahon, 'A new role for Irish Anglicans in the later nineteenth century: the HCMS and imperial opportunity', in C. O'Neill (ed.), *Irish elites in the nineteenth century* (Dublin, 2013), 225, 227–30.
6 P. Comerford, 'Success or failure? Church of Ireland overseas missions', based on a lecture given at NUI Maynooth, 3 March, 2008. Available at http://revpatrickcomerford.blogspot.com/2008/03/success-or-failure-church-of-ireland.html, accessed 4 November 2014.
7 A. Holmes, 'The shaping of Irish Presbyterian attitudes to mission, 1790–1840', *Journal of Ecclesiastical History*, 57, 4 (2006), 711–37.

attached to the sister church in Scotland, received the heartiest support from church leaders, and it was under its auspices that the first Irish Presbyterian 'foreign' missionaries went abroad, both to Jamaica: the Seceder Hope Waddell in 1829, and the Synod of Ulster's Thomas Leslie in 1835.[8]

Yet while the auxiliaries to the large voluntary mission societies continued to have a presence in Ireland, and particularly Ulster, for many decades afterwards, their membership became less overwhelmingly Presbyterian. By the 1890s, the LMS Belfast branch, for one, appeared to be dominated by members of Donegall Street Independent Church.[9] The union of the Presbyterian synods in 1840 had in fact precipitated a very different kind of organisational structure, which was neither an auxiliary branch of a denominational society, as the Irish SPG and HCMS were, nor a cross-denominational voluntary society, independent of any one church's governing structure. Instead, the model provided by the Church of Scotland was followed, and a series of discrete missions were created within the church itself by its ruling body, the General Assembly. These eventually included a Foreign Mission, a Home Mission targeted at converting Irish Catholics, a Jewish Mission and a Colonial Mission, which, until the end of the nineteenth century and the gradual decline of the Home Mission, attracted enthusiasm, measured by financial support and missionary volunteers, in that order.[10]

Missionaries of the Irish Presbyterian Church thus found themselves working right across the world: in Europe and the Middle East, in Manchuria and in Gujarat, as well as in the usual settler colonies. This extensive activity did not, however, constitute all Irish Presbyterian missionary activity. The Female Association for Promoting Christianity among the Women of the East, or Zenana Mission, was founded in Belfast in 1873 and, quite apart from the many wives who accompanied their missionary husbands, helped send 140 single women to China and India up to 1939.[11] Many individuals also continued to cross between the Irish and Scottish missionary structures, partly because the latter had an African presence first. This was epitomised by the Belfast Presbyterian Samuel Bill, who, through connections with the Scottish Missionary Society, was instrumental in founding the cross-denominational Qua Iboe Mission, which ultimately became the United Evangelical Church of Nigeria.[12]

8 B. Addley, 'Irish Presbyterian attitudes to mission before 1840', in J. Thompson (ed.), *Into all the world: a history of the overseas work of the Presbyterian Church in Ireland 1840–1990* (Belfast, 1990), 21.
9 Belfast News-Letter, 26 Mar. 1892; 24 Mar. 1894; 21 Mar. 1896.
10 S. Roddy, '"Not a duffer among them": the Colonial Mission of the Irish Presbyterian Church', in D. Dickson, J. Pyz and C. Shepard (eds.), *Irish classrooms and British empire. Imperial contexts in the origin of modern education* (Dublin, 2012), 144–56.
11 M. Hill, 'Gender, culture and "the spiritual empire": the Irish Protestant female missionary experience', *Women's History Review*, 16, 2 (2007), 205.
12 E. Doyle, 'The Qua Iboe Mission, 1887–1925', Ph.D. thesis, Queen's University, Belfast (2010).

31.2.3. Catholics

Although the latest of the three main Irish denominations on the overseas missionary scene, Irish Catholics made up for what they lacked in promptitude in sheer weight of numbers. Irish seminaries and female religious orders made unco-ordinated and piecemeal entrances into both the 'foreign' and what in this context is properly termed 'diaspora' mission fields from the 1830s, Catholic emancipation proving to be, as in other areas, a green light to action. Maynooth's mission to India, primarily in support of Irish Catholic soldiers in the colonial forces, was the most prominent, but, at the same time, groups of Irish Loreto, Presentation and Mercy sisters went variously to Mauritius, India and Newfoundland, establishing houses and, like the many male and female orders that came afterwards, often engaging in education, health or child welfare work.[13] The foundation of an Irish branch of the French-founded Association for the Propagation of the Faith (APF) in 1838 was the spur to a more formal missionary arrangement, however. Firstly, it helped alert many Irish priests to the idea of mission, and to the possibilities of joining burgeoning French missionary orders, including the Congregation of the Holy Ghost and the Society of African Missions.[14] Secondly, it led to the foundation of All Hallows College in Dublin in 1842. This missionary college, although established through the APF-inspired zeal of one man, Father John Hand, went on, even after his death in 1846, to send more than 1,500 priests around the world. The overwhelming majority were adopted by dioceses in the Irish emigrant world, particularly in North America and Australasia, although many, particularly in later years, also went to territories where non-Christians predominated.[15] Several other Irish diocesan seminaries, producing more priests than even increasingly orthodox Ireland could accommodate, supplemented this provision to the diaspora.

With All Hallows thus occupied in supplying Irish migrant communities, missions to non-Christians as a formal, distinctive enterprise began in earnest in the Irish Catholic Church only in the early twentieth century: 1916, when the Maynooth Mission to China was begun by Fathers Edward Galvin and John Blowick, is widely agreed to be the key starting point. The French influence was again evident in the structure taken by the new movement. The 'Maynooth Mission' was in fact christened the Missionary Society of St Columban, and, once approved by the Vatican, the society set up a seminary base in Ireland to supply it with missionaries, and to help drum up financial support for its activities. These eventually extended beyond the original Hanyang base in China to encompass missions throughout south-east Asia, South and Central America

---

13 E. M. Hogan, *The Irish missionary movement: a historical survey 1830–1980* (Dublin, 1990), 16–17.
14 Ibid., 62–88.
15 K. Condon, *The missionary college of All Hallows, 1842–1891* (Dublin, 1986).

and beyond.[16] Within two decades of the Columbans' formation, they were followed by several more societies: the related Columban Missionary Sisters (1922), the Sisters of the Holy Rosary (1924), St Patrick's Missionary Society, also known as the Kiltegan Fathers (1932) and the Medical Missionaries of Mary (1937). These societies eventually had hundreds of missionaries each, working across all continents.

Thus, each of the churches in Ireland contributed to what was clearly an extensive Irish element within the Christian missionary 'golden age' in the modern era. Whether it was humbly stated or gloriously proclaimed by the organisations themselves, it is very clear that Irish missionaries had a discernible impact on their host countries: many schools, hospitals and other institutions providing secular development services to otherwise deprived communities attest to that. Moreover, the fact that many of the organisations endure to this day, with vastly decreased Irish recruitment and diminishing Irish lay interest in their activities, but with an increasing reliance on staffing by local recruits in the mission fields, denotes a certain amount of 'success' on the missionaries' own, religious conversionist terms. A broader historical canvas might well tell us that Islam, not Christianity, 'was widely the winner' arising out of the modern peak of Christian missions,[17] but gauging success, by whatever measure, ought not to be our sole reason for studying missionary history.

31.3.   Themes in Irish Missionary History

Indeed, there are far more complicated and interesting questions that arise within Irish missionary history. Perhaps the most prominent in recent historiography has been the relationship between Irish Christian missions and the British empire, a sub-set of a burgeoning wider interest in what is now usually agreed to be Ireland's uniquely bifurcated identity: up to 1921 at least, it was at once 'colonial' in the nature of its governance and in some of its political sympathies, and 'imperial' in the extent of and enthusiasm behind both Protestant and Catholic involvement in the administration, defence and peopling of the empire.[18] The role of Irish missionaries, of whatever denomination, in the empire has thus been a contested one. To what extent, historians ask, did Irish missionaries collude with and reinforce secular British imperialism and to what extent did they empower indigenous populations to resist and eventually overcome their imperial masters? If the answer to this question is that there is a spectrum between these two

---

16 N. Collins, *The splendid cause: the missionary society of St Columban 1916–1954* (Dublin, 2009).

17 C. A. Bayly, *The birth of the modern world 1780–1914* (Oxford, 2004), 345; N. Atkin and F. Tallett, *Priests, prelates and people: a history of European Catholicism since 1750* (London, 2003), 188–93.

18 K. Jeffery, *An Irish empire? Aspects of Ireland and the British empire* (Manchester, 1996); D. Fitzpatrick, 'Ireland and the empire', in A. Porter (ed.), *The Oxford history of the British empire, vol. III: The nineteenth century* (Oxford, 1999), 495–521.

points, then it must be noted that Irish Protestant and Catholic missionaries are often assumed to occupy very different positions upon it. In some Irish writing there is a twin perception that since Protestant missionaries owed their allegiance to the secular power, they were closer to the 'collusion' end, while Catholic missionaries, in the surprising words of the post-colonial critic Declan Kiberd, are absolved because they 'had no ulterior political imperial motive, such as disfigured other European efforts'.[19]

It is certainly the case that Irish Protestant missionaries, like their British counterparts, spoke a language of 'spiritual imperialism' that assumed the inherent validity of European rule over the rest of the world, and that there were among them some individuals who occasionally put that case in overtly nationalistic and political terms. Yet Irish Catholic missionaries were equally prone to making the same claims of providential, national religious empire-building, and as Oliver Rafferty has recently shown, were just as conscious that British secular expansionism often directly and indirectly facilitated their work.[20] More generally, the presence of an 'ulterior political imperial motive' among Christian missionaries as a body is one that, as a recent volume on French missions contends,[21] most historians of missions would question. If the dichotomy in political interests between the aggressively secular French state and its country's Catholic missions, and between the Protestant British state and Ireland's Catholic missions is readily apparent, many scholars of British Protestant missionaries would equally argue that the relationship between 'bible and flag' was never entirely cosy. As Brian Stanley, Susan Thorne, Andrew Porter and others have noted, Protestant missionaries (Irish included) often found themselves radically at odds with British colonial authorities, even if stances could vary across personnel, territories, denominations and time period.

Moreover, if twentieth-century Irish Catholic 'foreign' missions can stake a claim, as Kiberd suggests, to have helped hasten decolonisation by identifying with 'the struggles of native people for self-development', and particularly through the provision of education, then they are hardly unique in that. Indeed, the most prolific historian of Irish Catholic missions, Edmund Hogan, has noted that Irish missionaries generally 'engaged in education not as a *planned strategy* but because they worked mainly in the British colonies, where missionaries were expected to supply educational needs'.[22] There was also, clearly, a direct evangelising motive behind education provision, and the political results of missionary education for post-colonial Africa are not clear-cut. Irish Catholic missionary enthusiasts used to be apt to note that Zimbabwe's first Prime Minister (now

19 D. Kiberd, 'Dancing at Lughnasa', *Irish Review*, 27 (2001), 27; see also D. Kiberd, *Inventing Ireland: the literature of the modern nation* (London, 1995), 558; D. Kiberd, *The Irish writer and the world* (Cambridge, 2005), 15.
20 S. Roddy, 'Spiritual imperialism and the mission of the Irish race: the Catholic Church and emigration from nineteenth-century Ireland', *Irish Historical Studies*, 38, 152 (2013), 600–19; O. Rafferty, 'The Catholic Church, Ireland and the British empire, 1800–1921', *Historical Research*, 84, 224 (2011), 288–309.
21 J. P. Daughton and O. White, *In God's empire: French missionaries in the modern world* (Oxford, 2012), 11.
22 Hogan, *Irish missionary movement*, 163.

long-reigning dictator), Robert Mugabe, was educated by Irish Jesuits and that he spoke generously of his teachers. Nelson Mandela, conversely, was ambivalent about his time at a university first founded by the Free Church of Scotland. Less provocative examples might be used, but the purpose is to demonstrate the essential truth that all western Christian missionary schools, Irish Protestant and Catholic ones included, occupied highly ambiguous places in both the colonisation and the decolonisation processes. In the striking words of Donald Akenson, 'they teach shame and discipline, introduce new gods, destroy old cultures, provide tools for dealing with the advancing Europeans and, simultaneously, seduce the indigene into following European ways'.[23]

This concept of 'cultural imperialism' or 'colonisation of consciousness', first elucidated in the pioneering anthropological studies of missions by Jean and John Comaroff, has been challenged in recent years by historians of mission, some of whom, perhaps rightly, advocate an approach that is less politically charged and acknowledges the fact that western and non-western societies were often in dialogue rather than in conflict through missions.[24] But while it is true that the religions that resulted from missionary endeavour were often in practice indigenous co-productions, incorporating elements of pre-existing local ritual and belief as well as Christian orthodoxies, this cannot entirely counter Akenson's criticism. For example, Irish Catholic priests in India in the 1830s and 1840s may have shown a measured sensitivity to the local culture that saw many of them adopt native dress and learn local languages while simultaneously bypassing the iniquitous caste system, but they also, as Barry Crosbie has argued, imposed a particularly 'Irish' form of Catholicism, defined as one in which priest and peasants in the parish formed a strong social bond, and the priest became a spokesman for their grievances.[25] That is arguably a rather benign reading of this 'social bond', which, as we know, could also have its negative, controlling side. Simply put, if historians are now able to uncover and critique the long-term social and psychological results of this system in Ireland itself, it is surely right to be prepared to do the same in missionary territories. As even a recent, popular and more or less celebratory account of Irish Catholic foreign missions has acknowledged, the abuse of power (in all its manifestations) in the missionary field is 'a timebomb'.[26]

In many ways these are issues that historians of all countries' overseas missions must confront. But the 'Irishness' of missions is a question worth examining in its own right.

23 D. H. Akenson, *An Irish history of civilization, vol. II* (Montreal, 2006), 491. See also K. Kenny, 'The Irish in the empire', in K. Kenny (ed.), *Ireland and the British empire* (Oxford, 2004), 119–21.

24 J. Comaroff and J. Comaroff, *Of revelation and revolution, vol I: Christianity, colonialism, and consciousness in South Africa* (Chicago, 1991); R. Dunch, 'Beyond cultural imperialism: cultural theory, Christian missions, and global modernity', *History and Theory*, 41, 3 (2002), 301–25; N. Etherington, 'Missions and empire revisited', *Social Sciences and Missions*, 24, 2 (2011), 171–90.

25 B. Crosbie, *Irish imperial networks: migration, social communication and exchange in nineteenth-century India* (Cambridge, 2011), 153.

26 J. Humphreys, *God's entrepreneurs: how Irish missionaries tried to change the world* (Dublin, 2010), 180.

What might that mean? Contemporary commentators certainly found it useful to emphasise the Irish origins of missions in some contexts. During Home Rule debates, Irish Protestants suggested that their missions in the colonies were vital to maintaining the Protestant character of the empire, and crucially, to defending it against an onslaught of Catholicism, since, they noted, they had already had ample practice – if not an enormous degree of success – in doing just that in Ireland.[27] Similarly, it could be argued that early Irish Catholic missionaries, in particular, were prepared for their task by coming from a church which, for all its Roman orthodoxy, retained vestiges of earlier folk beliefs, as, for example, divergent official and popular reactions to the apparitions at Knock in 1879 demonstrated. For Irish clergy, managing a gradual neutralisation of 'magic' within the Irish peasant's melange of beliefs and practices was perhaps preparation for what they regarded as a similar exercise among indigenous peoples in foreign climes. The broader notion that Irish Christians were uniquely fitted for the missionary field must remain moot, however, since it would require significantly more research to substantiate. It also has to contend with the parallel sense, common in all denominations, that, in novelist John McGahern's phrase, many missionaries were instead seen as the 'second-raters' of their churches, and missionary work as the preserve of those from a lower socio-economic background, an insinuation that invites the suggestion that Irish missionary effort was not necessarily the cross-class meeting ground that, for example, British missionary enterprise has sometimes been deemed.[28]

Yet, if the claims of Kiberd and other scholars to a particular Irish suitability to missionary work are difficult to sustain, the persistence of such claims, even in modified form, perhaps does tell us something important about the 'Irishness' of Irish missions. It is at least possible to say that in the twentieth century missionary endeavour had an unambiguous impact on Irish Catholic self-conception. Indeed, some have retrospectively seen the date of the foundation of the Maynooth Mission to China as significant; it was a religious 1916 to sit alongside the political, and the beginning of a parallel 'missionary nationalism' which informed the dominant sense of the Irish 'self' in the early decades of the new southern state.[29] In her analysis of Irish Catholic missionary magazines of the period, Fiona Bateman has argued that, far from seeing the point of view of the colonised, missionaries engaged in an 'othering' of those among whom they worked, through which they were able to strengthen the definition of themselves and their Irish co-religionists as 'civilised' in contrast to a non-Catholic, 'uncivilised',

27 *The Church of Ireland and the present crisis: report of the special meeting of the General Synod, holden at Dublin, March 23, 1886* (Dublin, 1886), 14–15; D. Hempton and M. Hill, *Evangelical Protestantism in Ulster society, 1740–1890* (London, 1992), 182.

28 J. McGahern, *The dark* (London, 1965), 49; see P. Kavanagh, *The green fool* (London, 1975), 125 for an oblique suggestion that foreign missionaries came from poorer backgrounds. J. Cox, *The British missionary enterprise since 1700* (London, 2007), 100.

29 B. Fanning, *Racism and social change in the Republic of Ireland* (Manchester, 2002), 16.

even 'savage' Other.[30] The cultural geographer Denis Linehan has similarly noted that the material culture of early twentieth-century Irish Catholic and Protestant missions – including hugely popular exhibitions of 'exotic' artefacts and magazines containing maps of Africa measured out in 'Irelands' – 'operated as a framing mechanism to align the relationship between the Irish and "the Other"', wherein the voices of Africans were largely absent.[31] Moreover, while there is a strong case for saying that a later, post-colonial generation of Irish Catholic missionaries were responsible for channelling their supporters' enthusiasm into a more secular humanitarian advocacy on which Ireland now partly likes to base its international reputation, that advocacy was, again, not necessarily unique to Ireland, nor is it or should it be beyond critical appraisal.[32]

31.4. Whither Irish Missionary History?

The above represents only a fraction of the problems thrown up by Irish missionary history. Yet empire, identity and humanitarianism are hardly esoteric concerns; indeed, they demonstrate the degree to which missions matter within the broader field of Irish social history. There are other significant issues, a number of which have had some recognition but would certainly bear further exploration. Many speak to subjects found elsewhere in this volume, but could also offer something new to the field of global missionary history. Gender – in terms both of constructions of masculinities and of female empowerment – has been widely considered within Catholic and Protestant missions, although rarely across denominational lines in comparative fashion; Irish case studies may offer that possibly illuminating opportunity.[33] Linked to that, the significance of the family in Protestant missionary life has also been identified, and assumed, for obvious reasons, to be less relevant to Catholic missionary life; but there is surely potential for historical interrogation of the transnational, extended missionary family that has inspired such stellar literary treatment. In a country that, north and south, remained startlingly uncosmopolitan and experienced relatively little return migration until recent decades, the roving missionary who made periodic home visits represents a potentially valuable historical witness to (as well as actor in) both changes in Ireland's relationship with the wider world and changes within Ireland itself. Not least, it is worth asking seriously what the presence of so many Irish-trained clergy around the world

---

30 F. Bateman, 'The spiritual empire: Irish Catholic missionary discourse in the twentieth century', Ph.D. thesis, NUI Galway (2003), 14–17.

31 D. Linehan, 'Irish empire: assembling the geographical imagination of Irish missionaries in Africa', *Cultural Geographies*, 21, 429 (2014), 441.

32 K. O'Sullivan, *Ireland, Africa and the end of empire: small state identity in the Cold War, 1955–75* (Manchester, 2012), 11.

33 M. Hill, 'Gender, culture and "the spiritual empire": The Irish Protestant female missionary experience', *Women's History Review*, 16, 2 (2007), 185–208.

meant for the Catholic Church in Ireland. Moreover, alternative – or, just as valuable, corroborating – Irish conceptions of the body, understandings of the mechanics and meanings of religious faith and attitudes towards modernity may well be lying dormant within vast and varied missionary archives, each awaiting its historians.

This admittedly partial agenda goes some way towards answering the question as to where we should place the history of Irish missions, and where it might be headed. Missions used to be the marginal concern of antiquarians focused on medieval monks; from around the 1970s until the early 1990s, the field was dominated by what amounted to hagiographies of more modern missionaries, which found their chief audience in supporters and members of missionary agencies. In somewhat modified form, such works still persist, albeit with dwindling interest. But in the past thirty years, there has also been a minor flowering of scholarship influenced by increased interest in the history of missions elsewhere. However, there is no reason for that new scholarship to be narrowly focused, either on particular organisations or on particular individuals. More spadework in the archives of individual missionary agencies is obviously necessary, but the goal should not simply be to produce a succession of slightly more critical versions of the older institutional chronicles. Rather, cross-cutting themes, wide-ranging questions and theoretically engaged research in multiple archives are required from researchers.

It is also important that such examinations do not merely replicate in an Irish context work that has already been done in a French, British or other national context. Ireland's history may not be 'exceptional', the term commonly used in collective self-flagellation by historians (and indeed, sometimes in straightforward flagellation of others), but it is certainly, like all nations' histories, unique. The very particular circumstances that led to its churches taking part in the global missionary movement in the modern era can certainly contribute to a wider, transnational historiography of that movement and the empires in which it operated, if historians of Ireland continue to demonstrate that they are prepared to do so. Glib, exceptionalist assumptions about an inherent Irish missionary anti-imperialism or acceptance of older tropes about Ireland's providential 'spiritual empire' are unhelpful, but there is surely a place for exploring the 'exceptional' in Irish missionary history through new research and genuine insight.

FURTHER READING

Ballantyne, T. 'Religion, difference and the limits of British imperial history', *Victorian Studies*, 47, 3 (2005), 427–55.

Ballantyne, T. 'The sinews of empire: Ireland, India and the construction of British colonial knowledge', in T. McDonough (ed.), *Was Ireland a colony? Economics, politics and culture in nineteenth-century Ireland* (Dublin, 2005), 145–61.

Barr, C. P. '*Imperium in imperio*: Irish episcopal imperialism in the nineteenth century', *English Historical Review*, 123, 502 (2008), 611–50.

Bateman, F. 'Defining the heathen in Ireland and Africa: two similar discourses a century apart', *Social Sciences and Missions*, 21, 1 (2008), 73–96.

Bateman, F. 'Ireland and the Nigeria–Biafra War: local connections to a distant conflict', *New Hibernia Review*, 16, 1 (2012), 48–67.

Bateman, F. 'An Irish missionary in India: Thomas Gavan Duffy and "the catechist of Kil-Arni"', in T. Foley and M. O'Connor (eds.), *Ireland and India: colonies, culture and empire* (Dublin, 2006), 117–28.

Bayly, C. A. 'Ireland, India and the empire, 1780–1914', *Transactions of the Royal Historical Society*, 6th ser., 10 (2000), 377–98.

Blyth, R. J. and K. Jeffery (eds.). *The British empire and its contested pasts* (Dublin, 2009).

Brown, S. J. 'Foreign missions: a survey', *Studies: An Irish Quarterly*, 15, 57 (Mar. 1926), 105–20.

Brown, S. J. *Providence and empire: religion, politics and society in the United Kingdom, 1815–1914* (Harlow, 2008).

Carey, H. M. (ed.). *Empires of religion* (Basingstoke, 2008).

Carey, H. M. 'Religion and the "evil empire"', *Journal of Religious History*, 32 (2008), 179–92.

Cleall, E. *Missionary discourses of difference: negotiating Otherness in the British empire, 1840–1900* (Basingstoke, 2012).

Clery, J. 'Amongst empires: a short history of Ireland and empire studies in international context', *Éire-Ireland*, 42, 1–2 (2007), 11–57.

Comerford, P. and R. O'Leary. ' "Heroism and zeal": pioneers of the Irish Christian missions to China', in J. McCormack (ed.), *China and the Irish* (Dublin, 2009), 73–87.

Conlan, P. 'Missions and missionaries', in E. Bhreathnach, J. MacMahon and J. McCafferty (eds.), *The Irish Franciscans, 1534–1990* (Dublin, 2009), 271–86.

Cooke, C. 'The modern Irish missionary movement', *Archivium Hibernicum*, 35 (1980), 234–46.

Copland, I. 'Christianity as an arm of empire: the ambiguous case of India under the Company, c.1813–1858', *Historical Journal*, 49, 4 (2006), 1025–54.

Curtis, S. A. *Civilizing habits: women missionaries and the revival of French empire* (Oxford, 2010).

Darch, J. H. *Missionary imperialists? Missionaries, government and the growth of the British empire in the tropics, 1860–1885* (Eugene, 2009).

Daughton, J. P. *An empire divided: religion, republicanism, and the making of French colonialism, 1880–1914* (Oxford, 2006).

Dowling, M. 'Irish Baptists: home mission and denominational home rule in the nineteenth and twentieth centuries', in I. M. Randall and A. R. Cross (eds.), *Baptists and mission: papers from the Fourth International Conference on Baptist Studies* (Milton Keynes, 2007), 42–63.

Elbourne, E. *Blood ground: colonialism, missions and the contest for Christianity in the Cape Colony and Britain, 1799–1853* (Montreal, 2002).

Elbourne, E. 'Religion in the British empire', in S. Stockwell (ed.), *The British empire: themes and perspectives* (Oxford, 2008), 131–56.

Etherington, N. (ed.). *Missions and empire* (Oxford, 2005).

Fairbairn, M. 'Missionary sisters of St Columban', *Studies: An Irish Quarterly*, 36 (1947), 451–60.

Forristal, D. *Edel Quinn, 1907–1944* (Dublin, 1994).

Friel, B. *Dancing at Lughnasa* (London, 1998).

Gaughan, J. A. *Olivia Mary Taaffe, 1832–1918: foundress of St Joseph's Young Priests Society* (Dublin, 1995).

Gilley, S. 'Catholicism in Ireland', in H. McLeod and W. Ustorf (eds.), *The decline of Christendom in western Europe, 1750–2000* (Cambridge, 2003), 99–112.

Gilley, S. 'Catholicism, Ireland, and the Irish diaspora', in S. Gilley and B. Stanley (eds.), *The Cambridge history of Christianity, vol. VIII: World Christianities c.1815–c.1914* (Cambridge, 2006), 250–9.

Gilley, S. 'The Roman Catholic Church and the nineteenth-century Irish diaspora', *Journal of Ecclesiastical History*, 35, 2 (1984), 188–207.

Hally, C. 'A hundred years of Irish missionary effort', *The Furrow*, 22, 6 (1971), 335–49.

Harkness, D. 'Ireland', in R. W. Winks (ed.), *The Oxford history of the British empire: historiography* (Oxford, 1999), 495–521.

Hill, M. 'Gender, culture and "the spiritual empire": the Irish Protestant female missionary experience', *Women's History Review*, 16, 2 (2007), 185–208.

Hogan, E. M. *Catholic missionaries and Liberia: a study of Christian enterprise in West Africa, 1842–1949* (Cork, 1981).

Hogan, E. M. 'The Congregation of the Holy Ghost and the evolution of the modern Irish missionary movement', *Catholic Historical Review*, 70 (1984), 1–13.

Hogan, E. M. 'The motivation of the modern Irish missionary movement 1912–1939', *Journal of Religion in Africa*, 10 (1979), 157–73.

Hogan, E. M. 'Origins of the modern Irish missionary movement: the "Missions Africaines de Lyons" in Cork 1876–1883', *Journal of the Cork Historical and Archaeological Society*, 86 (1981), 43–52.

Keaney, M. *They brought the good news: modern Irish missionaries* (Dublin, 1980).

Kelleher, D. 'From Westmeath to Peru full circle: memoirs of a Westmeath missionary in Sicuani, Cuzco', *Irish Migration Studies in Latin America*, 4, 4 (2006), 199–205.

Kerr, D. A. 'Under the Union flag: the Catholic Church in Ireland, 1800–1870', in *Ireland after the Union* (Oxford, 1989), 23–43.

KilBride, C. and D. Raftery. *The voyage out: Infant Jesus Sisters, Ireland, 1909–2009* (Dublin, 2009).

Kinealy, C. 'At home with the empire: the example of Ireland', in C. Hall and S. O. Rose (eds.), *At home with the empire: metropolitan culture and the imperial world* (Cambridge, 2006), 77–100.

Kinealy, C. 'Was Ireland a colony? The evidence of the Great Famine', in T. McDonough (ed.), *Was Ireland a colony? Economics, politics and culture in nineteenth-century Ireland* (Dublin, 2005), 48–65.

Kirk, M. D. 'Mother Cecilia Maher and the St Leo's mission to New Zealand', *Carloviana*, 60 (2011), 79–80.

Laheen, K. 'The letters of an Irish brother, Edward Sinnott S.J., from Calcutta, Part 2, 1837–43', *Collectanea Hibernica*, 48 (2006), 129–66.

Larkin, E. 'The beginning of the Irish effort to provide for the Roman Catholic foreign missions before the famine', in T. Dunne and L. M. Geary (eds.), *History and the public sphere: essays in honour of John A. Murphy* (Cork, 2005), 83–99.

Larkin, E. *The Roman Catholic Church and the creation of the modern Irish state* (Dublin, 1975).

Lynch, I. C. *Beyond faith and adventure: Irish missionaries in Nigeria tell their extraordinary story* (Dublin, 2006).

McGlade, J. *The missions: Africa and the Orient* (Dublin, 1967).

MacKenzie, J. 'Irish, Scottish, Welsh and English worlds? The historiography of a four-nations approach to the history of the British empire', in C. Hall and K. McClelland (eds.), *Race, nation and empire: making histories, 1750 to the present* (Manchester, 2009).

Marshall, W. 'Missionary work and the Church of Ireland', in C. Costecalde and B. M. Walker (eds.), *The Church of Ireland: an illustrated history* (Dublin, 2013), 92–5.

Martin, F. X. and C. O'Reilly. *The Irish Augustinians in Rome, 1656–1994 and Irish Augustinian missions throughout the world* (Dublin, 1994).

May, A. J. *Welsh missionaries and British imperialism: the empire of clouds in north-east India* (Manchester, 2012).

Meehan, D. 'Maynooth and the missions', *Irish Ecclesiastical Record*, 66 (1945), 224–37.

Morgan, H. 'Empire-building: an uncomfortable Irish heritage', *Linen Hall Review*, 10, 2 (1993), 8–11.

Moynagh, J. 'The Society of St Patrick for Foreign Missions', *Irish Ecclesiastical Record*, 64 (1944), 107–14.

Murphy, D. *A history of Irish emigrant and missionary education* (Dublin, 2000).

Murphy, J. H. *Abject loyalty: nationalism and monarchy in Ireland during the reign of Queen Victoria* (Cork, 2001).

Needham, C. 'Irish missions to Africa', *Irish Ecclesiastical Record*, 95 (1961), 167–75.

Nugent, A. 'Irish Benedictines in Africa', in M. Browne and C. N. Ó Clabaigh (eds.), *The Irish Benedictines: a history* (Blackrock, 2005), 202–10.

O'Connor, E. *SMA missionaries of northern Nigeria, 1907–1934* (Abuja, 2007).

O'Cuilinn, P. C. 'St Patrick's Missionary Society (the Kiltegan Fathers)', *Carloviana*, 58 (2009), 53–5.

O'Farrell, P. *Ireland's English question: Anglo-Irish relations, 1534–1970* (Oxford, 1971).

O'Neill, H. 'The foreign aid policy of Ireland', in P. Hoebink and O. Stokke (eds.), *Perspectives on European development cooperation: policy and performance of individual donor countries and the EU* (London, 2005), 303–35.

O'Shea, M. *Owen Maginn: a missionary's story* (Cork, 2009).

Oliver, M. *Love is a light burden: the life of Mother Mary Gonzaga Barry* (London, 1950).

Porter, A. 'Church history, history of Christianity, religious history: some reflections on British missionary enterprise since the late eighteenth century', *Church History*, 71, 3 (2002), 555–84.

Porter, A. '"Commerce and Christianity": The rise and fall of a nineteenth-century missionary slogan', *Historical Journal*, 28, 3 (1985), 597–621.

Porter, A. '"Cultural imperialism" and Protestant missionary enterprise, 1780–1914', *Journal of Imperial and Commonwealth History*, 25, 3 (1997), 367–91.

Porter, A. 'Missions and empire, c.1873–1914', in S. Gilley and B. Stanley (eds.), *The Cambridge history of Christianity, vol. VIII: World Christianities c.1815–c.1914* (Cambridge, 2006), 560–75.

Porter, A. 'Religion and empire: British expansion in the long nineteenth century, 1780–1914', *Journal of Imperial and Commonwealth History*, 20, 3 (1992), 370–90.

Porter, A. 'Religion, missionary enthusiasm, and empire', in A. Porter (ed.), *The Oxford history of the British empire, vol. III: The nineteenth century* (Oxford, 1999), 222–46.

Porter, B. *Critics of empire: British radical attitudes to colonialism in Africa, 1895–1914* (London, 1968).

Railton, N. M. '"The dreamy mazes of millenarianism": William Graham and the Irish Presbyterian mission to German Jews', in C. Gribben and A. R. Holmes (eds.), *Protestant millennialism, evangelicalism and Irish society, 1790–2005* (Basingstoke, 2006), 174–201.

Robertson, J. 'The Leprosy Asylum in India: 1886–1947', *Journal of the History of Medicine and Allied Sciences*, 64, 4 (2009), 474–517.

Roddy, S. *Population, providence and empire: the churches and emigration from nineteenth-century Ireland* (Manchester, 2014).

Semple, R. A. 'Missionary manhood: professionalism, belief and masculinity in the nineteenth-century British imperial field', *Journal of Imperial and Commonwealth History*, 36, 3 (2008), 397–415.

Smyth, B. T. *The Chinese batch: the Maynooth mission to China, origins, 1911–1920* (Dublin, 1994).

Stanley, B. *The Bible and the flag: Protestant missions and British imperialism in the nineteenth and twentieth centuries* (Leicester, 1990).

Stanley, B. '"Commerce and Christianity": providence theory, the missionary movement, and the imperialism of free trade, 1842–1860', *Historical Journal*, 26, 1 (1983), 71–94.

Stuart, J. *British missionaries and the end of empire: east, central, and southern Africa, 1939–64* (Grand Rapids, 2011).

Sullivan, T. 'Serving the spiritual needs of the Irish diaspora in nineteenth-century America', *Breifne: Journal of Cumann Seanchais Bhréifne*, 11, 44 (2008), 631–45.

Thorne, S. '"The conversion of Englishmen and the conversion of the world inseparable": missionary imperialism and the language of class in early industrial Britain', in F. Cooper and A. L. Stoler (eds.), *Tensions of empire: colonial cultures in a bourgeois world* (London, 1997), 238–62.

Thorne, S. 'Imperial pieties', *History Workshop Journal*, 63, 1 (2007), 319–28.

Thorne, S. 'Religion and empire at home', in C. Hall and S. O. Rose (eds.), *At home with the empire: metropolitan culture and the imperial world* (Cambridge, 2006), 143–65.

Twells, A. *The civilising mission and the English middle class, 1792–1850: the 'heathen' at home and overseas* (Basingstoke, 2009).

Tyrrell, I. R. *Reforming the world: the creation of America's moral empire* (Oxford, 2010).

Ussher, J. *Father Fahy: a biography of Anthony Dominic Fahy, O.P.: an Irish missionary in Argentina, 1805–1871* (Buenos Aires, 2005).

Walsh, O. 'Sketches of missionary life: Alexander Robert Crawford in Manchuria', in O. Walsh (ed.), *Ireland abroad: politics and professions in the nineteenth century* (Dublin, 2003), 132–46.

Williams, C. P. '"Too peculiarly Anglican": the role of the established church in Ireland as a negative model in the development of the Church Missionary Society's commitment to independent native churches, 1856–1872', in W. J. Sheils and D. Wood (eds.), *The churches, Ireland and the Irish*, Studies in Church History 25 (Oxford, 1989), 299–310.

Wolffe, J. *God and greater Britain: religion and national life in Britain and Ireland 1843–1945* (London, 1994).

32 Cultural Transmission, Irish Associational Culture and the 'Marching' Tradition

D. A. J. MacPherson

32.1. Introduction

St Patrick's Day parades have so often been a barometer of Irish identity, one day which reflects the shifting meanings of Irishness across the globe. The New York parade in 2015 was no different. Indeed, the controversial appearance in the parade, for the first time, of an LGBTQ organisation marked the culmination of decades of debate about how Irishness is (and should) be represented through the St Patrick's Day celebration. The Out@NBCUniversal group became the first gay participants officially sanctioned by the parade organisers. Representing the event's television broadcaster, the hundred or so employees of NBC who marched in 2015 were the first LGBTQ representatives to join the parade since the organising committee, led largely by the Ancient Order of Hibernians (AOH), decided to ban the Irish Lesbian and Gay Organisation (ILGO) from marching in 1991. That year, the ILGO did manage to march, but under the auspices of Division 7 of the Manhattan AOH. In protest against the decision to ban the ILGO from the main parade, Mayor David Dinkins walked with the ILGO and was pelted with beer cans by a crowd whose sympathies lay emphatically with the parade organisers.[1] Despite being the only LGBTQ group allowed to march in 2015, the appearance of Out@NBCUniversal was significant, then, in marking a shift towards the greater

1 K. Kenny, *The American Irish: a history* (Harlow, 2000), 237–8.

acceptance of homosexuality in the Irish diaspora.[2] More importantly, the debate about LGBTQ representation at the NYC parade reveals the great diversity of Irish identities throughout the world. While the New York parade was dominated during the 1990s and 2000s by a socially conservative (and explicitly Catholic) vision of Irishness, others reflected a greater plurality. In New York itself, since 2000 the 'St Pat's for All' parade in Queens has welcomed 'all to celebrate Irish heritage and culture regardless of race, gender, creed or sexual orientation'.[3] In Ireland, Fintan O'Toole has led criticism of the New York parade's exclusion of the ILGO and his spat in the *Irish Times* in March 1998 with historian Marion Casey reflects what Mary Hickman has termed 'the heterogeneous formation' of the Irish diaspora.[4] Since 1998, the Birmingham St Patrick's parade has invited the Irish LGBTQ group Cáirde le Chéile ('Friends Together') to march, reflecting the way in which the Irish community in the city has been integrated into broader celebrations of diversity and the extent to which, as James Moran argues, 'the future dynamism of the parade, and perhaps the event's access to corporate and local government funding, depends on continuing to celebrate what is distinctly Irish whilst at the same time developing a cross-community appeal'.[5]

St Patrick's Day parades, then, indicate the ways in which Irish diasporic identity is fractured and hybrid in nature and how, through the process of migration, Irish identity changes. Irish associational culture at home and abroad was shaped by this one key shared social function: diaspora. This chapter examines the transmission of Irish identities across the globe during the nineteenth and twentieth centuries, focusing on how Irish migrants used associational culture to retain, maintain and create new forms of Irish identities. In particular, this chapter explores how migrant associations created diasporic connections between home and abroad. This process of cultural transmission – of migrants taking their identities with them as part of their metaphorical baggage – is fundamentally diasporic, in that these identities are shaped as much by abroad as by home and by the interplay and interchange between two or multiple locations.

---

2 T. Schlossberg, 'St Patrick's Day parade includes first gay group, but dismay remains', *New York Times*, 17 March 2015. Out@NBCUniversal faced considerable hostility from within the LGBTQ community for marching. Groups such as Irish Queers were 'completely appalled by OUT@NBC, the corporate gay/straight/marketing alliance that's marching in the antigay parade to the exclusion of the actual Irish queer groups who have been shoved aside for the last quarter century'. See 'Irish Queers give it back to OUT@NBC', available at http://irishqueers.blogspot.co.uk/2015/03/irish-queers-gives-it-back-to-outnbc.html, accessed 4 June 2015. The role of NBC in the NYC parade was splendidly satirised in the television show *30 Rock*, in which the main protagonist, a fictional NBC producer, Liz Lemon, expresses her distaste for the whole affair by wearing head-to-toe orange. See 'St Patrick's Day', *30 Rock*, aired 15 March 2012.

3 'St Pats for All', available at www.stpatsforall.com/aboutus.html, accessed 4 June 2015.

4 M. J. Hickman, 'Reflecting on gender, generation and ethnicity in celebrating St Patrick's Day in London', in D. A. J. MacPherson and M. J. Hickman (eds.), *Women and Irish diaspora identities: theories, concepts and new perspectives* (Manchester, 2014), 113–14.

5 J. Moran, *Irish Birmingham: a history* (Liverpool, 2010), 229–30.

This chapter begins by outlining some of these theoretical contexts – largely focused on the concept of diaspora, but also drawing on some comparative perspectives, especially with the Scottish diaspora. Reflecting the standard Orange and Green traditions of Irish associational cultures, what interests us here is not necessarily the Irish origins of, say, the Orange Order, but instead the cultural transmission of these ideas and identities across the globe. The focus of this chapter, then, falls on exploring how diasporic connections are maintained through Orange and Green associational activity. The example of the Orange Order in Scotland and Canada will be used to demonstrate how Irish Protestant identities were transmitted across the globe, while the Green tradition of associational activity will be explored through the social networks established by organisations such as the Ancient Order of Hibernians, the Gaelic League and Irish county associations, largely using illustrations drawn from Britain and North America. These organisations were instrumental in creating diasporic connections, linking migrants 'back home' and to other locations across the world, creating new forms of Irish identities which reflected both where migrants were from and where they made new homes. These hybrid identities, of course, changed over time, often as a result of events in Ireland. One of the key arguments of this chapter is that the high point of Irish associational culture abroad parallels the period of greatest debate about Irish identity, roughly from 1880 through to 1920 — and that this is the case precisely because of the diasporic character of these organisations.

The chapter also briefly examines the Irish 'marching tradition'. Of course, Irish associational culture and the 'marching tradition' are deeply interrelated. I argue, however, that marching and parading are just the public and most visible tips of the Irish identities 'iceberg': looming vastly underneath the surface is an immense underpinning of associations, clubs, societies and the rest which articulate Irishness in a deeper, more complex way than dressing up and parading through the streets. So, while the chapter concludes with a brief consideration of the differing status of St Patrick's Day parades and Orange marches and how they reflect certain aspects of Irish identities, diasporic and otherwise, the core of the chapter focuses on the diasporic function of Irish associational culture.

32.2. The Diaspora as a Concept

Diaspora is one of the defining categories of Irish social history, and its very salience helps us to understand how Irish social history is different. The term diaspora has been a somewhat problematic term for historians, who have rightly demanded definitional rigour when it is used to analyse the past. In 2003, Kevin Kenny outlined some of the problems with the adoption of the term 'diaspora' in Irish ethnic and migration studies. Surveying the broadening out of its definition from classical dispersion and exile from homeland to encompass any type of migration or ethnic identity, Kenny called for a more precise usage of the term that focused on exploring the transnational connections between migrants and the 'home' country and placing this in a comparative framework with other ethnic groups. Kenny attached particular analytical value to exploring the notion of an Irish 'diasporic sensibility', in which the Irish abroad considered themselves to be connected through some measure of common, shared identity, providing examples of Irish nationalist political and trade union activity which demonstrated such a relationship between migrant community and home.[6] Kenny's critique of the term 'diaspora' is largely based on the recent broadening of the traditional usage of the concept by one school of thought within diaspora studies – what Rogers Brubaker has termed 'the diaspora "diaspora"'.[7]

Other historians have echoed Kenny's sceptical and cautious use of the term 'diaspora'. Drawing together three leading historians of Irish migration, a 'symposium' in the journal *Irish Economic and Social History* examined how Irish emigration could be explored through the analytical framework of diaspora. Don MacRaild echoed many of Kenny's concerns, arguing that historians should concentrate on finding evidence to demonstrate the existence of networks of communication that facilitated and maintained a diasporic consciousness among Irish migrants.[8] Enda Delaney discussed the need to avoid any labelling of the Irish diaspora as a unitary identity, emphasising the necessity in recognising the diversity of Irishness abroad and its complex, 'ambiguous' relationship with the notion of homeland.[9]

Such an approach, focused on mentalities and a multiplicity of Irish identities, indicates ways in which historians can engage with broader theoretical discussions of diaspora. Cultural anthropologists have argued since the 1990s that the term diaspora captures the way in which people can live their lives in many different locations, be they physical or imagined, and in doing so experience a sense of identity and subjectivity that is also multiple and hybrid. In their recent book *Diaspora and hybridity*, Virinder Kalra, Raminder Kaur and John Hutnyk argue that it is more helpful to think of diaspora less as a group of people and more as a process through which migrants can connect places of residence to 'intimate or material connections to other places'.[10] They demonstrate how the work of Stuart Hall and Paul Gilroy is important to an understanding of diaspora that stresses the multiple belongings of identity, where it is possible to be *from* one place but *of* many others. Avtar Brah's concept of 'diaspora space' captures the hybrid

6 K. Kenny, 'Diaspora and comparison: the global Irish as a case study', *Journal of American History*, 90 (2003), 143, 150.

7 R. Brubaker, 'The diaspora "diaspora"', *Ethnic and Racial Studies*, 28, 1 (2005), 1–19.

8 D. M. MacRaild, '"Diaspora" and "transnationalism": theory and evidence in explanation of the Irish worldwide', *Irish Economic and Social History*, 33 (2006), 51–8.

9 E. Delaney, 'The Irish diaspora', *Irish Economic and Social History*, 33 (2006), 45.

10 V. S. Kalra, R. Kaur and J. Hutnyk, *Diaspora and hybridity* (London, 2005), 29.

nature of diasporic identity that connects these multiple locations. Brah suggests that in the process of the encounter and mixing of different migrant identities with those of the long-term settled, a place of settlement such as Britain becomes a diaspora space in which 'the genealogies of dispersion' are intertwined with 'those of "staying put".[11]

The term 'diaspora' has now been pinned down sufficiently for it to carry significant analytical heft. In particular Kevin Kenny defines diaspora with admirable clarity, nailing down how it should be used as an explanatory tool in migration history. He argues that 'Diaspora is best approached not as a social entity that can be measured but as an idea that helps explain the world migration creates.'[12] For Kenny, the term diaspora explains the social world of the migrant that has roots in multiple locations — where the migrant is from, and then both where the migrant ends up and where others from the migrant's point of departure end up, and the connections that then form between all of these. In my research, I have attempted to find examples of how Irish Protestant women used the associational culture of the Orange Order in this kind of way – so, how the organisation creates diasporic connections between women from the same ethnic group in different locations. Diasporic connections are, therefore, part of a continuum: it is not just about how the homeland shapes the social world of the migrant abroad, but the active connections that those migrants create with home – and, perhaps most intriguingly, how home itself, and those who do not become migrants are shaped by diaspora and are part of this diasporic continuum.

To what extent, though, can the Irish practice and experience of diaspora be considered different to other forms of diasporic identity and organisation? While there are many examples of migrants thinking and feeling diasporically, the Scottish diaspora stands out as a particularly useful point of comparison. Here, we have a similar migrant population, in terms of both scale and diasporic desire to maintain meaningful connections 'back home'. Tanja Bueltmann's study of Scottish associational culture in New Zealand examines the impressive network of clubs and societies established by migrant Scots who had a strong 'orientation to homeland', one of the core criteria of 'diaspora' identified in her recent work with Andrew Hinson and Graeme Morton.[13] Caledonian and St Andrew's societies proliferated across the globe during the nineteenth century, attracting Scots (largely men) who wished to maintain a sense of Scottish ethnic identity and some kind of emotional connection 'back home'. This sense of being part of a connected network of diasporan Scots was emphasised in letter writing and newspaper culture. For example, publications such as the *Celtic Monthly* and the *Celtic Magazine* functioned as a means of imaginatively connecting Scots scattered across the globe,

---

11 A. Brah, *Cartographies of diaspora: contesting identities* (London, 1996), 209.
12 K. Kenny, *Diaspora: a very short introduction* (Oxford, 2013), 1.
13 T. Bueltmann, A. Hinson and G. Morton, *The Scottish diaspora* (Edinburgh, 2013), 128.

'inspiring "many happy thoughts when one hears of the dear Highland homeland".[14] Similarly, the Scottish Mothers' Union facilitated diasporic connection between branches in Alloa in Scotland and Hatiatai in New Zealand, through letter writing and visits back home during the 1930s.[15] The use of print culture and return visits certainly echoes some of the Irish diasporic behaviour examined later in this chapter. However, as both Bueltmann and Angela McCarthy point out, in New Zealand 'expressions of Scottishness [were] predominantly cultural while Irishness had a political tenor'.[16] Scottish diasporic associational culture was different, then, because it was not as closely tied to more political forms of identity, such as those manifested in the Orange and Green organisations which form the focus of this chapter. Equally, while Scottish diasporic connection was facilitated by print culture, it is in the Irish example that we see newspapers being used as an instrument *par excellence* of diasporic communication. And, finally, while the periodisation of Scottish associational culture abroad parallels that of the Irish diaspora (with the high point of both falling at the end of the nineteenth and beginning of the twentieth century), it is the salience of political expressions of Irish identity which have continued to drive membership trends in broader diasporic associationalism, as we see in the work of Eric Kaufmann on the Orange Order in Scotland and Canada.[17] It is this greater political tinge of Irish associational culture which then supercharges Irish diasporic connections and the cultural transmission of Irish identities and, therefore, distinguishes the Irish diaspora from others.

32.3. Green Associationalism

While the other two organisations examined in this section – the Gaelic League and the Irish county associations – were more clearly cultural in their articulations of Irish diasporic identity, the political dimension to Irish associational culture was keenly felt in the third example – the Ancient Order of the Hibernians (AOH). Writing in 1923 after his fall from influence in Irish nationalist circles, William O'Brien described the AOH as 'a Catholic Orangeism in green paint'[18] (see Figure 34.1, p. 592). The AOH stands as a fine example of how Catholic and nationalist Irish identities were culturally transmitted and how this process was facilitated by diasporic connection. While O'Brien's tart remark was made in response to Joe Devlin's use of the organisation as his 'personal political vehicle'

---

14 T. Bueltmann, *Scottish ethnicity and the making of New Zealand society, 1850–1930* (Edinburgh, 2011), 194.
15 Ibid., 201.
16 A. McCarthy, *Scottishness and Irishness in New Zealand since 1840* (Manchester, 2011), 210.
17 E. Kaufmann, 'The Orange Order in Ontario, Newfoundland, Scotland and Northern Ireland: a macro-social analysis', in D. Wilson (ed.), *The Orange Order in Canada* (Dublin, 2007), 42–68.
18 W. O'Brien, *The Irish Revolution and how it came about* (London, 1923), 31–2, quoted in A. C. Hepburn, *Catholic Belfast and nationalist Ireland in the era of Joe Devlin 1871–1934* (Oxford, 2008), 90.

in Belfast, the AOH had a much longer pedigree as a diasporic organisation. Derived from the merging of the St Patrick's Fraternal Society of New York with Ribbonmen from Schuylkill County, Pennsylvania, the AOH was formed in New York City in 1838. Kevin Kenny argues that the AOH was a 'peaceful fraternal transatlantic outgrowth of Ribbonism rather than a violent conspiratorial one', emphasising how the violence of the Molly Maguires (long associated with the AOH) was more a product of 'local industrial conditions' in Pennsylvania. In examining its roots in the USA, Kenny emphasises the importance of local Irish links to the AOH, with most members in Pennsylvania coming from Donegal, an example of the type of translocal connection which often characterises the Irish diaspora.[19] The evolution of the AOH into a 'sort of Irish Catholic freemasonry combining nostalgia with benevolence'[20] was marked throughout the diaspora, from the USA to Canada and England, and in all locations there was a sense of 'homeland orientation'. In England, John Belchem's work on Liverpool has outlined how the AOH grew from the Liverpool Hibernian Burial Society, functioning as a 'model for the expansion of Catholic collective mutuality throughout the Irish diaspora', while also providing 'convenient cover' for continuing Ribbonist links with Ireland. Following the failed rising in 1848, the Liverpool middle classes were eager to break the link between nationalism, Ribbonism and the pub, shifting the emphasis of Irish associationalism in the city from 'bibulous conviviality, oath-taking rituals and collective mutuality to cultural nationalism'.[21] It was not until the eve of the First World War, however, that the AOH gained serious traction among the Catholic Irish community in Liverpool, benefiting first from the reunification of the organisation in 1898 and then from the National Insurance Act in 1911, which allowed the AOH to tie collective mutuality to ethnic identity. The AOH was not, however, the most significant Catholic Irish organisation in the city, as the Irish National Foresters (INF) continued to claim the allegiance of most Irish migrants: at a counter-demonstration to the Ulster Unionists' 'Ulster Day' in September 1912, the INF mustered 8,000 members, while the AOH could command just 3,000.[22]

Across the Atlantic, the AOH developed apace towards the end of the nineteenth century. Following its reunification in 1898, it could boast more than 100,000 members in the USA. Tim Meagher's study of the Irish community in Worcester, Massachusetts, provides an intriguing example of how the AOH flourished during the 1890s. The first branch was formed in the city during the 1860s, drawing most of its members from

19 K. Kenny, *Making sense of the Molly Maguires* (Oxford, 1998), 17–18, 26.

20 Hepburn, *Catholic Belfast and nationalist Ireland*, 90.

21 J. Belchem, *Merseypride: essays in Liverpool exceptionalism* (Liverpool, 2000), 76, 97.

22 J. Belchem, *Irish, Catholic and Scouse: the history of the Liverpool-Irish, 1800–1939* (Liverpool, 2007), 119–20. The INF was also significant in the central belt of Scotland. See J. Bradley, 'Wearing the green: a history of nationalist demonstrations among the diaspora in Scotland', in T. G. Fraser (ed.), *The Irish parading tradition* (Basingstoke, 2000), 114–15.

semi-skilled or unskilled Irish immigrant workers. From a promising start, the organisation stalled in the face of Worcester's strident temperance culture and because its promotion of Irish ethnic culture was 'out of step with the times' in which accommodation with broader American society was key. The 1890s, however, saw a significant upturn in the fortunes of Worcester's AOH, claiming more than 2,500 members by 1901. The AOH was at the forefront of efforts to revive Irish culture, language and sport and it is here that the influence of events and ideas in Ireland is clear, in terms of inspiration, activities and personnel.[23]

The diasporic connection found in Worcester, MA, was also echoed in the activism of the AOH north of the border in Canada. Here, too, we find a combination of cultural and political revival in Ireland driving forward the cultural transmission of Irishness abroad. Formed in the 1880s, the AOH in Toronto became a 'vehicle for social respectability and Catholic devotion', cultivating an ethnic Irishness which kept a keen 'eye on Irish political developments'.[24] The AOH in Toronto, like their counterparts in Worcester, also displayed a keen sense of diasporic connection back to Ireland through their associational culture. The Toronto AOH played a key role in promoting Irish culture and language throughout Ontario. At their 1904 convention, the Toronto AOH resolved to campaign for the introduction of the Irish language into the Ontario provincial Separate Schools system.[25] Two years later, the Toronto AOH's commitment to promoting an Irish identity was underlined by the visit of the founder of the Gaelic League, Douglas Hyde. Described by Willie Jenkins as a 'diasporic beachhead of Ireland's Gaelic Revival', Hyde spoke in Massey Hall in May 1906 to a large audience, raising $1,000 towards the founding of a branch of the Gaelic League in the city.[26] The Toronto AOH also held expansive St Patrick's Day celebrations, which combined cultural expressions of Irish identity with a sense of 'due attention to the politics of the homeland'. At the beginning of the twentieth century, Toronto Hibernians invited a number of militant republican Irish-American speakers to their St Patrick's Day events, including such notable Clan na Gaelers as John T. Keating and O'Neill Ryan. However, following the renewed fortunes of the Irish Parliamentary Party in placing a Home Rule Bill at the top of the British political agenda in 1912, the Toronto AOH used the St Patrick's Day event to promote more constitutionally minded speakers. In 1912, the French-Canadian nationalist Henri Bourassa spoke to the AOH about his loyalty to both British institutions and the Catholic Church, capturing the greater ambivalence of

23 T. Meagher, *Inventing Irish America: generation, class, and ethnic identity in a New England city, 1880–1928* (Notre Dame, 2001), 170–2, 250.
24 W. Jenkins, *Between raid and rebellion: the Irish in Buffalo and Toronto, 1867–1916* (Montreal and Kingston, Ont., 2013), 298, 308.
25 R. McLaughlin, *Irish Canadian conflict and the struggle for Irish independence, 1912–1925* (Toronto, 2013), 59.
26 Jenkins, *Between raid and rebellion*, 323–4.

Canadian Irish nationalism, certainly in comparison with their brasher brothers (and sisters) in the USA.[27] For Jenkins, then, the activism of organisations such as the AOH in North America functioned as 'nodes on the global Irish diasporic map' through which Irish identity was 'made and remade at the local level'. This 'diasporic imagination', of imaginatively conceiving of their positions as migrants in a Greater British (and, arguably, a 'Greater Irish') world who had meaningful connections to both their homeland and other diasporan Irish throughout the globe, can be traced through the AOH, through their promotion of an Irish associational culture which helped migrants sustain their sense of Irishness.[28]

The decline of Irish diasporic associationalism following the First World War led to a realignment of Irish ethnic activism away from overt politics and cultural politics to a variety of 'softer' forms of expressing Irish identity. During the post-Second World War boom in Irish migration to Britain, Irish associational culture flourished in the cities and towns of England and Scotland. In particular, Irish dance halls became a very popular way of socialising for Irish migrants during the 1950s and 1960s, with clubs such as the Shamrock in Birmingham functioning as a hub of communal Irish migrant life. As Enda Delaney argues, these Irish dance halls were 'the place to meet potential Irish spouses, catch up on the news from home, chat with friends, or simply have some fun in the reassuring company of fellow migrants'.[29] In her research on Irish nurses in post-war Britain, Louise Ryan details how the dance halls of the Holloway Road became particular sites for the construction of Irish identities in London. Maura, one of the Irish nurses interviewed, talked about the Tower club, where 'all the Irish went', despite the warnings of her 'very English' matron about the 'roughness' of such an Irish space.[30] Equally, county associations were important in providing spaces in which Irish migrants could articulate a sense of identity. Here, though, the local and regional identities of these Irish migrants were emphasised, indicating how diasporic connection could be tethered to geographical specific locations, rather than the abstract nation state. Marc Scully has written about how an Irish county identity became an important marker of 'authenticity' among Irish migrants in Britain. In particular, Scully identifies St Patrick's Day parades as particular sites in which such translocal diasporic identities can be articulated, providing examples of the County Offaly float at the 2009 London St Patrick's Day event and its designation of politicians Brian Cowan and Barack Obama as 'Bright Intelligent Fella's [sic] From Offaly'.[31]

27 Ibid., 325.
28 Ibid., 181.
29 E. Delaney, *The Irish in post-war Britain* (Oxford, 2007), 171.
30 L. Ryan, 'Who do you think you are? Irish nurses encountering ethnicity and constructing identity in Britain', *Ethnic and Racial Studies*, 30, 3 (2007), 423.
31 M. Scully, 'BIFFOs, jackeens and Dagenham Yanks: county identity, "authenticity" and the Irish diaspora', *Irish Studies Review*, 21, 2 (2013), 144.

County associations and dance halls were all part of a broader process, then, by which the associational culture of Irish migrants lost much of its political edge over the course of the twentieth century. As Mo Moulton argues in her study of the interwar Irish in England, Irish associational activity abroad became less political and distinctly more cultural: 'The Irish Question was removed from the volatile realm of politics and reassigned to the rich interwar landscape of domestic and associational life, where Irishness could be safely reinterpreted as an enthusiasm, a heritage, or a leisure activity, rather than a public identity for which men and women would be prepared to die.'[32]

32.4. Orange Associational Culture

Much like their green counterparts, the Orange Order provided an institutional framework for the cultural transmission of Irish Protestant identities across the globe. The Orange Order began as an Irish Protestant society in rural County Armagh, following the Battle of the Diamond against the Catholic 'Defenders' on 21 September 1795. By the beginning of the nineteenth century, the organisation had consolidated its position as a loyalist, anti-Catholic bulwark against revolution in Ireland and had begun to spread across the rest of the British Isles.[33] Following the suppression of the United Irishmen rebellion in 1798, returning militiamen swiftly brought Orangeism to both Scotland and England. A year after the Irish rising, Orange lodges were formed in Maybole, Ayrshire and spread quickly to Glasgow and Argyll.[34] Further south, Manchester and Salford volunteers returned from Ireland to establish an Orange bridgehead in Lancashire, with lodges soon appearing in many of the textile towns of the north-west.[35] Across the Atlantic in Canada, a military lodge was most likely formed in Halifax as early as 1799, developing as Irish migrants settled across the frontiers of the new society.[36] From this transatlantic cultural transfer, the Orange Order soon spread to all corners of the British world (not simply limited to the boundaries of the empire), establishing, as Don MacRaild has shown, 'a palpable institutional framework for diverse loyalists: from soldiers manning colonial frontiers to migrants in Britain, Canada, the USA and Australasia.'[37] (For an example, see Figure 28.1, p. 488.)

What is intriguing about the Orange Order is that, despite being a brotherhood, the institution attracted significant numbers of women as well as men, in all parts of the

32 M. Moulton, *Ireland and the Irish in interwar England* (Cambridge, 2014), 4.
33 D. MacRaild, *Faith, fraternity and fighting: the Orange Order and Irish migrants in northern England, c.1850–1920* (Liverpool, 2005), 1–3.
34 E. McFarland, *Protestants first: Orangeism in nineteenth-century Scotland* (Edinburgh, 1990), 49; MacRaild, *Faith, fraternity and fighting*, 37.
35 MacRaild, *Faith, fraternity and fighting*, 37–9.
36 C. Houston and W. Smyth, *The sash Canada wore: a historical geography of the Orange Order in Canada* (Toronto, 1980), 16.
37 D. MacRaild, *The Irish diaspora in Britain, 1750–1939* (Basingstoke, 2011), 210.

globe. Moreover, as female lodges grew in England (from the 1850s), Canada (from the 1890s) and Scotland (from 1909), Orangewomen were just as diasporic in their thoughts, feelings and associational activity as their male counterparts. Building on Kenny's notion of diaspora with which we opened this chapter, Irish Protestant women used the associational culture of the Orange Order in a similar way, creating diasporic connections between women from the same ethnic group in different locations. In this way, diasporic connections are part of a continuum, where the social world of the migrant is shaped not only by the 'homeland' but also by the active connections that those migrants create with home. Perhaps most intriguingly, the experience of Orangewomen demonstrates how the homeland itself, and those who do not become migrants, are shaped by diaspora and are part of this diasporic continuum. Avtar Brah's concept of 'diaspora space' captures the hybrid nature of diasporic identity that connects these multiple locations. Brah suggests that in the process of the encounter and mixing of different migrant identities with those of the long-term settled, a place of settlement such as Britain becomes a diaspora space in which 'the genealogies of dispersion' are intertwined with 'those of "staying put"'.[38] My research modifies Brah's notion of diaspora space, to include those who do not become migrants. In cities such as Toronto and Glasgow, Orangewomen who do not travel are connected to their Orange sisters and brethren across the globe, making 'diaspora spaces', not because of the mixing of different migrant identities, but through the physical and imaginative connections of the Orange Order throughout the world.

The Orange Order held a distinct diasporic function and mentality, which was reflected in the organisation's role in the migration process and its members' awareness that they were part of a global, networked Orange world. MacRaild's work is important for demonstrating that Orangemen had a 'diaspora consciousness' from the mid-nineteenth century onwards, which was articulated through the Order's international Triennial Conference (established in 1865), the pages of the *Belfast Weekly News*, and through the migration process itself.[39] In particular, MacRaild notes the important role played by the *Belfast Weekly News* in creating transnational, diasporic networks that connected Orangemen across the globe. The *Belfast Weekly News* was the weekly edition of the *Belfast News-letter* and contained reports of meetings in Orange outposts throughout the world. MacRaild describes how the paper functioned as 'some kind of chatroom'[40] for Orangemen overseas during the Victorian and Edwardian periods, providing 'a vital conduit of communication between diasporic lodges and the homeland of Ireland'.[41] Orangewomen also thought diasporically and this gendered diasporic

---

38 Brah, *Cartographies of diaspora*, 209.
39 MacRaild, *Faith, fraternity and fighting*, 296.
40 Ibid., 308.
41 D. MacRaild, '"Diaspora" and "transnationalism": theory and evidence in explanation of the Irish world-wide', *Irish Economic and Social History*, 38, 1 (2006), 57.

consciousness extended well into the twentieth century and beyond the Atlantic world. While during the earlier Victorian period examined by MacRaild it is clear that Orange diasporic thinking was largely a male preserve, during the nineteenth and twentieth centuries women also shared this diasporic consciousness with their Orange brethren. Orangewomen were also keen networkers, playing a role in the migration process and in the maintenance of connections between Orange outposts. While women were not quite as prominent as Orangemen in the organisation's formal and public diasporic networks through such events as the Triennial Conference, Orangewomen in Scotland and across the British empire were equally adept as men in utilising the *Belfast Weekly News* to communicate with their Orange sisters across the globe.[42] Moreover, Orangewomen continued to think diasporically well into the twentieth century, although their sense of Irish identity underwent a similar process of transformation during this period as their counterparts in nationalist and Catholic Irish associationalism.[43]

This section concludes, then, with a couple of examples of how the Orange Order transmitted aspects of Irish identity, and how this functioned diasporically. Firstly, we can illustrate how ethnic print culture was used by Orangewomen abroad to express an aspect of their Irish Protestant identity with a song.

> I got it when I was in Tyrone,
>   And I'll get it to the last,
>   I've got it here in Glasgow,
>   And I've got it in Belfast.
> You may talk about your sporting games
>   Or anything you choose,
> But each Thursday night sure I delight
> In my 'Belfast Weekly News'.

Sister Lendrum from the women's Orange lodge in Bridgeton, in the east end of Glasgow, 'rendered this song in dashing style' at their monthly meeting in September 1913, during the height of the third Home Rule Bill crisis. While the political crisis in Ireland was foremost in their discussions that night, the social event that followed their meeting filled their Bridgeton headquarters with this song, articulating these Orangewomen's awareness that they were part of a much broader world of Orangeism. Stretching from their lodge room in Scotland, back to many Orangewomen's origins in Ireland and on to destinations throughout the British world, these women felt themselves to be part of an Orange diaspora, shaped by the material experience of migration and by the imagined community of global Orangeism.

---

42 MacRaild, *Faith, fraternity and fighting*, 308.

43 See D. A. J. MacPherson, 'Irish Protestant women and diaspora: Orangewomen in Canada, c.1890–1930', in MacPherson and Hickman, *Women and Irish diaspora identities*, 168–85.

The diasporic consciousness of Orangewomen is further demonstrated by the examples of return visits to the 'old country', often in the context of the Orange Order's Triennial Conference. Established in 1865, this event drew Orangemen and, on occasion, women from across the Orange world to key sites of Orangeism, such as Belfast, Toronto, Glasgow and other locations.[44] The Triennial Conference held in London during 1926 attracted a number of senior members of the Ladies' Orange Benevolent Association (LOBA). At a meeting of the 'Daughters of Portadown' lodge in Toronto, the Grand Mistress, Sister Kennedy, spoke fondly of her visit to the 'old country' for the Triennial, where she visited lodges in England, Scotland and Ireland and went to the Twelfth July parade in Belfast.[45] Kennedy was accompanied by her successor as Grand Mistress, Mrs Stewart Adrian, from Craik, Saskatchewan, who spoke of her official role in representing the LOBA at the London Triennial.[46] After the Triennial meeting, Adrian joined her 'Scotch brothers and sisters' for a parade on 10 July and the Twelfth celebrations in Belfast two days later.[47] The Triennial Conference meeting was, then, one of the most visible expressions of the Orange Order's diasporic nature and it is important to recognise that Canadian women took part during the 1920s and 1930s and felt connected to their Orange sisters across the globe through such an event.

32.5.   Conclusion

To return to the theme of parades with which we opened this chapter, the Orange Order's marching tradition was highly developed, and the key date in the Orange calendar — the Twelfth of July — matched (and often surpassed) St Patrick's Day as a public manifestation of Irish diasporic identity. The Orange Order's parades on the Twelfth are rather different affairs, though. They are the very public manifestation of the Orange Order's continuing relative associational strength, although attaining nowhere near the heights of the Victorian or Edwardian era when tens of thousands of Orangemen and women marched through the streets of Liverpool or Toronto. However, attempts to transform the Twelfth into a St Patrick's Day-style 'Orange Fest' have had limited effect – the element of carnival and inclusivity that largely characterise St Patrick's celebration have not translated well to an event that retains its fundamental connection to the sectarian associational culture of the Orange Order. In fact, the most recent and high-profile manifestation of Orange culture has been the pro-Union march through Edinburgh shortly before the Scottish independence referendum in 2014. The eagerness

44 For the functioning of the Triennial Council, see MacRaild, 'Networks, communication and the Irish Protestant diaspora', 317–18.
45 'Daughters of Portadown observe 11th anniversary', *Sentinel*, 30 Sept. 1926.
46 'Saskatchewan ladies elect Mrs J. L. Spence R. W. Grand Mistress', *Sentinel*, 17 Mar. 1927.
47 'M. W. Grand Mistress is honored by Toronto past Mistresses', *Sentinel*, 21 July 1927.

with which mainstream politicians distanced themselves from the parade tells us all about the continuing problems faced by Orange associational culture.

At the conclusion of the intense political debate over the position of Scotland within the Union in September 2014, Orangewomen once more played a key role in making a case for their worldview, indicating the longevity of some of the Orange, imperial and Protestant sentiments at the heart of Orange associational culture. Taking to the streets of Edinburgh in their thousands, Orangemen and Orangewomen marched to make the case for a 'No' vote in the Scottish referendum.[48] As a number of commentators remarked at the time, this seemed to be the 'last gasp of a dying empire'. Sir Tom Devine, in famously coming out as a supporter of Scottish independence, drew on recent history to argue that a British identity had been eclipsed in Scotland, not least because the institutions which had supported it — the British empire and Protestantism — no longer held their traditional sway in society.[49] However, the seemingly lost world of Orangeism on display in Edinburgh in September 2014 continued to have some relevance for sections of Scottish society, given the narrow 'No' vote. And it is this world, of Protestantism and empire, of conventional gender ideologies and women's public activism, which came to prominence through the women's Orange Order in England, Scotland and Canada between the mid-Victorian era and the beginning of the Second World War.

In both Orange and Green Irish traditions, then, associational culture has been at the heart of the cultural transmission of Irish identities abroad. Irish associational culture has been particularly adept at functioning diasporically, maintaining meaningful connections between the Irish homeland and the diasporan Irish, scattered across the globe. While the content of these diasporic connections has changed over time — with a gradual shift away from more political articulations of Irishness as the twentieth century progressed, certainly from the 1920s onwards, towards more cultural manifestations of Irishness — the way in which Irish migrants maintain diasporic identities through associational culture remains strong well into the twenty-first century.

FURTHER READING

Belchem, J. *Irish, Catholic and Scouse: the history of the Liverpool-Irish, 1800–1939* (Liverpool, 2007).

Bueltmann, T., A. Hinson and G. Morton. *The Scottish diaspora* (Edinburgh, 2013).

48 'Scottish independence: thousands of Orange Order supporters march through Edinburgh', *The Independent*, 13 Sept. 2014.

49 T. Devine, 'How history turned against Tory-voting Scotland', *The Guardian*, 14 Sept. 2014.

Cronin, M. and D. Adair. *The wearing of the green: a history of St Patrick's Day* (London, 2001).

Delaney, E. *The Irish in post-war Britain* (Oxford, 2007).

Devine, T. *To the ends of the earth: Scotland's global diaspora, 1750–2010* (Harmondsworth, 2011).

Fraser, T. (ed.). *Following the drum: the Irish parading tradition* (Basingstoke, 2000).

Gabaccia, D. *Italy's many diasporas* (London, 2003).

Gilroy, P. '"It ain't where you're from; it's where you're at …"': the dialectics of diasporic identification', *Third Text*, 5 (1991), 3–16.

Hall, S. 'Cultural identity and diaspora', in J. Rutherford (ed.), *Identity: community, culture, difference* (London, 1990), 222–38.

Harland-Jacobs, J. '"Maintaining the connexion": Orangeism in the British North Atlantic world, 1795–1844', *Atlantic Studies*, 5 (2008), 27–49.

Jenkins, W. *Between raid and rebellion: the Irish in Buffalo and Toronto, 1867–1916* (Montreal and Kingston, Ont., 2013).

Kenny, K. *The American Irish: a history* (Harlow, 2000).

Kenny, K. *Diaspora: a very short introduction* (Oxford, 2013).

MacPherson, D. A. J. and M. J. Hickman (eds.). *Women and Irish diaspora identities: theories, concepts and new perspectives* (Manchester, 2014).

MacRaild, D. *Faith, fraternity and fighting: the Orange Order and Irish migrants in northern England, c.1850–1920* (Liverpool, 2005).

MacRaild, D. *The Irish diaspora in Britain, 1750–1939* (Basingstoke, 2011).

MacRaild, D. 'Networks, communication and the Irish Protestant diaspora in northern England, c.1860–1914', *Immigrants and Minorities*, 23 (2005), 311–37.

Meagher, T. *Inventing Irish America: generation, class, and ethnic identity in a New England city, 1880–1928* (Notre Dame, 2001).

Moran, J. *Irish Birmingham: a history* (Liverpool, 2010).

Moulton, M. *Ireland and the Irish in interwar England* (Cambridge, 2014).

Mulligan, A. 'Countering exclusion: the "St Pats for All" parade', *Gender, Place and Culture*, 15, 2 (2008), 153–67.

33 Migration and Integration since 1991

Irial Glynn

33.1. Introduction

Most people associate Ireland's migration history with emigration but the country has an infrequently referenced but rich immigration history. For example, approximately 100,000 English-, Scottish- and Welsh-born people lived on the island following partition – 50,000 in the Free State and 50,000 in Northern Ireland. Around the same time, the island contained significant pockets of Litvak Jews, especially in Dublin, and smaller groups of Italians, French and German immigrants. Improvements in the Irish economy and the country's entry in to the European Economic Community (EEC) encouraged more west European immigrants to move to Ireland, with the amount of people born in the seven other EEC countries, excluding Ireland and the UK, tripling between 1971 and 1991. None the less, in comparison with other west European countries, Ireland remained a country remarkably untouched by post-war immigration.[1]

Until the 1990s, immigration to Ireland[2] consisted mostly of Irish emigrants returning home and a small number of Britons moving across the Irish Sea – often for love.[3]

This research was supported by a Marie Curie Intra-European Fellowship within the 7th European Community Framework Programme.

1 For more information about Ireland's immigration history prior to 1991, see Chapter 26 in this volume and I. Glynn, 'Returnees, forgotten foreigners and new immigrants: tracing the migratory movement into Ireland since the late nineteenth century', in N. Whelehan (ed.), *Transnational perspectives in modern Irish history: beyond the island* (London, 2015), 224–50.

2 Ireland here refers to the Republic of Ireland.

3 Pete Lunn and Tony Fahey record that 'Less than one-third of UK nationals who are in couples [in the Republic of Ireland] are partnered with other UK nationals … the majority of those who partner with other nationalities do so with Irish people – possibly, in the majority of instances, as partners or spouses of former Irish emigrants who returned to Ireland.' See P. Lunn and T. Fahey, *Households and family structures in Ireland: a detailed statistical analysis of census 2006* (Dublin, 2011), 27.

With no pressing need for foreign workers owing to a largely stagnant economy, Ireland never attracted significant numbers of immigrants after independence. Since 1991, however, the country has undergone an enormous change as it came to contain a larger proportion of immigrants than many western European states that had experienced extensive immigration for fifty years or more. By 2011, 17 per cent of the population had been born abroad while 12 per cent of the population were citizens of other countries.[4] Fewer than 55,000 people resident in the state in 1991 were born outside Ireland or the UK; by 2011 this had risen to more than 460,000.[5] Other western European states, such as Italy, Portugal and Greece, had experienced similar transitions from countries of emigration to countries of immigration but not on the same scale as Ireland. Spain, which experienced a comparable construction boom – and subsequent bust – harboured the most similarities with Ireland, but many of its immigrants came from the country's former colonies in Latin America.[6] The vast majority of Ireland's immigrant population came from other EU countries. This further distinguished Ireland from its EU counterparts, since most European states' immigrants came from outside the EU.[7] Northern Ireland also experienced a notable increase in immigration after 1991, but not to the same extent as its southern counterpart, with the percentage of the population born outside Ireland or the UK rising from 1.6 per cent in 2001 to 4.5 per cent by 2011.[8]

The first part of this chapter provides a chronological overview of the dramatic demographic changes that have taken place since 1991. Three main categories of immigrants have arrived in Ireland in the past twenty-five years: asylum seekers who applied for refugee status; non-EU migrants who entered on work, family or student visas; and EU citizens who did not require any visa to enter and stay in the country. In the late 1990s and early 2000s, asylum seekers attracted a lot of political, media and public attention because of the huge rise that occurred in annual applications and because of the responsibility that the state had towards housing these people. They represent an important feature of the immigration landscape since most applicants came from outside the EU and more than 90,000 arrived since 1991. Asylum applications began to fall in the early 2000s just as the scale of labour immigration markedly increased. Owing to the perceived need for more labour, Ireland, along with only the UK and Sweden from the 'old' EU15 member states, imposed no restrictions on citizens entering its labour force from the ten accession states that joined the EU in 2004. Whilst

4 Central Statistics Office (CSO), *This is Ireland: highlights from census 2011, part 1* (Dublin, 2012), 30.

5 Data for 1991 and 2011 come from the CSO's censuses.

6 M. Izquierdo, J. F. Jimeno and A. Lacuesta, 'Spain: from immigration to emigration?', Documentos de Trabajo 1503, Banco de España (2015).

7 See F. McGinnity, E. Quinn, G. Kingston and P. O'Connell, *Annual monitoring report on integration 2013* (Dublin, 2014), 5.

8 A. Krausova and C. Vargas-Silva, *Briefing: Northern Ireland: Census Profile* (Oxford, 2014), 4.

Sweden received modest inward migration owing to its regulated labour market and its demand for a limited amount of skilled migrant workers, the UK and Ireland played host to sustained and sizeable immigration from these new EU states.[9] The second part of the chapter examines how the island has adapted to its increasingly multicultural make-up. It charts successive governments' reluctance to introduce integration strategies and their preference instead for bestowing such tasks on schools, local authorities and NGOs. The positives, such as the absence, as yet, of any successful anti-immigration political party, will be highlighted, as will some of the negatives, such as sustained discrimination towards certain minorities, notably black immigrants. The chapter ends by briefly examining migration trends that followed the economic crisis in 2008, when Irish citizens began to emigrate in notable numbers but immigration of foreign citizens continued, albeit on a lesser scale.

33.2.   A Demographic Revolution

In 1994, Colm Tóibín published a non-fiction account of his travels around Catholic Europe.[10] In his chapter on Croagh Patrick, he described the scene in Westport on a Saturday evening in July: 'The place was full of young people and the evening was still warm … Everywhere there was a sense of plenty, of security, of ease.' Yet, Tóibín urged caution, for 'you could make the mistake that it was prosperous here; you could mistake the atmosphere in a market town on a summer's night, if you did not know that emigration had decimated Ireland in the previous five years'.[11] As described already in detail in previous chapters, the island has a long history of emigration. Economic difficulties caused extensive emigration to occur from Ireland once again in the 1980s. During the early 1990s, Ireland remained the only country in the EU15 to experience a negative net migration rate.[12] From the mid-1990s onward, by contrast, a remarkable transformation began to occur as the country experienced unprecedented immigration on the back of sustained economic growth. Many of the 1980s' generation of Irish emigrants began to return and they were increasingly joined by immigrants from around the world. Asylum seekers became the first group to capture political and public attention.

When debating the formation of a new Irish asylum policy in 1995, to replace the outdated 1935 Aliens Act, politicians adopted a remarkably progressive stance. Every party represented in the Dáil voiced its support for the formation of a compassionate

---

9 C. Devitt, 'Varieties of capitalism, variation in labour immigration', *Journal of Ethnic and Migration Studies*, 37, 4 (2011), 579–96, 588.

10 C. Tóibín, *The sign of the cross: travels in Catholic Europe* (London, 1994).

11 Ibid., 54.

12 M. Ruhs and E. Quinn, *Ireland: from rapid immigration to recession* (Washington, 2009), 2.

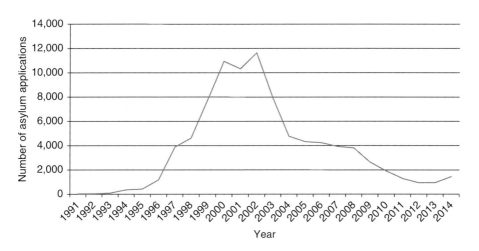

Figure 33.1 Asylum applications in Ireland, 1992–2014.
Source: Office of the Refugee Applications Commissioner.

asylum policy, with many referencing the parallels between Irish emigration and the arrival of people seeking sanctuary in Ireland. Reflecting this stance, one opposition Fianna Fáil politician remarked that the status of refugees 'should strike a chord with every man, woman and child here who has any grasp of Irish history' because of 'our history books being littered with the names and deeds of those driven from our country out of fear of persecution'.[13] Although asylum applications had increased from just thirty-one in 1991 to more than 400 by 1995, they remained remarkably low when compared with elsewhere in western Europe. But by 1997, numbers had risen almost tenfold to nearly 4,000, and they grew further to more than 10,000 by 2000 (as demonstrated in Figure 33.1). This represented a remarkable turnaround and caused bemusement in Irish society. Some of the theories put forward in the media to explain the arrival of immigrants included Ireland's growing international profile caused by successful football campaigns at consecutive World Cups, Mary Robinson's performance as president, the spread of Irish aid workers globally, the internet, the IRA ceasefire and the global diffusion of Irish pubs.[14] In the late 1990s, asylum applications actually outnumbered new work permits provided to labour migrants. A huge backlog of asylum applications began to build up as a result of a lack of state infrastructures to process applications. Later discussions on asylum never replicated the magnanimity of the 1995 debates referenced above, as Ireland attempted to put in place harsher policies commensurate with its European neighbours, especially those of the UK. Inevitably, this

13 John O'Donoghue, *Dáil Éireann*, 19 Oct. 1995, vol. 457.
14 See 'Sharp rise in the number of refugees seeking asylum', *Irish Times*, 24 May 1996; 'Only surprise is how long refugee influx has taken to happen here', *Irish Times*, 17 May 1997; 'Dublin now main target for gangs trafficking in people', *Irish Times*, 26 May 1997.

led to the imposition of a much more organised but parsimonious system whereby the state placed new applicants in accommodation centres, akin to hostels, across the country and provided them with food and a negligible weekly allowance. Asylum seekers had until then converged mainly around Ireland's largest cities but from 2000 onwards, they began to appear in suburbs, towns and villages around the country – to the chagrin of some.[15]

The new direct provision system did not lead to any notable decrease in applications. This was partly because of the inability of Irish state authorities to deport parents of an Irish child. In contrast to other EU countries, children born in Ireland then had the right to Irish citizenship from birth (discussed further below). Because of the right of the child to belong to a family, as enshrined in the constitution, the Supreme Court ruled that the foreign parents of an Irish child were 'entitled, on their children's behalf, to choose the place of residence of their minor children. As the children themselves are entitled to remain in the country of their nationality, so too may the parents lawfully choose such residence on the children's behalf.'[16] In 2001 and 2002, almost 13,000 asylum seekers applied to remain in Ireland on such a basis.[17] The state successfully challenged this position in a January 2003 Supreme Court ruling but a perceived ambiguity in that judgment caused the state to put a referendum on the matter to the public in June 2004. The 2002 Chen case at the European Court of Justice, when a Chinese couple received the right to reside in the UK because their daughter qualified for Irish citizenship on account of her birth in Belfast, also contributed to the government's efforts to close this perceived loophole.[18] The Citizenship Referendum, which the public voted in favour of comprehensively by a ratio of almost 4:1, caused the establishment of legislation that stipulated that a person born on the island of Ireland to non-Irish nationals was only entitled to citizenship if one of his/her parents had resided legally in the country for three of the previous four years.[19] As part of this change, the government decided to grant permission to reside in the country to all the parents of children born

15 See, for example, 'South-east reacts angrily to prospect of a sudden influx of asylum-seekers', *Irish Times*, 8 Apr. 2000; 'Most refugees "hoodlums" says Healy-Rae's son', *Irish Independent*, 15 Apr. 2000; 'Suspected arson at hotel blocks refugees' arrival', *Irish Independent*, 26 Apr. 2000; 'Ballsbridge challenge to refugees centre back in court this week', *Irish Times*, 24 Apr. 2000.

16 *Fajujoni v. Minister for Justice*, Supreme Court, 8 Dec. 1989. Taken from D. Cubie and F. Ryan, *Immigration, refugee and citizenship law in Ireland: cases and materials* (Dublin, 2004), 255–6.

17 See John O'Donoghue, Dáil Éireann, vol. 549, 21 Feb. 2002 and Michael McDowell, Dáil Éireann, vol. 584, 5 May 2004.

18 See *Kunqian Catherine Zhu and Man Lavette Chen v. Secretary of State for the Home Department*, European Court of Justice, 19 Oct. 2004 for more details.

19 Section 6A(1) Irish Nationality and Citizenship Act 2004; see also J. Handoll, 'Ireland', in R. Bauböck, E. Ersbøll, K. Groenendijk and H. Waldrauch (eds.), *Acquisition and loss of nationality, vol. II: country analyses* (Amsterdam, 2006), 289–328, 311.

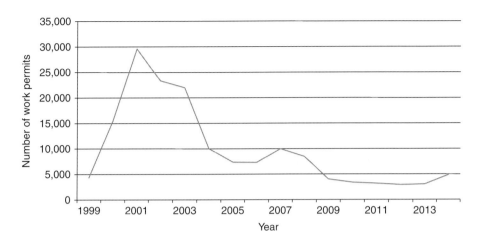

Figure 33.2 New work permits issued in Ireland, 1999–2014.
Source: Department of Jobs, Enterprise and Innovation.

in Ireland by 31 December 2004. Consequently, nearly 16,700 asylum seekers received leave to remain on this basis.[20]

Asylum became less prominent throughout the 2000s – partly as a consequence of decreasing annual asylum applications, but mostly because of the incredible volume of economic immigration that took place throughout the decade, which effectively dwarfed asylum figures. In a similar fashion to what had happened in various western European states during the 1950s and 1960s, Ireland's enormous intake of immigrants occurred mostly as a direct response to an acute shortage of labour generated by conditions of rapid domestic economic growth. The amount of people in employment, for example, rose from approximately 1.5 million in 1996 to over 2 million just ten years later. Unemployment dropped from more than 15 per cent in 1993 to just above 4 per cent by 2000.

Until 2003, local employers could essentially recruit as many non-EU workers as they wished, from whatever countries they wanted, and for any job, regardless of the skill level required.[21] With no 'mother-country' ties to former colonies, Ireland received migrants from an enormous range of countries. None the less, Europeans from non-EU countries dominated. The top seven countries for work permits in 2002, for instance, consisted of, in order, Latvia, Lithuania, the Philippines, Poland, Romania, South Africa and Ukraine.[22] Approximately three of four work permits were for low-skilled

20 See Michael McDowell, Dáil Éireann, vol. 622, 27 June 2006.
21 M. Ruhs, *Managing the immigration and employment of non-EU nationals in Ireland*, Studies in Public Policy (Dublin, 2005), xii.
22 Calculated from the Department of Jobs, Enterprise and Innovation statistics.

and low-paid jobs.[23] The services sector, particularly catering, dominated the figures. Permits for the agriculture industry also featured prominently. Health-care workers, many of whom came in the form of nurses and carers from the Philippines, comprised a significant part of the breakdown. The number of new work permits issued annually rose rapidly after 1999 before decreasing markedly, especially from 2004 onward owing to the welcome afforded to citizens of the ten states that joined the EU that year (see Figure 33.2).

In 2002, only approximately 8,000 nationals from the ten countries due to join the EU in 2004 officially resided in Ireland.[24] What occurred following the accession of these states on 1 April 2004 marked the most significant demographic transformation in the modern history of the state. Between 2004 and 2007, almost 400,000 people from the EU10 registered to work in Ireland.[25] Many arrived with the goal of earning and saving money for better futures for themselves and their families at home, but a substantial number remained, with the amount of immigrants resident in the state almost doubling between 2002 and 2006.

Migrants from Poland, the largest new EU member state, featured most prominently amongst newcomers. Indeed, more came from Poland than from all the nine other new EU member states combined. Immigration from EU15 countries also rose in the same period, but it remained minuscule compared with the inflow from the accession states. By 2006, for example, roughly the same number of Lithuanians lived in Ireland as Germans, French and Italians combined – the three EU15 countries with the largest immigrant populations in Ireland at the time, excluding the UK.[26] The UK immigrant population did rise in the 2000s, but only by 8.5 per cent between 2002 and 2011, whereas the number of Poles went from approximately 2,000 to more than 122,000 in the same period to overtake British citizens as the largest immigrant group in the country (see Figure 33.3). Although Ireland did not open up its labour market to Romania and Bulgaria on their accession to the EU in 2007, by 2011 more than 17,000 Romanians resided in the country.[27]

As a result of Ireland's liberal labour policy for citizens of the 'EU10', its work permit scheme for non-EU citizens became more selective from 2003 onward. Various occupational categories became ineligible for permits, including many construction-related jobs, and employers were encouraged to give preference to migrant workers from the accession states.[28] While some countries saw a drop in permits, such as South Africa

---

23 Ruhs, *Managing the immigration and employment of non-EU nationals in Ireland*, xii.
24 Calculated from figures presented in CSO, *Census 2011 profile 6: migration and diversity* (Dublin, 2012), 7.
25 Calculated from CSO, *Foreign nationals: PPSN allocations, employment and social welfare activity, 2009* (Dublin, 2011), 4.
26 See CSO, *Census 2011 profile 6: migration and diversity*, 7.
27 Ibid.
28 Ruhs and Quinn, 'Ireland: from rapid immigration to recession'.

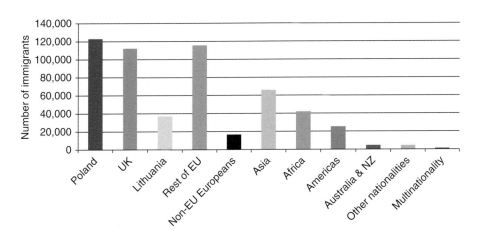

Figure 33.3 Immigrants in Ireland by nationality, 2011.
Source: CSO.

and European countries outside the EU, others saw notable rises, such as Brazil and especially India, the latter of which became the top non-European country for work permits ahead of the Philippines. None the less, significant numbers came in other forms, such as student migrants. Additionally, in a similar manner to what occurred with those from the EU10, immigrants from outside the EU began to put down roots in Ireland through family reunification.

The onset of the economic recession in late 2008 encouraged some migrants to leave. Nevertheless, in a similar vein to what happened with immigrants in western European countries in the 1970s following the oil price shocks, most immigrants chose to remain in the country. Consequently, Ireland's immigrant population continued to rise, albeit not on the same scale as the years immediately after the expansion of the EU. Nevertheless, the number of people entering the country in 2014 matched the figure for 2003 (see Figure 33.4).

Unbeknown to many residents, Belfast has housed a substantial number of Chinese, Indian and Pakistani migrants since the 1960s.[29] But Northern Ireland did not go through the same dramatic demographic change as the Republic of Ireland after 1991. The persistence of hostilities, a stuttering economy and the fact that a quarter of third-level students attended university in Britain (with most not returning) meant that Northern Ireland's net migration remained negative throughout the 1990s.[30] Following

29 A. Lee, "'Are you a Catholic Chinese or a Protestant Chinese?'": Belfast's ethnic minorities and the sectarian divide', *City: Analysis of Urban Trends, Culture, Theory, Policy, Action*, 18, 4–5 (2014), 476–87.
30 See figures contained in J. Devlin Trew, *Leaving the north: migration and memory, Northern Ireland, 1921–2011* (Liverpool, 2013), 31. For more about student migration from Northern Ireland, see K. Purcell, P. Elias, R. Davies and N. Walton, *Northern Ireland's graduates: the classes of '95 and '99* (Belfast, 2005).

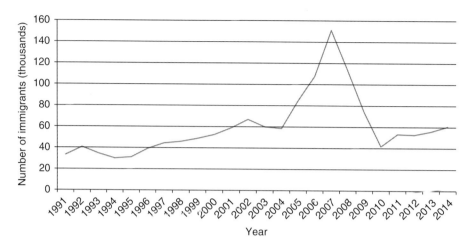

Figure 33.4 Immigration to Ireland, 1991–2014 (in thousands)
Source: CSO, Annual Population and Migration Estimates.

the signing of the Good Friday Agreement in Belfast in 1998, the return of peace to Northern Ireland led to an improving economy and the slow but sustained inflow of immigrants. The food-processing industry began to recruit Portuguese workers and hospitals began to hire nurses from India and the Philippines.[31] The entry of the accession state countries in 2004 resulted in more extensive immigration taking place. Between 2001 and 2011, the size of the population born outside the UK or Ireland increased almost threefold, from 27,226 to 81,314. After the UK and Ireland, the most common country of birth of residents in 2011 was Poland, with nearly 20,000 residents, followed by Lithuania.[32] Northern Ireland did not experience comparable economic growth to England or the Republic of Ireland during the 2000s and therefore did not receive a comparable inflow of immigrants. Despite not feeling the effects of the financial crisis as starkly as the southern part of the island, its rate of immigration has remained relatively low in recent years.[33]

33.3.   Integration in Ireland

The island of Ireland has experienced significant changes in the past twenty-five years. Peace returned after thirty bloody years. The power of the Catholic Church diminished considerably as a result of continuous sexual abuse scandals and increasing

31 R. Russell, *Migration in Northern Ireland: an update*, NI Assembly Research and Information Service research paper (Belfast, 2012).
32 Krausova and Vargas-Silva, 'Northern Ireland: census profile', 4.
33 'Northern Ireland's rate of immigrant arrivals is lowest in UK', *Belfast Telegraph*, 9 Aug. 2013.

secularisation. Unprecedented economic growth in the Republic of Ireland from the mid-1990s to 2007 was followed by an extraordinary economic collapse that brought about a temporary loss of sovereignty. During the same period, extensive immigration resulted in the formation of a more ethnically, racially, nationally, linguistically and religiously diverse island than ever before. In contrast to the situation in many west European states, immigrants in Ireland have come from an extensive variety of states and have settled throughout the country, not just in the major cities. But how have these newcomers 'integrated'? That is, have immigrants been able to participate in society at the same level as native citizens?

Eugenio Biagini and Andrew Holmes have already outlined in this volume that Ireland contained a number of minorities before the 1990s, most notably Protestants, Jews and Travellers (see Chapters 6 and 26). Many of these groups experienced discrimination at times.[34] Identity-based opposition and resource-based opposition also emerged after 1991 in relation to immigrants, particularly towards asylum seekers. One study published at the end of 2000 found that approximately two-thirds of asylum seekers experienced racism, rising to 87 per cent among black asylum seekers.[35] Another contemporary survey found that, when questioned, a large group of Irish teenagers felt that well-dressed asylum seekers and refugees abused the Irish welfare system or pursued criminal activities.[36] The decision to place asylum seekers in Direct Provision and provide them with a small weekly allowance (€19.50 a week for an adult and €9.10 for a child, which remained the same from 2000 to 2015) caused further difficulties. According to the sociologist Steve Loyal, asylum seekers became Ireland's most disempowered social group, lacking the right to work and proper access to education and training: 'Their presence marks the nadir of the putative values of the Celtic Tiger: they are marginalised, excluded, poor and, in many respects, they lack freedom.'[37] One legal scholar claimed that Ireland's asylum practices contravened international and European law.[38] The Irish Ombudsman in 2013 also highlighted the problems caused by asylum seekers frequently having to live for prolonged periods in poor quality

34 For more general information about the discrimination of minorities in Irish history, see R. Lentin and R. McVeigh (eds.), *Racism and anti-racism in Ireland* (Belfast, 2002); B. Fanning, *Racism and social change in the Republic of Ireland* (Manchester, 2012); B. Rolston and M. Shannon, *Encounters: how racism came to Ireland* (Belfast, 2002).

35 S. Casey and M. O'Connell, 'Pain and prejudice: assessing the experience of racism in Ireland', in M. MacLachlan and M. O'Connell (eds.), *Cultivating pluralism: psychological, social and cultural perspectives on a changing Ireland* (Dublin, 2000), 19–48.

36 A. Keogh, 'Talking about the other: a view of how secondary school pupils construct opinion about refugees and asylum seekers', in MacLachlan and O'Connell, *Cultivating pluralism*, 123–36.

37 S. Loyal, 'Welcome to the Celtic Tiger: racism, immigration and the State', in C. Coulter and S. Colman (eds.), *The end of Irish history? Critical reflections on the Celtic Tiger* (Manchester, 2003), 74–94, at 79.

38 C. Breen, 'The policy of Direct Provision in Ireland: a violation of asylum seekers' right to an adequate standard of housing', *International Journal of Refugee Law*, 20, 4 (2008), 611–36.

accommodation, arguing that it was 'damaging to the health, welfare and life-chances of those who must endure them'.[39]

The first large-scale representative survey of immigrants' experiences of racism in Ireland, carried out in 2005, found that asylum seekers experienced more discrimination than work permit holders. It also revealed that black Africans, most of whom came to Ireland originally as asylum seekers, 'experienced a particularly high level of racial harassment on the street and in public transport, relative to other migrants'. North Africans, Asians and Europeans from outside the EU experienced much lower levels of discrimination.[40] A 2011 Immigrant Council of Ireland report confirmed the greater likelihood of black respondents to be subject to racist violence, harassment and anti-social behaviour than other groups.[41]

Irish governments have occasionally put in place measures to combat the growth of racism. In 1998, the National Consultative Committee on Racism and Interculturalism (NCCRI) was established to promote anti-racism and dialogue between state actors and immigrant organisations. In early 2001 the government established a public awareness programme, the Know Racism campaign, to address racism and endeavour to promote a more inclusive society. The NCCRI later helped to prepare the National Action Plan against Racism (2005–8), which was designed to provide strategic direction to combat racism and develop a more inclusive and intercultural society in Ireland. Under the plan, support was provided for the development of a number of national and local strategies promoting greater integration in the workplace, the police service, the health service, the education system, the arts and within local authorities.

In 2006, the National Economic and Social Council (NESC) released the first major official state publication examining the effects of immigration on Ireland. The report argued that 'the main role of national or state governments in respect of integration should be to exercise policy leadership'.[42] The report provided five critical guidelines to help improve Ireland's integration policies, in which it advised the government to: create a compelling rationale for immigration; establish complementary policies to further integration; expand the capacity of local government agencies and NGOs to 'plan, organise and deliver integration services'; privilege social interaction over common values; and focus on a long-term strategy for immigration.[43]

39 E. O'Reilly, *Studies* 102, No.406 (Summer 2013).
40 F. McGinnity, P. J. O'Connell, E. Quinn and J. William, *Migrants' experience of racism and discrimination in Ireland* (Dublin, 2006), 64.
41 Immigrant Council of Ireland, *Taking racism seriously: migrants' experiences of violence, harassment and anti-social behaviour in the Dublin area* (Dublin, 2011). See also Fanning, *Racism and social change in the Republic of Ireland*, 212.
42 NESC, *Managing migration in Ireland: a social and economic analysis* (Dublin, 2006), 173.
43 Ibid., 171–3.

Following the general election in May 2007, a new 'Programme for Government' document contained a number of commitments related to the suggestions put forward in the 2006 NESC report and incorporated the Common Basic Principles of Integration agreed at EU level. These included plans to develop a national integration policy and to establish a junior ministry in charge of integration. In 2008, the newly established Minister of State for Integration launched an important report entitled *Migration nation*. Drawing on Ireland's emigration past, the minister, Conor Lenihan, affirmed that Ireland had a 'unique moral, intellectual and practical capability to adapt to the experience of inward migration'. He noted that the key challenge facing the government and Irish society was 'the imperative to integrate people of much [*sic*] different culture, ethnicity, language and religion so that they become the new Irish citizens of the 21st century'.[44] The report once again demonstrated the state's adoption of an intercultural approach to immigration rather than a multicultural one; that is, the report called for continual dialogue and interaction between immigrant groups and the Irish state to create unity and effectuate successful integration.[45]

Migration nation envisaged, amongst other aims, the establishment of: (1) a pathway to citizenship for immigrants; (2) funding to support diversity strategies for local authorities; (3) enhanced legislative measures to tackle discrimination; (4) new structures to promote integration; and (5) more targeted support for dealing with diversity in schools, especially language support.[46] Unfortunately, many of these plans were scuppered by the economic crisis that took hold later that same year. As the state grappled to cope with the fallout from the various economic and social problems resulting from the effects of the crisis, many of the suggested integration proposals were abandoned. The government closed the NCCRI in late 2008, leading to, in Bryan Fanning's opinion, 'a policy leadership vacuum in driving institutional responsiveness to racism'.[47] The Cross-Departmental Group on Migrant Integration, established in early 2008 and comprising senior civil servants, met only sporadically after its inception. The new government that came to power in February 2011 abolished the state ministry for integration and in its place founded the Office for the Promotion of Migrant Integration, attached to the Department of Justice and Equality but with a cross-departmental mandate. The 2012 Annual Monitoring Report recommended that the Office 'should be funded and

44 Office of the Minister for Integration, *Migration nation: statement on integration strategy and diversity management* (Dublin, 2008), 7–8.
45 It is no accident that 'intercultural' appears twelve times in the report but 'multicultural' fails to warrant a mention. Meer and Modood argue that instead of interculturalism 'being positively contrasted with multiculturalism', it should actually be considered 'as complementary to multiculturalism'. See N. Meer and T. Modood, 'How does interculturalism contrast with multiculturalism?', *Journal of Intercultural Studies*, 33, 2 (2012), 175–96 for further details.
46 Office of the Minister for Integration, *Migration nation*, 9.
47 Fanning, *Racism and social change in the Republic of Ireland*, 234.

empowered to play a more active role in the co-ordination of integration in Ireland'.[48] However, that same office suffered substantial cuts in subsequent funding reductions.

The *Migration nation* report underlined the importance that local authorities and NGOs had for providing services to immigrants. In recent years, most Irish local authorities have published integration strategies. As a consequence of extensive consultation, often through various community and ethnic focus groups, increasing emphasis began to be placed on providing language training, access to employment, education and health care, and there was a real impetus to put in place strategies that would result in joint community participation between immigrants and Irish people and groups.[49] But local authorities have also been hit hard by substantial decreases in state funding for integration measures since the onset of the recession. In 2010, local authorities received more than €1.2 million to promote integration measures, but this fell dramatically in 2011 to just over €180,000 and remained less than €200,000 in 2014.[50] NGOs have faced an analogous predicament. State funding for migrant-related NGOs fell from €2.8 million in 2008 to less than €1 million by 2013. Similarly, the amount of state funding provided for sports bodies, whose importance was continually underlined in *Migration nation*, has fallen from more than half a million in 2008 to just €35,000 in 2013.[51] Simultaneously, a number of prominent philanthropic organisations, most notably Atlantic Philanthropies and the One Foundation, also slowly started to pull out of the sector after years of extremely generous support.

The only notable change in integration policy that occurred since the economic crisis was the marked increase in non-EU nationals attaining Irish citizenship through naturalisation. Between February 2011 and April 2015, 85,000 immigrants became Irish citizens.[52] They became naturalised at one of the many citizenship ceremonies introduced by the Fine Gael–Labour coalition in June 2011, in which large numbers of participants took a symbolic oath of fidelity to the Irish nation and loyalty to the Irish state. Previously, successful applicants had received their citizenship certificate in the District Court. Thousands of Irish-born children with foreign parents also gained Irish citizenship, particularly before 2004 because of the stipulation in the Irish constitution,

48 F. McGinnity, E. Quinn, G. Kingston and P. J. O'Connell, *Annual Monitoring Report on Integration 2012* (Dublin, 2013), 2.
49 See, for example, Clare County Council, *Strategy for the coordination of services to the immigrant communities in County Clare: strategic actions 2009–2012* (Ennis, 2009); Kerry County Development Board, *Kerry integration strategy 2010–2012* (Tralee, 2010); Limerick Integration Working Group, *Integrating Limerick: integration plan 2010–2012 for Limerick City and County* (Limerick, 2010); F. O'Reilly et al., *County Monaghan: A profile of cultural diversity* (Monaghan, 2010).
50 McGinnity et al., *Annual monitoring report on integration 2013*, 16.
51 Ibid.
52 Speech by Aodhán Ó Ríordáin TD, Minister of State with responsibility for New Communities, Culture and Equality, Citizenship Ceremony, Dublin, 10 April 2015.

amended after the Good Friday Agreement, that it was 'the entitlement and birthright of every person born in the island of Ireland, which includes its islands and seas, to be part of the Irish nation'.[53] As previously noted, the 2004 Citizenship Referendum rescinded this right as Ireland became a country of *jus sanguinis* rather than *jus soli*. Nevertheless, thousands of migrants had claimed Irish citizenship for their children before the referendum, resulting in the establishment of mixed Irish nationality households, that is, families and households containing Irish citizens and citizens from elsewhere: 77 per cent of Nigerian households and approximately 50 per cent of Filipino households, for example, contained at least one Irish national in 2011.[54] Households containing citizens from the EU, in contrast, rarely included Irish citizens, presumably because EU citizenship confers many of the same rights that come with Irish citizenship. Ireland has received significant praise for its active citizenship policy from the European Integration Monitor.[55] Its performance under the other three core indicators used to assess integration in the EU as set out in the Zaragoza Declaration – education, employment and social inclusion – was more mixed.

The make-up of children attending Irish schools has changed enormously in recent times. Most schools in Ireland had been divided along religious lines, with Catholics going to Catholic schools and Protestants attending Church of Ireland schools. But over a short period of time, Irish schools came to contain children from religiously, ethnically and culturally diverse backgrounds. The state's main reaction to such a transformation was to provide language-support teachers to help non-native English speaking immigrants to adapt to the classroom as quickly as possible.[56] Considering that immigrants whose first language is not English scored significantly lower in some of the OECD's PISA indicators than Irish students in 2009, but improved substantially in 2012, the Department of Education's focus is understandable and appears to be leading to significant improvements.[57]

Apart from these initiatives, the state has taken a backseat with regard to how schools manage their more heterogeneous environment, encouraging individual schools to decide how best to adapt to their new compositions.[58] As a result, many teachers and schools have continued to communicate predominantly 'Catholic, white and Gaelic' curriculums and have failed to 'recognise and acknowledge the new expressions of

---

53 Article 2, Constitution of Ireland 1937 (as amended by the Nineteenth Amendment to the Constitutions Act 1998).

54 Calculated from figures presented in CSO, *Census 2011 profile 6: migration and diversity*, 17.

55 McGinnity *et al.*, *Annual monitoring report on integration 2013*, iii.

56 K. Kitching, 'An excavation of the racialised politics of viability underpinning education policy in Ireland', *Irish Educational Studies*, 29, 3 (2010), 213–29, at 220.

57 McGinnity *et al.*, *Annual monitoring report on integration 2013*, 31–3.

58 D. Devine, 'Welcome to the Celtic Tiger? Teacher responses to immigration and increasing ethnic diversity in Irish schools', *International Studies in Sociology of Education* 15, 1 (2005), 49–70, at 65–6.

race, culture and religion' in their classrooms.[59] This was particularly true for schools based in certain areas of Dublin. Although immigrants represented approximately one in ten students in Irish schools in 2013, four out of five children from immigrant backgrounds were concentrated in less than a quarter of the state's primary schools, raising concerns about possible ethnic segregation.[60] The heaviest concentration of immigrants in Dublin was in the inner city and the north-west suburbs around Blanchardstown.[61] This was largely due to these areas containing a surplus of private rented accommodation at affordable prices, since only approximately a quarter of immigrants lived in dwellings owned by their households (whereas more than three-quarters of Irish citizens lived in properties owned by their households).[62] According to Fahey and Fanning, the clustering of immigrants in certain areas of Dublin might not be all negative. Instead of causing increased social-spatial inequality, the build-up of large groups of immigrants in certain deprived areas has provided a social lift to these areas. It has also resulted in an improvement in the education profile of these areas because of the impressive human capital that many immigrants had on arrival.[63]

In relation to employment, immigrants earned substantially less than their Irish peers, most notably those from the newer EU member states.[64] Immigrants also experienced significant discrimination in recruitment.[65] In addition, immigrants were harder hit by the crisis than Irish citizens in terms of job losses, with unemployment rates higher for newcomers than natives, although by late 2014 the gap between the two had declined to roughly pre-crisis rates (see Figure 33.5). Nevertheless, this does not tell the full story. Certain immigrants had lower unemployment rates than Irish citizens, most notably EU15 nationals, excluding those from the UK. Other immigrant groups had considerably higher unemployment rates, however, such as UK citizens and those from the newer EU states. This may be because the sectors in which these immigrants worked, such as the services industry and construction, felt the brunt of the consumer decline and building collapse that followed the economic downturn in 2008. Yet it also highlights that certain migrants were 'in less favourable labour market

59 M. Parker-Jenkins and M. Masterson, 'No longer "Catholic, white and Gaelic": schools in Ireland coming to terms with cultural diversity', *Irish Educational Studies* 32, 4 (2013), 477–92.
60 'Census figures raise concerns of ethnic segregation in schools', *Irish Times*, 25 Feb. 2015.
61 T. Fahey and B. Fanning, 'Immigration and socio-spatial segregation in Dublin, 1996–2006', *Urban Studies* 32, 4 (2010), 1625–42, at 1633.
62 McGinnity *et al.*, *Annual monitoring report on integration 2013*, 41.
63 Fahey and Fanning, 'Immigration and socio-spatial segregation in Dublin, 1996–2006', 1641.
64 A. Barrett, S. McGuinness and M. O'Brien, 'The immigrant earnings disadvantage across the earnings and skills distributions: the case of immigrants from the EU's new member states', *British Journal of Industrial Relations* 50, 3 (2012), 457–81.
65 F. McGinnity, J. Nelson, P. Lunn and E. Quinn, *Discrimination in recruitment: evidence from a field experiment* (Dublin, 2009).

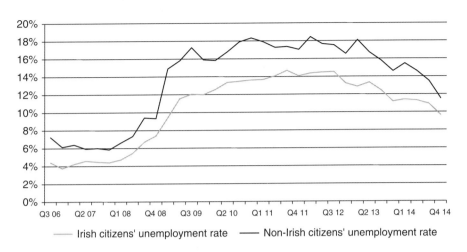

Figure 33.5 Percentage of labour market unemployed by nationality, 2006–14.
Source: CSO.

situations in the period before the recession' than their Irish counterparts.[66] What stands out, however, is the rate of joblessness of African citizens resident in Ireland, with the European Integration Monitor recording that almost 30 per cent of Africans in the labour force were unemployed in early 2013 – more than double the rate of Irish citizens.[67] Presumably, this has since reduced as a result of the upturn in economic fortunes that Ireland experienced from 2013 onward, but it still raises critical questions about racism, discrimination and social inclusion.

Some potentially positive developments have emerged in recent years. The *Irish Human Rights and Equality Commission Act* (2014) established the Irish Human Rights and Equality Commission, an independent body to replace the dissolved Equality Authority and the Irish Human Rights Commission. In the same year, the government instigated a cross-departmental review of Ireland's integration strategy, led by the Office for the Promotion of Migrant Integration. The results of this review are eagerly awaited but considering some of the delays and problems that have emerged in the 2000s relating to the state's attitude to integration, it remains unclear how successful this new initiative will be. The authors of the *Annual monitoring report on integration*, however, were under no illusions as to the urgency for action: '[T]he Government needs to name integration as an important objective of its economic and social policies, rather than deferring dialogue until such a time as large-scale problems evolve.'[68]

---

66 A. Barrett and E. Kelly, 'The impact of Ireland's recession on the labour market outcomes of its immigrants', *European Journal of Population/Revue européenne de démographie*, 28, 1 (2012), 91–111, at 93.
67 McGinnity *et al.*, *Annual monitoring report on integration 2013*, 21.
68 McGinnity *et al.*, *Annual monitoring report on integration 2012*, 2.

On a more positive note, Ireland still lacks an anti-immigration political party. In February 2002 all the major Irish parliamentary parties agreed to sign an anti-racism election protocol, which forbade the use of racist material or remarks by candidates and party workers and demanded sensibility in discussing race-related issues.[69] The signing of the anti-racism protocol by all of the main political parties meant that the subject of immigration rarely made its way into pre-election discussions. Anti-immigration political candidates, such as Áine Ní Chonaill of the Immigration Control Platform, failed miserably to garner votes in the 1997 and 2002 elections.[70] Eoin O'Malley has posited that Sinn Féin is the Irish party that most closely resembles anti-immigration parties in Europe in terms of its nationalist, populist and authoritarian characteristics. But it remains resolutely leftist and pro-immigrant, partly because it represents a minority constituency in Northern Ireland that has itself suffered considerable discrimination.[71]

Northern Ireland, despite having a much smaller concentration of immigrants than the Republic of Ireland, has encountered much more worrying instances of racism and discrimination. Hainsworth noted in 1998 that there had been a 'tendency to neglect, ignore or minimise the problems experienced by ethnic minorities in the province' due to the concentration on ending the Troubles.[72] This came to the fore as peace returned to Northern Ireland and the number of immigrants slowly increased. Continuous racist incidents in the 2000s resulted in Northern Ireland being unenviably referred to by some international media outlets as 'the racist capital of Europe'.[73] In 2009, international attention returned to Northern Ireland after a hundred Roma evacuated their south Belfast homes after suffering repeated intimidation.[74] The Northern Ireland government's 2005 *Racial equality strategy* plainly failed and the subsequent inability of the two largest political parties, the Democratic Unionist Party and Sinn Féin, to agree a joint policy to tackle the matter 'allowed government departments and agencies to evade their responsibilities in a public policy vacuum'.[75] Pointedly, Knox has argued that the Northern Ireland 'government must face up to the fact that locating migrant workers in working-class loyalist areas has merely provided an opportunity for *sectarian* gangs to engage in *racist* hate crime, a "transferable skill"'.[76]

---

69 'Dáil parties sign election protocol against racism', *Irish Times*, 8 Feb. 2002.

70 Interestingly, Ní Chonaill initially also wanted to reduce the amount of British and German nationals buying holiday homes in Ireland. See 'Candidate warns on effect of migrant influx', *Irish Times*, 27 May 1997 and 'Anti-immigrant candidates perform poorly', *Irish Times*, 20 May 2002.

71 E. O'Malley, 'Why is there no radical right party in Ireland?', *West European Politics* 31, 5 (2008), 960–77, at 974; cf. S. Garner, 'Ireland and immigration: explaining the absence of the far right', *Patterns of Prejudice* 41, 2 (2007), 109–30.

72 P. Hainsworth, *Divided society: ethnic minorities and racism in Northern Ireland* (London, 1998), 3, quoted in C. Knox, 'Tackling racism in Northern Ireland: "the race hate capital of Europe"', *Journal of Social Policy*, 40 (2011), 387–412.

73 'Race hate on rise in NI', *BBC News Online*, 13 Jan. 2004.

74 H. McDonald, 'Belfast Romanians rehoused after race attacks', *The Guardian*, 17 June 2009.

75 Knox, 'Tackling racism in Northern Ireland', 409.

76 Ibid., 410, emphasis in original.

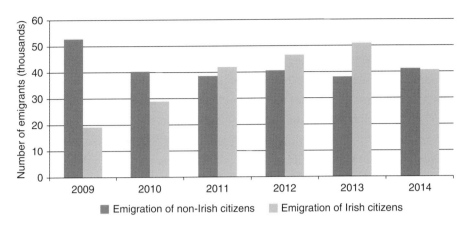

Figure 33.6 Emigration by nationality, 2009–14 (in thousands).
Source: CSO.

33.4. Mixed Migration

In the aftermath of the 2008 recession and mounting unemployment, extensive emigration returned to Ireland. In contrast to previous emigration, almost half of the people
leaving the country post-crisis were foreign citizens – something that did not happen
previously because Ireland was not host to such a diverse population (see Figure 33.6).
Indeed, sizeable immigration and extensive emigration have taken place simultaneously, resulting in Ireland becoming a country of mixed migration. Irish emigrants
went to a much more diverse range of countries than in the 1950s or the 1980s, with
Australia, Canada and the Gulf States attracting significant portions of those leaving. These emigrants were also more skilled than their earlier counterparts, as well
as their peers who stayed.[77] By contrast, those who did not complete their secondary
school education or attain an equivalent qualification were significantly underrepre-
sented among emigrants when compared with the Irish population within the same
age cohorts.

It remains difficult to determine whether recent emigration by Irish citizens has been
to Ireland's advantage or disadvantage. In the short term, emigration seems to have
benefited the Irish economy. While 47 per cent of Irish emigrants in recent years had
full-time jobs prior to leaving, 53 per cent were unemployed, underemployed or recent
graduates, and most would presumably have been in search of full-time employment
had they remained.[78] Therefore, emigration helped to substantially reduce national

77 I. Glynn, 'Just one of the "PIIGS" or a European outlier? Studying Irish emigration from a comparative perspective', *Irish Journal of Sociology* 23, 2 (2015), 93–113.
78 I. Glynn, T. Kelly and P. Mac Éinrí, *Irish emigration in an age of austerity* (Cork, 2013), 40.

unemployment figures and, consequently, the payment of social protection. This was particularly true for those previously employed in the construction industry, who made up 17 per cent of recent Irish emigrants. Yet there are various societal factors at stake that are somewhat underplayed in the economics literature. There may be economic gains but simultaneous societal losses. Moving may prove advantageous to migrants but not to their families and communities left behind. One nationally representative study, for instance, found that 'depressive symptoms and feelings of loneliness increase among the parents of migrant children', particularly among mothers.[79] The long-term effects for the state remain unclear and may depend on what proportion of emigrants return in the near future.

Skilled migrants might return with much needed capital, dynamism and experience garnered abroad that should benefit the economy and society. Or they might not. Ireland's economic situation and the availability of jobs were the two most common factors that influenced the chances of emigrants returning home, according to one survey.[80] By 2014, the Irish economy was growing at a faster rate than any other country in the EU and at more than three times the European average.[81] In 2015, unemployment dropped to less than 10 per cent for the first time since late 2008. If the Irish economy continues to improve, emigration may decrease and the number of people returning may rise, as occurred during the late 1990s and early 2000s, when large numbers of emigrants who had left in the 1980s moved back.

33.5.   Conclusion

In contrast to most of the other contributions to this volume, this chapter has provided an overview of a relatively contemporary development, the long-term effects of which are still uncertain. Immigrants have spread far and wide across Irish cities, towns and villages. In 2011, they comprised more than 10 per cent of the population in the vast majority of counties. Almost one in five inhabitants of some cities, such as Galway and Dublin, were immigrants and in more than twenty-five towns around the country, immigrants made up more than one in four residents.[82] Consequently, immigration has touched almost all aspects of Irish society. So far, Irish society appears to have adapted quite well to the arrival of such extensive numbers of newcomers, although the obstacles facing some immigrants, most notably black Africans, are much more prevalent

79 See I. Mosca and A. Barrett, 'The impact of adult child emigration on the mental health of older parents', IZA Discussion Paper 8037 (2014).

80 Glynn *et al.*, *Irish emigration in an age of austerity*, 102.

81 RTÉ, 'Ireland set to top euro zone growth table this year and next', 24 Nov. 2014, Available online at www.rte .ie/news/business/2014/1104/656805-eu-growth-forecasts/, last accessed 24 March 2015.

82 CSO, *Census 2011 profile 6: migration and diversity*, 10–11.

than those facing others, such as eastern Europeans. Public hostility towards immigration remains muted, partly because of mainstream political parties' tendency to refrain from discussing the issue. Whether the public and political atmosphere continues in this way in the future remains to be seen. The decision by the majority of immigrants to remain in the country since the economic downturn in 2008 demonstrates that although immigration has not played a prominent role in Ireland's modern history, it is set to play a significant part in the island's future.

FURTHER READING

CSO. *Census 2011 profile 6: migration and diversity* (Dublin, 2012).

Devine, D. 'Welcome to the Celtic Tiger? Teacher responses to immigration and increasing ethnic diversity in Irish schools', *International Studies in Sociology of Education*, 15, 1 (2005), 49–70.

Fahey, T. and B. Fanning. 'Immigration and socio-spatial segregation in Dublin, 1996–2006', *Urban Studies*, 47, 8 (2010), 1625–42.

Fanning, B. *Racism and social change in the Republic of Ireland* (Manchester, 2012).

Glynn, I., T. Kelly and P. Mac Éinrí. *Irish emigration in an age of austerity* (Cork, 2013).

Knox, C. 'Tackling racism in Northern Ireland: "the race hate capital of Europe"', *Journal of Social Policy*, 40 (2011), 387–412.

Mac Éinrí, P. and A. White. 'Immigration into the Republic of Ireland: a bibliography of recent research', *Irish Geography* 41, 2 (2008), 151–79.

National Economic and Social Council (NESC). *Managing migration in Ireland: a social and economic analysis* (Dublin, 2006).

Office of the Minister for Integration. *Migration nation: statement on integration strategy and diversity management* (Dublin, 2008).

O'Malley, E. 'Why is there no radical right party in Ireland?', *West European Politics* 31, 5 (2008), 960–77.

Epilogue: Remembering and Forgetting in Modern Irish History

Guy Beiner and Eunan O'Halpin

I   The Formation of Modern Irish Memory, *c.*1740–1914
Guy Beiner

The long nineteenth century saw the formation of *modern* Irish memory, although the nature of its novelty is open to debate, as it maintained a continuous dialogue with its traditional roots. A preliminary period from the mid-eighteenth to the mid-nineteenth century has been identified by Joep Leerssen – following the German school of history of concepts (*Begriffsgeschichte*) pioneered by Reinhart Koselleck – as a *Sattelzeit*, which accommodated the Anglicisation and modernisation of what had formerly been a predominantly Gaelic society. In particular, antiquarian fascination with the distant past played a key role in re-adapting native bodies of knowledge for Anglo-Irish readerships, whether in the music collecting of Edward Bunting, the song translations of Charlotte Brooke or the writings of Samuel Ferguson, to name but a few. This concept of cultural transition is useful for understanding the changes in memorial practices, which came about through reinvention, rather than simple invention and imposition from above, of Irish traditions.[1]

A record of remembrance in the countryside at the time of the transformation was captured between 1824 and 1842 by the Ordnance Survey, which, under the supervision

---

1 J. Leerssen, *Hidden Ireland, public sphere* (Galway and Dublin, 2002). For the role of antiquarian revivalism in reshaping Irish memory see J. Leerssen, *Mere Irish and Fíor Ghael* (2nd edn, Cork, 1996); J. Leerssen, *Remembrance and imagination: patterns in the historical and literary representation of Ireland in the nineteenth century* (Cork, 1996).

of the noted antiquarian George Petrie, sent out fieldworkers, among them the illustrious Gaelic scholars John O'Donovan and Eugene O'Curry, to compile detailed memoirs of local customs, originally designed as supplements for the topographical maps. Characteristically, the agents of change also engaged in documentation and preservation of traditional memory.[2] Whereas the loss of Irish language has been poignantly decried by Alan Titley as 'the Great Forgetting', the modernisation of Ireland was not a straightforward linear progression from a largely Irish-speaking traditional culture, steeped in memory, to an English-speaking capitalist society, supposedly clouded by amnesia. It should be acknowledged that the Irish language maintained a substantial presence well into the nineteenth century. Moreover, during the cultural revival of the fin de siècle, language enthusiasts such as Douglas Hyde collected folk traditions in Irish in order to make them available as a resource for a modern national society. Overall, the increase in literacy in English did not necessarily eradicate oral traditions. Examination of popular print reveals that it functioned as a vehicle for reworking memories, which then fed back into oral culture.[3]

In a defiant response to the unremitting colonisation drive of the early modern era, a flourish of Gaelic poetry readapted literary forms and tropes from earlier periods to lionise the Stuart dynasty. After the defeat of James II by William III at the battles of the Boyne and Aughrim, vernacular Jacobitism continued to thrive, despite the repression of the penal laws. It was expressed in toasts, prophecies, seditious chapbook prose, and most prominently in the *aisling* (vision) genre of Gaelic poetry, which depicted allegorical scenes of a woman in distress awaiting salvation. Explicit yearnings for deliverance of the 'Irish tribes' (*clanna Gael*) through the downfall of 'foreigners' (*Gaill*) and Protestant 'heretics' (*eiricigh*) gave vent to a subversive embittered Catholic memory of dispossession.[4] However, exclusion from official culture consigned many of the people's experiences of the eighteenth century to obscurity. Such is the case, for example, of the devastating famine caused by the 'Great Frost' of 1740–1, which left only a faint impression, recorded in a few rare poems. The inability to make an imprint on what would develop into a national collective memory meant that the designation of this catastrophe in folk memory as *blian an áir* (the year of carnage) would merge

---

2 G. M. Doherty, *The Irish Ordnance Survey: history, culture and memory* (Dublin, 2006); S. Ó Cadhla, *Civilizing Ireland: Ordnance Survey 1824–1842: ethnography, cartography, translation* (Dublin, 2007).

3 A. Titley, 'The Great Forgetting', in O. Frawley (ed.), *Memory Ireland, vol. I: History and modernity* (Syracuse, 2011), 221–8; N. M. Wolf, *An Irish-speaking island: state, religion, community, and the linguistic landscape in Ireland, 1770–1870* (Madison, WI, 2014); J. Egleson Dunleavy and G. W. Dunleavy, *Douglas Hyde: a maker of modern Ireland* (Berkeley, 1991); N. Ó Ciosáin, *Print and popular culture in Ireland, 1750–1850* (Basingstoke, 1997).

4 B. Ó Buachalla, *Aisling Ghéar: Na Stíobhartaigh agus an tAos Léinn, 1603–1788* (Dublin, 1996); for a partial English précis see B. Ó Buachalla, 'Irish Jacobite poetry', *Irish Review*, 12 (1992), 40–9. See also É. Ó Ciardha, *Ireland and the Jacobite cause, 1685–1766: a fatal attachment* (Dublin, 2002).

with remembrance of other calamities and its historical specificities would largely be forgotten.[5]

The cultural legacy of Jacobitism, which had run its course as a political movement with the deaths in 1766 of James Francis Edward Stuart (the 'Old Pretender') and in 1788 of his son Charles Edward Stuart (the 'Young Pretender'), would later reappear in recycled forms. Its persistence in popular memory is apparent in the demotic letters of intimidation and retribution that have been generically attributed to Whiteboyism, but actually reflect a variety of regional causes espoused at different times by violent agrarian secret societies (such as the Whiteboys, Oakboys, Rightboys, Steelboys, Defenders, Terry Alts, Rockites, Ribbonmen and Molly Maguires). Under the surface, Irish rural culture seethed with bitter memories of struggles for tenant rights and disputes over ownership of land, which would be harnessed to great effect in the Land War of the late nineteenth century. More openly, the expectations of quasi-messianic deliverance that had been cultivated by Jacobitism were revived in the first half of the nineteenth century in the popular mythologising of Daniel O'Connell as the Liberator and 'Uncrowned King' (*an rí gan choróin*) of Catholic Ireland. While tapping into the reservoir of Gaelic traditions and regenerating its evocative imagery, O'Connellite mass politics made effective use of modern communication media (not least, newspapers) to reclaim the public sphere. Consequently, O'Connell was remembered in Irish folklore traditions more than any other historical figure.[6]

The French Revolution, which introduced new commemorative practices in place of those of the *ancien régime*, had considerable influence in reshaping Irish memory. Theobald Wolfe Tone hailed Tom Paine's *Rights of Man* as 'the Koran of Blefescu', in a coded reference to its impact on Belfast, where the fall of the Bastille was commemorated in 1791 and again in 1792. In their endeavours to bring the ideology of republicanism to the Irish village, the propaganda of the underground society of the United Irishmen was designed to appeal to local sensibilities. The 'literary mischief' that marked their politicisation of popular culture was effectively disseminated in the radical newspapers the *Northern Star* and the *Press* (up until their suppression), as well as in the various editions of the popular song book *Paddy's resource*. In addition, the United Irishmen

---

5 D. Dickson, *Arctic Ireland: the extraordinary story of the Great Frost and forgotten famine of 1740–41* (Belfast, 1997); C. Ó Gráda and D. Ó Muirithe, 'The famine of 1740–41: representations in Gaelic poetry', *Éire-Ireland*, 45, 3–4 (2010), 41–62; L. Collins, 'The frosty winters of Ireland: poems of climate crisis 1739–41', *Journal of Ecocriticism*, 5, 2 (2013), 1–11.

6 R. uí Ógáin, *Immortal Dan: Daniel O'Connell in Irish folk tradition* (Dublin, 1995); see also G. Ó Tuathaigh, 'Gaelic Ireland, popular politics and Daniel O'Connell', *Journal of the Galway Archaeological and Historical Society*, 34 (1974), 21–34; C. Ó Danachair, 'Dónall Ó Conaill I mBéalabh na nDaoine', *Studia Hibernica*, 14 (1974), 40–66; D. Ó Muirithe, 'O'Connell in Irish folk tradition', in M. R. O'Connell (ed.), *Daniel O'Connell: political pioneer* (Dublin, 1991), 72–85; G. Owens, 'Nationalism without words: symbolism and ritual behaviour in the repeal "monster meetings" of 1843–5', in J. S. Donnelly jr and K. A. Miller (eds.), *Irish popular culture 1750–1850* (Dublin, 1998), 242–70.

made innovative use of a broad range of oral and literary forms, which included use of traditional genres, such as catechisms, sermons and seditious toasts. They also staged demonstrations of propaganda by deed that emulated familiar folk practices, such as communal harvesting of the fields of political prisoners.[7] The alliance of the United Irishmen with the agrarian secret society of the Defenders required the grafting of the universal ideals of Jacobinism on the sectarian millenarianism of Jacobitism, leaving lasting memories of clandestine activities that combined modern and traditional elements. In the early twentieth century, it was still remembered in County Mayo how a poor labourer known locally as Paidin a' Choga (*Páidín an Chogaidh* – 'Paddy of the War'), on account of his having rallied in his youth to support the French expeditionary force that landed in Killala in 1798, requested that a piper play the Jacobite anthem 'The white cockade' at his funeral.[8]

In contrast, loyalist memory relied on previously established traditions that commemorated the victories of Protestants over Catholics in the seventeenth century. Alongside the official events and public sculpture sponsored by Dublin Castle, popular Anglo-Irish celebrations of the cult of William of Orange and the Hanoverian succession, organised annually by dedicated loyalist societies (such as the Boyne, Aughrim and Culloden societies), were significantly boosted by the golden jubilee of the Battle of the Boyne in 1740. The co-option of these commemorations in the late 1770s and early 1780s by the Volunteers, whose demands for legislative reforms were publicised in print, backed up by military-style parades, trumpeted in patriotic toasts and songs and marketed through an array of souvenirs, demonstrated the potential of mobilising memorialisation for political purposes, inspiring both republicans and loyalists in the 1790s. Militant loyalism, which was mobilised into yeomanry corps to confront the danger of rebellion, found its vanguard with the founding in 1795 of the Orange Order (originally the Orange Society), an organisation that was zealously devoted to championing the 'glorious memory' of William III. The counter-insurgency measures of the late 1790s, which included the suppression of the oppositional press and the incarceration, execution and exile of many of the radicals, were also an attempt to silence the republican counter-memory propagated by the United Irishmen. [9]

Following the passing of the Act of Union, silencing would also be directed against Orangeism. The Orange Order was proscribed by the authorities in the early nineteenth century, on account of its blatant sectarianism, but in the 1860s enjoyed a popular revival,

7 J. S. Donnelly jr, 'Propagating the cause of the United Irishmen', *Studies*, 69, 273 (1980), 5–23; K. Whelan, *The tree of liberty: radicalism, Catholicism and the construction of Irish identity 1760–1830* (Cork, 1996), 59–96.
8 R. Francis Hayes, *The last invasion of Ireland: when Connacht rose* (Dublin, 1937), 222.
9 J. Kelly, '"The glorious and immortal memory": commemoration and Protestant identity in Ireland 1660–1800', *Proceedings of the Royal Irish Academy, Section C*, 94C, 2 (1994), 25–52; P. Higgins, *A nation of politicians: gender, patriotism, and political culture in late eighteenth-century Ireland* (Madison, WI, 2010); J. R. Hill, 'National festivals, the state and "Protestant Ascendancy" in Ireland, 1790–1829', *Irish Historical Studies*, 24 (1984), 30–51.

associated with the populist activism of William Johnston of Ballykilbeg, County Down. A more respectable conservative establishment assumed leadership over the Orange Order's lower-class Protestant membership and formalised its sporadic grassroots memorial practices into 'The Twelfth' (12 July being the date, according to the Gregorian calendar, of the Battle of the Boyne, which had been originally commemorated on 1 July OS). This would become the central commemorative festival of unionism.[10]

As the nineteenth century progressed, unionist celebration of iconic triumphs was increasingly confronted by nationalist remembrance of defeat and victimhood. Remembrance of the failed rebellions of 1798 and 1803 established the foundations for a pantheon of republican heroes, who would be evoked in the prose, poetry and music of Thomas Moore and lauded in the flamboyant romantic nationalism of the Young Ireland movement.[11] The rising assertiveness of nationalism challenged the dominance of British and imperial commemoration. Competition over the erection of public memorial sites commenced with the unveiling of monuments for Daniel O'Connell in Limerick (1857), Ennis (1865) and ultimately Dublin (1882), where the ceremony was reputedly attended by a crowd of half a million. The statue for the Young Irelander William Smith O'Brien, unveiled in Dublin in 1870, heralded the inauguration of monuments commemorating violent resistance to British rule.[12]

The interface of traditional memorial practices and modern media ensured that the Great Famine in the mid-nineteenth century was not buried in silence. Numerous documented oral traditions and literary representations reflect the magnitude of the trauma, with pervasive cross-fertilisation between folklore and literary sources. Mass emigration, however, entailed a drain of memory, as the social frameworks that sustained remembrance at home were not always available overseas. At the same time, emigrant letters and occasional return immigration could incidentally offer resources for revitalising memory in Ireland at a personal level, as relatives were reminded of stories that had been preserved and embellished abroad. The politicisation of the memory of the famine in the influential writings of John Mitchel and other polemicists (who cast the blame for the catastrophe on the policies of the English government) did not permeate all that deeply into local folk memory but was embraced none the less by Irish nationalist popular culture and adopted as a founding myth of Irish-American diasporic memory.[13]

---

10 D. Bryan, *Orange parades: the politics of ritual, tradition, and control* (London, 2000), 29–43.

11 M. H. Thuente, *The harp re-strung: the United Irishmen and the rise of Irish literary nationalism* (Syracuse, 1994).

12 J. Hill, 'Ideology and cultural production: nationalism and the public monument in mid nineteenth-century Ireland', in T. Foley and S. Ryder (eds.), *Ideology and Ireland in the nineteenth century* (Dublin, 1998), 55–68. For surveys of the erection of monuments, see J. Hill, *Irish public sculpture: a history* (Dublin, 1998); P. Murphy, *Nineteenth-century Irish sculpture: native genius reaffirmed* (New Haven, 2010).

13 C. Morash, *Writing the Irish famine* (Oxford, 1995); M. Cronin, 'Oral history, oral tradition and the Great Famine', in C. Noack, L. Janssen and V. Comerford (eds.), *Holodomor and Gorta Mór: histories, memories and representations of famine in Ukraine and Ireland* (London, 2015), 231–44.

In the second half of the nineteenth century, transatlantic Fenianism skilfully manip-
ulated commemorative rituals to develop an elaborate cult of political martyrdom, manifested in public funerals, monuments, ballads, memorabilia, and a voluminous body of
cheap publications. *Speeches from the dock*, originally published in 1867 and reissued
in multiple editions, was a seminal text in this nationalist hagiography, which began by
paying tribute to Wolfe Tone and listed a near-apostolic succession of revered figures. In
inverse proportion to its actual importance as a historical event, the controversial execution of the Manchester Martyrs (three Fenians convicted for the death of an English
policeman in a prisoner rescue operation) became a cornerstone of republican remembrance, marked annually on 23 November. These memorial rituals, as well as those that
had been dedicated to O'Connell, were put to use in the carefully planned nationalist
funerary procession for 'the chief', Charles Stewart Parnell (11 October 1891), which
was attended by more than 100,000 spectators, and were repeated on a smaller scale in
annual 'Ivy Day' commemorations of Parnell's death (6 October).[14]

Contestation over memory in the public sphere reached an apex at the turn of
the century. On the background of the Home Rule crises and a diminishing sense
of Protestant ascendancy, the self-confidence of loyalist commemoration was punc-
tured by growing anxieties. These were exacerbated by the triumphalist flaunting
of grievances exhibited in the parades of fraternal nationalist organisations, such as
the Irish National Foresters or the more vigilant Ancient Order of Hibernians. On
the other hand, the celebrations in 1897 of Queen Victoria's diamond jubilee, which,
like previous royal visits, demonstrated the prevalence of a popular undercurrent of
passive loyalism also shared by Catholics, aroused the ire of radical nationalists. In
response, the centenary of the 1798 rebellion, celebrated by nationalist communities
throughout Ireland and the Irish diaspora, was a mass demonstration of counter-
commemoration. The organisation of countless commemorative gatherings and the
dedication of numerous monuments brought together nationalists of all hues and
shades, including republicans, constitutionalists (from both wings of the Parnell split
in the Irish Parliamentary Party), revivalists of language (Gaelic League) and sports
(Gaelic Athletics Association), the Catholic Church, as well as socialists (including
James Connolly, who had moved to Dublin from Scotland three years earlier) and radical female activists (most notably Maud Gonne, Alice Milligan and Ethna Carbery).

---

14 D. G. Boyce, "'A gallous story and a dirty deed": political martyrdom in Ireland since 1867', in Y. Alexander
and A. O'Day (eds.), *Ireland's terrorist dilemma* (Dordrecht, Boston and Lancaster, 1986), 7–27; G. Owens,
'Constructing the martyrs: the Manchester executions and the nationalist imagination', in L. W. McBride (ed.),
Images, icons, and the Irish nationalist imagination (Dublin, 1999), 18–36; O. McGee, '"God save Ireland":
Manchester-martyr demonstrations in Dublin, 1867–1916', *Éire-Ireland*, 36, 3–4 (2001), 39–66; G. Beiner,
'Fenianism and the martyrdom–terrorism nexus in Ireland before independence', in D. Janes and A. Houen
(eds.), *Martyrdom and terrorism: pre-modern to contemporary perspectives* (Oxford, 2014), 199–220.

Figure 34.1 Ancient Order of Hibernians Pipe Band, *c.* 1930. Image courtesy of the Deputy Keeper of the Records, Public Record Office of Northern Ireland, Ref: D2886/0/7.

The orchestration of the 1798 centennial by central committees through a network of local '98 clubs named after heroic patrons, the ubiquity of statuomania (which extended beyond the areas that had actually been touched by the rebellion), and the activism of Catholic members on the boards of local administration in passing resolutions for renaming of streets to commemorate nationalist heroes, all give the impression that this was an essentially modern manifestation of 'invention of tradition', designed solely for contemporary political purposes. This conclusion would seem to comply with Eric Hobsbawm's seminal thesis on the mass-production of traditions in late modern Europe. However, such an interpretation underestimates the potency of local subcultures of social remembrance, which conditioned the reception of metropolitan discourses emanating from Dublin. At a provincial level, commemoration was brokered through the involvement of local mediators – school teachers, parish priests, newspaper editors and local politicians – who negotiated between vernacular traditions and nationalist initiatives. Attempts to introduce from above new configurations of memory were often rejected or readapted to comply with existing patterns of social memory. Violent clashes erupted in Ulster, where unionism had become entrenched along sectarian lines. Attempts of nationalists (who, at a membership level, were mainly Catholics) to publicly celebrate the 1798 rebellion were opposed by loyalist Protestants, who had developed a culture of social forgetting. The Presbyterians of Antrim and Down preserved memories of their ancestors' membership in the United Irishmen but objected to commemoration in public.[15]

Above all, engagement with the intense preoccupation with remembrance during the 1798 centenary was a formative experience for a young generation of radicals. The unveiling in 1911 of the monument for Parnell in Dublin (dedicated in 1899) denoted the completion of a symbolic reappropriation of public spaces that prepared the way for the Irish Revolution. Significantly, the revolution was triggered by the symbolic takeover of the Dublin GPO in Easter 1916, in what would become a founding myth of independent Ireland. This was also a time of reconfiguration of unionist memorial culture. Resistance to the Third Home Rule Bill under the dynamic leadership of Edward Carson and James Craig produced a new set of myths (centred on the mass signing of the Ulster Covenant on Ulster Day, 28 September 1912, the formation of the Ulster Volunteers Force in 1913 and the Larne gun-running in April 1914) that would blend with earlier loyalist traditions, which had taken root over the previous century. Unionist remembrance would also be recharged in 1916, with the adoption of the memory of the decimation of the 36th (Ulster) Division at the Battle of the Somme as a founding myth for Northern Ireland (unwittingly emulating the nationalist trope of 'triumph of defeat').[16]

Over the entire period, folk memory offered an alternative vernacular historiography. Oral traditions often recalled events which were unrecognised in the overtly political chronology of mainstream Irish history. A telling example can be found in the many accounts remembered across the isle of the exceptionally fierce windstorm of 6 January 1839, known as the 'Night of the Big Wind' (*Oíche na Gaoithe Móire*). Official acceptance of these recollections as qualification for those who lacked documentation to benefit from the state old-age pension system, introduced by the Asquith administration in 1909, illustrates the continuing interplay between tradition and modernity in Irish memory as it entered the twentieth century.

15 J. H. Murphy, *Abject loyalty: nationalism and monarchy in Ireland during the reign of Queen Victoria* (Washington, DC, 2001); T. O'Keefe, 'The 1898 efforts to celebrate the United Irishmen: the '98 centennial', *Éire-Ireland*, 23 (1988), 51–73; T. O'Keefe, '"Who fears to speak of '98?": the rhetoric and rituals of the United Irishmen centennial, 1898', *Éire-Ireland*, 27 (1992), 67–91; G. Beiner, 'Modes of memory: forgetting and remembering 1798', in Frawley, *Memory Ireland, vol. I*, 66–82; cf. E. Hobsbawm, 'Mass-producing traditions: Europe, 1870–1914', in E. Hobsbawm and T. Ranger (eds.), *The Invention of Tradition* (Cambridge, 1983), 263–307.
16 A. Jackson, 'Unionist myths 1912–1985', *Past and Present*, 136, 1 (August 1992), 164–85; G. Beiner, 'Between trauma and triumphalism: the Easter Rising, the Somme, and the crux of deep memory in modern Ireland', *Journal of British Studies*, 46, 2 (2007), 366–89.

II Commemoration and Memorialisation in Independent Ireland   Eunan O'Halpin

Independent Ireland's essays in commemoration have seldom been commended by historians. David Fitzpatrick has described 'a chronicle of embarrassment' about commemoration during the first two decades of independence, as successive governments sought to navigate the sensitivities of their followers, their former enemies, the general public and the people in between – ex-servicemen and the Protestant minority.[17] Studies of the fiftieth anniversary of the 1916 Rising have uncovered the combination of uncertainty, unease and residual triumphalism with which ministers, officials and some sections of civil society made plans for the golden jubilee, although Mary Daly, Margaret O'Callaghan and Roisín Higgins have argued robustly that on balance the 1966 celebrations were 'an attempt by the Irish government to unite its citizens behind 1916 as the formative founding moment in the history of an independent Irish state' and part of a drive for national modernisation, after decades of official diffidence during which commemoration was largely the preserve of anti-state republicans.[18] Roy Foster has pointed out that the bicentenary of the 1798 rebellion, planned in a spirit of optimism and reconciliation just as the Northern Ireland peace process approached its first fruition, included many publicly funded commemorative activities of doubtful historical or cultural merit, cross-fertilised with the intrusive and aggressive germ of tourism promotion.[19]

Anne Dolan has written vividly of the uncertainty with which the pro-Anglo-Irish Treaty Cosgrave government and its anti-Treaty successor each handled the issue of commemoration of the War of Independence and civil war during the first decades of independence, particularly in respect of memorials for the fallen.[20] The Cosgrave government was no more fortunate with its efforts to commission a cenotaph for Arthur Griffith, Michael Collins and Kevin O'Higgins, an enterprise which limped along for years owing to poor planning and execution, the damp Irish climate, and endless disputes about cost overruns and moneys owed. (It was not to be the last such mess: as late as 1984 officials in Belfast fumed at an excessive bill for a Stormont memorial to

---

17 D. Fitzpatrick, 'Commemoration in the Irish Free State: a chronicle of embarrassment', in I. McBride (ed.), *History and memory in modern Ireland* (Cambridge, 1997), 184–203.

18 M. E. Daly and M. O'Callaghan, 'Introduction', in Daly and O'Callaghan (eds.), *1916 in 1966: commemorating the Easter Rising* (Dublin, 2008), 7; R. Higgins, *Transforming 1916: meaning, memory and the fiftieth anniversary of the Easter Rising* (Cork, 2012), 203.

19 Roy Foster, *Luck and the Irish: a brief history of change, 1970–2000* (London, 2008).

20 A. Dolan, *Commemorating the Irish civil war: history and memory, 1923–2000* (Cambridge, 2003).

the unionist politician Edgar Graham, murdered by the IRA in 1983, 'a gross departure from the estimated cost', before deciding to compromise by paying '50 per cent ... i.e. £68 plus £10.40 VAT').[21] The new state's first stab at a historical review of progress since independence, the *Saorstát Éireann Official Handbook* published just as the Cosgrave government left office in 1932, was decidedly tentative. Professor Eoin MacNéill contributed a chapter covering the span of Irish history from Roman times to the twentieth century in just twenty-two pages. This compressed account, which made no reference to his or any other politician's revolutionary activities, was not without error: MacNeill dated the Anglo-Irish truce to June 1921, and abruptly closed his text just a sentence later with 'the Treaty to which the Irish Free State owes its existence'. He did not mention the civil war of 1922/3, during which he served as a Free State minister and in which his anti-Treaty son Brian was killed by Free State troops.[22]

Ireland is of course not the only state, nor its citizens and the wider Irish nationalist diaspora the only people, which struggle with commemoration, forgetting, remembering and recontextualising formative events, processes and individuals. Commemoration and memorialisation are often assigned, or acquire, an overtly political character in states which emerged into independence through revolution or disaggregation during the twentieth century, and which experienced serious internal conflict. Longer-established states also encounter difficulties, controversy and contradictions dealing with the past. One majority's day of celebration is a minority's day of sorrow. As recently as 2008 Australia issued an apology for 'past mistreatment' of indigenous peoples since European colonisation began in the 1790s: it was time to 'turn a new page ... by righting the wrongs of the past and so moving forward with confidence'.[23] Soon after, the Canadian and the United States legislatures did much the same in respect of their indigenous populations.[24] In Britain, provision of a memorial to the 55,000 aircrew who died serving in the Royal Air Force's Bomber Command took more than seventy years, and remains controversial: *The Observer*'s architecture critic waxed indignant on moral as well as aesthetic grounds: inflicting mass civilian deaths was 'a hard subject to memorialise'. He deplored the absence of 'some nuance, some recognition of moral complexity, some regret, some invitation to reflection'.[25] Britain entirely omitted to mark the centenary of its greatest crisis in civil/military relations since the Glorious Revolution of 1688,

---

21 Public Record Office of Northern Ireland, NIA-1-3-9A_1984-04-06, accessed via http://cain.ulst.ac.uk/cgi-bin/PRONI/pronidbase.pl?field=year&text=1984, minutes by Whiteside and Kennedy, 6 and 9 April 1984.
22 E. MacNeill, 'History', in *Saorstát Eireann official handbook* (Dublin, 1932), 63.
23 Prime Minister Kevin Rudd, House of Representatives, 13 Feb. 2008, available at www.australia.gov.au/sites/default/files/global_site/library/videos/National_Apology_Speech-48kbps_mono.mp3, accessed 22 April 2015.
24 M. Tager, 'Apologies to indigenous people in comparative perspective', *International Indigenous Policy Journal*, 5, 4 (Oct. 2014), 1–18; 'US lawmakers apologize for slavery, Jim Crow', www.npr.org/templates/story/story.php?storyId=93059465, accessed 19 April 2015.
25 Rowan Moore, writing in *The Observer*, 24 June 2012.

the Curragh mutiny of March 1914: the only commemorative function was an Irish academic exercise.[26] In 2015 the Turkish government chose to distort rather than clarify the historical record of the Dardanelles campaign, shifting the centenary commemoration of victory by five weeks to distract attention from the centenary of the Armenian genocide, a dark episode of Turkish history with which the Turkish state has yet to come to grips, and portraying the multi-ethnic Ottoman forces as exclusively Muslim.[27]

The acerbic Conor Cruise O'Brien and others argued that the fiftieth anniversary celebrations of 1916 contributed to the outbreak of political violence in Northern Ireland in 1969 by appearing to relegitimise armed struggle, yet that is hard to square with the record. The Belfast government certainly feared IRA attacks to mark the anniversary, beseeching London in December 1965 to take preventative action. But, perhaps in subconscious homage to 1916, when the Belfast Volunteer leader Denis McCullough reluctantly obeyed the 'mad' instructions of Pearse and 'especially James Connolly that "we were to fire no shot in Ulster"', the IRA attempted nothing of note.[28] The police reported 'fewer than the normal number of minor incidents' over the Easter weekend.[29] O'Brien would have done better to reflect instead on the mindset of Ulster loyalists: it was they, not republicans, who took to political violence between 1966 and 1969, provoked less by commemoration of 1916 than by the growth of the Northern Ireland civil rights movement.[30] In 1968 the British ambassador, commenting on economic modernisation, wrote that the 1966 commemorations had signalled the effective end of civil war politics. He predicted the rapid emergence of a party system based on 'differing views of economic and social problems, rather than on commitments to an unreal and outdated historical interpretation of the events of 1922'.[31]

The varying critiques of official Irish commemorative enterprises suggest an underlying immaturity, or justified embarrassment at the way in which past conflicts have been used to justify republican violence since the late 1960s. But, particularly after 1969, the state was in a very difficult position: celebrate twentieth-century Ireland's revolutionary history and risk being accused of promoting the legitimacy of the physical force tradition over that of non-violent politics, and thereby of stirring the Northern Ireland pot; or steer away from all but the most unavoidable or uncontroversial anniversaries, acknowledging them only in minimalist fashion, and be accused of forgetting those

---

26 A podcast of proceedings can be seen at www.tcd.ie/decade-commemoration/events/archive/curragh-mutiny/, accessed 9 September 2016.

27 *Irish Times*, 17 Apr. 2015 and *Daily News* (Istanbul), 20 Apr. 2015.

28 Military Archives of Ireland, Military Service Pensions, WMSP34REF55173, McCullough letter received 12 Nov. 1937.

29 *The Times*, 12 Apr. 1966.

30 Higgins, *Transforming 1916*, 91–112; E. O'Halpin, '"A poor thing but our own": the Joint Intelligence Committee and Ireland, 1965–1972', *Intelligence and National Security*, 23, 5 (2008), 658–80.

31 The National Archives (TNA), FCO33/571, Sir Andrew Gilchrist to London, 23 Oct. 1968.

who fought to make Ireland free. From the mid-1970s until 1998, the latter was the course chosen. State commemorations of the Rising and subsequent events were low-key and largely civilian in character and language. They could also be somewhat slapdash: a chaotic function to mark the seventy-fifth anniversary of the first meeting of Dáil Éireann in Dublin's Mansion House took place three months late in April 1994.[32] The one confident star in the commemorative firmament was the annual rally at Béal na mBlath at which Michael Collins was mourned and extolled. Until 2010 this was an exclusively pro-Treaty affair although Collins had also long been mourned by republicans, suggesting that the civil war divide was never all that absolute. In 1944 Mike Quill, an anti-Treaty veteran, lamented the fact that 'the recognised leaders … Liam Lynch, RIP, and Michael Collins, RIP, were killed not by the headhunters of Java, but, unfortunately, by Irishmen dressed in the uniform of Patrick Pearce [sic]'.[33] In the wake of the massively influential Tim Pat Coogan biography of Collins and the eponymous 1996 film, other parties and groups, including Sinn Féin which for a time sold Michael Collins mugs on its website, also now lay claim to his mantle.[34]

The Good Friday Agreement of 1998 radically altered the terms of Irish official commemorative activity. The state became markedly less diffident about commemorations generally, and set out to claim national ownership of what might otherwise have been simply anti-state republican events, such as the disinterment and reburial in 2001 of the 'Mountjoy Ten', executed and buried in the prison in 1920–1.[35] The state also increasingly emphasised inclusiveness in commemoration, a useful concept in contemporary public life but one which has its drawbacks: some commemorations belong emphatically to one community or political tradition, national or local, and not to another.

It has sometimes been argued that the new Ireland was neglectful if not sometimes downright hostile towards the commemoration of those who died fighting in British colours. On this the evidence is mixed. Republicans were certainly antagonistic and, particularly in the 1920s and early 1930s, they disrupted Armistice Day marches, services and the associated 'Poppy Day' fundraising. But most such world war commemorative exercises passed off peacefully, if without state encouragement or involvement.[36] It was not only republicans who viewed those commemorations as inherently political. Archbishop John Bernard, the Provost of Trinity College whose son John had perished at Gallipoli in 1915, wrote an almost ecstatic round-robin letter after Armistice

---

32 *Irish Press*, 27 Apr. 1994; *Dáil Debates*, vol. 557, no. 1, col. 10, 2 Nov. 2002. I was present as a great-grandson of P.J. Moloney TD of Tipperary.

33 New York University, Tamiment Library, Gerald O'Reilly papers, box 1, folder 15, Quill to Dan Breen TD, 17 Nov. 1944. Michael Quill (1905–66) became an important trade unionist in New York.

34 T. P. Coogan, *Michael Collins: a biography* (London, 1990). The film *Michael Collins*, directed by Neil Jordan, was released in 1996.

35 I was one of the relatives who carried Kevin Barry's remains during proceedings in Mountjoy.

36 Fitzpatrick, 'Commemoration in the Irish Free State', 193–4.

Day in 1924, when an estimated 70,000 people congregated to view a commemorative Celtic cross which was en route to Flanders: 'the spirit of Imperialism is undoubtedly alive in Southern Ireland to a degree which has not been appreciated in England'.[37] By the 1990s commemoration of the Irish who fell in the world wars had been almost completely depoliticised in independent Ireland, with the introduction in 1986 of a 'National Day of Commemoration' on the Sunday nearest 11 July (the anniversary of the Anglo-Irish truce of 1921), but not in Northern Ireland, as the Provisional IRA's murderous bombing of civilians at the Enniskillen war memorial on Armistice Day 1987 demonstrated. In December 1998 President Mary McAleese, Queen Elizabeth II and Prince Albert of the Belgians jointly unveiled the Irish Peace Tower at Messines commemorating Irishmen who died during the First World War. This marked a decisive shift from the non-committal 'civic tolerance' hitherto accorded commemoration of Irish involvement in the First World War towards its inclusion in a broader national narrative.[38] Important in itself, the act turned out to be a prelude to the remarkable occasion in May 2011 when Queen Elizabeth visited the Garden of Remembrance in Dublin and bowed her head before a monument commemorating those who had died fighting for independence between 1916 and 1921. The legitimacy of commemoration of Ireland's world war dead in parallel with its independence fighters is no longer in doubt.

The Irish state faces other commemorative challenges. Recent decades have seen a new imperative to memorialise collectivities such as victims of the Great Famine; unnamed, unbaptised infants who died in mother and baby homes and were buried in unmarked graves; and survivors of institutional care home abuse. Partly as a by-product of the Northern Ireland peace process, both the British and Irish governments have become accustomed to apologising for the inactions or failures of long-gone administrations. In 1997 Prime Minister Tony Blair expressed regret for British mishandling of the Great Famine, although it is hard to believe that an independent Irish administration would have performed any better, and in 2010 Prime Minister David Cameron made a fulsome apology for the killing of civilians in Derry in January 1972: 'it is clear from the [Saville] inquiry's authoritative conclusions that the events of Bloody Sunday were in no way justified'.[39] Irish governments have also acknowledged historic failings. In 1997 Taoiseach John Bruton expressed regret for Ireland's reluctance to succour European Jews fleeing Nazi persecution in the 1930s and 1940s. In 1999 Taoiseach Bertie Ahern issued an apology to people who as children had been entrusted to the care of residential institutions, and in 2013 the Minister for Defence apologised for the

---

37 British Library, Bernard papers Add. MSS 52781, Bernard to Lord Midleton, 12 Nov. 1924.
38 J. Horne, 'Our war, our history', in J. Horne (ed.), *Our war: Ireland and the Great War* (Dublin, 2008), 13.
39 *The Guardian*, 15 June 2010.

state's allegedly vindictive treatment of men who had deserted the Irish defence forces during the Second World War to fight for Britain.[40]

We must note that it was not only the civil war victors who found acts of commemoration and memorialisation problematic. Anti-state republicans struggled to cope with a range of commemorative issues. Recitation of the heroism and sacrifice of the republican fallen between 1916 and 1923, and of the brutality of their British and Irish oppressors, was an important element in asserting the legitimacy of continued pursuit of the republican millennium. On the other hand, practical problems arose for republicans just as they did for the state. As early as 1925, the Kerry IRA warned about 'Anniversaries. Last year these were held so often – practically every Sunday and Holyday – that in the end they were beginning to lose their effect.'[41] This had serious implications not only for public support, but for revenue for organisations such as the Irish Republican Prisoners Dependants Fund (IRPDF) which supported the families of IRA prisoners.[42] And money was badly needed: a familiar narrative of halfpence, pence and disallowed items quickly developed when relatives sought funeral expenses for their lost sons. Patrick Daly, father of one of eight IRA prisoners murdered at Ballyseedy bridge on 7 March 1923, listed 'funeral expences [sic] £10 coffin £3 hearse, priests £3, creaps [sic] £2, habits ets [sic] £1, bell tolls 7s/6d', and the mother of a Knocknagoshel republican sought expenses including 'groceries, bread, tobacco, pipes, candles etc. for wake £2/2s/8d' and '£12/7s/9d' for drink, but neither claimant was fully reimbursed. The IRPDF would allow only '£16 per funeral … they do not pay for such things as wreaths etc', nor for a commemorative cross at Ballyseedy, and the Kerry IRA were so dilatory in forwarding relatives' funeral claims that there was almost no money left to meet them. Cork, quicker off the mark than their Kerry neighbours, got more than three times as much.[43]

Commemorative activities were closely bound up with the pursuit of practical state recognition of service and sacrifice. In 1934 the County Cork 'Old IRA Men's Association' called for new legislation 'to provide for all Old IRA men in distress', and later intervened with the Mallow sugar beet factory 'on behalf of T Murphy's candidature for Storekeeper.'[44]

Splits in anti-Treaty republicanism in succeeding years and decades compounded the problem of commemoration overload. Sacred sites such as Wolfe Tone's grave at

---

40 *Irish Times*, 12 May 1999, 7 May 2013.
41 Kerry County Library, Con Casey papers, P36A/1/53, Kerry County Command to IRA GHQ, 30 Jan. 1925.
42 My grandmother Kathy Barry (1896–1969) was general secretary of the fund from 1922 to 1924. See her papers P94 in University College Dublin Archives.
43 Kerry County Archives, Con Casey papers, P36/8/14 and 25, IRA HQ to O/C Kerry, 2 Oct. and 24 Nov. 1924, and O/C Kerry to GHQ, 13 Dec. 1924.
44 Cork Archives Institute, Old IRA Men's Association (Cork County), U342, minutes of meetings, 14 Apr. 1934 and 6 Dec. 1935.

Bodenstown, the resting places of the 1916 leaders at Arbour Hill and lesser-known burial plots such as that of Liam Mellows in Wexford are still visited each year by different factions within the squabbling republican family, from Eamon de Valera's once-hegemonic Fianna Fáil to mainstream Sinn Féin to the purists of Republican Sinn Féin and other splinter groups who denounce everyone save themselves as sell-outs and traitors.[45] In 1970 Kevin Barry's niece, a republican activist in San Francisco, was relieved to miss the unveiling of a monument on the fiftieth anniversary of his execution: 'I saw in the *Irish Press* that Dev [de Valera] attended … so am glad I was not home for it'.[46] In 1971 the Provisional IRA threatened to prevent a Fianna Fáil march to commemorate the fiftieth anniversary of the murder of three War of Independence IRA volunteers in Kerry, but instead avoided trouble by staging their own commemoration a few hours later.[47] The Provisionals could be more tolerant when they were in charge: on 8 April 1973 I accompanied my grandfather Jim Moloney to a rally outside Fermoy, County Cork, to mark the fiftieth anniversary of the death of the anti-Treaty commander Liam Lynch. A raggle-taggle pipe band battled against a noisy wind before the attendance was addressed over a crackly loudspeaker by the leading republican Daithí Ó Conaill, who roundly condemned the Irish state and its politicians. Amongst those attending were Fianna Fáil men Ruairi Brugha TD, David Andrews TD and his father, Dr C. S. Andrews, none of whom turned a hair as they and their party were denounced as British hirelings (although their colleague Des O'Malley TD later complained that Ó Conaill should be behind bars).[48] Afterwards everyone adjourned to a pub.

Control of sites of memory posed practical as well as political problems. In 1995 the long-established republican National Graves Association (NGA) assumed responsibility for a 1798 statue in Tralee. Their motives were scarcely pluralist:

> We are very conscious … of a sudden interest being shown in the memorials to our Republican dead by people who up to now had no interest whatsoever in anything National. Even the Great Famine is being used for commercial gain … I am only interested in the future when neither of us is around any more to care for these memorials.[49]

There was 'a very great danger of these memorials falling into the wrong hands'.[50] Money was also a significant issue in erecting memorials: it was in desperately short

45 Fianna Fáil leader Micheál Martin, interviewed at Bodenstown by *Newstalk106FM*, 19 Oct. 2014. In December 2012 the leaders of Fianna Fáil, Sinn Féin and Republican Sinn Féin each spoke at Mellows's grave to mark the ninetieth anniversary of his execution during the civil war.

46 *Irish Press*, 2 Nov. 1970; Judy Moloney to her sister Helen, 9 Nov. 1970 (private collection, copy in my possession).

47 *The Kerryman*, 8 and 22 May 1971.

48 *Irish Press*, 9 and 14 Apr. 1973; C. S. Andrews, *Dublin made me: an autobiography* (Dublin, 1979), 29; F. O'Donoghue, *No other law* (Dublin, 1954), 261, 272, 297.

49 Kerry County Library, Con Casey papers, P36/9/44, M. Ni Chearnaigh to Casey, 27 Mar. 1995.

50 Kerry County Library, Con Casey papers, P36/9/46, M. Ni Chearnaigh to Casey, 26 Apr. 1995.

supply in the new Ireland, and veterans' groups customarily turned to émigrés to help. A priest in New York offered a tart defence of his fundraising efforts for a Kilkenny War of Independence monument: 'It is just as difficult to get a dollar out of the people here as it is to get a shilling out of the people at home … a thousand dollars is still a lot of money even in America.'[51] The American Irish diaspora remained a key source of funds for republicans: in 1971 IRA veteran Tom Barry's plan to raise money for the IRA at Easter Rising commemorations in New York foundered: his doctor was 'adamant that I am not to travel'.[52]

Sheer poverty also played a limiting part in commemoration. In 1936 Birmingham-based Tommy Ryan, who 'helped to produce the *Irish War News* etc etc etc in 1916', suggested to Diarmuid Lynch that he 'ask the "Easter Week Association" for some assistance to enable me to be present at the Dublin twentieth celebration': Lynch replied regretfully that no suitable fund existed, but enclosed 'a small contribution from myself and only wish it could be more'.[53]

Historical exploration of the Irish Revolution was hampered until 1986 by the inaccessibility of official records, although from the early 1970s the University College Dublin Archives became a repository for crucial collections including the Richard Mulcahy IRA GHQ papers. But great sensitivities remained in localities: an elderly Leitrim man interviewed in 1979 was apprehensive about his opinion that a local Protestant shot as a spy in 1921 was 'an innocent man … He was. It'd be awful if that came out, do you know I'd get killed.'[54] The release in 2003 of the Bureau of Military History witness statements and in 2006 of the 1911 census and the initiation in 2014 of the phased release of more than 300,000 military service pensions files has enabled far more research than hitherto into the Irish state's attitude towards its own violent origins. The recent opening of more than 70,000 medals files will deepen knowledge further.[55] Historians hitherto used the evidence of Department of Finance records to castigate parsimonious bureaucrats in matters of memorialisation and commemoration as well as in the granting of pensions. Officials who put a figure on a grieving widow's loss are easy targets for accusations of heartless penny-pinching.[56] Yet the extraordinarily detailed military service pension records disclose less an animus against the needy and deserving than a determination to

---

51 New York University, Tamiment Library, James Comerford papers, Box 2, Folder 'Associations – various 1965–1981', Father Séan Reid (New York) to Captain Padraig Quinn (Kilkenny), 9 Apr. 1947.
52 Cork Archives Institute, SM701, Jack McCarthy papers, Barry to McCarthy, 25 Jan. 1971.
53 National Library of Ireland, Diarmuid Lynch papers, MS11131, Tommy Ryan letter, 2 Apr. 1936 and Lynch to Ryan, 4 Apr. 1936.
54 Leitrim County Library, Ballinamore, Oral History Collection tape no. 78 (Larry Moran, interviewed 12 Dec. 1979).
55 C. Crowe (ed.), *Guide to the military service (1916–1923) pensions collection* (Dublin, 2012); speech by Taoiseach Enda Kenny TD, General Post Office, Dublin, 16 Jan. 2014.
56 A. Dolan, *Commemorating the Irish civil war* (Cambridge, 2005), 119.

grant precisely whatever was due under the relevant legislation. Tom Barry's case is unusual: his records show that he was ultimately granted a larger pension than prescribed under the regulations, despite being badly caught out in a lie, because of his exceptional fighting record, a point missed in recent discussions of his case.[57]

Launching the state's '2016 Commemoration' programme, Taoiseach Enda Kenny remarked that being Irish 'is more complicated, more diverse – indeed more interesting – than we might sometimes like to think. We need to appreciate the subtle inter-reliance and relationships between different traditions on this island. We do not need to be afraid of differences – but to embrace diversity.'[58] Historians have an altogether separate task, not to build a unitary and agreed all-island Irish narrative for present and future use, but to explore the past and its relationship to the present through the medium of records and memory as well as of contemporary words and actions. The stock of historical resources for the political and social history of the Irish Revolution has grown a great deal since 1966 and will grow still further. It remains to be seen what new uses historians will make of them.

FURTHER READING

Andrews, C. *Dublin made me: an autobiography* (Dublin, 1979).

Beiner, G. 'Between trauma and triumphalism: the Easter Rising, the Somme, and the crux of deep memory in modern Ireland', *Journal of British Studies*, 46, 2 (2007), 366–89.

Beiner, G. 'Fenianism and the martyrdom–terrorism nexus in Ireland before independence', in D. Janes and A. Houen (eds.), *Martyrdom and terrorism: pre-modern to contemporary perspectives* (Oxford, 2014), 199–220.

Boyce, D.G. '"A gallous story and a dirty deed": political martyrdom in Ireland since 1867', in Y. Alexander and A. O'Day (eds.), *Ireland's terrorist dilemma* (Dordrecht, Boston and Lancaster, 1986), 7–27.

Bryan, D. *Orange parades: the politics of ritual, tradition, and control* (London, 2000), 29–43.

Coogan, T. P. *Michael Collins: a biography* (London, 1990).

Cronin, M. 'Oral history, oral tradition and the Great Famine', in C. Noack, L. Janssen and V. Comerford (eds.), *Holodomor and Gorta Mór: histories, memories and representations of famine in Ukraine and Ireland* (London, 2015), 231–44.

Daly, M.E. and M. O'Callaghan (eds.). *1916 in 1966: commemorating the Easter Rising* (Dublin, 2008).

Doherty, G. M. *The Irish Ordnance Survey: history, culture and memory* (Dublin, 2006).

---

57 M. Ryan, *Tom Barry: IRA freedom fighter* (Cork, 2003), 228; D. Ferriter, *A nation and not a rabble: the Irish Revolution 1913–1923* (London, 2015), 319–20. Barry's pension application MSP34REF57456 is available on the Military Archives of Ireland website at http://mspcsearch.militaryarchives.ie/, accessed 10 September 2016.
58 Speech by Enda Kenny TD, GPO, 12 Nov. 2014.

Dolan, A. *Commemorating the Irish Civil War: history and memory, 1923–2000* (Cambridge, 2005).

Fitzpatrick, D. 'Commemoration in the Irish Free State: a chronicle of embarrassment', in I. McBride (ed.), *History and memory in modern Ireland* (Cambridge, 1997), 184–203.

Foster, R. *Luck and the Irish: a brief history of change, 1970–2000* (London, 2008).

Frawley, O. (ed.) *Memory Ireland*, 3 vols. (Syracuse, 2010–14).

Hill, J. *Irish public sculpture: a history* (Dublin, 1998).

Hill, J. R. 'National festivals, the state and "Protestant Ascendancy" in Ireland, 1790–1829', *Irish Historical Studies*, 24 (1984), 30–51.

Hobsbawm, E. J. 'Mass-producing traditions: Europe, 1870–1914', in E. J. Hobsbawm and T. O. Ranger (eds.), *The invention of tradition* (Cambridge, 1983), 263–307.

Horne, J. (ed.). *Our war: Ireland and the Great War* (Dublin, 2008).

Jackson, A. 'Unionist myths 1912–1985', *Past and Present*, 136, 1 (1992), 164–85.

Kelly, J. '"The glorious and immortal memory": commemoration and Protestant identity in Ireland 1660–1800', *Proceedings of the Royal Irish Academy, Section C*, 94C, 2 (1994), 25–52.

Leerssen, J. *Mere Irish and Fíor Ghael* (2nd edn, Cork, 1996).

Leerssen, J. *Remembrance and imagination: patterns in the historical and literary representation of Ireland in the nineteenth century* (Cork, 1996).

McGee, O. '"God save Ireland": Manchester-martyr demonstrations in Dublin, 1867–1916', *Éire-Ireland*, 36, 3–4 (2001), 39–66.

Murphy, J. H. *Abject loyalty: nationalism and monarchy in Ireland during the reign of Queen Victoria* (Washington, DC, 2001).

Murphy, P. *Nineteenth-century Irish sculpture: native genius reaffirmed* (New Haven, 2010).

Ó Buachalla, B. *Aisling Ghéar: Na Stíobhartaigh agus an tAos Léinn, 1603–1788* (Dublin, 1996).

Ó Ciosáin, N. *Print and popular culture in Ireland, 1750–1850* (Basingstoke, 1997).

Ó Gráda, C. *Black '47 and beyond: the Great Irish Famine in history, economy, and memory* (Princeton, 1999).

O'Halpin, E. 'The military service pensions project and Irish history: a personal perspective', in *Guide to the military service (1916–1923) pensions collection* (Dublin, 2012), 144–55.

O'Halpin, E. '"A poor thing but our own": the Joint Intelligence Committee and Ireland, 1965–1972', *Intelligence and National Security*, 23, 5 (2008), 658–80.

O'Keefe, T. '"Who fears to speak of '98?": the rhetoric and rituals of the United Irishmen centennial, 1898', *Éire-Ireland*, 27 (1992), 67–91.

Owens, G. 'Constructing the martyrs: the Manchester executions and the nationalist imagination', in L.W. McBride (ed.), *Images, icons, and the Irish nationalist imagination* (Dublin, 1999), 18–36.

Ryan, M. *Tom Barry: IRA freedom fighter* (Cork, 2003).

uí Ógáin, R. *Immortal Dan: Daniel O'Connell in Irish folk tradition* (Dublin, 1995).

Whelan, K. *The tree of liberty: radicalism, Catholicism and the construction of Irish identity 1760–1830* (Cork, 1996), 59–96.

Appendix: Mapping Ireland's Changing Demography, 1834–2002

Niall Cunningham and Ian Gregory

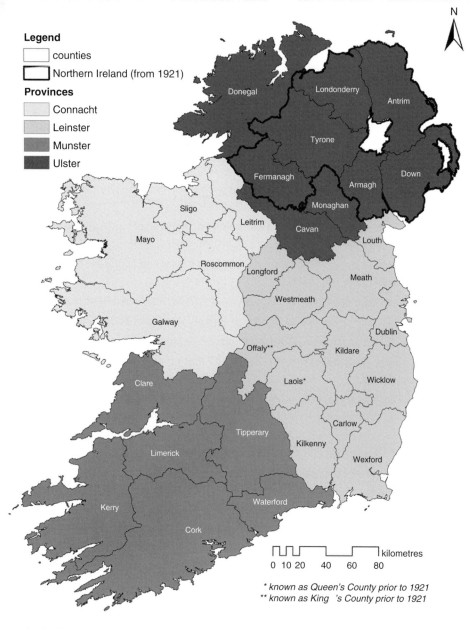

Legend
- counties
- Northern Ireland (from 1921)

Provinces
- Connacht
- Leinster
- Munster
- Ulster

* known as Queen's County prior to 1921
** known as King's County prior to 1921

1. Ireland's administrative units: counties and provinces

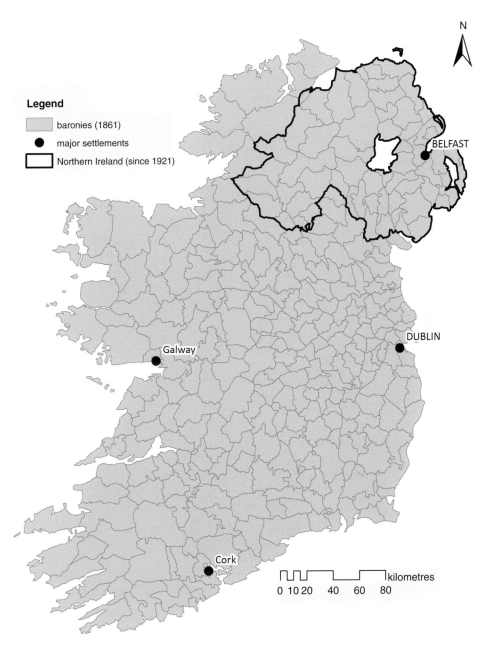

N

Legend

baronies (1861)

● major settlements

Northern Ireland (since 1921)

BELFAST

DUBLIN

Galway

Cork

kilometres
0 10 20 40 60 80

2. Ireland's administrative units: baronies. Baronies were an important administrative unit used by the census and other sources in the nineteenth century

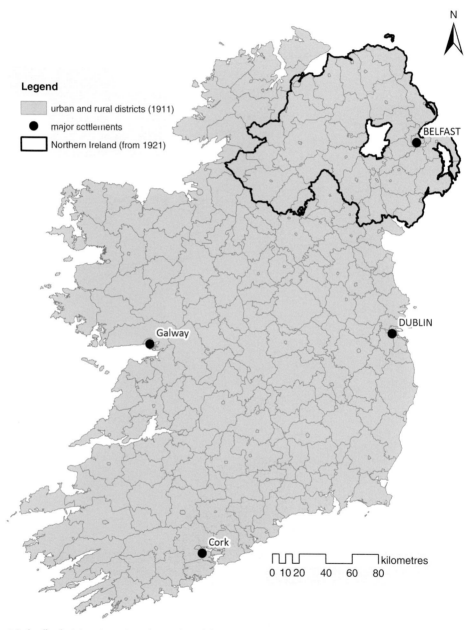

3. Ireland's administrative units: urban and rural districts. Urban and rural districts replaced baronies in the twentieth century

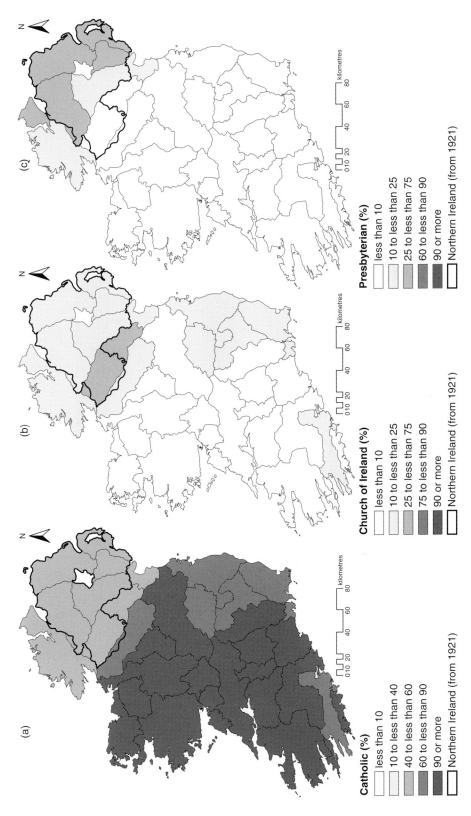

Catholic (%)

- ☐ less than 10
- ☐ 10 to less than 40
- ☐ 40 to less than 60
- ☐ 60 to less than 90
- ■ 90 or more
- ☐ Northern Ireland (from 1921)

Church of Ireland (%)

- ☐ less than 10
- ☐ 10 to less than 25
- ☐ 25 to less than 75
- ☐ 75 to less than 90
- ■ 90 or more
- ☐ Northern Ireland (from 1921)

Presbyterian (%)

- ☐ less than 10
- ☐ 10 to less than 25
- ☐ 25 to less than 75
- ☐ 60 to less than 90
- ■ 90 or more
- ☐ Northern Ireland (from 1921)

4. (a) Catholic, (b) Church of Ireland and (c) Presbyterian populations as a percentage share of the entire population at Church of Ireland diocese level in 1834

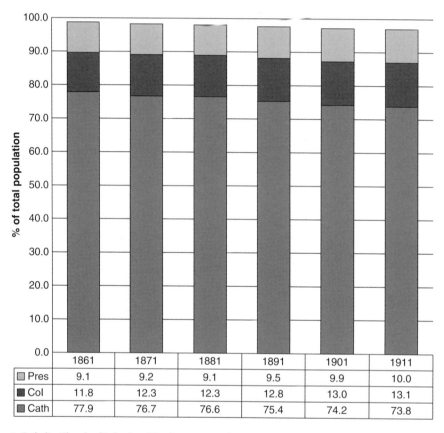

	1861	1871	1881	1891	1901	1911
Pres	9.1	9.2	9.1	9.5	9.9	10.0
Col	11.8	12.3	12.3	12.8	13.0	13.1
Cath	77.9	76.7	76.6	75.4	74.2	73.8

5. Catholic, Church of Ireland and Presbyterian populations, 1861–1911

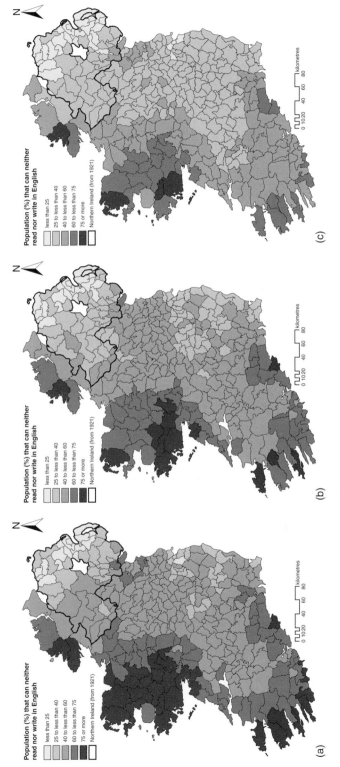

6. Illiteracy in English at barony level in (a) 1841, (b) 1851 and (c) 1861

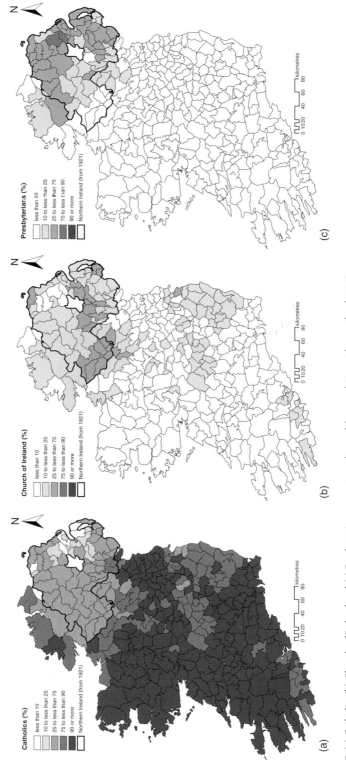

7. (a) Catholic, (b) Church of Ireland and (c) Presbyterian: percentage share of the population at barony level, 1861

Catholics (%)
less than 10
10 to less than 25
25 to less than 75
75 to less than 90
90 or more
Northern Ireland (from 1921)

Church of Ireland (%)
less than 10
10 to less than 25
25 to less than 75
75 to less than 90
90 or more
Northern Ireland (from 1921)

Presbyterians (%)
less than 10
10 to less than 25
25 to less than 75
75 to less than 90
90 or more
Northern Ireland (from 1921)

(a)

(b)

(c)

kilometres
0 1020 40 60 80

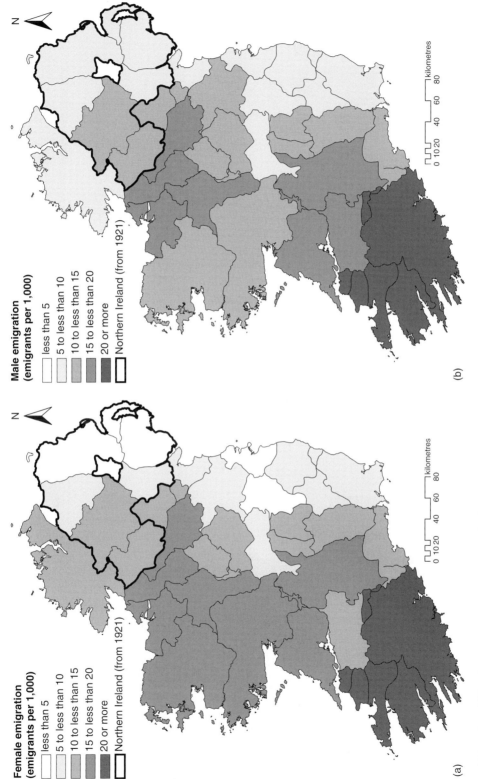

**Female emigration
(emigrants per 1,000)**

- less than 5
- 5 to less than 10
- 10 to less than 15
- 15 to less than 20
- 20 or more
- Northern Ireland (from 1921)

N

kilometres
0 10 20 40 60 80

(a)

**Male emigration
(emigrants per 1,000)**

- less than 5
- 5 to less than 10
- 10 to less than 15
- 15 to less than 20
- 20 or more
- Northern Ireland (from 1921)

N

kilometres
0 10 20 40 60 80

(b)

8. (a) Female and (b) male emigration per 1,000 at county level, 1881

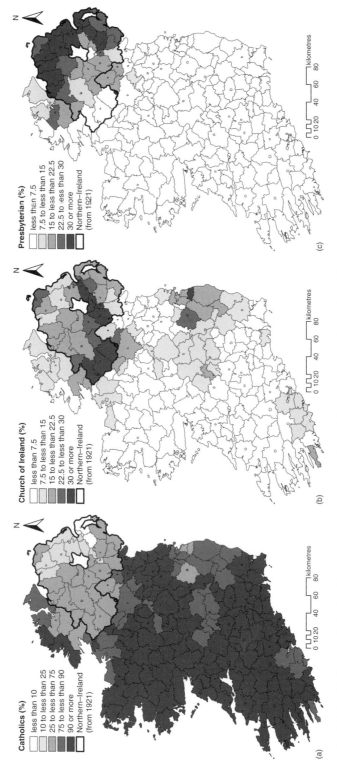

9. (a) Catholic, (b) Church of Ireland and (c) Presbyterians: percentage share of the population at urban and rural district level, 1911

Catholics (%)
- less than 10
- 10 to less than 25
- 25 to less than 75
- 75 to less than 90
- 90 or more
- Northern–Ireland (from 1921)

0 10 20 40 60 80 kilometres

(a)

Church of Ireland (%)
- less than 7.5
- 7.5 to less than 15
- 15 to less than 22.5
- 22.5 to less than 30
- 30 or more
- Northern–Ireland (from 1921)

0 10 20 40 60 80 kilometres

(b)

Presbyterian (%)
- less then 7.5
- 7.5 to less than 15
- 15 to less than 22.5
- 22.5 to ess than 30
- 30 or more
- Northern–Ireland (from 1921)

0 10 20 40 60 80 kilometres

(c)

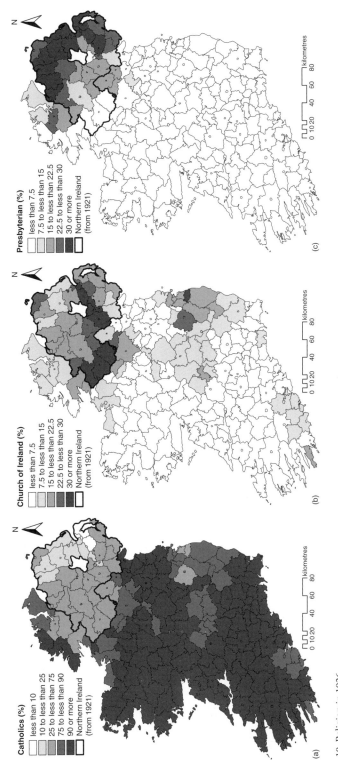

Catholics (%)

less than 10
10 to less than 25
25 to less than 75
75 to less than 90
90 or more
Northern Ireland (from 1921)

(a)

0 10 20   40   60   80
kilometres

Church of Ireland (%)

less than 7.5
7.5 to less than 15
15 to less than 22.5
22.5 to less than 30
30 or more
Northern Ireland (from 1921)

(b)

0 10 20   40   60   80
kilometres

Presbyterian (%)

less than 7.5
7.5 to less than 15
15 to less than 22.5
22.5 to less than 30
30 or more
Northern Ireland (from 1921)

(c)

0 10 20   40   60   80
kilometres

10. Religion in 1926

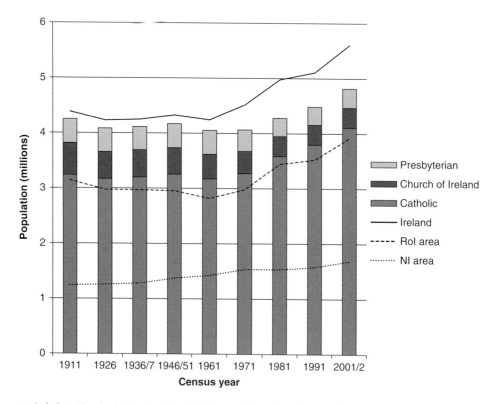

11. Catholics, Church of Ireland and Presbyterian populations, 1911–2001, and total populations for the Northern Ireland, Republic of Ireland and island of Ireland areas, 1911–2001

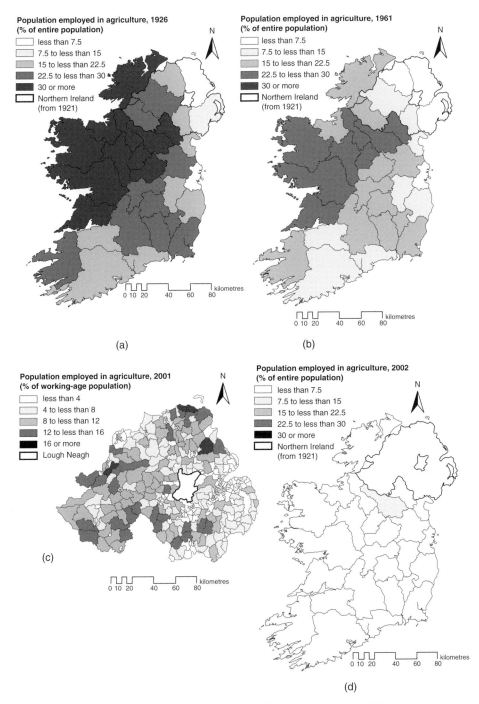

12. Population employed in agriculture, (a) 1926, (b) 1961, (c) 2002 (I) and (d) 2001 (NI) (percentage shares of entire population in 1926 and 1961, percentage shares of working-age population in 2001/2)

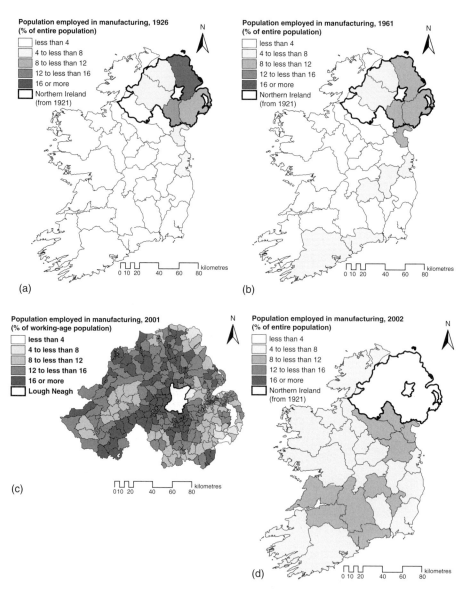

13. Population employed in manufacturing, (a) 1926, (b) 1961, (c) 2002 (I) and (d) 2001 (NI) (percentage shares of entire population in 1926 and 1961, percentage shares of working-age population in 2001/2)

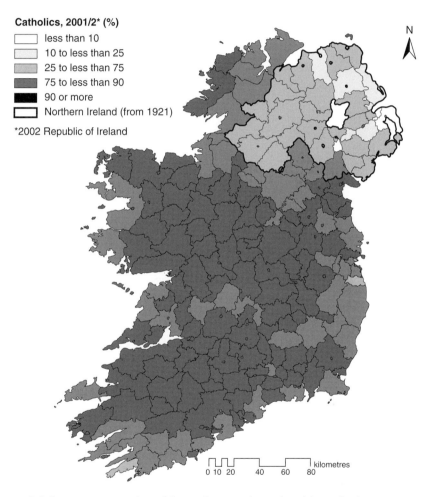

Catholics, 2001/2* (%)

- less than 10
- 10 to less than 25
- 25 to less than 75
- 75 to less than 90
- 90 or more
- Northern Ireland (from 1921)

*2002 Republic of Ireland

N

kilometres
0 10 20   40   60   80

14. Catholics as a percentage share of the population at urban and rural district level, 2001 (NI)/2002 (I)

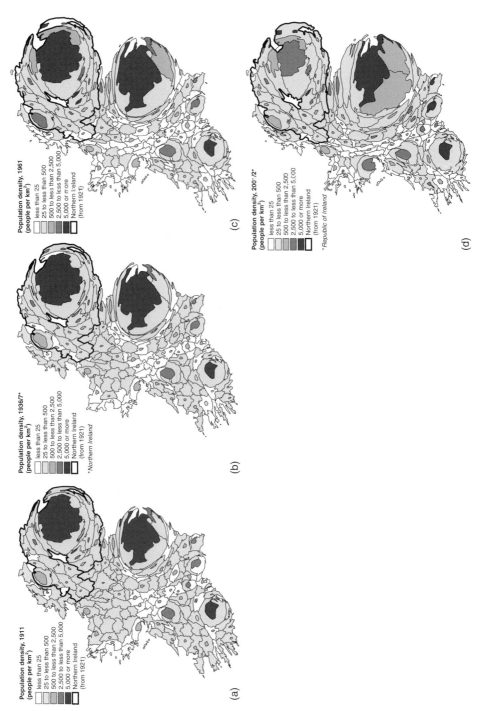

Population density, 1911
(people per km²)

- less than 25
- 25 to less than 500
- 500 to less than 2,500
- 2,500 to less than 5,000
- 5,000 or more
- Northern Ireland
  (from 1921)

(a)

Population density, 1936/7*
(people per km²)

- less than 25
- 25 to less than 500
- 500 to less than 2,500
- 2,500 to less than 5,000
- 5,000 or more
- Northern Ireland
  (from 1921)

Northern Ireland

(b)

Population density, 1961
(people per km²)

- less than 25
- 25 to less than 500
- 500 to less than 2,500
- 2,500 to less than 5,000
- 5,000 or more
- Northern Ireland
  (from 1921)

(c)

Population density, 2001/2*
(people per km²)

- less than 25
- 25 to less than 500
- 500 to less than 2,500
- 2,500 to less than 5,000
- 5,000 or more
- Northern Ireland
  (from 1921)

Republic of Ireland

(d)

15. Gastner-Newman population density cartograms at urban and rural district level for (a) 1911, (b) 1936 (I)/1937 (NI), (c) 1961 and (d) 2001 (NI)/2002 (I)

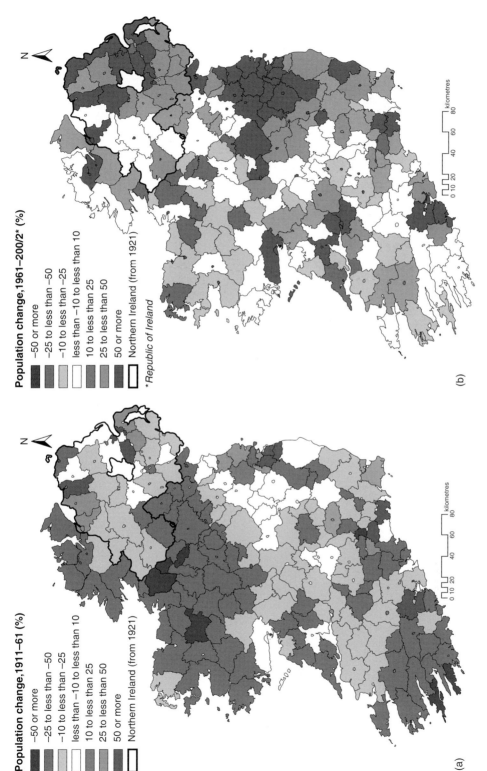

Population change,1911–61 (%)

–50 or more
–25 to less than –50
–10 to less than –25
less than –10 to less than 10
10 to less than 25
25 to less than 50
50 or more
Northern Ireland (from 1921)

N

(a)

0 10 20 40 60 80
kilometres

Population change,1961–200/2* (%)

–50 or more
–25 to less than –50
–10 to less than –25
less than –10 to less than 10
10 to less than 25
25 to less than 50
50 or more
Northern Ireland (from 1921)

Republic of Ireland

N

(b)

0 10 20 40 60 80
kilometres

16. Population change at urban and rural district level in (a) 1911–61 and (b) 1961–2001/2

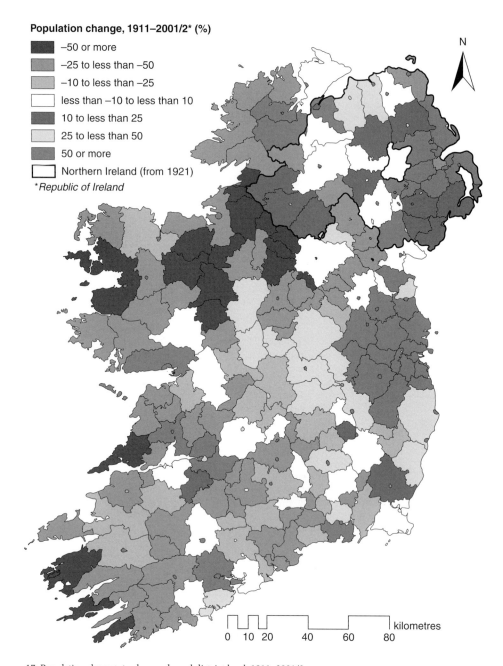

Population change, 1911–2001/2* (%)

- −50 or more
- −25 to less than −50
- −10 to less than −25
- less than −10 to less than 10
- 10 to less than 25
- 25 to less than 50
- 50 or more
- Northern Ireland (from 1921)

*Republic of Ireland

17. Population change at urban and rural district level, 1911–2001/2

Index